Advanced Guide to
Linux Networking and Security

Ed Sawicki
Nicholas Wells

THOMSON
COURSE TECHNOLOGY

Australia • Canada • Mexico • Singapore • Spain • United Kingdom • United States

Advanced Guide to Linux Networking and Security

is published by Thomson Course Technology.

Managing Editor:
William Pitkin III

Senior Product Manager:
Tricia Boyle

Developmental Editor:
Dan Seiter

Production Editor:
Summer Hughes, Elena Montillo

Manufacturing Coordinator:
George Morrison

Product Marketing Manager:
Guy Baskaran

Associate Product Manager:
Sarah Santoro

Editorial Assistant:
Jennifer Smith

Cover Design:
Laura Rickenbach

Compositor:
GEX Publishing Services

Copy Editor:
Susan Forsyth

Proofreader:
Karen Annett

Indexer:
Elizabeth Cunningham

Disclaimer
Course Technology reserves the right to revise this publication and make changes from time to time in its content without notice.

ISBN 1-4188-3539-0

BRIEF Contents

TABLE OF
Contents

CHAPTER THREE
Configuring Client Services   95

CHAPTER FOUR
Using Simple Network Services   141

Preface

Linux has become the operating system of choice for applications that require advanced networking capabilities or high levels of security. Linux leads the industry in advanced networking capabilities. This is obvious if you need to deploy IPv6, for example. Support for IPv6 is highly evolved in Linux, but is either absent from non-UNIX operating system platforms or is in the early stages.

Linux supports all the network devices you'll likely encounter, including any flavor of Ethernet (including wireless), Token-Ring, FDDI, ATM, Frame Relay, ISDN, USB, FireWire, traditional serial and parallel interfaces, and even ARCnet. It supports all the protocols you'll likely ever need: IPv4 and the usual associated protocols (TCP, UDP, ARP, and so on), IPv6, AppleTalk, Novell's IPX/SPX, X.25, AX25 (for radio amateurs), PPP, SLIP, PLIP, VoIP, and more. It supports networking techniques such as multicasting, network address translation (NAT), traffic shaping, transparent proxies, IP and IPX over IP tunneling, server clustering, and more.

The open source nature of Linux and Linux applications encourages the discovery and reporting of security issues through peer review and the rapid distribution of fixes. The past few years have shown that the open source model results in more secure systems, given the relatively small number of successful attacks against Linux systems in spite of the high number of reported problems. Linux-based systems are a clear choice for applications in which systems must be secure.

Linux systems are more secure than commercial, non-UNIX operating systems for many reasons:

Filesystem Structure

Linux, like UNIX, follows a tradition of structuring a filesystem so that related files are kept together in the same directories. Programs (binaries) are kept in different directories than data files. Binaries that should only be used by the superuser are kept in different directories than binaries used by all users. Data files that are static are kept in different directories than files that are dynamic.

By placing related files in their own directories, system administrators can use security tools such as ownership, permissions, attributes, access control lists, and mount options to better protect the files. Some implementations of Linux systems carry this concept further by making portions of the filesystem immutable if they contain static files. You can't attack what you can't modify.

Daemons and Services

When running Linux daemons, the system administrator chooses the user the daemon runs as. Administrators who are focused on security tend to create separate user accounts for every daemon they run. Each of these user accounts has its permissions in the filesystem set so the daemon only has access to files and directories that are absolutely required. A successful attack against a vulnerable daemon tends to affect only that portion of the filesystem. Other parts of the filesystem are insulated from the attack.

Jails

If an attack against a vulnerable daemon is successful, the attacker may be able to access or affect portions of the filesystem to which the daemon's user account has permissions. If more than one daemon must run as the same user, daemons that are not vulnerable may still be affected by the attack. The solution is to confine daemons to the portion of the filesystem to which they require access. They'll have no access to other portions of the filesystem, even though they might have permissions there. Confining daemon access is accomplished with the `chroot` feature of Linux, and is often called "putting a daemon in jail."

Virtual Machines

Linux daemons vary in the degree of trust that administrators have in them. Once a daemon has had more than a few security problems, experienced administrators no longer trust it and seek alternatives. Security problems in `sendmail`, for example, caused many administrators to adopt alternatives such as `qmail`, Postfix, and Exim, which have a better security architecture.

If administrators must run a daemon they don't trust, they tend to put it on another computer to isolate it from the daemons they do trust. Linux supports a form of virtual machine called User Mode Linux (UML) that allows an administrator to run an untrustworthy daemon on the same computer with relative safety. The daemon runs inside the UML, which is running another independent copy of Linux.

If the vulnerable daemon running in the UML is successfully attacked, everything outside of the UML is insulated from the attack. More than one UML can run on the same computer, thus allowing more than one untrustworthy daemon, each insulated from the others. To keep resource consumption down and to minimize the possibility of attack, UMLs can run minimal Linux configurations.

Firewall

The Linux firewall has functionality that rivals expensive commercial firewalls. It allows for fine-grained control over stateless and stateful packet filtering. It is extensible, allowing new filtering capabilities to be added as the need arises. In fact, many commercial firewalls are now based on Linux.

Advanced Security

Linux has advanced security features of which many system administrators are unaware. For example, a feature called POSIX Capabilities allows an administrator to limit the capabilities of his system. He can prevent the kernel from loading modules that were not loaded at boot time. He can limit processes and the signals they send to other processes. Processes that are not running as root may be able to bind to TCP and UDP ports below 1024. The list goes on and on.

In addition to the technical reasons why Linux is secure, the Linux culture encourages security as well. The Linux and UNIX communities have fostered an appreciation for security at every level—from the programmer who builds security into her application to the system administrator who uses every tool in his bag of impressive security tricks. Linux-based systems are more secure because we want them to be and we have the tools to do it.

Linux Certification

This book is the second in a set, the first being *Guide to Linux Installation and System Administration*. To get the most from this volume, you should be comfortable with Linux. You should have installed it before, and have experience using a Linux command line and graphical environment to execute programs, manage user accounts, and use a Linux filesystem. With that foundation, this book teaches you the basics of Linux networking and security. One aim of the material presented is to prepare you to pass a Linux certification exam, which demonstrates to potential employers that you have mastered important theoretical and practical knowledge about Linux-based networking and security.

Several certification programs for Linux are available. This book provides enough material for you to pass Linux Professional Institute (LPI) Level 1 and Level 2 certification. The other Linux certifications are not covered explicitly, but so much material is common to all certifications that this book should serve as an effective study guide for these as well. The exception is the Red Hat Certified Engineer certification, which is specific to Red Hat's Linux products. It requires additional study of Red Hat's version of Linux before you take the hands-on certification exam.

Appendix A provides the most current information about the LPI certification objectives at the time of this writing. References tie each objective to a particular section of this book.

The Intended Audience

This book is intended for students and professionals who need to understand computer networking and security technology in the context of a Linux-based server. The focus is practical, with hands-on descriptions of many programs and Web sites used by working system administrators. This book is ideal as a text for networking courses as long as students have some background in operating systems and are comfortable with a Linux or UNIX command line. The text and pedagogical features are designed to provide an interactive learning experience, so that further self-study of Internet and computer industry resources will prepare readers for more advanced education or work assignments in network administration and network security management. Each chapter includes Hands-On Projects that lead readers through various tasks in a step-by-step fashion. Each chapter also contains Case Projects that place readers in the role of problem solver, requiring them to apply concepts presented in the chapter to a situation that might occur in a real-life work environment.

Chapter Descriptions

Chapter 1, "Networking Fundamentals," introduces networking technology, including the hardware components of networking and basic networking theory. The chapter also introduces the basic networking protocols used in Linux, such as the TCP/IP suite and routing concepts.

Chapter 2, "Configuring Basic Networking," describes how networking devices are used in Linux and how to use both command-line and graphical utilities to configure network addresses and basic routing. CIDR notation and the new ip command are covered. Basic command-line utilities used to test networks are also presented.

Chapter 3, "Configuring Client Services," describes how to set up name resolution, dial-in network access, and remote graphical access using the X Window system. Basic concepts behind Web browsers and e-mail clients are explained and commonly used products are reviewed.

Chapter 4, "Using Simple Network Services," discusses Linux network daemons and shows how to set up a Linux superserver to handle a variety of incoming network service requests. Some of the more basic services are described, along with key administrative functions that can rely on networking, such as logging and printing.

Chapter 5, "Configuring File-sharing Services," discusses file sharing technologies that are supported on Linux: the Network File System (NFS), the File Transfer Protocol (FTP), and the Server Message Block (SMB) protocol used by Microsoft Windows systems.

Chapter 6, "Configuring Major Network Services," discusses four network services for which Linux is well-known: Domain Name Services (DNS), dynamic packet routing, e-mail service using `sendmail`, and Web services using the Apache Web server.

Chapter 7, "Security, Ethics, and Privacy," introduces the second half of the book by describing the landscape of network security and its relationship to ethics in the profession of system or network administration. The chapter also covers privacy of personal information as a legal issue and as a concern for network administrators.

Chapter 8, "File Security," discusses filesystem security mechanisms such as ownership, permissions, attributes, and access control lists (ACLs). It also covers running daemons in a `chroot` environment, loopback filesystems, monitoring log files, and checking for unauthorized file modifications.

Chapter 9, "User Security," describes how network administrators can safeguard user account information and help users act wisely to enhance system security. The chapter also explains software tools and security policies that are designed to aid user security.

Chapter 10, "Cryptography," discusses cryptographic systems, digital certificates, certificate authorities, and data encryption technologies, illustrating basic concepts and describing what protocols are currently used to secure network data. Commonly used Linux encryption tools are also covered in some detail.

Chapter 11, "Network Security Fundamentals," examines types of network security breaches, how to configure a Linux firewall, how to set up NAT, port forwarding, redirection, encrypting network traffic using SSL, tunneling protocols, and VPNs.

Chapter 12, "Security Tools," continues the discussion of network security by focusing on attackers' techniques and how to overcome them using intrusion detection systems and various vulnerability assessment utilities.

Appendix A, "Linux Certification Objectives," provides a list of objectives for the Linux Professional Institute (LPI) certification programs, with references from each objective to the section of this book that covers the material in that objective.

Appendix B, "Command Summary," provides a table with all Linux command-line utilities, server daemons, and graphical programs described in this book and in the companion volume.

Features

To help you fully understand networking concepts, this book includes many features designed to enhance your learning experience.

- **Chapter Objectives**.   Each chapter begins with a detailed list of the concepts to be mastered in that chapter. The list provides you with both a quick reference to the chapter's contents and a useful study aid.

- **Illustrations and Tables**.   Numerous illustrations of networking concepts, protocol layouts, and security methods help you to visualize and better understand technical concepts. In addition, tables provide concise references on essential topics such as command options and online information resources.

- **Chapter Summaries**.   Each chapter's text is followed by a summary of the concepts introduced in that chapter. These summaries provide a helpful way to recap and revisit the ideas covered in each chapter.

- **Key Terms**.   Terms that were introduced with boldfaced text in a chapter are listed in the Key Terms section at the end of the chapter. This method helps you check your understanding of all new terms.

- **Review Questions**.   A list of review questions is included to reinforce the ideas introduced in each chapter. Answering these questions ensures that you have mastered the important concepts.

- **Hands-On Projects**.   Although it is important to understand the theory behind the Linux operating system, nothing can improve upon real-world experience. To this end, each chapter includes numerous Hands-On Projects to provide practical implementation experience and real-world solutions.

- **Case Projects**.   To complete these exercises at the end of each chapter, you must draw on common sense and your knowledge of the technical topics covered to that point in the book. Your goal for each project is to find answers to problems like those you will face as a network administrator.

Text and Graphic Conventions

Wherever appropriate, additional information and exercises have been added to this book to help you better understand the topic at hand. Icons throughout the text alert you to additional materials. The icons used in this textbook are described below.

The Note icon draws your attention to additional helpful material related to the subject being described.

Tips based on the author's experience provide extra information about how to attack a problem or what to do in real-world situations.

The Caution icon warns you about potential mistakes or problems and explains how to avoid them.

Each Hands-On Project in this book is preceded by a special icon and a description of the exercise.

The Case Projects icon marks case projects, which are more involved, scenario-based assignments. In these extensive case examples, you are asked to implement independently what you have learned.

INSTRUCTOR'S MATERIALS

The following additional materials are available when this book is used in a classroom setting. All of the supplements available with this book are provided to the instructor on a single CD-ROM.

Instructor's Manual. The Instructor's Manual that accompanies this textbook includes lecture notes and additional instructional materials to assist in class preparation. These materials include suggestions for classroom activities, discussion topics, and additional projects. A 14- and 16-week sample syllabus is also provided.

ExamView®. This textbook is accompanied by ExamView, a powerful testing software package that allows instructors to create and administer printed, computer (LAN-based), and Internet exams. ExamView includes hundreds of questions that correspond to the topics covered in this text, enabling students to generate detailed study guides that include page references for further review. The computer-based and Internet testing components allow students to take exams at their computers and save the instructor time by grading each exam automatically.

PowerPoint presentations. This book comes with Microsoft PowerPoint slides for each chapter. These are included as a teaching aid for classroom presentation, to be made available to students on the network for chapter review, or to be printed for classroom distribution. Instructors, please feel free to add your own slides for additional topics you introduce to the class.

Figure files. All of the figures and tables in the book are reproduced on the Instructor's Resource CD, in bitmap format. Similar to the PowerPoint presentations, these are included as a teaching aid for classroom presentation, to make available to students for review, or to be printed for classroom distribution.

Solution files. Solutions to all end-of-chapter materials, including review questions and case projects, are provided for instructors.

Read This Before You Begin

The Hands-On Projects in this book help you to apply what you have learned about Linux networking and security. The following section lists the minimum hardware and software requirements that allow you to complete the projects. In addition, students must have administrator privileges on their workstations to complete many of the projects.

Although this book includes a copy of Fedora Core 3, the Linux certification programs that the book tracks are not focused on a particular Linux distribution. The information in the book applies in most cases to all current Linux distributions, such as Debian and its many derivative distributions—Gentoo, Mandriva (formerly Mandrake), SuSE, and many others. Exceptions can occur in some of the programs used as examples and in the location of certain files in the directory structure. In these cases, Fedora Core is used as an example to give readers notice that non-Fedora Core systems may differ. In particular, many of the projects rely on Fedora Core; this allows the projects to be more complex than would be possible if they were aimed at the lowest common denominator among all versions of Linux.

Minimum Lab Requirements

- **Hardware**
  - Each student workstation and each server computer require at least 128 MB of RAM, an Intel Pentium or compatible processor running at 200 MHz or higher, and a minimum of 1.5 GB of free space on the hard disk. More hard disk space is useful, but 1.5 GB will allow all critical network services to be installed.
  - The computer should also have a network interface. Ethernet is assumed throughout the book, but other interfaces, such as Token-Ring, will work equally well.
  - Many Hands-On Projects assume that all workstations are networked together. This can be done with simple Ethernet hubs or switches. No particular cabling system or speed requirements apply, as long as workstations can communicate with each other to experiment with networking and security protocols and programs.
  - Several Hands-On Projects assume that student workstations can access the Internet to research topics and products. Care should be taken that security is not compromised in allowing workstations to access the Internet through a larger organizational LAN. The tools and techniques used in the Hands-On Projects, if taken to extremes, could make LAN administrators quite unhappy.

- **Red Hat® Linux® Fedora Core 3 Software**
  - This book contains a copy of Red Hat® Linux® Fedora Core 3 Software. When you install it, it's best to choose a server configuration.

At the time this book was being developed, Red Hat Linux Fedora Core 3 was the current software version. At the time the book went to print, Fedora Core 4 was unavailable.

Core 3 is provided with the book. However, if you prefer to use Core 4, you should find that the vast majority of projects will work.

We will post information about any exceptions to this as we learn of them. You will be able to find these updates on *www.course.com*.

ACKNOWLEDGMENTS

Writing a book is easier when you have skilled people assisting you. Several people assisted with this book.

Nick Wells, the author of the First Edition of this book, was my first Linux mentor. He conducted classes and seminars that I organized in 1998, and I sat in on his sessions. This helped bootstrap me into the Linux world faster than if I had done it alone. He also introduced me to Course Technology, for which I'm grateful. Nick updated Chapter 7 for this edition.

This book was influenced by David May. David is a software designer with unconventional ideas about how computer systems generally and Linux specifically should be built and managed. He and I have spent hundreds of hours discussing and arguing ideas for significantly better ways to deploy, manage, and secure Linux-based systems. As a result, David designed a radically new approach that I call Sealed Systems. Some of these ideas changed the way I think about Linux systems, and have made it into this book.

The senior editor for this series is Will Pitkin, who convinced me to write the book even though my house had been significantly damaged by fire a month earlier. Had the book been with another publisher, I probably would have declined. My project manager, Tricia Boyle, kept me on track when my natural tendency is to lament about monopolies and the politics of the computer industry. Most of my interaction was with the development editor, Dan Seiter, who did an excellent job of polishing my prose and keeping an eye on the schedule.

My house was being rebuilt while I was writing this book. The demands on my time sometimes made it difficult to pay attention to detail. Fortunately, Shawn Day and John Freitas carefully tested the projects and checked all example commands and output for proper syntax. Their work is appreciated, and their pride in a quality job is obvious. Summer Hughes and Elena Montillo were the production editors, ironing out the final kinks.

My editors recruited four fellow instructors to review the material as writing progressed. Their input was invaluable in tailoring the material to students' needs, based on their many years of classroom experience. My thanks go to each of them:

- Tim Chappell   Dona Ana Branch Community College

- Jason Eckert   Trios College

- Ray Esparza   Glendale Community College

- Richard Tibbs   Radford University

Thanks to my consulting customers, David Cannon and Kimberly Virostek, who regularly challenge me with interesting networking scenarios and have indirectly contributed to this book.

I also thank the students who have attended my classes and seminars over the years, and whose questions drove me to learn the technical detail that has found its way into this book.

Most important is my family. Thanks to my wife Merryl for bearing the brunt of coordinating reconstruction of our house while I was busy writing, to my son Mark for being a pal, and to my daughter Beth for being the independent woman I always hoped she would be.

Feedback and Bonus Material

Given the popularity of Linux, there will likely be a Third Edition of this book in the future. The changes from the First Edition were substantial and were based in part on feedback from reviewers and readers. If you'd like to influence future editions of this book, send your feedback to ed@alcpress.com.

Not all the material I hoped to include made it into the book. To compensate, I set up a Web site that includes bonus material. You can access the site at *http://netsecure.alcpress.com.*

1

NETWORKING FUNDAMENTALS

> **After reading this chapter and completing the exercises, you will be able to:**
>
> ♦ Explain the purposes and evolution of computer networking
>
> ♦ Identify common types of network hardware
>
> ♦ Describe how network software operates
>
> ♦ Identify and describe the functions of the TCP/IP protocol suite
>
> ♦ Define network routing and describe the purpose of popular routing protocols

In this chapter, you will learn basic information about computer networks—knowledge that will prepare you to support and use the networking capability within the Linux operating system. This chapter describes the purposes and development of networking, then outlines the physical components that make up a network: the cables and computer parts that make it work. The second part of this chapter describes networking software in general terms and introduces you to the protocols—rules of operation—used by the most popular types of networks. Although this chapter does not explain networking hardware and protocols in great depth, it does give you a foundation for configuring Linux networking in the next chapter. You will learn more about networking protocols as specific services are configured later in this book.

THE EVOLUTION OF NETWORKED COMPUTERS

The need to share information and resources is essential for businesses and organizations. Mainframe computers in the 1940s and 1950s were very expensive, and only big companies and governments could afford one. Back then, networking meant locating the terminals and printers remote from the mainframe.

As computers became less expensive and companies owned many, the need to network them arose. Computer networks provide several advantages, including the following:

- Sharing information instantly without using a transportable medium such as a 3.5-inch disk or printout

- Automating data-processing tasks that involve multiple computer systems

- Making more efficient use of resources; networking allows multiple people to use a computer, printer, or other resource even from a distance

Three historical trends have contributed to the multitude of network-capable systems you work with today:

- Networking capability was added to personal computers as the usefulness of networking became apparent and its cost dropped.

- Network servers based on UNIX became less expensive.

- The Internet grew explosively and became widely accessible.

NOTE   Most of the larger computers connected to the Internet, even early on, were running the UNIX operating system. Because Linux is modeled after UNIX, the networking standards used by the Internet from its inception were also built in to Linux from *its* inception. When designers of other operating systems (such as Microsoft Windows or Macintosh OS) want to include Internet features, they must do so by adding UNIX or Linux features. Linux, you might say, has native support for the Internet.

The **Internet** is a collection of many networks around the world that are linked together. Communications on the Internet are based on specific protocols or rules of communication. These protocols are not proprietary to any vendor and are referred to as open protocols or Internet protocols. When Internet use became widespread, organizations also began using Internet protocols on their internal networks. Many proprietary protocols have given way to open protocols.

Computers can share information and resources in three general configurations: terminal connections, client/server computing, and peer-to-peer computing. Each of these types is explained in the following sections.

Terminal Networks

Terminal networks were the earliest type of computer network. A **terminal** network consists of a central computer or host with numerous terminals connected. A terminal consists of a keyboard and screen that allow a user to send keystrokes to the computer, and the computer sends responses to the terminal screen. Terminals are also referred to as **dumb terminals** or glass teletypes. Figure 1-1 shows several terminals connected to a single computer.

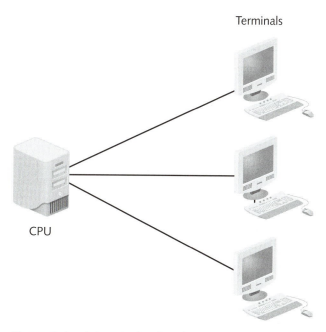

Terminals

CPU

Figure 1-1 A terminal network

The terminal is not a computer. It does not run any programs. All programs run on the central computer no matter how many terminals are attached. Terminals usually connect to computers via serial interfaces and communicate at relatively low speeds, such as 19,200 bits per second. Linux supports terminal networks and can easily function as the central computer.

Marketplace enthusiasm for personal computers has significantly diminished the demand for terminals, so terminals cost almost as much as PCs. A Wyse 55 terminal costs about $400. PCs can function as terminals if they run **terminal emulation** programs. Many terminal emulation programs are available for Linux.

Many people think of terminals and terminal networks as being old fashioned and out of date, and that they no longer exist. Not only do they still exist, but they are also generally immune to the problems that plague personal computer-based networks. Terminals cannot be attacked by viruses, do not need their hardware updated every few years, and do not need software upgrades, among other things.

Client/Server Computing

In **client/server** computing, every user has his own computer for running programs. The computers are connected in a network so users can share resources, such as files, printers, databases, and Internet connections. Computers that provide shared resources are called servers. A **server** is a computer or a software program that provides information or services.

A **client** is a computer or software program that requests information or services from the server. For example, when you use a Web browser, it is acting as a client. You request information from a Web server. The server returns that information to your client program—your Web browser. Figure 1-2 shows this interaction.

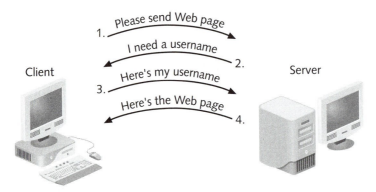

Figure 1-2   Client/server interaction to retrieve a Web page

You will see the terms "client" and "server" throughout this book. Your Linux system can act as a client *or* a server, depending on the software that you choose to run. In fact, a Linux system might act as a client for some programs and a server for other programs at the same time.

A Linux system can even act as both client and server to *itself*. Linux is a multitasking operating system. Suppose that one task running on your computer is a Web server, running in the background, and another task on the same computer is a Web browser. You enter a command in the browser requesting data from your own computer. The transfer of data from Web server to Web browser is a client/server network transaction, even though the data never leaves your computer.

Peer-to-Peer Networking

Peer-to-peer networks are different from client/server networks in one simple way. A typical client/server network has a small number of servers being used by a larger number of clients. In **peer-to-peer networks**, all computers may function as both clients and servers.

Most operating systems, including Linux and Windows, can run client programs *and* server programs. They do not require a centralized server to provide access to data or shared printers. This is called peer-to-peer networking. Each computer on the network is a *peer*, or equal to the other computers, and has the ability to initiate communications, respond to requests for information, and interact with users independent of other computer systems. Client/server networks are centralized. Peer-to-peer networks are decentralized.

Linux can be configured to operate in either client/server or peer-to-peer networks.

NETWORK HARDWARE

To learn about the components that make up a modern network, suppose that you work in a small medical office that wants to network its computers. You want to use a server running Linux to hold everyone's files and give everyone access to a shared printer. Figure 1-3 shows the systems that are involved in this project.

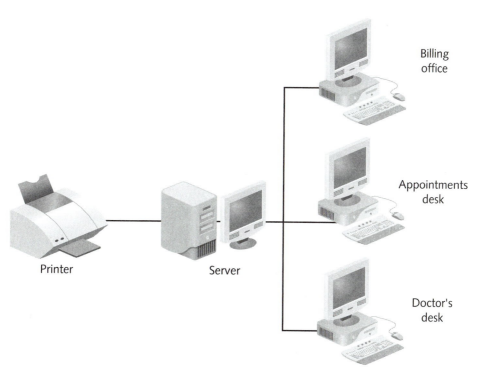

Figure 1-3 Small medical office network

You have two related questions to answer:

1. What hardware is needed to connect the computers into a network?
2. What software is needed to make the network function as you intend?

This section covers the first question, and you will explore the second question later in this chapter and throughout this book.

Ethernet is the most common method of networking computers, so you can assume its use for this example and throughout the rest of the book.

NOTE

Each computer requires a network **interface** that connects the computer with the network. Most modern computers have an Ethernet interface built in to them. Older computers don't have built-in network interfaces, so you must add one. Adding Ethernet to an older computer is simple. You add a **network interface card** or **NIC** (also called a network adapter or network card). You use a cable unless the network is wireless. Figure 1-4 shows typical NICs that plug in to the computer's PCI bus.

Figure 1-4   Typical NICs

Each computer on the network is called a **host**, regardless of whether it functions as a workstation or server.

NOTE

You also need a hub or a switch to connect multiple computers with the server. A **hub** is a wiring center to which multiple computers connect. Figure 1-5 shows how all the computers connect to the hub. A hub is inexpensive and unintelligent. If more computers will be added to the network in the future, you can improve network efficiency by using a switch, which is similar to a hub but more intelligent. **Switches** reduce network congestion on busy networks.

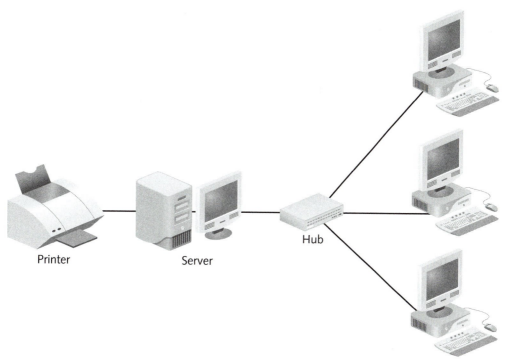

Figure 1-5   A small office network with a hub

NOTE This book does not cover all of the possible ways of physically connecting computers via cables and other devices. To be more thoroughly versed in physical networking, review a book such as *Network+ Guide to Networks* by Tamara Dean, published by Course Technology.

Units

This book uses units of measure that comply with the International System of Units or SI. Because this is a book about networking, units that express data rate will be used most. The basic unit of data rate is bits per second, which is properly abbreviated b/s—not bps. Data rates can be big numbers, so you use prefixes such as kilo, as in kilobits per second, which is abbreviated **kb/s**. Megabits per second is abbreviated as Mb/s and gigabits per second is Gb/s. Note that kb/s has a lowercase 'k,' while the other prefixes use uppercase.

Many people in the computer industry are confused about data rate and its units of measure, abbreviations, and prefixes. This is understandable, given that computer memory is measured in binary-oriented units. A kilobyte of computer memory is 1024 bytes, not 1000. The problem is that people think all computer industry units that use prefixes are binary, including data rate. They think that 1 kb/s equals 1024 b/s and 1 Mb/s equals 1024 kb/s. This is wrong. One Mb/s equals 1000 kb/s.

The prefix "kilo" means 1000 everywhere, except in the computer industry and only when binary-oriented devices, such as memory, are involved.

NOTE

Data rate should always be expressed in decimal units. A 10-Mb/s Ethernet runs at 10,000,000 b/s, not 10,240,000 b/s. For more detail on the International System of Units and prefixes, visit *physics.nist.gov/cuu/Units/binary.html*.

Networking Technologies

Before you buy any network hardware for your medical office network, you must decide what type of networking technology you will use. The most widely used technology is called Ethernet. **Ethernet** is a networking standard developed in the 1970s by Xerox, Intel, and Digital Equipment Corporation and standardized by the IEEE (Institute of Electrical and Electronics Engineers) as IEEE 802.3.

Three common variations of Ethernet are available, with differences based primarily on speed: 10 Mb/s Ethernet, 100 Mb/s Fast Ethernet, and 1000 Mb/s Gigabit Ethernet (abbreviated GbE). The speed or **bandwidth** determines the amount of information that can be transmitted. It is usually expressed in megabits per second (**Mb/s**). One megabit is one million bits. Ethernet transmits at 10, 100, or 1000 Mb/s.

The 1000-Mb/s speed can also be specified as one gigabit per second (**Gb/s**). One Gb/s equates to 1000 Mb/s.

NOTE

Many of today's computers include an Ethernet interface capable of running at all three speeds. The interface chooses its speed by negotiating with the device to which it's connected—typically an Ethernet switch. If one computer connected to the switch cannot operate as fast as the others, it forces all computers to run at the lower speed unless the switch allows for different speeds.

Most notebook computers are now equipped with wireless Ethernet in addition to the normal wired Ethernet interface. As the name implies, wireless Ethernet doesn't use cables to connect hosts to the network. Wireless Ethernet uses radio waves to communicate.

Wireless Ethernet is used for mobile applications, where a wired connection is not available. It can also be used where networking cables are difficult or impossible to install, such as outdoors or in historic buildings.

Wireless Ethernet can be set up in one of two ways. In a peer-to-peer arrangement (often called ad hoc mode), each computer communicates directly with the others. The other arrangement uses a wireless access point that is equivalent to the hub or switch in a wired

Ethernet. Figure 1-6 shows how the medical office could be set up with wireless Ethernet that uses an access point.

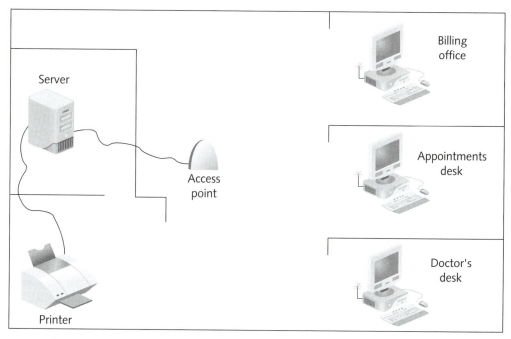

Figure 1-6   A wireless LAN (WLAN)

Wireless networks tend to be less reliable than wired networks because signal quality can be degraded by barriers such as concrete, metal walls, and floors, or by devices generating electromagnetic interference. Wireless networks tend to be less secure than wired networks because communications can be more easily intercepted. In an office setting, it's best to use wired Ethernet. Only use wireless Ethernet when connecting to a wired network is not possible.

For reference, Table 1-1 lists popular network technologies and shows their relative speeds. Remember that new products and technologies will make this table obsolete.

Table 1-1   Major networking technologies for local area networks

Technology	Speed	Comments
Ethernet	10, 100, and 1000 Mb/s	Inexpensive and easy to install
10 **Gigabit Ethernet**	10 Gb/s	Quite expensive; Linux has relatively few drivers for these cards
Token-Ring	4 or 16 Mb/s	Some networks can run at 20 or 40 Mb/s

Table 1-1 Major networking technologies for local area networks (continued)

Technology	Speed	Comments
Fiber Distributed Data Interface (FDDI)	100 Mb/s	Highly reliable because of its fault-tolerant features; used in network backbone applications
Asynchronous Transfer Mode (ATM)	155 Mb/s	Expensive and specialized; 622 Mb/s ATM is under development
Wireless LAN (WLAN)	11 Mb/s	802.11b (Wi-Fi) networks are popular; newer 802.11a and 802.11g products will operate at 54 Mb/s

Cabling a Network

Except for wireless Ethernet, the network technologies mentioned in the previous section use two primary types of cable or media: unshielded twisted pair (UTP) and fiber optics. However, other media were popular in the past and might still be used today. These are included in Figure 1-7 and described in the following list.

- **Unshielded twisted pair (UTP)** is made up of four pairs of wires encased in plastic insulation. UTP comes in six categories, with Category6 or CAT6 being the highest quality, and supports the highest speed. CAT5 and CAT6 are most widely used with Ethernet. Even the highest-quality UTP is inexpensive compared with other media. If you install CAT6 cables for an Ethernet 10/100 network, for example, you could later upgrade the network to Gigabit Ethernet without rewiring the office. UTP cables are susceptible to interference from strong electrical signals and may not be the best media choice in an environment with heavy electrical machinery.

- **Shielded twisted pair (STP)** is very similar to UTP but includes a metallic shield around the wires. This protects the network signal from outside electromagnetic interference, but makes STP cables more expensive than equivalent-quality UTP. STP may still be used in environments in which a lot of interference is expected from other electrical or electronic equipment.

- **Fiber-optic** cable is a high-end medium that uses light pulses rather than electrical pulses to transmit data. It is capable of very high speeds and is immune to electromagnetic interference. Fiber-optic cable is the most secure medium, nearly impossible to eavesdrop on. However, it is more expensive than the other wiring types and greater care must be taken during installation.

- **Coaxial cable (coax)** was a popular medium from the 1960s through the 1980s, but now has been overtaken by UTP. Early implementations of 10-Mb/s Ethernet used thick coax for 10Base5 Ethernet and thin coax (sometimes called ThinNet) for 10Base2 Ethernet. Coaxial cable is also used in CATV systems. You use it if you have a **cable modem**.

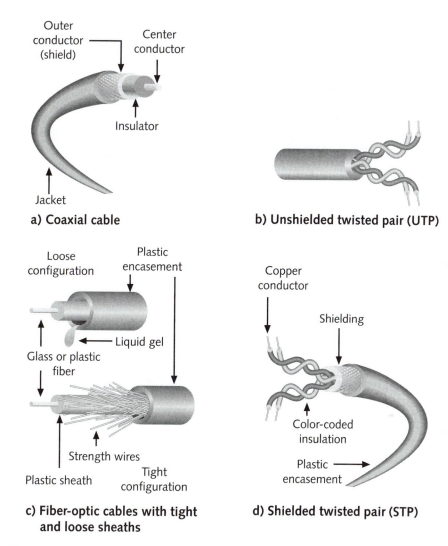

a) Coaxial cable

b) Unshielded twisted pair (UTP)

c) Fiber-optic cables with tight and loose sheaths

d) Shielded twisted pair (STP)

Figure 1-7   Networking cables

Last Mile Options

In addition to LAN cabling options is the **last mile connection**, or the connection between your LAN and the Internet or other high-speed network. This refers to the connection that begins at the home or office, goes through the local neighborhood, and ends at an Internet service provider (ISP) or other fast service provider. The connections that make up the nation's data-transmission infrastructure are generally very fast and well established, but the last mile connections that link these high-speed transmission lines to the home or office vary tremendously in speed and availability. Table 1–2 shows some of the last mile connections currently available. Cost increases proportionally to speed in these options; a dial-up modem can cost as little as $50, and a fiber-optic OC connection can cost millions.

Table 1-2   Last mile connections

Transmission Type	Speed	Typical Use/Comments	Time to Transmit Contents of One 680-MB CD-ROM (Hours:Minutes)
Dial-up modem	56 kb/s	Home	26:53
Integrated Services Digital Network (ISDN)	128 kb/s	Home or office; used for modem connectivity	12:5
Cable modem	5 Mb/s to 512 Mb/s	Home	3:2 to 0:18
Digital subscriber line (DSL)	128 kb/s to 1.544 Mb/s	Home; a relatively new digital telephone service that can be added to existing telephone lines in some areas	12:5 to 0:58
T-1	1.544 Mb/s	Home	0:58
T-3	44.736 Mb/s	Large companies, ISP	0:2
OC-1	52 Mb/s	ISP to regional ISP	8 seconds
OC-256	13.271 Gb/s	Major Internet backbone; uses fiber-optic cable	Less than 1 second

In addition to these wired last mile technologies, **fixed wireless** solutions are also popular. Fixed wireless uses transceivers and antennas mounted on buildings to transmit up to 18 miles, and they are cheaper to install than fiber-optic systems. This eliminates having to pay for dedicated circuits between offices. Traditional fixed wireless systems use commercial hardware and are expensive. "Homebrew" fixed wireless solutions can be engineered using Linux and off-the-shelf wireless Ethernet hardware.

Fixed wireless requires clear line of sight between sender and receiver. Not only must the two antennas be able to see each other, but there must also not be any obstructions within a conical-shaped area known as the Fresnel Zone. For more information, perform an Internet search for "Fresnel Zone."

Fixed wireless can be disrupted by rain, snow, and fog. Transmissions may be susceptible to eavesdropping. Of course, after reading this book, you will know how to protect all of the data on your network from eavesdroppers!

So far, you've seen many of the components that would likely be used to create a small office network. You must select a networking technology, which defines the types of interfaces you install and, to some extent, the cabling you use. The combination of Ethernet interfaces and

UTP cable is a common choice for a small office network. How you cable the network depends on the environment in which you're working. Finally, last mile technologies allow you to get an Internet connection at your home or office.

Before turning to the software aspects of networking, the following sections consider the physical arrangement, or topologies, of networks.

Network Topologies

Network **topology** is the *shape* of the network—how networked computers are connected together. There are two types of topologies: physical and logical. Rarely does a network technology use the same physical and logical topology. For example, a 10Base-T Ethernet is a physical star topology but a logical bus topology.

There are three common physical topologies:

- A **star topology**, in which computers connect to a central point, usually a hub or switch, as shown in Figure 1-8. This is the most common physical topology. Any Ethernet that uses twisted pair or fiber-optic cabling is a physical star, as is Token-Ring.

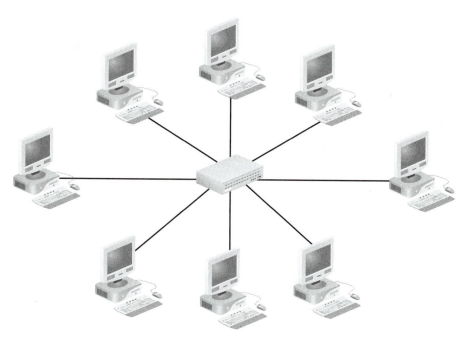

Figure 1-8   Star topology

- A **bus topology**, in which computers are connected to the same cable, as shown in Figure 1-9. Ethernets that use coaxial cable are examples of a physical bus.

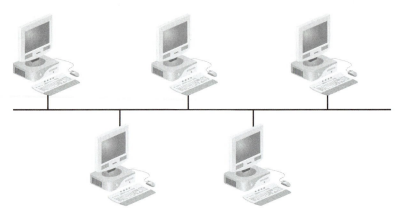

Figure 1-9   Bus topology

- A **ring topology**, in which computers are linked into a circular shape, as shown in Figure 1-10. This is the least common physical topology. FDDI is a good example.

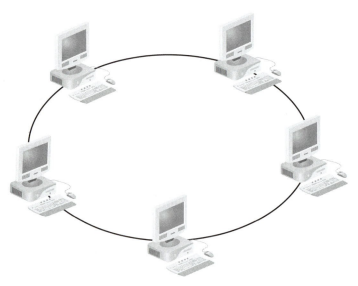

Figure 1-10   Ring topology

There are two common logical topologies:

- A bus topology, in which packets sent over the medium are received by all hosts at the same time. You can think of this as a broadcast topology—any sender is heard by everyone simultaneously. All Ethernets are logical buses. Wireless networks that use radio are typically buses.

- A ring topology, in which packets are sent from one host to its adjacent neighbor. The neighbor relays the packets to other hosts. Token-Ring, FDDI, and **ARCnet** are examples of logical rings.

An exception to these points occurs when you use switches with Ethernet. Although the Ethernet interfaces think they're operating in a logical bus topology environment, the switches change the logical topology to a switched point-to-point topology. Switched point-to-point is similar to the telephone network. Connections between two communicating machines are made through the network when they're needed.

Frames and Packets

When data flows over a network, it is organized into blocks of data called either frames or packets. The term "frame" is used when referring to network technologies like Ethernet and Token-Ring. The term "**packet**" is used when referring to protocols. This is described in more detail later.

Packets are of different sizes, depending on the amount of data to be moved and the network type being used. The maximum size for a packet is called the **maximum transmission unit (MTU)**. The MTU for Ethernet is 1500 bytes. The MTU for FDDI is 4470 bytes. A packet can be smaller than the MTU, but it can't be larger. If more data must be sent, additional packets are used.

Each packet is organized into a header and payload. The **payload** is the data transferred from one computer to another. The **header** is a structured collection of information that defines how the packet should be handled. For example, a header may include addresses, sequence numbers, and error-checking information.

Throughput

Throughput refers to how much payload information can be delivered. It is expressed in units such as kb/s and Mb/s. Your Ethernet may run at 100 Mb/s, but its average throughput is usually lower because of overhead and congestion. A busy network might squander its bandwidth on aborted attempts to deliver packets (caused by **collisions** or buffer-full conditions) and protocol overhead, resulting in reduced throughput. The solution for busy networks is to keep them from getting too busy by paying attention to the network topology.

Contention

Logical bus topologies allow network hosts to use a method of accessing the network called contention. With contention, all hosts have equal access to the network and can use the network whenever it's idle. If two or more hosts try to use the network at the same time, a collision occurs and the hosts must negotiate for which goes first. This is a time-costly procedure that steals bandwidth from the network. Collisions are infrequent when the network is lightly used.

Ethernet uses a contention technique called Carrier Sense Multiple Access/Collision Detection or CSMA/CD. When use is high, collisions can occur and bandwidth is lost. This means that you'll never be able to take full advantage of Ethernet's bandwidth. A conservative estimate is that Ethernet has a maximum throughput equal to about half the data rate. A 100-Mb/s Fast Ethernet yields about 50 Mb/s of throughput. When you use Ethernet switches, you'll likely do better.

Token-passing

A more efficient method for hosts to access a network is called token-passing, which uses a **token** to signal hosts that it's their turn to send. It is used to create a logical ring topology that can be used with any physical topology. Token-Ring and ARCNET are examples of token-passing. Hosts take their turn sending on the network based on either their address or their placement in a physical ring. Collisions don't occur regardless of how much the network is used.

There are time-costly procedures when hosts enter or leave the ring, but these should be relatively rare events. A token-passing network that is overused will still be a problem, but bandwidth won't be lost to time-costly collision recovery.

Segmentation

The problem of bandwidth being lost to network congestion can be eased by reducing the amount of traffic a network must move. The simplest way of doing this is to divide the network into smaller parts. This is often called segmentation because each smaller network has its own network **segment**. If the network uses Ethernet, each segment has its own hub or switch. Ethernet switches use a form of segmentation to reduce the possibility of collisions.

Segmentation alone doesn't necessarily reduce overall traffic on any one segment significantly. Each segment should include computers that access the same resources or communicate with each other. For example, suppose your company has two departments: Sales and Engineering. Each department would use its own segment. If each department has its own server and Sales people don't frequently exchange data with Engineering people, overall traffic on each segment would be reduced.

Segmented networks may use different technologies and topologies. One segment may be Ethernet and another may be Token-Ring. Practical reasons for this include compatibility with existing equipment and avoiding the high cost of rewiring buildings for newer cabling systems. Dissimilar topologies are connected with bridges or routers. The distinction between these is made clear in Chapter 6.

NETWORK SOFTWARE

All of the networking hardware you've been learning about isn't much use without the software to control it. A network-capable operating system is needed. Linux has excellent network support.

A **protocol** is a formalized set of rules for communication. In diplomatic circles, a person from one country learns how those from another nation act to communicate effectively with them. In the same way, a computer protocol allows one computer or device to communicate effectively with any other that uses the same protocol. Each protocol was designed for a specific purpose—that's why there are so many of them.

Before exploring the multitude of protocols, the following sections step back and look at some conceptual models of networking.

Conceptual Models of Networking

When computer makers first networked their computers, there were no standards for how this was to be done. This created significant problems when computers from different vendors had to be connected together. To bring order to this chaos, the International Organization for Standardization (ISO) developed the **Open Systems Interconnection (OSI) reference model**. The OSI model defines seven layers of network functionality that standard protocols would implement. Figure 1-11 shows the OSI model.

- The *Physical layer* represents the hardware used to send information over network media, such as a cable.

- The *Data Link layer* sends data over the media. It may also be concerned about detecting and correcting errors. It will need to support an addressing scheme if more than two computers are expected to use the media. Use the term "frame" when referring to the blocks of data sent at this layer.

- The *Network layer* finds the best route for packets that must be transferred between different networks. The Network layer gets the data from both the Physical and Data Link layers so that it can "translate" between different network types. Use the term "packet" when referring to the blocks of data sent at this layer and higher layers.

- The *Transport layer* sets up connections between specific computers across the network. It's concerned about end-to-end delivery assurances, such as missing packets, packets arriving out of order, and flow control (ensuring that a sender doesn't send more data than the receiver can handle).

- The *Session layer* manages network connections at a more abstract level than the Transport layer.

- The *Presentation layer* handles data representation issues such as adapting screen data to fit on a different geometry display.

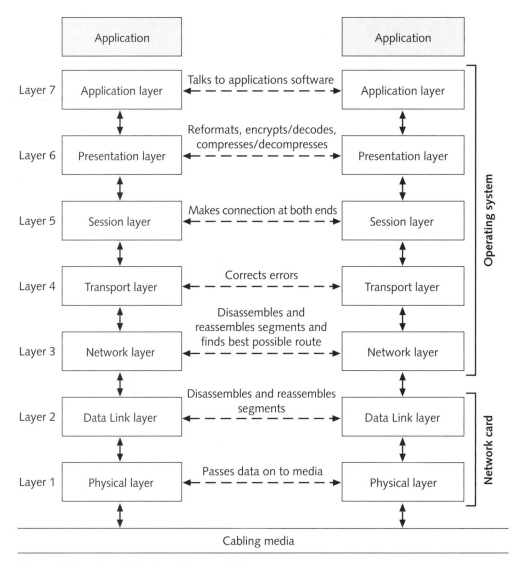

Figure 1-11 The OSI networking model

- The *Application layer* communicates with any application, such as a Web browser, that wants to use the network. It uses protocols from the lower layers to move data across the network to another application that can understand what is being sent.

The OSI reference model doesn't translate exactly for all networks. Internet-related protocols don't have formal Session or Presentation layers, though they may have the functionality of these layers. For the Internet and all TCP/IP-based networks, another networking reference model is used. It's called the **Internet model** or **TCP/IP model**. Linux is designed around this model, so understanding the Internet networking model is important for understanding Linux networking. The Internet model uses four layers, and each layer has specific protocols associated with it:

- The *Application layer* is the same as in the OSI model. Many protocols fit in this layer, such as DNS, HTTP, IMAP, POP3, and SMTP.

- The *Transport layer* is the same as in the OSI model. TCP and UDP are the important protocols in this layer.

- The *Internet layer* is the same as the Network layer of the OSI model. IP is the main protocol in this layer.

- The *Link layer* or *Network Access layer* combines the Physical and Data Link layers of the OSI model. It includes physical hardware and protocols such as Ethernet and Token-Ring.

Figure 1-12 shows the layers of the Internet model with the principal protocols used in each. Above these layers in the figure are applications that rely on the networking protocols. Below these layers are the physical media.

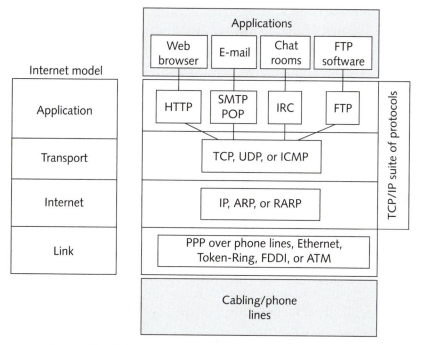

Figure 1-12   The TCP/IP suite of protocols within the Internet networking model

Before exploring specific protocols, the following example examines how these layers operate in general terms.

1. A Web browser wants to send a piece of data via HTTP. The data is generated by the application program and passed to the Application layer.

2. The Application layer packages the data in an HTTP packet and sends it to the Transport layer, specifying that it should be sent via the TCP protocol.

3. The Transport layer adds a TCP header to the packet and sends it to the Internet layer, specifying that it should be sent via the IP protocol.

4. The Internet layer adds an IP header to the packet and passes it to the Link layer.

5. The Link layer—Ethernet in this example—locates the MAC address and the physical address of the computer to which the packet is addressed, then adds its own header information and sends the packet out "on the wire" as a series of electrical impulses.

6. The Link layer on the Web server sees that the packet indicates its MAC address as a destination, so it grabs the packet, examines its Ethernet header information, then passes it to the Internet layer on the server.

7. The Internet layer examines the IP header, notes that the packet was sent using TCP, strips away the IP header, and sends the packet to the Transport layer.

8. The Transport layer examines the TCP header, sends back a packet to the client saying that this packet has been received correctly, strips away the TCP header, and sends the packet to the Application layer.

9. The Application layer examines the HTTP header, processes it, strips it away, and sends the remaining data (the payload) to the Web server.

10. The Web server reads the payload of the packet, prepares a response to the client request, and starts the whole process again.

The software for maintaining each protocol is often called a **protocol stack**. A protocol stack is software designed to receive data in a specific format from a higher-level protocol and transmit it to a lower-level protocol.

THE TCP/IP PROTOCOL SUITE

Most of the protocols that you'll learn about in this book are closely tied to the Internet and are based on the TCP/IP protocol suite. Most are Internet standards or RFCs. Internet protocols become standards by first being proposed by a person or team. Often, these are experienced software developers or engineers. A document called a **Request for Comments (RFC)** is written first. The RFC defines the protocol. Other experts around the world comment on the information in the RFC document, which is then revised several times to build on the suggestions received. Eventually, many people come to rely on the RFC as the standard definition of the new protocol.

All RFC documents are available (and searchable) on the Web site *www.rfc-editor.org*. There are about 4000 RFCs on this site. In a Hands-On Project at the end of this chapter, you'll explore this site.

This section looks at some of these protocols in more detail so that you'll understand their use as you learn about configuring networking on Linux in the next chapter. We'll start with the lowest level: the hardware.

NOTE Remember that this chapter provides only an overview with a few key networking details, just enough to get you started without overwhelming you with new terms at the outset.

As you would likely guess by now, each type of hardware has its own protocol to manage communication with other hardware of that type. For example, a Token-Ring network interface "speaks" the Token-Ring protocol, so it can send data over a cable to other Token-Ring interfaces. Because Ethernet is the most widely used protocol, this book focuses on Ethernet hardware.

NOTE Throughout this book, you will see notes about using other types of networks, such as Token-Ring, ATM, or FDDI. In addition, specific sections in later chapters are devoted to dial-up connections using modems.

Every Ethernet card has a unique address assigned by the manufacturer, called its **Media Access Control (MAC) address**, or simply its **hardware address**. Each manufacturer of Ethernet cards has a different range of numbers assigned to ensure that every Ethernet MAC address in the world is unique. MAC addresses are 48-bit binary values expressed in hexadecimal notation, like this: A1-67-CE-14-55-3C. Linux allows you to override this address if you want.

When one host on an Ethernet wants to communicate with another host, it must obtain the MAC address of the destination host. To obtain this MAC address, the host broadcasts a message to the entire network segment using the **Address Resolution Protocol (ARP)**. The message says, in effect, "I need the MAC address of the computer having the IP address aa.bb.cc.dd." All of the hosts on the network segment see the ARP request. The host that has the requested IP address responds with its MAC address directly to the computer that sent the ARP request. The host then stores, or caches, that correspondence between MAC address and IP address so that it won't need to repeat the ARP request later.

With the correct MAC address available, the Link layer can prepare packets from the IP stack and send them out on the network via Ethernet frames.

Figure 1-13 shows the Ethernet frame format. The Source Address field contains the sender's MAC address. The Destination Address field contains the receiver's MAC address. The Type field contains a value that indicates the type of payload the frame is carrying, or, if the value is less than 1501, the length of the frame. The Information field contains the payload. The FCS is the Frame Check Sequence, which contains a 32-bit value used to check the frame for errors at the receiver.

Preamble 64 bits	Destination Address 48 bits	Source Address 48 bits	Type 16 bits	Information 46-1500 bytes	FCS 32 bits

Figure 1-13　The Ethernet frame format

The Internet Protocol

The **Internet Protocol (IP)** is the foundation for transporting data across most Linux networks as well as the Internet. Although IP was designed decades ago and has in some ways been stretched past its original design, it still serves us well, as millions of systems around the world rely on it.

When learning about a new protocol, reviewing the structure and components of the header for that protocol can tell you a lot about how it's used and what it is capable of. The IP header is shown schematically in Figure 1-14. Each row is 4 bytes (32 bits). A typical IP header is 20 bytes long, though. Because the Options field at the end is optional, the length can vary.

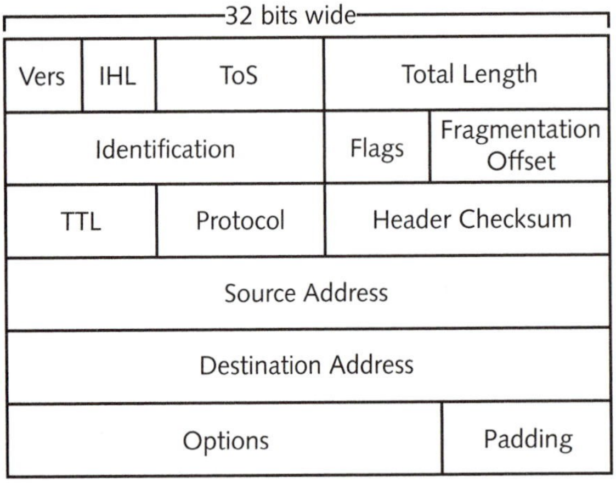

```
|-----------------32 bits wide-----------------|
```

Vers	IHL	ToS	Total Length	
Identification			Flags	Fragmentation Offset
TTL		Protocol	Header Checksum	
Source Address				
Destination Address				
Options			Padding	

Figure 1-14　The header fields of an IP packet

The *Version Number* field identifies the version of the IP protocol carried by this packet. Most IP packets are version 4. Version 6 is also being deployed.

The *IP Header Length (IHL)* field defines how many bytes are in the header, normally 20. This field is used in conjunction with the Total Length field.

The *Type of Service (ToS)* field is used to designate how the packet should be processed or routed. Some options include maximizing throughput, maximizing reliability, and minimizing cost. Few routers are able to do anything with this field. Most are not capable of keeping track of which route provides the highest reliability, lowest cost, and so on. This field is normally ignored.

The next three fields are used together: *Identification, Flags,* and *Fragmentation Offset.* These fields allow IP packets to be routed on networks that have a smaller MTU than the network that created the packet. For example, suppose you are using an Ethernet with an MTU of 1500 bytes. You exchange information with another Ethernet in a distant office, but to reach that network, your data must pass through two routers and an intermediate network that uses an MTU of 256 bytes. Figure 1-15 shows a schematic representation of this situation.

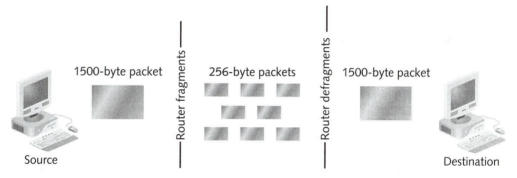

Figure 1-15   Fragmentation occurring when an intervening network has a smaller MTU

Each IP packet from your network must be broken into pieces to be transmitted on the intermediate network. This is called **fragmentation**. The Identification field provides each packet with a unique number so that the pieces of that packet can be reassembled. The Flags signal when more pieces of the indicated packet are still to arrive. The Fragmentation Offset identifies where in the original packet the current piece fits.

Fragmentation occurs regularly on larger networks with many diverse segments. It allows us to share data between networks with different packet sizes, but it adds a significant amount of overhead, including the following:

- Space wasted in partially filled packets because the payload size of an IP packet may not match exactly the payload size of the smaller packets

- Extra data needed to send multiple headers—one for each fragment of the original IP packet

- CPU time spent breaking a packet into pieces and then correctly reassembling it

Designing your networks to minimize fragmentation will improve your network performance.

Time to Live (TTL) ensures that a packet doesn't get lost and wander about the network forever, consuming bandwidth. The sender sets the TTL field to a numeric value, such as 64. The value is decremented each time the packet passes through a router. If the packet has not reached the destination host before the value reaches zero, the last router destroys the packet.

The *Protocol* field indicates which protocol layer should receive the payload of the IP packet. A numeric code identifies the protocol. The most common are TCP, UDP, and ICMP.

The **Header checksum** field is used to ensure the integrity of the header information. By using this field as a mathematical check of the contents of the other fields, the system receiving the packet can tell whether any data in the header has become corrupted.

The *Source Address* and *Destination Address* fields indicate the IP address of the computer that created the packet (the source) and the computer to which the packet is being sent (the destination).

Options are seldom used. The *Padding* field ensures that, if options are used, the header ends on a 32-bit boundary. The Padding field contains zeros.

IP Addressing

IP assigns a unique address to every host on the Internet. By referring to its **IP address**, you can contact any computer that is connected to the Internet or any network, no matter where it is located (as long as your routing is set up correctly, as described later).

Both an IP address and a MAC address are assigned to each network interface. The IP address is a worldwide address that can be used with any type of networking technology; it is passed around the Internet and used to identify a host. A MAC address is the address of the Ethernet interface. It is used within a single network segment to locate a host. ARP maps an IP address to a MAC address for "final delivery" of a packet that has arrived at its destination network.

IP addresses are assigned by a central Internet authority to ensure that each network host has a unique address. If you choose an IP address at random, you'll probably be unable to communicate via the Internet. ISPs are assigned blocks of addresses that they then assign to their customers. Your school or organization probably has a block of addresses assigned. The system administrator can assign you an address from that block.

In an environment that is isolated from all other networks, you can use whatever IP addresses you choose.

NOTE

An IP address is assigned to each network interface in a host. Each address is 32 bits long, made up of four 8-bit numbers separated by periods. The largest possible 8-bit number is 11111111, or 255 in decimal, and the largest possible IP address in decimal is 255.255.255.255. You've probably seen many of these addresses; for example, 192.168.12.254 is a valid IP address. The **dotted-quad** (also called **dotted-decimal**) **notation** shown here—four numbers separated by periods—is commonly used to write IP addresses.

An IP address has two parts, though you wouldn't know by looking at it. The first part of the address is a **network ID** and the last part is a **host ID**. Each network on the Internet has a unique ID, and within each network, each host has a unique ID. Setting off the network as a separate ID makes it possible to find computers all over the world. A simple way to view this is to think of the first three numbers as the network ID and the last number as the host ID, so 192.168.12.254 consists of a network ID (192.168.12.0) and a host ID (254). Whenever you refer to a network ID, you should use a full IP address (all four numbers), but fill in the host ID portion with all zeros. In this case, the last number is the host ID, so in stating the network ID, you would insert a zero in that place. The computer named by this address uses the full IP address of 192.168.12.254; other computers on the same network segment would have a different last number. One might use the address 192.168.12.34, for example.

Reserved Addresses

Some IP addresses are reserved.

- Addresses beginning with 127 are reserved for the local **loopback interface**. The address of the local loopback interface is 127.0.0.1 regardless of operating system. Packets sent to that address never leave the computer. Note that all the other addresses from 127.0.0.2 to 127.255.255.254 may be used for special purposes within the computer.

- An address that has all zeros for its host ID portion refers to the address of the network.

- An address that has all ones for its host ID portion refers to the broadcast address of the network.

- Three address ranges are designated for private use: 10.0.0.0 to 10.255.255.255, 172.16.0.0 to 172.31.255.255, and 192.168.0.0 to 192.168.255.255. Whenever you use these IP addresses, packets should never be routed to the Internet. Private addresses are used on networks that either do not connect to the Internet or use Network Address Translation or NAT to do so.

- Addresses in the range of 169.254.0.0 to 169.254.255.255 are used for Zeroconf or Link-Local addresses. These are used when hosts are configured to fetch addresses from a DHCP server but a server is not available. The host negotiates a Link-Local address. More information is at *www.zeroconf.org*.

NOTE

You don't need permission to use a private IP address on your local network segment. Most of the examples in this book use a private network IP address.

Most networks use one of a few standard network addressing systems, so you rarely need to get out your calculator. But you must still determine how large the network ID and host ID are, based on the networking space assigned to you by your ISP and the number of hosts you want to support in each segment of your network. In addition, the networking software must have some way to know what part of an IP address is the network ID and what part is the host ID. Two methods are used to show this:

- A **subnet mask** is a series of numbers that looks like an IP address but contains 1s for the network ID portion of the address and 0s for the host ID portion of the address. For example, the subnet mask 255.255.255.0 has 24 bits of 1s, so it indicates a 24-bit network ID, and 8 bits of 0s, for an 8-bit host ID. You need to provide a network mask when you configure networking, although a default may be provided by the network configuration tool.

- A prefix length indicator written after a computer's IP address indicates the number of bits used for the network ID. This notation is called **Classless Interdomain Routing** or **CIDR** (pronounced cider) **format**. For example, 192.168.12.254/24 indicates that 24 bits of the address are the network ID and the remaining 8 bits are the host ID. CIDR notation is the preferred way of expressing IP addresses, even though much software doesn't yet support it.

You can use either a subnet mask or CIDR format to indicate a classless address. You will see examples of both throughout this book. Classful addressing was used for many years and many network configuration tools are still based on it, even though networks are now classless.

To help you become familiar with the standard network IDs, Table 1-3 shows commonly used prefix lengths with corresponding network masks.

Table 1-3   Host IDs with varying network prefix lengths

Maximum Number of Hosts	Network Prefix Length	Corresponding Subnet Mask
2	/30	255.255.255.252
6	/29	255.255.255.248
14	/28	255.255.255.240
30	/27	255.255.255.224
62	/26	255.255.255.192
126	/25	255.255.255.128
254	/24	255.255.255.0
510	/23	255.255.254.0
1022	/22	255.255.252.0
2046	/21	255.255.248.0

Broadcasting

In the list of reserved IP addresses in the previous section, recall that when the host ID is all ones, the address is a **broadcast address** for that network. That is, if a host sends a packet to 192.168.12.255, the packet is delivered to all hosts on that network.

A broadcast message is used chiefly for system administration purposes, such as informing everyone that a server is about to shut down. When a packet has a destination address that matches the network broadcast address, every host on the network grabs that packet and passes it to the next higher layer of the networking stack—normally TCP or UDP.

Sometimes a host wants to send a broadcast message to its network, but does not know the address of its network. In this case, it uses the broadcast address 255.255.255.255. Any packet that has this IP address is picked up by every host on the network.

Packets sent to broadcast addresses should *not* be routed outside their network. It would not make sense to do so because hosts on other networks would not receive them. In addition, broadcast packets that go beyond their network can be used by crackers to consume bandwidth on other networks—a denial-of-service attack.

Multicasting

Another type of IP addressing, called **multicasting**, allows a computer to send a packet to multiple specific hosts. To understand why this is valuable, consider this example: You have created a large report that you need to distribute to 5000 hosts around the world. You can't use a broadcast address because most of the hosts are located on separate networks. You would have to send 5000 copies of the report, one to each host. If the report is 22 MB in size, that totals 110,000 MB, or 110 GB of data that must be transmitted.

Multicasting allows you to send a single copy of the report to the Internet with a multicast address that represents the group of all the destination IP addresses. Each router that intercepted the report's packets would determine whether hosts on its networks were part of the destination group and pass those packets on as needed. The report would be replicated (duplicated) at points near the destination hosts, instead of being sent entirely from a central source. This is the idea behind multicasting.

Multicasting is not supported by the entire Internet yet. It requires that routers support multicasting, and not all do. A portion of the Internet that does support multicasting is called MBONE. You can learn more about MBONE by conducting an Internet search for the term. Two sites of interest are *www.savetz.com/mbone* and *graphics.stanford.edu/papers/mbone*.

IPv6

The current version of IP (IPv4) supports roughly 3.7 billion unique addresses. That must have seemed more than sufficient when IPv4 was developed. But because of the incredible growth of the Internet and the many new types of devices that are connecting to the Internet, IPv4 is slowly running out of address space. To cope with this and other technical limitations, a new version of IP, called **IPv6**, has been developed.

The most interesting feature of IPv6 is that it uses 128 bits for addressing, rather than 32 bits. Because each additional bit doubles the number of possible addresses, IPv6 supports over 100 undecillion addresses (a 1 followed by 38 zeros). To represent such a large address space, a hexadecimal-based notation is used. Here's an example of an IPv6 address:

```
ED16:0000:0000:0000:7514:9BCA:EAA8:1989
```

IPv6 addresses normally have numerous contiguous zeros, so there's an abbreviated syntax that removes the zeros. Here's the same IPv6 address as shown previously, but with the zeros removed:

```
ED16::7514:9BCA:EAA8:1989
```

IPv4 addresses will be around for many years even after the conversion to IPv6. IPv6 packets need a way to embed IPv4 addresses. This is done by placing the 32-bit IPv4 address at the end of the IPv6 address. You can then use a mixed notation, as in this example:

```
AD26::4515:AB22:192.168.0.1
```

IPv6 has numerous other enhancements to make multicasting more workable, to allow dynamic configuration of networks, and to allow routers to make more intelligent routing decisions.

IPv6 doesn't throw IPv4 out the window; it just extends its technology and usefulness. ISPs will still assign IP addresses, network and host IDs will still be used, and networks will still become overburdened and slow because of too much traffic. But IPv6 prepares the Internet for the future by upgrading and fixing technical issues that were making it harder to keep networks properly configured and running well. In addition, networking software must be upgraded to support IPv6. Beyond the IP stack itself, upper-layer protocol stacks, such as TCP, must undergo some change to benefit from what IPv6 can offer.

IPv6 is up and running now. You can read all about it, install it on your Linux system, and try it out. But you'll be in the minority. It is not yet widely deployed. Islands of IPv6 are cropping up as people experiment and switch over to the newer, more powerful protocol. Just as there is MBONE for multicasting, there is a 6BONE for IPv6. Over time, the backbone of the Internet will change to IPv6 and eventually islands of IPv4 will remain. At that point, you won't need a 4BONE because IPv6 is compatible with IPv4 packets. You can learn more about IPv6 on Linux by reading the Linux IPv6 HOWTO at *www.tldp.org*.

ICMP

The **Internet Control Message Protocol** or **ICMP** is confusing. Some people consider it a Network-layer protocol—a necessary adjunct to IP. Others consider it a Transport-layer protocol because its data is carried by IP—it appears to be the next layer up from IP. Because its functionality is closely tied to IP and has little or none of the functionality of transport protocols, in this book you can consider ICMP a Network-layer protocol.

ICMP can be thought of as the portion of IP that handles error conditions and testing. The ICMP packet header includes these fields, as shown in Figure 1-16:

- *Type* and *Code* (one byte each) to identify the message being sent
- *Checksum* to verify the integrity of the ICMP packet
- *Sequence number* to order a series of ICMP packets

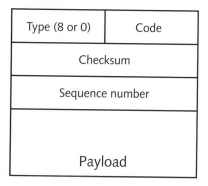

Figure 1-16   Structure of an ICMP packet

The Type field is the most significant—it determines the function of the packet. Common types are Destination Unreachable, Router Advertisement, Time Exceeded, Timestamp, and Traceroute. Some types, such as Destination Unreachable, use the Code field for additional information.

Most of these ICMP message types are handled automatically by IP; a person doesn't generally get involved. Two ICMP types are meant to be used by people—Echo and Echo Reply. These are used by ping programs to test for connectivity between two hosts. Ping commands can include numerous parameters to test for various issues such as timing, routing, and packet fragmentation.

Transport Protocols

In the Internet networking model, the Transport layer focuses on providing a foundation for applications to operate. It provides end-to-end packet delivery services. In the Internet model, the two transport protocols are TCP and UDP. TCP is a connection-oriented protocol and UDP is connectionless.

Connection-oriented and Connectionless

Transport-layer protocols can be connection-oriented or connectionless. A **connection-oriented** protocol must first establish a logical connection between the two communicating hosts before they can exchange data. Thereafter, many packets can be exchanged. All packets are checked for errors and any bad packets are re-sent. Packets that arrive out of order are put in the right order before being delivered to the application program. When the hosts are finished exchanging data, the logical connection is terminated. Connection-oriented protocols offer high delivery assurance.

A **connectionless** protocol sends each packet as an independent (atomic) unit. It has no relationship with any previously sent packet or with any packet sent in the future. A logical connection does not have to be established before the hosts can exchange packets. If a packet is lost en route, the protocol does not recognize the loss and does nothing about it. Connectionless protocols provide low delivery assurance.

It may seem that connection-oriented protocols are the better deal and should be used all the time, but that's not the case. Connectionless protocols have less overhead and fewer delays. Some applications would suffer from time-costly error recovery procedures. For example, listening to a digital audio stream sent over the Internet is better when it is sent connectionless. Infrequent packet errors may not be noticeable by users, but taking the time to recover from them would be.

Ports

Suppose two hosts are communicating using two application protocols, such as HTTP and SMTP. There needs to be some way to direct the HTTP packets to the Web programs and the SMTP packets to the mail programs. Transport-layer protocols handle this by using their own addressing. These addresses are called ports. Each TCP or UDP packet includes a source port and a destination port. The **source port** identifies the application that sent the packet. The **destination port** identifies the application that is to receive the packet.

NOTE

IP addresses identify computers, whereas ports identify the application on the computer that needs the information.

Ports are 16-bit numbers that range from 0 to 65,535. Standard protocols or services have their own port number. For example, Web servers normally use port 80, the default port for HTTP. Mail servers use port 25 for SMTP and port 110 for POP3. Port assignments are made by the Internet Assigned Numbers Authority or IANA. Refer to *www.iana.org/assignments/port-numbers* for a complete list.

There are three ranges of port numbers:

0–1023	Well-known ports
1024–49,151	Registered ports
49,152–65,535	Dynamic or private ports

The well-known ports and registered ports should be used by servers. The dynamic or private ports should be used by clients. Unfortunately, these rules are frequently broken. For example, both Windows and Linux are normally configured so clients incorrectly use registered ports instead of dynamic ports. You pay the price in subtle ways. For example, firewalls cannot provide as much protection as they could when it's uncertain whether packets are coming from clients or servers.

Fortunately, it's easy to configure Linux to use the right ports. This is covered in Chapter 2. It's not so easy with Windows.

The mapping of services to default port numbers is done via the /etc/services file. Programs may refer to this file to determine which port to use for a particular network service. A few lines from the file are shown here:

```
ftp-data     20/tcp
ftp-data     20/udp
ftp          21/tcp
ftp          21/udp
telnet       23/tcp
telnet       23/udp
smtp         25/tcp      mail
smtp         25/udp      mail
```

Each line in /etc/services consists of a service name, a port/protocol block, and any aliases (alternative names) for the service, such as the alias "mail" for the smtp lines in the example. An optional comment may follow the aliases. Although most services use either TCP or UDP as a transport protocol, /etc/services includes a line for both.

If you need to add a service to the file, you can use any text editor to add a line. If you're uncertain about what port number to use, refer to the IANA Web page mentioned earlier in this section.

You can choose to use different port numbers for your servers, but you'll have to tell users about it. For example, if you run your Web server on port 8008, you must tell users that their Web browser must refer to port 8008 by using a URL like this: *www.myserver.com:8008*.

Transmission Control Protocol

The **Transmission Control Protocol** or **TCP** is a connection-oriented transport protocol. Many of the services you are likely to use regularly on the Internet rely on TCP as their transport protocol. These include HTTP (Web), SMTP/POP3/IMAP (e-mail), FTP (file transfers), and many others.

The structure of a TCP packet header is shown in Figure 1-17. Each of the fields is described in the following list.

- *Source port* is the port assigned to the application that created this data.

- *Destination port* is the port assigned to the application that should receive this data. (We hope that an application will be waiting to receive it!)

- *Sequence number* identifies the position within the stream of data for the data in this packet. This allows the TCP stack on the destination computer to reassemble packets in the correct order (because of routing, the packets could arrive out of order). It also allows TCP to see if any packets are missing and request that they be re-sent.

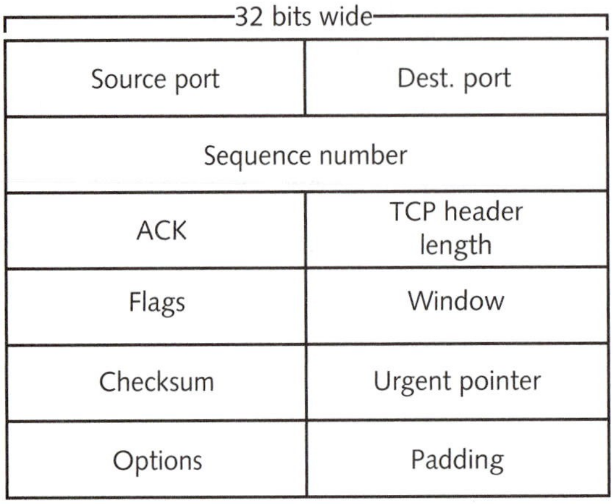

32 bits wide	
Source port	Dest. port
Sequence number	
ACK	TCP header length
Flags	Window
Checksum	Urgent pointer
Options	Padding

Figure 1-17   The fields in the header of a TCP datagram

- *Acknowledgment number (ACK)* confirms that a specific packet was received correctly.

- *TCP header length* defines the length in bytes of the TCP header information. The TCP header is variable because of the Options field (though that field is rarely used).

- *Flags* contains codes that indicate special actions such as starting or ending a TCP connection. These codes are single bits with the names SYN, ACK, FIN, RESET, PUSH, and URGENT. This part of the header also defines the length of the TCP header, which can vary based on the number of options included with the packet.

- *Window* refers to the sliding window size, which defines how many packets the receiving computer is ready to receive and process.

- *Checksum* provides a mathematical method of verifying the integrity of the data contained in the TCP packet. Unlike IP, the checksum in TCP is used to verify the integrity of the payload data, not just the header.

- *Urgent pointer* indicates a range within the payload of the packet where urgent data begins.

- *Options* can define special actions for the TCP stack, but this field is very rarely used.

- *Padding* is used, as in IP, to fill the header up to a 32-bit boundary.

Remember that payload is a flexible term: It refers to whatever a specific protocol needs to transmit. That is, the full TCP packet, both headers and payload, becomes the payload portion of an IP packet. The IP stack takes the TCP packet, adds its own IP header, and passes it on to Ethernet or another Link-layer protocol stack. At the destination computer, the IP stack strips off the IP headers, examines them to find that TCP is the indicated protocol for the payload, and then hands the payload off to the TCP stack. The TCP stack then does the same thing, reviewing the TCP headers and handing the remaining payload to an Application-level protocol.

A computer establishes a TCP connection with another host by using a **three-way handshake**. This is a three-packet sequence as shown in Figure 1-18, where a client connects to a server. The client initiates the handshake by sending a TCP packet with the SYN bit set. The server indicates its willingness to connect by sending the client a TCP packet with the SYN and ACK bits set. Finally, the client acknowledges by sending a TCP packet with the ACK bit set. The TCP connection is now in place and the client and server can exchange packets.

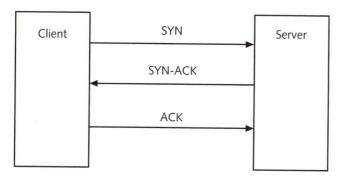

Figure 1-18   A three-way handshake

Either host can tear down the connection in one of two ways. First, the host can send a TCP packet with the FIN bit set. The other host acknowledges this by sending a TCP packet with the ACK bit set. Alternatively, a host can send a TCP packet with the RESET bit set. This is a brute force method that needs no acknowledgment by the other host.

User Datagram Protocol

The **User Datagram Protocol** or **UDP** is a connectionless transport protocol. UDP has low overhead: only 8 bytes per header, plus no network traffic is used for sending acknowledgments. UDP is used by applications that can deal with missing packets or packets arriving out of order. Examples of applications that use UDP include **name servers** and network management utilities, where overhead needs to be low.

Packets sent using a connectionless protocol such as UDP are also referred to as **datagrams**.

TIP

The UDP header includes only four fields. No options are available, so no padding is needed:

- *Source port* to identify the application that is sending the data
- *Destination port* to identify the application that should receive the data
- *Message length* to indicate how many bytes are in the packet
- *Checksum* to correct for network transmission errors

Application Protocols

Application protocols are used by application programs to move data across a network. Table 1-4 lists some of the application protocols that you will read about throughout this book, along with their commonly used port numbers.

Table 1-4   Application protocols commonly used in Linux

Protocol	Purpose	Commonly Used Port
File Transfer Protocol (FTP)	Transfers files from a server to a client	20 (data) 21 (control information)
Secure Shell (SSH)	Creates an encrypted terminal session	22
Network News Transport Protocol (NNTP)	Transfers newsgroup postings from central news servers to other news servers and end users	119
Simple Mail Transport Protocol (SMTP)	Transfers e-mail messages from one host to another	25
Domain Name Service (DNS)	Answers questions about named entities on the network	53
Hypertext Transfer Protocol (HTTP)	Transfers documents from a Web server to client browsers	80
Post Office Protocol 3 (POP3)	Transfers e-mail messages stored on a server to a client for viewing	110

ROUTING CONCEPTS

Most of the discussion so far in this chapter assumes that you are working with a single network segment. Many new issues arise when you need to connect multiple network segments, a more common situation than a single, isolated network segment.

To illustrate some of the issues that arise with connecting network segments, consider the network segments shown in Figure 1-19. Each network segment has a network ID assigned to it. To send packets from Host A to Host B requires that the packets pass through two network segments.

In Figure 1-19, suppose Host A wants to send a packet to Host B. The IP packet contains a destination IP address that refers to a different network from the one on which Host A is located. Because of this, the network stacks on Host A know that the packet must be sent to a **router**—a computer that is connected to more than one network and can forward packets between networks. To **forward** a packet is to transmit it to a different network from the one where it originated. A router is sometimes called a **gateway**, though the term has another more specific meaning, which you will explore in later chapters.

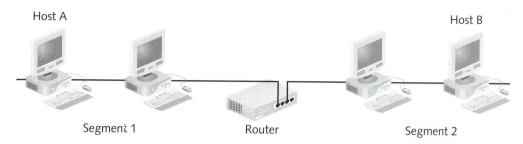

Figure 1-19   Multiple network segments with a router

When you configure Linux networking, you specify the IP address of a computer that can act as a **default router** to other networks. (This is also called the **default gateway** in some Linux documentation.) This is the router used when a packet is addressed to a host that is outside the source host's network. The default router may be connected to just one other network, as in Figure 1–19, or it may provide access to the entire Internet. In any case, the packet from Host A isn't destined for Network A, so it has to go to the router for further processing.

The **default route** is an IP address configured on a host computer that identifies the computer to which packets should be sent when their network is not otherwise known to the host. In Figure 1–20, you see two networks inside an organization, connected by a router. For Host A, the router is configured as the default gateway: Packets addressed to the other internal network are sent on by the router to that network. For the router itself, Host G is an upstream router, or a gateway to networks beyond the organization. Host G is connected only to the router and to the Internet. If a packet arrives at the router and is destined for neither network Segment X nor Segment Y, it is sent by the router to Host G for further routing to the Internet, where it is eventually routed to its correct destination.

Routers use a routing table and a routing algorithm (also called a routing engine) to decide where to send packets. A **routing table** is a listing that contains at least three things:

- The network ID for which a route is being stored, which lets the router identify the network IDs it knows how to reach

- The network interface through which the network ID can be reached; for example, some networks might be reachable through the Ethernet card and others through a dial-in modem connection to the Internet

- The IP address of the upstream router that handles the listed network ID; this field is called the gateway in the output of several Linux commands because it provides a gateway to other networks

Routing tables may contain additional information to help make the best routing decisions. The **routing algorithm** or **routing engine** is software that determines how to process a packet that is sent to the router. The routing engine uses the routing table as data to help make a good routing decision. Routing tables are populated (filled with entries) in two ways.

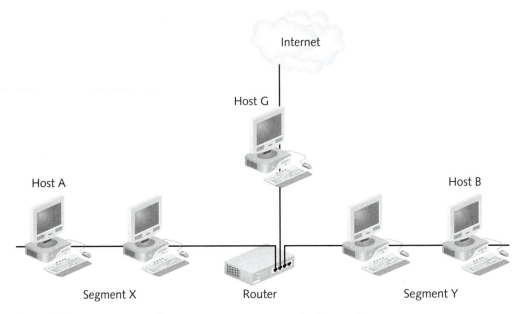

Figure 1-20   A router with a separate gateway to the Internet

- Manually, by a system administrator (such as you) entering a route by which packets can reach a named network ID. This can be done in Linux using the `route` or `ip` commands or a variety of graphical tools that you'll begin exploring in Chapter 2.

- Automatically, by a protocol designed specifically to keep track of how packets are flowing through a network and report that information to a router. The most commonly used routing protocols within organizational networks are the **Routing Information Protocol (RIP)** and the **Open Shortest Path First (OSPF)** protocol. Routing table entries are cached so that they are available for use in routing future packets.

As you configure Linux networking on your system in Chapter 2, you will learn how to use the `route` command to set up manual routes. Every system must act as a router because it must know how to handle packets sent to IP addresses outside the local network. A typical host has a very basic routing engine and expects only manually configured routing table information.

Linux can also act as an automatic router. You might think of this as a "real" router because its goal is to forward traffic between network segments rather than just routing the packets generated by a single host. The Linux program `routed` uses RIP to gather routing information automatically. In later chapters, you'll learn more about routing protocols and setting up Linux routing.

CHAPTER SUMMARY

- By networking computers, users can work more efficiently by sharing data instantly, automating tasks, and using expensive resources more efficiently.

- A terminal acts simply as a remote keyboard and monitor for a system, whereas client/server computing assumes that both systems are intelligent. Although many Linux programs use client/server techniques, Linux is designed for peer-to-peer networking.

- Networking hardware uses various technologies such as Ethernet to send electrical signals over transmission media—cables or wireless systems. Each collection of data is called a packet (or a datagram for connectionless protocols such as UDP).

- Bandwidth of various types of physical networking ranges from just a few kb/s to several Gb/s, though throughput—the amount of useful data received by a remote user—is a better measure of the value of a network in the eyes of most end users.

- Network topologies define the physical and logical layout of a network. Bus, star, and ring network designs are common choices.

- Many types of transmission media are available, such as UTP, fiber optics, and wireless systems.

- Modern networks use different layers of software to handle the different aspects of managing a network connection. Software that handles a networking task is designed around a protocol, or well-defined communication system for that task.

- The OSI and Internet models are two important conceptual layered models of networking.

- Protocols are defined by RFC documents, which are created by technical experts and posted on the Internet for review and comment.

- IP is focused on packet delivery based on source and destination IP addresses.

- IP addressing can be defined with or without using address classes (A, B, C). When classes are not used, a network prefix length must be specified. In either case, an IP address always consists of a network ID and a host ID.

- Fragmentation allows packets with different MTU sizes to be routed across intermediate networks. But fragmentation introduces several inefficiencies and so should be avoided whenever possible.

- Broadcasting and multicasting provide methods of sending IP packets to multiple hosts simultaneously.

- IPv6 provides more addresses and many additional features than IPv4. It is slowly replacing the existing IPv4 infrastructure of the Internet.

- Networking protocols can be connection-oriented or connectionless. Connection-oriented protocols like TCP provide guaranteed delivery of data between two hosts.

❑ TCP and UDP are Transport-layer protocols. TCP is connection-oriented, providing high delivery assurances. UDP is connectionless, providing low delivery assurances.

❑ Many application protocols are used as part of network-aware programs, such as Web servers and e-mail servers.

❑ Routers move packets between network segments. Each router maintains a routing table to identify how to reach various networks. The routing table is filled either by manual entries or by automatic entries generated by a routing protocol such as RIP or OSPF.

KEY TERMS

Address Resolution Protocol (ARP) — A protocol that broadcasts a message to an entire network segment to obtain a host's MAC address.

ARCnet — An older token-passing network technology that has lost a great deal of its former popularity. ARCnet is reliable, but slower than more modern networking technologies like Token-Ring or Ethernet.

Asynchronous Transfer Mode (ATM) — A networking technology used for the Internet backbone or other specialized high-speed networks. It is fast (currently 155 Mb/s with 622 Mb/s under development) but also expensive.

bandwidth — The amount of information that a network technology can transmit; usually expressed in bits per second (b/s).

broadcast address — An IP address in which the host ID consists of all ones, which causes the packet to be sent to every host on the named network.

bus topology — A network topology design in which computers are connected to a single length of cable.

cable modem — A device that supports high-speed networking through a cable television connection, with the cable TV company acting as the ISP.

Classless Interdomain Routing (CIDR) format — A method of indicating the network prefix length of an IP address by writing it with a slash following the address (for example, 192.168.14.45/24).

client — A computer or software program that requests information or service from a server and then processes or acts on the information it receives.

client/server — A model of computing in which information is shared between networked systems by multiple clients requesting information from a server.

coaxial cable (coax) — A network transmission medium (a cable) made up of a single, thick copper wire encased in thick plastic and foil layers of insulation. Coax is used mostly for video signals, though many people now have Internet access available via a cable modem using coax cable.

collision — The result when two or more Ethernet packets attempt to use an Ethernet cable at the same time.

connectionless — A protocol that sends packets without regard to whether they are correctly received by the destination computer. IP and UDP are examples.

connection-oriented — A protocol that keeps track of which packets have been correctly received by the destination computer, resending those that are not received, managing the flow of packets, and reporting errors.

datagram — A network packet sent over a connectionless protocol such as UDP.

default gateway — *See* default router.

default route — An IP address configured on a host computer that identifies the computer to which packets should be sent when their network is not known to the host.

default router — The router to which a packet is sent if a host has no idea where else to send it. Also called the *default gateway*.

destination port — A port that identifies the application that is to receive the packet.

digital subscriber line (DSL) — A relatively new digital telephone service that can be added to existing telephone lines in some areas; used for relatively fast Internet connections.

Domain Name Service (DNS) — The name normally used to refer to the name service used by the Internet (BIND).

dotted-quad (dotted-decimal) notation — A method of writing IP addresses as four numbers separated by periods.

dumb terminal — *See* terminal.

Ethernet — An international networking standard developed in the 1970s by Xerox, Intel, and Digital Equipment Corporation (now part of Compaq Computer Corp.).

Fiber Distributed Data Interface (FDDI) — A networking technology that uses fiber-optic cable in a dual-ring topology. It is highly reliable, but not installed much now because it is slower and more expensive than newer Ethernet technologies.

fiber-optic — A network transmission medium (a cable) made of glass or plastic to transmit light signals; it is capable of extremely fast transmission speeds, immune from electromagnetic interference, and highly secure. It is also very expensive to install.

fixed wireless — A wireless network communication technology that relies on small transceivers mounted on buildings; it is normally used to connect multiple offices in the same city.

forward — The process of sending a packet to a different network than the one from where it originated.

fragmentation — The process of breaking up an IP packet into multiple smaller packets for transmission on a different type of network.

gateway — Generally, a router that can forward packets to other network segments. Also, the default router that acts as a "gateway" or exit point to reach networks outside of a local segment. Also, more technically, a system that can translate between protocols at the Transport and Application layers of a network.

Gb/s — Gigabits per second. 1 Gb/s is 1024 Mb/s or roughly a billion bits per second.

Gigabit Ethernet — An Ethernet networking technology that can transmit data at either 1 Gb/s or 10 Gb/s.

hardware address — *See* Media Access Control (MAC) address.

header — The highly structured information within a packet that defines how the network stacks should handle the packet.

Header checksum — A numeric code within an IP packet header used to ensure the integrity of the header information.

host — A device on the network, such as a workstation, server, or printer.

host ID — The part of an IP address that designates the host to which the address refers within a certain network.

hub — A device used as a wiring center that allows cables from multiple computers to be concentrated into a single network connection.

Integrated Services Digital Network (ISDN) — A type of telephone service that provides digital signals for higher-speed network connectivity than standard modems.

interface — A computer's networking port or connection.

Internet — A collection of many networks around the world that are linked together via high-speed networking connections.

Internet Control Message Protocol (ICMP) — A protocol used by IP to transmit control and error data about IP traffic on a network. Most widely known as the basis of the `ping` utility, which uses ICMP Echo and Echo-request commands.

Internet model — A conceptual model of networking that divides protocols into four layers based on their function. This is the model used by Linux.

Internet Protocol (IP) — The foundation protocol for transporting data across most Linux networks as well as the Internet.

IP address — A numbering scheme that allows each computer in the world that wants to use the Internet (or just IP) to have a unique ID number.

IPv6 — The new version of IP that uses 128 bits for addresses instead of 32 bits, and adds numerous other features, including dynamic configuration capabilities, better security options, and more intelligent packet routing. Using IPv6 requires many changes to other protocols, as well as generally more sophistication in networking hardware and software.

kb/s — Kilobits per second. 1 kb/s is 1000 bits per second.

last mile connection — The connection between a LAN within a home or office and the Internet or other high-speed network.

loopback interface — Any IP address beginning with 127 (127.0.0.1 is normally used). This address is used only within a computer for testing the network stacks. No packet with a 127 address is ever sent out of the local computer.

maximum transmission unit (MTU) — The maximum size for a packet on a given type of network.

Mb/s — Megabits per second. 1 Mb/s is 1000 kb/s, or exactly one million bits per second.

Media Access Control (MAC) address — A unique address assigned to (and programmed into) each Ethernet card in the world.

multicasting — An IP addressing system in which one computer can address a packet to multiple specific hosts.

name server — A computer running name service software that can translate from IP addresses to names and vice versa.

network ID — The part of an IP address that designates the network to which the address refers.

network interface card (NIC) — A hardware device used to connect a computer to a network.

Open Shortest Path First (OSPF) — A protocol that automatically fills routing tables with information about how to reach networks.

Open Systems Interconnection (OSI) reference model — A reference model that divides networking into seven conceptual layers, each assigned a specific task. The OSI model is the basis for much of modern networking theory and system design.

packet — A small collection of data with identifying information (headers) that is destined for or coming from a network.

payload — The data that a network packet is transferring. Packets are divided into a header and payload.

peer-to-peer network — A model of networking in which all computers on the network are peers and have the ability to initiate communications, respond to requests for information, and interact with users independent of other computer systems.

protocol — A formalized system of rules for communication.

protocol stack — The software for maintaining a network protocol. A stack may refer to a single protocol capability or to the collection of protocols supported by a host or server.

Request for Comments (RFC) — A document describing a protocol or other technical advance, written by a technical expert and posted on the Internet for review. It then becomes the accepted definition for the protocol or standard it describes.

ring topology — A network topology design in which multiple computers are linked into a circular shape.

router — A device that connects multiple network segments, translating data formats as needed by forwarding packets between segments; also the software program on a computer used for this purpose.

routing algorithm — The software that determines how to process a packet that is sent to the router for forwarding; also called a *routing engine*.

routing engine — *See* routing algorithm.

Routing Information Protocol (RIP) — A protocol that automatically fills routing tables with information about how to reach networks.

routing table — A listing within a router containing network IDs, the network interface by which packets can reach that network, and the IP address of the next router to which the packet should be sent.

segment — A part of a network whose traffic has been isolated from other parts of the network to improve the efficiency of the network as a whole. Each segment's network traffic is only "seen" within that segment unless it is destined for a host outside the segment.

server — A computer or software program that provides information or services of some type to clients.

shielded twisted pair (STP) — A type of network transmission media (a cable) made up of several pairs of wires encased in foil-wrapped insulation to block interference by electromagnetic radiation.

source port — A port that identifies the application that sent the packet.

star topology — A network topology design in which multiple computers connect to a single center point, usually a hub or a switch.

subnet mask — A set of numbers similar in appearance to an IP address, used to denote how many bits of an IP address are part of the network ID. Any bit set (1, not 0) in the subnet mask is part of the network ID; used for class-based IP addressing.

switch — A device used to connect other networking devices (such as hosts or printers) into a larger network using built-in intelligence to decide which network packets should be sent to which parts of the network.

TCP/IP model — *See* Internet model.

terminal — A screen and keyboard attached to a computer, usually at a distance from the computer. Multiple terminals attached to the same computer allow multiple people to access the computer at the same time; also known as *dumb terminal*.

terminal emulation — A software program that allows a personal computer (or other intelligent device) to act like a terminal in connecting to another computer.

three-way handshake — A procedure used by TCP to establish a connection.

throughput — The amount of useful payload information that can be transmitted on a network.

Time to Live (TTL) — A counter within an IP packet header that determines how many hops (routers) a packet can pass through before being discarded as "destination unreachable."

token — An electronic code that is passed from computer to computer to identify which computer on the network has the right to send out a packet at that moment. Used by certain types of networks such as Token-Ring.

Token-Ring — A popular networking technology developed by IBM in the early 1980s. It uses a token-passing technique.

topology — A shape or ordering applied to the connections between systems on a network.

Transmission Control Protocol (TCP) — A widely used connection-oriented Transport-layer protocol. TCP is the transport mechanism for many popular Internet services such as FTP, SMTP, and HTTP (Web) traffic.

unshielded twisted pair (UTP) — A type of network transmission medium (a cable) made up of four pairs of wires encased in plastic insulation. UTP comes in six categories, with Category 6 or CAT6 being the highest quality, and supports the highest speed.

User Datagram Protocol (UDP) — A fast, connectionless Transport-layer protocol.

wireless LAN (WLAN) — A wireless network designed to be used within a small radius of a central transceiver.

REVIEW QUESTIONS

1. By maintaining state information, the _____ protocol is able to _____ .

   a. TCP; guarantee packet delivery by tracking packet acknowledgments
   b. ICMP; report errors in IP transmissions
   c. TCP; avoid the need to use a checksum field
   d. IP; retransmit packets that are dropped by routing processes

2. The unit kb/s refers to:

   a. a quantity of exactly 1000 bits
   b. a data rate of 1000 bits sent each second
   c. a quantity of exactly 1024 bits
   d. a data rate of 1024 bits sent each second

3. Each Ethernet card has a number assigned to it by the manufacturer. This is called the:

   a. NIC Header checksum
   b. Ethernet cyclic redundancy check
   c. Data Link protocol
   d. Media Access Control (MAC) address

4. A UDP packet is also called:

   a. an envelope
   b. a datagram
   c. a nybble
   d. a fresnel

5. Assuming you have moved into a new building that already contains CAT5 UTP cable to each office, which of the following network technologies might you choose to set up the new network?

   a. FDDI, because the cost of existing cabling could be deducted from the total cost of the project
   b. a wireless system, in case you need to expand the network to off-site locations
   c. not Ethernet, because the star configuration required for Ethernet would not be feasible using UTP cable
   d. Ethernet, because the existing cable could provide a high-speed network without the expense of rewiring

6. Each entry in a routing table consists of at least the following three items:

   a. a network ID, a checksum, and the interface through which the network can be reached

   b. a default fault for the local network segment, a header for the routing protocol being used, and optional flags

   c. a network ID, a network interface, and the IP address of the next hop router

   d. a network ID, a network interface, and a routing engine

7. Which of the following IP addresses indicates a 24-bit network ID with a CIDR-format network prefix?

   a. 192.168.14.5/24

   b. 192.168.14.8/255.255.255.0

   c. 192.168.14.0/8

   d. 192.168.14.24/255.255.240.0

8. Name services such as DNS are used to:

   a. translate between human-readable domain names and IP addresses

   b. translate headers between levels of the network architecture

   c. assign packet IDs to each session initiated by the TCP stack

   d. locate services available on the worldwide Internet

9. A default route is normally defined at the same time Linux networking is configured on any host. This allows Linux to:

   a. accumulate routing table information passed on by a routing protocol such as RIP

   b. avoid duplicate packets being sent to the local segment and to the correct remote segment

   c. respond automatically to ISP requests for routing information

   d. act as a router, sending packets addressed to other segments to the "gateway" out of the local segment

10. Multiple network segments are often better than one large network segment because:

    a. A single large segment does not have to bear all the network traffic of an entire organization.

    b. Parts of a network can be configured with different networking hardware or security features.

    c. Routers can defragment packets more efficiently because the segments are smaller.

    d. a, b, and c

    e. only a and c

    f. only a and b

1

11. If an IP stack does not have the MAC address of the system it needs to communicate with, it must:

   a. Send the packet in question to the default router, which has the MAC address for the system noted in the destination IP address.

   b. Consult the routing engine tables to obtain the correct IP address, which includes the MAC address as well.

   c. Consider fragmenting the packet so that it can travel across intermediate network segments without the use of standard IP header information.

   d. Use ARP to obtain the MAC address directly, caching it for future communications with the same remote system.

12. The ICMP protocol:

   a. maps MAC addresses to IP addresses

   b. handles TCP keep-alive requests

   c. manages IP connection-oriented state information

   d. reports IP error conditions and is used for testing

13. Packets for any networking layer consist of:

   a. a collision field and a Header checksum field

   b. a header and payload

   c. both TCP and UDP headers

   d. fragmentation offsets, if required by intervening segments with a smaller MTU

14. The broadcast IP address for a local network is:

   a. a method of distributing a packet from one source host to multiple, specifically named destination hosts

   b. 255.255.255.255

   c. dependent on the routing protocol

   d. the appropriate network prefix with the host ID set to all zeros

15. Ports are used by TCP and UDP to:

   a. attach security information to lower-level IP packets

   b. autoconfigure TCP header information

   c. identify a remote host by a specific Ethernet hardware address

   d. provide an application-to-application path for network packets

16. Some applications prefer to use UDP instead of TCP, even though TCP provides guaranteed packet delivery, because:

   a. UDP has lower network overhead, with smaller packet headers and less computation for packet tracking.

   b. UDP is able to interact more directly with the IP protocol, thus providing better throughput than TCP.

   c. UDP is a more secure protocol for Internet traffic.

   d. UDP prevents fragmentation by creating smaller default packets for IP to hand off to the local network segment.

17. The TTL field in an IP packet is used to:

   a. hold a "hop counter" that is decremented each time a packet passes through a router

   b. provide error checking for the packet

   c. keep track numerically of a sequence of packets that were fragmented to pass through an intermediate segment with a smaller MTU

   d. identify the upper-layer protocol that the payload should be handed to after IP packet headers are stripped off for processing

18. A dumb terminal is called "dumb" because it:

   a. typically has no storage device, such as a hard drive

   b. is not connected to the Internet

   c. cannot understand natural language queries

   d. does not have a CPU that can process data received from another computer

19. The software that provides network protocol capabilities on a system is called, in general terms:

   a. the protocol stack

   b. the routing engine

   c. the routing algorithm

   d. the fragmentation offset

20. Connectionless protocols are used when:

   a. The HTTP protocol is the only one you'll be using.

   b. Guaranteed delivery of packets is managed by an application rather than a Transport-layer network protocol.

   c. Full state information must be maintained for network connection.

   d. IPv6 may be required at a future date.

21. A network's topology defines its:

   a. logical and physical layout

   b. networking layers

   c. application port configurations

   d. IP addressing headers

22. What is the name of the procedure TCP uses to establish a connection?
    a. CIDR
    b. three-way handshake
    c. datagram
    d. token-passing

23. The chief advantages of using fiber-optic cable include:
    a. ability to upgrade the cabling to new topologies as faster networking technologies make FDDI obsolete
    b. limited bend radius and high tensile strength
    c. low cost compared to CAT6 UTP
    d. imperviousness to electromagnetic interference and difficulty of eavesdropping

24. Terminal emulation is available in many operating systems via:
    a. popular software programs like minicom in Linux or HyperTerminal in Windows
    b. hardware add-ons such as FireWire cards
    c. dumb terminals in the typical computer lab
    d. the IP and TCP networking stacks

25. A CIDR-formatted address indicates:
    a. The information has been cached as a MAC address.
    b. A broadcast address must be used to reach the host.
    c. A network prefix length has been appended to the IP address.
    d. A subnet mask has been appended to the IP address.

HANDS-ON PROJECTS

HANDS-ON
PROJECTS

Project 1-1

In this project, you review RFC documents for some of the protocols described in this chapter. To complete this project, you need a Web browser with an Internet connection.

1. Start your Web browser and enter the address *www.rfc-editor.org*.

2. Click the link to search for an RFC.

3. Search for RFC number 792.

4. Click the result returned by your search to view RFC 792.

5. After RFC 792 is downloaded, browse through it. What are the purposes of this protocol as outlined in the Introduction? How many message types are supported by this protocol?

6. Press the browser's **Back** button twice to return to the Searching and Retrieving screen.

7. Enter **HTTP** in the search text field.

8. On the right side, select **Search: RFC**; **RFC Contents via: HTTP**; and **Show Abstract: On**.

9. Click **Search**.

10. Review the results screen. Select one that looks interesting and click its link to read more about it. RFC 2616 is the main HTTP protocol definition standard.

Project 1-2

In this project, you calculate the address size needed for a small network. You need a pencil and paper to complete this project.

1. For this project, suppose you anticipate a network segment size of a maximum of 50 hosts. Using the information earlier in the chapter, find the number of binary bits required to represent that many hosts by seeing what power of 2 will reach or exceed 50.

   a. You know that 2^6 (2 X 2 X 2 X 2 X 2 X 2) = 64, and that 64-2 = 62. The host ID for your segment needs to be 6 bits long. Seven bits will provide space for 128-2=126 hosts, which is more than you need; 5 bits will only allow 32-2 = 30 hosts, which is not enough.

   b. Because 6 bits are needed for the host ID, 32-6, or 26 bits of a 32-bit IP address, remain for use as the network ID. So you will add a /26 after the IP address to indicate the network prefix length.

   c. Suppose that you are using a private network address, 192.168, as your IP address range. A sample address might be 192.168.1.104/26. By reviewing the bit values in the last number, 104, you see that they are:

   0 1 1 0 1 0 0 0

   The far left two bits are part of the network ID. Only the last 6 bits form the host ID. The host ID here includes bits valued at 8 and 32, so the host ID value is 40.

2. Refer to the "Reserved Addresses" section in this chapter and determine what classful-style subnet mask would correspond to a 26-bit network prefix length.

Project 1-3

In this project, you research wireless Ethernet on the Web. To complete this project, you need a Web browser with an Internet connection.

1. Start your Web browser and enter the address *www.google.com*.

2. Enter **802.11** and press **Enter**.

3. Choose a few of the results and click the links. Become familiar with the various types of wireless Ethernet, such as 802.11a, 802.11b, and 802.11g.

4. Go back to the Google window and enter **802.11 security**. Press **Enter**.

5. Choose a few of the results and click the links. Become familiar with the various security features and problems of wireless Ethernet, such as WEP.

6. Go back to the Google window and enter **war driving**. Press **Enter**.

7. Choose a few of the results and click the links. Learn what war driving means, and learn the software tools used to crack wireless networks.

CASE PROJECTS

CASE PROJECTS

Case Project 1-1

You have been asked to consult for a medium-sized federal government agency. The agency is opening a new office because its current office is overcrowded. You are told that the agency will be renting space in a standard office building. The building is about eight years old and was originally wired with UTP cable, though you aren't told any more details about the state of the existing wiring.

1. Some pieces of this puzzle are still missing. What questions will you want to ask of the agency directors and of the technical people assigned to the project before beginning your analysis for network design? If some of that information is not directly available from them, what steps will you take to obtain the data you need to make a solid analysis of the situation and create a preliminary design?

2. What assumptions might you make about this project based on who your client is? How will those assumptions fit into your design?

3. After turning in your first draft, you are informed that this office will be hosting a Web site that will contain a publicly downloadable video clip library and photo archive from government projects that the agency has directed over the past 10 years or so. How will your network design need to change? If a great deal of change is needed, how might you have planned your original design to make it fit the new requirements more easily? What trade-offs does that force you to make?

4. Visit the site *www.6bone.net* and review the description documents regarding IPv6. Does IPv6 sound like a good fit for this project? Why or why not?

2

CONFIGURING BASIC NETWORKING

After reading this chapter and completing the exercises, you will be able to:

♦ Describe how network interfaces are initialized

♦ Configure network interfaces using scripts and text-mode utilities

♦ Configure Linux networking using popular graphical utilities

♦ Effectively use networking utilities to test a network and troubleshoot networking problems

♦ Understand the IPX and AppleTalk protocols

In this chapter, you will learn how the networking principles in Chapter 1 are implemented in Linux, and how to configure Linux networking. This configuration can be accomplished using simple command-line tools or any of several graphical tools. Modern Linux distributions typically include at least one graphical tool.

In the second part of this chapter, you will learn about the basic networking utilities—most of which are command-line tools—and how to test and troubleshoot a network using these tools. Finally, you will learn a little more about other protocols that are occasionally used in Linux to connect with other types of networks. These protocols include IPX and AppleTalk.

INITIALIZING NETWORK INTERFACES

When Linux boots up, it will probably recognize your network interface hardware, install the appropriate drivers, and configure the interfaces so they're ready to use. When it doesn't happen this way, you'll have to troubleshoot to find out why. Troubleshooting requires that you know how to identify network hardware and load the drivers.

The first step is to see whether Linux recognized the interface hardware when it booted up. If you're running a Linux kernel earlier than 2.6, you have to look in the /proc/net/dev file to see the interfaces. The lines in this file are too long to display in the limited space on this page. Look at the file on your system by entering this command:

```
cat /proc/net/dev
```

You'll see the interface names, such as lo and eth0, at the start of each of the displayed lines. You can ignore the rest of the lines.

If you're running a 2.6 kernel or later, you can more easily see the network interface names listed in the /sys/class/net directory. Here's an example of what you'll see if you display the contents of this directory:

```
eth0 eth1 lo
```

This shows that there are two physical Ethernet interfaces (eth0 and eth1) and a local loopback interface (lo). If you know that your computer has a network interface but you don't see its name in one of these files, it means the interface driver is not loaded.

Interface Names

Network interfaces have default names. The first Ethernet interface is called **eth0**, the second is called eth1, and so on. Token-Ring interfaces are called tr0, tr1, and so on. Table 2-1 provides a partial list of networking interfaces used by Linux.

Table 2-1   Examples of Linux interface names

Interface Name	Description
eth0	Ethernet interface
tr0	Token-Ring interface
lo	Local loopback interface
ppp0	Point-to-Point Protocol
slip	Serial Line Internet Protocol
plip	Parallel Line Internet Protocol
arc0	ARCnet interface
fddi0	FDDI interface
dlci0	Frame relay interface
ippp0	Integrated Services Digital Network (ISDN) modem

You can change the interface names to suit your taste by using the **ip** program. You'll have to be logged on as root to make changes. If you want to rename the eth0 interface, you must first take the interface down:

```
ip link set eth0 down
```

change its name:

```
ip link set eth0 name inside
```

then bring the renamed interface back up:

```
ip link set inside up
```

You can display information about the renamed interfaces by using either the ip or the ifconfig programs. Here's an example of using the ip program:

```
ip link show inside
2:  inside: <BROADCAST,MULTICAST,UP> mtu 1500 qdisc
pfifo_fast qlen 1000
        link/ether 00:01:02:ed:b3:bb brd ff:ff:ff:ff:ff:ff
```

Here's an example of using the ifconfig program:

```
ifconfig inside
inside  Link encap:Ethernet HWaddr 00:01:02:ED:B3:BB
        inet addr:192.168.1.1 Bcast:192.168.1.255
Mask:255.255.255.0
        UP BROADCAST RUNNING MULTICAST MTU:1500 Metric:1
        RX packets:421 errors:0 dropped:0 overruns:0 frame:0
        TX packets:19 errors:0 dropped:0 overruns:0 carrier:0
        collisions:0 txqueuelen:100
        RX bytes:49814 (48.6 Kb) TX bytes:1434 (1.4 Kb)
        Interrupt:11 Base address:0x1400
```

Most Linux users and programmers do not rename their interfaces and many do not know that you can. Consequently, some programs that refer to network interfaces by name only recognize the default names.

Multiple Interfaces

If your computer has only one Ethernet interface, there's no doubt that it will be called eth0. If the computer has two or more interfaces, you face the challenge of determining which of the physical connectors belongs to eth0, which belongs to eth1, and so on. When Linux boots up, it locates the interfaces and loads drivers for them. The order in which the drivers are loaded determines the interface naming.

Normally, you have no choice about which of the interfaces is detected first and, consequently, the names of the physical interfaces. The order in which the interfaces are detected is determined by your computer's Plug and Play logic in the case of PCI interfaces and by hardware settings (base I/O address) in the case of non-Plug and Play interfaces, such as ISA bus cards.

The most reliable way of determining which connectors belong to which interface names is to connect another computer to each interface and see if the computers can ping one another. After you've determined which physical connectors are associated with the interface names and you connect the appropriate cables, they should stay the same when you reboot as long as you do nothing to change the way the interfaces are detected.

Adding a new interface to your computer can cause existing interfaces to be renamed when the system boots up. Whenever you add another interface, you should verify that the connectors are still associated with the same interface names. If you don't, you won't be the first person to spend hours troubleshooting a problem that is solved by moving the cables to the proper connectors.

Interface Drivers

Network interfaces use device drivers that are implemented as kernel modules. The modules are usually loaded at system start-up but can be loaded or unloaded while Linux is running. You can see which modules are loaded with the **lsmod** command. You'll see a list of modules displayed that include those needed to support the interface. Here's an example of a module used to support Intel Gigabit Ethernet interfaces:

```
e1000          76956    2    (autoclean)
```

How do you know that the e1000 module is used by Intel Gigabit Ethernet interfaces? You learn it with experience. Until you have that experience, you should use Internet search engines, such as Google, to find out. Before you use Google, you must know what network interface you have. If you purchased a network interface card and plugged it in to your computer, you probably know the manufacturer and model. If the interface is built in to your computer, such as a notebook computer, you might not know.

You can see what interfaces are inside your computer by running the lspci program. Look for one or more lines that contain the words *Ethernet controller* (in the case of Ethernet). The following is an example of one such line:

```
0000:00:04.0 Ethernet controller: Silicon Integrated Systems
[SiS] SiS900 PCI Ethernet
```

You can then use Google to search for *sis900 ethernet linux*. The SiS900 Ethernet page will probably appear at the top of the list. Click the link and the page will tell you about the SiS900 driver. With this information, you can try loading the driver (module) by using the modprobe program:

```
modprobe sis900
```

The **modprobe** command automatically handles dependencies. It loads any other modules that are required. The module initializes the interface hardware. If everything is successful, the command prompt returns after the modprobe command with no additional output. No news is good news.

The **insmod** command also loads kernel modules but it doesn't handle dependencies. The modprobe command is usually the better choice.

Chances are good that the driver/module will load properly and you'll see the interface name appear in the /sys/class/net directory or when you run the **ifconfig** or **ip link** commands. One problem you might have is that the module is not present on your system. The obvious solution is to locate a copy of the module by doing another Google search, downloading it, and installing it on your system.

Kernel modules are located in a directory somewhere below the **/lib/modules** directory. The exact location varies according to your Linux distribution and the kernel version you are using. On a Fedora Core system, the interface modules are in the directory:

```
/lib/modules/2.6.10-1.766_FC3/kernel/drivers/net
```

When you load a kernel module, you don't need to specify the path to the module's directory. The modprobe command is aware of the location of the modules on your system. You also don't need to include the ".o" or ".ko" file extension that you see in the modules' filenames. All you need is the name of the module, as shown in the following examples.

Interface drivers do not need to be implemented as kernel modules. You can recompile the kernel with the drivers compiled into a monolithic kernel. Directions for doing this are provided in Chapter 4 of the *Guide to Linux Installation and Administration* (Course Technology, ISBN 0-619-13095-4) or the kernel-HOWTO document on *www.tldp.org*.

ISA Bus Interfaces

Network interfaces that are **ISA bus** cards might require that you specify details such as the I/O address, interrupt number, and DMA channel. You can specify these as command-line parameters with the modprobe command. For example, to specify interrupt 15 and I/O address 300:

```
modprobe ne2000 irq=15 io=0x300
```

Alternatively, you can specify them in a configuration file that modprobe uses. This file may be called /etc/modprobe.conf or /etc/modules.conf. Older Linux systems may use the /etc/conf.modules file. The file might look like this:

```
alias eth0 3c59x
options 3c59x irq=15 io=0x300
```

The statements that you can include in this file, and their syntax, are documented in the man page for the appropriate configuration file. For a system that uses /etc/modules.conf, refer to the modules.conf man page.

Some modules allow parameters that are unique to the network hardware. To learn about the parameters that may be applicable to the module you need to use, refer to the kernel documentation at *www.tldp.org/HOWTO/Module-HOWTO*. This document includes a list of networking modules and their valid parameters.

Special-purpose Interfaces

Some of the interface names in Table 2-1 are for special purposes and are described in more detail here:

- **Point-to-Point Protocol (PPP)**—This protocol connects two hosts together. PPP can operate over several types of hardware. The most common use of PPP is to create a network connection over a modem to reach an Internet service provider (ISP). Depending on the type of connection you have, you might have something like PPP over Ethernet. For example, if you are using a digital subscriber line (DSL) or a cable modem from your telephone or cable television company (acting as your ISP), you might be connecting a special modem to your Ethernet card and creating a PPP connection to the ISP. PPP is covered in detail in Chapter 3.

- **Serial Line Internet Protocol (SLIP)**—You can use this protocol to transmit network data over a serial port, rather than a special networking cable. SLIP is used with a modem to connect to an ISP, but has been superseded by PPP, which is more flexible. SLIP is still fully supported in Linux.

- **Parallel Line Internet Protocol (PLIP)**—Similar to SLIP, this protocol uses a parallel port as a network interface. PLIP allows you to connect two computers using a parallel cable. Because this is a parallel interface, bytes are sent—not a serial bit stream. The data rate depends on the speed of both parallel ports, but can reach about 20 kB/s.

- **Integrated Services Digital Network (ISDN)**—This is a special type of telephone service that is widely used in Europe. ISDN is available in much of the United States, but is less favored now that DSL and cable modems provide faster service for lower cost. (ISDN provides 128- or 144-kb/s bandwidth, compared to speeds up to 10 times that or more for DSL and cable modems.) ISDN cards work like modems, using a PPP-type networking device. Linux has good ISDN support. Detailed information, including a list of ISDN hardware supported by Linux, is available at *www.isdn4linux.de/faq*.

- Several other types of high-speed networking connections are supported by Linux, though a complete explanation of them is beyond the scope of this book. For example, you can use a **frame relay** card to connect to an ISP using a **T-1** line from your telephone company. T-1 provides a speed of 1.544 Mb/s, usually for a few hundred dollars per month. A **T-3** line provides 45 Mb/s, but usually costs many thousands of dollars per month.

CONFIGURING NETWORKING WITH COMMAND-LINE UTILITIES

2

Linux distributions use the same commands and similar scripts to configure and control networking. The two traditional commands are `ifconfig` and `route`. These are replaced by the newer `ip` command; the `ip` program is part of the new IPROUTE2 package.

Using the `ifconfig` Command

The `ifconfig` program is the traditional way of viewing and controlling network interfaces. If you enter the `ifconfig` command with no command-line parameters, you'll see a list of all the interfaces that have drivers loaded and their status:

```
ifconfig
eth0 Link encap:Ethernet HWaddr 00:10:5A:9E:9D:6F
     inet addr:192.168.100.10 Bcast:192.168.100.255 Mask:255.255.255.0
     UP BROADCAST RUNNING MULTICAST MTU:1500 Metric:1
     RX packets:421 errors:0 dropped:0 overruns:0 frame:0
     TX packets:19 errors:0 dropped:0 overruns:0 carrier:0
     collisions:0 txqueuelen:100
     RX bytes:49814 (48.6 Kb) TX bytes:1434 (1.4 Kb)
     Interrupt:11 Base address:0x1400

lo   Link encap:Local Loopback
     inet addr:127.0.0.1 Mask:255.0.0.0
     UP LOOPBACK RUNNING MTU:16436 Metric:1
     RX packets:52 errors:0 dropped:0 overruns:0 frame:0
     TX packets:52 errors:0 dropped:0 overruns:0 carrier:0
     collisions:0 txqueuelen:0
     RX bytes:3428 (3.3 Kb) TX bytes:3428 (3.3 Kb)
```

If you haven't yet loaded a kernel module for your interface, it will not appear in the output. You should still see the loopback interface, as indicated by the **lo** in the left column of the output. The loopback interface doesn't exist physically—it's a logical interface used for testing and by daemons or applications for communicating within the computer. The loopback interface typically uses the 127.0.0.1 IP address.

The status information may seem cryptic. Here's an explanation.

- `Link encap`—Stands for link encapsulation. For Ethernet interfaces, it typically shows "Ethernet."

- `HWaddr`—Indicates the hardware address or MAC address of the interface.

- `inet addr`—Indicates the IPv4 address of the interface.

- `Bcast`—Indicates the broadcast address of the interface.

- `Mask`—Indicates the subnet or network mask of the interface.

- `UP`—Indicates the interface is up. You can take the interface down with an `ifconfig` command.

- BROADCAST—Indicates that the interface supports broadcasting.

- MULTICAST—Indicates that the interface supports multicasting.

- LOOPBACK—Indicates the interface is a loopback device.

- MTU—Stands for maximum transmission unit—the maximum size of a frame (packet) the interface supports. The MTU for Ethernet always defaults to 1500, though you could change it to avoid fragmentation if most of your traffic had to pass through a network segment with a smaller MTU.

- **Metric**—Determines the cost of a route that uses this interface. It is normally set to 1, but it can be set to a higher value to make the route less attractive. It is used for routing purposes.

- RX packets—Indicates the number of packets that have been received while the interface has been up.

- TX packets—Indicates the number of packets that have been transmitted while the interface has been up.

- collisions—The number of specific collision errors (remember that Ethernet packets collide if multiple NICs try to use the cable at the same instant).

- txqueuelen—Indicates how many packets the network interface can store for transmission while waiting to actually send the packets on a busy network.

- RX bytes:—Indicates the number of bytes that have been received by the interface. Following that number, you may see another number in parentheses that displays the same information in a more convenient unit, such as MB for megabytes. Recent versions of the ifconfig program display MiB, which stands for mibibytes—a measure of megabytes that is based on binary, not decimal. A mibibyte is 1,048,576 bytes, not 1,000,000.

- TX bytes—Indicates the number of bytes that have been transmitted by the interface.

- Interrupt—Indicates the interrupt or IRQ of the interface hardware.

- Base address—Indicates the I/O address of the interface hardware.

- Memory: The memory address range of the interface hardware. This is not displayed if the hardware does not use memory for communicating with the operating system.

You can display the status of only one interface by specifying it like this:

```
ifconfig eth0
```

You can configure and control an interface by specifying the interface name followed by an option. For example, this command stops the eth0 interface:

```
ifconfig eth0 down
```

To start it again, enter this command:

```
ifconfig eth0 up
```

You can configure the interface IP settings like this:

```
ifconfig eth0 192.168.0.1 netmask 255.255.255.0 broadcast
192.168.0.255
```

You can use numerous options with `ifconfig`. Refer to the man page for more details.

NOTE

When you change the status of an interface that is used to reach your default gateway, the default gateway is deleted. It has to be configured again with the `route` or `ip` command.

Using the `route` Command

The **route** program is the traditional way to view and configure the routing table. The routing table determines where packets are to be sent so they can reach their destination. Using the `route` command with no parameters displays the routing table. Here's an example for a host with one Ethernet interface (eth0), an IP address of 10.0.1.1, and a subnet mask of 255.255.255.0:

```
route
Kernel IP routing table
Destination   Gateway     Genmask        Flags Metric Ref Use Iface
10.0.1.0      *           255.255.255.0  U     0      0   0   eth0
127.0.0.0     *           255.0.0.0      U     0      0   0   lo
default       10.0.1.3    0.0.0.0        UG    0      0   0   eth0
```

The output consists of three lines (after the column headings):

- A line defining where to send traffic for the 10.0.1.0 network—the network to which this computer is directly connected.

- A line defining where to send traffic for the 127.0.0.0 network—the loopback interface.

- A line defining where to send any packet with a destination address on a network other than the two just mentioned. These packets must go to the gateway because this system doesn't know how to reach any other networks.

Now look at the columns in the output of the `route` command:

- `Destination`—The network or host to which the routing table entry applies. If the destination address of an IP packet is part of the network listed on a line, that entry will be used to route the packet.

- `Gateway`—The IP address of the host that should receive a packet destined for the specified network. An asterisk (*) is displayed to indicate which network the host is a part of; no routing is needed.

- `Genmask`—The network mask of the routing table entry. The entry for the default gateway is supposed to be 0.0.0.0.

- `Flags`—The nine single-letter flags that indicate information about this routing table entry. A `U` indicates that the route is up; a `G` indicates that the route refers to a gateway. An `H` indicates that the route refers to a host. The other six flags are only displayed when the host is running a dynamic routing protocol.

- `Metric`—The number of hops this route represents.

- `Ref`—The number of references made to this route. This is not used by Linux.

- `Use`—The number of times this route has been looked up by the routing software. This gives a rough measure of how much traffic is headed for the specified network.

- `Iface`—The interface on which packets destined for the specified network should be sent.

NOTE

In the following examples of the `route` command's output, the Ref and Use columns are not shown to save space on the page.

The routing table is normally handled automatically. When an interface is assigned an IP address, the Linux kernel determines the network address and an entry for that network is placed in the routing table. Look at the following example. Assume that no interfaces are active (up). The routing table is empty:

```
route
Kernel IP routing table
Destination  Gateway     Genmask          Flags Metric Iface
```

Bring up the `eth0` interface and assign it an IP address of 10.0.1.3 and a mask of 255.255.255.0 (a /24 network):

```
ifconfig eth0 10.0.1.3 netmask 255.255.255.0
```

Here's what happens to the routing table:

```
route
Kernel IP routing table
Destination  Gateway     Genmask          Flags Metric Iface
10.0.1.0     *           255.255.255.0 U      0       eth0
```

The Linux kernel automatically determined the network address is 10.0.1.0 and created the routing table entry. It did not create an entry for the default gateway because it has no way to automatically determine the address of the gateway. This must be done manually or by a script. Assuming the gateway address is 10.0.1.1, here's the syntax of the `route` command that adds a default gateway into the routing table:

```
route add default gw 10.0.1.1
```

The default gateway is added to the routing table:

```
route
Kernel IP routing table
Destination  Gateway     Genmask       Flags Metric Iface
10.0.1.0     *           255.255.255.0 U     0      eth0
default      10.0.1.1    0.0.0.0       UG    0      eth0
```

Figure 2-1 shows a typical routing scenario. It shows a network with two Ethernet segments that connect to the local router—Host C. Host C also has an interface that connects to the Internet via an ISP's router. Host A and B have their default gateway set to 10.0.1.1. Host D has its default gateway set to 10.0.2.1. Host C also has a default gateway setting that points to the ISP's router—69.30.87.1.

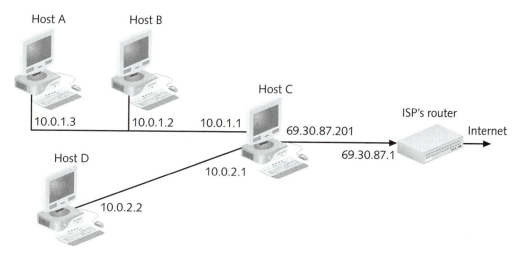

Figure 2-1   A two-segment network with an Internet connection

This example is relatively simple with regard to the routing table. You just need to ensure that all hosts point to the correct default router. The Linux kernel determines the rest. Things are more complex with networks that have more than one gateway. Figure 2-2 shows that Host B is now a router—the gateway to the Internet instead of Host C. Yet, Host C is still a router. It connects networks 10.0.1.0 and 10.0.2.0 together.

To what should Host A's default gateway be set? If it's set to 10.0.1.2, it will be able to reach the Internet but it won't be able to reach network 10.0.2.0. If it's set to 10.0.1.1, it will be able to reach network 10.0.2.0 but it won't be able to reach the Internet.

The solution is to add another route to the host's routing table. Its default gateway will be set to 10.0.1.2. Another route is needed for network 10.0.2.0. You can add this route with this command:

```
route add -net 10.0.2.0 netmask 255.255.255.0 gw 10.0.1.1 dev eth0
```

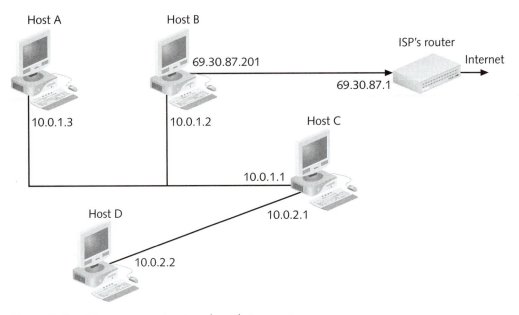

Figure 2-2   A two-segment network with two gateways

Host A can now reach the Internet and network 10.0.2.0. Its routing table now includes two gateways:

```
route
Kernel IP routing table
Destination  Gateway       Genmask          Flags Metric Iface
10.0.1.0     *             255.255.255.0 U       0      eth0
10.0.2.0     10.0.1.1      255.255.255.0 UG      0      eth0
default      10.0.1.2      0.0.0.0          UG      0      eth0
```

Host B has its default gateway set to 69.30.87.1—the ISP's router. However, it doesn't know about network 10.0.2.0. It also needs to have another route added to its routing table, just like Host A. The `route` command is the same as for Host A. Host B's routing table also has two gateways:

```
route
Kernel IP routing table
Destination  Gateway       Genmask          Flags Metric Iface
10.0.1.0     *             255.255.255.0 U       0      eth0
10.0.2.0     10.0.1.1      255.255.255.0 UG      0      eth0
default      69.30.87.1    0.0.0.0          UG      0      eth0
```

Host C already has routes for networks 10.0.1.0 and 10.0.2.0. The only change is to set its default gateway to 10.0.1.2 so it can reach the Internet. The change from Figure 2-1 to Figure 2-2 is invisible to Host D, which uses the same routing table as before.

Using the `ip` Command

The `ip` command is a recent addition to Linux. It is part of the IPROUTE2 package that most distributions now include. It's meant to be a replacement for the `ifconfig`, `route`, and `arp` commands. These excerpts from the Linux Advanced Routing & Traffic Control HOWTO explain why:

- *Most Linux distributions ... use the arp, ifconfig, and route commands. While these tools work, they show some unexpected behavior under Linux 2.2 and up.*

- *As new networking concepts have been invented, people have found ways to plaster them on top of the existing framework...This constant layering of cruft has led to networking code that is filled with strange behavior...*

One of the best features of the `ip` command is that it allows you to use CIDR notation. This was covered in Chapter 1 to a degree, but this section takes a closer look at it. The classful notation that `ifconfig` requires is awkward—you need to specify three parameters to ensure that you've properly configured an interface: IP address, subnet mask, and broadcast address. The following is an `ifconfig` command that illustrates this using a subnetted address:

```
ifconfig eth0 10.1.1.204 netmask 255.255.255.248 broadcast 10.1.1.207
```

This is a lot to remember and a lot to type. The following is the equivalent `ip` command using CIDR notation:

```
ip addr add 10.1.1.204/29 dev eth0
```

Instead of three parameters, there's only one: 10.1.1.204/29. From this single piece of information, the network address and the broadcast address are easily derived.

You can use the `ip` program to work with the routing table—eliminating the need for the `route` program. To display the routing table, use the `ip route` command:

```
ip route
10.1.1.200/29 dev eth0 proto kernel scope link src 10.1.1.204
default via 10.1.1.201 dev eth0
```

The second line that starts with `default` is the default gateway. You can add a default route with a command like this:

```
ip route add default dev eth0 via 10.1.1.201
```

The `ip` program does not display interface statistics, such as the number of packets transmitted and received, unless you ask for them:

```
ip -statistics link dev eth0
eth0: <BROADCAST,MULTICAST,UP> mtu 1500 qdisc pfifo_fast qlen 1000
link/ether 00:11:43:35:c0:cc brd 00:00:00:00:00:00
RX: bytes  packets  errors  dropped  overrun mcast
1578604995 12828220 7       0        0       0
```

```
TX: bytes   packets  errors  dropped  carrier collsns
212168783   217086443 0       0        0       0
```

The `ip` program has much more functionality that's not described here. You can refer to the `ip` man page for more detail, but it's not easy reading. You might have better results searching the Internet for tutorial information on the command.

Adding IP Addresses to Interfaces

Sometimes you need to assign more than one IP address to an interface. This is often called **IP aliasing**. You'll read about a practical application for this in Chapter 6. You have two ways to add addresses to interfaces that are quite different from one another. One way uses the `ifconfig` program and the other uses the `ip` program.

When you use `ifconfig`, the aliases have names. The names are typically created by appending a colon followed by a number to the interface name. If the interface is `eth0`, the first alias would be called `eth0:0`. The second alias would be `eth0:1` and so on. The following is an example of creating an alias using `ifconfig`:

```
ifconfig eth0:0 10.0.0.2 netmask 255.0.0.0 broadcast
10.255.255.255
```

When you run the `ifconfig` program with no command-line parameters, you can see both the `eth0` interface and the `eth0:0` interface. Alias names do not have to use a number following the interface name. You could use a short string of alphabetic characters such as this:

```
ifconfig eth0:web1 10.0.0.2 netmask 255.0.0.0 broadcast
10.255.255.255
```

However, some programmers do not know that you can do this. Consequently, some programs do not work with aliases that don't use numbers.

When you use the `ip` program to create aliases, the aliases do not have names. You simply add an IP address to the interface. The following command is equivalent to the previous examples:

```
ip addr 10.0.0.3/8 dev eth0
```

When you create aliases using `ip`, they do not appear in an `ifconfig` listing. However, Linux knows about these aliases and uses them. If you create an alias using `ifconfig`, you can see it in an `ip` listing.

Using the `ip` command is generally the better way to create aliases.

PCMCIA and PC Card Interfaces

Mobile computers can use PCMCIA cards or PC Cards for their network interfaces. These interfaces are hot-pluggable—they can be inserted and removed anytime you want. Linux needs to be able to load and unload their drivers on the fly. When Linux support for these hot-pluggable devices was introduced, there was no generic hotplug mechanism. So, a hotplug mechanism that used scripts and configuration files specific to PCMCIA and PC Cards was developed.

Kernel modules for the cards are kept in a directory separate from the non-hotplug interfaces. On a Fedora Core system, these interface modules are in the directory:

```
/lib/modules/2.6.10-1.766_FC3/kernel/drivers/net/pcmcia
```

These cards have their own configuration files and scripts in the /etc/pcmcia directory. To use a PCMCIA or PC Card interface, edit the /etc/pcmcia/network.opts file. Then create a hotplug event by removing and inserting the card. The scripts should run and activate the interface with the settings you placed in the network.opts file. If this doesn't work, you have some troubleshooting on your hands. This may involve having to deal with the details of card services. You can visit the Linux PCMCIA Information Page at *http://pcmcia-cs.sourceforge.net* for more information.

NOTE   PCMCIA Card Services allow you to create named configurations that let the interface behave differently depending on whether you're at home, in the office, or elsewhere.

Since PCMCIA and PC Card interface support was integrated into Linux, interfaces based on USB and FireWire have been introduced. These are also hot-pluggable devices. We need a more generic and intelligent hotplug system. The new /sys filesystem that was introduced with kernel version 2.6 now makes this possible, and work is progressing at a rapid rate. Sometime in the future, the /etc/pcmcia directory will go away.

Wireless Interfaces

Wireless interfaces, such as wireless Ethernet, have their own unique capabilities and requirements. They have a radio receiver and transmitter that need to be configured and monitored. Instead of adding wireless support to programs like ifconfig, additional wireless-specific programs were developed. These are **iwconfig** and iwlist.

The iwconfig program is the primary tool for configuring wireless interfaces. It is used to display and configure parameters that are peculiar to wireless interfaces, such as frequency, transmit power, data rate, encryption key, and selecting between ad hoc or access point mode. You still need to use the ifconfig or ip program to set the interface's network parameters, such as IP address.

The iwconfig syntax is:

```
iwconfig interface option
```

where *interface* is the name of the interface and *option* is one of the following:

- `essid` *name*—Sets the Extended Service Set Identifier or ESSID. This is the name of the overall wireless network, which might consist of more than one cell. This is needed so a user can roam between cells. The name is case sensitive and limited to 32 characters.

- `nwid` *name*—Sets the network ID of the cell. This is needed only if the WLAN is running in ad hoc mode. If you use an access point, you don't need to define the network ID.

- `freq` *number*—Sets the transmitter's frequency. You can enter the frequency in Hz but you'll want to use the G suffix (2.46 G) instead.

- `mode` *mode*—Sets the operating mode of the interface, where *mode* can be Ad-Hoc, Managed, Master, Repeater, Secondary, Monitor, and Auto.

- `ap` *x*—Sets the access point to be used, where *x* is the MAC address of the access point you prefer or *any* chooses the best access point.

- `key` *key*—Sets the encryption key, where *key* is in a numeric form using hex digits (1234-5678-90ab or 1234567890ab) or in string form (s:mysecretkey). If you need to use more than one key, refer to the `iwconfig` man page.

Not all `iwconfig` options are shown here. Refer to the `iwconfig` man page for the lesser-used options.

The `iwlist` program displays detailed information about the interface's radio. The syntax is:

`iwlist` *interface option*

where *interface* is the name of the interface and *option* is one of these:

- `event`—Lists the wireless events supported by the interface

- `frequency`—Lists the interface's available frequencies

- `key`—Lists the encryption key sizes that the interface supports

- `power`—Lists the power management attributes and modes

- `rate`—Lists the data rates supported

- `retry`—Lists the transmit retry limits

- `scanning`—Lists the access points and ad hoc cells that are in range

- `txpower`—Lists the transmit power levels the interface supports

Using `proc`

You can view and set many network configuration parameters by using the **proc filesystem**. This is a virtual filesystem that allows you to view and modify kernel settings. Many network-related parameters can only be modified by using the proc filesystem. To view the proc filesystem, go to the /proc directory. All the files and directories you see there don't exist on your hard disk. They are kernel settings made to look like a filesystem's directory structure so you can use ordinary text-oriented tools to view and set them.

For example, enter the command cat /proc/cpuinfo. You see information regarding your computer's CPU. Network-related kernel settings are in two /proc directories: /proc/net and /proc/sys/net. The /proc/net directory structure contains status information—you can only view this information. The /proc/sys/net directory structure contains network-related settings that you can modify.

You can tell which proc files you can modify by doing a long directory listing. For example, enter ls -l /proc/net/ and you see entries like this:

```
-r--r--r-- 1 root root 0 Feb 25 09:28 anycast6
```

If you're up to speed on Linux/UNIX permissions, you can see that you only have read access to this "file." Permissions are covered in a later chapter. If you look at files in the /proc/sys/net directory structure, you see that the root user has write permission to the files there.

To see how you can modify network parameters, enter cat /proc/sys/net/ipv4/ip_local_port_range. For a default Fedora Core installation, you see this:

```
32768     61000
```

These numbers are the lower and upper limits for the pool of port numbers that the kernel assigns to TCP and UDP clients. In Chapter 1, you discovered that these are called dynamic ports and learned that the proper range is from 49,152 to 65,535. Fedora Core and most other Linux distributions don't use the proper range. You can fix this by setting the proper values using this command:

```
echo "49152 65535" > /proc/sys/net/ipv4/ip_local_port_range
```

The change takes place immediately. Verify that this worked by entering cat /proc/sys/net/ipv4/ip_local_port_range and noticing that the proper numbers are displayed. All new client connections will now use ports from this range. Existing connections will continue to use the ports assigned to them in the past.

The change is made to the running kernel. If you reboot your computer, the change will be lost. You must put the echo command into one of the start-up scripts to have it take effect when you boot your computer. The /etc/rc.d/rclocal script is one such script. It runs after all other start-up scripts.

Another proc setting that you should know about is /proc/sys/net/ipv4/ip_forward. This needs to be set to 1 if you have more than one interface and you want to route packets between the interfaces (you want the computer to behave as a router). Your Linux distribution probably sets this automatically, but if it doesn't you'll have problems. You can set it with this command:

```
echo "1" > /proc/sys/net/ipv4/ip_forward
```

Many network-related files are in the proc filesystem. The filenames and subdirectories you see vary depending on the features compiled into the kernel and the kernel modules that are loaded. You'll take a look at other proc settings throughout this book.

Using ARP

In Chapter 1, you learned about the Address Resolution Protocol (ARP), which obtains the hardware address of a host given its IP address. Now that you are more familiar with the route command, you can try the **arp** command. You'll use the arp command mainly for troubleshooting network problems.

The ARP protocol maintains a table in memory called the **ARP cache**, which is a mapping of IP addresses to interface hardware addresses. You can view the ARP table with the command arp –a (the "a" is for "all"):

```
arp-a
fire.course.com (10.0.1.1) at 00:0D:87:F0:76:1A (ether) on eth0
igor.course.com (10.0.1.3) at 00:40:63:C2:8A:64 (ether) on eth0
```

The first entry says that the host whose name is *fire.course.com* and IP address is 10.0.1.1 has an Ethernet interface with a MAC address of 00:0D:87:F0:76:1A. The second entry says that the host whose name is *igor.course.com* and IP address is 10.0.1.3 has an Ethernet interface with a MAC address of 00:40:63:C2:8A:64.

ARP table entries are dynamic and are discarded if not referenced within two minutes. You can see this by pinging some hosts on your network and on the Internet. Then run the arp –a command and note the entries. Wait a few minutes and run the arp –a command again. You'll see that some of the table entries have been deleted.

You can use the arp command to add an entry manually, but there are few practical reasons for doing so.

System Networking Scripts

Linux distributions provide numerous scripts and configuration files to set up your interfaces and to make starting and stopping the interfaces easy. The networking scripts follow the model used for most system services on UNIX-based computers. The simplistic view is that networking on most Linux distributions is controlled by a single script: /etc/init.d /network or a similar name. You can start up networking with this command:

/etc/rc.d/init.d/network start

Using this command stops networking:

/etc/rc.d/init.d/network stop

These two steps are combined with this command:

/etc/rc.d/init.d/network restart

Elegant though it might be, this grand network script begs the question: How does it do all of this? The answer is that more scripts and configuration files lie behind the scenes. All of these are located in the directory **/etc/sysconfig**, under the subdirectories network-scripts and in the file networking.

The network-scripts subdirectory contains scripts that start and stop individual network interfaces. In that directory, you see two main scripts called **ifup** and **ifdown**. These are used to control more common interfaces such as localhost and Ethernet. Other specialized scripts can also be found in the subdirectory for interfaces, such as IPv6, PPP, or ISDN.

A question should be forming in your mind: Why use a script instead of just the up and down options with ifconfig? The short answer is this: The scripts can be more intelligent in handling the network interfaces. For example, they can check whether a firewall configuration needs to be adjusted, whether a wireless interface is involved, whether default routes must be updated, and so forth. You can obtain the more complex answer if you have any experience with shell scripts: Open the files in a text editor and study them.

Scripts that control individual network interfaces do not contain the actual configuration data. That information is stored in separate files in the /etc/sysconfig/network-scripts subdirectory according to the name of the interface. The file you're most likely to see is /etc/sysconfig/network-scripts/ifcfg-eth0, which contains information to configure the first Ethernet interface. The contents of that file are shown here:

```
DEVICE=eth0
BOOTPROTO=static
BROADCAST=192.168.100.255
IPADDR=192.168.100.10
NETMASK=255.255.255.0
NETWORK=192.168.100.0
ONBOOT=yes
```

NOTE

If you are using DHCP to obtain IP address information, your ifcfg-eth0 file will look different from the one shown here.

With this file, you can finally see how the data to configure the interface is actually stored. If you were to change the IP address in this file and use the command /etc/rc.d/init.d/network restart, the IP address of your system would be changed. Most Linux systems add graphical configuration utilities to let you change IP addresses, add network interfaces, and so forth. Behind the scenes, those utilities may be changing the data files and using the system scripts that control networking.

An earlier section in this chapter discussed how to add an IP address to an interface. This was called IP aliasing and you learned how to do it with the ifconfig and ip commands. The scripts used by Fedora Core are designed around all aliases having a name. This makes the `ifconfig` command the better one to use in these scripts. The scripts would have to be redesigned to make use of the `ip` command.

To add an IP alias, you create a new file in the `/etc/sysconfig/network-scripts` directory with the name `ifcfg-eth0:0`. The easiest way is to copy the existing file `ifcfg-eth0`. Then change the values of the `DEVICE` and `IPADDR` lines to refer to `eth0:0` and the new IP address. Now restart networking to make the additional IP address automatically active. Every time you start up Linux, the additional IP address is started. To stop this, delete the additional file that you created and restart networking. This experiment is one of the Hands-On Projects at the end of this chapter.

CONFIGURING NETWORKING USING GRAPHICAL TOOLS

A good system administrator knows how things work "under the hood," rather than just relying on the basic tools. By knowing about the networking scripts and the `ifconfig`, `route`, and `ip` commands, you'll have a better grasp of how to diagnose any problems that arise on your network. You'll also be better prepared to do well on a Linux certification test. After you understand these things, however, you might find it easier to use graphical tools to configure your network. Every major version of Linux includes graphical utilities to help you manage networking. This section describes the utilities included with some popular versions of Linux.

Fedora Core includes the graphical **Network Configuration Tool** for managing network interfaces. Start the tool from the graphical menu of the GNOME desktop by choosing Applications, System Settings, and then Network. You can also start it from a command line by entering the utility name: **neat**. Figure 2-3 shows the main screen of this tool.

NOTE

This section only explores the Hardware and Devices tabs. The Hosts and DNS tabs are covered later.

When the tool starts, the Devices tab is selected. It displays a list of each Linux networking device name and its status. Select one of the interfaces and click Edit. You'll see the Ethernet Device window shown in Figure 2-4. The General tab allows you to perform the following tasks:

- Activate the interface when the computer boots up. Normally, this is enabled.
- Allow all users to control the interface. Normally, this is not enabled because of security concerns about giving users such power.
- Enable IPv6 for the interface. Enable this only if you need IPv6 support.

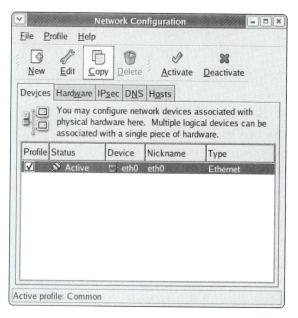

Figure 2-3   The main screen of the Fedora Core Network Configuration Tool

- Choose to obtain an IP address lease from a DHCP or BOOTP server. You'll learn about DHCP in Chapter 3.

- Choose to use a static IP address and gateway.

The Route tab of the Ethernet Device window lets you define a list of static routes that will take effect when you start or restart networking. You should only need to do this if you have nonstandard routing needs caused by working on a large network with multiple gateways or points through which you can reach the Internet. The Hardware Device tab is ill-named. It actually allows you to define IP aliases for the interfaces. Click OK to return to the main screen.

The Hardware tab of the Network Configuration Tool (see Figure 2-5) shows a list similar to the Devices tab, but the manufacturer and model of the interface are shown. Click Edit to reveal the Network Adapters Configuration window (see Figure 2-6), which allows you to configure the hardware settings for the interface. Click New to define another interface. You can select the type of hardware for which you want to add support to the kernel. The supported options are Ethernet, Token-Ring, ISDN, Modem, and Wireless. Linux supports many other types of networking, but the options shown are the ones you can manage using this utility. To configure others, you must use the command line.

After you make any changes in the dialog boxes of the neat utility, click the OK button to close each dialog box. Then click the Close Window button and confirm that you want to save your changes and update the system with the new information you've entered.

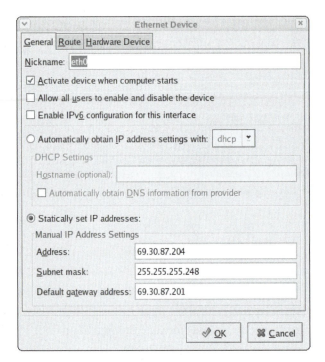

Figure 2-4   The Ethernet Device window in the Fedora Core Network Configuration Tool

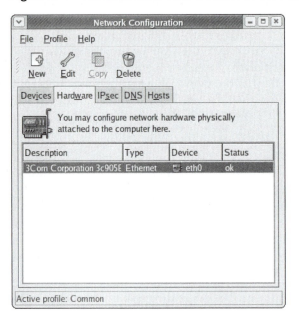

Figure 2-5   The Hardware tab of the Fedora Core Network Configuration Tool

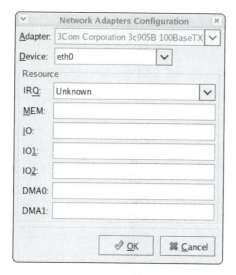

Figure 2-6   The Network Adapters Configuration window

Another popular graphical configuration program is **Webmin**, a Web browser-based program. When you start Webmin, you're starting a tiny Web server that runs on a high-numbered TCP port—usually 10,000. You then point your Web browser at that port and Webmin answers. It first requires that you log on. Thereafter, you can configure most aspects of Linux, including networking.

Webmin works with most versions of Linux as well as most versions of UNIX. If you or your IT staff need to maintain Linux and UNIX computers, Webmin allows different OS platforms to be managed by a common program with a common user interface. Training costs are reduced.

Webmin is extensible with modules. Anyone can write Webmin modules to add needed functionality. For example, if Webmin provides DNS support for BIND but not for another DNS server, someone can write a Webmin module for the other DNS server. Webmin and Webmin modules are written primarily in Perl.

Webmin is a moving target—its user interface changes periodically. Therefore, you should refer to the Webmin Web site (*www.webmin.com*) for more details. You should download Webmin from the Web site, install it, and practice using it.

USING BASIC NETWORKING UTILITIES

With basic networking running smoothly on your Linux system, you're ready to begin exploring the utilities and applications that make it useful. This section provides a description of three popular utilities that you should become familiar with as troubleshooting and informational tools. For each, a brief summary and a few examples are provided. To learn more, you should experiment with these utilities (the projects at the end of this chapter are a good place to start) and review the online man page documentation when questions arise about how to use them.

The Telnet Remote Logon Utility

Telnet is a terminal emulator program. It allows you to log on to a remote computer as if you were sitting at that computer's terminal (keyboard and screen). After you are logged on, you can view any files that your user account permits you to view. You can also execute any command, including changing or deleting files, as long as you have the permissions to do so. Telnet is also used for troubleshooting network problems.

NOTE   Telnet is a convenient program, but a warning is in order: Telnet packets are not encrypted or encoded to prevent eavesdropping. Everything you do in Telnet can easily be viewed by anyone connected to the same network. You should use the ssh program when eavesdropping could be a problem.

To use Telnet as a terminal emulator program, you must connect to a host running a Telnet server (daemon). The details of setting up clients and servers are discussed in Chapters 4 and 5. Many Linux systems already have a Telnet server running (though this is considered a security risk). All Linux systems have a Telnet client installed, as do most Windows systems.

The telnet command in Linux requires you to enter the host name or IP address to which you want to connect. If a connection can be made—that is, if a Telnet server on that host accepts your client's request for a connection—then you are prompted to enter a username and password. After logging on, you see a command prompt as if you were sitting at the remote computer.

If you want to try a Telnet session from Windows, launch the Telnet program included with some Windows versions or obtain a free Telnet program. (You can search on a site such as *www.tucows.com* for free Windows Telnet client software.) Graphical Telnet programs generally ask for the following information:

- The remote host to which you want to connect. For this field, you can enter an IP address or a host name.

- The port number to which you want to connect. By default, the Telnet port—23—is used. You can choose other ports for testing or experimentation as you learn about other services.

- The type of dumb terminal that you want the software to emulate. A standard choice would be a **VT100** terminal. Hundreds of dumb terminal models exist, but VT100 is widely supported.

- You might be asked to enter a username and password, which is sent to the remote host as part of your logon. The Telnet program typically requests that this information be saved, so you don't have to enter it each time you connect to the same remote host. Figure 2-7 shows a Telnet session being started in the Windows Telnet program. (Depending on your version of Windows, the program may differ slightly from that shown in the figure.)

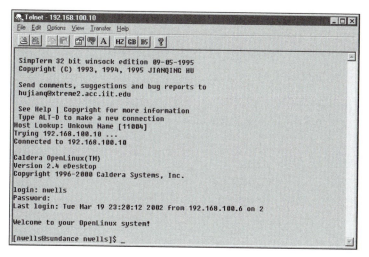

Figure 2-7   The Windows Telnet program with a session in progress

Using `ping` for System Testing

In Chapter 1, you learned about the echo message type in the ICMP protocol. ICMP is used to send status or error messages about an IP connection; echo is used to send test packets to see whether a remote host can be reached. The utility that you use to send ICMP echo packets is called **ping**.

To use ping, just include the host name or address of the host that you want to contact. For example:

```
ping 198.60.22.20
```

This command sends a series of ICMP echo packets to the host with the IP address 198.60.22.20. If the host is reachable, the IP stack on that host responds with a message saying "I'm here," and your system displays a message to show that the remote host is "alive." Another packet is sent every second until you stop the ping program. The resulting listing looks like this:

```
PING 198.60.22.20 from 64.24.90.213 : 56(84) bytes of data.
64 bytes from 198.60.22.20: icmp_seq=0 ttl=244 time=319.537 msec
64 bytes from 198.60.22.20: icmp_seq=1 ttl=244 time=299.984 msec
64 bytes from 198.60.22.20: icmp_seq=2 ttl=244 time=299.994 msec
64 bytes from 198.60.22.20: icmp_seq=3 ttl=244 time=300.008 msec
64 bytes from 198.60.22.20: icmp_seq=4 ttl=244 time=280.005 msec
64 bytes from 198.60.22.20: icmp_seq=5 ttl=244 time=280.006 msec
64 bytes from 198.60.22.20: icmp_seq=6 ttl=244 time=279.998 msec
--- 198.60.22.20 ping statistics ---
7 packets transmitted, 7 packets received, 0% packet loss
   round-trip min/avg/max/mdev =
   279.998/291.298/319.537/10.805 ms
```

When you press Ctrl+C to end the `ping` program, it calculates the statistics that are printed at the end of the listing. It's common to use a series of `ping` commands to test networking. By using these commands in the order given here, you can identify at what point a problem occurs.

NOTE

The `ping` command on a Windows system simply sends four echo packets and then stops; note that in Linux, `ping` continues until you press Ctrl+C.

- Ping `127.0.0.1` to check that the internal networking stacks are functioning and that networking is enabled in the Linux kernel.

- Ping your own IP address to check that your networking card is configured as expected.

- Ping the IP address of another host on your local network segment to check that your Ethernet card and cable are functioning correctly.

- Ping the IP address of a host on another network segment close by to check that the default gateway or basic routing tables (depending on the complexity of your network) are correctly configured.

- Ping an IP address beyond your organization to check that distant routers are able to work with those in your organization in getting traffic to and from the Internet or other distant networks.

You can also use `ping` with a host name, as you did in the previous example. Ping your own host name to see that it can be resolved (converted into an IP address). Then ping the host name for another host on your local network segment, then of a distant host or Internet site. Chapter 3 explores this further, but the basic idea is the same: Ping to hosts farther and farther away from your system. If something stops working, you know where the error occurred. For example, if you can ping other hosts within your local network segment but not on any other segments, you know that your packet cannot get outside the local segment. This might be caused by bad cabling between segments, a lack of IP forwarding at the router, a bad routing table entry, a firewall entry blocking your traffic, or a few other things. Pinging lets you know where to start looking.

Several types of attacks in the past have relied on the `ping` command. One example is the "flood ping," which sends many `ping` commands in rapid succession, overwhelming the server that tries to respond to them. Another example is the "ping of death," in which a single `ping` command with a very large payload is sent to a server; the payload overflows the memory space allocated to receive ICMP packets and corrupts other parts of the server's memory. Because of attacks like these, many hosts on the Internet completely block pings originating from anywhere outside their organization.

NOTE

Find a few Internet sites (universities are a good bet) that respond to pings so you can use them for troubleshooting.

2

Notice the parts of the `ping` output from the listing shown previously. They include the following:

- The number of bytes sent in the packet. You can change this using a command-line option.

- The host name (if you included one) and IP address of the host you are pinging.

- A sequence number, starting with 0. ICMP assigns the number and simply keeps counting up sequentially.

- The Time to Live (TTL) of the ICMP packet. This is the number of routers that the packet can pass through before being discarded. The default here—224—is quite high.

- The time elapsed between sending the ICMP echo packet and when it returns. In this example, you see a time of about 280 milliseconds (shown as msecs). This time gets shorter as the host you're pinging gets closer. Try pinging within your local network to see much shorter times.

- The statistics shown after you press Ctrl+C include minimum, maximum, and average time to get a response, plus the number of packets for which no response was received (typically zero percent if you reached the host at all).

The `ping` command has numerous command-line options that let you set parameters, such as the number of packets to send before automatically stopping, the time to wait between each packet (the default is one second), the size of packet to send (the default is 64 bytes), and other specialized features that are useful for debugging routing problems. For example, the `-R` option lists all of the intervening routers that your ping packet passed through to reach the destination host. (This is similar to the `traceroute` command described next.)

Using `traceroute` to Examine Routing Patterns

When the information provided by `ping` is not enough to help you figure out a routing problem, `traceroute` is the logical next step. The **traceroute** command carefully identifies each router (each hop) between you and another host. This lets you see the path your packets are taking and how long each hop takes. Sample output from the command `traceroute 198.60.22.77` is shown here:

```
1 192.168.100.5 (192.168.100.5) 2.922 ms 9.798 ms 19.928 ms
2 wdc2-dial7.popsite.net (64.24.80.232) 219.817 ms 199.408
  ms 199.944 ms
3 wdc2-dial7.popsite.net (64.24.80.232) 199.930 ms 209.430
  ms 199.942 ms
4 wdc2-core1.popsite.net (64.24.80.225) 199.995 ms 199.461
  ms 199.923 ms
```

```
 5 wdc1-core1-p1-0.starnetusa.net (64.24.80.1) 200.004
   ms 199.437 ms 189.952 ms
 6 wdc3-core1-pos2-0.starnetusa.net (216.126.145.122)
   199.987 ms 199.401 ms 199.952 ms
 7 jsy1-core1-a3-0-2.starnetusa.net (216.126.145.105)
   220.021 ms 949.325 ms 900.048 ms
 8 chi1-core1-s4-0.starnetusa.net (216.126.145.113) 1619.974
   ms 3579.417 ms *
 9 * sjc1-core1-a3-0-2.starnetusa.net (216.126.146.18)
   2045.692 ms 319.424 ms
10 pao1-core1-p6-0.starnetusa.net (216.126.145.97) 360.012
   ms 319.415 ms 339.969 ms
11 xmission-paix.xmission.com (198.32.176.42) 289.961
   ms 1049.435 ms 949.921 ms
12 xmission-paix.xmission.com (204.228.132.29) 819.957
   ms 309.562 ms 309.941 ms
13 core-border.xmission.com (166.70.4.10) 309.973
   ms 309.580 ms 309.887 ms
14 ftp.xmission.com (198.60.22.77) 309.989
   ms 319.627 ms 309.934 ms
```

Each line is numbered. In this example, it took 14 hops to get from our host to the 198.60.22.77 host. The IP address is shown for each router along the way, along with the router's host name if it has one. Three timing values are shown after the IP address for each router. Traceroute sends three "probe packets" and shows the length of time that each took to respond. If an asterisk (*) appears in the listing, the router did not respond within the default time limit of five seconds. Traceroute tries a maximum of 30 hops to reach a destination, though you can change that number using a command-line parameter.

Traceroute relies on the TTL field and ICMP "packet timed out" messages to move step-by-step through the Internet to reach the host in which you are interested. Because not all systems follow standard practices in using these features, some lines of the traceroute output may contain nothing but three asterisks. In most cases, however, traceroute is a very useful tool for diagnosing problems such as the following:

- Where a packet stops. You try to reach a certain host, but because of bad routing information, it reaches a certain point on the Internet and doesn't go any farther. The output of traceroute shows you the last router reached by the packet.

- Where a packet slows down. Your connectivity to a certain site seems unusually slow. Traceroute indicates the time to receive a response from each router. The one that takes an inordinate amount of time to respond deserves special attention.

Other problems are possible, of course, but these are two common uses for traceroute. Command-line options in traceroute include setting the maximum number of routers to try, limiting the time to wait for each response, and indicating that packets cannot be fragmented, which can help you diagnose problems related to packet fragmentation between different types of networks (as discussed in Chapter 1).

Some administrators block `traceroute` packets at their routers, firewalls, and servers because they perceive them as a security threat. It's common for `traceroute` to stop displaying hops when the `traceroute` packet reaches the destination network.

Troubleshooting Network Connections

This may surprise you, but you have learned enough already about Linux networking to troubleshoot a variety of problems. Networking can become very complex, and you have not yet delved into many of the hardware issues that could arise (such as cabling problems). Table 2-2, however, lists some common networking problems that you can diagnose and troubleshoot with the tools covered so far. This list will be expanded with other trouble-shooting tables as you learn more about different aspects of networking, such as DNS in Chapter 3.

Table 2-2   Basic networking troubleshooting review

Trouble	Things to Check
Networking doesn't appear to function at all	Use the `ifconfig` command to see whether networking is up and running; if not, try the network script in `/etc/rc.d/init.d`. (Remember to check things that seem obvious: Is the cable plugged into the Ethernet card? Is an Ethernet card installed? Is the cable plugged into the wall or a hub?)
Network script doesn't appear to work	Use the `lsmod` command to see whether any network modules are installed in the kernel. If not, use `modprobe` as described in this chapter or a graphical utility to install the right kernel module for your networking card.
Can't ping any other systems on the local network segment	Check the cables; check with `ifconfig` to see whether a valid IP address has been assigned; check the routing tables to see that a route is listed for the local network.
Can't ping any system on another segment within the organization	Check the cables at the hub or server room; check with `ifconfig` to see whether a valid IP address is assigned and how that address compares with those of the other network segment (is there a conflict?); does the routing table include a route for the other network that refers to an intermediate router if necessary?
Traffic to another segment seems very slow	Check the routing table to see whether the most direct route is defined; check whether another system has the same IP address assigned; review the output of the `ifconfig` command to see whether a large number of collisions are occurring—if so, the network may be overloaded; check `ifconfig` output to see whether a large number of errors are occurring—if so, the NIC may be defective; review whether fragmentation problems between the two segments could be slowing down traffic; use `traceroute` to see at what point the transmission slows down significantly.

OTHER NETWORKING PROTOCOLS

In later chapters, you will learn a lot about many different protocols designed for different types of information sharing. But two lower-level protocols deserve mention in the same context as the discussion of TCP/IP and routing. These are IPX and AppleTalk.

IPX

The **Internetwork Packet Exchange (IPX)** protocol was designed by Novell Inc. in the early 1980s for use in its NetWare server product. IPX was the dominant protocol on local area networks from about 1985 through the mid-1990s because NetWare was the dominant server operating system for businesses using personal computers. People ask why Novell chose to use its own proprietary protocol rather than use the standard TCP/IP protocol suite. IPX is based on the Xerox Network System (XNS) protocol because, in the early 1980s, it was not clear to anyone that TCP/IP would become so popular more than a decade later.

In the early to mid-1990s, Novell added TCP/IP support to NetWare and customers converted from IPX. TCP/IP is the protocol of the Internet and is perceived as a superior protocol. However, many networks still run IPX and you might have to integrate Linux into them.

If you work with NetWare, you can use Linux as a client to communicate with NetWare servers. You can also have Linux route IPX network traffic. For more information on setting up IPX on Linux, review the IPX HOWTO document at *www.tldp.org/HOWTO/IPX-HOWTO.html*.

Apple Networking

AppleTalk is the name of the networking protocol used by Macintosh computers. Anyone who has used the Macintosh might wonder about the complex maneuvers needed to set up a PC network (running Windows or Linux). Macs and AppleTalk provide simple plug-and-play networking. But that simplicity doesn't scale to something like the worldwide Internet, so AppleTalk is used on small local networks.

On Linux, you can install the **Netatalk** package to allow Macintosh computers to have a Linux server show up on the Mac desktop as an available shared resource. Another program called `afpfs` lets Linux users access Macintosh resources. However, `afpfs` is not currently being developed and is not supported by the latest Linux kernels.

To get started, carefully review the Netatalk HOWTO document and download the appropriate software as directed. See *www.anders.com/projects/netatalk/* for details.

The latest version of the Macintosh operating system, OS X, supports TCP/IP-based protocols and Microsoft SMB networking as well as AppleTalk. Mac users can choose how they want to network. They can access Linux servers running NFS, Samba, or Netatalk. If

2

you don't already have an AppleTalk network and your Macs support Ethernet, it's best to use NFS or Samba.

Mac users can also choose from a wide variety of applications. They can run native OS X applications, older applications written for Mac OS, X applications ported from Linux or UNIX, and most Windows applications via Apple's Virtual PC software. Mac OS X users have one of the most flexible and compatible desktop computers on the planet with a user interface more attractive than either Windows or Linux. Mac OS X on desktops and Linux servers in the back room are a very attractive combination.

CHAPTER SUMMARY

- ❏ Modern Linux distributions normally load support for network interfaces automatically without you having to get involved.

- ❏ Linux networking devices are created directly in the Linux kernel when a kernel module supporting a type of networking is loaded.

- ❏ Many types of networking are supported in Linux, though the most widely used is Ethernet.

- ❏ You can change the name of interfaces using the `ip` program.

- ❏ The `modprobe` command is used to add a networking module to the Linux kernel. The currently loaded kernel modules can be listed using the `lsmod` command.

- ❏ Sometimes, installing a kernel module requires that you include parameters to help the module locate or operate the networking hardware.

- ❏ The `ifconfig` command sets up a networking interface in the Linux kernel or displays the current setup for all configured interfaces.

- ❏ The `route` command establishes entries in the kernel IP routing table or displays the current routing table entries.

- ❏ The `arp` command lets you view the hardware address entries in the system's ARP cache. These entries are used by IP to route a packet to its final destination correctly.

- ❏ A number of networking scripts are used to streamline the configuration of Linux networking, making it more flexible and robust. The main networking control script is `/etc/rc.d/init.d/network`, or a script in a similar location.

- ❏ Networking configuration parameters are stored in files within the `/etc/sysconfig/network-scripts` subdirectory. These files can be edited directly, but are usually modified using a configuration tool of some sort, such as Webmin.

- ❏ IP aliasing occurs when multiple IP addresses are assigned to the same physical network interface (such as a single Ethernet card).

- ❏ Fedora Core includes a powerful Network Configuration Tool. Other Linux distributions use a variety of graphical tools to configure networking.

❑ The Telnet utility lets you connect to a remote host as if you were sitting at that host, but Telnet is not secure or encrypted and must be used with caution.

❑ Ping is a utility that uses the ICMP echo command to check whether a remote host is accessible and alive. Ping is a widely used tool for testing network connections, though some systems on the Internet do not respond to ping because of previous attacks that used this utility.

❑ The traceroute command displays each of the intervening routers between your host and another host you want to contact. Traceroute provides information that helps troubleshoot problems connecting to a remote host or with slow connections.

❑ IPX is a useful protocol that originated with Novell's NetWare operating system. It is supported in Linux, though not widely used.

❑ AppleTalk is supported in Linux via the Netatalk package, which you can add to Linux so that a Macintosh computer can see and access Linux resources.

Key Terms

/etc/sysconfig — The directory in which networking configuration files and scripts are stored, specifically in the subdirectory network-scripts and the file networking.

/lib/modules — The directory in which all of the available kernel modules for Linux are stored.

afpfs — A software package that lets Linux users access Macintosh resources. This software is still available for download, but because it is not currently being developed, is not supported by the latest Linux kernels.

AppleTalk — The networking protocol used by Apple Macintosh computers. AppleTalk is supported in Linux via the Netatalk package.

arp — A command that displays or alters the contents of the ARP cache. Used mainly for troubleshooting network connectivity.

ARP cache — A list of IP address-to-hardware mappings maintained by the ARP protocol to assist in routing packets.

eth0 — The device name in Linux for the first Ethernet card installed in a host.

frame relay — A technology used to provide dedicated high-speed Internet connectivity via telephone wires.

ifconfig — The interface configuration utility that configures a networking interface within the Linux kernel or that lists all currently configured network interfaces.

ifdown — The script used to shut down individual networking interfaces. Generally used by other scripts such as /etc/rc.d/init.d/network rather than directly by a user.

ifup — The script used to start individual networking interfaces. Generally used by other scripts such as /etc/rc.d/init.d/network rather than directly by a user.

insmod — The command used to install a module into a running Linux kernel. It can include parameters that provide additional information to the module being installed.

2

Integrated Services Digital Network (ISDN) — A special type of telephone service, widely used in Europe, that provides 128- or 144-kb/s bandwidth.

Internetwork Packet Exchange (IPX) — A protocol designed by Novell Inc. based on an older protocol called the Xerox Network System (XNS) protocol. IPX was the dominant protocol on local area networks for many years and is fully supported in Linux. It uses the network hardware address as a host ID, thus simplifying network configuration.

ip — A program that allows you to change interface names.

IP aliasing — A networking feature that allows a single physical interface to have more than one IP address assigned to it.

ip link — A utility that lists currently configured network interfaces.

ISA bus — The Industry Standard Architecture bus that was developed by IBM in the early 1980s and included in early personal computers. It is also called the AT bus. The ISA bus is obsolete.

iwconfig — The interface configuration utility specific to wireless interfaces.

lo — The device name of the loopback network device.

lsmod — The command used to list the modules that are loaded in your kernel at that moment.

metric — A value assigned to a network interface to guide dynamic routing decisions about when to use that interface. A higher metric means an interface is less likely to be used if other interfaces are also available.

modprobe — The command to load a kernel module while automatically checking for and loading dependent modules.

neat — The command-line invocation of the Network Configuration Tool.

Netatalk — A software package for Linux that allows Macintosh computers to recognize Linux (have it show up on the Mac desktop as an available shared resource).

Network Configuration Tool — A graphical interface provided in Fedora Core that is used to manage network interfaces. It can be started from the command line using neat.

Parallel Line Internet Protocol (PLIP) — A protocol that relies on a parallel port to transmit network data, often to connect two computers in a simple, inexpensive network.

ping — The utility used to send ICMP echo packets for network testing.

Point-to-Point Protocol (PPP) — A protocol that allows a host to tie directly to a single computer, making a network of two systems. PPP is used most often with a modem providing the underlying physical connection to the second computer.

proc filesystem — A virtual filesystem that allows you to view and modify kernel settings.

route — A command that displays or configures the routing table within the Linux kernel.

Serial Line Internet Protocol (SLIP) — A protocol that relies on a serial port as the underlying physical connection used to transmit network data, usually over a modem to an ISP.

T-1 — A high-speed transmission format (1.544 Mb/s) available through your local telephone company, usually for a few hundred dollars per month.

T-3 — A high-speed transmission format (45 Mb/s) available through your local telephone company, usually for several thousand dollars per month.

Telnet — A terminal emulator program that allows a user to log on to a remote computer as if sitting at that computer's keyboard.

traceroute — A command used to list each router (each hop) that a packet passes through between a source host and a destination host.

VT100 — The most widely supported dumb terminal standard.

Webmin — A browser-based utility that can manage many system functions, including network configuration.

Review Questions

1. A key advantage of IPX over IP is that:

   a. IPX does not require configuration of a host ID because it uses the network hardware address.

   b. Even IPv6 does not provide as large an address space as IPX.

   c. Linux has stronger support for IPX than for ICMP.

   d. IPX routing relies on RIP instead of just the `route` command.

2. Networking devices differ from other Linux devices in that:

   a. Networking devices use a different set of major and minor device numbers than devices that do not rely on kernel modules.

   b. Networking devices can transmit data much faster than other types of devices.

   c. Networking devices are not directly visible in the `/dev` subdirectory, but are created on the fly when a networking device module is loaded into the kernel.

   d. Networking devices can only be accessed via shell scripts.

3. Modprobe is preferable to `insmod` for loading modules because:

   a. Modprobe allows you to include module parameters on the command line and `insmod` does not.

   b. Modprobe loads any dependent modules automatically before the requested module.

   c. Insmod is not supported in all versions of Linux, but `modprobe` is.

   d. Insmod can interfere with operation of the `ifconfig` command on Token-Ring systems.

4. From the Hardware tab in Webmin, what is the next step to reconfigure the IP addresses of a network interface?

   a. Choose the Network Configuration icon.

   b. Choose the Network Interfaces icon.

   c. Select the hardware interface for which you want to enter new IP addresses.

   d. Select whether you want to modify the active interface parameters or the boot-up interface parameters.

5. Which of the following directories is most likely to contain kernel modules for net-working devices?

   a. /lib/modules/networking

   b. /etc/sysconfig/network-scripts

   c. /proc/sys/net

   d. /lib/modules/2.4.7-10/kernel/drivers/net

6. When using Telnet, you might refer to VT100 because it is:

   a. a standard protocol designation used by Telnet

   b. the port used by default to connect to the Telnet server

   c. the most commonly used terminal emulation standard

   d. the speed at which terminal emulator connections are typically handled

7. In which circumstance would kernel parameters most likely be needed to make a NIC function correctly in Linux?

   a. You are using an older ISA NIC that has a special feature allowing automatic IRQ mapping in software.

   b. You are using a brand-new PCI NIC that is identical to an established model.

   c. The documentation with your new NIC explains that Windows-based software is provided to help you configure the card.

   d. You want to do IP aliases and IP forwarding on your network.

8. Explain the difference between the TX packets and TX bytes lines in the output of ifconfig.

9. Which is not a valid ifconfig command?

   a. ifconfig eth0 up

   b. ifconfig eth0 192.168.100.1 netmask 255.255.255.0 broadcast 255.255.255.0

   c. ifconfig

   d. ifconfig eth0 if-up

10. Which information field is not part of the output of the route command?

   a. the gateway to reach the specified network

   b. the MAC address of the interface used to transfer packets to the specified network

   c. the interface through which the specified network can be reached

   d. the network address to which each routing table entry applies

11. Which statement is true about the following command?

    ```
    route add -net 192.168.20.0 netmask 255.255.255.0 gw
    192.168.10.1 dev eth0
    ```
    a. It is valid and defines the router that can reach network 192.168.20.0.
    b. It is valid and defines a default gateway for all traffic not destined for network 192.168.20.0.
    c. It is invalid because it does not specify the host IP address of the source of the packets to be routed.
    d. It is invalid in format because it lacks needed dashes before command-line options.

12. The PLIP networking device refers to:
    a. Protocol Layer Internet Proxy activity
    b. ProxyARP Layered Internet Protocol transmissions
    c. Parallel Line Internet Protocol support
    d. multiple, parallel SLIP channels

13. Distinguish between RARP and InARP.

14. You would use the `arp` command to:
    a. send a hardware address to a remote host per an ARP protocol request
    b. turn on and off ARP functionality for your network
    c. collect host name-to-IP address mappings for each of the hosts on your local network
    d. view or modify the ARP cache containing hardware address-to-IP address mappings

15. Scripts such as `/etc/rc.d/init.d/network` and their corresponding data files are used to control networking because:
    a. Using `ifconfig` and `route` is too complicated for the average user.
    b. The `ifconfig` and `route` commands alone don't complete the network configuration.
    c. Using scripts allows flexibility and power in managing multiple interfaces, firewall settings, and peripheral requirements that involve many diverse parts of Linux.
    d. By relying on scripts, graphical utilities can create a more user-friendly environment that makes system administrators more efficient.

16. The correct device designation for an IP alias to the first Ethernet card is:
    a. `eth00`
    b. `eth0:0`
    c. `Ethernet II`
    d. `eth1:0`

2

17. In the Network Configuration Tool (neat), the Hardware tab includes:

    a. a list of all networking hardware for which a module is currently installed

    b. a list of all available networking modules in Fedora Core

    c. a list of parameters that are available for currently installed modules

    d. the IP addresses of each installed hardware interface

18. The loopback device is assigned the IP address:

    a. 255.255.255.0

    b. 127.0.0.1

    c. 127.0.0.0

    d. any IP address beginning with 192.168

19. IP forwarding is enabled by which command?

    a. `ifconfig eth0 ip_forward`

    b. `arp ip_forward`

    c. `route add default ip_forward -net 192.168.10.0 netmask 255.255.255.0`

    d. `echo 1 > /proc/sys/net/ipv4/ip_forward`

20. Which utility cannot be used to configure network interfaces?

    a. `ip`

    b. `ifconfig`

    c. `route`

    d. `ping`

21. Telnet is considered dangerous because:

    a. It provides access to networking stacks, to which only the root user should have access.

    b. It transmits data—including passwords—without encrypting them, so anyone on the network can see them by using special software.

    c. It causes an increased number of Ethernet collisions by ramping up network traffic with broadcast messages to the local network segment.

    d. It requires that a user provide a password to gain access to a remote system.

22. `Ping` is used to test networking connections by:

    a. trying to contact systems that are progressively farther from your host to see if any networking problems occur

    b. flooding the network with traffic to see if it has sufficient bandwidth

    c. testing whether remote servers are configured to respond to ICMP echo-request packets

    d. noting the route that packets take when responding that they are "alive"

23. Traceroute is a useful troubleshooting tool because:

    a. All data sent by traceroute is fully encrypted, so it can be used safely on open networks.

    b. It reports the ARP cache of each system it contacts.

    c. It reports each router that a packet passes through to a destination IP address, along with the time needed to reach that router.

    d. It uses UDP to report errors generated by the IP stack of intermittent routers that may be misconfigured and slow down packets as they traverse large networks.

24. If you cannot ping a host on a different segment of your local network, you probably wouldn't bother checking:

    a. the cable connections at the hub or in the server room

    b. whether ifconfig indicates that the host has a valid IP address that does not conflict with any other host on the network

    c. whether the routing tables of the host and the router include the proper entries to tie the segments together

    d. whether the ping command was subject to fragmentation by the router in trying to reach the other segment

25. Define what the Netatalk package does for a Linux system.

HANDS-ON PROJECTS

In the following projects, you experiment with the networking configuration of your host. You must be aware that changing your IP address causes your networking to cease functioning correctly. It may also cause someone else's networking to cease functioning! Check with your instructor or system administrator before completing these projects. In addition, note that standard file locations are used when discussing networking files. Some Linux systems may place these files in slightly different subdirectories. You should be able to locate them by exploring the /etc subdirectory or asking someone who is familiar with your Linux distribution.

HANDS-ON PROJECTS

Project 2-1

In this project, you explore the Address Resolution Protocol on your host. To complete this project, you should have a network connection configured with at least one other host on the network. An Internet connection is used for the last part of the project, but is not strictly necessary.

1. From any Linux command line, enter this command:

```
arp -a
```

2

This displays the contents of the ARP cache on your Linux system. The result may be nothing—the cache is probably empty at this point if you have not done any networking in the last few minutes. Each entry is saved only for about two minutes.

2. If the ARP cache is not empty, note the contents carefully. See if you can identify a neighbor on the network (in your computer lab, for example) that is not listed in the output of the command. Obtain that neighbor's IP address.

3. Ping your neighbor using a command such as the following (substitute the neighbor's IP address for 192.168.100.45):

```
ping 192.168.100.45
```

You can press Ctrl+C to end the `ping` command.

NOTE

4. Run the `arp` command a second time:

```
arp -a
```

Do you see your neighbor's system listed (as indicated by an IP address that you recognize)?

5. Ping an Internet site such as 155.99.1.2 or 192.20.4.70.

6. Run **arp -a** again. Why is no additional entry included for the new site that you pinged?

**HANDS-ON
PROJECTS**

Project 2-2

For this project, you need a system running Linux with Internet access on which you can log on as `root`. You should open a command-line window to complete this project.

1. Obtain the IP address of a host (not your own) within your computer lab or your organization, but not on the Internet.

2. Execute the `traceroute` command using this IP address and note the times displayed for reaching each point on that route to that host.

3. Locate a business that is headquartered or located near you, such as a bank in your city or the local government Web site. (Don't choose your own school or organization. You may want to ask your instructor for a suggestion or use an Internet search site to help you find the Internet address for the entity you select.)

4. Use a `traceroute` command to see how packets reach that site from your host. If your system has DNS configured already, feel free to use a command such as this, rather than using only an IP address:

```
traceroute www.uva.edu
```

For some sites, you might see a number of asterisks instead of the times you expect to see. Review the man page for traceroute to learn what these indicate.

NOTE

5. You are likely to see a long list of unusual names for the routers that the packets pass through to reach someone's site close to you. Can you identify where these routers are physically located by their names (that is, which city and state they are located in)?

6. Why might a packet travel so far to get across town? How could the routing be improved?

Project 2-3

HANDS-ON PROJECTS

For this project, you need a system running Linux with Internet access. You should open a command-line window to complete this project. After each step shown, make a note about what its successful completion indicates about your network. To complete the last few steps (as indicated), you need to have root access and your instructor's permission, as these steps might create a heavy load on your network.

1. Run the **ifconfig** command to view your networking devices. See that you have both lo and eth0 devices configured.

2. Ping your loopback device using its IP address.

3. Ping your own IP address.

4. If you are working in a classroom or computer lab, ask your neighbor for her IP address, then ping her host.

5. If your instructor gives you permission to continue, make sure you are logged on as root.

6. Use the **ping** command with the **-f** option, for flood. This sends pings (ICMP echo-request packets) as quickly as possible. Each period that is printed on your screen after you execute this command indicates one dropped packet (because the host being pinged cannot respond quickly enough).

7. If possible, have your neighbor try to complete a networking task such as opening a browser window and viewing a graphically intensive page. The flood ping places a heavy load on the network and should be used with caution. This is why some system administrators block pings, and why you will want to learn in Chapter 11 how to do the same yourself.

Project 2-4

To complete this project, you must have a network interface on your computer. It is useful but not necessary to have other computers on the network. You must be logged on as `root` and open a command-line window to complete this project.

1. Using either the `ifconfig` or `ip` program, note the IP address and the broadcast address of your computer's network interface.

2. By default, Linux responds to pings. You can verify this by using the `ping` program to ping your interface. Enter the command **ping –c 1** *1.2.3.4*, but substitute your IP address for 1.2.3.4. The `-c 1` option limits the pings to one—normally it will ping continuously. You see output similar to this:

```
PING 1.2.3.4 (1.2.3.4): 56 data bytes
64 bytes from 1.2.3.4: icmp_seq-0 ttl=64 time=0.1 ms

--- 1.2.3.4 ping Statistics ---
1 packets transmitted, 1 packets received, 0% packet loss
```

3. If there is another computer on your network that you (or a lab partner) can use, try pinging your computer's IP address. The other computer should display output similar to that in Step 2.

4. You can disable your computer from responding to pings without having to configure a firewall. Enter the following command:

   echo "1">/proc/sys/net/ipv4/icmp_echo_ignore_all

5. Enter the command **ping –c 1** *1.2.3.4* again. This time, your computer does not respond to the ping. The last line of the output will be this:

   ```
   1 packets transmitted, 0 packets received, 100% packet loss
   ```

6. Enable pings with the following command. You should be able to ping your computer and have it respond.

   echo "0">/proc/sys/net/ipv4/icmp_echo_ignore_all

7. By default, Linux responds to broadcast pings. If you specified the broadcast address in your command, all Linux computers on your network might respond. Enter **ping –c 1** *1.2.3.255*, substituting your computer's broadcast address for 1.2.3.255. Your computer will respond to the ping, but other computers on your network might as well. You'll see output similar to the following if another computer responds:

```
PING 1.2.3.4 (1.2.3.4): 56 data bytes
64 bytes from 1.2.3.4: icmp seq-0 ttl=64 time=0.1 ms
64 bytes from 1.2.3.7: icmp seq-0 ttl=64 time=0.1 ms

--- 1.2.3.4 ping Statistics ---
1 packets transmitted, 1 packets received, +1 duplicates, 0%
packet loss
```

8. You can disable your computer's ability to respond to broadcast pings without disabling its ability to respond to normal (specific) pings. Enter the command **echo "1">/proc/sys/net/ipv4/icmp_echo_ignore_broadcasts**. Your computer will no longer respond to broadcast pings. Enter the command **ping –c 1 *1.2.3.255***, substituting your computer's broadcast address for 1.2.3.255. You won't get a response from your computer, but other computers on your network may respond.

9. You can still ping your computer with a specific ping. Enter the command **ping –c 1 *1.2.3.4***. Your computer will respond.

10. Of course, you can disable both broadcast and specific pings. Enter the command **echo "0">/proc/sys/net/ipv4/icmp_echo_ignore_broadcasts** to enable your computer to once again respond to broadcast pings.

NOTE

By default, Windows computers do not respond to broadcast pings. If you have Windows computers on your network, they will not respond when you ping the network's broadcast address.

HANDS-ON PROJECTS

Project 2-5

For this project, you need to be connected to an Ethernet and have the permission of your instructor and a static IP address assignment to use when creating an IP alias. You must be logged on as root to complete this project.

1. Run the **ifconfig** command to see that you have eth0 configured.

2. Change to the directory: /etc/sysconfig/network-scripts:

   ```
   cd /etc/sysconfig/network-scripts
   ```

3. Copy the configuration file for the eth0 interface as a basis for creating a new interface called eth0:0, which is an IP alias to the same physical Ethernet card.

   ```
   cp ifcfg-eth0 ifcfg-eth0:0
   ```

4. Open the file ifcfg-eth0:0 in a text editor.

5. Change the DEVICE parameter from eth0 to read **eth0:0** instead.

6. Change the IPADDR parameter to reflect the new IP address provided by your instructor. Remember, if you simply choose a random IP address, you might cause networking problems for others in your lab or on the Internet.

7. Restart networking by running the network script with start and stop (or restart on some Linux distributions):

   ```
   /etc/rc.d/init.d/network stop
   /etc/rc.d/init.d/network start
   ```

8. Run the **ifconfig** command. Notice that you now have a new interface, eth0:0.

2

9. Ping the IP address of `eth0`. Ping the IP address of `eth0:0`. In later chapters, you will learn how you can use an IP alias to make management of multiple Web sites easier.

10. Return to the `/etc/sysconfig/network-scripts` directory if you have left it:

   cd /etc/sysconfig/network-scripts

11. Delete the file you created, confirming the deletion if prompted:

   rm ifcfg-eth0:0

12. Restart networking a second time:

   /etc/rc.d/init.d/network stop
   /etc/rc.d/init.d/network start

13. Run the **ifconfig** command to verify that you once again have only two networking devices: `lo` and `eth0`.

CASE PROJECTS

CASE PROJECTS

Case Project 2-1

You have been hired as a consultant by the law firm of Snow, Sleet, and Hale, based in Fairbanks, Alaska. The firm has been in business for many years, but is just now realizing the need to upgrade its information technology infrastructure. The firm consists of three offices, two in Fairbanks and one in Juneau. The Fairbanks headquarters is the largest office, with 40 attorneys plus a support staff of paralegals, secretaries, librarians, and others. They are divided into two practice groups, one for environmental work and another for energy work relating to oil, natural gas, hydrothermal, and hydroelectric. The work of the two groups doesn't intermingle much, though the attorneys from the two groups occasionally have a common client. All staff members share e-mail, of course, and occasionally need to access the same files. The managing partner tells you that she isn't ready to provide Internet access to the company as a whole. (A few attorneys have a private modem connection for legal research, but you needn't be concerned about that yet.) The second Fairbanks office is located about two miles away from headquarters. It consists of 10 lawyers who also do energy work, almost exclusively for a large company that occupies the same building. The Juneau office is relatively new and focuses on government-related work at the state capitol. It consists of seven lawyers and a few support staff.

Based on the volume of network traffic you anticipate over the next four years or so, you have already decided to use standard 100-Mb/s Ethernet cards in each computer, with new CAT6 cabling throughout the office. You have also planned for a high-speed connection among all three offices (don't worry about the specifics of the connection at this point).

1. Your immediate question is how to set up the three offices to make the best use of the network bandwidth so that everyone has fast access to the information they use most, with perhaps slower access to information they need less often. Diagram the

network segments as you would arrange them, noting your reasons for the arrangement. Within the parameters described previously, you can assume a physical arrangement of personnel within each office so that it suits your plan. Try to plan for the placement of hubs and routers, as well as how segments are arranged. Consider also these questions: What questions would you ask the managing partner about future growth plans before solidifying your network arrangement? What contingency plans could you make based on her responses? This scenario leaves many questions unanswered that will be addressed in future chapters. What additional questions come to mind that you may not have adequate information to answer yet?

2. Snow, Sleet, and Hale has merged with another firm: Sand & Son, located in Amarillo, Texas. Sand & Son is an energy law firm of 10 attorneys serving mainly oil companies. The two firms have several common clients and feel the merger will strengthen their position among clients seeking energy law specialists. Sand & Son has a fairly new office network for its 10 lawyers and staff. It runs on Token-Ring at 4 Mb/s. They have no Internet access. Assuming that you set up a high-speed network connection between Texas and Alaska, how will you incorporate Sand & Son into the existing corporate network? How will the need to integrate this office affect existing network topology? Will you need additional routers? Will you need to reconfigure anyone's IP addresses? What about possible packet fragmentation and slow data transfers between offices? What other problems might the Token-Ring network pose?

3. One year later, the managing partner accepts your recommendation. The entire firm must have Internet access to work effectively for its clients. Make some simple assumptions about the costs of different types of connections such as a modem or a dedicated circuit, then consider questions such as these: How can you add Internet access to your network design? How many connection points do you anticipate? What new problems arise because of how you set up the segments and routing? Would you have been better off setting things up differently if you had known that this new requirement would come up, or would it have made things too inefficient in the intervening year?

# CHAPTER 3

CONFIGURING CLIENT SERVICES

**After reading this chapter and completing the
exercises, you will be able to:**

♦ Understand name services, including DNS

♦ Understand the DHCP client service

♦ Configure dial-up network access using PPP

♦ Understand the LDAP client service

♦ Use remote graphical applications and remote dial-up authentication

♦ Use common client tools such as Linux Web browsers and e-mail clients

In this chapter, you will learn how to configure network client services, such as DNS and DHCP, which rely on the networking technologies you learned about in Chapters 1 and 2.

The first part of this chapter describes tasks that must be accomplished prior to using common networking applications. For example, you will learn about setting up DNS name resolution, so you can use names instead of IP addresses to refer to hosts on your local network and on the Internet. You'll also learn about the DHCP client service.

In the second part of the chapter, you will learn about specific Linux client services that let you view Web pages, run graphical applications, get your e-mail, or remotely execute Linux commands on another computer.

NAME SERVICES

Most people who use computers wouldn't do well if they had to remember IP addresses to specify Web sites and to send e-mail. They do better with names such as *yahoo.com* or *amazon.com*. These are often called domain names. A domain is a collection of computers that can be accessed using a common name such as a company or school name.

Name services map domain names to information such as IP addresses. A name service is an Application-layer program that lets a computer provide a name and receive back information about that name. A computer can also provide an IP address and receive back a name. The process of having a name server answer queries about a name or IP address is called name resolution. A name server is a computer running software that provides name services.

The hosts File

The simplest form of a name service is the **/etc/hosts** file. It contains a table of names and IP addresses. Each text line in the file is a row in the table. A sample file is shown here:

```
127.0.0.1          localhost.xmission.com localhost
192.168.1.35       sundance.xmission.com
```

The first line is the loopback address of the host. The second line is the host name and address. You can add other names and addresses to the file:

```
127.0.0.1          localhost.xmission.com localhost
192.168.1.35       sundance.xmission.com
198.80.146.30      www.course.com
69.30.87.202       www.alcpress.com
66.35.250.177      www.linux.com
```

When you have a small network, you can create a hosts file that contains all the hosts that anyone on the network needs to access. You can copy that file to every host so they can all resolve the same names. Each time a host needs to convert a domain name to an IP address, it can find the needed information on the local hard disk.

 Some networks use DHCP to assign dynamic IP addresses to hosts. You shouldn't put these addresses in the /etc/hosts file because they may change.

CAUTION

When you enter the name *www.linux.com* in your Web browser, the first thing the browser does is to send a request to the resolver asking "What is the IP address of the server *www.linux.com*?" The resolver searches the hosts file and responds with the address. The Web browser can initiate a network connection using that address.

Given the size of the Internet, it would be impractical to administer a hosts file that contained all the names you might ever use. There needs to be a more manageable and scalable name service. Welcome to DNS.

3

DNS Names

The most popular name service on the Internet is the Domain Name Service or DNS. This section describes how to configure the client portion of DNS so a Linux system can access a DNS server. Chapter 6 describes how to configure your computer to be a DNS server.

The term **domain name** loosely refers to the name of multiple hosts on the Internet that are referred to collectively, such as *ibm.com* or *utah.edu*. Within each domain, you have names that refer to hosts and services. For example, there may be a host called *server1.ibm.com* and services called *www.ibm.com* and *mail.ibm.com*. This can be confusing because it's perfectly valid to have a host called *www.ibm.com* that's running a Web service you access with a URL containing *www.ibm.com*. Don't be concerned about this distinction; in the world of DNS, all names are just that—names.

Domain names are hierarchical—there are levels. The top level is called the top-level domain or TLD. The TLD is intended to represent the type of organization using the name. For example, the most widely known TLD is .com, which is supposed to be used by commercial organizations. In practice, the .com TLD is used by any kind of organization, including individuals, who register a name. Because of this, the .com TLD has lost its significance. Similarly, the .net TLD is supposed to be used by Internet service providers, but anyone can register a .net name.

Some TLDs are enforced. Only colleges and universities can register a name in the .edu TLD. Only organizations created by international treaty, such as the United Nations, can register a name in the .int TLD. The United States military enforces the use of the .mil TLD. Presumably, you must be a museum to use .museum.

There are more than 200 TLDs that represent countries. These are two-letter names such as .us for the United States and .ca for Canada.

Table 3-1 shows the common top-level domains.

Table 3-1 Examples of top-level domains

Top-Level Domain Name	Example	Description
.biz	www.escrubber.biz	Businesses
.com	www.ibm.com	Commercial organizations
.edu	www.ucla.edu	Postsecondary educational institutions
.gov	www.state.gov	U.S. federal government
.int	www.un.int	International treaty organizations
.info	www.medicine.info	Sites that provide information
.mil	www.army.mil	U.S. military
.museum	index.museum	Museums
.name	www.smith.name	People names—usually family names
.org	www.un.org	Nonprofit organizations
.net	www.internic.net	Network service providers
.pro	www.index.pro	Professionals

To see all the country-specific codes, visit *www.iso.org* and do a Standards Search for ISO-3166.

NOTE

When you register a domain name, you choose a TLD in which to register it. For example, the publisher of this book registered the domain name *course.com* and the author registered *alcpress.com*. In these two examples, the names *course* and *alcpress* are second-level domain names or SLDs. The combination of a TLD and an SLD forms a domain name. Thus, the general form of a domain name is SLD.TLD.

Organizations and individuals who register and use domain names commonly use third-level domain names. You don't abbreviate this term because it would conflict with the top-level domain name. We'll refer to third-level and lower domain names as simply *names*. The general forms of a DNS name are name.SLD.TLD, name.name.SLD.TLD, name.name.name.SLD.TLD, and so on. Here are examples from the domain names in Table 3-1:

```
www.course.com
www.alcpress.com
```

In both these examples, the third-level name is *www*. When the third-level name is the name of a computer or host, the name is called a **host name**. Many administrators use arbitrary names for their hosts, such as the names of plants, cities, planets, bands, inventors, poets, and so on. In a name like *igor.alcpress.com*, *igor* is the host name, *alcpress.com* is the domain name, and *igor.alcpress.com* is the **fully qualified domain name** or **FQDN**. When the DNS name includes the SLD.TLD portion, it is called an FQDN.

Domain names can include all letters of the English alphabet, digits 0 through 9, and the dash (-). Uppercase and lowercase never matter when using domain names (unlike most of Linux). *Course.com* is identical to *COURSE.COM* and *course.COM*.

TIP

Next, you'll learn how to set up Linux so that it can query a DNS server to resolve DNS names.

Configuring the DNS Resolver Manually

The **resolver** is the client part of DNS. It makes requests to a DNS server on behalf of programs running on your system. Programs such as a Web browser automatically use the resolver in Linux to resolve domain names into IP addresses.

If you included a DNS server address when installing Linux, the resolver should already be configured. You can test it by pinging another system using a host name instead of an IP address. For example, enter "`ping www.novell.com.`"

TIP

The resolver is configured by a single file in Linux: **/etc/resolv.conf** (notice that "resolve" is missing an "e" in the filename). You configure the resolver by storing the IP address of one or more DNS servers in the `resolv.conf` file, preceded by the keyword `nameserver`. You can use any DNS server on the Internet that allows you access, but the closer the server is to your local network segment, the faster the responses are to resolver requests. You can include up to three DNS servers in `resolv.conf`, each on a separate line. The resolver tries to reach each of the servers in the order you list them until a request succeeds. Here's an example of a `resolv.conf` file:

```
nameserver 198.60.22.2
nameserver 10.21.105.1
```

NOTE

The resolver is not a program or a daemon. It is a library. You cannot see the resolver running using the `ps` command.

You can include other items in `resolv.conf`, such as the domain name of which your host is a part. This information helps the resolver determine how to create fully qualified names when the query does not specify a fully qualified name. For example, suppose the `resolv.conf` file looks like this:

```
domain course.com
nameserver 198.60.22.2
nameserver 10.21.105.1
```

If you were to run this command:

```
ping www
```

the resolver knows the name *www* is not fully qualified. It adds the domain string to the name, producing the fully qualified name *www.course.com*. It is this name that's sent in a query to the name server.

There can only be one domain statement in the `resolv.conf` file, and it can have only one domain name. If you operate in an environment in which there are numerous domain names, you can use the `search` statement instead. The `search` statement can have many domain names, but they must all be on a single line and separated by white space (spaces and tabs). On most Linux systems, you can list up to six domains. The following is an example.

```
search abc.com cbs.com nbc.com
nameserver 198.60.22.2
nameserver 10.21.105.1
```

If you were to run the command *ping www*, the resolver would first build the fully qualified name *www.abc.com* and send this in a query to the name server. If the name didn't exist, the resolver would next build the name *www.cbs.com* and query the name server again. It would do this until a name resolved or it tried all the domains in the `search` statement.

You can change the resolv.conf file with any text editor. This configuration file is checked before each query, so if you make a change in /etc/resolv.conf, you don't need to take any other action for the change to take effect.

There are additional statements that you can include in the resolv.conf file, but most are for advanced features that you don't typically need. Refer to the man page for resolv.conf to learn about them.

Related to the /etc/resolv.conf and /etc/hosts files is the **/etc/host.conf** file. This file's main purpose is to specify the order in which names are resolved. This file typically contains a single line:

order hosts,bind

This line tells the resolver to check the /etc/hosts file first when a name must be resolved. If the name is not listed in /etc/hosts, the resolver uses the configuration in resolv.conf to query a DNS server. The word *bind* in the statement refers to the most popular DNS software, called BIND. Checking the /etc/hosts file first and DNS second is the most practical way of resolving names. You could check DNS first and the /etc/hosts file second by switching the order of the words in the order statement. However, the practical reasons for doing this are elusive.

The /etc/host.conf file has been made obsolete by another configuration file: **/etc/nsswitch.conf**. This file functions much like /etc/host.conf but is also used by other programs, such as NIS (defined below). It also includes more options for where information can be obtained, rather than just /etc/hosts or a DNS server. A sample excerpt from a nsswitch.conf file from Fedora Core is shown with the comments removed:

```
passwd:      files
shadow:      files
group:       files
hosts:       files dns
ethers:      files
netmasks:    files
networks:    files
protocols:   files
rpc:         files
services:    files
netgroup:    files
publickey:   nisplus
automount:   files
aliases:     files nisplus
```

The line beginning with hosts: controls how the resolver handles name resolution. It first looks in the local file (/etc/hosts), and then it tries DNS. This is equivalent to the functionality provided by the /etc/host.conf file.

TIP   The **Network Information System (NIS)** protocol and the more advanced **NIS+** protocol let hosts share configuration information across a network, so that only one master configuration file need be supported for a number of hosts. Linux supports NIS and NIS+, but they are not discussed further in this book. To learn more about them, search for the NIS HOWTO document at *www.linuxdocs.org*.

3

Configuring the DNS Resolver Graphically

If you prefer a graphical configuration tool for configuring the resolver, you can use a number of graphical utilities, including those described in Chapter 2 for network configuration.

In Fedora Core, the same Network Administration Tool you used in Chapter 2 also manages the contents of the /etc/hosts and /etc/resolv.conf files. To use it, start the program by choosing Applications, then System Settings, and then Network from the GNOME desktop menu. When the main Network Configuration window opens, choose the Hosts tab. From this tab, you can use the New button to enter new combinations of IP addresses and host names to store in your /etc/hosts file. Remember that any names you store here can be accessed without contacting a DNS server.

To configure the /etc/resolv.conf file, choose the DNS tab. This tab displays your FQDN host name, plus the contents of your /etc/resolv.conf file. The host name of your system is stored in the /etc/sysconfig/network file, which is then read by the /etc/rc.d/init.d/network script. You can modify it by entering a new value in the host name or domain fields of the DNS tab.

CAUTION   Don't casually modify your host name or domain name. That information is probably also stored on a DNS server somewhere. If you change it, other systems may not be able to reach you.

The three possible DNS servers are listed in the Primary, Secondary, and Tertiary (Third) DNS fields. Enter IP addresses here as needed. The search line in resolv.conf is controlled by the DNS search path entry. None of the options described in the resolv.conf man page can be added to the file using this graphical screen. For reference, Figure 3-1 shows the DNS tab.

Figure 3-1   DNS information

Using DHCP

The **Dynamic Host Configuration Protocol (DHCP)** is a service that automatically assigns IP addresses and other network configuration information (called **leases**) to clients on a network. DHCP is backward compatible with the **BOOTP** system that has long been used by diskless workstations to obtain network configuration. Using DHCP involves installing a DHCP server on your network and configuring client computers to use a DHCP client program.

Using DHCP can reduce network administration. Instead of having to visit each client computer to change a network setting, the setting can be changed at the DHCP server. Clients will use the new setting the next time they have to renew their lease.

A Linux DHCP server can be used by DHCP clients regardless of the operating system the clients run. It's common for a Linux DHCP server to be used by Windows desktop computers.

DHCP Client

The DHCP client program communicates with a DHCP server on your network to obtain a lease. You can run the client program anytime to fetch a lease. It doesn't matter that the interface is normally configured for static addresses. Suppose you use your notebook computer at work and it's normally configured to use a static IP address. When you take your notebook into meetings held in the conference room, your static IP address does not work there. You must fetch an address from DHCP instead. Just run the DHCP client program in the conference room and your static address will be overridden. When you get back to your desk, you'll have to restore your static IP address, but that's easy. You learned how to do this in Chapter 2.

There are three popular DHCP client programs: **dhcpcd**, **dhclient**, and **pump**. Linux distributions typically include one of the three. Fedora Core includes dhclient. This section focuses on this client. You can run the dhclient program without specifying any command-line parameters and it will use a default configuration. The default configuration is appropriate for computers with a single network interface and when it's acceptable for the DHCP server to override any network settings that exist before dhclient runs.

If your computer has more than one interface or you need to control which network settings dhclient is allowed to change, you must either specify options on the command line or create the /etc/dhclient.conf configuration file. Refer to the man page for dhclient to learn about command-line options. Refer to the dhclient.conf man page to learn about configuration statements that are placed in the /etc/dhclient.conf file.

In Fedora Core, you configure an interface to use DHCP using the graphical Network Configuration Tool. Choose the Devices tab and then select the device that you want to configure for DHCP. Then choose Edit. The Ethernet Device dialog box opens, as shown in Figure 3-2. Click the radio button labeled "Automatically obtain IP address settings with" followed by a list box. Choose DHCP from this list and then click OK. Notice that you can also choose whether you use DNS information provided by the DHCP server. When you close the main window of the Network Configuration Tool, confirm that you want to save your changes. DHCP is now activated.

Note that you have less control over the DHCP client when you use the graphical tools. After DHCP is configured, it can take a minute or two for the DHCP client to obtain an IP address and activate the network interface. If you run the ifconfig or ip program and see 0.0.0.0 for the IP address, DHCP has not yet obtained an IP address. Wait a few moments and try ifconfig again to see whether a valid IP address is shown.

Figure 3-2   Ethernet Device dialog box

Dial-up Network Access Using PPP

In Chapter 2, you learned about PPP, the Point-to-Point Protocol, which is one method of making a network connection between two hosts. Because PPP is widely used to connect to the Internet via a modem, it deserves special attention. Fortunately, Linux vendors have also given it special attention and provided a number of easy-to-use graphical tools for setting up PPP connections.

PPP differs from traditional dial-up terminal connections. When you call in to a remote computer using a terminal emulator program such as **minicom**, the program simply sends characters over the modem to be interpreted by the Telnet server on the remote computer. In contrast, using PPP establishes a low-level network protocol over which other programs can communicate with the remote computer independent of one another. PPP includes features that make it more secure, flexible, and dependable than a terminal emulation setup. Of course, that's exactly why people use PPP; it allows your computer to download files, run multiple networking programs simultaneously, run graphical programs, and, in general, act like an independent node on the network rather than a terminal to a distant CPU.

Setting up PPP used to be quite a challenge. It involved the following steps:

1. Identify your modem's serial port and make certain it functions correctly, perhaps by using a program such as minicom to call a remote computer and test the modem.

2. Set up a `ppp-options` file to instruct the PPP daemon (the PPP server) how to operate.

3. Create a script for the `chat` program. The `chat` program uses this script to send commands to the modem. The script tells `chat` to watch for text such as "ssword" coming in on the modem. This would indicate that a password is being requested by the remote computer, and `chat` should respond accordingly.

4. Have the script launch the PPP server program, `pppd`, using the correct options file and command-line parameters.

Using a `chat` script and a PPP options file was considered challenging under ideal conditions. Troubleshooting it was difficult, and the interaction of multiple components (the modem, `chat`, `pppd`, the remote computer's logon program, and the remote computer's `pppd`) made it generally an unpleasant topic among new users of Linux.

In addition, standard PPP was not secure because the username and password you used to connect to the remote computer were stored in the `chat` script file, and then passed over the modem to the remote computer. Two advances improved the security of PPP. One is the **Password Authentication Protocol (PAP)**, which stores pairs of usernames and passwords in a file (`/etc/ppp/pap-secrets`) that only the root user can access. They are still passed over the modem (where others might be able to eavesdrop), but at least they are more secure on the local host. (Security is discussed in more detail in later chapters.)

The more advanced type of security is called **Challenge Handshake Authentication Protocol (CHAP)**. CHAP never sends your password across the modem to the remote computer. Instead, the remote computer selects a random string, encrypts it with a user's password, and sends it to the host that is trying to authenticate for PPP. The host uses the password stored in the CHAP file (`/etc/ppp/chap-secrets`) and sends back the random string. By showing that it can decode the string, it demonstrates that it has the correct password for the user.

NOTE

Most ISPs provide PPP connections, and nearly all of these ISPs use PAP or CHAP, rather than the older-style scripts.

PPP Connections Using `wvdial`

In response to the difficulty of using PPP, several new projects have appeared in recent years that make it easy to connect using PPP. One of these is a text-mode utility called **wvdial**. This program detects how to configure the modem and how to respond to queries from the remote server to establish a connection with the basic information you provide (such as the phone number of the ISP, the username, and the corresponding password). You can learn more about the WvDial project by visiting *http://open.nit.ca/* and examining the Project Info list. The wvdial utility is installed by default on most distributions. Use the `locate` command to see if wvdial is installed on your system.

One potential problem with Linux dial-up networking is that most modems today are not real modems. They're hardware devices that require a program running on the computer to make them behave as modems. These devices are called Winmodems because they used to work only on Microsoft Windows. The Linux community has managed to get many, but not all, of these devices to work with Linux. Those that do work are called Linmodems. Search for the Linmodem-HOWTO on the Internet for more details.

One advantage of wvdial is that you can easily use it from a command line on a server without using a graphical interface. To use wvdial, first run the wvdialconf program. This program finds your modem and detects how to operate it (regardless of whether it uses standard commands, for example). It then creates the configuration file that the wvdial program uses to actually connect to a remote host. The format of the wvdialconf command includes the name of the configuration file to be created, as shown here:

```
wvdialconf   /etc/wvdial.conf
```

After running wvdialconf, open the /etc/wvdial.conf file in a text editor and enter your ISP information (phone number, username, and password). Then, you can connect to your ISP by executing wvdial (with no options). The Defaults section shown in the following sample file defines the ISP information. Every line except the username, password, and phone number was generated by wvdialconf. If you run the wvdialconf program again, it checks and updates the information within /etc/wvdial.conf, but doesn't disturb the details you entered.

```
[Dialer Defaults]
Modem = /dev/ttyS2
Baud = 115200
Init1 = ATZ
SetVolume = 1
Dial Command = ATDT
Init4 = ATM1L2
Username = nwells
Password = secretpassword
Phone = 703-437-0900
Stupid mode = 0
```

Because many people work with multiple ISP accounts, you might use a more complex `wvdial.conf` file than the previous example. The `wvdial` program lets you set up multiple ISP accounts in the `wvdial.conf` configuration file and choose which connection you want to initiate each time you start the program. For each account, the file can contain a `Dialer` section; you connect to that account by entering `wvdial` followed by the account name. For example, within `wvdial.conf`, one section might look like this:

```
[Dialer usnet]
Username = nwells@nd.us.net
Password = topsecretpassword
Phone = 801-997-5599
Inherits = Dialer Defaults
Stupid mode = 0
```

The `Stupid mode = 0` setting in the last line indicates that `wvdial` should start PPP immediately after the remote server answers, without waiting for specific instructions to start it. A few ISPs require this setting to connect successfully, but by default, it is not used. To connect using the settings in this section, enter this command:

```
wvdial usnet
```

Automating PPP with `diald`

Many users who rely on a modem for a dial-up connection must balance the hassle of starting and stopping their connection (even using a convenient program like `rp3` or a script) with the need to keep down ISP charges or keep a home telephone line open for other uses. Moreover, when a modem is used to connect several users on a LAN to a single Internet connection, those users may not know how to make the connection or have access to the computer where the modem is located.

The **diald** program lets a dial-up connection remain active only when needed, disconnects after a specified period of inactivity, and automatically reconnects when anyone makes a request to an Internet site. Although this is a highly useful set of features, the program only recently became stable enough to use on production systems, so you won't find it included with most Linux distributions. You can learn more by visiting *diald.sourceforge.net*. "Stable," however, does not mean "easy to use"; `diald` is difficult to configure.

The `diald` program works by setting up a "fake" network interface (a proxy interface) as the default gateway. Whenever network traffic is routed to that interface, `diald` establishes a PPP connection and changes the default gateway to that network interface. The `diald` program monitors the packets that are coming to the proxy interface to determine whether they warrant starting the dial-up connection. You can set configuration parameters such as how long the connection should remain active without any activity or when the connection should not be established even if network traffic appears to justify it.

The difficulty in using `diald` is that it relies on the "old-fashioned" method of configuring PPP: using logon scripts, `chat` scripts, and manually configured security files (such as `/etc/ppp/chap-secrets`). In addition, `diald` uses a number of complex, text-based configuration files to set its operating parameters. The program is flexible and powerful, but challenging to set up unless you feel quite comfortable with all the topics discussed in Chapters 1 and 2, plus PPP dial-up scripting.

The easiest way to set up `diald` is to locate an RPM or Debian format software package for your version of Linux (check *www.rpmfind.net*). Such a package includes configuration files designed to interact with other parts of your specific Linux distribution. However, because few preconfigured packages are available for `diald`, you may need to download the source code, compile it, and configure the following files in `/etc/diald/`:

- `diald.conf`—Contains all standard operation parameters. Note that in the `diald` documentation, this file is often referred to by its name in previous versions of `diald`, which was `diald.options`.

- `standard.filter`—Indicates how different types of network traffic are handled; for example, whether they cause the connection to come up or keep it up after it is established.

- `diald.connect`—Contains the instructions for starting a PPP connection using a script written for the `chat` program located in `/etc/chatscripts`.

- `ip-up` and `ip-down`—Executes these optional scripts each time the link is initiated or dropped.

- `addroute` and `delroute`—Resets routing if anything more complex than a single interface is being managed by `diald` (in which case, the routing changes made by `diald` are adequate, and these additional scripts are not needed).

Man pages are provided for the `diald` program and several of the supporting programs (such as `diald-control`). You can learn more by reviewing either the FAQ file under the Documentation link on *diald.sourceforge.net* or the `diald` HOWTO document, available on *www.linuxdocs.org*. (This second document includes sample scenarios for connecting within recent versions of Debian, Slackware, and SuSE Linux.)

UNDERSTANDING LDAP

On a single host, you can easily review the contents of configuration files or a graphical utility to learn about your system. On larger networks, knowing "what's out there" can become a real problem. Both system administrators and users often need to know more about a network resource than is readily apparent. These resources might include users (user accounts), services provided by hosts, printers, and many others.

The solution to this lack of information is to create a **directory service**: a database of information about resources that can be accessed by people on a network. Several international standards have emerged for creation of just such a directory. One of these is **X.500**. A popular commercial implementation of a directory service is Novell Directory Services (NDS) or eDirectory. Another similar model is the Lightweight Directory, which you can access using the **Lightweight Directory Access Protocol (LDAP)**. Although LDAP is too large a topic to explore in depth here, a review of its core concepts can prepare you to retrieve the LDAP documentation and begin using it. Linux typically uses the free **OpenLDAP** server. You can learn about this server and LDAP in general by visiting *www.openldap.org*.

Directories such as X.500 and LDAP are organized as inverted trees of information. Each level of the tree consists of **objects**, or **nodes**. At the bottom of the tree, the objects are **leaf objects**; at a higher level, they are **container objects** because they contain other objects (below them in the tree). Figure 3-3 illustrates how these object types are used in a Novell Directory Services tree. Each object is created based on a **class**; the class defines the type of resource that the object represents, such as a printer, a user, or a company. Each class has a definition that includes **attributes** to specify information about that type of object. Each leaf object in the tree has a name, called its **common name**. The **schema** is the collection of all the possible object classes and their attributes that the directory supports. The directory tree itself contains data mapped out using those classes and attributes.

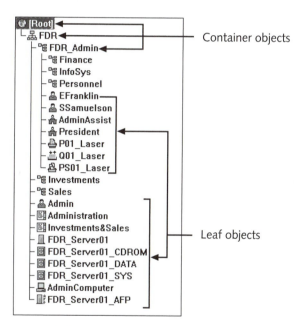

Figure 3-3   Container and leaf objects in a Novell Directory Services tree

To use a directory, you use client software (the `ldapsearch` program is one text-mode LDAP client in Linux) to traverse the tree, looking for the information you need within the database. For example, think of the top of the tree as having a label; call it Top for our purposes. Underneath Top are a number of other objects, each representing a country; these are objects with a class of country. Each country object has useful attributes that define a country, such as name, principal languages, international telephone codes, and so on. When you see the object named Latvia, you can use your LDAP client to query the attributes of that country object.

More likely, you will continue down the tree. Each country object is a container that holds many organization objects. An organization object has certain attributes, including a name, and is also a container that may have resources such as user objects, printer objects, group membership objects, and many other classes of objects.

You refer to an object in the directory tree using a formalized set of identifiers. For example, a user named Luis Rodriguez working at IBM in Mexico might be referred to using this designation:

```
cn=Luis Rodriguez, o=IBM, c=MX
```

This is the **distinguished name (DN)** of the user-class object representing this person. The DN is the complete path to an object within the directory tree. The *cn* in the preceding text stands for common name. The *o* stands for organization. The *c* stands for country. After you know how to refer to this object (perhaps by browsing the directory tree until you find it), you can query for the attributes of the object to learn Luis's e-mail address or phone number, if he had made those publicly readable. Figure 3-4 shows how a portion of an LDAP directory tree might appear.

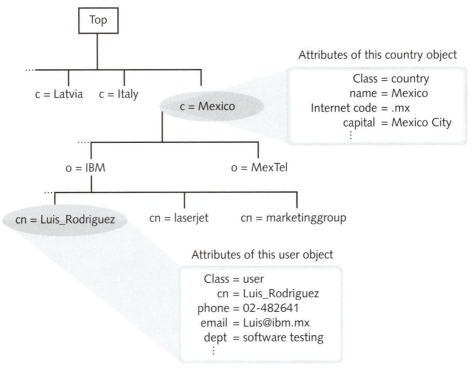

Figure 3-4   A simple LDAP directory tree

You should get the sense from this brief outline that directory services is a large and complex topic. LDAP is just one of the available directory services, though it continues to grow in popularity. The OpenLDAP server included with most Linux distributions lets you set up a local directory service. In Fedora, the `openldap` and `openldap-clients` packages are installed by default in some configurations. These provide both the client and server software. You can immediately begin using the client without setting up the server by sending queries to a public LDAP server. The following is an example of using the `ldapsearch` command to access the Bundespost (the German Post Office) LDAP server:

```
ldapsearch -x -h x500.bund.de -b o=Bund,c=DE
'(mail=heinrich*)' cn mail
```

This produces a listing of anyone at the Bundespost whose e-mail address begins with heinrich. This is a long and complex command. Unless you're an LDAP administrator, you're not expected to use these commands. Programs that you use talk to LDAP servers—you don't. LDAP is like SQL—you can use SQL queries directly but most people use programs that prepare SQL queries.

 Other LDAP clients include KLDAP for KDE and GQ for GNOME.

NOTE

Many programs can access LDAP. Most e-mail programs that have local phone books, such as Mozilla Thunderbird, also support LDAP-based phone books. There are PAM modules that allow you to log on to Linux computers, where user credentials are in LDAP. PowerDNS is a DNS server that can use LDAP for storing zone file information.

If you're looking to implement LDAP in your company but you want to start on a small scale, a project to implement a company-wide phone book is a good starting place.

RUNNING APPLICATIONS REMOTELY

After you have a network connection to a system running Linux, you can execute programs remotely in several ways. This section explores running both graphical and text-based programs remotely between Linux and Windows hosts.

Using X for Remote Graphical Applications

The Linux graphical environment—the X Window System or just X—provides a feature that few other systems can emulate: It separates the computational parts of a program from the part that collects keystrokes and mouse movement and displays program output. This allows you to run the program on one host but collect input (keyboard and mouse) and display output on a different computer. This is very similar to the terminal concept described in Chapter 1, except that the program is graphical—and the whole system is much more complex!

For example, suppose you have a program installed on a host named paris, but you are working on a host named rome. You don't want to install the program on rome, but you need to use it. X allows you to log on to paris and start the program with an additional instruction: "Display the program on rome and get input from rome." The program then starts running on paris but appears on the screen of rome. If the computer is powerful enough, dozens of users can log on to paris and launch programs that are displayed on computers across the network. This setup is illustrated in Figure 3-5.

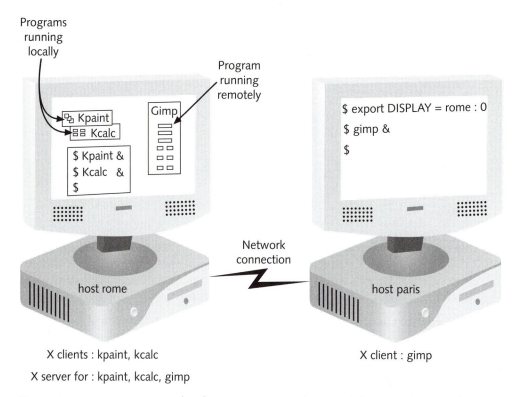

Figure 3-5   Executing a graphical program on one host and displaying it on another host

To begin using remote X execution, you must learn two terms that may be counter-intuitive:

- The program running on a host is the **X client**.
- The screen, keyboard, and mouse of the system on which the program is remotely displayed are those of the **X server**.

Each system uses an environment variable called **DISPLAY** that contains a host name and a screen number to define where each X client should display its windows and collect its input. Normally, your DISPLAY variable contains only a **sequence number** and perhaps a **screen number** (both zero), and so by default X displays programs on your local host. (Some systems might have multiple displays, in which case the zeros would not always be used for the local host.) The results of the echo command to show the variable's value indicate this. (Here, only a sequence number is shown; your system might display :0.0 for both a sequence number and a screen number.)

```
echo $DISPLAY
:0
```

You can change the DISPLAY variable manually. Suppose you log on to rome using a program such as Telnet and then enter these commands (in the default Linux bash shell):

```
DISPLAY="rome.mynet.com:0.0"
export DISPLAY
```

Now, every graphical program is displayed on rome rather than paris. You can also include the display information on the command line when you start a graphical program. The format of this option is the same for all graphical programs. For example, instead of starting the gimp graphical program like this:

```
gimp &
```

Start it with the **--display** option, like this:

```
gimp --display "rome.mynet.com:0.0" &
```

The --display option overrides the DISPLAY environment variable.

> **TIP**
> Each user on a system has a different set of environment variables, so all users can log on and have the programs they run displayed on different remote hosts.

Before an X client can display its windows on a remote host, the remote host must be configured to allow other computers to use its X server. You can do this in two ways: one easy and insecure, the other more difficult, but more secure.

xhost Authentication

The easy method is to use the **xhost** program on the host where you want the X client to display its output, specifying the host that is allowed to use the local X server. To use xhost, you include the host name of the computer that you want to allow to display. For example, if you are logged on to host rome and want to allow X clients from host paris to use rome as an X server (to display on and get input from rome), use the following command:

```
xhost +paris.mynet.com
```

When you are finished running the program, you can remove paris from the list of authorized hosts using this command:

```
xhost -paris.mynet.com
```

CAUTION

You commonly see xhost used without a host name, as xhost +, which allows any host to use your system as an X server. This is highly insecure and allows anyone to start a program and have it show up on your screen. It also allows a clever user to capture the keystrokes you are entering as you work. Use xhost − to disable all access, then use specific host names to add hosts that you want to allow to use your system as an X server.

These steps summarize the process of remotely executing a graphical program:

1. Open a command-line window on your host.

2. Enter the xhost command with the name of the host that will run the X client.

3. Log on to the remote host.

4. Start the program with the --display command-line option referring to your host (or set the DISPLAY environment variable if you intend to run multiple programs).

The X client program appears on your local screen.

CAUTION

You will quickly notice that the X protocol uses a lot of network bandwidth. Various compression methods can ease this, but be aware that running graphical applications remotely uses much more bandwidth than running text applications remotely.

xauth Authentication

Even when used with a host name, the xhost command is not terribly secure because it permits *any* user on the named host to use your host as an X server. The **xauth** system prevents that problem by requiring that an X client present a specific token (a long number) to the X server to be granted access to use that X server. The common term for a numeric token of this sort is a **cookie**, and the xauth system uses a number that is also called the **MIT Magic Cookie**. The xauth process works like this:

1. Suppose you start a program on host paris that is to be displayed on host rome (rome is running the remote X server). The program you execute on paris examines the **.Xauthority** file in your home directory on paris to see whether a token is given for the remote host rome.

2. Assuming that a token is available (you must put it there yourself, as you'll learn next), it is sent to rome using the X network protocol, as paris tries to initiate a connection to use the X server on rome.

3. The X server on rome looks in *its* .Xauthority file for a token that corresponds to host paris. If it finds one, it allows the connection to proceed. If not, the connection is refused and the program on paris will not run (because it has been instructed to use rome for its display and rome won't allow that).

The .Xauthority files mentioned in this process are stored in a user's home directory. So, each user must have the necessary tokens to use another user's X server. Of course, the most common situation is that you have accounts on two systems and you copy the token between your home directories so that you can run and display programs on any of the systems to which you have access. In any case, xauth is designed to be a user-to-user security system, rather than a host-to-host security system.

> **NOTE**
> To use the xauth security method, you must start the X Window System with the option auth-- and the name of the authority file to use, $HOME/. Xauthority. This is the normal authority file by default in most modern Linux systems, but if yours uses a different authority file, you should examine the startx script that is typically used to launch X. Alternatively, if you are running with a graphical logon, the configuration you need to alter is in the display manager file. For example, the .Xauthority file is specified in Red Hat Linux as part of the gdm.conf file in /etc/X11/gdm.

You can see the .Xauthority file in your home directory using the ls -a command (it's a hidden file). To view or alter the file's contents, you use the xauth program, which you can start from any command line. From the xauth prompt, you enter commands to manage the tokens stored for your use on the X server. A few helpful commands include help to show all the xauth commands, list to list all the tokens currently stored, and add to place a token into the authority file for use by a remote host.

The authority file should always include a token for the host where you are working. A new token is generated each time you log on to X. If your file doesn't include a token for your local host, use the generate command within xauth to create one. Below, you see xauth launched, followed by the list command to show all the known tokens on host rome.

```
[root@rome root]# xauth
Using authority file /root/.Xauthority
xauth> list
rome.xmission.com/unix:0  MIT-MAGIC-COOKIE-1
  6da29c0a7399aa179c90cba39426dd5f
rome.xmission.com:0  MIT-MAGIC-COOKIE-1
6da29c0a7399aa179c90cba39426dd5f
xauth>
```

If you have a file like this one and you want host paris to be able to use rome as an X server (that is, to display programs on it), you must get the information from this file into the .Xauthority file on paris. After you have done this, paris has a valid token to send to rome so that rome can allow paris to connect for remote program display.

You can accomplish this in several ways, from writing down the information on a piece of paper (which is rarely done by Linux pros) to using a program like `telnet`, `rlogin` (described later in this chapter), or `ssh` (described in Chapter 11) to log on to one machine while sitting at the other, then copy and paste the information between two windows. For example, you could follow these steps:

1. Open two Xterm windows in your graphical environment on the X server host (the host that you want to display programs—rome in the previous example).

2. In the first window, start `xauth` and use `list` to display the known tokens.

3. Switch to the other window and log on to the remote host on which you will run the X client programs (paris in the previous example).

4. Start `xauth` on the remote system.

5. In the first window, click and drag the line containing the token for the X server host. Click Edit on the menu bar, and then click Copy.

6. Switch to the second window, type `add`, then choose Paste from the Edit menu of the Xterm window. The text of the token is pasted on the line containing the `add` command.

7. Make sure the `add` command has the correct format, then press Enter. Use `list` to make sure the token is included correctly.

8. Type `exit` in both windows to close the `xauth` program.

NOTE As a review of what you've already learned, think about why you can log on as part of Step 3, even though you don't have access for graphical program display. What are the differences between these two things?

The `add` command referred to looks something like this (with the token taken from your own file):

```
add rome.xmission.com:0  MIT-MAGIC-COOKIE-1
6da29c0a7399aa179c90cba39426dd5f
```

Don't be surprised if the remote display of graphical applications doesn't work correctly on your first attempt. The many components of X can make it difficult to configure. If you are having problems, be certain that your `DISPLAY` variable is correctly set. Check with your system administrator to see if X was started with the `-nolisten tcp` argument, which stops it from listening for remote connections. Make certain that the host name you have specified is reachable on the network (try `ping`, for example). Check again that the tokens in the two `.Xauthority` files match and that some problem such as an expired token is not interfering with your efforts. Finally, review the man pages (for X, `xauth`, and others) and HOWTO documents related to X to see what else might be preventing your setup from functioning as expected.

Using XDMCP for Remote Graphical Terminals

Many Linux systems are now configured during installation to use a graphical logon screen automatically, so users don't see text-mode displays by default. The graphical logon screen is presented by a display manager. The commonly used programs are xdm, gdm, and kdm (for X generally, GNOME, and KDE, respectively). You can typically explore the configuration files for these programs in the subdirectories of /etc/X11. These files tell the display manager what logon screen to display, how to respond to shutdown commands, and many other options.

One feature of a display manager is its ability to display the logon screen on a remote computer so that a user can begin running Linux programs without first logging on using Telnet or another text-based program. The display manager presents a logon screen, the user logs on, and the Linux desktop (GNOME, KDE, or another interface) appears, ready for the user to launch programs graphically. This capability is especially useful when you are running X server software on a non-Linux computer. For example, many users running Windows have an X server program such as X-Win32 or Hummingbird Exceed. This program allows a program (an X client) running on a remote Linux system to be displayed on a Windows desktop and to collect its keyboard and mouse input from that system. Figure 3-6 shows a Windows computer running an X server; the figure displays the output of a clock program that is running on a Linux server.

Linux running a
clock program

Windows running
an X server

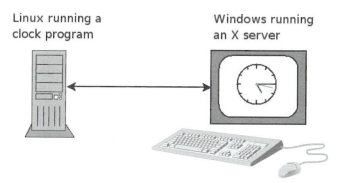

Figure 3-6   Windows computer running an X server

To have a graphical logon display appear on an X server, you must configure the display manager control protocol, **XDMCP**. XDMCP is not a secure protocol, so it is turned off by default on most Linux distributions. To enable it, you must change the configuration so that the components of X and the display manager can use network connections. This is not especially difficult, but the process varies among Linux versions because each sets up X configuration in a slightly different way. The following steps outline how to enable XDMCP on Fedora Core, including comments that should assist you on other versions of Linux. However, because this book has limited space to devote to XDMCP here, you are advised to review the HOWTO documents for XDMCP, XDM, and X if you have difficulty making this process work.

1. Make the X Font Server, `xfs`, use a network connection. Open the file `/etc/X11/fs/config`. Comment out the `no-listen=tcp` line, and add the line `port=7100`. On other systems, you might instead need to alter the line in `/etc/rc.d/init.d/xfs` that begins with `daemon` so that the port specified is 7100 instead of −1.

2. Allow hosts to communicate with the display manager. Open the file `/etc/X11/xdm/Xaccess` and remove the comment sign (#) from the line starting with "*" and indicating "any host can get a logon window."

3. Enable the XDMCP protocol within the display manager configuration file. Open the file `/etc/X11/gdm/gdm.conf`, find the `Enable` line within the [XDMCP] section, and change it from `False` to `True`. Be certain that a line within this section indicates `Port=177`.

4. Be certain that the file permissions (the mode) of `/etc/X11/xdm/Xsetup_0` is `755`.

5. Be certain that the file `/etc/X11/xorg.conf` includes the line `FontPath "unix/:7100"`.

6. Restart the X Window System to be certain the configuration files have been reread.

7. On the remote X server (including a Windows host running X-Win32 or a similar program), provide the host name or IP address of the Linux host, or use the XDMCP-broadcast method to try to reach the Linux display manager. If all works as it should, the X server displays a Linux-like graphical logon screen after a few moments.

Using r-Utilities for Remote Execution

The **r-utilities** (*r* is for "remote") allow you to access remote hosts to run programs, transfer files, or perform other functions within a trusted network environment. Of course, few networks are really trustworthy, and so using the r-utilities is a security risk. There are secure alternatives to all the r-utilities, such as SSH and SFTP. Whenever possible, use them instead. Table 3-2 presents the r-utilities and their functions.

Table 3-2   Commonly used r-utilities

Utility Name	Description
rwho	List the users who are logged on all hosts attached to the local network (hosts that have the r-utilities networking features activated)
ruptime	List all hosts attached to the local network (that are using r-utilities) with the uptime for each
rlogin	Log on to a remote host; very similar to Telnet, but uses the r-utilities authentication methods
rsh	Execute a command on a remote computer without logging on
rcp	Copy one or more files between different computers (the local computer and a remote computer or between two remote computers)

NOTE The r-utilities rely on Remote Procedure Call (rpc) networking, which you will learn about in more detail in Chapter 5 as part of the Network File System discussion. You must have `rpc` and the `portmapper` application installed to use r-utilities.

3

WEB AND E-MAIL CLIENTS

Most computer users have some experience with the World Wide Web and with electronic mail (e-mail). This section describes the client programs available in Linux for using these two services.

Web Browsers

The earliest graphical Web browser, NCSA Mosaic, was a simple program when it first appeared in the early 1990s. Its freely available code became the basis for all modern browsers. It displayed Web pages with text and graphics described by HTML codes. Everyone using the Web would see the same thing when browsing pages. There were few, if any, serious security problems. Then vendors started making Web browsers. The Web will never again be simple, compatible, and safe to use.

The dominant browser vendors were Netscape and Microsoft. They competed with one another by adding features to their browsers at a dizzying pace, trying to upstage the other. Standards and compatibility were ignored. Browsers became much more complex as they were called upon to support additional types of content and features such as JavaScript, CGI programs, Cascading Style Sheets (CSS), client-side image maps, Java, ActiveX, Flash, Shockwave, QuickTime, and streaming audio and video.

This complexity led to compatibility problems. Web site administrators couldn't afford to develop Web content that worked well with both browsers, so they had to pick sides. They put browser logos and "This site is best viewed with" messages on their pages. This forced browser users to either pick sides as well or install both browsers.

This complexity also led to serious security issues, though Microsoft's browser has had the bulk of the more serious problems.

Microsoft included its Internet Explorer browser with Windows at no additional charge, whereas Netscape sold its browser. This prompted Netscape to declare its browser code to be open source in 1999. Part of this code is the rendering engine that Netscape calls Gecko. The Gecko engine is the basis for many open source Web browsers that run on Linux.

Linux Browsers

Many browsers are available for Linux (and other operating systems) thanks to Netscape's contribution of its code base. The most popular Linux browser is **Mozilla** Firefox by far. There's also the classic Mozilla that rolls Web browsing, e-mail, newsgroups, and Web page authoring into one package. The free Netscape browsers are still available but their popularity is declining.

The Firefox and Mozilla browsers are based on Gecko, and so are many other Linux browsers such as Galeon and Dillo. Because all of these browsers are based on Gecko, any Web page you visit with any of these browsers should be rendered the same. If Web pages said "This site is best viewed with Gecko," it would cover a lot of browsers.

The file-browsing programs for the KDE and GNOME graphical desktops also function as Web browsers. The GNOME Nautilus and KDE Konqueror programs are both based on Gecko.

Configuring graphical Web browsers in Linux is usually the same as configuring Windows browsers. You click an item in one of the menus called Configuration or Options, which exposes a configuration menu or a window with tabs. However, an open source Web browser like Firefox could have hundreds of optional plug-ins installed. How do you configure them all?

If you enter the about:config URL, Firefox displays a page of several hundred configuration parameters. Double-click any of the parameters to change the values. This is a reasonable way of handling configuration when there are far too many parameters for a menu system.

The Firefox browser has a capability of which most people are unaware. Firefox is based on XUL—the Extensible User-interface Language. With XUL, you can completely redefine the Firefox graphical user interface. For example, you can eliminate all or most of the user interface if you want to run Firefox in a kiosk application. You can lock down the user interface so users can only do the things that you want them to do.

Lynx and Links

You're in your company's cold and noisy computer room, working on a Linux server. You need to download a program from a Web site on the Internet and install it on the server. The server has no mouse and may not even have X installed. A graphical Web browser is out. What do you do?

You use a nongraphical (text-based) Web browser. Two are popular: **Lynx** and **Links**. Both support HTML tables, frames, forms, bookmarks, language support, SSL, FTP, proxies, cookies, and other features that graphical browsers support. Links can be configured to invoke a graphical viewer when you ask it to display an image.

Because these browsers do not have to render graphical pages, they are very fast. If you think that Web pages that include lots of graphics and advertisements are an assault on your senses and you crave the serenity of plain text, these browsers are for you.

Lynx is installed by default by many popular Linux distributions. Fedora Core installs Links by default. Figure 3-7 shows a Lynx screen. Compared to graphical browsers, Lynx keyboard commands take more practice to use effectively, but again, using the program to navigate Web pages becomes very fast once you are comfortable with Lynx.

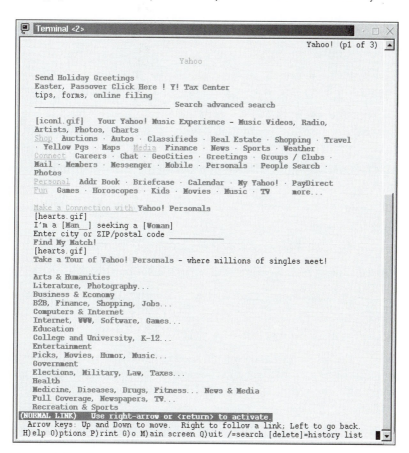

Figure 3-7   The Lynx text-based Web browser

To start Lynx, enter `lynx` on any command line, followed by a Web page address. For example:

```
lynx www.yahoo.com
```

> or

```
lynx http://www.yahoo.com
```

Use the up and down arrow keys to move between links on the Web page. Use the right arrow key to go to the link. Use the left arrow key to go back. To move between screens of text without reference to links on the page, use the Page Up and Page Down keys. Many other keys for different browser functions are displayed at the bottom of the Lynx screen. To exit Lynx, you can use the q key (then confirm with y) or just press Ctrl+C.

Understanding E-Mail

E-mail is one of the most widely used Internet services and is a complicated subject. In Chapter 6, you will learn how to set up a basic e-mail server in Linux. This section focuses on e-mail client-side programs.

The protocol by which e-mail is transferred on the Internet is called **Simple Mail Transfer Protocol** or **SMTP**. E-mail-related programs are divided into three categories:

- **Mail Transfer Agent** or **MTA**—A program that moves e-mail messages from one server on the Internet to another. When the term "e-mail server" is used, it generally means an MTA.

- **Mail Delivery Agent** or **MDA**—A program that places e-mail in a user's mailbox so that it can be read.

- **Mail User Agent** or **MUA**—A program that displays and manages e-mail messages for a user.

The process of sending and receiving e-mail works something like this:

1. You use a Mail User Agent to create an e-mail message.

2. The MUA hands the message to a Mail Transfer Agent.

3. The sender's MTA contacts the recipient's MTA. This involves DNS. The message is transferred between the MTAs using SMTP.

4. The recipient's MTA hands off the message to the Mail Delivery Agent, which uses a set of rules to deliver the message to the mailbox of the recipient. In many cases, the MTA acts as the MDA, placing the message directly in the mailbox.

5. When the user is ready to read e-mail, she starts an MUA, which accesses the mailbox and displays the messages that have been received.

One assumption behind this process is that e-mail servers are always available—always turned on and always connected to the Internet. Users can come and go as they choose, but the server is always available to accept a message that might arrive from another server.

On most Linux systems, all users have e-mail accounts. Your e-mail is placed either in the **/var/spool/mail** directory in a file corresponding to your username or it is placed in a directory structure below your home directory. If your account name is nwells, your e-mail inbox may be the /var/spool/mail/nwells file or directories beneath /home/ nwells/Maildir. Placing messages in the inbox is done by whatever MDA or MTA you

3

are using. No special action is required to make e-mail "work" on Linux. In fact, even if you are not running any sort of e-mail server, many system administration programs send messages to the root user by writing directly to the mailbox file `/var/spool/mail/root`. You can open this file in any text editor to see the raw format of Internet e-mail messages. After the messages are stored in that file, the user can use an MUA to read the message.

> When you create additional e-mail folders (beyond your default inbox), they are separate files in your home directory. Messages in these folders are not stored in `/var/spool/mail`.

Because many of you don't leave your computers on all the time, you rely on a remote e-mail server to receive your messages. This might be a central e-mail server for an organization or a server at an ISP site. When you feel like it, you turn on your computer and use an MUA (an e-mail client) to retrieve your e-mail messages. You typically do this in one of three ways:

- Use the **Post Office Protocol 3 (POP3)** via a POP3 server (acting as an MDA) to download all the messages to your computer.

- Use the **Internet Message Access Protocol (IMAP)** (again, using an IMAP server acting as an MDA) to view messages on the remote server, never storing them on your local computer.

- Use a Web browser to view, delete, and create messages that are stored on a remote server.

When you use POP3 to download messages to your own host, you can indicate whether the messages should be saved on the e-mail server or deleted. Normally, you would choose to delete them so that they don't continue to take up space on the e-mail server. You might choose not to delete them on the server if you are working on a system that you don't normally use for e-mail.

After the e-mail messages are downloaded, you can read them at any time (without a network connection), extract attached files, back up the messages to another location, or delete them.

When you use IMAP to view e-mail messages on the remote e-mail server, no storage space is required on your local computer, and the messages can be backed up or otherwise managed by a system administrator for all of the users who have e-mail on that server. The advantage to this method is that people are less likely to "erase their mailbox" and lose all of their messages because they are always controlled by the system administrator. A user can always download files attached to messages or print the messages on paper if needed.

There are minor downsides to IMAP. A system administrator who has a technical problem might lose everyone's e-mail, not just e-mail for one person. Because e-mail messages are stored on the server, users have little incentive to clean their mailboxes periodically.

This potential downside of IMAP must be balanced, however, with an organization's policies regarding e-mail. For example, a company may have an explicit policy that management is allowed to review any e-mail sent or received by an employee using company equipment. IMAP makes this policy straightforward to implement.

Many users now rely on e-mail that they access via a Web browser, using the same concept as the IMAP model. A Web-mail program on the e-mail server constructs Web pages that present lists of e-mail messages, the text of a selected message, and so on. The user clicks links within the page that causes the Web browser to send requests to the e-mail server such as "Send a list of message titles," "Display message number 127," or "Send the file attached to message 73." These are the same types of messages that an IMAP e-mail client would send to an IMAP server.

You can view e-mail without using POP3 or IMAP. If you log on to the host on which the messages are stored (where the MDA has placed them), either directly or using Telnet, ssh, or another program, you can use an e-mail client that simply reads your mailbox file in /var/spool/mail. Later in this section, you'll learn about e-mail clients that read e-mail in just this way.

Using an E-Mail Filter: Procmail

One special MDA you should be aware of is **Procmail**. Whereas POP3 and IMAP servers simply deliver e-mail as requested by a POP3 or IMAP-capable e-mail client, Procmail acts as a filter, typically in conjunction with an MTA, though it can act alone on a mailbox that is already full of messages. Procmail processes e-mail based on characteristics that you define. Typically, it is used to delete unwanted messages automatically or to store specific message types in different mail folders. Procmail is difficult to configure, but it is a great way to delete junk e-mail and automatically sort your mailbox if you have a large number of incoming e-mail messages.

Procmail is installed by default on many Linux systems and is available in convenient rpm or deb package format if you need to install it. Procmail can be started manually, but more commonly it is configured to operate as part of an e-mail server on the same system, filtering messages as they are placed in your inbox file. Procmail checks for both a system–wide Procmail configuration file, **/etc/procmailrc**, and a per-user configuration file, **.procmailrc**, stored in a user's home directory. Each of these files can contain **recipes**, or formulas for examining an e-mail message and taking an action if it matches certain criteria. In most configurations, such as for Red Hat Linux, Procmail begins working as soon as you create a .procmailrc file. This means that you should not create a file of that name in your home directory until you have completed all the recipes you want to use and carefully reviewed them, perhaps saving your work under a different name until you are ready to activate the recipes.

> **TIP**
> Many users create each recipe in a separate file and then refer to them within `.procmailrc` using the INCLUDERC directive. This allows you to disable or modify each recipe quickly and individually without examining an entire `.procmailrc` file.

The first part of a `.procmailrc` file contains environment variables to guide Procmail's work. For example, you might include the MAILDIR variable to specify a working directory for Procmail; all nonabsolute paths in the `.procmailrc` file then refer to that directory.

The format for a Procmail recipe is daunting at first glance, but need not be complicated when you first use the program. The syntax of each recipe is as follows:

```
:0<flags>: <lockfile>
* <condition-character> <condition-1>
* <condition-character> <condition-2>
* <condition-character> <condition-N>
<action-character><action >
```

Each recipe starts with a colon followed by a zero. A flag may follow to indicate a special type of recipe. The second colon tells Procmail to "lock" the message so that more than one process can't try to alter it at the same time. A default `lockfile` name is used for this purpose unless you specify one. Locking is a good precaution on busy systems, but it does add a fair amount of overhead when you have many recipes or many messages for Procmail to process.

Within the recipe, one or more conditions are listed, each starting with an asterisk. If no conditions are listed, all messages "match" and the recipe is applied to them. If multiple conditions are listed, a message must match all of them for the recipe to be applied. After checking the conditions, matching messages are processed according to the action character and action. This action line is often just the name of a file where the message should be stored (or `/dev/null` if the message should be discarded). If the action delivers the message to another user or to a mailbox file, no other recipes are examined for that message. If the action does not deliver the message, the remaining recipes are checked for a match against the message until one recipe delivers the message.

More than a dozen possible flags are listed in the `procmailrc` man page, but basic recipes don't need any flags. Likewise, you won't need a lot of characters in condition lines. These conditions let you do things like check the size of a message (in bytes) or negate a condition (a condition is satisfied if it *does not* match the description on that line). The condition itself uses regular expression matching to check all the text within a message. To use Procmail effectively, you should be quite familiar with using regular expressions. For example, suppose you keep getting junk e-mail from the domain *getrichquick.com*. To match any e-mail with a From: header that included the word *getrichquick*, you could use this condition line:

```
* ^From: *getrichquick*
```

The ^ character ties the "From" text to the beginning of the line. You could check multiple headers for an address:

```
* ^(To|Cc|From) *course.com
```

Following one or more conditions, you specify the action to take on matching messages. If no action character is specified, the e-mail is saved to the filename given. You can add a "!" to send the message to the named e-mail address, or a "|" to pipe the message text to another program. You can also use { } to enclose additional recipes for nested processing.

TIP

Be very careful about simply sending messages to /dev/null as your action. Instead, write junk e-mail to a file and check a few times to see if good e-mail is being discarded because of an imprecise recipe. After you have determined that the recipe is reliable, you can change it to delete messages permanently by using /dev/null instead of a filename.

A small sample .procmailrc file is shown below, based on Red Hat documentation. It sets a variable for the file where junk e-mail is stored (to be checked and then deleted if no good messages are caught in the Spam Web). Three types of messages are caught in this set of recipes: those with no valid To: header, those with more than 15 recipients (this may delete good e-mail!), and those without a valid Message-ID header. Of course, you could create more specific filters to catch the type of spam you are receiving, either based on the From: header, the Subject: header, or other characteristics that you notice about the junk e-mail.

```
SPAM=discard
0:
* To??^$
$SPAM
:0:
*
^(To|CC):.*,.*,.*,.*,.*,.*,.*,.*,.*,.*,.*,.*,.*,.*,
$SPAM
:0:
* ^Message-Id:.*<[^@]*>
$SPAM
```

Text-based E-Mail Clients

The most basic Linux e-mail client (MUA) is called **mail**. You can use the `mail` program to send an e-mail message from the command line or to read all the messages stored in your local mailbox. The `mail` program only reads local files; it doesn't use POP3 or IMAP.

To use `mail` to send a message from the command line, use the `-s` option to indicate a subject, followed by the e-mail address of the recipient. For example, enter a command like this:

```
mail -s "Question about your schedule" tom@mail.house.gov
```

You then enter the text of the message on multiple lines as needed, pressing Ctrl+D when you have finished. If you enter the command `mail` without anything after it, the `mail` program displays all of the messages in your e-mail inbox and starts its interactive mode. You can enter ? to see a list of commands.

Two other text-based e-mail clients that have been around for years are **pine** and **elm**. Both of these operate on locally stored mailbox files, but are very fast and powerful at managing your e-mail if you don't rely on viewing attached graphics files. System administrators who prefer a command-line interface typically use `mail`, `pine`, or `elm` for their e-mail. These programs are not installed by default on most systems, but are available for you to install, either from the CD that accompanied your Linux product or by downloading the software package or source code.

You can start both `elm` and `pine` from any command line. The first time you run them, they set up directories to hold their files. Somewhat cryptic messages at the bottom of the screen indicate the keys to use for core functionality, with a help screen available that lists all the possible commands. Figure 3-8 shows a screen from `elm`. Messages are listed with a few commonly used commands below. Single-key commands make `elm` efficient after you have memorized the keystrokes you need.

Figure 3-8   The `elm` text-mode e-mail reader

Graphical E-Mail Clients

Most desktop computer users prefer a graphical e-mail program. Numerous graphical e-mail client programs are available for Linux. Mozilla Thunderbird, Evolution, and KMail are among the most popular. All of these programs use POP3 or IMAP to retrieve messages from an e-mail server. They all have similar capabilities and are configured in similar ways. If you know how to use one, moving to another is not difficult. This section briefly covers Thunderbird configuration.

When you run Thunderbird the first time, it runs the account setup wizard, in which you enter information, such as your account name, e-mail address, mail servers, and so on. Thereafter, you configure Thunderbird by choosing the Tools menu and clicking either Account Settings or Options.

You can also download and install a plug-in that gives you the same about:config configuration mechanism as Firefox.

CHAPTER SUMMARY

- ❑ The client portion of the Domain Name Service (DNS) is called the resolver. It is configured by placing the IP address of name servers in the /etc/resolv.conf file. Several graphical utilities are available to help with configuration.

- ❑ A fully qualified domain name (FQDN) consists of a host name plus the domain of which the host is a part. The term "domain name" is also used casually to refer to FQDNs.

- ❑ The /etc/hosts file can also be used to resolve a domain name and an IP address. The /etc/host.conf or /etc/nsswitch.conf files determine the order in which the resolver looks to various sources to resolve IP addresses.

- ❑ The Dynamic Host Configuration Protocol (DHCP) allows clients to configure IP networking automatically by receiving network address information from a DHCP server, which hands out (leases) addresses to clients on a network.

- ❑ Most versions of Linux include at least one of the three common DHCP clients: pump, dhcpcd, and dhclient. The DHCP client is normally configured using a graphical interface such as YaST in SuSE Linux or the Red Hat Network Administration Tool.

- ❑ Point-to-Point Protocol (PPP) is a popular method of making network connections via a modem. Configuring PPP connections is now easily done using graphical utilities such as rp3-config.

- ❑ PPP security is typically provided by the Password Authentication Protocol (PAP) or the Challenge Handshake Authentication Protocol (CHAP).

- ❑ The wvdial utility can configure and manage a PPP connection from the command line.

3

❏ The `diald` program automates use of a dial-up connection via PPP, connecting automatically when network traffic requires the connection, and dropping the connection when traffic drops off.

❏ The Lightweight Directory Access Protocol (LDAP) provides a directory service that lets users query a worldwide database for information on resources (companies and individuals). Each object within the hierarchical LDAP database is composed of attributes that describe the characteristics of the resource that the object represents.

❏ The OpenLDAP server is provided with most Linux distributions.

❏ X can execute graphical programs remotely by referring to the `DISPLAY` variable or the `--display` command-line option. Two methods of authenticating users who want to remotely display applications include `xhost` and `xauth`, the latter being much more secure.

❏ XDMCP lets users on remote X servers obtain a graphical logon screen and begin using X clients on Linux without first logging on to Linux using a program like Telnet.

❏ The r-utilities provide a convenient way to execute commands on, or copy files between, remote hosts when working in a trusted network environment.

❏ Many Web browsers are available for Linux. The most popular are the text-mode browser, Lynx, and the graphical browsers Mozilla and Netscape Communicator. Most other Linux browsers do not have full capabilities for the latest HTML documents, XML, Java, and so on.

❏ Internet e-mail relies on a Mail Transfer Agent (MTA), typically called a mail server, to move messages between hosts on the Internet. A Mail Delivery Agent (MDA) may process mail as it is delivered to a user's mailbox file. Finally, a user relies on a Mail User Agent (MUA) to read messages and send new e-mail.

❏ MUAs can either read local mail files (including the default mailbox in `/var/spool/mail/username`) or use the POP3 or IMAP protocols to retrieve messages from a central server.

❏ The Procmail program processes e-mail messages using recipes, which may result in e-mail being moved to new e-mail folders or discarded.

❏ Many other Linux e-mail clients are popular, including text-based programs for reading local mail files, such as `elm` and `pine`; the POP client `fetchmail`; graphical programs such as those provided in Netscape Communicator and Mozilla; plus stand-alone graphical programs.

KEY TERMS

.procmailrc — The configuration file for individual Procmail users. *See also* `/etc/procmailrc`.

.Xauthority — The file that contains tokens (cookies) used by the `xauth` security system for displaying graphical programs.

/etc/host.conf — The file that specifies the order in which the resolver should consult resources to resolve the host name to an IP address.

/etc/hosts — The file used to store IP addresses and corresponding domain names for hosts, usually those frequently accessed on a local network.

/etc/nsswitch.conf — The file that defines the order in which the resolver and many other programs use various local or network resources to obtain configuration information.

/etc/procmailrc — The system wide configuration file for Procmail. *See also* .procmailrc.

/etc/resolv.conf — The file that configures the Linux resolver.

/var/spool/mail — The default directory for e-mail inboxes on most Linux systems.

attribute — A discrete data element that is part of an object within a directory service database such as LDAP.

BOOTP — A protocol used by diskless workstations (prior to DHCP being available) that allowed them to obtain network configuration instructions.

Challenge Handshake Authentication Protocol (CHAP) — A security method used by PPP. CHAP maintains username and password data locally but never sends it to the remote computer.

class — A definition for a type of object within a directory service database such as LDAP. The class defines the attributes of an object as well as its place within a directory service tree.

common name — The name assigned to a leaf object in a directory service database such as LDAP.

container object — Within a directory service database such as LDAP, an object that can have one or more subordinate objects "below it" in the data structure. *See also* leaf object.

cookie — A token, or long number, used as an identifier by a program such as a Web browser or the xauth X Window System security program.

dhclient — One of the most widely used Linux DHCP client daemons.

dhcpcd — One of the most widely used Linux DHCP client daemons.

diald — A program that manages PPP dial-up connections, initiating a connection only when needed by network traffic and disconnecting when the connection is no longer needed.

directory service — A database of information about network resources (or other resources) that can be accessed by people throughout a network.

--display — An option supported by all graphical programs that defines the X server on which the program's output should be shown and from which input should be collected. Overrides the DISPLAY environment variable.

DISPLAY — An environment variable that controls the display of graphical programs in X.

distinguished name (DN) — The complete path to an object within the directory tree, traversing (and naming) all the container objects above that object.

domain name — A name applied to multiple hosts on the Internet that are referred to collectively, such as *ibm.com* or *utah.edu.*

Dynamic Host Configuration Protocol (DHCP) — A protocol that allows a server to hand out IP addresses automatically to clients on a network.

elm — A powerful text-based e-mail client (MUA) for reading locally stored e-mail folders.

3

fully qualified domain name (FQDN) — The complete or official name of a network host, including the name of the domain of which the host is a part. More casually, a domain name.

host name — The name assigned to a host on a network.

Internet Message Access Protocol (IMAP) — A protocol used to interact with a user's e-mail messages that are stored on a remote server, as with many popular Web portals that allow e-mail access via a Web browser.

ldapsearch — A text-mode LDAP client in Linux.

leaf object — Within a directory service database such as LDAP, an object that cannot have subordinate objects "below it" in the data structure. *See also* container object.

lease — The action a DHCP server takes in assigning an IP address to a client for a specific length of time.

Lightweight Directory Access Protocol (LDAP) — A protocol for accessing the lightweight directory service.

Links — A text-based Web browser.

Lynx — A text-based Web browser.

mail — A very basic text-mode e-mail client (MUA) for Linux.

Mail Delivery Agent (MDA) — A program that places e-mail in a user's mailbox so that it can be read. This function is often subsumed by an MTA.

Mail Transfer Agent (MTA) — A program that moves e-mail messages from one server on the Internet to another. Also called an e-mail server.

Mail User Agent (MUA) — A program that displays and manages e-mail messages for a user.

minicom — A terminal emulator program used to connect to a remote computer using a modem.

MIT Magic Cookie — The name given to a cookie used by the xauth program for X display authentication.

Mozilla — A popular graphical Linux Web browser that began as an open source version of Netscape Navigator.

Network Information System (NIS) — A protocol that lets hosts share configuration information across a network, so that only one master configuration file need be supported for a number of hosts. *See also* NIS+.

NIS+ — A more advanced version of the NIS protocol. *See also* NIS.

node — A data element within a directory service database such as LDAP. Also called an object.

object — A data element within a directory service database such as LDAP. Also called a node.

OpenLDAP — The most widely used LDAP server on Linux systems.

Password Authentication Protocol (PAP) — A security method used with PPP. PAP stores pairs of usernames and passwords in a local file and transmits them over the Internet for review by an ISP.

pine — A powerful, text-based e-mail client (MUA) for reading locally stored e-mail folders.

Post Office Protocol 3 (POP3) — A protocol used to download a single user's e-mail messages that are stored on a remote e-mail server.

Procmail — A special Mail Delivery Agent (MDA) that filters e-mail messages.

pump — One of the most widely used Linux DHCP client daemons.

rcp — A utility that allows a user to copy files between two hosts. Either or both of the hosts can be remote to the host on which `rcp` is executed.

recipe — A formula used by Procmail to filter or examine an e-mail message and take an action if it matches the given criteria.

resolver — The client portion of DNS, which makes requests to a DNS server so that other programs on a host can use the IP address of a named server to make a network connection.

rlogin — A utility that allows a user to log on to another host, much like the `telnet` command.

rsh — A utility that allows a user to execute a command on a remote host without logging on to that host.

r-utilities — Short for "remote utilities," the programs that allow a user to access remote hosts to run programs, transfer files, or perform other functions within a trusted network.

schema — The collection of all the possible object classes and their attributes that a directory service supports.

screen number — A number used as part of the `DISPLAY` environment variable for remotely running graphical programs. Most systems have only a single X Window System session, referred to as screen number 0. The screen number is the second zero (the first is the sequence number) in the standard format `:0.0`.

sequence number — The sequential number of the screen on which a graphical program is displayed. Used as part of the `DISPLAY` environment variable for remotely running graphical programs. Its value is zero (indicated by `:0`) except on multimonitor systems.

Simple Mail Transfer Protocol (SMTP) — The protocol by which e-mail is transferred on the Internet.

wvdial — A text-mode utility that allows users to configure and initiate dial-up connections easily using PPP.

X client — A graphical program running on a host. *See also* X server.

X server — The screen where a graphical program is remotely displayed (and the keyboard and mouse of that system). *See also* X client.

X.500 — A widely known international standard for a directory service.

xauth — A security system for managing the display of graphical programs on remote computers by sharing a numeric token called a cookie; also the program used in Linux to manage this security system and the numeric cookies associated with it.

XDMCP — A protocol that allows remote hosts to use X running on a Linux system to provide a graphical logon display.

xhost — A program that can control access by X clients to an X server for display of graphical programs. The `xhost` program is not a secure system.

REVIEW QUESTIONS

1. Based on the top-level domains you have learned about, which of the following is not a correctly formed FQDN?

   a. *ftp.state.va.us*

   b. *red.marketing.lockheed.com*

   c. *www.ge.dns*

   d. *www.af.mil*

2. The Linux resolver:

   a. resolves a DNS name to an IP address and vice versa

   b. resolves conflicts between multiple IP addresses on the same host

   c. resolves contention between Ethernet packets on a network cable

   d. resolves authorization issues for X clients using `xauth`

3. Which of the following is not a valid configuration file discussed in this chapter?

   a. `/etc/host.conf`

   b. `/etc/nsswitch.conf`

   c. `/etc/resolve.conf`

   d. `/etc/hosts`

4. Two widely used PPP authentication (security) mechanisms are:

   a. PAP and POP3

   b. CHAP and UUCP

   c. DHCP and IMAP

   d. PAP and CHAP

5. To use the `wvdial` utility, you would first use which of the following programs to create a basic configuration file?

   a. `ppp-options`

   b. `rp3-config`

   c. `diald`

   d. `wvdialconf`

6. Before initiating a dial-up connection using `rp3`, you must:

   a. Create a valid chat script.

   b. Create all necessary `diald` configuration files.

   c. Define accounts using `rp3-config` or KDE tools.

   d. Use `wvdial` to check the `ifconfig` settings for `ppp0`.

7. Commonly used Linux DHCP clients include:

    a. `dhcpd`, `pump`, and `dhclient`

    b. `dhcp.conf`, `dhclient`, and `fetchmail`

    c. `dhcpd`, `pump`, and `bootp`

    d. `dhcpcd`, `dhclient`, and `pump`

8. Which statement is valid?

    a. A DHCP lease can assign an IP address based on a MAC address.

    b. A DHCP server requires a valid Linux DHCP client to request an IP address.

    c. DHCP is not compatible with Windows clients.

    d. Addresses assigned by DHCP include only the host IP address and netmask.

9. If you are working with an LDAP database, the following would be best described as what: `cn=Tomas_Trevino.o=Ferrari.c=Italy`.

    a. an FQDN

    b. an object class

    c. an object's common name

    d. an object's distinguished name

10. Describe at least one advantage and one disadvantage of using `xauth` instead of `xhost`.

11. The `DISPLAY` environment variable:

    a. is used only by `xhost`, not by `xauth`

    b. must be used in conjunction with the `--display` command-line option

    c. is only used when connecting via Telnet or `ssh`

    d. often includes a screen number and sequence number with the host name

12. Which of these is NOT a valid top-level domain name?

    a. .pro

    b. .museum

    c. .church

    d. .int

13. The advantage of CHAP over PAP for PPP is that:

    a. CHAP is much faster than PAP over slow modem connections.

    b. CHAP never sends passwords over the network, but PAP does.

    c. CHAP can be configured graphically, but PAP cannot.

    d. CHAP is only useful for terminal programs like minicom, not for PPP.

14. The function of `diald` is to:

    a. Automatically initiate and drop dial-up connections to match network traffic.

    b. Automatically detect and configure modems and account settings for dial-up connections.

    c. Automatically set up routes and IP addresses provided by a remote (ISP) host.

    d. Create a secure dial-up environment in which UUCP can operate.

15. The `/etc/hosts` file is checked before contacting a DNS server only if:

    a. The `/etc/host.conf` or `/etc/nsswitch` file says to use `/etc/hosts` first.

    b. A DNS server cannot be contacted.

    c. The `search` keyword in `/etc/resolv.conf` indicates a local domain name.

    d. A graphical tool was used to configure both `/etc/resolv.conf` and `/etc/hosts`.

16. Which browser is text-based rather than graphical?

    a. Mozilla

    b. Opera

    c. Galeon

    d. Lynx

17. Which protocol is used to transfer messages between two MTAs?

    a. SMTP

    b. POP

    c. IMAP

    d. PPP

18. Thunderbird can be used as an:

    a. MTA

    b. MUA

    c. MDA

    d. MTU

19. Setting up an e-mail account for a Linux user requires:

    a. nothing; all users automatically have e-mail inboxes in `/var/spool/mail`

    b. setting up a valid MUA with a local inbox file

    c. configuring the MTA to recognize each user on the system

    d. using either POP3 or IMAP to download messages from a remote server

20. A key difference between POP3 and IMAP is that:

    a. POP3 can be used on DHCP-capable systems, but IMAP should not.

    b. POP3 downloads all messages, but IMAP does not.

    c. POP3 support is available in Netscape, but IMAP is not supported.

    d. POP3 is considered secure; IMAP is not.

21. The Procmail program uses recipes to:

    a. Define which users can access e-mail remotely using POP3.

    b. Automate downloading of messages using either POP3 or IMAP.

    c. Take actions on (filter) messages based on their content.

    d. Configure basic MTA functionality.

22. Each object within an LDAP directory service database:

    a. is based on a class, which defines the attributes of that object

    b. must be a leaf node to have valid attributes

    c. includes an organization and country code

    d. is referred to using an FQDN or, more commonly, a domain name

23. Describe the difference between the terms X client and X server when using X to display programs remotely.

24. Three text-based Linux e-mail clients are:

    a. `mail`, `elm`, `pine`

    b. `mail`, Procmail, KMail

    c. MTA, MDA, MUA

    d. POP3, IMAP, SMTP

Hands-On Projects

HANDS-ON PROJECTS

Project 3-1

To complete this project, you need a functioning Linux system with the Lynx browser installed (on some systems, it is not installed by default). You should also have Internet access and permission to write files on the local system. You do not need root access.

1. Open a command-line window or go to a virtual console.

2. Lynx has several dozen command-line options controlling its functions. Start the Lynx browser with the **-dump** option to dump the referenced Web page to STDOUT. Include a redirection operator to store the Web page to a file. Here is an example, but you can choose any URL you want:

```
lynx -dump http://www.linuxapps.com > ~/linuxapps_home.html
```

3. Use **-dump** again, but instead of storing the results to a file, pipe them through another Linux command. For example, search for a specific word with `grep`. Here is one example that searches the home page of the FreshMeat open source developer site for the word "Webmin". If a Webmin update is listed on the FreshMeat home page, a line of text will be printed on your screen; otherwise, nothing will appear:

```
lynx -dump http://www.freshmeat.net | grep Webmin
```

4. Start Lynx again with the following URL:

```
lynx www.yahoo.com
```

5. Answer the question about accepting cookies by entering **A**. Use the **Page Up** and **Page Down** keys to look through the document.

6. Press the **/** (forward slash) key to initiate a search. Type the word **movies** and press **Enter**.

7. Press **Enter** or the **right arrow** key to jump to the selected Movies link on this Web page.

8. After scanning the page, press the **left arrow** key to move back to the previous page (like the Back button in a graphical browser).

9. Press **Ctrl+C** to exit Lynx.

HANDS-ON PROJECTS

Project 3-2

To complete this project, you need a working Linux system.

1. Log on to Linux and open a command-line window.

2. Enter the following command to send an e-mail message to your own user account (substitute your username as indicated).

```
mail -s "An e-mail test" username
```

3. When you press **Enter** after the preceding command, you do not see a new command prompt. Instead, you enter the text of your message on the blank line, pressing **Enter** as needed for new lines of the message. Press **Ctrl+D** when you have finished entering the text of your message. Press **Enter** at the CC: prompt.

4. Use any e-mail client you prefer to view the e-mail message that you just sent to yourself.

5. You can use `mail` to send thousands of messages with a single command. Suppose you have created a file called `namelist` containing thousands of e-mail addresses, one per line, and another file called `message_file` containing the text of an e-mail message you want to send to each e-mail address. The following command sends the contents of `message_file` to every e-mail address in `namelist` by using the `cat` command within single quotes to effectively insert the entire contents of `namelist` as a parameter specifying e-mail recipients for the `mail` command:

```
mail -s "Association Newsletter for August" 'cat namelist'
< message_file
```

Project 3-3

To complete this project, you need a Web browser with access to the Internet. This project focuses on how you can learn more about a topic in this chapter, using LDAP as an example.

1. Open your browser and go to the site *www.rfc-editor.org*.

2. Choose the **RFC Search** link at the top of the page.

3. Enter **LDAP** and choose **RFC** as the search area. Click the **Search** button. When the list appears, review the titles. Select any that look interesting and review them.

4. Now go to the page *www.linuxdocs.org*.

5. Enter **LDAP** as a search term.

6. From the results that appear, choose the **LDAP Linux HOWTO** document.

7. Can you find the section that describes how to use LDAP for the Netscape Address Book?

8. Now go to the page *www.linuxworld.com*. This is a commercial online Linux magazine.

9. Review the titles of the articles that appear. Choose one that looks like it would contain an introduction to LDAP. Click that link and review the article.

10. Finally, go to the page *www.openldap.org*.

11. Choose the link to the **OpenLDAP Admin Guide** and review the contents. Do you see the different components of the Linux OpenLDAP server listed?

Project 3-4

To complete this project, you need root access to a Linux system that can reach the Internet. For each of the `ping` commands described in this project, you only need to let two or three response lines of `ping` appear before pressing Ctrl+C to interrupt and continue with the next step.

1. Open a command-line window.

2. Choose a site that allows you to ping it and execute the `ping` command to see that it is alive. We've used the University of Utah as an example:

```
ping www.utah.edu
```

3. As the ping packets are returned, note how the domain name and a corresponding IP address for the site are shown on each line. Write down the IP address.

4. Open the `/etc/hosts` file in a text editor and add a line like the following one to the end of the file. Then save the file. (Use the domain name and IP address that you used in Steps 2 and 3 if you prefer.)

```
155.99.1.2      www.utah.edu
```

5. Ping the same site again. This time the IP address is being taken from the /etc/ hosts file instead of DNS. Do you know why?

ping www.utah.edu

6. Open **/etc/hosts** again and change the IP address that you entered in Step 4. Save the file again. For example, change the line to read like this:

155.99.255.255   www.utah.edu

7. Ping the site a third time. This time it doesn't work, showing you that the hosts file is being referenced instead of a DNS server.

8. Open **/etc/hosts** a final time and delete the line that you added.

9. Ping the site a final time. Because a reference to the site is not included in /etc/ hosts, the resolver must use a DNS server to obtain an IP address, so ping works correctly again.

ping www.utah.edu

HANDS-ON PROJECTS

Project 3-5

To complete this project, you need a working Linux system with a graphical (X) display and a friend in your classroom or lab with a similar system. You will work as a team on this project.

1. Log on to Linux. Instead of using the xauth command interactively as the chapter text describes, use command-line options. Start with the list option (no dashes) to dump to the screen the cookies stored in your .Xauthority file.

xauth list

2. Now use the extract option to create output in the cookielist file that can be merged into another .Xauthority file. You must include the display for which cookies are being extracted, which would be :0 on most systems.

xauth extract cookielist :0

3. Give this file to your trusted friend (e-mail it, use FTP, copy it to a disk, or use whatever means you prefer).

4. Move to your friend's computer and copy the file containing the cookie from your system into your friend's home directory. (The easiest way to transfer the file, if you don't have all your networking services already set up, is to use the mcopy command to transfer the file to a 3.5-inch disk and then from the 3.5-inch disk to the other host.)

5. On your friend's computer, execute the following command, inserting the filename containing the cookie from your system. This command merges the xauth cookies from the named file into the .Xauthority file on your friend's system.

xauth merge cookielist

6. On your friend's system, execute the following command to start a graphical program. You can use any graphical program that is installed, but be certain to substitute your own host name where the command says `hostname`. (You might try `xcalc` or `netscape` if `kpaint` is not installed.)

```
kpaint --display hostname:0.0
```

You and your friend should see the program appear on your system.

7. Move back to your system and execute the following command, substituting the program name if you used a different program in Step 6.

```
ps aux|grep kpaint
```

You see that the program that appears on your system's screen is not running on your system; it is running on your friend's system.

8. Close the program by pressing **Ctrl+C** on your friend's system or choosing **Exit** from the **File** menu on your screen.

Though you trust your friend, the next time you log out of X and log on again, a new `xauth` cookie is generated automatically, so your friend will not be able to use your system as an X server unless you hand over your cookie again.

CASE PROJECTS

CASE PROJECTS

Case Project 3-1

You are still consulting for the law firm of Snow, Sleet, and Hale in Alaska. The firm is doing well, with very little employee turnover. Because of the static nature of the network information, you are considering taking some steps to reduce the burden on the firm's system administrator.

1. Would you consider relying on an `/etc/hosts` file instead of a DNS server for the firm? For just one office? What are the costs and benefits of doing this?

2. Would you consider using DHCP instead of assigning IP addresses statically? Would you do this throughout the firm? If so, would you use a separate DHCP server in each office? What are the trade-offs you must consider in deciding this?

3. The firm has been using a proprietary e-mail system but is considering relying solely on Internet e-mail in the future. Describe how you might set up their e-mail system so that they can reliably and securely exchange e-mail within the company and have access to the Internet. Although you have not studied e-mail servers yet, consider what you have learned in this chapter to decide how the benefits and features of the POP3, IMAP, PPP, and UUCP protocols might be relevant. Where would you store e-mail for each office? How would you allow users to download or view it? How would you transfer messages between offices and to and from the Internet? Based on your initial plan, can you foresee cost, performance, or security concerns that may arise initially, or that may arise as the volume of e-mail increases (as it always does)?

4

USING SIMPLE NETWORK SERVICES

After reading this chapter and completing the exercises, you will be able to:

♦ Understand network daemons

♦ Configure "superservers" to handle multiple network services

♦ Set up administrative services such as logging and printing

♦ Use simple network information services such as `finger` and `talk`

♦ Understand basic mailing list and news server configurations

The Linux services that you have learned about so far have been mostly client-oriented, such as e-mail clients, Web browsers, and the DNS resolver. In this chapter, you will begin to learn about server software that runs on Linux. This chapter explores a number of network services that are part of most Linux systems, including both administrative services that help to maintain a working server and specialized information services for users or system administrators. The services described in this chapter are not the "famous" ones, like Web, FTP, and e-mail (those are covered in Chapters 5 and 6). Instead, the administrative services in this chapter include such things as logging, printing, time services, and network management.

The basic information services described in this chapter will help you understand how Linux network services operate. You will learn here about `finger`, `talk` (which is like Internet chat), and `whois`. In addition, you will learn how to set up mailing lists to manage e-mail in a large group and the core concepts behind setting up a news server to facilitate newsgroup postings by the users on your network.

NETWORK DAEMONS

Most Linux systems deployed in businesses are dedicated servers, providing numerous services, such as Web access, e-mail, DNS, file sharing, and printer sharing. All of these services are implemented as daemons. A Linux daemon is similar to a Windows service. Daemons are programs that are typically started by the system and are not associated with a user's terminal. You can recognize most daemons because their names usually end in a "d," such as inetd. The following partial output from the ps ax command shows daemons running on a system:

```
PID TTY       STAT    TIME  COMMAND
   1 ?        S       0:06  init [3]
   2 ?        SW      0:00  [keventd]
   3 ?        SWN     0:00  [ksoftirqd_CPU0]
   4 ?        SW      0:00  [kswapd]
   5 ?        SW      0:00  [bdflush]
   6 ?        SW      0:00  [kupdated]
  10 ?        SW      0:00  [mdrecoveryd]
  11 ?        SW      0:00  [kjournald]
  25 ?        SW      0:00  [kjournald]
  26 ?        SW      0:00  [kjournald]
  27 ?        SW      0:00  [kjournald]
  41 ?        SW      0:00  [khubd]
  93 ?        S       0:00  /usr/sbin/syslogd
  96 ?        S       0:00  /usr/sbin/klogd -c 3 -x
  98 ?        S       0:00  /usr/sbin/inetd
 107 ?        S       0:00  /usr/sbin/sshd
 119 ?        S       0:07  /usr/sbin/named
 121 ?        SL      0:00  /usr/sbin/ntpd
 199 ?        S       0:00  /usr/sbin/crond
 201 ?        S       0:00  [atd]
1347 ?        S       0:00  /usr/sbin/sshd
1363 ?        S       0:00  /usr/sbin/httpd
1364 ?        S       0:00  [httpd]
1365 ?        S       0:00  [httpd]
1366 ?        S       0:00  [httpd]
1367 ?        S       0:00  [httpd]
1368 ?        S       0:00  [httpd]
```

Notice that the TTY column shows question marks in every line. This means that a terminal is not associated with the daemons. All the daemons were launched by the system at start-up. You could start a daemon from a terminal sometime after the system starts up. If you do, you may see a TTY for that daemon. However, daemons are not written to communicate with a user terminal even if they are run by a user. You typically communicate with a daemon by modifying its configuration and sending it signals.

To cause a daemon to reread its configuration and reconfigure itself, you typically send it a SIGHUP signal using either the `kill` or `killall` command. Here's an example of reconfiguring the `syslogd` daemon using the `killall` command and an abbreviation for the SIGHUP signal:

```
killall -HUP syslogd
```

This command reconfigures the `syslogd` daemon without stopping `syslogd` services. The daemon reconfigures itself while still performing its function. Non-UNIX operating systems typically cannot do this. You must stop their services and restart them for configuration changes to take effect. A few Linux daemons also behave this way. The `dhcpd` daemon is a good example.

You can stop a daemon by sending it a SIGTERM signal:

```
killall -TERM inetd
```

If a daemon ever crashes (normally a rare event) and does not respond to signals, you can usually stop it with the SIGKILL signal. In the following example, the `kill` program requires that the daemon's PID is specified—not its name:

```
kill 201 -KILL
```

 NOTE You can get more information about signals and the use of the `kill` and `killall` commands from a basic Linux book, such as the *Guide to Linux Installation and Administration* (Course Technology, ISBN 0-619-13095-4).

Daemons consume system resources such as memory, disk space, and file descriptors (such as file handles in DOS and Windows). Various daemons have dramatically different resource requirements. The Telnet daemon, for example, is relatively lightweight. Its file size on disk is about 33 kilobytes. By comparison, the Apache Web server's daemon can be over a megabyte, and numerous Apache daemons are running all the time.

 NOTE You can't tell from a program's file size on disk how many system resources it will consume. The program may use libraries as the Telnet daemon does. Telnet uses the `libc` and `libutil` libraries, so it could consume vast resources—but it doesn't.

The UNIX/Linux security model requires that any daemon that binds itself to (connects to) TCP or UDP ports below 1024 (well-known ports) must run as the root user. This means that only the system or the root user can run these daemons. Daemons that bind to ports higher than 1023 may be run by other users. Many Linux daemons that bind to well-known ports initially run as root, but after binding to the port, switch themselves to another user so they're less of a security risk.

DAEMONS ON DEMAND

On a Linux system running many services, client requests for each service are unlikely to arrive at regular intervals. Some services may be accessed infrequently. Instead of having the daemons for infrequently accessed services running all the time, you could choose to load these daemons only when there is demand for them. This would reduce the system resources consumed by idle daemons.

Daemons can be loaded on demand using software called **superservers** that listen on multiple network ports and start the appropriate service when a client requests a connection for that port or, in the case of UDP, a datagram arrives. Two popular superserver programs are `inetd` (Internet daemon) and `xinetd` (extended Internet daemon or Internet Super Daemon). One of these superservers is installed on your Linux system. You can tell which one you have by examining the `/etc` directory for the superserver configuration file. If you're running `inetd`, you'll see the `inetd.conf` file. If you're running `xinetd`, you'll see a `xinetd.conf` file.

Many daemons can be configured to run in a stand-alone mode or with a superserver. When a daemon runs stand-alone, we sometimes refer to the daemon as being *daemonized*. The Apache Web server was originally designed to run either stand-alone or using a superserver. In time, people realized that it was a poor idea to run Apache on demand because of its rather large size. Loading Apache on demand is too time-costly, so modern versions of Apache will no longer run with a superserver.

So, superservers are only useful when the daemons are not too large. But suppose they're small, like the Telnet daemon. A small daemon is less likely to consume significant system resources, so there may be little penalty if you run it stand-alone. Under what conditions, then, do superservers make sense?

In addition to launching daemons on demand, superservers provide access control. You can control who is allowed to access your daemons on a per-daemon basis. Of course, access can also be controlled with firewall rules. You may prefer to do all your access control in your firewall and none in your superserver.

You could easily come to the conclusion that superservers are not useful and choose not to use them. After all, memory and disk space are relatively inexpensive and you can configure your kernel for more file descriptors. The choice of whether to use a superserver is often a personal one. The decision may be out of your hands, however, if you must run a daemon that is written to run in a superserver environment and cannot be easily configured for stand-alone operation.

Using `inetd` and TCP Wrappers

The `inetd` program is the original superserver. It is extremely simple. It monitors TCP and UDP ports and launches programs to handle connections on these ports. The **TCP Wrappers** program, called **tcpd**, provides logging and access control for these incoming connections. Each is configured by different files.

NOTE

Inetd is not installed on Fedora Core. It uses the xinetd superserver.

You configure inetd by editing the /etc/inetd.conf file. Here's an example of the file's contents:

```
ftp     stream tcp nowait root /usr/sbin/tcpd in.ftpd -l -a
telnet  stream tcp nowait root /usr/sbin/tcpd in.telnetd
pop3    stream tcp nowait root /usr/sbin/tcpd ipop3d
imap    stream tcp nowait root /usr/sbin/tcpd imapd
```

- The first field is the service name, which must correspond to a service name in /etc/services. The service name tells inetd which port to listen to.

- The second field indicates the type of connection that is made. It will be stream for TCP connections and dgram (short for "datagram") for UDP connections.

- The third field is tcp in all the example lines. The other choice is udp. The second and third fields seem to duplicate each other.

- The fourth field is either wait or nowait. When a packet arrives at the port being listened to, this field determines whether inetd waits for that packet to be processed before watching that port again, or immediately hands the packet to a server and goes back to listening for more packets on that port. The value nowait is typical here because it allows many more client requests to be processed in a shorter time.

- The fifth field indicates the user ID that inetd should use when it starts a server program to handle an incoming packet. For many services, this must be root. If the server is capable of running as another user, you can improve your system security by creating a user account specifically for that server and entering that username in this field instead of root.

- The sixth field indicates the program that inetd should launch when a packet arrives at the port specified by this service name.

In the first line of the example, this is the sixth field:

```
/usr/sbin/tcpd in.ftpd -l -a
```

The program that runs is the tcpd program. This is TCP Wrappers. If it decides that the incoming connection should be allowed, it spawns the in.ftpd daemon and passes it the -l and -a options on the command line. It also logs the request. If TCP Wrappers denies the request, it is simply dropped. This is illustrated in Figure 4-1.

TCP Wrappers traditionally uses two configuration files: **/etc/hosts.allow** and **/etc/hosts.deny**. An extended syntax allows you to use only the hosts.allow file. This is described later.

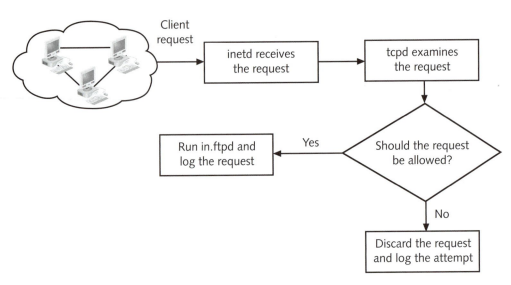

Figure 4-1 Processing incoming client requests through TCP Wrappers

The interaction of the `hosts.allow` and `hosts.deny` files in controlling access to network services is shown in Figure 4-2. Getting started with these files is easy, but be aware that you should test the configuration carefully before relying on it. This flexibility in configuration means that you may not be configuring exactly what you *think* you are configuring! The format is simple. You list a daemon name followed by the host name or IP address that should be allowed or denied access to that daemon, as follows:

```
in.telnetd:    192.168.1.12
```

NOTE You must use the precise name of the daemon. It's the name you would see in a `ps` listing when the daemon is running. If you're a programmer, it's the `arg0` value.

Instead of specifying an IP address or a host name, you can use the keywords `ALL` and `EXCEPT`. For example, suppose the `hosts.deny` file contains this line:

```
in.telnetd:    ALL
```

And the `hosts.allow` file contains this line:

```
in.telnetd:    192.168.
```

This indicates that only users whose IP addresses begin with 192.168 are allowed to access the Telnet server. Similarly, suppose the `hosts.allow` file contains this line:

```
in.telnetd:    *.myplace.net EXCEPT ns.myplace.net
```

4

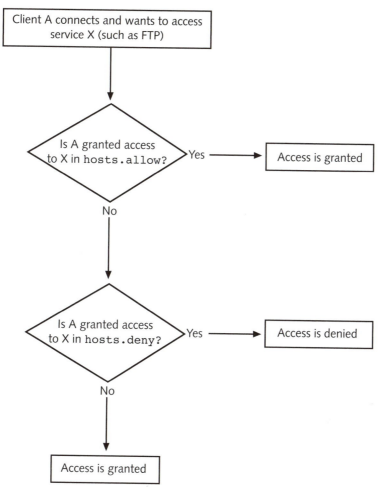

Figure 4-2   Controlling access via `hosts.allow` and `hosts.deny`

This indicates that users from the *myplace.net* domain name, except the name server (*ns.myplace.net*), are allowed to use Telnet. Of course, these examples only touch upon the complexity of the assignments you can create. The ALL and EXCEPT keywords (plus several others) can be used in the first field as well to protect a number of fields at the same time. For example, the `hosts.deny` file can contain the following line to block access to all daemons for all users:

```
ALL:      ALL
```

It's important to understand that the default action of `tcpd` is to allow access. The `hosts.allow` file is checked first, and if an entry matching a pending connection request is found, the connection is accepted. If no entry is found, `hosts.deny` is checked. If an entry is found there, the connection is denied; otherwise, it is accepted. The most secure configuration is to block all daemons to all users, and then in `hosts.allow` to specifically allow any daemon you want users to have access to, with corresponding IP addresses, hosts, or even an ALL designation.

Whenever you make a change in the inetd.conf file, you must restart the inetd program using the system script with a command like this:

```
/etc/rc.d/init.d/inetd restart
```

You can also use either the kill or killall command to send a reinitialize signal to the daemon, causing it to reread its configuration file. An example of each command is shown here:

```
kill -HUP 'cat /var/run/inetd'
killall -HUP inetd
```

TCP Wrappers supports user-specific entries in the hosts.allow and hosts.deny files, as well as advanced options such as returning a message to the client initiating the connection. To learn about these options, carefully review the man page for hosts.allow and hosts.deny using this command:

```
man 5 hosts_access
```

TIP   Another way to view this information is with the pinfo command, which presents man pages in a color-coded format with hypertext links to other documents referenced in the man page. Use this command: pinfo hosts_access.

If the notion of having separate files for allow and deny conditions seems silly to you, an extended syntax allows you to configure tcpd with a single configuration file that contains DENY and ALLOW statements. Here's an example:

```
in.telnetd:     *.myplace.net EXCEPT ns.myplace.net ALLOW
ALL: ALL: DENY
```

You can learn more about this extended syntax from the hosts_options man page.

Most of tcpd's functionality is in the libwrap library. Programs besides tcpd can and do use the libwrap library. This means that they can also use the hosts.allow and hosts.deny files for access control even though they're not controlled by inetd.

Using xinetd

The xinetd program is a superserver with greatly enhanced functionality. It is included with Fedora Core. It has one configuration file, /etc/xinetd.conf, that refers to the contents of the /etc/xinetd.d directory. Within that directory, each service is configured by a separate file. A sample file, /etc/xinetd.d/wu-ftpd, is shown here:

```
# default: on
# description: The wu-ftpd FTP server serves FTP
    connections. It uses \
```

```
#       normal, unencrypted usernames and passwords for authentication.
service ftp
{
        socket_type         = stream
        wait                = no
        user                = root
        server              = /usr/sbin/in.ftpd
        server_args         = -l -a
        log_on_success      += DURATION USERID
        log_on_failure      += USERID
        nice                = 10
        disable             = yes
}
```

The format of each file in /etc/xinetd.d names a service, as in the preceding service line. Brackets then enclose options that apply to that service. Some of these options match those for the inetd.conf file, such as socket_type, user, and server. Several other options extend the functionality of xinetd beyond what the older inetd program offers. For example, various logging options are provided to determine what information xinetd writes to the system log when a connection is attempted, and several security options are available to control access to services. For example, the parameters only_from, no_access, access_time, and deny_time determine which hosts can access a service and when they can access it.

The extensive man page for xinetd.conf describes its available options. One particular option to note is the disable option. Several services in Fedora Core Linux are fully configured but are disabled, so no connections are accepted. You can enable them by changing the line in the appropriate configuration file to disable=no. (The logic of the disable=no statement seems reversed to some users.)

You should also restart xinetd after making any changes to the configuration files within /etc/xinetd.d (or to /etc/xinetd.conf itself). You can use the script in /etc/rc.d/init.d or the kill command, but be careful with the kill command so that you send the right signal and don't simply stop the superserver. The authors of xinetd were wary of intruders changing access settings and then restarting xinetd using a standard SIGHUP restart signal. Instead, to restart xinetd you must send a SIGUSR2 signal. Either of the following example commands can do this:

```
kill -SIGUSR2 'cat /var/run/xinetd.pid'
killall -USR2 xinetd
```

Exploring Network Testing Services

The inetd and xinetd servers support several network services that are internal to the superserver—that is, no other server programs are launched. These services are used to test the network and the operation of the superserver, including experimenting with the security settings using a service that doesn't pose much threat. (Still, production sites normally shut down these services to avoid any possible security holes.) These services are typically disabled by default; to use them you must change the `disable=yes` line in the appropriate file in `/etc/xinetd.d` to `disable=no` or remove the comment character from the beginning of the appropriate line in `/etc/inetd.conf`.

Five of the testing services are described here. You can use any one of them (after enabling it) by using Telnet to connect to the indicated port. You can do this locally to explore these functions, or connect to any remote host on which the service is enabled and to which your host has been granted access. For example, this command starts the `chargen` service on the local host:

```
telnet localhost 19
```

NOTE

If your system is configured to block access to unnecessary services, you will receive an error when using the preceding `telnet` command to test `chargen`.

Some of the services described here are explored in a Hands-On Project at the end of this chapter.

- The **echo** service on UDP or TCP port 7 repeats back to you whatever you type. This shows you that a remote host is correctly receiving the information that you type. No password is needed, and no processing is done on the text; it is simply parroted back to you. The Echo Protocol is described by RFC 862.

- The **chargen** service uses the Character Generator Protocol described by RFC 864. It uses UDP port 19 to return a stream of characters (the standard character set, in numeric order). The `chargen` service continues to issue this stream until you end the Telnet session.

- The **discard** service on UDP or TCP port 9 is like `/dev/null`. Anything you send to the port is discarded without any processing. The Discard Protocol is described in RFC 863.

- The **time** service on UDP or TCP port 37 returns a number corresponding to the current time and closes the connection. This number is returned in a program-readable format, which appears as random characters if you use this service from a command prompt. It may be useful within a program to collect the time from another host. The Time Protocol is described in RFC 868.

- The **daytime** service on UDP and TCP port 13 returns the current date and time in human-readable form, then closes the connection. For example, the response would look something like this: `02 APR 2003 23:17:02 EST`. The Daytime Protocol is described in RFC 867.

USING ADMINISTRATIVE SERVICES

You can use services such as echo, chargen, and daytime to test networking. Other services are used to provide administrative services for Linux, such as logging and printing. This section describes how those services operate.

Logging with logd

You are probably already familiar with the Linux logging facility, controlled by the two daemons klogd and syslogd (for kernel messages and all other messages, respectively). These programs are managed using standard scripts in /etc/rc.d/init.d. The logging function is configured via the file /etc/syslog.conf. Multiple types of messages from multiple types of programs are generated on a typical Linux system and passed to syslogd; messages from the Linux kernel are processed via klogd. The syslog.conf file supports four basic options for how a message is handled. These can be combined as you choose:

- Write the message to a file.

- Write the message to a pipe to which a filter program is listening. The filter program can do whatever it wants with the messages.

- Print the message on the terminal of one or more named users or all users. (Users must be logged on to receive a message designated for this type of delivery.)

- Forward the message over the network to another Linux system, where it is processed according to the syslog.conf file on that system. This is called remote logging.

This section focuses on remote logging. Log messages provide key information about how a system is operating and about how users are using system resources. Sending some or all logging messages to another host can improve security because intruders can't change the log files to hide their tracks. Storing log entries remotely also lets you track what has happened when a system dies and its log files are unavailable. For example, suppose you have a remote system that fails. If its log entries were written to your local server, you could see the log entries leading up to the failure without having to repair the remote server first.

The **syslogd** daemon uses the BSD syslog Protocol described by RFC 3164. It uses UDP port 514 to communicate with a syslogd on another system. This port must be listed in /etc/services (it is by default). By default, syslogd does not support remote transfer of log messages. To enable this feature, you must add the -r option to the command launching syslogd. You can best do this by editing the /etc/sysconfig/syslog file and adding the -r to the SYSLOG_OPTIONS line.

The `syslogd` program sends kernel messages to a remote host if so configured in `/etc/syslog.conf`, as described later in this chapter. You don't need to configure `klogd` specially.

After you start `syslogd` with the `-r` parameter, it watches the correct port and accepts incoming connections from remote logging daemons. You can check the man page for `syslogd` to see how to specify additional or multiple ports for `syslogd` to watch for incoming connections from remote `syslogd` daemons. Remember that for `syslogd` to communicate remotely, you must allow UDP traffic destined for port 514 to pass through any firewalls between the host producing log messages and the host you intend to receive them.

Now turn your attention to the host receiving the log messages. To configure one host to send log messages to another host, use the "@" symbol on the far right of the appropriate configuration line in `/etc/syslog.conf`. For example, suppose you originally had a configuration line such as this, which causes all kernel messages to be stored in the `/var/log/messages` file:

```
kern.*        /var/log/messages
```

By changing the line as shown here, the messages are logged on the host *london.myplace.net* (typically in the file `/var/log/messages` on the remote host, but that depends on how `syslog.conf` is set up on the remote host).

```
kern.*        @london.myplace.net
```

As a final note, if you set up remote logging, you should review the options available for `syslogd` in the man page. For example, the `-s` option lets you specify domain names to be stripped off before logging an event, and the `-x` option indicates that host names should not be dereferenced for remotely logged events (to avoid a deadlock if the DNS server is unavailable). These and several other `syslogd` options are designed to make remote logging more effective.

Printing with Linux

Printing in Linux uses networking by default. The assumption is that many hosts need to share printers. Network printing was developed decades ago, when printers were expensive and users had to share them. Even though printers are now inexpensive and users can have their own, there are still benefits to sharing. For example, if a multiuser application requires a standard form for printing certain output, an office staff should consider devoting a network printer to the form. This saves users from having to switch paper trays. Another example is implementing quotas. If you want to limit users to a certain number of printed pages a day, you should use a network printer.

Two network printing protocols are used with Linux. The older Line Printer Daemon Protocol is described by RFC 1179. The newer Internet Printing Protocol is described in RFCs 2566, 2567, 2568, and others. You may also want to refer to RFC 2569, called *Mapping Between LPD and IPP Protocols*.

NOTE This section deals with the networking aspects of Linux printing. For details on other printing issues, refer to a book that covers generic Linux printing, such as the *Guide to Linux Installation and Administration* (Course Technology, ISBN 0-619-13095-4).

The Line Printer Daemon Protocol is supported by Linux, all UNIX operating systems, NetWare, and Windows. Using this protocol, Linux can interoperate with other operating systems—a Linux desktop computer can print to a printer connected to a Windows computer and vice versa. On Linux and UNIX systems, this protocol is supported by these programs:

- `lpd`—Controls the line printer daemon
- `lpr`—Sends a print job to a print queue
- `lpq`—Displays the contents of the print queues
- `lprm`—Removes print jobs from print queues
- `lpc`—Controls the print queues

TIP Windows includes a different print sharing protocol by default: Server Message Block (SMB, described in Chapter 5). It's normally better to use SMB to print to Windows hosts.

The Line Printer Daemon Protocol uses TCP and the line printer daemon listens on port 515. It expects source ports to be within the range of 721 to 731.

To configure printing to a remote host, you set up the appropriate entry in the `/etc/printcap` file. This includes the following two lines:

```
:rm=printer.example.com:\
:rp=lazer:\
```

The line beginning with `:rm=` defines the remote host to print to, and `:rp=` defines the remote print queue to use. If you don't define a remote print queue when you create this printer definition, `lpd` uses the default print queue on the remote system.

Linux distributions include graphical tools to manage `printcap` entries.

For this printer definition to print successfully, you must specify a print queue that is valid on the remote host. You must also be granted permission to print on the remote host, although by default, no restrictions are placed on who can print remotely. Permissions are configured in `lpd` using the `/etc/lpd.conf` and `/etc/lpd.perms` files.

After you have defined a printer, the `lpd` print server accepts print jobs, spools them to a print queue directory, and sends them one at a time to the physical printer.

Whenever `lpd` sees that a print job is destined for a remote printer, it uses port 515 to connect to the `lpd` program running on that remote host. Assuming that no firewall is blocking communication and that `lpd` is running on the remote host, the remote copy of `lpd` accepts the connection, processes the print job being sent, and spools it to a local file as if it had originated on the local host (using its own `printcap` printer definitions).

The Internet Printing Protocol (IPP) is considered an experimental protocol, and it will probably be several more years before a standard is developed. This has not deterred vendors from coming up with IPP-based products. Linux has support for IPP in the form of the **Common UNIX Printing System** or **CUPS**. CUPS was built by a vendor (Easy Software Products), but the code is free software protected by the GNU Public License.

IPP currently uses HTTP version 1.1 running on TCP port 631 to communicate between CUPS clients and servers. This could change in the future, but using HTTP makes sense. Why create yet another application-specific protocol when a general-purpose protocol like HTTP easily does the job?

The current implementation of CUPS on Linux allows configuration via a Web browser. With the CUPS daemon (`cupsd`) running, point your browser to *http://localhost:631*. You see the main CUPS page, as shown in Figure 4-3.

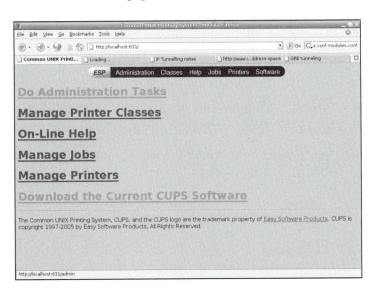

Figure 4-3 The main CUPS page

This page is the main menu. It has links to other pages where you configure classes, print jobs, and printers. Click the Do Administration Tasks link to see the Administration page, as shown in Figure 4-4.

For more information about CUPS, refer to its Web site at *www.cups.org*.

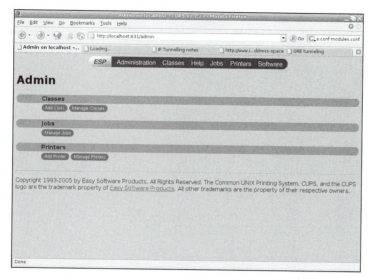

Figure 4-4 The CUPS Administration page

Configuring NTP Time Synchronization

Maintaining accurate and consistent time among all the hosts on a network is critical for some application programs and a relief to network users who would otherwise become confused by inconsistent date and time stamps on files, e-mail messages, and other material. For example, it may be important for a scheduling application to notify people 10 minutes before a meeting. If a host's time is off by 10 minutes, you may be late for your meeting.

To keep all hosts synchronized to a common and accurate time, you use a time synchronization protocol. The Internet's time synchronization protocol is the **Network Time Protocol** or **NTP**, described in RFC 1305. With NTP, timekeeping is a serious affair. NTP time is sent as a 64-bit value, where the first 32 bits represent the amount of time, in seconds, that have elapsed since midnight, January 1, 1900. This date is the NTP epoch. The remaining 32 bits represent the fractional part of the current second, which offers precision of 232 picoseconds. Chances are good that this precision is good enough for your applications. However, precise time may be useless to you if it's not accurate.

A hierarchy of NTP time servers exists to ensure that you have access to sources of time that are accurate enough for your purposes. Each level in the hierarchy is called a **stratum**. Higher strata provide accurate time to time servers at lower levels. The top level, stratum 1, consists of a few hundred time servers all over the world that synchronize their time to atomic clocks. Many of these time servers are operated by government agencies, such as the National Institutes of Standards and Technology (NIST) and the U.S. Naval Observatory.

Stratum 2 time servers synchronize their time to stratum 1 servers. Stratum 3 servers synchronize to stratum 2 servers, and so on. Figure 4-5 illustrates the basic structure of NTP server strata. The stratum 1 server in this diagram synchronizes to an atomic clock whose time is broadcast by a satellite. It must compensate for the significant propagation delay the satellite channel represents. If the satellite is geosynchronous, it's orbiting the earth at an altitude of about 22,300 miles with a delay of a few hundred milliseconds.

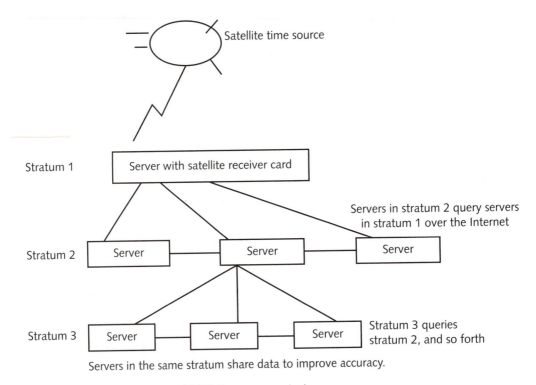

Figure 4-5   The structure of NTP time server strata

Servers at lower strata synchronize to higher-stratum servers (lower stratum numbers) but they may also synchronize amongst themselves, as shown in Figure 4-5. Servers at the same stratum that synchronize amongst themselves are called peers and rely on a form of majority logic called the Correctness Principle to decide which of the servers are accurate. For details on the Correctness Principle and other highly technical information about timekeeping, refer to *www.eecis.udel.edu/~mills/exec.html*.

NOTE   An NTP client is any host running NTP, and no other hosts query it for the correct time.

NTP is supported in Linux with the **ntpd** daemon. It is installed on most Linux systems by default. The same daemon is used on both NTP servers and clients. This means that an NTP client can behave like an NTP server just by changing its configuration file.

NOTE

The ntpd daemon's code has also been ported to other operating systems, such as Windows, NetWare, and OS X. NTP is a cross-platform application.

4

Before you can use ntpd, you must modify its configuration file, /etc/ntp.conf. This file should already exist. You need to modify the file to tell ntpd to which sources of time to synchronize. Assuming that you're not going to have peer time servers, you'll simply add some server lines to the file:

```
server ntp.ucsd.edu
server ntp1.kansas.net
server clock1.unc.edu
server tick.cs.unlv.edu
server ntp0.cornell.edu
```

Each server line specifies a server to which ntpd should synchronize. For best accuracy, you should have at least five servers. The NTP Web site, *www.ntp.org*, has links to lists of public stratum 1 and 2 NTP servers. Watch for the "Rules of Engagement" link and read the page. It will tell you why you should be careful and responsible in choosing the time servers to which you synchronize. You should synchronize to a server at a stratum that offers the accuracy you need—no more. You should not synchronize to stratum 1 servers unless you have a need for extremely accurate time. If stratum 1 servers become overloaded, their accuracy will suffer and their administrators will have to solve the problem in some way, such as denying access to the public.

The highest stratum you should synchronize to is stratum 2. Stratum 2 servers are still sources of very accurate and precise time—probably far better than your needs. You can afford to synchronize to lower-stratum servers, but there are no lists of public stratum 3 servers. To solve this problem, just synchronize to *www.pool.ntp.org*. This chooses a random time server operating at a random stratum from a pool of public time servers. More information about this pool is at the *http://ntp.isc.org/bin/view/Servers/NTPPoolServers* Web site. This Web page has a list of names you can use to synchronize to time servers that are geographically close to you for slightly better accuracy. If you're in the United States, here's an example of the server lines in your ntp.conf file:

```
server us.pool.ntp.org
server us.pool.ntp.org
server us.pool.ntp.org
server us.pool.ntp.org
server us.pool.ntp.org
server us.pool.ntp.org
```

Now that you've configured ntpd, there's one more thing to do before you can start it. You must ensure that your system's time is close to the current actual time. The ntpd daemon will refuse to synchronize to other time sources if its local time is off by more than 1000 seconds from the other servers. You can, of course, do this manually with the date command, as in this example:

```
date -s "03/06/2005 10:31"
```

When you boot your system, you need a way to synchronize automatically unless you're certain that your system will never be more than 1000 seconds off. The most common way to set time at boot-up is to use the ntpdate program. Here's an example of a command that will set your system time at boot-up:

```
ntpdate -s pool.ntp.org
```

You can include this command in your NTP script in /etc/rc.d/init.d. Make sure the script runs this command before it runs the ntpd daemon.

NOTE
Note that ntpd may be called **xntpd** on some Linux systems.

If ntpd is shut down or restarted, it saves information in the file specified in the driftfile line of the configuration file to calibrate its drift when it starts up again. Drift compensates for the error in the computer's internal clock.

A suite of utility programs is provided with the ntpd server. For example, ntpq gives you lots of detailed technical information about NTP. Here's just one example of its usage:

```
ntpq -pn
     remote           refid      st t when poll reach   delay   offset  jitter
==============================================================================
 127.127.1.0     127.127.1.0     10 l   62   64  377    0.000    0.000   0.008
+206.103.37.2    198.72.72.10     3 u  119 1024  377    1.405   -1.321   1.856
*206.103.37.3    131.216.1.218    3 u   38 1024  377    1.368   -0.423   0.572
```

This displays a list of the time servers to which the computer has connected. The far left character on each line is the tally code. If this code is a space, the server rejects this time server as unreachable. If the character is a plus sign, it means that this server's time is reasonable and is a candidate for use in the future. If the character is an asterisk, it means that this is the time server you are synchronized to currently. Numerous other tally codes are documented on the ntpq Web page at *www.eecis.udel.edu/~mills/ntp/*.

In this example, the server whose IP address is 206.103.37.3 is the server to which you're currently synchronized. It is synchronized to a server whose IP address is 131.216.1.218, and it is a stratum 3 server. This makes the 131.216.1.218 server a stratum 2 server. The offset column shows the difference between this server's time and your computer's time in milliseconds.

The `ntptrace` program traces a chain of NTP servers back to the primary (stratum 1) source. This only works if you allow UDP port 123 (for all these servers) through your firewall. Here's an example of the program's output:

```
localhost: stratum 5, offset 0.000061, synch distance 0.21452
fire.alcpress.com: stratum 4, offset 0.001103, synch distance
0.20074
216-9-0-66.lan.isomedia.com: stratum 3, offset 0.003461,
synch distance 0.10390
bigben.ucsd.edu: stratum 2, offset 0.004509, synch distance
0.05167
time.sdsc.edu: stratum 1, offset 0.004672, synch distance
0.00218, refid 'WWVB'
```

The computer running the `ntptrace` program is the local host, which is at stratum 5 in this example. You see the other four time server names in the far left field, along with their stratum number. The second field is the time offset between the time servers and the local host. The third field—the synchronization distance—is the estimated error relative to the primary source. The stratum 1 server also has a fourth field, the identifier of the reference clock. In this example, it is radio station WWVB operated by NIST in Boulder, Colorado.

The 32-bit number that NTP uses to measure seconds will reach its upper bounds (all ones) in the year 2036 and roll over to all zeros, bringing us back to the beginning of NTP time—midnight, January 1, 1900. Sometime before then, a solution must be agreed upon. The most likely solution is to declare a new epoch (the point in time to which NTP numbers are referenced). Instead of the midnight, January 1, 1900 epoch, a date in the future will be chosen.

Another solution is to replace NTP with a protocol that greatly extends the lifetime of an epoch. Dan Bernstein, a math professor at the University of Chicago, proposes TAI64, which uses a 64-bit value. You can read more about TAI64 from Bernstein's Web page at *http://cr.yp.to/proto/taiclock.txt*.

Supporting Clients with NTP

With a Linux NTP server running on your network, you're ready to offer time synchronization services to your client computers. If the client computers are running Linux or UNIX, you still use the `ntpd` daemon. However, the configuration file will be simpler and different from your NTP server. You'll use only one server statement (unless you have more than one NTP server) and you'll add the `iburst` option to the server line. Here's an example that assumes your NTP server's IP address is 10.0.0.25:

```
server 10.0.0.25 iburst
```

The `iburst` option allows the client's `ntpd` daemon to achieve time synchronization in about 10 seconds on average. Without this option, synchronization takes at least 10 minutes. Do not use the `iburst` option in the configuration file of your NTP server if you're synchronizing to public NTP servers. These servers may interpret your `ntpd` daemon's behavior as an attack.

If your clients are running Windows 2000 or later, it includes a time synchronization client. This client uses the **Simple Network Time Protocol** or **SNTP** protocol described by RFC 2030. SNTP is a subset of NTP that does not use the 32-bit value that provides for subsecond precision. SNTP precision allows accuracy no better than plus or minus one second—a far cry from NTP precision and accuracy. SNTP clients can access your Linux NTP server without difficulty.

If you're using Windows XP, you configure time synchronization by right-clicking the time in the lower-right corner of the screen. Select Adjust Date/Time from the menu. Click the Internet Time tab. You can turn on time synchronization by checking the "Automatically synchronize with an Internet time server" check box. Choose the time server to synchronize to by clicking the Server list box. By default, only the *time.windows.com* and *time.nist.gov* servers are in the list. To put your server in the list, you have to modify the Windows Registry. Using the `regedit` program, go here:

```
HKEY_LOCAL_MACHINE\Software\Microsoft\Windows\CurrentVersion
\DateTime\Servers
```

You have to either modify one of the existing keys (change *time.windows.com* to your server name) or create another key so your server appears in the list.

Understanding SNMP on Linux

The **Simple Network Management Protocol** or **SNMP** is designed to give you feedback about how the components of your network are functioning. For example, you can use SNMP to determine whether routers are overloaded or whether software programs on remote servers have crashed. Using SNMP is a large and complex topic; you can research it further by visiting *http://linas.org/linux/NMS.html*. The link to the SNMP FAQ has a detailed discussion of the protocol, and the rest of the page describes numerous SNMP software tools that run on Linux. RFC 1067 is the basic reference document on SNMP (see *www.rfc-editor.org*).

SNMP uses a client/server architecture, but also uses other terms to describe its actions. An SNMP-aware program running on a host is called an **agent**. You configure the agent to watch for specific events on a host. Anytime such an event occurs, the agent collects the details. An SNMP **console** program gathers data from SNMP agents on the network for a system administrator's review. A console can also present SNMP data statistically as graphs or as summaries.

Allowing Dial-in Access with a PPP Server

In Chapter 3, you learned about setting up a Linux client to connect to a remote host using PPP, typically over a modem connection. The other side of the story is that a server somewhere must accept people calling in who want to connect using PPP. In this section, you learn the basics of setting up such a service on Linux. The same program, pppd, is used for both the client and server sides of a PPP connection; the only difference is who calls whom, and how pppd is configured.

NOTE

Configuring a dial-in PPP server, especially for use by multiple modems, is a complex task. Your computer is basically becoming an ISP when you set this up. The information in this section should get you started.

When you log on to Linux from a command line (as opposed to a graphical logon screen), a terminal program watches for your username and password, then passes them on to the logon program, which starts a command shell if they are acceptable. The command-line environment for Linux includes multiple virtual terminals (usually six) that you can switch to using the key combinations Ctrl+Alt+F1 through Ctrl+Alt+F6. Each of the virtual terminals is monitored by a program called **getty** or something similar such as **mgetty** or **mingetty**. These are different versions of a program that does the same thing: watches for someone logging on.

The getty program is managed by **init**, a master control program that the Linux kernel starts right after the system is started. The init program configuration is located in /etc/inittab. Part of this file includes configuration lines for each of the virtual terminals. A sample line from /etc/inittab is shown here:

```
1:2345:respawn:/sbin/mingetty tty1
```

To set up a PPP dial-in server, you must have a getty-type program that watches a modem; mgetty is typically used because it was designed with modems in mind. The mgetty program listens to a serial port instead of a virtual terminal. Whenever someone sends logon information via the modem, mgetty verifies its validity, then starts pppd using the parameters that initialize a valid network device. For example, if you have mgetty installed on your Linux system, you can add a line like the following one to the end of /etc/inittab to have mgetty watch the modem on the first serial port (device ttyS0) for incoming calls.

```
S1:2345:respawn:/sbin/mgetty -x 3 -s 57600 -D ttyS0
```

After making this change, you can restart the init program with this command:

```
kill -1 1
```

Or this command:

```
init 6
```

When another host calls the modem on your serial port, mgetty examines the characters sent by the remote host. If the host requests a PPP connection, mgetty starts pppd. To make this happen, however, you must configure mgetty to use the AutoPPP command by making certain that the following line appears in the /etc/mgetty+sendfax/login. config file (this command is case sensitive):

```
/AutoPPP/ - a_ppp /usr/sbin/pppd -detach
```

You can include other options in the pppd command, but they are normally stored in the /etc/ppp/options file. The options file contains configuration parameters that apply to every copy of pppd running on your system. Each individual modem can also have a configuration file with parameters that only apply when pppd is used for that device. For example, a modem attached to the first serial port would use the file /etc/ppp/options. ttyS0. If you use a multiport serial card to attach multiple modems to your Linux system, you would create multiple options files, one for each modem device. This allows you to specify an IP address to use for each client that calls in. The main file, /etc/ppp/options, might look like this:

```
name sundance   # the name of my server
require-pap     # require PAP authentication
refuse-chap     # don't permit CHAP authentication
proxyarp        # let clients use proxy ARP
login           # authenticate the dial-
                    in user to the local /etc/passwd file
netmask 255.255.255.0
# send this network mask to the dial-in client
idle 600
# disconnect if this modem sits idle for 600 seconds
asyncmap 200a0000    # convert special characters XON, XO
                        FF, and ^]
crtscts         # Use hardware flow control
modem           # Use standard modem control signals
```

Some additional options are useful if Windows clients are dialing in to your Linux PPP server. See the pppd man page for more information on these options. If you want to assign the IP address to a dial-in client, the /etc/ppp/options.ttyS0 file must contain a line like the following. This "range" causes the address 192.168.150.1 to be assigned to any client dialing into the modem on ttyS0.

```
192.168.150.0:192.168.150.1
```

PPP creates a single point-to-point connection between your host and the dial-in host. For any packets to reach the rest of the network, you must have IP forwarding enabled on your host.

If this basic configuration does not function for you, check the log files for `pppd` and `mgetty` (such as `/var/log/mgetty.log.ttyS0`) and review the documentation for `pppd` or the PPP HOWTO document on *www.linuxdocs.org*. PPP is complex, but provides a very useful service for many small and medium networks.

4

USING BASIC INFORMATION SERVICES

In this section, you will learn about a few additional services that provide simple network information or communications capability. As indicated in the text that follows, many of these services are not enabled by default after a standard Linux installation because they are not considered highly secure. You can change the settings to experiment with them or have them active as a regular part of your network.

Communicating with `talk`

Linux and UNIX systems had functionality like Internet "chat" long before chat was as popular as it is now. The **talk** program uses the **talkd** daemon to let you initiate a real-time conversation with another user who is logged on a remote host that is also running the `talkd` daemon. The `talkd` daemon uses UDP on port 517 to communicate with remote hosts. You must enable this service in `/etc/inetd.conf` or `/etc/xinetd.d/talk` as appropriate; your Linux installation may not have this enabled by default. Be certain you restart the superserver if you make changes to its configuration file before trying out `talkd`.

To use `talkd`, use the `talk` program with the username and host name that you want to contact. For example, suppose you are logged on as nwells at host london. Your friend is logged on as abutler on host dublin. You can enter the following command to initiate a chat session using `talkd`:

```
talk abutler@dublin
```

You do not use the fully qualified domain name (FQDN) because you're on the same local network as your friend, so Linux adds the domain name by default, yielding the correct FQDN for the remote host. If firewalls are not in the way, you can use `talkd` across the Internet to any host in the world using an FQDN.

When you enter the preceding command, the `talk` program "takes over" your window and displays messages as it tries to establish a connection with the remote user. Meanwhile, the `talkd` daemon on dublin checks whether abutler is logged on. If she is not, a message on london informs you of that, and you can press any key to exit `talk`. If she is logged on, however, `talkd` displays a message on her screen:

```
Message from Talk_Daemon@london.myplace.net at 22:52
talk: Connection requested by nwells@london.myplace.net.
talk: respond with: talk nwells@london.myplace.net
```

This message is repeated once per minute until abutler either responds with a `talk` command or nwells cancels the `talk` command with Ctrl+C. Assuming that abutler enters the `talk` command as prompted, the two-way communication is initiated and the command-line window on both screens is split, with you typing in the top half of the screen and abutler's responses appearing in the bottom half of the screen. Each line appears as soon as it is typed.

You can use Ctrl+P and Ctrl+N to scroll up or down, respectively, and review the text of the conversation. If you want to stop people from bothering you with talk requests, use the **mesg** command to disable access to your command-line window:

```
mesg n
```

Using this command is a good idea anytime you are working with a full-screen program such as `elm` or `pine` for e-mail.

If you generally work at a graphical display rather than a character-mode screen, you can still access `talkd` functionality using a graphical tool such as Ktalk (for KDE). (The actual program name is `ktalkdlg`.)

Linux also supports a number of popular chat-style systems for communicating across the Internet. Table 4-1 summarizes some of the programs that are available for various chat and messaging systems.

Table 4-1   Linux chat programs for various messenger systems

Program Name	Description
B-Chat	A Yahoo! Messenger client for GNOME
EveryBuddy	A Universal Instant Messaging client supporting America Online Messenger (AIM), I Seek You (ICQ), Yahoo! Messenger, and Microsoft Network Chat
Gabber	A client for the open source Instant Messaging system, Jabber
GAIM	An AIM client for GNOME; plug-ins support ICQ, Yahoo! Messenger, Microsoft Network Chat, Internet Relay Chat (IRC), Jabber, Napster, and Zephyr
Kchat	A basic chat program for KDE (use with the `chatserver` package)

Table 4-1   Linux chat programs for various messenger systems (continued)

Program Name	Description
Kicq	A KDE client for ICQ chatting
Kit	An AIM client for KDE
Kmerlin	A KDE client for Microsoft Network Chat
Kntalk	A KDE client for the `ntalk` chat protocol
Kopete	A plug-in-based multiprotocol messaging client for KDE
Ksirc	An IRC chat client for KDE
KYIM	A Yahoo! Messenger client for KDE
Licq	A widely used ICQ chat client
meko	A client for the Say2 chat protocol
Qirc	A basic IRC chat client
QtChat	A KDE client for Yahoo! Chat

Using `finger` to Collect User Information

For you to use `talk`, the user you want to contact must be logged on. The **finger** program provides a quick method of determining whether that is the case. The `finger` program uses the `finger` protocol via the `in.fingerd` daemon. The `finger` program also provides information such as how long a user has been logged on and the user's full name. After `finger` is enabled in `/etc/inetd.conf` or `/etc/xinetd.d/finger`, the superserver watches for incoming `finger` queries on port 79 and sends them to the `in.fingerd` daemon.

You initiate a `finger` query from a command line using the username of the person you want to learn about and the host name, if that user account is not on the same host from which you are working. For example, if you want to learn about jthomas, who has an account on the same host where you are logged on, you can use this command:

```
finger jthomas
```

The resulting output from the `finger` program (via the `in.fingerd` daemon) looks like this:

```
Login: jthomas                    Name: Juan Thomas
Directory: /home/jthomas          Shell: /bin/bash
On since Wed Apr 3 19:41 (EST) on tty1  11 minutes 52
   seconds idle
On since Wed Apr 3 19:37 (EST) on pts/0 from :0
   56 minutes 44 seconds idle
On since Wed Apr 3 19:39 (EST) on pts/1 from :0
Mail last read Wed Apr 3 19:42 2006 (EST)
No Plan.
```

If jthomas is located on another host, include the host name in "e-mail" format, like one of the following examples, depending on whether you are fingering the account from within the same domain:

```
finger jthomas@sophia
finger jthomas@sophia.myplace.net
```

In any case, the finger protocol must be enabled with in.fingerd running, and traffic to port 79 must be allowed by any intervening firewalls. The finger protocol is less used nowadays, partly because there are other methods of learning about each other via the Internet, and partly because finger has presented several gaping security holes in past years.

On a system supporting finger, any user can create a hidden file called .plan in her home directory. When finger is used, it sends the contents of the .plan file in addition to the account information. The .plan file can be as long as you like. This lets a user provide information such as a mailing address using finger. The contents of two other files, .project and .pgp, are also sent in response to any finger request. The .pgp file is used to provide the user's public encryption key (as described in Chapter 8). The .project file is limited to one line and is intended to tell others on what project the user is currently working. Sample finger output that includes a .plan file might look like this:

```
Login: jthomas             Name: Juan Thomas
Directory: /home/jthomas    Shell: /bin/bash
On since Wed Apr 3 19:41 (EST) on tty2   13 minutes 35
  seconds idle
No mail.
Plan:
123 Elm Street
Washington, DC 20023
```

If your system administrator likes finger, but you prefer that no one use it to learn about your activities, create a **.nofinger** file in your home directory and make it visible to the finger daemon. The finger program should then report nothing about you, including your existence as a valid user on the system. The following commands can set up .nofinger, but test it before relying on it for privacy if finger is active on your host:

```
touch ~/.nofinger
chmod o+x ~
chmod 644 ~/.nofinger
```

The .nofinger file only works to block finger queries originating on systems other than your own.

TIP

As with talk, you can use a graphical client to execute a finger query. The **kfinger** program for KDE actually includes both finger and talk capabilities. The kfinger program is part of the kdenetwork package and, therefore, should be installed on any system with KDE. Figure 4-6 shows the main window of kfinger.

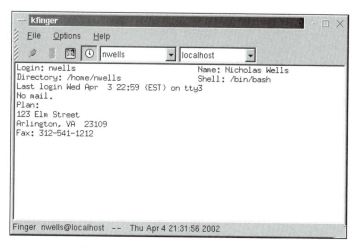

Figure 4-6   The main window of `kfinger`

Collecting Server Information with `whois`

Next, we return for a moment to the world of the DNS server. To maintain a semblance of order in the computer world, all domain names are registered, as noted in previous chapters. Previously, a single entity handled all registration, but now many companies register domain names. Information about each domain name is stored in a database maintained by the domain registrar. The **whois** utility queries that database to learn about a specific domain.

Learning about a domain is usually a two-step process. First, you use the `whois` command with the domain in which you are interested. This causes `whois` to query the main `whois` server, called *whois.internic.net*. The results of this query tell you which registrar will have more detailed information about the domain in which you're interested. For example, suppose you want to know about Brigham Young University's domain, *byu.edu*. You begin with a command to query the *whois.internic.net* server (shown in bold). The results are shown after the command.

```
$ whois byu.edu
Whois Server Version 1.3

Domain names in the .com, .net, and .org domains can now
be registered with many different competing registrars. Go to
http://www.internic.net for detailed information.

   Domain Name: BYU.EDU
   Registrar: EDUCAUSE
   Whois Server: whois.educause.net
   Referral URL: http://www.educause.edu/edudomain
   Name Server: NS1.WESTNET.NET
   Name Server: NS1.BYU.EDU
   Name Server: NS2.BYU.EDU
   Updated Date: 25-jan-2006
```

```
>>> Last update of whois database: Wed, 3 Apr 2006
   16:58:13 EST <<<
```

The Registry database contains ONLY .COM, .NET, .ORG, .EDU
domains and Registrars.

This is helpful, but not as detailed as you might like. Notice the lines in the output that refer you to the Registrar and another whois server. You can use that whois server in another whois command with the -h option to get further details about the domain. Here is the second step, with the output shown after the command. (You can see all the commentary as well as the details about the domain; notice what you *cannot* use whois information for.)

```
$ whois -h whois.educause.net byu.edu
This Registry database contains ONLY .EDU domains.
The data in the EDUCAUSE Whois database is provided
by EDUCAUSE for information purposes in order to
assist in the process of obtaining information about
or related to .edu domain registration records.

The EDUCAUSE Whois database is authoritative for the
.EDU domain.

A Web interface for the .EDU EDUCAUSE Whois Server is
available at: http://whois.educause.net

By submitting a Whois query, you agree that this
information will not be used to allow, enable, or
otherwise support the transmission of unsolicited
commercial advertising or solicitations via e-mail.

You may use "%" as a wildcard in your search. For
further information regarding the use of this WHOIS
server, please type: help


_____


Domain Name: BYU.EDU

Registrant:
  Brigham Young University
  290 FB
  Provo, UT 84602
  UNITED STATES

Contacts:

  Administrative Contact:
  Kelly C. McDonald
  Brigham Young University
  Information Systems Services
```

```
167 TMCB
Provo, UT 84602
UNITED STATES
(801) 378-5025
kcm@byu.edu


Technical Contact:
Brigham Young University
159 TMCB
Provo, UT 84602
UNITED STATES
(801) 378-7782
dnsmaster@byu.edu


Name Servers:
  NS1.BYU.EDU      128.187.22.200
  NS2.BYU.ED       128.187.22.202
  NS1.WESTNET.NET

Domain record activated:     19-Jan-1987
Domain record last updated:  14-Dec-2001
```

Now you have some truly useful information: the name, address, phone, and e-mail address of a real person. You also have the IP addresses of the name servers for this domain, which you can use after reading Chapter 6 to glean further information about how this domain is configured or why it is not operating as expected.

The whois utility is straightforward and doesn't have other options besides -h. You can, however, use the whois help command to learn about extended queries you can make based on available information in the network information database.

Linux Telephony

A special type of "information service" that Linux can manage is your telephone system. The term **telephony** typically refers to having a computer interact with a telephone in such a way that it can be an answering machine, route and track calls, act as a voice recorder, and so on. Millions of dollars are spent by companies each year to set up telephony systems to track incoming customer phone calls and manage employee use of extensive telephone switches. Linux has some support for special hardware cards that allow you to connect phone lines directly to your computer, then manage and track calls using Linux software.

Using Linux as a fax server is a simple but useful form of telephony, and Linux supports several free and commercial fax server packages. These include HylaFax, eFax, sendfax (with mgetty), and a number of graphical programs to configure and maintain these utilities.

The best way to begin exploring this still-emerging topic in the Linux world is to search the Internet for "linux telephony." Numerous sites for telephony hardware and open source telephony software are available. Table 4-2 lists a few telephony-related Linux software packages. Figure 4-7 shows a screen from gPhoneMan as an example of the information that telephony software can provide. You can perform an Internet search to learn more about this program and download a copy of it.

Table 4-2   Telephony-related software for Linux

Package Name	Description
KmsgModem	Retrieves messages and faxes from a U.S. Robotics (USR) Message Modem
KAlcatel	Manages Alcatel 50x and 70x mobile phones
Voxpak	Plays, edits, and otherwise manages voice and fax messages
KMLOVoice	Processes voice messages received using the ELSA™ MicroLink™ Office modem
KAM2	Serves as an answering machine for ISDN cards
gPhoneMan	Serves as a generic phone manager for tracking calls

Figure 4-7   gPhoneMan tracks incoming and outgoing calls

A related but distinct topic that sometimes is categorized as telephony is the use of IP as a protocol and the Internet as a transport medium for long-distance telephone calls. This process is more commonly called **Voice over IP**, or **VoIP**. The idea is this: An Internet connection lets you connect to servers all over the world without additional charges via the routers that make up the Internet backbone. By digitizing a voice collected via a microphone and sending it as a stream of IP packets to a destination host, you can talk to people around the world without using long-distance telephone services.

Of course, Internet packet routing was not designed for this type of real-time transfer, as the sound quality of many VoIP products demonstrate. However, many products are now available, including stand-alone Internet phones that plug into a standard phone jack but actually call a local ISP to complete long-distance calls. This technology continues to evolve and improve, especially with the increasing speed of the Internet backbone and better last mile connectivity to homes using DSL, cable modems, and other broadband technologies. Also, the need to retool much of the Internet infrastructure to use IPv6 provides an opportunity for other new protocols like VoIP to gain a foothold over older, more established systems.

Another telephony application is video and audio conferencing, which was made popular by Microsoft NetMeeting. The open source equivalent is GnomeMeeting (*www.gnomemeeting.org*). These applications are based on the ITU H.323 teleconferencing protocols, which are implemented on Linux by the OpenH323 Project (*www.openh323.org*).

NOTE   Linux software for VoIP includes the Kphone and linphone packages.

4

UNDERSTANDING MAILING LISTS AND NEWS SERVERS

In this section, you will learn more about sharing information with other users, either on your local network or around the world. Two popular methods of sharing information with a large group are mailing lists or newsgroups. Each is organized to fulfill different purposes, as you will see.

A **mailing list** enables a group of users to share information on an ongoing basis via e-mail. Mailing lists are topically oriented. Some are designed to send announcements to members of the list, such as for Linux security issues, for new museum exhibits, or for class schedule changes. Others are designed to allow all members of the mailing list to send messages to each other, such as a list that includes all developers of a new software project, or all members of an extended family. The concept behind a mailing list is that when you send an e-mail message (post it) to the e-mail list, the **mailing list manager (MLM)** software sends your message to all users on the list. A single MLM can manage thousands of users subscribed to hundreds of different lists on a single Linux server.

You become a member of a mailing list by subscribing. When you subscribe, the mailing-list software adds your e-mail address to the list. You can unsubscribe later if you decide you no longer want to receive such messages. The sections that follow on specific mailing list packages describe how to subscribe and unsubscribe.

The advantage of mailing-list software is that it automates subscribing, unsubscribing, and sending all the messages so an individual doesn't have to spend the time to manage a (sometimes) huge list of users. Conversely, some e-mail lists are moderated. A moderated e-mail list is one that you can join only if the person managing the list (the list administrator) approves your subscription, or one for which each message posted to the list must be approved by or originate from the administrator.

TIP   A note of caution: Don't accidentally send a message to all members of a mailing list when you intend to send a message only to the administrator of the mailing list or to a single member of the list. Check the To: and Cc: lines of your message before you send it!

Most MLM packages allow the owner of a list (a user designated as the manager of the list) to create digests—summaries of all messages posted to the list during a day or week. Users can elect to receive a digest instead of all the individual e-mail messages. Archiving options are also provided, as well as commands to help users control what e-mail they receive, such as suspending message delivery while on vacation.

Newsgroups differ from mailing lists in several ways. First, they are not e-mail messages, so they are not handled by an e-mail server using SMTP. Instead, newsgroup messages (postings) are transferred using the **Network News Transport Protocol (NNTP)**. Newsgroup postings are more like a giant bulletin board; instead of subscribing, you provide the name of a newsgroup server to a news client (as described in the sections that follow) and you may see hundreds of messages that you can read. Newsgroups are more free form than mailing lists—the term anarchy comes to mind. Although a few newsgroups dedicated to specific topics are moderated, most impose no control other than the flames (disparaging postings) between users.

Internet newsgroups are also referred to as **Usenet news** or just net-news.

The following sections describe several popular software packages for setting up mailing lists and setting up a server for newsgroups.

Using majordomo for Mailing Lists

One of the most widely used MLM packages is called **majordomo**. The majordomo package is a collection of Perl scripts that interact with the sendmail mail server to create automated mailing lists. The majordomo package might be installed on your system already, or you can install it quickly using a software package such as rpm or deb. In either case, you need to configure majordomo before use by creating a user and group ID for majordomo, then using a program called wrapper (part of the majordomo package) to create a new mailing list with an administrative password, owner e-mail address, and description.

Visit *www.greatcircle.com/majordomo* to learn more about this program and to download additional resources.

Instructions for configuring majordomo are provided in the documentation directory. Because majordomo configuration can be complex and may require that you alter the configuration of the sendmail e-mail server, you should consider using a graphical tool to help you set it up.

For example, Webmin includes modules to configure `majordomo`. After launching Webmin, choose the Servers tab, then Majordomo List Manager. The first time you use this page, you must designate which user manages `majordomo` by entering an e-mail address in the Owner e-mail address field. You can then begin creating mailing lists using the "Add a new mailing list" link. Figure 4-8 shows the page on which you add a new mailing list.

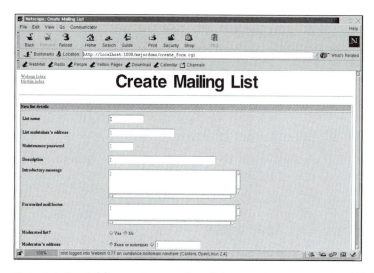

Figure 4-8 Adding a new mailing list to `majordomo` using Webmin

Each mailing list must have a person who acts as a managing user (also called the owner of the specific mailing list). When `majordomo` must report a problem, or when a user sends something to the "list owner" explicitly (using the e-mail address of *listname*-owner), the message goes to the username you specify in the Owner e-mail address field. You provide a password so that only the designated maintainer can alter the configuration of the list. You can also select to have the list moderated and name the list maintainer or another user as the moderator.

Part of `majordomo` configuration involves setting up aliases within `sendmail` for the mailing lists you create. This allows anyone on the Internet to send a message to the list name as a regular e-mail address and have `sendmail` correctly route the message to `majordomo`. For example, suppose you create a mailing list called linux-security on your host *rome.myplace.net*. Users all over the world can interact with that list by sending messages to linux-security@rome.myplace.net or linux-security-owner@rome.myplace.net.

If a user is unfamiliar with using an e-mail server, a message addressed to majordomo@rome.myplace.net with `help` as the body of the message shows the format and commands that the user can send to interact with `majordomo`. Similarly, sending the word `list` as the body of an e-mail message to majordomo@rome.myplace.net causes `majordomo` to send back a list of all the mailing lists being hosted on that server, so the user knows what addresses he can use to subscribe to a desired mailing list.

TIP

Some MLMs require that commands appear in the subject of an e-mail message; others (like majordomo) look in the body of an e-mail message for the command text.

After a mailing list is set up, the mailing list owner/maintainer can interact with majordomo using e-mail messages. For example, the maintainer could approve a new person being added to the list using a command like this:

```
approve maintainer-password subscribe linux-security
abutler@usnetworks.org
```

Some commands can be issued only by the list maintainer or moderator (and thus require that a password be included). Others are user commands, such as this one:

```
subscribe linux-security abutler@usnetworks.org
```

If no e-mail address is included in the command, majordomo assumes that the e-mail address of the sender (taken from the message headers) should be subscribed to the named mailing list.

Using Other Mailing List Managers

Although majordomo is widely used (and freely available), several other MLMs are also supported on Linux. These include the following:

- **LISTSERV** is the most widely used MLM in the world, with more than 100 million subscribers being served. LISTSERV is a commercial product available from L-Soft (*www.lsoft.com*). Although LISTSERV is expensive to purchase, a trial version with reduced functionality is available as well. The advantages of LIST-SERV include its scalability for huge mailing lists (numbering thousands of users or millions of e-mail messages), flexible security features, and a Web-based configuration and maintenance interface. For subscribers, using LISTSERV is similar to the majordomo functionality already described. For example, you send e-mail messages by including a command such as SUBSCRIBE linux-security.

- **ListProc** is another commercial MLM that features graphical configuration tools, security enhancements such as password-protected postings, digests and archives, and special features such as the ability to delete invalid e-mail addresses. You can learn more about ListProc by visiting the ListProc home page at *www.listproc.net*.

- **SmartList** is a free MLM that works in conjunction with procmail (described in Chapter 3) and sendmail (described in Chapter 6). SmartList includes features such as remote list maintenance, archiving, and message digests.

- **Mailman** is a free MLM with many standard list management features. It is managed via a Web browser interface.

TIP

Most MLMs include functionality designed to reduce the occurrence of **spam**—unwanted advertisements sent to a large number of recipients (that is, all the members of a mailing list). This is an important part of list management; mass e-mailers are always trying to find ways to reach more recipients, but an abundance of spam is the best way to offend list subscribers and make a mailing list worse than useless.

Understanding Linux News Servers

Newsgroup postings are passed around the Internet using NNTP. When you set up a news server, it receives news postings by getting a feed from another news server (generally a large ISP). Your news server downloads all the messages that the ISP news server has, and uploads messages generated by users at your site. As you probably know, there are thousands of newsgroups. Each can be included or excluded from your news server, either individually or by category. For example, many newsgroup postings include program files or pictures. You can exclude the newsgroups where these are posted to reduce the resources required by your news server.

The most widely used Linux news server software is Internet News server or **INN** (the news server daemon itself is innd). But for most networks, setting up a dedicated news server is not worth the effort. Unless many users (dozens or hundreds) need access to news postings, a better solution is to gain access to your ISP's news server. For reference, here are some potential problems associated with having your own news server the following:

- You need a lot of network bandwidth and storage space. A full news feed can consume 250 GB of storage *each day*. A news feed that excludes binaries and pictures would consume 2 to 3 GB each day. (Messages are typically stored for 10 days.)

- Configuration is difficult, including ongoing tuning requirements to keep the server functioning efficiently (and to avoid downtime from resource exhaustion).

- You may face policy questions regarding how newsgroups can be used within your organization, including issues such as which newsgroups can be accessed or the proper etiquette for postings to avoid complaints coming to you as the administrator of the news server.

If you still feel that your organization should have its own news server, the good news is that some Linux distributions (notably Fedora Core) include INN with most of the basic configuration already complete. This includes having a user account ("news") created for you; having the necessary configuration and spool directories set up (as described in the following list); and having cron scripts to manage some basic aspects of the news server automatically, such as hourly uploads of newly created postings. Starting from this foundation, your first steps in setting up a news server would be:

- Check that the two packages cleanfeed and inn are installed on your system. (Use the rpm -q command if you have Red Hat, Mandrake, or another rpm-based system.) Install them if they are not already installed.

- Contact your ISP to discuss using their news server as a news feed.

- Plan your news server, focusing on what newsgroups to include, what local newsgroups you might create (for use only within your organization), and how to store articles (how long and in what format, as described below).

- Consider the policies that you want users to follow and how to inform them of these policies (and monitor or punish prohibited activity if necessary).

The configuration files for INN are stored in /etc/news. You can review example configuration files in the documentation for INN (in Red Hat, for example, see /usr/share/doc/inn-2.3.2/). Newsgroup postings are stored in the spool directory, typically /var/spool/news.

Even with a system like Red Hat Linux, in which a lot of the work is done for you, you need to set up some information in the /etc/news/inn.conf file. For example, you must define parameters such as the address of the server that acts as your news feed, the address of your server, and your organization's name. A complete list of the many supported parameters is included in the man page for inn.conf.

To set up which newsgroups you want to include on your server, refer to the master list maintained by the Internet Software Consortium at *ftp://ftp.isc.org/pub/usenet/CONFIG/*. The newsgroups file contains a list of all standard newsgroups with a one-line description of each. The active file contains an abridged list of commonly included newsgroups. You should download both files and store them in /etc/news. (Download the compressed versions and then uncompress them.) Edit the active file to indicate which newsgroups you want to include on your news server.

Given the massive number of postings on a news server, the method you choose to store messages can greatly affect how you manage your system. By default, each message is stored in a separate file. A better solution is to configure the **compact news file system (CNFS)** method, which stores multiple messages in a single file. The file acts as a buffer; when the buffer becomes full, the oldest messages are deleted. This system lets you maintain messages for as long as possible without the risk of running out of disk storage and without administrator intervention to manage a large number of files.

As installed initially, INN allows all users with an account on the same host as the news server to access it. To allow other users on your network to access the news server, you need to configure the `/etc/news/readers.conf` file with details on who should be allowed to read the news. To enable this, be certain that no firewalls or similar obstacles block access to news (such as a proxy server that only allows HTTP to pass).

TIP
Two other news servers available for Linux are **C News** and **LeafNode** (see *www.leafnode.org*). Both programs are simpler to configure than INN, but are not intended for use on larger news sites.

Linux News Clients

Whether you set up your own news server or rely on your ISP's, Linux provides several good news clients that let you read newsgroup postings, either graphically or in text mode. Most full-featured Web browsers now include newsgroup browsing capabilities, but you can also choose from several stand-alone newsreaders.

To set up newsgroup access in the Netscape browser, consult the online help in your version of Netscape. Enter at least your name and organization, because without these, news servers won't accept message postings from you. Also, you must have at least one news server listed. Ask your ISP for the correct server name of a news server you can access. After you have configured Netscape, you can select the newsgroups that you want to subscribe to and review. Only messages for the newsgroups you select are downloaded to your system.

Both GNOME and KDE support multiple graphical newsreaders. Some are focused on posting binary (program) files, such as Gnewspost and Knewspost. Others are more generic, for reading and posting standard text messages. Either the **Knode** newsreader or krn, or both, come with most Linux distributions that include KDE. The initial configuration window that appears when you start using Knode is shown in Figure 4-9. For GNOME, the **Pan** newsreader is installed by default. The first time you use it, a set of configuration screens appears. Both Knode and Pan help you set up the same types of information that Netscape also requires before using newsgroups.

The most widely used text-mode newsreader is probably **trn**, the threaded newsreader. Because so many good graphical newsreaders are available, and perhaps because `trn` is so hard to learn, it is not installed by default on many systems.

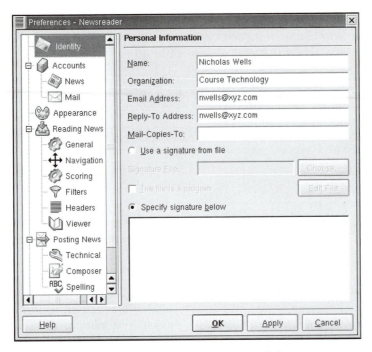

Figure 4-9   The initial configuration screen of the Knode newsreader

CHAPTER SUMMARY

❑ The superservers `inetd` and `xinetd` listen to numerous network ports and start network services when needed to respond to an incoming client request.

❑ Some network services, such as the Apache Web server and the `innd` news server, are not designed to be run by a superserver and should always be run stand-alone.

❑ Application-level security is provided for `inetd` via TCP Wrappers—the `tcpd` program. The `tcpd` program uses `hosts.allow` and `hosts.deny` as configuration files to control access to services. The `xinetd` configuration files include security functionality similar to `tcpd`.

❑ Ports are mapped to service names by the `/etc/services` file.

❑ Network testing services such as `chargen` and `echo` are provided by `inetd`.

❑ System logging can be done remotely using `syslogd` by enabling another host to receive `syslog` messages across the network and specifying a host in `/etc/syslog.conf`.

❑ Linux can print across the network using `lpd`. Printer definitions that specify remote hosts cause a local copy of `lpd` to contact `lpd` running on a remote host and forward the print job to that host.

❑ Time management in Linux is provided via NTP and the `ntpd` daemon. Although complex setups are possible, a simple two-line configuration file permits a host to retrieve time synchronization data from a time server.

- SNMP provides detailed information about what is happening on hosts on a network. An administrator configures SNMP agents to gather information, which is then requested by an SNMP console that processes and displays the data for the administrator.

- To configure Linux as a PPP server, use `mgetty` or a similar program to watch for incoming modem calls. The `mgetty` program launches `pppd`, which uses its option files to determine how to communicate with a dial-in client.

- The `talk` system lets users communicate in real time between two hosts. The `talk` system is generally used in text mode, but graphical clients are also available.

- Linux supports a number of chat-style messaging services such as Yahoo! Chat, America Online Instant Messenger (AIM), and Microsoft Network messaging.

- The `finger` program provides a small user account summary. If a user has created a `.plan` file, the contents of that file are also returned by the `finger` command.

- The `whois` command lets you query information about a domain name through the network information databases maintained by name registrars around the world.

- Linux telephony is a growing field that allows your computer to interact with voice telephone systems, acting as an answering machine and tracking or initiating calls.

- Voice over IP (VoIP) is a technology that allows you to make long-distance telephone calls by converting your voice to digitized packets transmitted via the Internet using IP.

- Mailing list management (MLM) software provides automated management of message delivery between a potentially large number of users. Popular MLM packages include `majordomo`, LISTSERV, and ListProc.

- Setting up a news server on Linux is possible, but maintaining such a server can entail a lot of work and system resources. A popular alternative is to use an ISP as a news server. Some versions of Linux include the INN news server with most configuration options preset.

- Many Web browsers include news-reading capability. Linux also supports a number of graphical and text-based news clients such as `krn` for KDE and `trn`, a text-based newsreader.

Key Terms

.nofinger — A file that, when created in a user's home directory, causes the `finger` program to display no information about that user.

.plan — A hidden file within a user's home directory, the contents of which the `finger` program displays when queried.

/etc/hosts.allow — The configuration file that defines services and hosts that should be permitted service by TCP Wrappers.

/etc/hosts.deny — The configuration file that defines services and hosts that should be denied service by TCP Wrappers.

agent — An SNMP-aware program running on a host. The client that collects data for analysis and transmission using other SNMP software.

C News — A Linux news server program designed for small networks with low newsgroup volume.

chargen — A network testing service provided by `inetd` on port 19. Whenever queried, `chargen` responds with a stream of characters (the standard character set, in numeric order).

Common UNIX Printing System (CUPS) — A replacement for older printing systems used by Linux. CUPS is based on the Internet Printing Protocol or IPP.

compact news file system (CNFS) — A method of storing newsgroup postings within INN using a single file as a buffer for holding multiple individual postings.

console — The SNMP program that collects and analyzes data from SNMP agents on a network.

daytime — A network testing service provided by `inetd` on port 13. Returns the current date and time in human-readable form.

discard — A network testing service provided by `inetd` on port 9. The `discard` service acts like `/dev/null`. Anything sent to the service is discarded without any processing.

echo — A network testing service provided by `inetd` on port 7. The `echo` service parrots back whatever it receives.

finger — A program that provides brief information about a user.

getty — A program (and a type of program) that monitors terminals for activity and processes it, generally to allow a user to log on.

inetd — The most widely used superserver program. *See also* `xinetd`.

init — The master control program that the Linux kernel starts right after the system is started.

INN — The most widely used news server software for Linux. Implemented by the `innd` daemon.

kfinger — A graphical version of `finger` (including `talk` protocol capability) for KDE.

Knode — A newsreader for KDE.

LeafNode — A Linux news server program designed for small networks with low newsgroup volume.

ListProc — A commercial mailing list manager (MLM). See *www.listproc.net*.

LISTSERV — The most widely used MLM in the world. A commercial product available from L-Soft (*www.lsoft.com*).

mailing list — A group of users who share information on an ongoing basis via e-mail using special management software.

mailing list manager (MLM) — A software package used to create and manage mailing lists, including collections of user information and the messages those users send.

Mailman — A free MLM with many standard list management features.

majordomo — One of the most widely used MLM packages. A free software package consisting of Perl scripts that interact with the `sendmail` e-mail server.

mesg — A command that disables access to the command-line window so that `talk` or other programs cannot interrupt a work session.

mgetty — A version of `getty` adapted to use with modems.

mingetty — A minimalist version of `getty`.

Network News Transport Protocol (NNTP) — The protocol used to transport newsgroup messages (postings).

Network Time Protocol (NTP) — A time management and synchronization protocol used by Linux. Implemented by the `ntpd` daemon.

ntpd — The Linux daemon that implements NTP. *See also* `xntpd`.

Pan — A newsreader for GNOME.

Simple Network Management Protocol (SNMP) — A protocol designed to provide feedback about how the components of a network are functioning.

Simple Network Time Protocol (SNTP) — A subset of NTP; it does not use the 32-bit value that provides for subsecond precision.

SmartList — A free mailing list manager that works in conjunction with `procmail` and `sendmail`.

spam — The unwanted advertisements sent to a large number of e-mail or newsgroup recipients.

stratum — A layer within the time server structure of NTP.

superserver — A program that listens on multiple network ports and starts appropriate network service daemons when a client connection arrives for that port. Also called a metaserver. The most widely used superserver program is `inetd`.

syslogd — The system logging daemon, which can use port 514 to communicate with `syslogd` on another system to provide remote logging capability.

talk — A program used with the `talkd` daemon to initiate and manage a real-time typed conversation with another user.

talkd — The daemon that implements the `talk` communication system.

tcpd (TCP Wrappers) — An application-level access control (security) program that examines incoming network connections when requested by a superserver, then compares the connection details to a configuration file to determine whether the connection is allowed.

telephony — The technology that lets a computer interact with a telephone in such a way that it can serve as an answering machine, call router, voice recorder, and so forth.

time — A network testing service provided by `inetd` on port 37. Returns a number corresponding to the current time in a program-readable format, which appears as unreadable characters on screen.

trn — The threaded newsreader, probably the most widely used text-mode newsreader for Linux.

Usenet news — Another name for Internet newsgroups.

Voice over IP (VoIP) — The use of IP as a protocol for transport of digitized voice packets, often as a medium for long-distance telephone calls over the Internet.

whois — A utility that queries an Internet database to learn about the person who manages a specific domain.

xinetd — A superserver with extended configuration options. Standard on Red Hat Linux instead of the more usual `inetd` program.

xntpd — A daemon used on some Linux systems to implement NTP. *See also* ntpd.

REVIEW QUESTIONS

1. Which of the following is a Linux daemon?
   a. telnet
   b. ftp
   c. cupsd
   d. grep

2. Daemons that may be run by ordinary users must use:
   a. any ports up to 65,535
   b. only those ports specified in /etc/services
   c. ports below 1024
   d. ports above 1023

3. The inetd superserver typically starts:
   a. TCP Wrappers
   b. an Internet service daemon such as in.ftpd
   c. pppd
   d. stand-alone services like a Web server

4. The nowait option within the inetd or xinetd configuration indicates:
   a. that ICMP packets should not respond to ping packets
   b. that additional copies of a service daemon can be started without waiting for the current copy to finish processing
   c. that TCP Wrappers should be used to process the client request
   d. that the UDP transport protocol should be used for the client request

5. TCP Wrappers is configured using:
   a. /etc/hosts
   b. /etc/inetd.conf
   c. /etc/hosts.allow and /etc/hosts.deny
   d. /etc/services

6. Select the meaning of the `in.telnetd 192.168.0` line within `/etc/hosts.allow`:

   a. Deny access to the Telnet service for all hosts on any network ID starting with 192.168.0.

   b. Permit access to the Telnet service for all hosts on any network ID starting with 192.168.0.

   c. Deny access to the Telnet service for any host except those on any network ID starting with 192.168.0.

   d. Permit access to the Telnet service for all hosts except those on any network ID starting with 192.168.0.

7. To enable remote logging using `syslogd`, you must:

   a. Use the `-r` option when starting `syslogd`.

   b. Include port 514 in `/etc/services` and allow traffic for that port through firewalls.

   c. Use an `@hostname` designation within `/etc/syslog.conf`.

   d. a and b

   e. a, b, and c

8. The `lpd` program allows Linux to:

   a. Manage print queues on remote print servers.

   b. Print to remote printers when properly defined in `/etc/printcap`.

   c. Connect to remote hosts using a modem.

   d. Access control agents used by management protocols.

9. Describe the arrangement of time servers in multiple strata as used for NTP.

10. An SNMP agent provides:

    a. detailed event information to an SNMP console

    b. analysis of multiple events from a range of hosts

    c. access to an SNMP console via a graphical interface

    d. configuration capability through either GNOME or KDE

11. The CUPS protocol uses:

    a. UDP port 80

    b. TCP port 80

    c. UDP port 631

    d. TCP port 631

12. Which program is used to listen for modem connections and start `pppd` when needed?

    a. `init`

    b. SNMP

    c. `mgetty`

    d. `majordomo`

13. IP addresses are usually assigned to multiple modems connected to a dial-in PPP server using:

    a. the `/etc/ppp/options` file

    b. information in the `/etc/mgetty+sendfax` configuration files

    c. parameters included in `/etc/inittab`

    d. individual `/etc/ppp/options` files named for each device (such as `ttyS0`)

14. To prevent `talkd` from interrupting a work session, you:

    a. Create a `.nofinger` file in your home directory.

    b. Issue the command `mesg n`.

    c. Delete any `.plan` file in your home directory.

    d. Use a graphical program such as Ktalk to initiate the session.

15. Name three Linux clients used for messaging or chatting.

16. Which piece of information about the queried user is not included in a standard reply to `finger`?

    a. the contents of the `.pgp` file in the user's home directory

    b. the full name of the user whose account is queried

    c. the user's home directory

    d. the contents of the `.nofinger` file

17. The main `whois` server, *whois.internic.net*:

    a. is the only place on the Internet where information about domain maintainers is stored

    b. is replicated at various sites around the world

    c. can refer you to other `whois` servers that can provide specific information on domains not provided by *whois.internic.net*

    d. must be specified with the `-h` parameter of the `whois` command

18. Briefly explain the difference between Linux telephony and Voice over IP technology.

19. Which of the following is the open source equivalent of Microsoft NetMeeting?

    a. GnomeMeeting

    b. LinMeeting

    c. X–Meeting

    d. H322–Meeting

20. A moderated mailing list refers to one that:

    a. only accepts postings via newsgroups

    b. requires that a list moderator approve subscriptions and/or message postings

    c. has been configured using LISTSERV

    d. uses a filter to prevent spam

21. Linux news servers include:

    a. Knode, `trn`, and `pan`

    b. INN, NTP, and SNMP

    c. `trn`, `elm`, and `majordomo`

    d. INN, C News, and LeafNode

22. Network testing services provided by `inetd` include:

    a. `chargen`, `daytime`, `echo`, and `discard`

    b. `mesg`, `chargen`, and SNMP

    c. `daytime`, `time`, `date`, and `echo`

    d. `getty`, `mgetty`, and `mingetty`

23. Using a server in stand-alone mode refers to:

    a. relying on information in `/etc/services` so that `inetd` can initiate it correctly

    b. not using a superserver to control the server

    c. testing the server by connecting only to `localhost`

    d. relying on TCP Wrappers for security rather than built-in security functions

24. Which of the following must be done as part of establishing a dial-in PPP server?

    a. Create an options file for `pppd`.

    b. Configure a `getty`-like program to monitor incoming modem calls.

    c. Establish AutoPPP to make `getty` launch `pppd`.

    d. Create a CHAP authentication file.

25. `Xinetd` must use TCP Wrappers if you want access control. True or False?

Hands-On Projects

HANDS-ON PROJECTS

Project 4-1

In this project, you establish a time server using NTP. To complete this project, you need root access to your Linux system and an Internet connection.

1. Log on as root and open a command-line window.

2. Be certain that the NTP server software is installed on your system. You can do this by looking for either `ntp` or `xntpd` in the directory `/etc/rc.d/init.d` or the corresponding system start-up script directory on your version of Linux. Or, you can search for the NTP package. This command will find an `rpm` package on most `rpm`-based versions of Linux:

   ```
   rpm -qa | grep ntp
   ```

3. Open a Web browser and go to *www.ntp.org*.

4. Select the **Public Time Server Lists** link.

5. Open the list of secondary time servers by clicking **Public NTP Secondary (stratum 2) Time Servers**. The list of servers is organized alphabetically, first by two-letter country code, then by state or province code. Locate the time servers in your state or province, or as close to you as possible. Carefully review the Access Policy field of each listing in your area to choose one that you can use.

6. Copy the information from the server you have selected. (Write it down or copy and paste it into a document that you can save.) The critical information is the IP address of the server and the e-mail address of the administrator, because in most cases you want to send an e-mail explaining your intention to use their time server.

7. Now configure your NTP daemon. See if you have an `/etc/ntp.conf` file already installed. If you do, open it and find the `server` line. Place the host name of the time server after the keyword `server`.

8. If you don't have an `ntp.conf` file, open a text editor and create one with the following two lines, substituting the host name of the server that you located previously.

   ```
   server [host name]
   driftfile /etc/ntp.drift
   ```

   Then create the `drift` file with this command:

   ```
   touch /etc/ntp.drift
   ```

9. With NTP configured, you are ready to restart the `ntpd` or `xntpd` daemon. Use a set of commands like this to do so:

   ```
   /etc/rc.d/init.d/ntpd stop
   /etc/rc.d/init.d/ntpd start
   ```

10. It will take several minutes to synchronize with the time server. Run the `ntptrace` program every few minutes. When your computer has synchronized to the time server, the `ntptrace` program will display the chain of time servers to the primary source.

Project 4-2

4

In this project, you use `whois` to look for information about a domain name. To complete this project, you need a working Linux system and an Internet connection.

For this project, you are helping a friend set up the new computer lab at Alexandria High School in northern Virginia. Because this will be a small lab, you want to have a couple of backup DNS servers that you can include in your configurations in case you need to stop your local DNS server for maintenance. You decide that Northern Virginia Community College (NVCC) probably wouldn't mind if you pointed to their site for your secondary and tertiary DNS servers.

1. You've seen two different URLs for the NVCC site. Try the first one, *nvcc.vccs.edu*, in a `whois` query. What result do you see?

2. If this didn't work, maybe you need to reference the `whois` server that is specific to the .edu domain. If you didn't do this in Step 1, use *whois.educause.net* and query again for *nvcc.vccs.edu*.

3. If this still didn't work, consider the address itself. It apparently refers to NVCC within some larger unit, VCCS—probably the Virginia Community College System, or something similar. With this theory in mind, try a query to the Educause `whois` server using just *vccs.edu*. What results do you see?

4. You are concerned that VCCS may not have direct authority over the NVCC servers, so you decide to try the other NVCC address to see if you can locate someone at that school. Run a `whois` query for *nv.cc.va.us*. (You might want to view both *www.nv.cc.va.us* and *www.nvcc.vccs.edu* in your Web browser first to check that they are valid domains.) Where did you query for *nv.cc.va.us*? What result did you see, and why did you get that result?

5. Concerned that you haven't been able to find the contact person yet at NVCC, you decide to try the University of Virginia site, *uva.edu*. Make this `whois` query. Sometimes a query directly to *whois.internic.net* connects directly to another `whois` server such as *educause.net*. At other times, you may need to specify *educause.net* as your `whois` server.

6. From the information listed, obtain the IP addresses of the DNS servers and the name, phone, and e-mail address of the contact person. You should check with the contact person as a courtesy before referencing their DNS servers.

Project 4-3

In this project, you experiment with the `finger` protocol. To complete this project, you need Fedora Core installed and root access to the system.

1. Log on as root and open a command-line window.

2. Verify that the finger-server package is installed using this command:

   `rpm -q finger-server`

3. Enable the finger-server configuration in `xinetd` by modifying the `disable` line in `/etc/xinetd.d/finger`.

4. Also enable the `daytime` and `chargen` services by modifying the `disable` line in `/etc/xinet.d/daytime` and within `/etc/xinetd.d/chargen`.

5. Restart `xinetd` to make your changes active.

6. Experiment with the `daytime` service by issuing a `telnet` command to the `daytime` port. Why might you want to use this network service?

   `telnet 127.0.0.1 13`

7. Experiment with the `chargen` service by issuing a `telnet` command to the `chargen` port. Why might this service be useful in testing your network?

   `telnet 127.0.0.1 19`

8. Use a text editor to create a `.plan` file within the home directory of your regular user account. Include information in the file such as a favorite saying or a list of your classes.

9. Set the permission of the `.plan` text file to `644` using `chmod`.

10. While still logged on as root, finger your regular user account. What information is returned by `finger`?

11. Find a friend in your classroom or computer lab who has participated in this project. Ask for their username and host name, then finger that username and host name. What result do you see?

Project 4-4

In this project, you explore the `xinetd` superserver configuration. Because `finger` is a convenient method of doing this, you may find Project 4-3 useful as background before doing this project; however, note that the options used here are part of the `xinetd` configuration and are not specific to `finger`. To complete this project, you need Fedora Core installed and root access to the system. You should work as a team with another student to complete this project; designate one of your systems as client and one as root, then work together as directed.

1. Determine the IP address (or host name if you have access to a DNS server) of the client system.

2. Log on as root on the server and open a command-line window.

3. If you have not already done so in Project 4-3, enable `finger` within the `/etc/xinetd.d` directory and restart `xinetd` to make the change take effect.

4. From the client, finger your regular user account on the server. You should see a basic `finger` reply.

5. On the server, edit the `finger` configuration file to add a `no_access` line that refers to the IP address of the client as in this example, but use the IP address for your client system:

   ```
   no_access = 192.168.100.10
   ```

6. Restart `xinetd` on the server, then finger your user account from the client. What is the result?

7. Add the following two lines to the `finger` configuration file on the server:

   ```
   log_type = FILE /tmp/fingerlog
   log_on_failure  += HOST
   ```

8. Restart `xinetd` on the server.

9. Create the log file using `touch`. How could you alter the `log_type` attribute to take advantage of the default system logging facilities? (See the `xinetd.conf` man page.)

10. Open a second command-line window and use the following command to watch the log during the next few steps:

    ```
    tail -f /tmp/fingerlog
    ```

11. From the client, finger your user account on the server again. What result do you see on the client? On the server?

12. Add the following line to the `finger` configuration file, but use the client's IP address:

    ```
    only_from = 192.168.100.10
    ```

13. Restart `xinetd`, then go to the client and finger your user account on the server again. What result do you see on the client? On the server? Which takes precedence, the `only_from` attribute or the `no_access` attribute?

14. Delete the `no_access` line from the `finger` configuration file, save the file, and restart `xinetd`.

15. From the client, finger your user account a final time. What result do you see? How could you alter the logging done in this case?

16. Remove all of the extra lines from the `finger` configuration file and restart `xinetd`.

Project 4-5

In this project, you learn more about some of the hardware options available to Linux as a dial-in PPP server. To complete this project, you need a Web browser with Internet access.

1. Stallion Technologies and Sangoma Technologies have supported Linux users of their hardware for many years. Go to the Stallion Technologies Web site at *www.stallion.com* and look for the EasyIO multiport serial adapter on the Products page. This is a basic card that lets you attach either four or eight modems through a single expansion slot. Stallion and others sell cards that support 256 or more modems.

2. Review the information on EasyIO. What is the stated maximum data rate per port?

3. Assume that the EasyIO product sounds appropriate for your needs, but you don't know if it has Linux support. Return to the home page of Stallion Technologies and search for a Linux driver for EasyIO by using the **download** link.

4. Within the listed drivers for the EasyIO product, is the Linux operating system shown? If so, what is the filename of the driver software provided?

5. With EasyIO selected as the modem port card, you also want a high-speed card to connect your PPP server to the Internet via a T-1 line. Visit the Sangoma Web site at *www.sangoma.com* to explore their networking products.

6. Look for WAN Cards under the **PRODUCTS** link. Can you see any cards that support T-1 connections?

7. Under SUPPORT you see a link for WanPipe for Linux. What does this refer to? Are the T-1 cards supported in Linux or not?

8. If it appears they are, what is the filename for the latest WanPipe software for Red Hat Linux 7.3 running on an SMP server?

CASE PROJECTS

Case Project 4-1

Returning once again to the law offices of Snow, Sleet, and Hale, you are thinking today about the services that the offices may need.

1. Of the basic network services you learned about in this chapter—finger, talk, chargen, echo, daytime, discard—which, if any, might be useful to the users on the law office network? Why did you select any that you did?

2. Lawyers use a lot of paper—even lawyers who specialize in environmental work. Nevertheless, why might you choose *not* to use lpd as your main remote printing mechanism for these offices? (*Hint:* Think about the clients that are printing.)

3. Would a PPP dial-in server be of use to these offices, either to employees working from home or as a connection between the different offices? What concerns would you have about using a PPP dial-in server for either use? If you feel that a PPP server is useful, what concerns would you have if the size of the firm doubled after you had set up the PPP server and dial-in clients?

4. A few attorneys have asked about using a mailing list to share information about legal topics and current clients of the firm. It sounds useful to you. Consider the following questions, including your reasons for each response: Which MLM would you likely use? Where would you host the mailing lists? Who would you make the maintainer of various lists? What security concerns would these lists raise? Given what you know about the size of the law firm and the volume of messages that you think it would generate, would newsgroups be a better option than a mailing list?

4

CONFIGURING FILE-SHARING SERVICES

After reading this chapter and completing the exercises, you will be able to:

♦ Configure an FTP server for anonymous or regular users

♦ Set up NFS file sharing between Linux and UNIX systems

♦ Use SMB to share files and printers with Windows-based PCs

In this chapter, you will explore different file-sharing technologies that let you exchange information with computers running Linux and a number of other operating systems.

Each of the file-sharing methods described in this chapter has strengths and weaknesses; you will learn to decide which technology to use based on the operating systems you are working with and the differing needs of your network.

RUNNING AN FTP SERVER

The **File Transfer Protocol (FTP)** has been used for decades to share files between networked computer systems. It was part of UNIX in the 1970s. Since then, FTP client and server programs have been developed for almost all available platforms. The need for separate FTP client programs has diminished because FTP has been integrated into modern Web browsers.

The primary use for FTP today is **anonymous FTP**. This allows any user to log on to an FTP server anonymously (without having a user account on the FTP server) and download files. Many servers on the Internet are dedicated solely to FTP, providing a repository of downloadable programs, images, documents, and so on.

When you have files that should only be accessible by certain users, you can also set up an FTP server that only allows access to "known" users.

Using an FTP Client

Accessing an FTP server requires an FTP client. There are character-based and graphical clients. Linux includes a text-mode FTP client called **ftp** that is covered here, but there are many text-mode clients that you'll probably like better. The **ncftp** program is one such client, which may already be installed on your Linux system.

Using the FTP client with an anonymous FTP server is simple. Just specify the server name, as in this example:

```
ftp ftp.ibiblio.org
```

If your system can connect to the FTP server (resolve the host name, and so on), you are prompted for a username and password. For a public FTP site, you should enter *anonymous* as your username. Then use your e-mail address as your password. Some systems won't let you log on without entering an e-mail address in a valid format, but most do not care what you enter. The information is logged, creating a record for the system administrator.

After you have logged on, you typically see a welcome message followed by the ftp> prompt. From this prompt, you can enter commands to interact with the FTP server. Table 5-1 shows a list of often-used FTP commands. When you are finished with the FTP client, enter bye to exit.

Table 5-1 Often-used commands in the text-mode FTP client

Command Name	Description
open	Initiates a connection to an FTP server.
close	Ends an FTP connection.
ls	Lists the contents of the current directory on the FTP server.
pwd	Displays the current directory you are working in on the FTP server.
cd	Changes to a new directory; follow the command with the directory name to which you want to switch.

Table 5-1 Often-used commands in the text-mode FTP client (continued)

Command Name	Description
get	Downloads a file; include a filename after the command; regular expressions (such as ? and *) are not allowed (use mget).
mget	Downloads a set of files. Include a filename that may include regular expression characters (such as ? or *) after the command name. You are prompted to answer Y or N to each matching filename to confirm whether you want to download it. To avoid this prompting, execute the prompt command.
put	Uploads files to the FTP server. On most FTP servers, this is only allowed for those with regular user accounts, not anonymous users. Include the name of the file you want to upload.
mput	Uploads multiple files from your system to the FTP server. Include a regular expression pattern to define the files you want to upload. You are prompted to answer Y or N for each matching file (unless you have issued the prompt command).
lcd	Changes the directory that you are working in on your local system (not on the FTP server); this is useful when you want to download files to a different directory from the one you were in when you started the FTP client.
prompt	Turns prompting off or on for downloading or uploading multiple files; enter the command alone to toggle between off and on, or include either on or off after the command.
binary	Sets the transfer mode to 8-bit. Everything but plaintext files should be transferred in binary mode; otherwise, you lose part of every byte in the file. If you download a program and it won't even run, this is often the cause. The ascii command changes to 7-bit mode for text files, though you can use binary mode to download them as well.
bye	Exits the FTP client.

5

If you prefer working in a graphical environment, you can use a Web browser to access FTP sites. For example, point your browser to *ftp://ftp.hq.nasa.gov*. The Web browser uses the name *anonymous* and your e-mail address to log on to the server and displays the main directory. The browser also creates HTML pages from the FTP server file listings on the fly as you change directories.

When you click a file, your browser will either try to display it or ask you where to save it. If you want to save the file but your browser displays it instead, this is easily solved. Instead of using the left mouse button when clicking the file link, right-click it. Then select Save Link As if you're using the Firefox browser. This option may have another name with another browser. You'll be prompted for a location to save the file, unless you configured your browser to always place file downloads in a certain place. Figure 5-1 shows a Netscape browser being used to access the NASA FTP site.

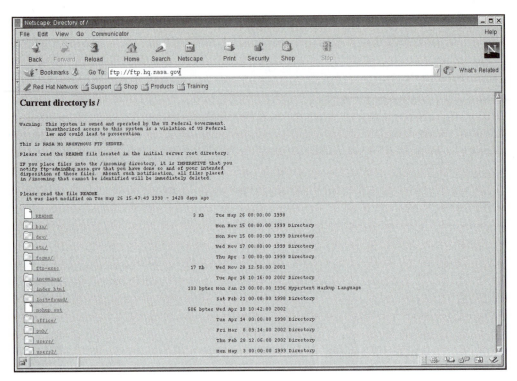

Figure 5-1 Using a browser to access a public FTP site

TIP

You can access FTP sites with real user accounts. Use the format *ftp:// username@ftp.servername.com/*. The browser prompts you for a password after making a connection. But beware: Your username and password are transferred in the clear (without encryption) across the network.

So far, you've used only the *anonymous* user account to access public FTP sites. If you have a user account on a remote server, and that server is running FTP server software, you can also log on with your user account and transfer files between your host and the remote host on which you have an account. Anonymous FTP servers restrict your access for security reasons, but when you log on using an FTP client to a server on which you have a regular user account, you can access all parts of the system, change filenames, and upload, download, and delete files—anything that you could do if you were logged on at the remote host using the same username. Of course, the FTP administrator may restrict which activities you can perform remotely, again for security reasons. You'll learn how to set these restrictions shortly.

Using a browser as your FTP client limits you to basic directory listings and file downloads, but several graphical FTP clients provide much more complete FTP functionality. One good example is the **gFTP** program, shown in Figure 5-2. You enter the host that you want to connect to, plus your username and password, in the fields at the top of the window. You can select to transfer files with either FTP, HTTP, or SSH (described in Chapter 8). The gFTP program is not specifically oriented toward anonymous FTP users—it has a number of options that are useful for regular users who access their accounts on multiple Linux systems. The Bookmarks menu even has a list of numerous Linux-related FTP sites for immediate access. The gFTP program is installed by default on Fedora Core and is widely available for other platforms.

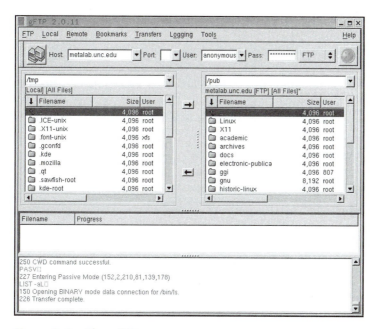

Figure 5-2   The gFTP program

  The fireFTP extension to the Firefox Web browser has a similar look and feel as gFTP. Another popular graphical FTP client is **IglooFTP**, which you can download free from *www.iglooftp.com*.

TIP

Introducing FTP Servers

One of the most widely used and most functional FTP servers is the Washington University FTP server, **wu-ftp**. There are other FTP servers that you'll probably like better, such as ncftpd and proftp. You will learn about wu-ftp here because you'll probably be asked questions about it on a Linux certification test.

The name of the wu-ftp server daemon is in.ftpd. On many Linux systems, the FTP server is installed and minimally configured by default.

TIP

A protocol similar to FTP is **Trivial FTP (TFTP)**. This protocol is supported by the server in.tftpd and various TFTP clients. It provides basic FTP-like services for special-purpose computing situations in which a full FTP configuration would take too much memory or disk space. One example is when a diskless workstation needs to download its operating system from a server during the boot process. TFTP provides the workstation with the functionality to download the needed files.

Setting up the FTP server is done via a number of configuration files. Table 5-2 lists the FTP server configuration files. By default, not all of these files are installed. The following sections walk you through the different files and how you might choose to set up your FTP server.

In addition to these configuration files, you need to be aware of the **anonymous user home directory**. Whenever you log on to an FTP server anonymously, you are not permitted to see the entire filesystem of the remote computer. Instead, you are limited to a working area—a subdirectory—in which all the downloadable files are stored. In most modern versions of Linux, this directory is either /home/ftp or /var/ftp.

Table 5-2 FTP server configuration files

FTP Configuration File	Description
/etc/ftpaccess	The main FTP configuration file; to use this file, the FTP server must be launched with the -a option (as it is by default in most Linux distributions).
/etc/**ftpusers**	A list of user accounts that are not allowed to log on via FTP. This file includes administrative accounts by default (such as bin, daemon, news, and mail). You can add any regular user accounts for which you want to block FTP access.
/etc/hosts.allow and /etc/hosts.deny	Because the FTP server is typically started via the inetd super-server, you should set up host- or domain-specific access controls for FTP in these files if you are using inetd (recall TCP Wrappers from Chapter 4).
/etc/inetd.conf	If you are using the inetd superserver, enable FTP in this file by removing the # sign in front of the line for the FTP service.
/etc/xinetd.d/wu-ftpd	For the xinetd superserver, set up host- and domain-specific access controls in this file. Also enable the service by changing disable=yes to disable=no and adding any logging attributes that you want to use.

As you explore /var/ftp, you will see a number of directories, such as /bin, /etc, and /lib. These resemble the root of your filesystem, though these subdirectories don't contain many files. They contain only the files required by the FTP server to continue operating without looking outside the /var/ftp directory structure. In technical terms, the FTP server does a "change-root" operation, using the chroot program, when you log on as anonymous. This means that the server "thinks" that /var/ftp is the root of the filesystem—it can't access any other parts of the hard disk. So, all of the libraries and other files that the server needs must be stored in the subdirectories of /var/ftp.

The key location for anonymous users is /var/ftp/pub (pub stands for "public"). This is the directory in which files for public download are stored. When you log on to a public FTP server such as *ftp.ibiblio.org*, you can immediately click the /pub directory to begin exploring what is available for download.

FTP is normally started via a superserver—either inetd or xinetd. You must enable the FTP service in either /etc/inetd.conf or /etc/xinetd.d/wu-ftp. Then restart the superserver to reread the configuration file. As soon as the superserver is watching for FTP connections, you can stop allowing connections using the command **ftpshut**. This command accepts parameters to define how long the server should continue accepting connections and to send a message to each connected user's screen. For example, to stop accepting FTP connections immediately and disconnect all FTP connections, use this command:

```
ftpshut now
```

The following command is a kinder method, which causes the FTP server to shut down at 9:00 p.m. and sends a warning message to all connected users:

```
ftpshut 21:00 "The FTP server will shut down at 9:00 p.m.
Please complete your work and disconnect."
```

The ftpshut command creates a file called shutmsg in /etc or in /var/ftp. (The filename is defined by the shutdown directive in /etc/ftpaccess.) When the superserver starts the FTP daemon for an incoming connection, the daemon checks for the presence of the shutmsg file. If it exists, the daemon prints the contents of shutmsg and closes the connection immediately.

Incredibly, there is no elegant way to allow the FTP daemon to run again. There's no counterpart to the ftpshut option to allow the server to start again. Many system administrators have had their FTP service down for hours or days trying to figure out how to get it running again. The answer? You must delete the shutmsg file:

```
rm /etc/shutmsg  /var/ftp/shutmsg
```

Setting Up FTP Configuration Files

Wu-ftp's main configuration file is the **ftpaccess** file in the /etc directory. You should think about the following three questions:

- Which users do you want to have access to the FTP server?
- When do you want them to have access?
- What do you want them to be able to do?

Let's start with the first question. FTP users are of three types:

- **Anonymous users**, as described already, use *ftp* or *anonymous* as their logon name. They are placed in the /var/ftp directory and have limited access to the system.

- **Real users**, as described already, log on using a regular Linux user account. They can work in any directory of the filesystem that they could access when logging on normally to Linux. You can restrict what they can do via FTP, however, to enhance your server's security.

- **Guest users** have regular Linux user accounts, but are more restricted in what they can do while logged on using FTP. They often are not allowed to log on at all except using FTP, and their FTP actions are limited.

You define a guest user with the guestuser directive. For example, suppose you created a user account for a colleague named John Lin. His Linux account name is jlin. Use this line within /etc/ftpaccess to make him a guest user when he logs on using FTP:

guestuser jlin

Note that this does not prevent John from logging on normally and having access to the system. Typically, you would modify the entry for jlin in the /etc/passwd file after creating the account so that he had no regular logon shell.

In addition to defining system users as guests for FTP purposes, you can create **classes of users**. This is optional, but it allows you to assign permissions within FTP based on a grouping that you define. Using classes can be confusing at first because the named classes that you create are independent of the distinctions for anonymous, real, and guest users. For example, you could define all users who log on from a certain address as being in the class *office*, whereas all others are in the class *other* (the class definitions are checked in the order listed within the file).

```
class office   real,guest,anonymous   192.168.100.0/24
class other    real,guest,anonymous   *
```

You'll use these classes shortly to define specific access rights. First, however, consider the messages that you want users to see on their screens during different parts of their FTP session. You can define several different message files that are automatically displayed by the FTP server at different points. Table 5-3 summarizes these files. You can use any, all, or none of these. Several are defined by default in most FTP configurations.

Table 5-3 Message files defined in `ftpaccess`

Configuration Keyword	Description	Example
banner	Displays the contents of the named file before prompting the user for a username and password; you must create the file in plaintext.	`banner /etc/ftpbanner.msg`
readme	Prints a message telling the user to read the contents of a file whose name matches the pattern given. The example causes FTP to print a message stating "Please read the *filename* file" if any file matching the pattern README* exists in the root directory (`/var/ftp`). The second example provides the same type of notice message if any file matching the name README* exists in any directory that the user changes into using the `cd` command. (The contents of the named file are not displayed; the user must open the file to view it.)	`readme README* login` `readme README* cwd=*`
greeting	Sets how much information is displayed when first connecting to the FTP server (such as the date, time, and version of the FTP server software); options for this keyword include full, brief, or terse.	`greeting terse`

message	Displays the contents of the named file when the user logs on (using `login`, the first example) or enters a directory (`cwd=`, the second example).	`message /etc/ftpwelcome.msg`
		`    login`
		`message .message cwd=*`

You can control which file actions an FTP user is permitted to perform using a series of directives naming the file action, followed by `yes` or `no`, followed by the classes of user to which the directive applies. You can use the predefined classes (real, guest, or anonymous), or you can use a class that you have defined, such as *office* and *other* in the previous examples. Table 5-4 shows how these directives are used.

Table 5-4   File action directives within `ftpaccess`

Command Keyword	Description	Example
chmod	Controls whether the user can change the file permission of files on the FTP server	`chmod no anonymous`
delete	Controls whether the user can delete/remove files on the FTP server	`delete yes class=office`
overwrite	Controls whether the user can overwrite existing files	`overwrite no anonymous,guest`
rename	Controls whether the user can change the name of files	`rename no anonymous,guest`
umask	Controls whether the user can issue the `umask` command to set the default file permissions assigned to files	`umask yes class=office`
compress	Controls whether the user can compress files for faster transfers; typically, all users are allowed to do this	`compress yes all`
tar	Controls whether the user can `tar` files together for more convenient multifile transfers; typically, all users are allowed to do this	`tar yes all`

It's normal to have several lines setting permissions for different groups using the directives in Table 5-4. In addition to these file-related directives, the upload, noretrieve, and allow-retrieve directives control how users can download and upload files. The syntax of these directives is more complicated than the syntax of those in Table 5-4. For the upload directive, the format is as follows:

```
upload root-directory upload-directory permission user-ID
group-ID umask directory-rights
```

An example is shown here:

```
upload /var/ftp /incoming yes ftp ftp 0666 nodirs
```

This example allows users to upload files in the /incoming directory. This directory name is relative to the /var/ftp directory, so it is actually /var/ftp/incoming. The yes indicates that uploading is permitted. (You could have multiple upload directives setting yes and no permission for various subdirectories.) Files uploaded into the directory are assigned the user ID of ftp and the group ID of ftp, with the permissions of 0666. (This mode indicates read and write permissions for all users, and is displayed as rw-rw-rw- if you use the chmod a+rw filename command.) Finally, no directories can be created. (You could substitute the dirs keyword for nodirs in the previous command to permit directories to be created.)

You can control downloading using the noretrieve and allow-retrieve directives. These directives have several alternate formats, so reviewing a couple of examples is the best way to see how to use them. For reference, the syntax of noretrieve looks like this (items in square brackets are optional—allow-retrieve syntax is similar):

```
noretrieve [relative|absolute] [user-class]
    filename|directory
```

The following example gives a directory name that is absolute (starting with the true root of the Linux filesystem). It prohibits downloading any file in the /etc/ subdirectory by any guest or anonymous user.

```
noretrieve absolute guest,anonymous /etc
```

The following example includes only a list of filenames. No user is permitted to download any file with a name that matches either of the names given here.

```
noretrieve core stocks
```

You can effectively override the noretrieve directive using the allow-retrieve directive. It uses a very similar syntax, as this sample line shows:

```
allow-retrieve relative class=office /pub/reports/
    summary.txt
```

This example lets any user in the *office* class download the named file, which is given relative to the FTP root directory, even if the noretrieve directive would otherwise block the download.

It is critical to remember that when working with FTP permissions such as upload, allow-retrieve, and all the items in Table 5-4, the user must have permission within the Linux filesystem *in addition to* the permission of the FTP server, or an operation is not permitted. For example, if you use an upload directive to permit a real user to upload files to the FTP server, but that user account does not have permission to create files in a particular directory, the FTP server does not override Linux security. A user must have both permission within the filesystem (as set using the chmod command) *and* permission from the FTP server to complete a task.

To do FTP file uploads, users need write permissions in the directory. To do FTP file downloads, users need read permissions. Users need read and execute permissions to all directories and the write permission to directories that receive file uploads.

After you have decided which capabilities you want users to have on your FTP server, you may also want to restrict access in other ways. The limit directive lets you limit the number of users who are logged on at one time, by class, and lets you limit the days of the week and times of the day that they are permitted to log on. To limit the overall number of users allowed to log on, use the keyword Any with the limit directive. Here is an example:

```
limit other 50 Any /etc/ftplimit.msg
```

This example limits the number of users in the *other* class to 50 at a time. If one logs off, another can log on. The Any refers to the day and time; the limit always applies. The contents of the ftplimit.msg file are displayed for any user who is not allowed to log on because the limit is exceeded. You can use a time-of-day range, or a set of days of the week, instead of Any. For example, this line limits to 20 the number of users of class *office* who can log on on Saturday or Sunday:

```
limit office 20 SaSu /etc/ftplimit.msg
```

You can use the `file-limit` and `data-limit` directives to limit the number of files or number of bytes that a user can transfer in a single session. (The count for a user is reset when she logs off.) You can use the keywords `in`, `out`, or `total` to limit by uploading (`in`), downloading (`out`), or both combined (`total`). For example, the following line limits users of class *office* to downloading only 50 files per session:

```
file-limit out 50 office
```

The following line limits users in the *other* class to a total transfer (uploading and down-loading) of about 100 MB:

```
data-limit total 100000000 other
```

To limit the time that a user can be logged on, use the `limit-time` directive. The following example limits anonymous users to 60 minutes per session.

```
limit-time anonymous 60
```

Because FTP is usually started from a superserver, you can use the access control mechanisms of TCP Wrappers or `xinetd` configuration files to allow or block access based on host name, domain name, or IP address. FTP itself has a similar feature. This is useful if you are running FTP in stand-alone mode; it also may be more convenient if you are already working in the `/etc/ftpaccess` file. The `deny` directive denies access to specific host names, displaying the contents of the named file when access is denied.

```
deny hosta,hostb,hostc  /etc/ftpdeny.msg
```

Similarly, you can deny or allow access based on the username that is provided during logon. These directives work together with the `/etc/ftpusers` file (see Table 5-2). That is, a user must *not* be listed in `/etc/ftpusers`, and must also have a user ID and group ID that are allowed by the directives `allow-uid`, `allow-gid`, `deny-uid`, and `deny-gid`. A typical setting is to block all user IDs between 100 and 65534. The command to do this is shown here. (This alone does not block anonymous FTP access.)

```
deny-uid %100 %65534
```

You can also log all of the transfers that are managed by your FTP server. Transfers are logged to the file `/var/log/xfers`. The standard directive used in `ftpaccess` is:

```
log transfers anonymous,guest,real inbound,outbound
```

This directive causes both uploads and downloads (inbound and outbound) to be logged, no matter what type of user does the transfer. Software is available to analyze and create statistics from your `xfer` log file about how your FTP server is being used. For example, try the Ftp Logger Perl script or the Flog program, both of which you can download from *linux.tucows.com*. Connection attempts that fail are also logged by the FTP server in the system log file, usually in /var/log/messages. Examining these messages lets you know if someone is trying to break in to your system via FTP.

A few final options are not part of the broader categories covered so far, but are part of nearly every ftpaccess configuration file. The e-mail directive identifies where the FTP server should send messages when a problem arises or when the server simply needs to notify the administrator of something. A typical line looks like this:

e-mail root@myplace.net

Related to the limitation directives, the loginfails directive defines how many bad username and password combinations a user can enter before the connection is dropped by the FTP server. This slows down someone who is attempting to break in using FTP. The typical value is 5:

loginfails 5

A final directive that is included at the end of all default ftpaccess files is passwd-check, which defines how closely the FTP server pays attention to the password entered by an anonymous user. These users are asked to enter their e-mail address as a password. The first parameter after the directive can be none, which ignores the password; trivial, which checks that it contains an "@" character; or rfc822, which checks for a correctly formed e-mail address. The second parameter defines what action to take if the first parameter (if trivial or rfc822) is not met. It can be either warn, to simply tell the user that the password was not correctly formed, or enforce, to log the user off because a valid e-mail address was not entered. The typical line looks like this:

passwd-check rfc822 warn

You can view the documentation for wu-ftpd in the /usr/share/doc/ wu-ftpd-2.6.1 directory. In the examples folder, you can see the file ftpaccess. heavy for a more complex sample file than is included in this section. A graphical tool called kwuftpd lets you create an ftpaccess file, but it doesn't help a great deal unless you already understand the options presented in the dialog boxes.

The man page for ftpaccess contains further details on the directives presented in this section, plus dozens of other more esoteric directives. The ftpaccess file is normally installed as part of an FTP server package. Part of the file is shown next; you should recognize all of the directives included in this file.

```
e-mail root@localhost

# Allow 5 mistyped passwords
loginfails 5

# Notify the users of README files at login and when
# changing to a different directory
readme   README*     login
readme   README*     cwd=*
```

```
# Messages displayed to the user
message /welcome.msg              login
message .message                 cwd=*

# Allow on-the-fly compression and tarring
compress        yes              all
tar             yes              all

# Prevent anonymous users (and partially guest users)
# from executing dangerous commands
chmod      no      guest,anonymous
delete     no      anonymous
overwrite  no      anonymous
rename     no      anonymous

# Turn on logging to /var/log/xferlog
log transfers anonymous,guest,real inbound,outbound

# If /etc/shutmsg exists, don't allow logins
# see ftpshut man page
shutdown /etc/shutmsg

# Ask users to use their e-mail address as anonymous
# password
passwd-check rfc822 warn
```

FILE SHARING WITH NFS

The **Network File System (NFS)** was developed by Sun Microsystems in the 1980s to make multiple UNIX systems appear as a single large system. That is, hard disks located all over the network would appear as if they were local resources. For example, when you execute a command such as `ls /data/aircraft`, you might actually be viewing the contents of the `/parts/data/reports/aircraft` directory on a host located in the next room or in another county. This ability to interconnect systems seamlessly led to Sun's slogan "The Network Is the Computer".

System administrators regularly mount filesystems to make an additional hard disk partition appear in the local filesystem. For example, the following command makes the contents of a Windows partition on the second hard disk appear as the directory `/mnt/windows` on Linux:

```
mount -t vfat /dev/hdb1 /mnt/windows
```

NFS is used in the same way. It was designed for permanent, long-term connections that allow you to access remote filesystems as part of your regular user environment. Organizations use NFS for actions such as maintaining a centralized /home directory on a main server and mounting each user's home directory automatically using NFS when the user logs on. This makes system administration and backup of all users' data easier. NFS is often used with the Network Information System (NIS), referred to in Chapter 3. NIS allows a single database of user information on the network to provide logon information for multiple hosts.

NFS was designed with a trusted network in mind. You'd use it on your network but you wouldn't deploy it over the raw Internet.

NFS is a good way to share commonly used directories over a local network. For example, you might use NFS to share the /home directory, the /var/log directory, or the /var/spool/mail directory. By having the files from these directories in a single location, administration and security management can be simplified. Just be certain you have the network bandwidth to keep all the users on the network happy with the performance of these remote filesystems.

Running the NFS Daemons

The NFS protocol is implemented by several daemons, each handling a different set of tasks. These daemons are not started by default in Linux. You should start them yourself and set them to start automatically only after you have configured the NFS system, as described in this section.

NFS communication is built on the **Remote Procedure Call (RPC)** service. This service functions like a superserver: Programs are assigned an RPC number. A program called **portmap** watches for RPC requests from programs like the NFS daemons, then maps them to TCP or UDP ports to use the network. You can view the RPC number mappings in /etc/rpc. The portmap program is started by default on your Linux system to handle any requests from programs like the NFS daemons. If the portmap daemon is not running, NFS does not work.

NFS itself uses the **rpc.mountd** daemon to make new connections—that is, to mount a remote filesystem. The rpc.mountd command checks all the relevant permissions to see whether the mount is permitted. After a filesystem is mounted, the **nfsd** daemon handles file transfers based on the settings that the rpc.mountd daemon has validated. Some systems add one or two peripheral programs to help manage NFS-mounted filesystems. The first is rpc.rquotad, which permits tracking user disk space quotas for remotely mounted filesystems, just as you can on local Linux filesystems. The second is rpc.rstatd, which helps manage NFS-mounted filesystems when the remote NFS server crashes (or otherwise breaks its connection) and then comes up again.

All of these programs are normally started by a script in the /etc/rc.d/init.d directory. In some versions of Linux, they are listed individually by name; in others, they are grouped for management by a few scripts. For example, in Fedora Core, when you execute /etc/rc.d/init.d/nfs start, three daemons are started: rpc.mountd, nfsd, and rpc.rquotad. You start the rpc.rstatd daemon using the nfslock script in the same directory.

The `portmap` program that controls network access by the NFS server may use the TCP Wrappers program. You use the `/etc/hosts.allow` and `/etc/hosts.deny` files that you learned about in Chapter 4 to define which hosts have access to NFS. Within these files, use the service name `portmap` (not one of the NFS-specific daemons).

Accessing Remote NFS Filesystems

Acting as a client to an NFS server is straightforward: You use the `mount` command, as you would for any filesystem on a local hard disk partition. The only difference is the filesystem type you specify and a variety of options you can use.

You should already be familiar with the `mount` command and the use of the `/etc/fstab` file. Here's the syntax of a line in the `/etc/fstab` file for mounting NFS filesystems:

```
host:directory    mountpoint  nfs  options      0 0
```

The *host:directory* is the host name of the NFS server and the path to the directory to be shared. The *mountpoint* is a directory on your local Linux system. The options are the interesting part. The `mount` man page lists about 20 options specific to NFS filesystems, in addition to the many options that are applicable to all filesystem types. A few especially useful options are listed here:

- `rsize=8192,wsize=8192`—Used together, these options alter the default buffer size for NFS transfers. Using these options often improves performance because larger buffers allow more efficient data transfers.

- `ro` and `rw`—You can mount a filesystem as read-only (`ro`) or read-write (`rw`).

- `hard` or `soft`—You can **hard mount** an NFS filesystem, which means your programs waits—without limit—for the NFS server to respond. If the server goes down and then comes up again a while later, your program will continue without a hitch. Alternatively, you can **soft mount** an NFS filesystem, which means that NFS waits for a while and then gives up. The documentation recommends not using the `soft` option unless the NFS server you are working with is quite unreliable.

- `noauto`—This option causes the NFS filesystem not to be mounted automatically at system start-up.

Refer to the `mount` man page for other options. Here's an example of an NFS line in an `/etc/fstab` file:

```
rome:/home/public    /mnt/rome    nfs    rsize=8192,wsize=8192,rw,
noauto 0 0
```

You can have many different NFS filesystems in `/etc/fstab`, each listed on a separate line. As with other types of filesystems, after you have this information defined in `/etc/fstab`, you can use both the `mount` command and the `umount` command with just the remote directory or the local mount point. All of the information in `/etc/fstab` is applied to the command. For example, if the preceding line is included on your system, you can issue the following command to mount the NFS filesystem.

```
mount   /mnt/rome
```

Exporting Your Filesystems Using NFS

To make parts of your filesystem accessible over the network to other systems, you must have the NFS daemons running and you must allow NFS traffic to pass between the two hosts without a firewall blocking NFS packets. Beyond these requirements, you must set up the /etc/**exports** file to define which of your local directories you want to be accessible to remote users (that is, which directories are exported) and how each can be used.

After you have /etc/exports set up, run the **exportfs** command to activate the contents of /etc/exports, then start the NFS daemons using the scripts in /etc/rc.d/init.d.

The syntax of a line within /etc/exports is shown here. You can include multiple hostname(option) settings for the same directory, separating each by a space.

```
/directory-path     hostname(option,option,...)
```

The host name can be defined in several ways. You can use a complete host name to define a specific host; you can use a domain name to define all hosts within a domain; or you can use an IP address, either for a single host, a network, or part of a network. The exports man page lists all of the possible permutations.

An /etc/exports file can be as simple as this:

```
/projects
```

This /etc/exports file allows anyone who can reach your host via NFS to mount the /projects directory because no host name or access options are specified. Well, that's almost true. When you use an NFS client to access a remote filesystem, the NFS server must decide what user to treat you as, because you never "log on" or provide a password when you use the NFS client (as you saw in the previous discussion of the mount command). The default action is that the mount command sends your user ID and group ID on the client, and then the NFS server uses the same user ID and group ID on the server system. Your file permissions match those of the corresponding user and group. This is designed for a situation in which a single user has accounts on multiple systems, with the same user ID and group ID on each one.

This arrangement is not always easy to achieve, nor is it always appropriate. For this reason, you normally include options in /etc/exports to **map** incoming client user and group IDs to user and group IDs on the NFS server.

NFS uses a security concept called **squashing** to prevent a user from gaining access to a user account on the NFS server simply because the user has the same ID on the NFS client. The most important use of this concept is squashing the root account: You shouldn't have root access on the NFS server just because you have root access on an NFS client! Squashing of the root account is done automatically unless you use the `no_root_squash` option. One method of squashing incoming client user IDs is to define an anonymous user account and tell NFS to map all incoming users to that account. Thus, all NFS clients have access only to areas that you have specifically granted to this "anonymous" user. Reviewing a few examples should make the uses of this system apparent.

```
/ scout(rw,no_root_squash)
```

This line shows a very trusted host, scout, for which squashing is not used (remember, `root_squash` is the default action). The root user can thus have root access to the `/` directory on the NFS server. This type of entry would be used for a trusted network in which a single system administrator wanted to have complete access to multiple hosts' filesystems via NFS.

The next example assumes that everyone on the *myplace.net* domain has a user account with a matching user ID on the NFS server. All users are permitted to access the `/projects` directory, reading and writing according to the file permissions within `/projects` on the NFS server.

```
/projects *.myplace.net(rw)
```

In the following example, the `/pub` directory is available to all hosts (not naming any host is equivalent to using `*` as the host name), but the hosts can only mount `/pub` in read-only mode. The `all_squash` option causes all users on client systems to be mapped to a "nobody" user on the NFS server. This means that even if users were able to somehow create a file on the NFS server (via a security hole of some type), it would have a user ID of "nobody" and thus be less harmful than a file created by a valid user.

```
/pub (ro,all_squash)
```

In a final example, users on train01 can access `/home/testing` on the NFS server, but all users on train01 are mapped to user ID 150 and group ID 100, which you need to define in `/etc/passwd` and `/etc/group` on the host running the NFS server. All of these users have read-write access, but can only act as the named user, providing a good margin of safety for what they are actually allowed to do.

```
/home/testing train01(rw,all_squash,anonuid=150, anongid=100)
```

Again, the man page for `exports` has examples and descriptions of many other options than those explored here. The basics of defining sets of host names, mapping users between systems, and controlling read-only or read-write access should get you started with NFS.

TIP

Remember to run `exportfs` after making any changes to `/etc/exports`. This activates your changes and alerts you to any syntax errors in the file. (This program is run automatically each time you reboot your system.)

NOTE Avoid exporting / or /etc, or other sensitive directories on your system, unless you are very confident in your /etc/exports configuration. Always export the smallest portion of your filesystem that satisfies the needs of clients; don't just export / and assume everyone can find what they need. Such laziness invites trouble.

WINDOWS FILE AND PRINT INTEGRATION WITH SAMBA

5

Windows uses a file-sharing protocol called **Server Message Block (SMB)**. Later versions of Microsoft products use the name **Common Internet File System (CIFS)** for this protocol. This is a poor name because the CIFS protocol is rarely used over the Internet. Like NFS and almost every other remote filesystem protocol, it is not secure. CIFS may be common on LANs, but not over the Internet. This book refers to SMB.

The SMB protocol is a filesystem (Application layer) protocol that was designed to operate using an application programming interface or API called **NetBIOS.** NetBIOS stands for Network Basic Input Output System. NetBIOS was intended to be a local area networking extension to the IBM PC BIOS. SMB and NetBIOS were designed by IBM, Sytek, and Microsoft in the mid-1980s.

Originally, NetBIOS was tied to IBM's early LAN products: PC Network and Token-Ring. Computers on the network were given names, and clients connected to servers or other clients using these names. At the time, there was no centralized naming service. Computers would find one another using NetBIOS broadcasts. Broadcasts could not cross routers, so a NetBIOS-based network was limited in size.

To solve this scalability problem, NetBIOS packets were later carried by protocols that were routable, such as Novell's IPX and (what would later become) the industry standard, TCP/IP. A centralized naming service, called the Windows Internet Naming Service or **WINS**, was developed to map NetBIOS names to IP addresses. More recent versions of Windows now use DNS.

Regardless of which of these protocols and technologies are used, Windows resources that are available over the network are called **shares**. Most commonly, there are disk shares and printer shares.

To implement SMB and NetBIOS in Linux, you use the **Samba** suite of programs. The name "Samba" was chosen because the name resembles SMB but avoids using the Microsoft trademarked protocol name. Samba includes server programs that let your Linux computer operate as a Windows SMB server. It also includes client programs that let you connect to shares on Windows computers or other Linux computers running Samba.

The Samba server programs are as follows:

- smbd—Provides file and print services. One daemon is spawned for each client.
- nmbd—Provides NETBIOS name service and browsing service.

- winbindd—Provides winbind service; obtains user and group information from a Windows server. This program is not necessary for Samba to function.

The Samba client programs are as follows:

- findsmb—Displays a list of systems that respond to SMB name query requests and their IP address, NETBIOS name, workgroup/domain, and operating system
- net—Provides functionality similar to the Windows net commands
- nmblookup—Queries the network for NETBIOS names and displays the results
- pdbedit—Manages accounts in a SAM database
- rpcclient—Issues administrative commands using Microsoft RPCs
- smbcacls—Modifies access control lists (ACLs)
- smbclient—Connects to an SMB share and accesses files via a command prompt, similar to an FTP client; an SMB client
- smbcontrol—Sends control messages to smbd, nmbd, and winbindd daemons
- smbgroupedit—Sets up mappings between UNIX and Windows groups
- smbmount/smbumount—Mounts/unmounts SMB shares to a Linux filesystem mount point
- smbpasswd—Manages Samba user passwords
- smbspool—Sends a print job to a Samba printer
- smbstatus—Displays the current Samba connections, their open files, and any file locks
- smbtar—Provides a tar-like capability for SMB shares
- testparm—Checks the Samba configuration file for errors
- wbinfo—Displays information from the winbindd daemon

To use Samba, be certain that the samba, samba-common, samba-client, and samba-swat packages are installed in Fedora Core Linux, or similar packages in other versions of Linux. The easiest way to check for Samba on a system that uses rpm packages is with these three commands (in some systems, the packages are named for the protocol, and in some they are named for the suite of programs):

```
rpm -qa | grep smb
rpm -qa | grep samba
rpm -qa | grep swat
```

NOTE Strictly speaking, the samba-swat or swat package is optional. SWAT is the Samba Web Administration Tool. It's a Samba configuration tool described later in this section, but if you're new to Samba, it's the best way to learn about the capabilities of Samba.

TIP

The history of Samba development is a fascinating story of a few software developers in Australia (led by Andrew Tridgell) who reverse-engineered Microsoft's networking system; they had no intention initially to create software that would allow UNIX and Linux users all over the world to interact with Windows systems. You can read the full story at *www.samba.org*.

Using Samba Client Utilities

Samba client utility programs let you access shared Windows resources as if you used a Windows-based computer. Windows-based computers cannot tell that you are running Linux.

It's useful to know what SMB servers are running on your network. You can get a list of them by using the findsmb program that's included with newer versions of Samba. The following is one example of using it:

```
                                   *=DMB
                                   +=LMB
IP ADDR        NETBIOS NAME     WORKGROUP/OS/VERSION
---------------------------------------------------------------------
10.1.2.4       CASCADE         +[ED]  [Win 5.0]  [Win 2000 LAN Manager]
10.1.2.4       CASCADE         +[ED]  [Win 5.0]  [Win 2000 LAN Manager]
10.1.2.5       CASCADE          [ED]  [Win 5.0]  [Win 2000 LAN Manager]
10.1.2.5       CASCADE          [ED]  [Win 5.0]  [Win 2000 LAN Manager]
10.1.2.9       XFILES           [ED]  [Unix]  [Samba 3.0.9-1.2E.2]
10.1.2.26      ZEUS             [SUN]  [Win Server 2003]  [Win Server 2003 5.2]
10.1.2.28      WEB              [SUN]  [Win Server 2003]  [Win Server 2003 5.2]
10.1.2.31      STAFF            [SUN]  [Win 5.0]  [Win 2000 LAN  Manager]
10.1.2.35      ULTRASERVER      [SUN]  [Win NT 4.0]  [NT LAN Manager  4.0]
10.1.2.46      PCWIZARD         [SUN]  [Win 5.1]  [Win 2000 LAN  Manager]
10.1.2.53      TRACY            [SUN]  [Win 5.1]  [Win 2000 LAN  Manager]
10.1.2.65      DOCFILES         [SUN]  [Win 5.0]  [Win 2000 LAN  Manager]
10.1.2.72      SALES-EAST       [SUN]  [Win 5.1]  [Win 2000 LAN  Manager]
10.1.2.81      SALES-WEST       [SUN]  [Win NT 4.0]  [NT LAN Manager  4.0]
```

In the preceding example, *Windows* is abbreviated to *Win* so it would better fit on this page. You can see a list of shares for any of the servers by using the **smbclient** program. The following example uses the command smbclient -L 10.1.2.9. You'll be prompted for the password to the server.

```
Domain=[SUN] OS=[Unix] Server=[Samba 3.0.9-1.3E.2]

          Sharename        Type       Comment
          ---------        ----       -------
          net              Disk       Public Network Store
          queue            Disk       Print Queue
          IPC$             IPC        IPC Service (Linux Server)
          ADMIN$           IPC        IPC Service (Linux Server)
```

The smbclient utility can operate much like the FTP client. It is a command-line utility that lets you log on to a Windows host and interact using a series of commands much like the FTP commands.

To use the smbclient command, you need to know three things:

- The host name or IP address of the Windows system you want to contact. Use this with the -L option.

- Your username on that host. Use this with the -U option.

- The workgroup that the host is a part of (the command may work without this, but you improve your odds on a large network by including it). Use this with the -W option.

The command format to use is shown here. Notice that the options are case sensitive. Windows normally refers to workgroup names, so you may avoid potential problems if you do the same:

```
smbclient -L hostname -U username -W WORKGROUP
```

After you enter this command, you may have to wait a minute while smbclient finds the Windows system. There may be a wait even on a very small network, and it may be longer if you have only recently started one or both of the computers or are working on a larger network. At any rate, after a minute, you are prompted for the password (which does not appear on the screen as you enter it). The smbclient program then lists all the resources reported by the server you indicated. Sample output is shown here:

```
added interface ip=192.168.100.10 bcast=192.168.100.255 nmask=
255.255.255.0
Got a positive name query response from 192.168.100.6  ( 192.168.
100.6 )
Password: *******
Domain=[WELLS] OS=[Windows NT 4.0] Server=[NT LAN Manager 4.0]

          Sharename        Type       Comment
          ---------        ----       -------
          ADMIN$           Disk       Remote Admin
          IPC$             IPC        Remote IPC
          C$               Disk       Default share
          D$               Disk       Default share
```

E$	Disk	Default share
F$	Disk	Default share
V$	Disk	Default share
G$	Disk	Default share
HPLaserJ	Printer	HP LaserJet 4L
print$	Disk	Printer Drivers

Server	Comment
LONDON	
SUNDANCE	Samba Server

Workgroup	Master
WELLS	LONDON

NOTE Each version of Windows has variations, but the basic method of creating a shared resource in Windows is first to find the resource, such as a hard disk, subdirectory, or printer. For example, you can use My Computer or Windows Explorer to find the resource, then right-click the item and choose Properties. Within the Properties dialog box, choose the Sharing tab and set the appropriate fields to name the share and select who can access it. See your Windows documentation (or online help) for further information.

After you have identified the share to which you want to connect, you can issue a second `smbclient` command to begin using it. (If you already knew the share name, of course, you could begin with this step.) The format of the server name and share name are peculiar to Windows networking. Start with a double forward slash, followed by the server name, then a single forward slash, then the share name. For example, to connect to drive D—share D$—use this command:

`smbclient //london/D$ -U nwells`

Once again, you must enter the password for the user, then you see the `smb` prompt:

`smb: \>`

At this prompt, you can enter commands as you did in the FTP client. In fact, most of the commands you're likely to use are the same: get, put, ls, pwd, cd, mget, mput, and prompt. (See Table 5-1.) To exit `smbclient`, however, enter `exit`; `bye` doesn't work.

A few graphical tools are equivalent to `smbclient`, but the better way to graphically access Windows systems is to mount a Windows share as part of your Linux filesystem. This is done using the standard mount command using a filesystem type of **smbfs**—the SMB filesystem. When using a mount command to mount a Windows share, you include a username as an option with the o parameter. In some situations, you also want to include the password to fully automate the mount command during system start-up, for example. The command would then look like the following example, assuming you had already created a directory as the mount point:

```
mount -t smbfs -o username=nwells,password=coconuts
    //london/d$ /mnt/london_d
```

If Linux successfully makes a connection and the username and password are valid, the preceding command returns after a moment to the command line. At that point, you can access the directory /mnt/london_d as you would any other part of the Linux filesystem, including using any standard Linux graphical utilities to manage your files. Figure 5-3 shows a Linux desktop with the contents of a Windows share.

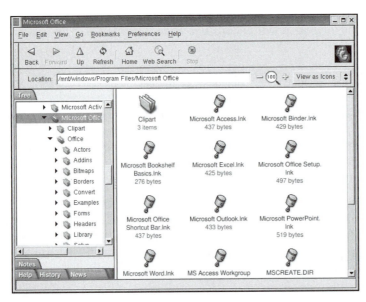

Figure 5-3   A mounted Windows share viewed within a Linux desktop

You can use additional options in your mount command. For example, you can mount the Windows share as read-only, define the user ID and group ID that all files will appear with in Linux, log on as a guest on Windows, or define the Windows workgroup name. Enter the command man smbmount to learn about these and other options.

In addition to accessing Windows files from Linux, you can print to a Windows printer. This is done using the **smbprint** command, but most users prefer that you define a regular Linux printer that routes print jobs transparently to the Windows printer. The easiest way to do this is with one of the modern graphical printer tools. One good example is Fedora's Printer Configuration Tool, which you can start by entering printconf-gui at a command line, or by choosing Applications, then System Settings, then Printing on the GNOME menu. This utility lets you create printer definitions that are stored in the **/etc/printcap** file (where all Linux printer definitions are stored) and manage print queues after they are created.

Within the Printer Configuration Tool, you can click the New button to begin creating a new printer definition. A series of dialog boxes guides you through the process. You can select Networked Windows (SMB) as the queue type to which you want the printer definition to refer. When you finish defining the printer, the Printer Configuration Tool shows the new printer in the list (see Figure 5-4). You can get detailed information about the new printer (WinPrinter in this example) by selecting it and clicking Edit. Figure 5-5 shows the screen that appears. Click the Queue type tab to see detailed connection-oriented information. In this example, the network printer is connected to a Linux computer running Samba. The procedure for using the `printconf-gui` program to add a networked Windows printer is the same, regardless of whether the printer is connected to Windows or Samba/Linux.

5

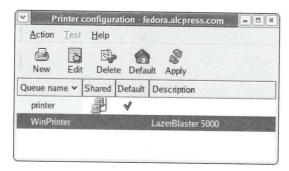

Figure 5-4   Selecting Windows as the printer type in the Fedora Core Printer Configuration Tool

If you're already experienced with Linux printing, you may wonder how this is done behind the scenes. The Printer Configuration Tool creates a definition in `/etc/printcap` that looks like the following code. Note how the `lp` line pipes the print job to the `smbprint` command. Review the `printcap` man page for details on the other items shown in this file:

```
# /etc/printcap
#
# DO NOT EDIT! MANUAL CHANGES WILL BE LOST!
# This file is autogenerated by printconf-backend during
    lpd init.
#
# Hand edited changes can be put in /etc/printcap.local,
    and will be included.

HPLJ:\
        :sh:\
        :ml=0:\
        :mx=0:\
        :sd=/var/spool/lpd/HPLJ:\
        :af=/var/spool/lpd/HPLJ/HPLJ.acct:\
        :lp=|/usr/share/printconf/util/smbprint:\
        :lpd_bounce=true:\
        :if=/usr/share/printconf/util/mf_wrapper:
```

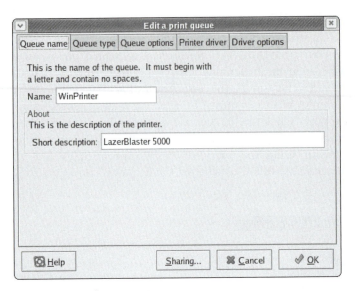

Figure 5-5 Editing a print queue

As part of the standard printer definitions, any printer tool can manage the print queues after this definition is created.

If your printing system is CUPS and the `smb.conf` file has the directives `printing = cups` and `printcap name = cups`, the `/etc/printcap` file is not modified and print jobs are sent directly to the CUPS API.

This section covered the major Samba client tools, but you can learn more about them by using the man pages.

NOTE

Setting Up a Samba Server

The Samba suite includes two server daemons: **nmbd**, which implements NetBIOS, and **smbd**, which implements SMB file and print sharing. Both of these daemons must be running to implement a Samba server, and both are managed using a single script in `/etc/rc.d/init.d`. On some systems, this script is called `smb`; on others, it is called `samba`. As soon as you have configured Samba as described in this section, you can start the server using this script and use `chkconfig` to make it start automatically whenever you boot Linux.

Samba configuration files are typically stored in /etc/samba, though the location may vary in different Linux distributions. The main configuration file is smb.conf. A sample or default smb.conf file is provided. You need to review this file and add your own settings before running the Samba server. A very basic smb.conf file is shown here, though the sample file on your system is filled with comments explaining numerous other options.

```
[global]
workgroup = MYPLACE
netbios name = sundance
server string = Samba on Linux posing as Windows 2000
hosts allow = 192.168.100.
printcap name = /etc/printcap
load printers = yes
printing = cups
log file = /var/log/samba.log
max log size = 0
security = user
encrypt passwords = yes
smb passwd file = /etc/samba/smbpasswd
socket options = TCP_NODELAY SO_RCVBUF=8192 SO_SNDBUF=8192
dns proxy = no

[homes]
comment = Home Directories
browseable = no
writable = yes

[printers]
comment = All Printers
path = /var/spool/samba
browseable = no
guest ok = no
printable = yes
```

The smb.conf file is divided into sections. The [global] section defines the overall operation of the server. Other sections define how the server handles shared resources: either the printers or specific filesystem "shares" (directories that you want to share). The [homes] and [printers] sections are standard names that refer to the home directories of each user who logs on and the Linux printers, respectively. You can create other sections to define other shares. Each line in the minimal smb.conf preceding sample file is explained here:

- *workgroup = MYPLACE*—The workgroup of which your Samba server is a part.

- *netbios name = sundance*—The host name of your Samba server. This line is normally commented out and defaults to the same name as your Linux host name, although it doesn't have to be because NetBIOS and WINS servers operate independently of DNS. If the names differ, however, be careful to keep track of them.

- *server string = Samba on Linux posing as Windows 2000*—This is the comment that appears in Windows when you access this Samba server. If you enter something like "Windows XP" here, no one can tell you are really running Samba on Linux.

- *hosts allow = 192.168.100.*—Which hosts the Samba server allows to access the server. This definition specifies all hosts on the network 192.168.100.0. You can specify this field in various ways. This field does not substitute for a good firewall.

- *printcap name = /etc/printcap*—Defines where Linux printers are defined, so that Samba can obtain a list of the printer names to present to clients. This can also be set to *cups*.

- *load printers = yes*—Printing is enabled by using yes here.

- *printing = cups*—The printing system used on your Linux system.

- *log file = /var/log/samba.log*—Samba sends log messages to this file. You can create per-client log files using the %m option as well.

- *max log size = 0*—With the maximum log size set to zero, no maximum is imposed. If you include a number, it defines a maximum size for the log file in KB. You should use a log rotation plan to avoid having overly large log files.

- *security = user*—Require each user to provide a username and password before accessing the Samba server.

- *encrypt passwords = yes*—User passwords must be encrypted for Samba to accept them. This is the standard choice because all newer Windows systems (Windows 98 and later) require encrypted passwords.

- *smb passwd file = /etc/samba/smbpasswd*—The list of user accounts to which Samba should refer.

- *socket options = TCP_NODELAY SO_RCVBUF=8192 SO_SNDBUF=8192*—How Samba uses TCP/IP for transporting data. The options shown here are a standard way to speed up transmissions. (You may recognize that they resemble the options used to speed up NFS as well.)

- *dns proxy = no*—Don't use DNS to resolve names; rely instead on Windows protocols.

- *[homes]*—Indicates the Windows share devoted to user home directories.

- *comment = Home Directories*—The share's contents.

- *browseable = no*—The share cannot be located by "browsing"; you must know the name of the share that you want (your own home directory in this case).

- *writable = yes*—Users can create or update files in their home directories.

- *[printers]*—The printing management section of Samba.

- *comment = All Printers*—The contents of this share.

- *path = /var/spool/samba*—A path where print jobs are spooled (stored).

- *browseable = no*—Printers are not browseable; you must know the name of the printer you want to access.

- *guest ok = no*—Guest users cannot print; only those who log on using a valid username and password can print.

- *printable = yes*—Yes, users can print!

Creating Samba Users

The user security model requires that each user must log on with a valid username and password before using a share on the Samba server. It's common to allow everyone with a Linux user account to also log on via Samba. Several utilities included with the Samba suite make this easy to implement. Assuming that you have created all your Linux user accounts, the following command creates a Samba password file for all your Linux users:

```
cat /etc/passwd | mksmbpasswd.sh > /etc/samba/smbpasswd
```

No passwords are transferred in this process; you must enter a password for each user (twice) using the `smbpasswd` command. For example, the following command lets you set the Samba password for user nwells in the `smbpasswd` file:

```
smbpasswd nwells
```

User nwells can then use that password to log on from a Windows system.

If you prefer not to use the user security model described so far, consider one of these values for the "security =" setting.

- *security=share* means that all users who log on to your Samba server have the same access, which you define in your configuration. Normally, you assign all Samba users to the Linux user "nobody," or a similar user account with few rights. This type of security is ideal for a Samba server that is acting solely as a print server.

- *security=server* is the same as *security=user*, except that you define another server that verifies the username and password. This system looks the same as *security=user* to the client, but lets you avoid setting up separate password files on every server if it doesn't make sense.

- *security=domain* lets you rely on a Windows NT domain server for user authentication. You still need to set up Linux user accounts before using this option, however.

Using SWAT to Configure SMB

The example `smb.conf` configuration file described previously contains only a fraction of the hundreds of options supported by Samba. Exploring them all can be a challenge, especially if you are new to Windows networking. Several graphical tools can help you configure Samba (check *www.kde.org* or *www.gnome.org*, for example), but the method of choice according to the developers of Samba is the SWAT tool. **SWAT** is a browser-based graphical interface that sets up the `smb.conf` file, restarts the Samba servers, and provides some status information on how the server is being used.

SWAT runs as a network service managed by the superserver. To use SWAT, the SWAT service must be included in your `/etc/services` file (it is on most modern Linux systems). The line in `/etc/services` should appear like this:

```
swat 901/tcp
```

You also must enable SWAT within your superserver configuration. Check either `/etc/inetd.conf` or `/etc/xinetd.d/swat` to make sure the service is enabled; the superserver can then start SWAT when a request arrives from your browser. You can use your browser from any system to reach SWAT and manage your Samba server. However, SWAT transfers are not encrypted, so unless you are using SWAT to manage Samba on the same machine, you risk exposing your root password to someone snooping around your network.

To access SWAT after you have the network capabilities configured, launch your Web browser and enter the URL *http://localhost:901/* (assuming you are configuring SWAT on your own machine). You are prompted for a username and password. You must enter the username `root` and the root password for your host. The initial SWAT page then appears, as shown in Figure 5-6.

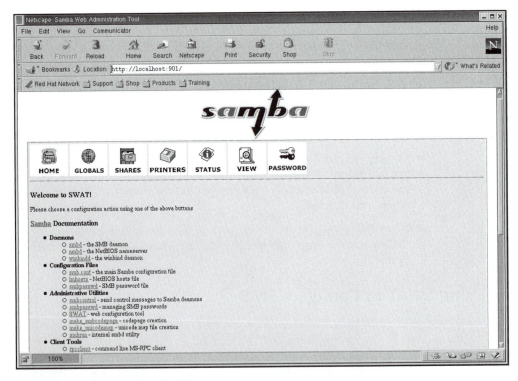

Figure 5-6 The opening SWAT page

NOTE SWAT modifies your /etc/smb.conf file. It may delete comment lines you have entered or rearrange the configuration lines in the file. If you have hand edited /etc/smb.conf, make a backup copy of it under a different name before using SWAT.

The great advantage of using SWAT is that you can learn about Samba as you configure it. If you haven't already, you should use SWAT at least to check (and possibly modify) the settings listed previously in the small example smb.conf file. Beyond that, you can view the SWAT pages to see what options are available. You begin using SWAT by clicking one of the buttons at the top of the page. For example, you can click Globals to alter the global server configuration, or Home to set up home directory shares. A page full of options then appears. Figure 5-7 shows the Globals options page.

5

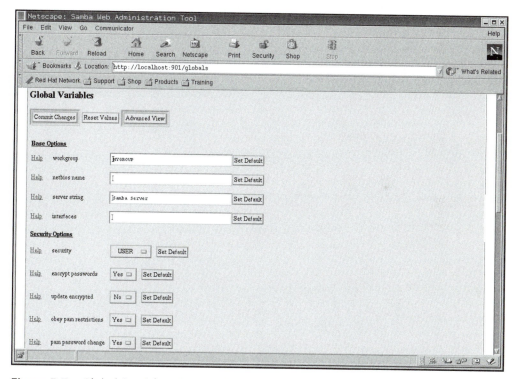

Figure 5-7   Global Samba options within SWAT

You can choose the Help link to the left of any option to see how it is used. Each Samba page initially includes the options that are most likely to be needed in a typical configuration. Review all of these options to consider what you might need to configure for your server. After you make changes, click the Commit Changes button at the top of each screen to update the Samba configuration file. When you're ready to explore in more depth, click the Advanced View button at the top of the page to expand it and list all the available options, including many that you will probably never need. But you can learn a lot by reviewing them!

> If you are curious, explore some of the 195 options included in the Advanced View of the Global section.

TIP

Within SWAT, you create new shares (directories that you want to make available to clients) using the Shares button at the top of the SWAT Web page. You enter a name for the new share and click the Create Share button. You can then select the share from the list box and click the Choose Share button to configure settings for that share.

The Status page shows you the state of the smbd, nmbd, and winbindd servers and lets you start or restart them using buttons on the Web page. Figure 5-8 shows this page. The bottom part of the page lists all the active client connections to the server.

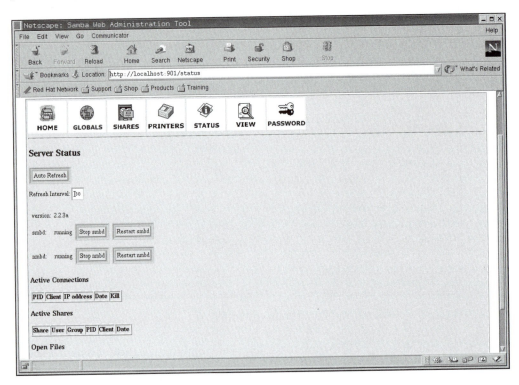

Figure 5-8   The SWAT Status page

The `smbstatus` command lets you see similar status information at any command line. A useful exercise is to review the files included with the various Samba packages to see what specialized utilities and documentation files are included.

Accessing Samba from Windows

After you have a Samba server up and running, you can access Linux files and print to Linux printers from any Windows-based host. All you need is the correct Windows networking configuration and a valid username and password. Although Windows networking can use various low-level networking protocols such as TCP/IP, IPX, and others, Samba uses only TCP/IP. To reach a Samba server from a Windows host, therefore, you should use the Networking icon on the Windows Control Panel to be certain the following components are installed:

- *A network adapter*—Windows should be able to recognize your NIC and have a valid driver for it. The network card is listed in the resources of the Network Configuration dialog box.

- *TCP/IP*—You should configure TCP/IP so that you have a valid IP address.

- *NetBEUI*—The optional **NetBEUI** protocol implements NetBIOS functionality on Windows systems. Both this and TCP/IP can be added using the Add button within the Network Configuration dialog box. In Windows NT, look on the Protocols tab. In Windows XP, click the WINS tab in the Advanced TCP/IP properties.

- *Client for Microsoft Networks*—This must also be installed. Again, you can add this if it's not already listed.

From your Windows desktop, you access a Samba server by double-clicking the Network Neighborhood (or My Network Places) icon and browsing to the appropriate workgroup. If you use Windows XP, double-click My Computer, and then click My Network Places. If you use an older version of Windows, you may have to choose Find, then select Computer on the Windows menu, and search for either the Samba server's name or even its IP address before Windows can locate the server (this is true particularly when you have just started Samba). After you see an icon for the server, you can double-click it to see a list of shares (after entering your username and password). Then double-click a share name to view its contents. Figure 5-9 shows a Windows desktop with a Samba server.

Figure 5-9   A Samba server viewed from Windows

CHAPTER SUMMARY

□ FTP is a widely used Internet protocol that was designed for efficient transfer of files from a server to multiple clients at diverse locations.

□ The anonymous feature of FTP makes it popular for public download archives. Many capabilities of the anonymous feature can be configured to control access to the FTP server.

□ To access an FTP server, you can use the text-mode client ftp, a graphical client such as gFTP or IglooFTP, or a Web browser.

□ The standard FTP server is wu-ftpd. It is configured using /etc/ftpaccess, logs file transfers to /var/log/xfer, and usually relies on the access control mechanism of the superserver that launches it, though ftpaccess can also include host-based access controls.

□ You can configure classes of users in ftpaccess, then assign permission to perform different file actions, or define other types of access limits using those user classes.

□ The Network File System (NFS) lets you access remote filesystems as part of your local directory structure by using the mount command. Numerous options control how a client mounts an NFS filesystem. These options are usually placed in the /etc/fstab file to simplify mounting and unmounting operations.

❑ An NFS server consists of several possible daemons. At the least, `nfsd` and `rpc.mountd` are required. NFS is not managed by a superserver, but instead uses the `portmap` program in conjunction with the remote procedure call (RPC) service.

❑ An NFS server is configured using the `/etc/exports` file, which defines which local directories are available for remote clients to mount. Each line in `/etc/exports` also defines which hosts can mount the directory and how the server should configure their access. This includes options such as user mapping and read-only versus read-write access.

❑ NFS relies on several layers of security, including the client `mount` command, the configuration of `/etc/exports`, and any restrictions in the `/etc/hosts.allow` and `/etc/hosts.deny` files using the `portmap` daemon name.

❑ Windows networking uses the NetBIOS and SMB (also called CIFS) protocols, both of which are implemented by the Samba suite in Linux.

❑ Using the Samba client utility `smbclient` and mounting Windows filesystems of type `smbfs` provide convenient access to shared resources. Most modern graphical Linux printer management tools also let you use the `smbprint` utility to automatically print to Windows printers.

❑ A simple Samba server configuration in `smb.conf` involves defining the server name, basic security options, and defining shares. Samba shares are viewed from Windows just like any Windows server.

❑ SWAT provides graphical configuration and administration functionality for Samba. Though it is not secure for use across a network, SWAT makes it easy to learn more about Samba through listing all available options with online help.

KEY TERMS

`/etc/printcap` — The file in which printer definitions are stored.

anonymous FTP — The use of FTP for public access via a common username, without a user-specific account on the FTP server.

anonymous user home directory — The directory on Linux that anonymous FTP users can access for downloading or uploading files. Typically either `/var/ftp` or `/home/ftp`.

anonymous users — The users logging on to an FTP server who do not have a regular Linux user account and are thus restricted to a specific area of the filesystem. *See* anonymous FTP.

classes of users — The practice of defining groups of potential FTP clients within an FTP server configuration to aid efficient server configuration.

Common Internet File System (CIFS) — The latest extended version of the SMB protocol, used by recent Microsoft operating systems and provided in Linux via the Samba suite.

`exportfs` — A command used to activate the contents of `/etc/exports`.

`exports` — The `/etc/exports` configuration file, which defines filesystems that NFS can make available to other hosts.

File Transfer Protocol (FTP) — A protocol used to share files between networked computer systems.

`ftp` — The most common text-based client program for accessing FTP servers.

`ftpaccess` — The main FTP server configuration file.

`ftpshut` — A command that causes the FTP server to stop allowing connections.

`ftpusers` — An FTP server configuration file listing user accounts that are not allowed to log on via FTP.

gFTP — A graphical FTP client. Installed by default on many Linux systems.

guest users — The users logging on to an FTP server who have a regular Linux user account, but are restricted in what they can do while logged on using FTP.

hard mount — A method of mounting an NFS filesystem that causes NFS to wait indefinitely for the NFS server to respond.

IglooFTP — A popular graphical FTP client.

map — The process of creating a correspondence between a user ID on an NFS client and user permissions on an NFS server.

`ncftp` — A text-based FTP client program similar to FTP, but newer and more refined.

NetBEUI — A protocol within Windows-based computers that implements NetBIOS functionality.

NetBIOS — A protocol that provides a network name resolution service, similar in concept to DNS. Used by Windows operating systems and provided as part of the Samba suite.

Network File System (NFS) — A protocol used to share filesystems on a network.

`nfsd` — A daemon that handles file transfers for a mounted NFS filesystem, based on the settings that the `rpc.mountd` daemon has validated.

`nmbd` — The daemon within the Samba suite that provides NetBIOS capability to Linux.

`portmap` — The program that watches for RPC requests (such as from NFS daemons) and creates the network connections to make them function.

real users — The users logging on to an FTP server who have a regular Linux user account.

Remote Procedure Call (RPC) — A protocol used to allow programs to communicate over a network. RPC acts almost as a superserver, watching for network requests from RPC-capable programs and transferring them to the appropriate transport protocol (such as TCP or UDP).

`rpc.mountd` — A daemon used as part of NFS to make new connections, mounting a remote filesystem after checking relevant permissions to see if the mount is permitted.

Samba — A suite of programs for Linux and many UNIX operating systems that permits these systems to support Windows protocols, such as SMB, CIFS, and NetBIOS.

Server Message Block (SMB) — The transport protocol used for file and print sharing by Windows systems and the Samba suite.

share — A Windows resource for shared use over a network.

`smbclient` — A utility that provides client access to Windows-based hosts or to Samba servers. Part of the Samba suite.

`smbd` — The daemon within the Samba suite that provides SMB capability to Linux.

`smbfs` — The filesystem type designation used to mount a Windows share as part of a Linux filesystem using the `mount` command.

smbprint — A command within the Samba suite that enables printing to a Windows printer over the network.

soft mount — A method of mounting an NFS filesystem that causes NFS to give up on an operation after waiting for a specified time.

squashing — A security concept used by NFS servers to prevent a user from gaining access to a filesystem on the NFS server simply by virtue of having the same user ID on the NFS client.

SWAT — A browser-based graphical configuration interface for setting up and managing the Samba SMB server.

Trivial FTP (TFTP) — A protocol similar to FTP, but designed for downloading an operating system over a network to boot a diskless workstation. Requires less memory and provides fewer features than standard FTP.

WINS — Acronym for Windows Internet Naming Service, a host-locating service for Windows systems, similar in function to a DNS server. The Samba suite can act as a WINS server or client.

wu-ftp — The Washington University FTP server. The name of the server daemon is in.ftpd.

REVIEW QUESTIONS

1. Describe how the purpose of FTP differs from the purpose of HTTP and SMTP.

2. Which of the following is not an FTP client program?

   a. gFTP

   b. ftp

   c. wu-ftpd

   d. ncftp

3. Within the standard FTP client program, you would use the prompt command to:

   a. prevent being prompted for confirmation before downloading a set of files using mget

   b. cause the server to prompt you if you were about to exceed your time limit or download size limit

   c. turn off prompting of help screens for new users

   d. change the format of the default command-line prompt within the utility

4. Which is a correctly formed URL to reach an FTP site within a standard Web browser?

   a. *http://nwells@ftp.myplace.net/*

   b. *ftp://nwells@in.ftpd/*

   c. *ftp://nwells@ftp.myplace.net/*

   d. *http://ftp.myplace/*

5. Assuming the FTP server is running in stand-alone mode, which file lists user accounts that are not allowed to access the FTP server?

   a. `/etc/ftpusers`

   b. `/etc/hosts.deny`

   c. `/etc/shutdown.msg`

   d. `/var/ftp/pub/ftpusers`

6. Describe the difference between a real user and a guest user when configuring an FTP server.

7. A filename given after the banner directive in `/etc/ftpaccess` will:

   a. cause the FTP server to alert the user to the presence of the file after logging on

   b. display the contents of the file to the client before logging on

   c. display the contents of the file to the client after logging on

   d. display the contents of the file to the client upon entering the `/etc` directory

8. Which of the following does not use RPC?

   a. NFS

   b. r-utilities

   c. `portmap`

   d. FTP

9. The two principal NFS daemons on Linux are:

   a. `rpc.mountd` and `nfsd`

   b. `portmap` and `rpc`

   c. `rpc.mountd` and `rpc.umountd`

   d. `fstab` and `exports`

10. Which is the valid line in `fstab` to configure mounting for an NFS filesystem on rome?

    a. `nfs rome:/home/public /mnt/rome rsize=8192,wsize=8192,rw, noauto 0 0`

    b. `rome:/home/public /nfs/rome rsize=8192,wsize=8192,rw,noauto 0 0`

    c. `rome:/home/public /mnt/rome rpc rsize=8192,wsize=8192,rw, nfs 0 0`

    d. `rome:/home/public /mnt/rome nfs rsize=8192,wsize=8192,rw, noauto 0 0`

    e. `nfs:/home/public /mnt/rome nfs rsize=8192,wsize=8192,rw, noauto 0 0`

11. Why is root squashing the default action on an NFS server?

12. Which is a validly formed configuration line in /etc/exports?

   a. (ro,all_squash)   /pub

   b. portmap   o=ro,all_squash

   c. /pub   host1(ro,all_squash)

   d. /pub   host1=ro,all_squash

13. How is inetd or xinetd configured to manage which hosts can access an NFS server?

   a. It isn't. NFS uses portmap, not the superserver, though /etc/hosts.allow and /etc/hosts.deny are still checked.

   b. It isn't. NFS uses host-specific configurations within /etc/fstab to control host access.

   c. by setting the appropriate host definitions for the nfsd daemon in /etc/hosts.allow and /etc/hosts.deny

   d. by relying on the xinetd parameters within the nfs file in the /etc/xinetd.d configuration

14. The passwords for Samba users are stored in which file?

   a. passwd

   b. smbmount

   c. smb.conf

   d. smbpasswd

15. Windows resources that are available over a network are called a:

   a. mount

   b. share

   c. fork

   d. cookie

16. Which vendor did NOT participate in the development of NetBIOS and SMB?

   a. Microsoft

   b. IBM

   c. Red Hat

   d. Sytek

17. The Samba suite can act as a WINS server on a Windows network, which is roughly equivalent to a _____ server for a Linux-only network.

   a. SMB

   b. NetBEUI

   c. FTP

   d. DNS

5

18. Which choice contains only protocols supported by the Samba suite?

    a. CIFS, SMB, NetBIOS

    b. CIFS, SMB, DNS

    c. SMBD, NMBD

    d. SMB, SWAT, FTP

19. The `smbclient` program most resembles which other program in this chapter?

    a. `exportfs`

    b. `ftpshut`

    c. `ftp`

    d. gFTP

20. To see a list of file and printer shares available on an SMB server, you would include that server name with the _____ parameter of the _____ command.

    a. `-S`, `smbfs`

    b. `-L`, `smbclient`

    c. `-S`, `smbclient`

    d. `-W`, `smbprint`

21. To mount a Windows share as part of your Linux filesystem, you:

    a. Use the `mount` command with the `-t` parameter set to `smbfs`.

    b. Rely on a graphical utility for convenient access.

    c. Use `smbclient` to download the desired files.

    d. Make certain that the `smbpasswd` file was first properly configured.

22. Which security model within the SMB server of Samba is most like anonymous FTP?

    a. server

    b. share

    c. user

    d. domain

23. What is the principal concern with using SWAT to configure the Samba suite across a network connection?

24. From which page of SWAT can you restart the `smbd` and `nmbd` server daemons?

    a. Global

    b. Shares

    c. Home

    d. Status

25. Which Linux command-line program can be used to display the names of the shares on an SMB server?

   a. `smbmount`

   b. `winmount`

   c. `smbclient`

   d. `getsmb`

5

HANDS-ON PROJECTS

**HANDS-ON
PROJECTS**

Project 5-1

In this project, you experiment with the FTP client program, `ftp`. The steps describe the procedure on Fedora Core 3, but the steps should be substantially equivalent on any Linux distribution running an FTP server. In particular, the `ftp` client program does not vary between distributions.

For this project, you should work in teams; one Linux system should be designated as the FTP server and the other as the FTP client. You should have root access to the FTP server system.

1. On the server, create a document tree for anonymous FTP testing using this command:

   `cp -r /usr/share/doc/pam-0.77/* /var/ftp/pub`

2. Make sure that the FTP server daemon is running by entering the following command:

   `/etc/init.d/vsftpd start`

3. On the client Linux system, log on with the `ftp` command using the name of the server system. Enter **ftp** as the username when prompted.

4. When prompted for your password, enter **ftp** as your username again, not your e-mail address.

5. Describe what happens.

6. Log off of the FTP client using the **bye** command, then start it again as in Step 2.

7. Use the username **anonymous** this time (it is equivalent to the username ftp).

8. When prompted, enter your e-mail address correctly as the password.

9. Enter the **help** command to see a list of `ftp` commands. Do you recognize many of these from your previous work at the Linux command line?

10. Choose a command that you haven't seen before and use the `help` command to see a one-line description of it. For example, if you want to learn about the `mdelete` command, enter:

    help mdelete

11. Change to the `/pub/html` directory on the FTP server. (This assumes you copied the files from the `pam-0.77` directory in Step 1.)

    cd pub/html

12. List the files in the directory. Next, retrieve a file from the directory by entering `get pam.html`. The file is downloaded to the client computer and placed in the current directory.

13. Choose a file and try to rename it with the `rename` command in FTP:

    rename pam.html david.html

14. Why can't you do it?

15. Log off of the client.

16. On the server, use the `tail` command to view the last few lines of the transfer log:

    tail /var/log/xferlog

    You should see an entry for the `pam.html` file you downloaded in Step 13.

17. Also on the server, use the `tail` command to view the last few lines of the system message log, `/var/log/messages`. What do you see? How does this relate to the steps you completed previously?

18. Delete the files you copied in Step 1.

**HANDS-ON
PROJECTS**

Project 5-2

In this project, you continue to experiment with FTP. The chapter text described the `wu-ftp` software because it is used by most UNIX-based FTP sites, and Linux certification programs still test your knowledge about it. However, Fedora Core 3 does not include `wu-ftpd`. It includes `vsftpd` instead, which is a more secure program.

The following steps describe the procedure on Fedora Core 3, but they should be substantially equivalent for any Linux distribution using `vsftpd` as the FTP server. To complete this project, you should have the FTP server and client programs installed and should have completed Project 5-1 so that you have a set of files in the `/var/ftp/pub` directory.

For this project you should work in teams; one Linux system should be designated as the FTP server and the other as the FTP client. You should have root access to the FTP server system.

1. On the server, edit the /etc/vsftpd/vsftpd.conf file. Modify the line that begins with #ftpd_banner to something like the following:

   ftpd_banner Welcome to the Simpleton Chamber of Commerce

   Note that you must remove the # at the start of the line.

2. Save the file and exit the text editor.

3. Restart the FTP server:

   killall -HUP vsftpd

4. On the client, create a temporary directory and then change to it.

   mkdir ~/temp
   cd ~/temp

5. Log on to the FTP server using the anonymous user. You'll see a line like the following one when you're prompted to log on:

   220 **Welcome to the Simpleton Chamber of Commerce**

6. Change to the /pub/html directory.

7. Turn off interactive mode by entering **prompt off**.

8. Download all the files in the html directory by entering **mget ***.

9. Exit the FTP client by entering **bye**.

10. Enter **ls** and notice that all the files from the FTP server are now in your local directory.

11. To read about the many configuration statements you can use to configure vsftpd, consult the vsftpd.conf man page.

12. Delete the directory you created in Step 4.

HANDS-ON PROJECTS

Project 5-3

In this project, you experiment with the NFS protocol. The steps describe the procedure on Fedora Core 3, but they should be substantially equivalent for any Linux distribution. To complete this project, you should have the NFS daemons installed.

For this project you should work in teams; one Linux system should be designated as the NFS server and the other as the NFS client. You should have root access to both systems.

1. On the server, edit the /etc/exports file and add the following lines, substituting the host name of your client system for *danielle*. One share is read-only and the other is read-write:

   ```
   /usr/share/doc    danielle(all_quash,ro)
   /tmp              danielle(all_quash,rw)
   ```

2. On the client, log on as root and create a mount point directory for the NFS server's /usr/share/doc directory:

   mkdir /mnt/docs

3. On the client, create a mount point directory for the NFS server's /tmp directory. The following example creates the mount point directory below the /mnt/docs directory:

   mkdir /mnt/docs/tmp

4. On the client, mount the /usr/share/doc share, substituting the name of your server for *chris*:

   mount chris:/usr/share/doc /mnt/docs

5. On the client, mount the /tmp share:

   mount chris:/tmp /mnt/docs/tmp

6. On the client, change to the /mnt/docs directory:

   cd /mnt/docs

7. You should be able to display all the files in the /usr/share/docs directory on the server with the ls command.

8. Try to create a file in the directory with a command such as **touch 123**. This should fail because the exports file on the server defines it as a read-only share.

9. Go to the /mnt/docs/tmp directory:

   cd /mnt/docs/tmp

10. Try to create a file in the directory with a command such as **touch 123**. This should work because the exports file on the server defines it as a read-write share.

11. Unmount the shares:

    cd /
    umount /mnt/docs/tmp
    umount /mnt/docs

12. On the server, remove the lines from the /etc/exports file that you added in Step 1.

HANDS-ON PROJECTS

Project 5-4

In this project, you experiment with printing using Samba. The steps describe the procedure on Fedora Core 3, but they should be substantially equivalent for any Linux distribution. To complete this project, you should have lpd installed and running, you should have Samba packages installed as described in the chapter text, and you should be familiar enough with the chapter materials to get Samba running as a server.

For this project, you should work in teams; one Linux system should be designated as the Samba server and the other as the Samba client. Your team should have root access to both systems.

1. On the server, use a printer configuration tool to set up a local Linux printer definition. The easiest way is to start the **printconf-gui** program, choose **New**, select a **LOCAL** printer type, and enter a name such as **printer1** to identify the printer. Complete this step even though you may not have a physical printer attached to your Linux system.

2. Also on the server, stop lpd from attempting to send print jobs queued to your new printer definition to a physical printer, in case one does not exist. Use the lpc command, like this:

lpc stop printer1

3. On the server, use the basic Samba configuration file shown in the chapter text, or similar settings, to get the Samba server up and running. Be certain you have a [printers] section. Create at least one user account to use for this project and assign it a password. You can use SWAT if you prefer not to hand edit the file.

4. On the client system, use the printconf-gui utility to define an SMB printer. Name the SMB printer definition printer2. Specify printer1 as the remote printer name on the Samba server; use the username, password, workgroup, or other data that you used to get the Samba server running.

5. On the client system, use the lpr command to print a text file to the SMB printer that you defined as printer2. You can use a graphical utility with a print function if you choose, but many Linux graphical programs do not list the available printers, so it may be easier to just print from a command line using a command like this one:

lpr -P printer2 /etc/termcap

6. Back on the server, use the lpq command to view the contents of the print queue for the local Linux printer that you defined as printer1. The command looks like this (you might also choose to try a graphical printer manager in KDE or GNOME):

lpq -P printer1

7. This shows that you have effectively printed from a Samba client to a Samba server; both sides acted as if the other side were a Windows-based host. Now use lprm to delete the print job on printer1.

8. Using the printconf-gui utility, delete the printer definitions that you created on the client and server.

5

Project 5-5

In this project, you experiment with Samba file transfers. The steps describe the procedure on Fedora Core 3, but they should be substantially equivalent for any Linux distribution. To complete this project, you should have Samba running as a server.

For this project, you should work in teams; one Linux system should be designated as the Samba server and the other as the Samba client. Your team should have root access to both systems.

1. Make certain the Samba server is running.

2. Log on to the SWAT Web page for your Samba server, as described in the chapter text. You can log on to the SWAT page with the *http://localhost:901/* address.

3. Within SWAT, alter the security method to be **share** and add a guest user account. To do this, click the **Globals** icon and change the Security item in the Security Options section.

4. On the Shares page, define a share called **Pub**.

5. Switch to a command prompt and copy some files to the directory that you defined as the location of the share. (Use the **cp -r** command.)

6. Log on to the client system and create a download directory.

7. From within the download directory that you created, log on to the Samba server using smbclient.

8. Download a few files from your /Pub file collection.

9. How does this process differ from using anonymous FTP? Is it easier to set up for the administrator? Does it seem easier for the end user? Does it seem more or less secure? If more secure, why might you still not use Samba?

10. Log off of the smbclient program and return to the server.

11. Review the contents of the log files you specified in your Samba server configuration (probably located in /var/log/samba). What information is recorded?

CASE PROJECTS

Case Project 5-1

Your work in Alaska has been such a success that word has spread. Island Associates, colleagues of Snow, Sleet, and Hale that are located in Los Angeles, want you to set up an FTP server for their maritime public records database, so that users around the country can download reports about how recently passed maritime laws might affect their rights.

1. They have given you the following rules for setting up the FTP server, based on their current Internet connectivity and security concerns.

   a. The individual reports are fairly small, but they don't think a user should be allowed to download more than 10 during one logon session, or a maximum of 10 MB of data.

   b. Anonymous FTP access should be restricted to 30 minutes per session.

   c. They have been having trouble with a group of users originating at the *no-law.org* domain, so you should block all access to that domain.

   Write the `ftpaccess` lines that will implement these rules. Refer to the `ftpaccess` man page for the correct directives and formatting. Don't include the entire `ftpaccess` file, but only the lines used to set up these requirements.

   ```
   file-limit out 10 all
   data-limit out 10000000 all
   limit-time anonymous 30
   deny no-law.org  /etc/deny.msg
   ```

2. Island Associates also wants all 15 of its staff to have access to the reports posted on the FTP site. They should be able to view the reports as part of their local filesystem rather than having to download them using FTP. This prevents having 15 copies of each report, which might lead to individual staff having different versions as the reports are updated. The office includes a central Linux server hosting the FTP server you created and several other network services. The server is *ftp.islandnet.com*. The office also has a Windows PC on each user's desk. Assume for a moment that each Windows PC has NFS client capabilities from previous configurations. Write out the configuration line(s) in `/etc/exports` to allow the users to mount and access the reports on the Linux server. Given that the reports are on the same server that is being used for anonymous FTP access, also write out a configuration for `/etc/hosts.allow` and `/etc/hosts.deny` to limit access to the server for the NFS server. Did you place all the reports in a single directory? Did you use the same directory as you did for anonymous FTP downloads? Why? Do you think you would use NFS if the Windows clients did not already have NFS clients installed? Why? If not, what would you use instead?

3. Island Associates has also asked for your help in setting up a small FTP server for reports originating from their branch office on Rarotonga in the Cook Islands. Because this will be a small server with limited resources, you decide to review other FTP servers to see how you can make the most effective use of the Rarotonga server. You are considering something that might combine several protocols, and maybe use Java or something similar to provide for remote administration of the server (the Cook Islands being a long flight from your office). Look up FTP servers on *www.sourceforge.net* or another Linux resources site that you prefer, and write a brief report on three programs that provide FTP server capabilities and that would be worth reviewing as a selection for this project. Include the advantages and risks associated with each program.

# CHAPTER 6

CONFIGURING MAJOR NETWORK SERVICES

After reading this chapter and completing the exercises, you will be able to:

♦ Expand the routing capabilities of your Linux server

♦ Understand the DHCP server

♦ Set up your own DNS name server

♦ Configure a basic e-mail server

♦ Understand how Linux can excel as a Web server

In this chapter, you will continue to explore network services that are commonly used on Linux systems. The previous chapter focused on file-sharing services. This chapter focuses on the services for which dedicated Linux servers are often used: routing, DNS, e-mail, and the Web.

In the first part of the chapter, you will learn about creating a Linux router with dynamic routing tables, building on the concepts you learned in Chapters 1 and 2. You will also learn about setting up a DNS server on Linux, so that you can resolve domain names without resorting to another DNS server on the Internet.

The second part of the chapter is devoted to e-mail server and Web server configuration. The discussion here will get you started with a basic configuration. Linux has a long tradition as a Web server platform; you'll learn how to set up a basic Web server and explore some of the many additional technologies that are available to expand a Web server's capability on Linux.

DYNAMIC ROUTING WITH ROUTING PROTOCOLS

In Chapter 2, you learned how routing is configured in the Linux kernel using the `route` command. You learned that each entry in the routing table contains the following elements:

- The target network or host to which the routing table entry applies; that is, the network or host that you can reach using the information in the entry.

- The network mask to use when calculating addresses for the target.

- The address of the next hop router, or, more simply put, the system to which packets are sent that are destined for the target network or host. (A **hop** refers to passing through a router to reach a final destination.)

- The network interface on which packets should be sent to reach the target network or host. For example, if there are three Ethernet cards installed, this part of the routing entry would specify one of those interfaces for each entry in the routing table.

The Linux kernel running on a given host uses the information in the routing table whenever packets arrive that have the host's MAC address (physical address of the network card) but another host's IP address. As long as IP forwarding is enabled, Linux routes packets to the next hop router until they eventually reach their destination.

The routing described thus far is called **static routing**. The routing table in your Linux kernel is assembled by entries in your start-up scripts or by `route` commands that you enter to update or modify the routing table. This is straightforward and effective for a small, reliable network, but static routing is not the best choice for larger networks and sometimes unreliable connections. In most routing situations, dynamic routing is used. **Dynamic routing** is the process of using a routing protocol to build and modify routing tables automatically based on information shared by the routers, without human intervention.

To see the value of dynamic routing, consider the networking configuration shown in Figure 6-1. Host Abe wants to reach host Bill. If static routing is used, Router 1 would have an entry showing that the Ethernet card connected directly to Router 2 was the correct way to reach host Bill. However, if something breaks the network connection between Router 1 and Router 2—for example, the phone connection is broken, or someone unplugs the wrong network cable in a server room—host Abe is unable to reach host Bill, even though host Bill *could* be reached via Router 3 and Router 4. With static routing, Router 1 can't find this out; a system administrator would need to learn of the problem, determine an alternate route, and enter the information at a command line. Later, when the problem was fixed, the original route directly to Router 2 would need to be entered in Router 1's routing table to keep the network operating as efficiently as possible.

On the other hand, if all four of the routers in Figure 6-1 are using a routing protocol, they will exchange information often about the networks that they are capable of reaching. Before a minute had passed, Router 3 would have informed Router 1 that packets for network A should be sent to it, passed on to Router 4, and then Router 2. Even on a large

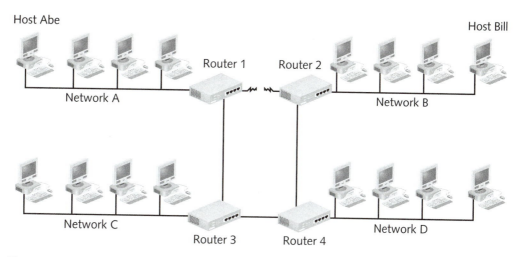

Figure 6-1   The need for dynamic routing

network, a well-configured routing protocol would have reestablished the connection between host Abe and host Bill via another route within a minute or two, without any administrator having to take action.

Many routing protocols are available, but only a few are widely used. Routing protocols are divided into two categories: interior and exterior. Although the difference can seem vague at the outset, loosely stated, **interior routing protocols** are those designed for routing packets among networks under your control. They route packets based on mathematical models. **Exterior routing protocols** are designed for routing packets between networks controlled by different organizations. They route packets based on administration policies, often controlled by how much a particular organization's routing information is trusted.

All routing protocols are designed to exchange information among routers. They use broadcast messages or other techniques to inform other routers of the networks that they know how to reach. For example, one router might send a message using a routing protocol that says, "I can reach network 198.60.12.0 in five hops." If another router sees that message and doesn't know how to reach the named network in four hops or less, it copies that information to its routing table. Then it can broadcast to other routers: "I can reach network 198.60.12.0 in six hops." (It adds one hop to reach the router from which it received the information.)

A packet typically passes through many routers (makes many hops) to reach its destination. You saw this when you experimented with the `traceroute` command in Chapter 2. In some routing protocols, the hop count is called the metric. In Chapter 2, however, you learned that a metric is an abstract numeric measure of how good a route is—a preference value as to whether a route should be selected if multiple routes are available.

All routing protocols have the same function: communicating among routers to find the most efficient route for network packets. Routing protocols are distinguished by the method they use to communicate routing information to other servers and the method they use to decide which route is best among several known routes. Several popular routing protocols are described in the sections that follow.

Routing Information Protocol (RIP) and `routed`

RIP, an interior routing protocol, is the oldest routing protocol still in common use. Its usefulness is limited to smaller networks or routing that is not highly complex. There are two versions of RIP: RIPv1 (version 1, described by RFC 1058) and RIPv2 (version 2, described by RFC 1723). RIPv1 does not provide support for classless IP addresses. RIPv2 does. Both versions of RIP can only handle routes with up to 15 hops between source and destination, making it unusable for networks the size of the Internet.

RIP defines the best route as the one with the lowest number of routers (hops) to reach the destination network. The cost of a route is a measure of how efficient it is; the route with the lowest cost should always be chosen. When RIP is started on a host (we'll call it Router 1), it broadcasts a request for routing information. Routers running RIP respond by sending all the entries from their routing table to Router 1. Router 1 populates its routing table with the entries it receives using a series of simple rules:

- If an entry refers to a network that is not in the routing table already, that route is added.
- If the **cost** (the number of hops) of a route is less than one already in its table, Router 1 substitutes the newly received route.
- If Router 1 receives a route with a cost of 15, the route is assumed to be unreachable and is deleted from Router 1's routing table.

RIP uses UDP port 520. It is implemented in Linux using a few daemons. The **routed** daemon is the most popular and is included with most Linux distributions. Other daemons are **gated**, **zebra**, and **bird**. To start `routed`, use the script in `/etc/rc.d/init.d` or start it directly using the command:

```
/usr/sbin/routed
```

The `routed` daemon immediately begins broadcasting requests for routing information and assembling routing table entries. `Routed` needs no command-line parameters and requires no configuration file. However, the default operation may not be to your liking. You can configure it with the `/etc/gateways` and `/etc/config/routed.options` files. Each line in the `/etc/gateways` file contains a routing table entry that looks like this example:

```
net 192.160.14.0 gateway 172.14.88.12 metric 1 active
```

The `net` and `gateway` numbers refer to the network ID and gateway used to reach that network. The `metric` is an initial "hop" value for the route. As you can see in the `/etc/gateways` example line, the network mask is not provided, so any network using classless IP addressing is unable to use the routing information correctly. Using RIP version 2 solves this one problem, but the better answer lies in using other routing protocols.

If you need to configure other aspects of `routed` operation, refer to the `routed` man page.

Open Shortest Path First (OSPF)

The Open Shortest Path First (OSPF) protocol is an interior routing protocol designed to work effectively even in very large networks. OSPF uses a technique called flooding. A router running OSPF periodically floods the network with everything it knows about its neighboring hosts. Other OSPF routers see information coming from other routers and use this data to intelligently construct a "chart" inside the router that defines the best way to reach the various networks. It's as if OSPF tries to let each router take the pulse of distant networks so that OSPF can determine which route to use for the most efficient connection from point A to point B.

To construct its virtual chart of networking connections, OSPF uses a mathematical technique formally called the Dijkstra Shortest Path First algorithm. OSPF is an open protocol (one everyone can use) that uses the Shortest Path First algorithm, hence its name.

OSPF uses a metric like RIP, but in OSPF the metric refers to how much better a given route is than other available routes to the same network. OSPF has no predefined limit on how many routers a packet can pass through to reach its destination. OSPF also lets you define authentication parameters to control which routers you accept routing data from, and lets you assign priorities to different routers on your network based on their capabilities (that is, you can send the most packets to the most powerful router on the fastest network connection available).

Relatively few Linux network administrators need to use OSPF. The larger, often nation-wide networks for which OSPF was designed generally rely on dedicated router hardware such as that provided by Cisco Systems. Nevertheless, Linux does support OSPF using a few daemons: `gated`, `zebra`, and `bird`. All of these daemons also support RIPv1 and RIPv2, and an external routing protocol called **Border Gateway Protocol (BGP)**.

The `gated` daemon used to be considered the replacement for `routed` because it also supports RIP. However, it was never protected by the general public license (GPL) or similar license and is now commercial software. Most Linux distributions will not include commercial software, requiring that you acquire it from the vendor. The home page for the `gated` daemon is *www.gated.org*. You should still know something about `gated` because Linux certification tests may still include it.

You configure `gated` using the file /etc/gated.conf. The format is similar to other configuration files, with sections devoted to each protocol you want to support and braces enclosing options for that protocol. To have `gated` run only RIP (not OSPF or BGP), use a simple /etc/gated.conf configuration file similar to this example:

```
rip yes  {
    broadcast;
    interface 192.168.10.3
        version 2
        multicast
        authentication simple "noSecrets";
};
```

6

This file causes gated to use RIP version 2, which supports classless IP addresses. The broadcast keyword indicates that the router should actively broadcast the routes that it knows about—it should participate in propagating RIP information with other RIP-capable routers on the network. The interface line defines a networking interface using the IP address of that interface. For that interface, multicast refers to how information is sent back to other RIP routers that request information. The simple authentication line defines a basic scheme for identifying routers on a common network. Numerous other examples and tips are provided in the complete gated documentation.

BGP

BGP is an external routing protocol designed for routing between major national networks. Initial configuration of BGP is not hard—that is, the configuration file is not long—but at this level, managing packet routing becomes very complex. In fact, some of the most highly specialized (and highly paid) Internet careers focus on the sometimes mundane task of keeping routers running efficiently.

To use BGP, you must have an autonomous system number to identify your organization to others with whom you will be exchanging routing information. You obtain this number from the Internet Assigned Names Authority (IANA). To learn more, visit *www.iana.org*, select Protocol Number Assignment Services, and scroll down to the section on autonomous system numbers, which is labeled "AS Numbers (Blocks of 1023 Numbers) (RFC 1930)."

BGP is implemented on Linux with the gated, zebra, and bird daemons.

Table 6-1 summarizes the routing protocols described in this section.

Table 6-1   Popular routing protocols

Protocol	Daemon	Comments
Routing Information Protocol (RIP)	routed, gated, zebra, and bird	The most basic interior routing protocol; of limited use because it does not support classless IP addresses
Routing Information Protocol (RIP) version 2	routed, gated, zebra, and bird	A popular interior routing protocol for small networks; supports classless IP addresses but does not scale well (for example, supports a maximum of 15 hops)
Open Shortest Path First (OSPF)	gated, zebra, and bird	The best choice for an interior routing protocol for small to large networks; scalable; distributes routing information by flooding the network periodically with all the routing information it has

Table 6-1 Popular routing protocols (continued)

Protocol	Daemon	Comments
Border Gateway Protocol (BGP)	`gated, zebra,` and `bird`	A widely used exterior routing protocol, used to route packets between organizations on the Internet and other very large networks; cannot be used until you obtain an autonomous system number from *www.iana.org*

DHCP SERVER

The DHCP server consists of the **dhcpd** daemon. You must configure it by creating or editing the /etc/dhcpd.conf file. This file contains information about the IP address ranges, lease times, broadcast address, gateway address, addresses of DNS servers, and many other options. Each time a client requests an IP address, the DHCP server is said to lease the address to the client for a specified time. After that time, the client must request a renewal of the lease, which may involve getting a different IP address. After being configured, however, the whole arrangement is transparent to the user on the client host. A sample dhcpd.conf file is shown here:

```
# Sample /etc/dhcpd.conf
default-lease-time 600;
max-lease-time 7200;
option subnet-mask 255.255.255.0;
option broadcast-address 192.168.1.255;
option routers 192.168.1.254;
option domain-name-servers 192.168.1.1, 192.168.1.2;
option domain-name "mydomain.org";

subnet 192.168.1.0 netmask 255.255.255.0 {
    range 192.168.1.10 192.168.1.100;
    range 192.168.1.150 192.168.1.200;
}
```

This file defines two ranges of addresses within the 192.168.1.0 network. Within these ranges, IP addresses are randomly assigned to any client that requests an address. You can tie a specific IP address to a specific host by using the MAC address of that host's Ethernet card. This is useful if you want to control the addresses of your servers using DHCP but the servers must have fixed addresses. The relevant portion of the configuration file looks like this:

```
host web {
    hardware ethernet c8:01:6a:3a:29:ff;
    fixed-address 192.168.1.5;
}
```

Many additional options are supported by dhcpd. You can refer to the dhcpd.conf man page for a list of these options. After you have the DHCP server configured, you can start it using the standard script in /etc/rc.d/init.d.

Recent versions of the DHCP server support a fault-tolerant configuration that allows more than one DHCP server to service a given network segment. This is documented in the dhcpd man page.

If you must have a graphical configuration tool for the DHCP server, you can use Webmin. Fedora Core does not have a graphical tool.

SETTING UP A DNS NAME SERVER

In Chapter 3, you learned how to configure the DNS resolver. This allows your computer to resolve DNS names of other Internet sites. If you run an Internet site, you'll need your own DNS names handled by DNS. Many people have their ISP provide them with DNS service, but better results can often be achieved by managing your own DNS. In this section, you will learn how to set up a DNS server on Linux.

DNS is central to the Internet. Every time someone enters a URL in a Web browser or an e-mail address in a mail client, a DNS server converts that name to one or more IP addresses, allowing the client system to send a packet directly to the remote server. The information in DNS can be thought of as an Internet-wide inverted hierarchical tree, as Figure 6-2 illustrates. The very top of the tree is called root and is represented by a period. The root is typically only referred to in regard to the **root name servers**—DNS servers that the organizations that run the Internet have designated as a starting point for DNS queries.

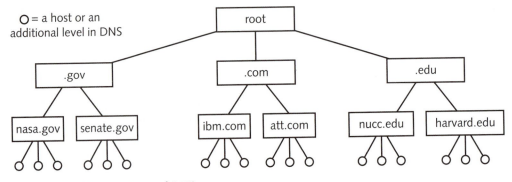

Figure 6-2   The structure of DNS

The last part of DNS names is referred to as the top-level domain or TLD. Common TLDs are the familiar .org, .com, .edu, .net, and about a dozen others. There are also more than 200 TLDs for countries, such as .us, .ca, and .ru. When you register a domain name, you must choose one of the TLDs for your name.

The following steps outline how the resolver on a host converts a DNS name to an IP address. Note that every DNS server caches, or stores, every DNS name-to-IP address resolution that it learns of. This example resolves the DNS name *alpha.nasa.gov*. This process is also illustrated in Figure 6-3.

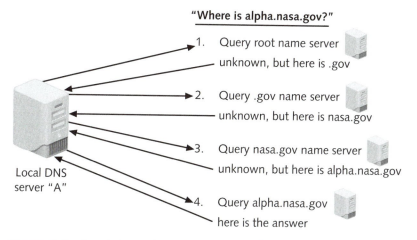

Figure 6-3   Resolving a domain to an IP address using DNS

1. The resolver on the client queries the DNS server that is configured in the /etc/resolv.conf file (call this DNS server A). If the client cannot reach any of the name servers listed in /etc/resolv.conf, the client gives up and the name cannot be resolved.

2. DNS server A receives the query from the client and checks both its own databases (stored in files on the DNS server, as you will soon see) and the names it has previously learned about and cached in memory. Not finding the requested domain anywhere, it looks to its list of root name servers (stored in memory, but taken from the DNS server configuration files described below) and sends the query to one of them.

3. The root name server receives the query and checks its cache. Seeing that it doesn't have the requested name, it says to DNS server A, in effect, "I don't know the IP address of *alpha.nasa.gov*, but I do know about the DNS server for the .gov domain. Try asking there."

4. DNS server A then asks the .gov DNS server the same question. The .gov DNS server responds, in effect, "I don't know the IP address of *alpha.nasa.gov*, but I do know the DNS server for the *nasa.gov* domain. Try asking there."

5. DNS server A asks the DNS server for *nasa.gov*, which checks its database of DNS records and responds, "The IP address of *alpha.nasa.gov* is 192.168.1.45."

Queries do not always involve all these steps. Some of these steps are skipped because of caching. Server A caches the DNS server address for the .gov domain the first time someone requests a .gov address. The *nasa.gov* DNS server caches most of the names within the *nasa.gov* domain, even if they are not permanently stored on the DNS server that you queried. Finally, if the example name were a Web site or some other frequently referenced location, the next time a query arrived for the same name, DNS server A would respond immediately with the in-cache information that it collected in the first query.

Anytime caching is used, you must consider how long information persists in the cache before it is considered too old and deleted. This is easily handled in DNS caches because each name has a time value called the Time to Live or TTL. The TTL specifies how long the name is allowed to be cached. For names that are not expected to change in the near future, the TTL can be set to a high value, such as one day. Names that could change at any time should have a shorter TTL, such as one hour or 10 minutes.

Another issue related to caching is the size of the DNS server's cache, which depends on the DNS software you use. The most popular software, BIND, expands its cache to fit all the records that must be cached. You can restrict the cache size with a statement in the BIND configuration file.

From the example steps given previously, you also get a sense that for each domain, a specific server is designated to provide answers about that domain. The root DNS servers are operated by the Internet Engineering Task Force (IETF), but a commercial domain such as the *ibm.com* domain is managed and controlled by IBM Corp. Likewise, if you obtain your own domain name, *mysmallbusiness.com*, you are in charge of maintaining DNS servers for that domain whether you operate the servers or someone else (your ISP) does. Without such a server, no one will be able to find your hosts and your domain name will have little value to you. The DNS servers for a domain provide authoritative information about that domain. These servers are often referred to as **authority servers**.

One of the authority servers is called a **master**. It is the one that you manage directly by editing the **zone file** for your domain. Other authority servers are **slaves**. Slaves periodically synchronize to the master by downloading a copy of the master's zone file.

It's a good idea for authority servers for a particular domain to be physically remote from one another. A power or Internet outage that affects one is less likely to affect the others.

 The terms "master" and "slave" are a sensitive issue for some people, so the terms "primary" and "secondary" may also be used when referring to DNS servers. The keywords used in the configuration files, however, are `master` and `slave`.

When DNS names are converted to IP addresses, this is called a **forward lookup**. When IP addresses are converted to a DNS name, this is called a **reverse lookup**.

Reverse lookups are commonly used to log information about requests. For example, later in this chapter you will learn about Web server logs. These logs normally have the IP address of each host requesting a Web page. Optionally, you can configure the Web server to store the DNS name of every requester by doing a reverse lookup on the IP address.

Reverse lookups are also used as a security measure to prevent **spoofing**. Spoofing occurs when a remote host masquerades as another host. Forward and reverse lookups, used together, can protect against spoofing by matching a remote host's IP address to its DNS name. Suppose a remote host sends a packet from 192.168.1.34. The server receiving the request does a reverse lookup on the address, and the answer is *waldo.arpa.net*. Next, a forward lookup on that name reveals that the IP address should be 10.244.13.2. The addresses don't match and the remote host is likely trying to spoof the server. The server can discard the request.

Reverse lookups use odd-looking queries. For example, a reverse lookup for the address 192.168.24.15 uses this query: 15.24.168.192.in-addr.arpa. The numbers in the IP address are reversed and the domain in-addr.arpa is appended.

> Many network administrators don't bother setting up reverse lookups. The penalty is that hosts on your network will be unable to contact some outside servers because those servers cannot check for spoofing.

Setting Up a Basic Name Server

Several Linux daemons behave as DNS servers. The most popular is called BIND—the Berkeley Internet Name Domain. Others include tinydns, PowerDNS, NSD, and MaraDNS. You'll need to know BIND if you take a Linux certification test, so it is the focus here.

BIND is a collection of programs that implement the DNS protocol. If you selected the name server component when installing Fedora Core Linux, the BIND daemon, called **named**, is installed. You will also have bind-conf, which provides a graphical configuration utility described later in this section; bind-utils, a collection of command-line utilities for querying name servers; and caching-nameserver, a set of simple configuration files that make named ready to run.

A **caching name server** is not an authority server. It simply queries other DNS servers and caches the results. By running your own caching name server, you ensure that all queries are cached close to your users and DNS performance is high. This is especially useful when slow data links, such as dial-up modems, are used.

> One program that can act *only* as a caching name server (it can't be an authority server) is dnscache, part of the djbdns package. It is much smaller and faster than named. You can find this package at *http://cr.yp.to*. It is not included in Linux distributions because its licensing is vague, though it is free to download and use.

Most Linux distributions include the named daemon. It is normally controlled via a system script in /etc/rc.d/init.d, though you must set up the configuration files as described in the following section before starting it. The latest version of BIND is version 9.

BIND is widely used, is difficult to configure properly, and occasionally suffers from security issues. This makes it vulnerable to attack. You must keep up to date with BIND security announcements and apply patches when they become available. If you're unwilling to do this, it's best to use a DNS server that is less likely to be successfully attacked. Tinydns (part of the djbdns package) is frequently used when DNS administrators need a more secure DNS server.

The basic /etc/named.conf file provided by the Fedora Core caching-nameserver package is a good place to start. An example file is shown here:

```
// generated by named-bootconf.pl

options {
        directory "/var/named";
        /*
         * If there is a firewall between you and name
         * servers you want to talk to, you might need
         * to uncomment the query-source directive
         * below. Previous versions of BIND always
         * asked questions using port 53, but BIND 8.1
         * uses an unprivileged port by default.
         */
        // query-source address * port 53;
};

//
// a caching only nameserver config
//
controls {
        inet 127.0.0.1 allow { localhost; } keys
        { rndckey; };
};
zone "." IN {
        type hint;
        file "named.ca";
};

zone "localhost" IN {
        type master;
        file "localhost.zone";
        allow-update { none; };
};

zone "0.0.127.in-addr.arpa" IN {
        type master;
        file "named.local";
        allow-update { none; };
};

include "/etc/rndc.key";
```

This file is divided into five sections: `options`, `controls`, three different `zones`, and an `include` line, which refers to the `rndc` security key file. The only non-comment line in the `options` section is the `directory` line, which identifies where all the `named`-related files are stored. This line is required. Each filename referred to in `named.conf` is relative to the directory `/var/named`. You can include many other options in this section, but only the `directory` line is critical at this point.

The `controls` section defines who can control the running name server using the `rndc` control program. Although you can start and stop the name server using the script in `/etc/rc.d/init.d`, the **rndc** control program is the preferred method of reinitializing the name server and handling various other administration tasks. It can control the name server remotely over a TCP network connection, but the `controls` section here permits only `localhost` to control the name server. To use `rndc`, an `rndc` key is used. The `controls` section refers to this key, which is specifically named in the `key` section of the file (via the `include` line at the end). The contents of the file are shown here:

```
key "rndckey" {
        algorithm        hmac-md5;
        secret
"LfuzfpIleaIDuyqzTHrOGnuAZDtyOvuOvFbaHXPU0sizqgnQEAJpII0UK  DIf";
};
```

To use `rndc`, the same key must be present on both the client and server end of the connection. Because only the `localhost` computer is allowed to use `rndc` in this configuration, this presents no problem. The `rndc` key for the server is stored in the `/etc/rndc.key` file shown previously; the key used by the client is stored in the `/etc/rndc.conf` file.

A **forwarding name server** forwards all queries to another name server for processing. This allows an administrator to concentrate queries from multiple DNS servers into just a few servers, taking advantage of the cached entries on those servers to reduce response times and lighten the load on your network. Forwarding can be implemented in the `options` section of the `named.conf` file by specifying the DNS server or servers to which queries should be forwarded:

```
forward first;
forwarders  {
     10.0.5.1;
     10.0.4.1;
}
```

The remaining sections of the `named.conf` file define three zones. A **zone** is a part of the DNS domain tree for which the DNS server has authority to provide information. Including a zone in `named.conf` indicates that information about that zone is provided in the files on the server. Other zones are accessed as described previously, and the results are stored in memory. Part of a zone might be delegated to another name server. For example, if name server B is authoritative for *ibm.com*, it might refer you to another name server for the *research.ibm.com* domain if *research.ibm.com* is not part of the zone of authority for name server B. The format of each zone section is shown here:

```
zone "domain-name" IN {
various options
};
```

The IN keyword indicates that this refers to an Internet-type zone. Other types of zones exist, but are historic—you are unlikely to use them. BIND assumes IN by default, so you do not have to include it. The three configuration lines you see in the zones defined in named.conf are type, file, and allow-update. The type line defines what type of information is provided for the named zone.

For the root zone, ".", a hints file is provided. The hints file, given in the file line, contains a list of the Internet root servers. The other two zones are master zones for the given domain. If you had agreed to act as a slave server for a friend, you would include a zone section for her domain with the type set to slave. The file line defines the local zone file where records for that zone are stored. Finally, the allow-update line defines which hosts can make dynamic changes to the zone. This is set to none, meaning that dynamic changes cannot be made. This is the most secure setting.

Both of the master zones in this file refer to localhost, which is the local loopback interface in the computer. One zone is for forward lookups and the other is for reverse lookups. You'll need an additional zone for your domain name. The following is an example for the network 192.168.24.0, for which *myplace.com* is the domain name. You can name the files anything you choose, but it's traditional to use the domain name and IP address, as shown here, to avoid confusion.

```
zone "myplace.com" IN {
      type master;
      file "myplace.com";
      allow-update { none; };
};

zone "24.168.192.in-addr.arpa" IN {
      type master;
      file "192.168.24.0";
      allow-update { none; };
};
```

The network IDs used in this chapter are private network IP addresses used only as examples. You should substitute your real addresses.

CAUTION

Next, you can examine the zone files. The first is the file containing a list of root name servers that is traditionally called named.ca, but it can be called whatever you like. The first few non-comment lines of this file are shown here:

```
.                        518400    NS    A.ROOT-SERVERS.NET.
A.ROOT-SERVERS.NET.      3600000   A     198.41.0.4
.                        518400    NS    B.ROOT-SERVERS.NET.
B.ROOT-SERVERS.NET.      3600000   A     128.9.0.107
.                        518400    NS    C.ROOT-SERVERS.NET.
C.ROOT-SERVERS.NET.      3600000   A     192.33.4.12
.                        518400    NS    D.ROOT-SERVERS.NET.
D.ROOT-SERVERS.NET.      3600000   A     128.8.10.90
.                        518400    NS    E.ROOT-SERVERS.NET.
E.ROOT-SERVERS.NET.      3600000   A     192.203.230.10
.                        518400    NS    F.ROOT-SERVERS.NET.
F.ROOT-SERVERS.NET.      3600000   A     192.5.5.241
.                        518400    NS    G.ROOT-SERVERS.NET.
G.ROOT-SERVERS.NET.      3600000   A     192.112.36.4
```

Each of these lines is a resource record. A **resource record** defines the answer given when its name is queried. Each resource record has this general format:

name   *time-to-live*   *type-of-record*   *information*

Two types of resource records are used in the named.ca file just shown: NS records and A records. An **NS record** defines the authoritative name server for the given zone. An **A record** defines the IP address for the given name. The first line in the file specifies that one of the authoritative name servers for the DNS root, ".", is A.ROOT-SERVERS.NET. The second line specifies its IP address as 198.41.0.4. The NS records specify a TTL of 518,400 seconds, or exactly six days. The A records specify a TTL of 3,600,000 seconds, or about 41 days.

The IP addresses of the root name servers change over time, so you should update this file every few months. The easiest way to keep this file up to date is to use the dig program, as in this example:

```
dig @f.root-servers.net  .  ns  > /var/named/named.ca
```

Next take a look at a master zone file for the domain *myplace.com*:

```
$TTL        86400
$ORIGIN     myplace.com.
@                   SOA  ns1.myplace.com.  beth.myplace.com. (
                          20050214            ; serial
                          3H                 ; refresh
                          15M                ; retry
                          1W                 ; expire
                          1D )               ; minimum

            NS        ns1.myplace.com.
            NS        ns1.yourplace.com.
```

```
                       A              192.68.24.15
                       MX     10    mail.myplace.com.
mail            A              192.168.24.30
ns1             A              192.168.24.40
www         A           192.168.24.15
```

Understanding zone files can be challenging. A single misplaced period can prevent a host name from resolving. You can review the comprehensive documentation on BIND in the directory /usr/share/doc/bind-*version#*/arm (the Administrator's Resource Manual).

In the previous example, the first two lines are directives. The $TTL directive indicates that the default Time to Live for all resource records is 86,400 seconds or 24 hours. The $ORIGIN directive specifies, in this case, the domain name. Any names in the file that are not fully qualified will have the $ORIGIN name appended to them. For example, the resource record for the name *mail* will become *mail.myplace.com* when the $ORIGIN is applied.

The **SOA record** (start of authority) describes how to use the information provided for this zone. The @ symbol used within a zone file indicates the current origin. The name *ns1.myplace.com* is the name of the master server. The name *beth.myplace.com* is the e-mail address to which questions should be sent regarding this DNS zone. The format of the e-mail address here is odd, because the @ symbol is replaced by a dot. Anyone looking at this file or the SOA record would know that *beth.myplace.com* is really *beth@myplace.com*.

The next four numeric values in the SOA record have to do with BIND zone transfers. A **zone transfer** occurs when a slave server requests a copy of the zone file and the master server sends it. The first number, labeled `serial` in the comments, is used to indicate whether the file has been altered and thus needs to be copied to a slave server. Traditionally, the format of the number is the year, month, and day when the zone file was last updated, followed by two digits to indicate the number of the change that day.

It is not necessary to use this format. You can use simple numbers. You can start with 1 when you create the zone file and increment the value by one whenever you make a change.

The slave server checks the serial number to see whether it is a higher number than the copy of the zone file it has. If it is a newer copy, the slave initiates a zone transfer. Every time you make a change to a zone file, you must update the serial number; if you don't, the update is ignored by the slave server.

The `refresh` interval (three hours here) defines how often the slave server checks to see if the master has been updated. If that check fails, the slave retries according to the `retry` interval (every 15 minutes here) until the `expire` interval has passed (one week here). At that point, the slave server stops answering queries for that zone.

The last number, labeled `minimum` in the comments, is the minimum TTL for the records in the file.

Whenever a record begins with white space, its name is the same name as the previous record. The NS, A, and MX records that immediately follow the SOA record start with white space, so their name is the same as the $ORIGIN.

The **MX record** specifies the mail exchanger for the zone. MX records are used by Mail Transfer Agents (MTAs) to find the correct e-mail server to contact when delivering e-mail to a recipient. The 10 before the name of the e-mail server indicates a preference value. You could have multiple MX records for a zone. If there was another MX record with a preference value of 20, MTAs would try to deliver mail to the mail exchanger with the lowest preference value. MTAs would only deliver mail to mail exchangers with higher preference values if lower-value mail exchangers were unavailable.

Another commonly used resource record type is the **CNAME record** (for canonical name), which is used to create an alias. For example, suppose you have a single server on your network that runs an FTP server, an e-mail server, and a Web server. You want to use names that correspond to these purposes, even though they all run on the same server. The following lines define an IP address for the main server using an A record, followed by aliases for ftp, mail, and www that refer to the main server.

```
main     A       192.168.24.1
ftp      CNAME   main
mail     CNAME   main
www      CNAME   main
```

CNAME records must refer to A records, not another CNAME record.

CAUTION

You can have resource records of the same type and the same name. A practical example may be that you have several Web servers containing identical information that handle a large volume of Web traffic. Each of the Web servers will have the same name but different IP addresses. When the server receives a query for the name *www.myplace.com*, named responds with four A records. The following lines illustrate such a configuration:

```
www     A     192.168.100.5
www     A     192.168.100.6
www     A     192.168.100.7
www     A     192.168.100.8
```

Next, let's briefly look at a reverse lookup file for a network 192.168.24.0:

```
$TTL      86400
$ORIGIN        24.168.192.in-addr.arpa.
@      SOA     ns1.myplace.com.  beth.myplace.com.  (
                             2005021400 ; Serial
                             28800      ; Refresh
                             14400      ; Retry
                             3600000    ; Expire
                             1D )    ; Minimum
       NS      ns1.myplace.com.
15     PTR     www.myplace.com.
30     PTR     mail.myplace.com.
```

```
40      PTR     ns1.myplace.com.
50      PTR     ed.myplace.com.
51      PTR     diana.myplace.com.
52      PTR     bj.myplace.com.
53      PTR     jim.myplace.com.
50      PTR     ken.myplace.com.
```

This zone file is similar to a forward lookup zone file except that most of the records are PTR records. A **PTR record** "points" to the name to which an IP address is assigned.

Table 6-2 summarizes the types of resource records presented in this section. Many others are supported, as well as dozens of options in the /etc/named.conf file. Setting up a DNS server can be challenging, but it is an important part of most administrators' work. All users rely on DNS; plus, DNS can present serious security holes if incorrectly configured. To learn more about setting up a DNS server, review the documentation in /usr/share/doc/bind-*version#* or a similar documentation directory on your distribution. Also review the man pages for named, named.conf, and the related utilities described in the following sections, such as dig and nsupdate.

Table 6-2   Common DNS resource record types

Resource Record Type	Defines:
A	An IP address associated with a name
CNAME	An alias for a name
MX	The mail exchanger: the host that accepts e-mail
NS	The authoritative name server for the given domain
PTR	The name associated with an IP address
SOA	The zone name, e-mail address of the administrator, and zone transfer parameters

Managing the named Server

After you have the /etc/named.conf configuration file and the appropriate zone files set up in /var/named, you can start the named daemon by entering /usr/sbin/named. More likely, you will want to use the script in /etc/rc.d/init.d. You can also use the same script to restart the server if you make changes to the files.

The rndc utility mentioned previously is provided with the BIND package and is used to control it from a command line without reloading. The rndc utility can operate over a network connection, but is used only locally by default.

You use the rndc command to reload configuration files, write out a status file, or perform other tasks, as described in the man page. The command you are most likely to use is the following one, to reload the /etc/named.conf configuration file and all zone files:

```
rndc reload
```

TIP If your name server does not seem to be working properly, one technique is to restart it and then review the messages in the system log: /var/log/ messages. The named daemon writes copious messages when a problem occurs in reading the configuration or zone files.

Using Command-line Utilities

Three popular programs are used for testing DNS: host, **nslookup**, and dig. The host program is useful for casual testing and for use in scripts. The nslookup and dig programs are used for more comprehensive testing but can also be used in scripts. The nslookup program is considered obsolete by many DNS experts, and dig should be used instead. Though obsolete, nslookup is still shipped with Windows (dig is not), so many people still use it.

Using host

A simple use of the **host** command is to do a forward lookup by entering a DNS name:

```
host igor.alcpress.com
igor.alcpress.com has address 69.30.87.202
```

You can do a reverse lookup by entering an IP address:

```
host 69.30.87.202
202.87.30.69.in-addr.arpa domain name pointer igor.alcpress.com
```

There are many command-line options. The –v option (verbose) produces more detailed output:

```
host -v igor.alcpress.com
Trying "igor.alcpress.com"
;; ->>HEADER<<- opcode: QUERY, status: NOERROR, id: 3578
;; flags: qr rd ra; QUERY: 1, ANSWER: 1, AUTHORITY: 0,
ADDITIONAL: 0

;; QUESTION SECTION:
;igor.alcpress.com.        IN    A

;; ANSWER SECTION:
igor.alcpress.com.   171   IN    A    69.30.87.202

Received 51 bytes from 69.30.87.201#53 in 0 ms
```

The –C option is useful for checking to see if all servers are running with the same copy of the zone file. It queries all name servers that are authoritative for a zone and displays their SOA records:

```
host -C lpi.org
Nameserver server1.moongroup.com:
    lpi.org SOA ns.starnix.com. dns.starnix.com. 2004091700 3600
1800 3600000 600
```

```
Nameserver ns.starnix.com:
     lpi.org SOA ns.starnix.com. dns.starnix.com. 2004091700 3600
1800 3600000 600
```

The serial number (2004091700) is the same for both servers, so you can assume they're using the same zone file.

Other command-line options for the host program are documented in the man page.

Using dig

The **dig** program lets you extract information from the zone files of DNS servers for domains in which you are interested. You can query for specific types of resource records, and you can direct your query to a specific DNS server, instead of always starting with the server listed in your /etc/resolv.conf file. A simple dig query looks like this:

dig www.npr.org

A more complex query looks like this:

dig @ns.xmission.com www.xmission.com any

This query goes directly to the DNS server *ns.xmission.com*, looking for information about *www.xmission.com*. It returns all types of records for that address, including NS, MX, A, CNAME, and other record types not included in this discussion. The output from the preceding command is shown here:

```
; <<>> DiG 9.1.3 <<>> @ns.xmission.com www.xmission.com
any
;; global options:  printcmd
;; Got answer:
;; ->>HEADER<<- opcode: QUERY, status: NOERROR, id: 2857
;; flags: qr aa rd ra; QUERY: 1, ANSWER: 2, AUTHORITY: 3,
ADDITIONAL: 4

;; QUESTION SECTION:
;www.xmission.com.            IN      ANY

;; ANSWER SECTION:
www.xmission.com.    3600   IN      MX      10 mail.xmission.com.
www.xmission.com.    3600   IN      A       198.60.22.4

;; AUTHORITY SECTION:
xmission.com.        3600   IN      NS      ns.xmission.com.
xmission.com.        3600   IN      NS      ns1.xmission.com.
xmission.com.        3600   IN      NS      ns2.xmission.com.

;; ADDITIONAL SECTION:
mail.xmission.com.   3600   IN      A       198.60.22.22
ns.xmission.com.     3600   IN      A       198.60.22.2
ns1.xmission.com.    3600   IN      A       198.60.22.22
ns2.xmission.com.    3600   IN      A       207.78.169.150
```

```
;; Query time: 381 msec
;; SERVER: 198.60.22.2#53(ns.xmission.com)
;; WHEN: Sat Apr 20 15:52:12 2002
;; MSG SIZE  rcvd: 188
```

The man page for dig describes the command-line options and output in full, but notice some of the features you see here:

- The first line shows the command you entered, so you can see what options created this output.

- A Question section summarizes what you asked for.

- An Answer section gives you the response data: the records corresponding to the requested domain name.

- An Authority section shows you the authoritative name servers for the domain of which the requested host is a part.

- The Additional section provides information that dig thinks might be useful.

- The summary information at the end shows how long this query took (381 milliseconds), which name server provided the information (including the IP address, port number, and FQDN), and the precise time of the query.

A utility that goes beyond dig and nslookup is **nsupdate**. This utility, referred to briefly earlier, lets you update zone files dynamically at the command line. It is an interactive utility with a separate command prompt. The following two sample commands remove all A records for a host and then add a new A record for that host:

```
nsupdate delete oldhost.example.com A
nsupdate add newhost.example.com 86400 A 172.16.1.1
```

See the nsupdate man page for further information on this utility.

You may sense at this point that you have only scratched the surface of DNS. Complex configurations, security and performance issues, and dozens of other topics can make DNS administration a full-time job for some networks. The documentation included in /usr/share/doc/bind-devel-*version*#/draft gives you some idea of the expansive nature of DNS. This folder contains working drafts by Internet engineers on topics such as refining DNS used with IPv6 (though IPv6 is already supported in named), using new security features such as DNSSEC, and relying on virtual domains to allow non-English speakers to access internationalized domain names without changing the English-only limitations of current DNS.

Using bindconf

A number of graphical utilities have been developed to help you configure the files described in this section. One of them is **bindconf**, which is part of the Fedora Core system-config-bind-2.0.3-1 package. You can start this program by entering bindconf at the command line. The main window of bindconf is shown in Figure 6-4.

It includes a line for each zone file, but immediately after you install Fedora Core, you only have localhost and localdomain forward zones and loopback-oriented reverse zones.

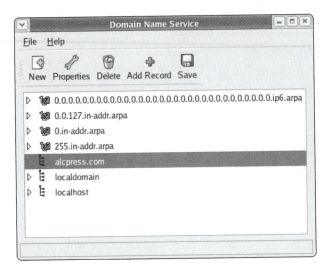

Figure 6-4   The main window of `bindconf`

From this window you can create a new zone by choosing New. In the dialog box that appears, you select whether to create a forward master zone, a reverse master zone, or a slave zone. Figure 6-5 shows this dialog box.

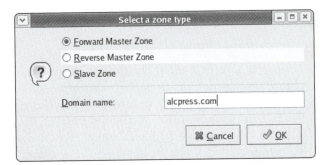

Figure 6-5   The Select a zone type dialog box in `bindconf`

NOTE   If you select Reverse Master Zone, the text box label changes to "IP Address (first 3 Octets)". This is acceptable if you're creating a reverse zone file for a /24 network, but is misleading if you want to create a reverse zone for a /16 network, for example. Ignore the label and enter the number of octets (bytes) that is appropriate for your zone.

When you select the appropriate zone type, you'll see a dialog box like the one in Figure 6-6. You'll see the same dialog box if you select the zone later from the main window. For forward DNS zones, the dialog box is labeled Name to IP Translations. The fields in the top part of the dialog box include the SOA record information, but you must manually change the serial number if you make a change. You access the refresh numbers for zone transfers via the Time Settings button.

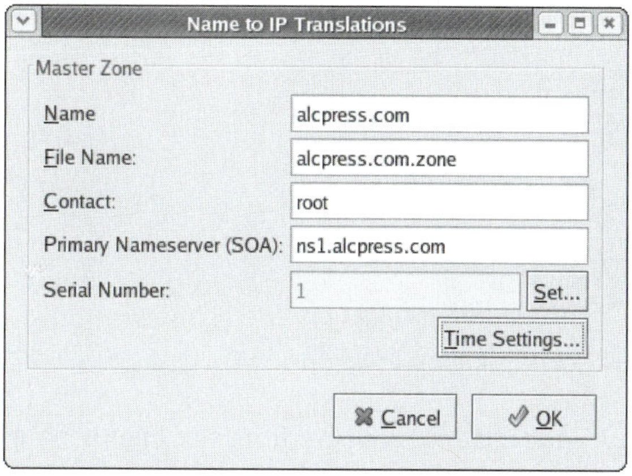

Figure 6-6 Editing forward zone information in bindconf

From the main bindconf window, you can select a zone and click the Add Record button to add a record to the zone. You see a screen like the one in Figure 6-7. Use the Host tab to create A records, the Alias tab to create CNAME records, the Nameserver tab to create NS records, and the Mail Exchange tab to create MX records.

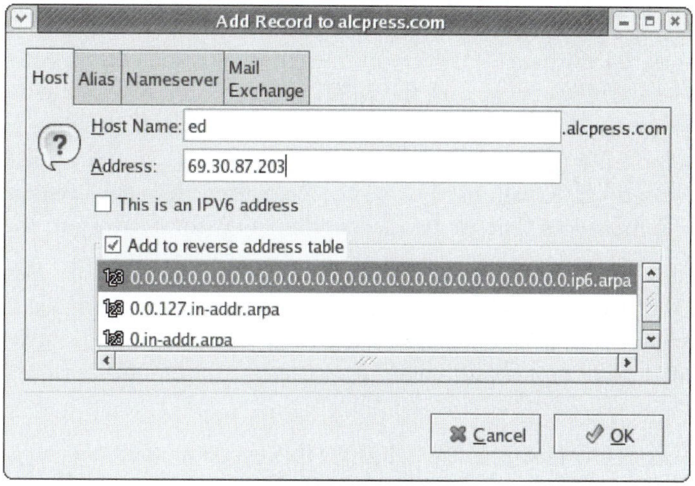

Figure 6-7 Adding a new record in bindconf

If you select a reverse DNS file in the main window of bindconf and then choose Edit, a different dialog box appears, as shown in Figure 6-8. The information here is similar to that used for the forward DNS files. The SOA information is shown at the bottom of the dialog box; IP addresses within the network ID and their corresponding names are listed at the top of the file.

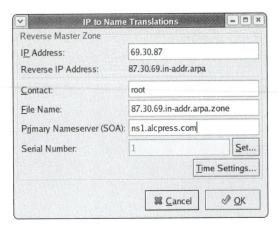

Figure 6-8   Editing a reverse DNS configuration in `bindconf`

After making any changes with `bindconf`, choose Save from the File menu to save your changes to the appropriate zone files.

Although `bindconf` is a handy tool for editing zone information and it avoids the problem of small typing errors causing big headaches for your DNS server, you should recognize that the tool is not useful unless you understand DNS. Also, this utility does not let you edit the main DNS configuration file, `named.conf`. At times, editing zone files with a text editor is best.

Configuring a Basic E-Mail Server

In Chapter 3, you learned how e-mail delivery on the Internet is structured. A Mail Transfer Agent (MTA) moves mail between servers; the MTA is commonly referred to as the e-mail server. A Mail Delivery Agent (MDA) such as `procmail` examines messages and delivers them to a user's mailbox file (such as `/var/spool/mail/nwells`). A Mail User Agent (MUA), such as Thunderbird, Kmail, `elm`, or `pine`, lets a user view the messages stored in the mailbox and create messages that are handed to the MTA for delivery to the recipient.

Earlier in this chapter, you also learned about a key component of how e-mail servers operate: They use DNS to request the mail exchanger for a recipient. For example, if you send an e-mail message to *quong@teranet.com*, your e-mail server must find out which server should receive e-mail destined for *teranet.com*. It does this by asking DNS for the MX record for *teranet.com*.

After the correct mail exchanger is located using DNS, your e-mail server can initiate a connection using SMTP and begin sending all messages destined for any domains that are handled by that mail exchanger.

SMTP has been extended since its original introduction, so you may see occasional references to the Extended Simple Mail Transfer Protocol, ESMTP. Most administrators just refer to SMTP.

E-Mail Servers

A number of e-mail servers are available for Linux. The classic and best known is `sendmail`. Most Linux distributions include `sendmail`, and it is often installed by default. Sendmail has had security problems, and many system and network administrators want a more secure alternative. A few popular alternatives have been designed specifically to be more secure than `sendmail`:

- Qmail (*www.qmail.org/top.html*)
- Postfix (*www.postfix.org*)
- Exim (*www.exim.org*)

Postfix is probably the most popular of these alternatives among Linux administrators, but Linux certification tests still ask about `sendmail`, so this section focuses on `sendmail`.

The `sendmail` program is installed on Fedora Core using three separate software packages. The `sendmail-8.13.1-2` package contains the `sendmail` daemon and is the only package that is required to use `sendmail`. The other two are `sendmail-cf-8.13.1-2`, which contains configuration examples and helper programs, and `sendmail-doc-8.13.1-2`, which contains documentation for the server. You should install all three if you intend to run `sendmail`. The `sendmail-doc` package is not installed automatically.

Sendmail is started using a standard script in `/etc/rc.d/init.d`. You can use the `start`, `stop`, `restart`, and `status` commands to control the daemon. The start-up parameters of `sendmail` are controlled by information stored in the `/etc/sysconfig/sendmail` file. By default, the file contains the following lines with Fedora Core:

```
DAEMON=yes
QUEUE=1h
```

The first statement instructs `sendmail` to run as a daemon. The parameter `QUEUE=1h` tells `sendmail` to attempt to send stored messages each hour.

Starting `sendmail` takes a few moments. If the start-up script hesitates rather than starting `sendmail`, check that your host name is correctly defined in your `/etc/hosts` file. By default, `sendmail` uses this to determine the host on which it is operating, information that it must have.

The operation of sendmail is configured using the file /etc/mail/sendmail.cf. You should review this file briefly using a read-only tool such as less so you won't accidentally change its contents. The sendmail.cf file is widely considered to be the most difficult configuration file to master. You can study the comments in this file and the documentation for sendmail to learn how the file is organized. Some administration tasks may require you to edit this file directly. The file README.cf acts as an online manual for the sendmail.cf file. It contains more than 3000 lines of text. This file is installed at /usr/share/doc/sendmail after you have installed the sendmail-doc package.

If people had to configure sendmail by editing the complicated sendmail.cf file, sendmail would not be popular. Most e-mail administrators instead edit a simpler configuration file, /etc/mail/sendmail.mc, and use the **m4** macro processor program to create the sendmail.cf file. After you create or modify the sendmail.cf file, you execute the following command (assuming the current directory is /etc/mail):

```
m4 sendmail.mc > sendmail.cf
```

Although the sendmail.mc file is simpler than the sendmail.cf file, it is still not easy to use. When you look at its contents, you'll see many lines that start or end with dnl. The text dnl stands for "delete to new line," and is used at the start of a line to indicate that the line is a comment. It is also used at the end of lines that contain commands. The lines that actually configure sendmail are not easy to understand.

The default configuration provided with Fedora Core gives you a workable sendmail server environment, but you must make a few changes to use it as an Internet e-mail server. The rest of this section describes those changes, as well as some of the key features of e-mail servers in general, as implemented in sendmail. For a more detailed treatment of setting up the sendmail.mc file, refer to the README.cf file in /usr/share/doc/sendmail.

Setting up a sendmail configuration file is difficult, but managing any e-mail server is an ongoing challenge because of the nature of the Internet and e-mail. The configuration file for an e-mail server must contend with issues such as these:

- Many programs on many types of hosts are creating e-mail messages. All of these messages must be standardized to some degree so that e-mail servers around the world can understand their contents enough to deliver them correctly. This is handled in part by the so-called "rewriting rules" that are a default part of every sendmail.cf file.

- An organization may include numerous SMTP-based e-mail servers. Yet most organizations want to have a single point (a single address) that manages e-mail reception, to avoid naming conflicts and to present a coherent image to the public.

- All users want to send and receive e-mail without restrictions, but **spam** (unsolicited, advertisement-related e-mail) has become a problem not only for users but for e-mail servers. Spam can clog an e-mail server and frustrate users if the administrator doesn't take steps to stem its flow.

- Users want flexibility in how they create and read their e-mail. They want to have access to it from various hosts, they want their messages to be delivered quickly, and they want to be able to use the program of their choice to work with e-mail. None of these demands are unreasonable, but some require extra work in light of the other issues that face the administrator of an e-mail server.

Before we discuss specific options in the `sendmail.mc` file, consider the following scenario. Suppose you manage the network for a technology company that includes 50 employees, most of whom are technically savvy and have Linux systems at their desk. Many users choose to run `sendmail` because it provides powerful user configuration options. You also have a central e-mail server that is always connected to the Internet. All users receive their e-mail from this server, either by downloading it using POP3 in an e-mail program such as Mozilla or Thunderbird, or by having the mail transferred in some other way to their system (as described shortly). Figure 6-9 illustrates this scenario.

Now let's review some key sections of the `sendmail.mc` file as it might relate to this scenario. To begin, the default settings allow `sendmail` to accept e-mail only from the local host. This is controlled via the DAEMON_OPTIONS directive. To make `sendmail` accept mail from the Internet, you must insert `dnl` at the beginning of that line so that other servers can connect to your copy of `sendmail`.

If you were configuring Host A in Figure 6-9, you might choose to configure `sendmail` to accept e-mail only from the main e-mail server. In this case, you would not put `dnl` at the beginning of the line. You would modify the line as shown in the following code:

```
DAEMON_OPTIONS('Port=smtp,Addr=192.168., Name=MTA')
```

None of your changes in `sendmail.mc` take effect until you save the file. Run `m4` to create a new `sendmail.cf` file, and restart `sendmail`. Don't do this until you have reviewed all of the information in this section, especially if you are connected to the Internet.

You can receive mail for multiple domains. If you have only a few domains, you can use a command similar to this:

```
Cwmyplace.net myplace.com myplace.org
```

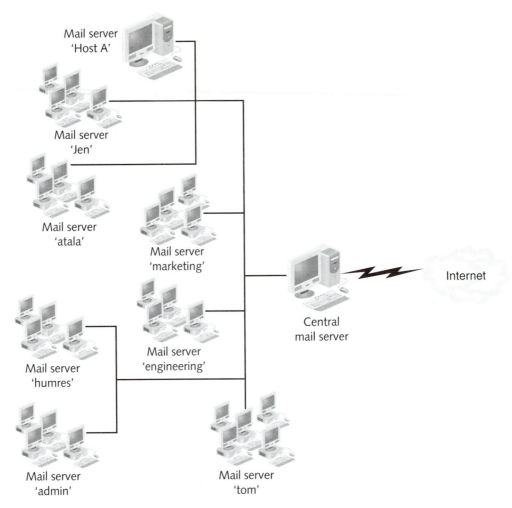

Figure 6-9   A corporate network with many e-mail servers

If you are hosting many domains, you can include the following line in the `sendmail.mc` file and list all the domains separately in the file `/etc/mail/local-host-names`:

`FEATURE(use_cw_file)dnl`

A common e-mail administration task is dealing with spam or messages you don't want to receive. One way of handling these messages is to use `sendmail`'s access database, which defines what to do with messages coming from various addresses. You can specify that the message be discarded without further action, accepted for delivery to the intended user, rejected with a message sent back to the sender, or any of several other options.

To use the access database, place entries in the `/etc/mail/access` file for mail that you want to handle specially. By default, the file contains a listing to indicate that e-mail from `localhost` should be relayed. (The overall settings of `sendmail` preempt this if you use the relay settings described previously.) Other examples that you could include in the access file are shown here:

```
spammers.net    DISCARD
unbelievableoffer.com    REJECT
```

The first line indicates that any message coming from *www.spammers.net* is discarded without further action. The second line prevents messages from *www.unbelievableoffer.com* from being delivered, but a message is returned to the sender stating that the message was not delivered. Generally, you should discard messages. Rejecting messages tells spammers that your e-mail address is valid. You can also include specific users. For example, if unwanted mail is originating from a particular user account, you can discard the mail by using the following line:

```
reduceyourmortgagedebt@aol.com    DISCARD
```

After you make a change to the access file, you must convert it to a database format so that `sendmail` can use it. The following command converts the `/etc/mail/access` text file into an `/etc/mail/access.db` database file that `sendmail` can use:

```
makemap hash /etc/mail/access < /etc/mail/access
```

NOTE The database format used in this example employs hashing techniques for fast retrieval of the information. An explanation of hashing is beyond the scope of this book.

As spam has become a larger problem, e-mail server administrators have taken more heavy-handed measures to protect their users from it. Many e-mail servers use **DNS Blacklists** or **dnsbls**. These are lists of sites that are known sources of spam. Adding the following line to the `sendmail.mc` file will use the *www.blackholes.mail-abuse.org* `dnsbl`:

```
FEATURE('dnsbl')dnl
```

You specify other `dnsbls` by specifying their names, like this:

```
FEATURE('dnsbl dnsbl.spammaster.net')dnl
```

You can use several `dnsbls` by adding multiple lines to the `sendmail.mc` file:

```
FEATURE('dnsbl bl.spamcop.net')dnl
FEATURE('dnsbl dnsbl.njabl.org')dnl
FEATURE('dnsbl sbl.spamhaus.org')dnl
```

The various `dnsbls` vary in how aggressively they list spam sites. Sites that send spam as well as non-spam messages are listed by some `dnsbls`, but not others. To learn which `dnsbls` are right for you, do some research on the Web. Use Google or another search engine to get started.

Using Forwarding and Aliases

In conjunction with the access database described previously, `sendmail` maintains a forwarding database. This lets you set up rules for how a user's e-mail is handled. A table of forwarding instructions is stored in the file `/etc/mail/virtusertable`. This table is useful for sites that accept e-mail for a number of different domains. For example, suppose you agree to act as the e-mail server for a user group with the domain name *sllug.org*. You want e-mail arriving for *sllug.org* to be redirected to the leader of the organization, who has an individual user account on your system. You could add the following line to the `virtusertable` file to set this up:

```
sllug.org jfreeman
```

Suppose that all e-mail for the support account on *sllug.org* should go to jfreeman, but he has moved his principal e-mail account to a different server. You agree to maintain his e-mail service for a time. The following line forwards all e-mail addressed to *support@sllug.org* to jfreeman's new e-mail address, which is not handled by your e-mail server:

```
support@sllug.org jfreeman@xmission.com
```

After you make changes in the `virtusertable` file, you must update the database using the following command, then restart `sendmail`:

```
makemap hash /etc/mail/virtusertable <
    /etc/mail/virtusertable
```

Forwarding that relies on a single domain name for the incoming message can also be accomplished using two other techniques. The first is the aliases file. An e-mail alias is another name that delivers e-mail messages to a user. This file contains a list of alternate names or e-mail addresses to which e-mail messages might be addressed. Each e-mail alias in this file is followed by text that defines what `sendmail` should do with a message so addressed. For example, suppose that your e-mail address is *kcarver@myplace.net*. Because different companies use specific formats for e-mail addresses, you also want to receive e-mail using the addresses *kim.carver@myplace.net*, *kim_carver@myplace.net*, and *kimc@myplace.net*. You can use such e-mail aliases if you include the following lines in `/etc/aliases`:

```
kim.carver: kcarver
kim_carver: kcarver
kimc: kcarver
```

In a large company, you need to be careful about the formats you use, because a person with a similar name might need to use an alias you have created as a real e-mail address. Aliases are also commonly used for assigning topical e-mail to a specific individual. For example, you can define a `webmaster` alias that sends e-mail to the accounts of Kim Carver and Thomas Jennings, who work at a company that helps manage your Web server:

```
webmaster: kcarver, tjennings@webstuff.com
```

You can include long lists of usernames in the `/etc/aliases` file, you can pipe messages to programs, you can include files containing e-mail addresses, and you can store messages directly to a file, all by varying the format of a line in `/etc/aliases`. Aliases can even be recursive; that is, they can build on themselves. For example, if you define a managers alias that includes five user accounts, you could then specify a webmaster alias that went to managers and to other user accounts. Aliases are the right tool for creating small mailing lists that don't change membership often. For larger, frequently changing lists, use a mailing list manager such as majordomo.

Each time you make a change in /etc/aliases, you must run the newaliases command to create a database of aliases that sendmail can use. This is done automatically each time sendmail is started, but you can rebuild the database with newaliases at any time without restarting sendmail.

Individual users can't alter the /etc/aliases file, but they can create a .forward file in their home directories. If sendmail finds a .forward file in a user's home directory, e-mail for that user is processed according to the text in .forward instead of simply being sent to the user's standard inbox in /var/spool/mail. Common uses of .forward include forwarding e-mail to another system when you prefer to receive your e-mail at another host (this method requires you to have a user account on the e-mail server) and piping your messages through a mail filter such as procmail. If you were on assignment with a subsidiary company for a month, you could include the following line in your .forward file:

kcarver@myplace_India.net

All e-mail that would have been delivered to your mailbox would instead be forwarded to the e-mail address given. What if you had a user account on the central e-mail server in Figure 6-9, used this file in your home directory, and used a forwarding feature in sendmail itself? The sendmail forwarding feature would forward your mail from the central server to your desktop system before it ever reached your local user account; all the mail would be at your desktop and none would reach you in India.

Watching sendmail Work

The sendmail daemon creates copious logs of what it does. Each message received and each message sent is logged along with daemon-specific messages about the server configuration, starting and stopping, and so on. These messages are written to the standard system logger, syslogd, based on the configuration in /etc/syslog.conf. In many Linux systems, these messages are written to /var/log/messages by default, along with log messages from many other programs. If you operate a busy sendmail mail server, you should alter the configuration of /etc/syslog.conf to store messages from the mail facility in a separate file. For example, the default setting in Fedora Core is to store messages from any mail server in /var/log/maillog.

You can also set sendmail to generate more or less debugging data in the logs using the -d command-line option. See the man page for sendmail to learn more about this. (The sendmail.cf and sendmail.mc files don't have man pages, but sendmail itself does. This man page describes only the start-up options for the daemon.)

In addition to learning about sendmail activity by reviewing the log files, you can use several other programs that keep you informed about the state of your e-mail server, such as:

- hoststat—Displays the status of hosts that have recently sent e-mail to your sendmail daemon. By default, information for a host is maintained for 30 minutes.

- mailq—Displays a list of messages queued and waiting to be sent. Messages wait in the queue if they are sent while you are not connected to the Internet, while sendmail waits for a domain name to be resolved, or when messages have not been accepted by a remote mail server (by default, sendmail tries again later).

- mailstats—Displays a summary of the amount of e-mail traffic that sendmail has handled. Fields in the output of mailstats include messages received, bytes received, messages sent, bytes sent, messages rejected, and messages discarded.

Table 6-3 summarizes the sendmail configuration files and utilities that are described in this section.

Table 6-3   Configuration files and utilities for sendmail

File or Utility	Description
sendmail.mc	A configuration file containing macro definitions used by the m4 program to create a sendmail.cf file
m4	The conversion utility that converts a sendmail.mc file into a sendmail.cf file
sendmail.cf	The configuration file that defines the operations of sendmail
sendmail.cw	An additional configuration file that defines the domains for which sendmail will accept e-mail messages
/etc/sysconfig/sendmail	A system configuration file that defines start-up parameters for sendmail; used by the start-up script in /etc/rc.d/init.d
sendmail	The sendmail daemon or e-mail server (MTA)
access	An optional configuration file that defines how sendmail should handle e-mail from the domains listed in the file; must be converted to an access.db file using the makemap utility
virtusertable	An optional configuration file that defines how sendmail should handle e-mail addressed to user accounts listed in the file; must be converted to a virtusertable.db file using the makemap utility
makemap	The utility used to convert plaintext files such as access and virtusertable into database format files that sendmail can process
aliases	Lists alternate e-mail addresses and the actual user account or filename that messages to each address should be delivered to

Table 6-3 Configuration files and utilities for `sendmail` (continued)

File or Utility	Description
`newaliases`	A utility that converts the `aliases` file into a database format that `sendmail` can process; must be executed after any change is made to the `aliases` file

CREATING A LINUX WEB SERVER

Tim Berners-Lee at the CERN laboratory on the French-Swiss border developed the Web as a way to help scientists exchange data in a variety of different formats. The Hypertext Transfer Protocol (HTTP) that he designed focused on real-time exchange of relatively small files between a server and numerous clients. At the time, many data formats were commonly used for information stored on Internet servers. The HTML document description language provided one way to create basic hyperlinked documents for exchange via HTTP-capable servers.

Although the Web was a hit with scientists, the explosive growth of the Web began with the development of a program called Mosaic at the National Center for Supercomputing Applications (*www.ncsa.uiuc.edu*). Mosaic was the first well-known graphical browser, as described in Chapter 3. NCSA also created one of the first Web servers; CERN created another. Today, millions of Web sites are running all over the world. To see more statistics about the Web, visit *wcp.oclc.org*, or visit *www.w3.org* and search on "statistics."

A **Web server** in Linux terminology is a daemon that accepts requests via HTTP and responds with the requested files. A basic Web server can be extremely simple in design: It accepts an HTTP request for a file, then it sends that file to the requester. As with other Internet services you have studied, the complexity comes when you begin to add security features, flexible configurations, support for many types of data, and many other features.

Although CERN and NCSA Web servers are still available, the most widely used Web server in the world today is Apache. Apache is included with every standard version of Linux and is installed by default on most of them. Many other Web servers are available for Linux, some basic and some complex. A few of them are listed here:

- *Boa* is a small, free Web server designed to be efficient without all the overhead (and features) of a server like Apache. (See *www.boa.org.*)

- *Servertec iServer* provides features focused on large sites, such as load balancing among multiple Web servers and the ability to interact easily with other types of servers, such as databases. (See *www.servertec.com.*)

- *Stronghold* is a secure server that is appropriate for running e-commerce applications on Linux. It is not free, but is based on Apache and includes source code. Stronghold was developed by C2Net, which is now owned by Red Hat Software. (See *www.redhat.com/software/stronghold/.*)

- *Zeus* includes a graphical administration interface and encryption (like Stronghold). It was designed for ISPs and is considered one of the fastest Web servers. (See *www.zeus.com/products/zeus.*)

If you want to know how popular various Web servers are, visit *www.netcraft.com/archives/web_server_survey.html*, which claims to have data on more than 59 million Web sites as of early 2005. Another source for Web server popularity is *www.biznix.org/surveys/*. This site restricts its survey to corporate Web sites.

Some of the features of Apache that make it popular include the following:

- A regular development cycle that keeps up with Web technology and provides a very reliable product

- Virtual hosting, which allows a single Web server to provide documents for multiple Web sites (multiple domain names)

- A modular design that lets Web administrators add and remove functionality to meet their site's needs

- Many security options and performance-tuning settings

- A broad support base, despite being free software (for example, see *www.apacheweek.com*)

Apache Versions

There are two current versions of Apache. Version 1.3 is the older version of Apache that is still being maintained. Version 2.0 is the newer version, in which most Apache development now takes place. The older version is still being maintained because some modules developed for it do not work with the newer version. Many Web sites rely on these modules. After these modules are rewritten for the new version, the older version will be retired.

If you're setting up an Apache Web server for the first time, use the newer version. If you later discover that you need to use a module that only works with the older version of Apache, you can either convert to the older version or run two copies of Apache on your computer—one old and one new. Converting between Apache versions is not difficult but you will need to make changes to the Apache configuration file to get it to work.

Running two copies of Apache is possible but it's unlikely that your Linux distribution makes it easy. You'll have to do your own engineering, such as creating another start-up script or modifying the existing one, directing the PIDs to different files, using two configuration files, using different directories for Web pages, logging to different log files, and so on. An experienced Linux administrator should be able to do this in a few hours, including doing the testing to ensure that it was done right.

One difference between the versions is how Apache creates children. With the older version, the parent process spawned child processes on demand, which is time-costly. The newer version lets you configure Apache so the parent process spawns child threads instead, which is less time-costly. Apache will appear to run faster under varying loads. It may not appear to be faster if the load is fairly constant.

Using threads may cause server applications (written in PHP, for example) to be unreliable. You might have to configure Apache for child processes even if you use the new Apache version. Newer versions of Apache support both child processes and child threads.

Controlling Apache

You start Apache from the standard script /etc/rc.d/init.d/httpd, but it may be running as part of your default system settings. The following example output shows how many Web server daemons are often running on a Linux system. Your output might look slightly different.

```
ps aux|grep httpd
root      279   0.0   3.3 4052 6392 ? S   Feb11  0:03  /usr/sbin/httpd
apache    280   0.0   3.4 4312 6516 ? S   Feb11  0:00  [httpd]
apache    281   0.0   3.4 4332 6516 ? S   Feb11  0:00  [httpd]
apache    282   0.0   3.4 4444 6516 ? S   Feb11  0:00  [httpd]
apache    283   0.0   3.4 4324 6516 ? S   Feb11  0:00  [httpd]
apache    284   0.0   3.4 4340 6516 ? S   Feb11  0:00  [httpd]
```

Notice that one of the httpd processes is owned by root (as indicated by the word root in the far left column of the first line). This is the parent process. The other processes are child processes or threads owned by user apache, a user account that has no access rights outside of the documents designated for the Web server to access. These additional processes were started by the parent process to handle incoming requests. (By default, some servers are running even when no requests are pending.)

The documents that the server sends to clients are stored in a directory of your choosing, but it is /var/www by default on Fedora Core systems.

Apache uses a configuration file called httpd.conf. On Fedora Core systems, it is stored in the /etc/httpd/conf directory. The file contains hundreds of configuration directives, along with comments describing most of them. Whenever you change the configuration file, you should restart Apache by using the script in /etc/rc.d/init.d. If you are working with an active Web site, however, restarting the server drops all the current client connections. A better method is to send the master httpd server a "reload" signal using this command:

```
kill -HUP `cat /var/run/httpd.pid'
```

NOTE

The character to the left of "cat" in the previous line of code is a grave accent mark. This key is left of the 1 key or left of the Spacebar on most keyboards.

Because the configuration file contains examples of all the directive types you are likely ever to need for Apache, exploring that file and reading its comments will give you a solid understanding of what Apache is capable of and how to take advantage of those capabilities. The online documentation provided at *www.apache.org* is also worth researching when you have questions about specific directives that you are considering using.

The directives in the first part of `httpd.conf` affect the global operation of Apache. Most are fine with their default values, but a few that are worth noting are mentioned here to illustrate important concepts in Apache configuration. In each case, all the comments that appear in the configuration file have been removed.

A connection to a Web site exists independent of the file being transferred. Apache can keep the connection active (alive) after sending a file, on the theory that a client that has requested one file is likely to request several. By using this **keepalive** feature, the client saves time in requesting additional files. Apache doesn't have to set up the connection for each file and overall performance is better. The following directives control how connections are kept alive:

```
KeepAlive Off
MaxKeepAliveRequests 100
KeepAliveTimeout 15
```

Change the `KeepAlive` directive to `On` if it is set to `Off`. The `MaxKeepAliveRequests` refers to the number of requests that a client can make during a single connection; a higher number yields better performance. However, if you have a limited number of connections because your server is overloaded, this directive may prevent someone from connecting to your Web site. The `KeepAliveTimeout` directive indicates a time in seconds that a connection will be maintained without activity. You can adjust this time based on how long you think visitors to your Web site pause between viewing one page and clicking a link to move to the next. You must balance performance from the client's perspective with having idle connections to your Web server.

Parents and Children

Apache uses a parent process to spawn additional child processes or threads (the Apache children) that handle client requests, but a series of directives controls how this is done. In general, Apache notes the number of client requests waiting to be handled. If it decides that more children are needed, it starts one child the first second, two the next second, and so forth until the client demand is met. You can control the number of children with these directives:

```
MinSpareServers 5
MaxSpareServers 20
StartServers 8
MaxClients 150
MaxRequestsPerChild 1000
```

The `MinSpareServers` directive specifies the minimum number of children that are idle—not servicing client requests. This directive allows a sudden burst of client requests to be handled quickly without the parent having to spawn more children—a time-costly affair. The MaxSpareServers directive specifies the maximum number of children that are idle. If the number of client requests decreases and there are many idle children, Apache kills all idle children except the number specified by the directive.

The StartServers directive specifies how many children should be spawned immediately when Apache is started. If you were to stop your server during a heavy load, and then restart it, the StartServers directive would cause Apache to immediately create the specified number of children. Apache won't have to spawn those children over time and have some clients not receive service.

The MaxClients directive imposes a limit on the number of clients that can connect to your server. This keeps Apache from spiraling out of control trying to start new servers to keep up with client demand if the machine's resources simply can't handle the load. You can adjust this number based on the expected traffic, your computer's memory, network bandwidth, and so on.

MaxRequestsPerChild defines how many requests (or connections, if you are using keepalives) a single copy of Apache will process. After the limit is reached, that copy of Apache will be stopped and a new copy will be started to replace it, if warranted. This is to prevent memory leaks in system libraries from causing the server to stop functioning after running for a long time. Linux does not seem to have library memory leaks, so you can set this directive to zero to disable this feature.

TIP When the genealogy Web site *www.familysearch.org* was first announced, organizers expected less than 1 million hits per day. The actual daily traffic when the site was opened was close to 8 million hits, slowing server performance to a crawl for several days until site administrators could ramp up the hardware to handle the traffic that had materialized immediately upon the site's opening.

Modules

Modules are a key feature of Apache. Many Apache features are implemented as loadable modules. You select the features you need by loading the modules that support these features. Each module is controlled by various directives that you include in the httpd. conf configuration file. Much like the Linux kernel, **Apache modules** can be included when you compile Apache from source code or they can be loaded on the fly as shared objects.

With Fedora Core, modules are stored in the /etc/httpd/modules directory. Examples of modules include mod_userdir to allow users to have their own home pages in their home directories, mod_autoindex to create attractive Web pages automatically from a directory listing, and mod_log_config to let you configure exactly what information is logged by Apache. More complex modules, which you won't use by default, include mod_speling (deliberately misspelled) to check the spelling of URLs so that you are more likely to get the page you intended, a series of mod_auth modules to provide authentication for client requests using a variety of methods, and mod_throttle to configure usage limits for various classes of incoming users.

NOTE The userdir module allows users to have personal Web pages that are stored in a directory below their home directory. By default, the directory is public_html. These pages are accessed with URLs that end in a tilde (~) followed by the user's Linux account name, such as *http://www.alcpress.com/~ed*.

The LoadModule directive defines a filename for a shared object as well as the programmatic function name of the module. The AddModule directive defines a code file for a module. The order in which AddModule directives appear is significant, as it indicates the order in which modules are loaded into Apache. If you want to use modules differently from the way they're used in the default Apache configuration, comment or uncomment the LoadModule and AddModule directives in the default httpd.conf file.

You can learn more about all available Apache modules by visiting *modules.apache.org*. This site lists hundreds of modules that you can download to add functionality to Apache. Some of the most important modules are mod_perl and mod_PHP, which enable Apache to run Perl and PHP scripts without loading a separate Perl or PHP interpreter. These features are so widely used that you see links to separate Web sites for them on the main *www.apache.org* Web site. Adding a Perl or PHP module does make Apache much larger, however.

Several other directives that control overall operation of Apache are described here.

- The User and Group directives define which user and group ID Apache operates under. While the master copy of Apache runs as root, other copies run as the user "apache," "nobody," or a similar user account. That way, if a browser request should somehow allow unexpected access to the system, the access is limited to what the named user (rather than the root user) could do.

- The ServerAdmin directive lists the e-mail address of a contact person who should be listed at the bottom of Apache-generated Web pages (for example, server error message pages that a user sees when a requested Web page does not exist).

- The ServerName directive defines the domain name to which Apache sends requests among virtual hosts (as described later in this section). This domain name is also reported back to the browser when responding to a request. This gives your site a consistent feel, despite the fact that multiple domain names may resolve to the same IP address.

- The DocumentRoot directive defines where documents for the Web server are stored. By default on Fedora Core this directory is /var/www/html.

Much of the httpd.conf file is organized into containers. A **container** is a special type of directive that activates other directives only if a condition is met or only within a particular context. One container example that appears several times in httpd.conf is the <directory> container. Each <directory> container starts with a <Directory> line and ends with a </Directory> line, similar to some HTML tags. The container defines how Apache handles requests for files within the named directory. The standard <directory> container for the default document root of Apache is shown here.

```
<Directory "/var/www/html">
    Options Indexes FollowSymLinks
    AllowOverride None
    Order allow,deny
    Allow from all
</Directory>
```

The Options line defines what types of files can be accessed in this directory.

- Indexes means that a Web page listing the contents of the directory is generated by Apache if no index.html file is available. (The DirectoryIndex directive defines the default filename index.html, which you can add to or change.)

- FollowSymLinks lets Apache follow a symbolic link in this directory to a file in another directory.

- Includes would allow Apache to process special statements within the text of files in this directory. These are called **server-side includes** (or **server-parsed documents**) and allow Apache to alter documents dynamically (as they are requested). This feature can add significantly to the load of a Web server. (It also presents security issues, as do many of the features listed here. See Chapter 12 for more information.)

- ExecCGI allows Apache to run a script in this directory and return the output of the script to the requesting browser.

- You could also use the All or None keywords after Options to use all of the above (for very open access) or none of the above (for very restrictive access).

The AllowOverride line defines which parts of the directory access information defined in this container can be changed if a configuration file called .htaccess is present in the named directory. (The file is called .htaccess by default—you can change the name.) Using .htaccess lets you allow multiple users to control their own subdirectories on a Web site, but AllowOverride lets you also limit their freedom to choose settings that might endanger the rest of the site. AllowOverride can use any of these keywords:

- FileInfo, which defines how different data types are handled

- Options, as described for the Options directive above

- AuthConfig, to control the authentication options by which a user must provide a username and password before accessing a file

- Limit, which is a separate container that can be included within a <directory> container to limit access to a file to a set of host names or IP addresses

- None or All provides a blanket answer, giving .htaccess no ability to change the configuration or letting it set everything differently

The `Order`, `Allow`, and `Deny` directives (`Deny` is not shown previously) define which hosts can access files in this directory. `Order` defines which is processed first, `Allow` directives or `Deny` directives. This is similar to what you have learned about the `/etc/hosts.allow` and `/etc/hosts.deny` files. For example, the following lines permit access only by hosts on the 192.168.0.0 network:

```
Order deny,allow
Allow from 192.168.
Deny from all
```

The following lines allow access to everyone except clients from the *trouble.net* domain:

```
Order allow,deny
Allow from all
Deny from trouble.net
```

Think carefully about what you want to achieve when you set up your access statements, and remember that Apache is not controlled by a superserver, nor does it rely on TCP Wrappers. Besides `httpd.conf`, the only access control mechanisms for your Web server are any firewalls that block packets at the network level (as described in the second part of this book).

In `httpd.conf`, you see several other examples of <directory> containers, <limit> containers, and other containers to help you understand how these are used. The information in a <directory> container applies to all subdirectories of the named directory unless another <directory> container defines different settings for the subdirectory.

The `Options` field mentions both server-side includes and scripts that Apache can execute, returning the output of the script as a document for the browser. Traditionally, scripts were kept in a separate directory that had the `ExecCGI` option set. More common now is the use of the `AddHandler` directive, which lets you specify that Apache should treat a file a particular way based on its file extension. For example, the following two directives define scripts as any file ending with .cgi, and server-side includes as any file ending with .shtml. Apache processes these files accordingly, no matter where they occur in the directory structure.

```
AddHandler cgi-script .cgi
AddHandler server-parsed .shtml
```

Of course, other factors may also be important. For example, Apache cannot execute a script file if the file does not have the execute file permission (the x bit) set. Likewise, it is possible to use more advanced directives to limit the type of server-side includes that Apache processes, beyond simply instructing Apache that .shtml files should be processed.

Virtual Hosts

Virtual hosting is the feature of Apache that lets a single Apache server handle more than one Web site. For example, if you operated a server for a large school district, you could host the Web sites for all of the schools in the district on one server running one copy of Apache. Each school is identified by its own name or URL and has its own Apache virtual host.

The documents for each virtual host are stored in a separate directory on the server. When you configure Apache for a virtual host, you specify the virtual host name and the directory where that virtual host stores its documents. When Apache receives an HTTP client request, one of the fields in the header contains the name of the virtual host that the user typed into his browser. Apache matches that name against its configuration to find the virtual host's document directory, called the DocumentRoot. This is called name-based virtual hosting and is the most common way of doing virtual hosting.

Within `httpd.conf`, you then specify the directive `NameVirtualHost` with the IP address used for virtual hosting. Apache examines any requests sent to that IP address to see what domain name is requested. You then specify a container such as the following for each of the Web sites that you want to host:

```
<VirtualHost *>
    ServerName www.mhcc.edu
    DocumentRoot /var/www/mhcc.edu
</VirtualHost>
```

This example contains the essential directives a virtual host needs. You can include many other directives. For example, you can configure this virtual host to use its own set of log files.

Setting up name-based virtual hosting requires that you also configure your DNS properly. You must set up your DNS server so all virtual host names resolve to Apache's IP address.

If a request arrives that does not specify one of the virtual hosts you defined, Apache does its best to determine which document tree to use, either the first listed or the default DocumentRoot directive that exists outside of any <VirtualHost> containers.

Virtual hosting can also be IP-based, where the virtual host is identified by its IP address. All IP-based virtual hosts need their own IP address. Because IP addresses can be a scarce commodity, IP-based virtual hosting is avoided. One situation in which you can't avoid it is when you configure Apache for secure Web pages using HTTPS, which is based on the Secure Sockets Layer (SSL). Any virtual host that uses SSL must be IP-based.

If you have more than one IP-based virtual host, you'll need to configure your network interface for multiple IP addresses. You learned how to do this in Chapter 2. DNS should refer each Web site name to the correct IP address.

The NameVirtualHost directive is not used for IP-based virtual hosting. Instead, you simply include the IP address in the <VirtualHost> container:

```
<VirtualHost 192.168.12.1>
    ServerName www.mhcc.edu
    DocumentRoot /var/www/mhcc.edu
</VirtualHost>
```

Apache supports many directives that are not discussed in this chapter. All directives are placed in the main configuration file, `httpd.conf`. Table 6-4 lists and describes the directives included in this chapter.

Table 6-4   A selection of Apache directives

Apache Directive (Sample Values in Italics)	Description
KeepAlive *Off*	Sets whether Apache keeps client connections open after responding to a request
MaxKeepAliveRequests *100*	Sets the maximum number of requests from a client via a single connection
KeepAliveTimeout *15*	Sets the length of time in seconds that a connection with a client will be kept open without a request arriving
MinSpareServers *5*	Sets the minimum number of idle copies of Apache to be kept running to handle incoming requests
MaxSpareServers *20*	Sets the maximum number of idle copies of Apache to be kept running to handle incoming requests
StartServers *8*	Sets the number of copies of Apache to start immediately after Apache is launched
MaxClients *150*	Sets the maximum number of clients that can be connected to Apache at the same time
MaxRequestsPerChild *1000*	Sets the maximum number of client requests to which a single copy of Apache can respond before being shut down as a precaution against memory leaks
User *apache*	Sets the username under which copies of Apache run
Group *apache*	Sets the group name under which copies of Apache run
ServerAdmin *webmaster@mydomain.com*	Sets the e-mail address to be added to Web pages generated by Apache
ServerName *www.mydomain.com*	Sets the server name that Apache associates with Web pages within a given set of documents
DocumentRoot *"/var/www/html"*	Sets the directory where Web pages are located; all client requests are relative to this directory
<Directory *"/var/www/html">*	Defines characteristics/directives that apply only to files contained in the named directory or its subdirectories
Options Indexes *FollowSymLinks*	Sets access options that apply to Web pages; used within a <Directory> container
AllowOverride *None*	Sets access options that can be overridden by a configuration file located in a subordinate directory
Order *allow,deny*	Defines the order in which the Allow and Deny directives are processed
Allow from *192.168.10.10*	Sets domains or IP addresses from which access is permitted
Deny from *trouble.net*	Sets domains or IP addresses from which access is not permitted
DirectoryIndex	Defines the filenames for which Apache searches as default documents when a client requests a directory name rather than a filename
AddHandler *cgi-script .cgi*	Sets a file extension that has special meaning to Apache, such as an executable script

Table 6-4   A selection of Apache directives (continued)

Apache Directive (Sample Values in Italics)	Description
`NameVirtualHost`	Sets an IP address for which queries must use settings in a matching <VirtualHost> container
`<VirtualHost 192.168.12.1>`	Sets up a virtual host, with all the directives in the <VirtualHost> container applying only to requests to that host

CHAPTER SUMMARY

- Routing tables guide the Linux kernel in sending packets to their final destination on distant networks. These tables can be constructed manually or dynamically with the help of routing protocols.

- Interior routing protocols are used within an organization using mathematical algorithms to determine how to route packets. RIP and OSPF are examples of popular interior routing protocols.

- Exterior routing protocols are used for routing packets among organizations, based on policy decisions about which specific sources of routing information are to be trusted—and how much. BGP is an example of an exterior routing protocol.

- The `routed` daemon implements the RIP routing protocol in Linux. RIP is only appropriate for small networks, but `routed` is easy to use and has no required configuration settings.

- OSPF is a more sophisticated interior routing protocol. It builds a chart of the status of all routers that it knows of, determining the best route based on more detailed criteria than RIP.

- The `gated` daemon is commercial software that supports RIP version 2 with classless addressing, OSPF, and BGP on Linux. It must be carefully configured, but provides a powerful, cross-protocol routing engine for dedicated Linux routers.

- DNS is an Internet-wide information hierarchy used to provide name-to-address matching (called forward lookups) and address-to-name matching (called reverse lookups, or reverse DNS).

- Queries about a given name begin with one of the Internet's root DNS servers, unless the host making the query has already cached information about where to find part of such data, such as the location of an authoritative DNS server for the .com domain.

- A zone is a part of a domain about which a particular DNS server is authorized to provide information. Most DNS servers provide information on several zones; each zone should have at least one master DNS server and one slave DNS server as a backup. The slave receives updated information from the master via a zone transfer.

❏ Reverse DNS provides a security mechanism that is widely used to prevent unauthorized users from completing queries to various network services. Many servers do not accept a connection if a reverse DNS lookup fails.

❏ Setting up a simple caching name server to forward DNS queries to another name server makes efficient use of network bandwidth for many small networks.

❏ The DNS protocol is implemented in Linux by the named daemon, which is part of the BIND collection of programs. The named daemon is configured by the /etc/named.conf file, which refers to data files typically stored in /var/named.

❏ Resource records hold information about a name within a zone that a client can receive through a query. Resource records include A records for an IP address, CNAME records for an alias to the canonical name, PTR records for reverse DNS "pointers" to map an IP address to a name, MX records to define a zone's mail exchanger, the start of authority (SOA) record, and many others.

❏ The SOA record defines how to reach the DNS administrator for a zone. It also includes a serial number to track updated zone information and several parameters governing zone transfers for that zone.

❏ The bindconf utility is one of many utilities that let you configure named, after you understand the configuration options and structure of the zone files.

❏ The host, nslookup, and dig commands let you query a DNS server from the command line using numerous options to determine exactly how a DNS server is configured and how default queries function.

❏ The nsupdate utility lets you update DNS zone files over a network, on the fly, if this feature is properly configured in /etc/named.conf.

❏ Popular Linux e-mail servers include sendmail, Qmail, Postfix, and Exim. Sendmail is the most widely used e-mail server and is available both as free software and as a commercial product.

❏ Start-up options for sendmail are configured via /etc/sysconfig/sendmail, but sendmail is most often configured through the /etc/sendmail.cf file. This file is extremely complex.

❏ Spam is a source of great concern and annoyance to e-mail server administrators. E-mail servers provide many features to control spam, including relay configuration options, access lists, forwarding features, and DNS Blacklists.

❏ Aliases are a popular way to redirect e-mail or create small mailing lists via sendmail. They are stored in /etc/aliases and are activated using the newaliases command.

❏ Apache is the most widely used Web server and is included with all standard Linux distributions. It is configured using the httpd.conf file.

❏ When you start Apache, a parent process spawns child processes or threads to handle client requests. Configuration directives define how Apache handles its children.

- Apache functionality is extensible by loadable modules, which are configured using directives in `httpd.conf`. Many additional modules are available for special purposes.

- Apache has fine-grained access controls. You can specify access controls on a per-host, per-directory, and per-file basis.

- Apache supports advanced features like virtual hosting and proxy services.

KEY TERMS

6

A record — A line (a record) within a DNS zone file that provides the IP address for the given host.

Apache module — A functionality for the Apache Web server that can be independently loaded on the fly as a shared object.

authority servers — The DNS servers that are authoritative for particular domains and zones.

bindconf — A graphical utility used to configure zone files.

bird — An open source routing daemon that supports RIPv1, RIPv2, OSPF, and BGP.

Border Gateway Protocol (BGP) — A widely used external routing protocol.

caching name server — A DNS server that contains no preconfigured information on domains (except `localhost`), but simply queries other DNS servers and caches the results.

CNAME record — A line (record) in a DNS zone file that defines an alias for a given name.

container — A special type of Apache configuration directive that activates other directives only if a condition is met or only within a particular context.

cost — A measure of how efficient a route is. The route with the lowest cost should always be chosen, other things being equal.

dhcpd — The most widely used Linux DHCP server daemon.

dig — A utility used to query specific DNS servers for specific resource records.

DNS Blacklist (dnsbl) — A list of IP addresses that are known principally as sources of spam and whose messages can be blocked automatically by mail servers such as `sendmail`.

dynamic routing — The process of collecting and updating routing table information automatically using a routing protocol.

exterior routing protocols — The routing protocols designed for routing packets between networks controlled by different organizations; packets are routed based on administrative policies, which are often controlled by how much a particular organization's routing information is trusted.

forward lookup — The process of using DNS to convert a domain name to an IP address.

forwarding name server — A DNS server that forwards all queries to another name server for processing.

gated — The Linux program that implements OSPF, BGP, and RIPv2 (with classless addressing).

hop — A pass through a router.

host — A utility used to query specific DNS servers for specific resource records.

interior routing protocols — The routing protocols designed for routing packets among networks controlled by a single organization; packets are routed based on mathematical models.

keepalive — The process of maintaining an active network connection after sending a file, based on the theory that a client that has requested one file is likely to request several.

m4 — A program that converts a text file containing configuration parameters into a complete `sendmail.cf` file.

master — The authoritative name server for a zone, typically containing database files that provide IP addresses for hosts within that zone.

MX record — A line (record) in a DNS zone file that defines the mail exchanger for the named host. MX records are used by Mail Transfer Agents (MTAs) to find the correct e-mail server to contact when delivering e-mail to a recipient.

named — The Linux program that implements the DNS protocol to create a DNS server; part of the BIND collection of programs.

NS record — A line (a record) within a DNS zone file that defines the authoritative name server for the given domain.

nslookup — A utility used to query DNS servers for resource records.

nsupdate — A utility used to update zone files dynamically at the command line.

PTR record — A line (record) in a DNS zone file that maps an address to a name. Used for reverse DNS lookups.

resource record — The information about a name that a DNS server can provide to answer queries. Example resource records include the A record to associate an IP address and host name, the MX record to define a host's mail exchanger, and the PTR record to associate a host name with an IP address for reverse DNS lookups.

reverse lookup — The process of using DNS to obtain the name that corresponds to an IP address.

rndc — A control program used to manage the `named` daemon.

root name servers — The DNS servers designated as a starting point for DNS queries.

routed — The Linux program that implements the Routing Information Protocol (RIP).

server-parsed documents — *See* server-side includes.

server-side includes — The statements within a text file that are processed on the fly by a Web server when that document is requested.

slave — A backup to a master DNS server, containing the same database files as the master DNS server.

SOA record — The first line (record) in a DNS zone file. Defines the start of authority for the information in the file, describing how to use the information provided for this zone, including a serial number for updates and refresh periods for zone transfers to slave DNS servers.

spam — Unsolicited, advertisement-related e-mail.

spoofing — A technique used by a malicious user to act as another person when contacting a server.

static routing — The process of assembling a routing table via entries in start-up scripts or by manually entered `route` commands.

virtual hosting — A feature of the Apache Web server that lets a single copy of Apache serve documents for several Web sites (several domains).

Web server — A daemon that accepts requests via HTTP and responds with the requested files.

zebra — An open source routing daemon that supports RIPv1, RIPv2, OSPF, and BGP.

zone — A part of the DNS domain tree for which a particular DNS server has authority to provide information.

zone files — The files referred to in named.conf that contain detailed information about specific zones; the information that a DNS query seeks.

zone transfer — The process of exchanging information between a master DNS server and a slave DNS server.

6

REVIEW QUESTIONS

1. The purpose of a routing protocol is to:
   a. Route packets across multiple network segments.
   b. Facilitate the exchange of routing table entries among routers.
   c. Make static routing easier to configure on multiple hosts.
   d. Avoid the need to use DNS in larger networks.

2. An exterior routing protocol uses _____ to determine how to route packets.
   a. mathematical algorithms
   b. a DNS root server
   c. BGP
   d. policies that may be based on the trust accorded the host providing routing data

3. A primary disadvantage of using RIP as an interior routing protocol for larger organizational networks is that RIP:
   a. can only accommodate a maximum of 15 hops between source and destination
   b. relies on class-based network masks, even in version 2
   c. does not have a long history as a stable protocol
   d. is not as popular as OSPF

4. Explain how the metric differs between OSPF and RIP.

5. Which protocols does zebra support?
   a. RIP, OSPF, DNS
   b. BGP, RIP, OSPF
   c. SMTP, OSPF, RIP
   d. BGP, OSPF

6. Which statement best describes how a DNS domain name is resolved?

   a. through a recursive tree-walking algorithm starting at a root name server

   b. by relying on cached information stored at multiple DNS servers

   c. because of the master/slave backup relationship of authoritative zone files

   d. due to the common practice of forwarding queries to make the local DNS server more efficient

7. Zone files are transferred from the master server to the slave server using:

   a. a reverse lookup

   b. spoofing

   c. caching

   d. a zone transfer

8. Which is a valid reverse DNS domain name for the network ID 198.165.24.0?

   a. 24.165.198.in-addr.arpa

   b. 0.24.165.198

   c. 198.165.24.0

   d. 198.165.24.in-addr.arpa

9. What is the advantage of using forwarded DNS requests when using a slow Internet connection?

10. Describe the difference between A and CNAME resource records.

11. What is the result of not updating the serial number in an SOA record when making changes to a zone file?

    a. When named is restarted, it will not recognize the updated information.

    b. DNS queries to the master DNS server for the domain cannot produce valid results.

    c. The rndc command cannot function properly.

    d. Zone transfers will not update secondary servers, thinking no update is necessary.

12. The $TTL directive in a zone file defines:

    a. the default Time to Live in a DNS cache for the resource records defined in that file

    b. the Time to Live assigned to the SOA record within that file

    c. the Time to Live for packets used to query that DNS server

    d. the Time to Live for any forwarded queries, if forwarding is enabled in /etc/named.conf

13. Multiple MX records assigned to a zone indicate that:

    a. The zone's only valid mail exchanger can be accessed via multiple IP addresses.

    b. Multiple e-mail servers are able to receive messages for users in that zone.

   c. The authoritative name server for the zone has not been correctly defined.

   d. The mail server is likely mentioned in at least one CNAME record.

14. The _____ utility is the preferred tool for querying name servers for administrative or troubleshooting purposes.

   a. `nslookup`

   b. `bindconf`

   c. `dig`

   d. `host`

15. When using the `dig` utility, describe what the "@" symbol before a host name indicates.

16. The configuration file used by the `sendmail` MTA is:

   a. `/usr/share/doc/sendmail-9.1.3/README.cf`

   b. `/etc/mail/access.db`

   c. `/etc/sendmail.cf`

   d. `/etc/mail/sendmail.cw`

17. Features in a master configuration file are converted to a file that `sendmail` can use via the _____ program.

   a. `m4`

   b. `dnl`

   c. `procmail`

   d. `newaliases`

18. Describe some of the options in the `sendmail.mc` file.

19. Describe the difference between discarding a message and rejecting a message.

20. Modules allow the Apache Web server to:

   a. Interact cleanly with the Linux kernel.

   b. Load and unload functionality by recompiling Apache.

   c. Use LoadModule and AddModule directives to make new functionality part of Apache.

   d. Use LoadModule to specify programs that are loaded when a user requests a certain Web document.

21. Apache can maintain open network connections with clients, expecting that they will make additional requests. This is called:

   a. load balancing via round-robin DNS lookups

   b. the KeepAlive feature

   c. host-based authentication

   d. virtual connections

22. Server-parsed documents are:

    a. documents stored on the Web server that Apache examines/processes at the moment they are requested by a client

    b. module information files that Apache examines/processes when the server starts

    c. document files that Apache can preload into memory to speed responses to browser queries

    d. another name for virtual-hosted documents

23. Using IP-based virtual hosting requires that you:

    a. Load additional modules in your copy of Apache.

    b. Include all relevant virtual-host names in /etc/hosts.

    c. Define which remote server holds the document tree for each hosted site.

    d. Configure DNS to refer each domain name to the appropriate IP address configured on your host.

24. Name an Apache directive that assists in managing the traffic load on a busy Web server.

25. Which protocol is used for e-commerce applications with Apache?

Hands-On Projects

HANDS-ON PROJECTS

Project 6-1

In this project, you set up and test a caching, forwarding name server using BIND. This project assumes that you're using Fedora Core, but it will probably work using any Linux distribution that has BIND installed. To complete this project, you should have Fedora Core installed, with networking established, root access to the system, and an Internet connection.

1. Log on as root and open a command-line window.

2. Check that the following packages are installed. Each package name will be followed by a version number (*Hint*: rpm -qa|grep bind).

   ```
   bind
   bind-utils
   caching-nameserver
   ```

3. Start the name server using the named script in /etc/rc.d/init.d.

4. Enter ***dig www.sony.com*** to get the IP address of Sony's Web server. You have not changed your /etc/resolv.conf file, so your previously configured DNS server will still be used.

5. Notice the Query time: and SERVER: lines in the last part of the output of dig.

6. Try out your caching name server with this command:

   dig @localhost www.sony.com

7. Notice the same two lines at the end of the output. How do they differ?

8. Why was the time not faster than in Step 5?

9. Enter this command again:

   dig @localhost www.sony.com

10. Notice the Query time value. Why is it different?

11. Open the /etc/named.conf file in a text editor.

12. Within the options section near the top of the file, right after the line directory "/var/named", insert the following lines. Substitute the IP address of your primary DNS name server at your ISP for the IP address shown here:

    forward first;
    forwarders { 198.60.22.2; };

13. Save the file and exit the editor.

14. Run the **named-checkconf** command to see whether any syntax errors were introduced as you edited the configuration file. If so, correct them. If there are no errors, nothing will be displayed.

15. Reload the configuration using the following command (you may see a warning message about the name key, which you can safely ignore for this project):

    rndc reload

16. Select another domain name for testing. You should select one that others in your class have not selected and that you would not expect to have been visited often; a somewhat obscure domain name is better for this test. Use dig with your local host to query for the domain you selected:

    dig @localhost www.cern.org

17. Notice how long the query time is, given near the end of dig's response.

18. Perform the same query again. How does the query time differ? Where is the information being taken from? What advantage does forwarding have over simply using a caching name server?

19. If you want, you can change the /etc/resolv.conf setting of your local system to refer to **127.0.0.1**, so that your local DNS server is always used for name resolution. If you choose to do this, use the following command to make named start each time your system is started:

    chkconfig --level 35 named on

Project 6-2

In this project, you check the contents of remote name servers using the `dig` command. To complete this project, you should have Linux installed, the `dig` program installed, networking established, and an Internet connection.

Sometimes the results from name resolution are unexpected. This can be caused by several factors, such as a poorly configured DNS server, a DNS server without a slave that temporarily goes down, or a slow propagation of a change in a DNS file. In this project, you query step-by-step through several name servers to get a complete name resolution. This project uses the domain name *nasa.gov*, but feel free to experiment on any domain name after you understand the process being illustrated.

1. Log on as root and open a command-line window.

2. Query your local name server for the authority name servers for the .gov top-level domain.

   dig gov. NS

3. You should see an ANSWER section that lists the authority servers for the .gov domain. There are many servers listed. Here are three of them:

   ```
   gov.      140337   IN    NS    g.gov.zoneedit.com
   gov.      140337   IN    NS    f.gov.zoneedit.com
   gov.      140337   IN    NS    e.gov.zoneedit.com
   ```

4. From the list of .gov authority servers, choose one. Query this authority server for the second-level domain name *nasa.gov*.

   dig @f.gov.zoneedit.com nasa.gov. NS

5. You should see an AUTHORITY section that lists the authority servers:

   ```
   nasa.gov.     140337   IN    NS    NASANS1.nasa.gov.
   nasa.gov.     140337   IN    NS    NASANS3.nasa.gov.
   nasa.gov.     140337   IN    NS    NASANS4.nasa.gov.
   ```

6. From the list of *nasa.gov* authority servers, choose one. Query this authority server for the third-level domain name *hq.nasa.gov*.

   dig @nasans1.nasa.gov hq.nasa.gov. NS

7. You should see an ANSWER section that lists the authority servers for *hq.nasa.gov*. You see that two of the servers are the same as in Step 5 and one is new:

   ```
   hq.nasa.gov.     7200   IN    NS    NASANS1.nasa.gov.
   hq.nasa.gov.     7200   IN    NS    NASANS4.nasa.gov.
   hq.nasa.gov.     7200   IN    NS    ns3.hq.nasa.gov.
   ```

8. From the list of *hq.nasa.gov* authority servers, choose one. Query this authority server for the fourth-level domain name *mail.hq.nasa.gov*.

   dig @nasans1.nasa.gov mail.hq.nasa.gov. NS

9. There is no ANSWER section in the response. This probably means that *mail.hq. nasa.gov* is a host name that has no associated NS records. But it probably has an IP address. Let's see:

```
dig @nasans1.nasa.gov mail.hq.nasa.gov. A
```

10. It does have an IP address. In the ANSWER section, you see:

```
mail.hq.nasa.gov.    7200    IN    A    198.116.65.49
```

11. Are there other records for *mail.hq.nasa.gov*? Let's see:

```
dig @nasans1.nasa.gov mail.hq.nasa.gov. ANY
```

12. There are other records. The ANSWER section reveals:

```
mail.hq.nasa.gov.    7200    IN    A     198.116.65.49
mail.hq.nasa.gov.    7200    IN    MX     10 spamfw1.hq.nasa.gov.
mail.hq.nasa.gov.    7200    IN    MX     20 smtp.hq.nasa.gov.
```

13. There are two MX records associated with *mail.hq.nasa.gov*. Presumably you can send mail to someone@mail.hq.nasa.gov.

14. Look at the SERVER: line in the response, third from the bottom. This identifies the name server that responded to the query. See if you can locate this address in the ADDITIONAL section.

15. What is the name of the responding name server?

16. Look in the AUTHORITY section. Is the responding name server listed as being authoritative for *mail.hq.nasa.gov*?

17. What does this process tell you about the quality of the information you just obtained? How could you use this process if you were seeing unexpected results from standard DNS operations?

Project 6-3

HANDS-ON PROJECTS

In this project, you experiment with e-mail aliases and `sendmail`. To complete this project, you should have Linux installed, with root access to the system. For simplicity's sake, the directory names referred to are specific to the Fedora Core distribution, but most distributions should use the same location.

1. Log on as root and open a command-line window.

2. View the mail log using the following command. This will occupy the terminal window for the duration of this project:

```
tail -f /var/log/maillog
```

3. Use a text editor to add the following lines to the end of the /etc/aliases file.

```
supervisor:     root
spam:       /tmp/spamcan
```

4. Save the file and then execute the following command:

```
newaliases
```

5. Use a mail program to send a message to the address supervisor. The following command is one way to do this, sending the contents of a text file as the body of the message:

```
mail -s "testing aliases" supervisor < /etc/syslog.conf
```

6. Watch the window where the mail log is displayed.

7. When you see a line indicating that your message has been delivered, open an e-mail reading program to see that the message addressed to supervisor was delivered to root.

8. Send another e-mail message to spam. A sample command to do this is shown here:

```
mail -s "still testing aliases" spam </etc/syslog.conf
```

9. Watch the window where the mail log is displayed to see when the message has been delivered by sendmail.

10. Look in the /tmp directory to see whether the spamcan file was created.

11. Enter the command **mailstats** to see a summary of activity for your sendmail server. Have any messages been discarded (see the msgsdis column)? If not, what happened to the message addressed to spam?

Project 6-4

In this project, you create a virtual Web site using Apache. To complete this project, you should have Linux installed, with root access to the system. Though the directory names referred to are specific to Fedora Core, most other distributions will use similar locations for the files named.

1. Log on as root.

2. Start the Apache server with this command:

```
/etc/init.d/httpd start
```

3. Open a browser such as Mozilla or Thunderbird.

4. Enter the URL *http://localhost* to view the default page provided with Apache.

5. This default page is actually an error page. Fedora Core 3 displays this page when you have no /var/www/html/index.html file. Choose **File** on the menu bar, choose **Open File**, and select the file **/var/www/error/noindex.html**. How is viewing this file different from viewing the file in Step 4?

6. Create the following directories that will be used to store documents for the virtual host you will create: *www.virtualhome.com*.

```
mkdir  /var/www/blisbat
```

```
mkdir  /var/www/blisbat/html
mkdir  /var/www/blisbat/logs
```

7. Copy some example HTML files to your document tree. For example:

```
cp -xa /usr/share/doc/bind-9.2.4/arm/* /var/www/blisbat/html
```

8. Change the configuration of your Web server by adding the following lines to the end of the /etc/httpd/conf/httpd.conf file. Note that the BIND HTML files you copied in the previous step didn't have an index.html file. So, you'll tell Apache that its default Web page for this virtual host is the Bv9ARM.html file, using the DirectoryIndex directive.

```
NameVirtualHost *:80
<VirtualHost *:80>
    ServerAdmin webmaster@blisbat.com
    DocumentRoot /var/www/blisbat/html
    ServerName www.blisbat.com
    DirectoryIndex Bv9ARM.html
    ErrorLog /var/www/blisbat/logs/error_log
    CustomLog /var/www/blisbat/logs/access_log common
</VirtualHost>
```

9. Restart Apache with this command:

```
apachectl restart
```

10. Go back to your browser and load the following URL:

```
www.blisbat.com
```

11. Why didn't this work?

12. Edit the /etc/hosts file and add the following line:

```
127.0.0.1       www.blisbat.com
```

13. Return to your Web browser and try the URL again. Why does it work now without restarting the Web server?

14. Display the /var/www/blisbat/logs/access_log file with the less command to see a record of your browsing on your new virtual Web site:

```
less /var/www/blisbat/logs/access_log
```

15. Display the /var/www/blisbat/logs/error_log file with the less command to see a record of any errors:

```
less /var/www/blisbat/logs/error_log
```

NOTE
It's normal to see errors about a missing favicon.ico file. If you find this annoying, create a favicon.ico file with the touch favicon.ico command.

Project 6-5

In this project, you configure miscellaneous Apache features such as redirection and indexes. To complete this project, you should have completed Project 6-4 and should have Internet access. Though the directory names used in the steps are specific to the Fedora Core distribution, most other distributions use similar locations for the files.

1. Log on as root.

2. Using a Linux text editor, edit the `/etc/httpd/conf/httpd.conf` file. Go to the end of the file and add the following lines:

   ```
   <Directory "/var/www/blisbat/html" >
       AllowOverride FileInfo
       Options None
       Order allow,deny
       Allow from all
   </Directory>
   ```

3. Using your text editor, create a file called `.htaccess` in the `/var/www/blisbat/html` directory. Enter the following lines in the file:

   ```
   Redirect /ibm http://www.ibm.com
   Redirect /course http://www.course.com
   ```

4. Restart Apache by entering the following command:

   ```
   apachectl restart
   ```

5. Open a browser such as Mozilla or Thunderbird. Enter *www.blisbat.com/ibm*. The Redirect statement in the `.htaccess` file causes Apache to redirect your Web browser to the *www.ibm.com* site.

6. Enter *www.blisbat.com/course*. You should be redirected to the Course Technology Web site. Redirection is useful if content on one Web site is moved to another but you still want the content to be accessible with the old URLs.

7. Edit the `/etc/httpd/conf/httpd.conf` file by replacing the following line:

   ```
   DirectoryIndex Bv9ARM.html
   ```

   with this line:

   ```
   DirectoryIndex index.html
   ```

NOTE   (The following step is specific to Fedora Core. You will probably not have to perform it with other Linux distributions.)

8. Edit the `welcome.conf` file in the `/etc/httpd/conf.d` directory so that all the lines are commented out. They begin with a pound sign (#).

9. Restart Apache by entering the command **apachectl restart**.

10. Enter *www.blisbat.com* in your Web browser. Instead of seeing a Web page, you will see a screen with an error message because you have no index.html file in the /var/www/blisbat/html directory.

11. Using a text editor, edit the /etc/httpd/conf/httpd.conf file. Go to the part of the file shown in the following code and change the Options None line to **Options Indexes**:

```
<Directory "/var/www/blisbat/html" >
    AllowOverride FileInfo
    Options None
    Order allow,deny
    Allow from all
```

12. Restart Apache by entering the command **apachectl restart**.

13. Enter *www.blisbat.com* in your Web browser. You see a list of files in the /var/www/blisbat/html directory. Click the **Bv9ARM.html** file; you see the Web page you created in Project 6-4.

14. Reverse what you did in Step 8.

CASE PROJECTS

CASE PROJECTS

Case Project 6-1

A new client has signed up for a consulting contract. The client is an association of small businesses in Fairbanks, Alaska, that you met through your work at Snow, Sleet, and Hale. The association has about 50 members, most of whom are family business owners. They want to increase their business and are looking for ways that exposure via the Internet can help them. Snow, Sleet, and Hale have agreed with the association to let you place a separate server in its office so that it can hook into the Internet on the office connection (recent oil contracts have led them to install a T-3 line).

1. You plan to host a separate domain for each small business that chooses to participate in the association's promotional efforts. For each domain, you want to be able to handle incoming e-mail, provide a Web site and possibly an FTP site for some, and act as a master DNS server for the domain. Describe the configuration issues that you foresee with having up to 50 domains handled on the single server.

2. Describe how you will set up the DNS server for this multidomain host.

3. Several of the small business owners have approached you to ask how they can gather lists of e-mail addresses for people who may be interested in their products or services. The next chapter begins discussing related topics, but how do you feel about helping them gather e-mail addresses and sending out their promotional material? What advice would you give them? Would you send them to another "e-mail service bureau" to do the work of mailing? How might your actions affect your relations with the law firm? With the association (your new client)?

7

SECURITY, ETHICS, AND PRIVACY

After reading this chapter and completing the exercises, you will be able to:

- List typical security risks in modern networked computer systems
- Understand how to assess risk and create a security policy
- Describe the function of top security-awareness organizations
- Outline the role of the government in security and privacy
- Locate Linux products designed especially for security-conscious environments

In this chapter, you will begin to add the basics of computer security to your knowledge of Linux computer networking. This chapter discusses the environment in which system administrators work, the rules they abide by, and the consequences of their actions.

You will learn specifically about vulnerabilities of modern networked computer systems. Many of these may be familiar to you because of stories you have read about computer crimes. Familiarity with these weaknesses will help you understand the broad scope of computer security work.

You will also learn in this chapter about organizations that have a keen interest in security. These include professional groups that focus on security education for system administrators, as well as government groups that create policies or enforce laws to make computers more secure.

Finally, you will read about a few specialized versions of Linux that have a particular focus on security. Security-related *utilities*—rather than complete Linux distributions—are the focus of the remaining chapters of this book.

Introducing Computer Security and Privacy

To introduce the topics of computer security and privacy, consider a few news stories:

- On November 3, 1988, system administrators all over the United States found that their systems were running very slowly. Eventually, they realized that someone had released a worm into the Internet. A **worm** is like a virus. It is a self-replicating program that invades systems, duplicates itself, and then tries to reach out to infect other systems. This particular event became known as the Morris worm, after its creator, Robert Morris, Jr., then a student at Cornell University. It was the first major security incident that affected the entire Internet, and it scared many people because no one knew how to stop it. Morris had intended no harm, but a programming bug caused his worm to replicate many times faster than expected, slowing Internet systems all over the country to a crawl. Morris anonymously sent an e-mail describing how to stop the worm, but was eventually apprehended and received a sentence of three years probation and a large fine.

- In early 1998, during one of the more tense moments between India and Pakistan (both of which have nuclear weapons), a group of teens hacked into the computer system of the Bhabha Atomic Research Center in India and intercepted e-mail between physicists working there. They intended to do the same with a similar facility in Pakistan. The same group penetrated a nuclear facility in Turkey the next day.

- A rash of attacks in early 2000 that attempted to shut down the most popular Web sites—Yahoo!, eBay, Microsoft Network, and others—set the technology world on its ear. For several weeks, security experts scrambled to cope with a new type of security problem: a **denial-of-service (DoS) attack**, designed to shut down access to an Internet site by overwhelming it with bogus requests. You will learn more about this type of attack later in this chapter.

- In a similar series of incidents later that year, several high-profile Web sites were **defaced**, meaning that text or images on the home page were altered. These sites included NASA, the U.S. Department of Justice, the Central Intelligence Agency, and the White House.

- Kevin Mitnick, who was in the news for a time after being sentenced to six years in prison in 1994 for his cybercrime exploits, has since gained unauthorized access to military sites (including the North American Aerospace Defense Command), financial institutions, and numerous technology companies.

- In March 1997, a programmer in Sweden gained access to the 911 emergency response system in Florida, disabling emergency access for 11 counties. Similar events have occurred in other U.S. states.

- Carlos Felipe Salgado Jr. used a common system-administration technique called sniffing to collect more than 100,000 credit card numbers from online merchants. He was arrested in June 1997 as he tried to sell the numbers to undercover FBI agents.

Despite all of these hazards, Linux system administration and networking are fascinating topics. With Linux, there are thousands of exciting programs to explore and impressive capabilities with which to complete assignments at work or school. You have a worldwide community of enthusiastic supporters with whom you can learn and share experiences, and you have the operating system source code, which gives you unlimited flexibility in digging into the arcane workings of a modern operating system. Using Linux can be intellectually stimulating and a lot of fun.

But when the discussion turns to security, the tone is unlikely to be lighthearted. As the news stories about unauthorized computer access—computer crimes—vividly show, computer security is a serious matter. It suddenly ties the work you do on your Linux server to the entire world, and that world includes far too many people who would use your resources for their own ends.

7

Computer security is a large and specialized field, separate in some ways from the day-to-day operation of a network server. Security specialists must focus as much on the world outside the computer as on the technology and data they seek to protect. Unfortunately, security requires you to be paranoid about the world at large. The reason is straightforward enough: The more broadly a computer is networked, the more potential for access to that computer, and thus the more anonymous that access may become if not properly controlled. Broad—even anonymous—access represents the power of networked computers, but it also presents an opportunity for those with malicious intentions.

Two terms are commonly used to refer to people who break into computer systems: hacker and cracker. To Linux enthusiasts and many other technically astute people, the term "**hacker**" means only a technology expert who enjoys learning about the intricate workings of computer systems and software. The term is a compliment, reserved for those whose vast knowledge of a technology make them invaluable consultants, efficient troubleshooters, and effective programmers when a challenging new project arises.

A **cracker** is a person who breaks the law or ethical standards by accessing computer systems without authorization. Some crackers have malicious intentions and seek to damage or shut down hardware, to corrupt software programs, or to damage or destroy data. Other crackers are not malicious, but only want to test their skills by exploring areas that they are not authorized to enter; they don't intentionally damage systems or data, but they are still breaking the rules. These are the definitions used in this book. You can find nuances of these meanings, of course. Some maintain that a cracker must have malicious intent; for others, the term "hacker" is synonymous with criminal mischief.

Crackers form an underground community of Internet users. They use pseudonyms instead of their real names and often form groups bent on achieving a common goal, be it taking down sites with political views opposite their own, or simply having a good time at others' expense. Many crackers are young, from 15 to 18. Older crackers (late 20s or 30s) are more likely to work alone, to have a motivation beyond "let's see what I can get away with," and to have a truly impressive set of technical skills.

What does it mean when you read about someone breaking into a computer system, cracking a system, or, as some publications use the term, hacking into a computer system? It normally means that a user was able to attain remote access to a computer without authorization. Just as you can use Telnet in Linux to log on to a computer remotely and run commands or view files, nearly all operating systems have programs that permit some sort of remote control or remote access when connected to a network. If the operating system or the program itself is not carefully configured, anyone who knows the software well can gain remote access.

If you like a challenge, this might sound like the ultimate technical thrill-seeking: Pick a high-profile Web site and see whether you can gain access to the server through the holes in the system administrator's security. Then alter the Web site's home page to show the world what you were able to accomplish. This is exactly what was done to the White House site and others.

What crackers might not understand is that, even if they have no malicious intentions, this is not harmless fun. Their activities have consequences that crackers may not anticipate: People get fired, billions of dollars are wasted recovering from even "innocent" cracker exploits, and participants may be fined or even imprisoned. In fact, with the increasingly international scope of cracking activities and of terrorist threats, lives are at stake if crackers manipulate government and military computer sites. The Government Accounting Office, a research arm of the U.S. Congress, reports that 120 nations have information warfare programs. The purpose of such programs is to exploit vulnerabilities in computer security as a tool of war. The successful attacks on hundreds of (nonclassified) Pentagon servers in February 1998, masterminded by Israeli Ehud Tenenbaum, show that the dangers of poor security do not stop at national borders.

Accurate estimates of the damages caused by computer crime are hard to calculate, though useful statistics are available. Gathering accurate statistics is difficult for several reasons. First, computer break-ins are not always reported, either because they are not discovered or because they are discovered long after the break-in occurred, making prosecution difficult. Second, the company that was broken into may not want to risk negative publicity by reporting the incident; at the very least, they want to avoid inclusion in any statistics related to victimization. Finally, as described in reports by the U.S. Department of Justice, computer crimes are prosecuted using a number of different laws; matching a crime with a law is difficult. Even defining computer crime itself is a difficult task. Which of the following actions do you consider computer crime?

- Breaking into a bank's computer system and transferring funds from a major corporation's account to your own numbered bank account in another country

- Breaking into a bank's computer system and looking up the balances of your employer's bank accounts

- Breaking into a bank's Web server and adding an anonymous note to the bottom of their Web home page

- Breaking into a government or military server and sending e-mail to the system administrator explaining how you were able to break in

- Breaking into a server at your school and changing your grade on a midterm exam

- Breaking into your friend's computer and copying her music files onto your system (without damaging them on her system)

Although the likelihood of prosecution differs in these examples, every one of them could be called a crime if the organization or person whose system you broke into decided to press the issue. In simple terms, **computer crime** is unauthorized access to a computer system.

The Privacy Debate

You may wonder why privacy and ethics are grouped with security in this chapter (and on some Linux certification tests). Privacy makes computer security an issue of personal concern. Any personal information stored on a computer is threatened by someone cracking the system where it is stored.

Many books have been written about the immense amount of data that is stored for nearly every person in this country. (*Database Nation* by security expert Simon Garfinckel is one good example.) The government is naturally a major participant: The Internal Revenue Service has financial data, driver's license divisions have information about you, and vital records offices have family information such as birth and marriage records. Some of this data is publicly available, but much is not. Companies also maintain vast databases of personal information to help them market products more effectively. Billions of dollars are spent each year by companies that purchase mailing lists to track your exact spending habits and preferences. For example, anyone can contact a mailing list company and purchase a list of names and addresses for all computer professionals living in zip code 22046 who have an income of at least $80,000 per year, own a home, have at least two cars, two kids, work for the government, and have a college education. If you're willing to pay more, the information you receive can be even more detailed.

A great deal of personal information must be stored on computers to make government and businesses function efficiently—we would be annoyed with the results if they stopped doing so. However, because so much information about us is stored on computers, we all have a personal interest in security measures that are effective enough to prevent someone from stealing our credit card numbers, our medical files, or our military records. Ongoing debates pit the privacy advocates against those advocating a free flow of information or the need to maintain personal information in government or commercial databases. Who should be able to obtain your credit report (listing all your credit cards, balances, any late payments, loans applied for, mortgages, and so on)? Who should be allowed to obtain your medical records, with or without your permission? Who should be allowed to see copies of your old tax returns? How can a company that gathers information about you use that information?

NOTE Some of the laws regulating privacy issues include the Electronic Communications Privacy Act (U.S. Code, title 18, section 2701) and the Electronic Freedom of Information Act. To see these laws, you can visit *www.law.cornell.edu/uscode* and use the search function or the Title/Section fields halfway down the page.

Laws and government regulations have something to say about who can access your credit records, but when businesses are involved, the answers are uncertain. Companies can ask you for information about yourself; after they have that information, do you own it or do they? Can you tell them not to use it for marketing purposes? Can you tell them not to sell it to another company?

NOTE Some people are happy to share basic information about themselves, their preferences, and their habits, either electronically or by regular mail. They like receiving catalogs with products that interest them, and they like getting coupons and special offers. Companies gather and trade personal data primarily for this reason: to get their products to the people most likely to want them.

With the growth of the Web, many people became concerned with how their personal information was being used or resold. A company that hadn't made much money selling products on the Web could make a tidy profit by selling information on its customers to other companies. Now, every reputable Web site has a link to the company's privacy policy, either on the home page or the page where a user enters personal information, such as a shopping cart page. A **privacy policy** is a voluntary statement by a company about how it will and will not use data that it collects about users or customers. Figure 7-1 shows a good example of a privacy policy from the site *www.consumerreports.org*. This example is clearly worded and includes a link to the site's public security policy as well (the link is not visible in the figure).

The privacy policy is important to the system administrator because seeing that its terms are carried out may be his responsibility. Privacy policies are usually lengthy, but their contents are usually similar to one of the following:

- We don't collect or save any information about visitors to our Web site. Nothing but your IP address is logged, and that is used only collectively for statistical purposes in maintaining a viable Web site.

- We collect information to complete a sale or register users, but we do not share that information with any other company for any purpose, nor do we use that information to contact you about our products and services.

- We collect information on visitors to our site and use patterns in that information to determine whether you might be interested in some of our other products. If we think you might be interested, we will contact you with marketing information about that product. You can ask us not to contact you if you choose.

- We collect information about you and share that information with our partners who may have products that we think you would enjoy hearing about.

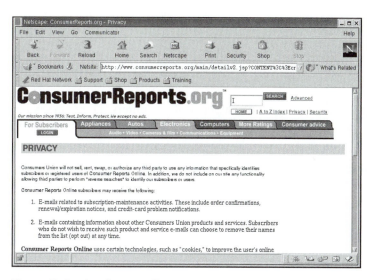

Figure 7-1 A privacy policy

One of the debates about privacy (and Internet marketing in general) is whether users should have to opt in or opt out. Using an **opt-in** scheme, you will not receive advertisements unless you specifically say "yes, put me on the mailing list." Much more common is the **opt-out** scheme, in which you receive advertisements (by e-mail, mail, telephone, fax, and so on) unless you contact a company and say "take me off the mailing list." By that time, of course, they may have sold your name to other companies who don't know that you have opted out. Also note that companies often speak of their "marketing partners." This usually just refers to other companies that have purchased your customer information, thinking that if you bought from company X, you are likely to enjoy their products also.

TIP If you are interested in privacy issues, visit the Electronic Privacy Information Center at *www.epic.org* and the Privacy section of the Electronic Frontier Foundation at *www.eff.org*.

Lawyers and marketing vice presidents are the people most likely to create a privacy policy. However, because system administrators have immediate access to data that is collected on an Internet site, they play a role in implementing the policy. As previously mentioned, privacy is the personal aspect of computer security: If you don't use adequate security measures to protect personal information collected by the Internet site you manage, a privacy policy assuring users of your good intentions and plans for their personal information is of little worth.

A company's privacy policy places an appropriate burden on the system administrator, the person best able to maintain privacy by properly securing the systems on which data is stored.

User Privacy

Computer users have a lot to lose as a result of poor security. The biggest threat is to their privacy; when private information can be harvested from computers, identity theft is highly likely.

People have choices when it comes to their personal computers. They can select computers, operating systems, and software that is less vulnerable. If particular software has had security problems for many years, users might decide to replace it.

When computer users work for a company, they lose that control. If a company decides to continue using software that has a rich history of security problems, employees can do little, although they have a personal stake. Employee records are frequently stored on computers that are connected to a network—computers that are easy to hack. The employer's security problems can become the employees' problems.

The problem will get worse. For example, many companies are considering the use of **biometrics** for user authentication. They're learning about the technology from companies that have biometric products to sell. These companies portray biometrics in a positive light, so decision makers might be unaware of the downside.

Biometrics, in the context of computer security, allows computer systems to accurately authenticate users based on their unique characteristics. Biometric-based computer security relies on the fact that no two people have the same fingerprint and retina pattern.

This might seem ideal, but the very thing that makes biometric security attractive can also make it unworkable. Fingerprints and retina patterns may be unique to individuals, but they are also permanent. You can't change your fingerprint or retina pattern, unlike a passphrase or security certificate.

Fingerprints are not private; you leave a trail of them every day. It's trivial for bad guys to get a copy of your fingerprint, so biometric-based security systems that use fingerprints are a bad idea. Retina patterns don't carry the same risk—you don't leave a trail of retina patterns as you move around. The problem is that fingerprint-based security devices are relatively cheap, but devices based on retina patterns are expensive. Many companies are likely to choose the less-expensive solution.

If your company installs biometric-based security products, you'll have to allow the company to take a copy of your fingerprint or retina pattern. This creates serious issues:

- What happens if you refuse to surrender your biometric? Can you be fired?
- Who owns the digitized information—you or the employer?
- Is biometric data subject to trademark and copyright law?
- What happens to your biometric data when you leave the company? Does the employer need to keep a copy after you leave?
- Can ex-employees demand an audit of the employer's computer system to ensure that their private information has been deleted?

- What happens if your data is replicated across system backups?

- If thieves steal your biometric data and use it in the commission of a crime, how might you be affected?

- Will the technology ever exist to transfer an electronic copy of a fingerprint to a material surface, such as that of a gun, knife, or bank vault?

- Will your biometric data be stored in databases? Your personal information can often be sold to anyone who can pay the fee.

Ethics and System Administrators

Many professionals have a code of ethics. Doctors take the Hippocratic Oath, government officials must uphold national or state constitutions, and lawyers have codes of professional responsibility as well as ethical guidelines. Ethical standards are not the same as laws; ethics revolves around the question of doing the right thing at the right time, for the right reason.

The details of every possible ethical difficulty can't be written out like the laws of the land. Instead, codes of conduct, or ethical guidelines, outline the principles that members of a profession follow. They use these principles to make decisions when difficult situations arise. Ethical codes are based on both philosophy and religion; they are moral guidelines that make society pleasant and livable for everyone. They often play an important role when a great deal of trust is placed in a professional by people who have little or no knowledge of the specialized work of that professional. For doctors and lawyers, this is obvious. For system administrators, it is at least obvious to you, though perhaps not to your employer or to your "customers"—the end users who you support.

The more networked the world becomes—the more dependent on the Internet, on computerized databases, and on digital communications—the more we all depend on the men and women who are the gatekeepers of those systems. Furthermore, the complexity of those systems, like human physiology or the U.S. legal code, is beyond the comprehension of people who are not dedicated to making sense of it. For example, though the president of General Electric has no idea how to maintain a Web site or how to extract statistical sales information from an e-commerce application, the entire company relies on such information.

Consider the privacy policies that are used on Web sites, the information that they safeguard, and the security concerns mentioned previously. The person entrusted with the keys to all of these critical components of business and government operation is the system administrator. Remember that trust and power go together. System administrators are necessarily trusted because no one else has their abilities. Likewise, the position holds a tremendous amount of power—often out of proportion to its salary or prestige. This is because of the information that the system administrator controls. As a system administrator, take the trust of your employer very seriously. The more you validate that trust over time, the more you will find satisfaction in your work and the more you will be rewarded for it.

NOTE

Not all employers recognize the value of a skilled system administrator, but it is never appropriate to take revenge on a bad employer by violating their trust. You still have responsibilities to internal and external customers, as well as your own integrity, to consider. Move on to another employer if necessary. Your best revenge will be your former employer's difficulty in replacing you.

Very few people set out to act unethically—to break rules of conduct that can lead to embarrassment, loss of position, or even criminal prosecution. However, time pressure and conflicting goals can cause people to make decisions that they later regret. Ethics codes were developed to define the role of system administrators in an organization and to increase the respectability and raise standards of behavior in the profession. After all, it is always easier to make a decision before the pressure is on. As you review the ethics codes for system administrators and other technical positions, you should think about difficult situations that might arise and how you would or should respond to them. When challenges do arise, you will already have reasoned out your response and will not be tempted to make a decision you would later regret.

Many professional organizations support system administrators. You might be familiar already with the SAIR/GNU organization for Linux and GNU software certification (see *www.linuxcertification.org*) and the Linux Professional Institute (see *www.lpi.org*).

Other organizations are not specific to Linux. The largest professional group for system administrators is the System Administrators Guild (SAGE). SAGE is part of the Advanced Computing Systems Association, which goes by the name USENIX (see *www.sage.org* and *www.usenix.org*). SAGE has thousands of members and sponsors regular technical conferences (sometimes with product trade shows attached) dedicated to current system administration topics on a variety of operating system platforms (though SAGE and USENIX are noted fans of Linux and UNIX generally). The main conference, called LISA, moves to a different city each year. The SAGE Web site provides details on upcoming conferences.

The SAGE Web site includes the SAGE Code of Ethics, created by Lee Damon, and information about the SAGE Ethics Working Group. Members of SAGE are expected to abide by the code, which is reprinted next. (You can find it online at *www.sage.org/ethics.mm.*)

"We as professional system administrators do hereby commit ourselves to the highest standards of ethical and professional conduct, and agree to be guided by this code of ethics, and encourage every system administrator to do the same.

- *Professionalism* — I will maintain professional conduct in the workplace, and will not allow personal feelings or beliefs to cause me to treat people unfairly or unprofessionally.

- *Personal Integrity* — I will be honest in my professional dealings, and forthcoming about my competence and the impact of my mistakes. I will seek assistance from others when required. I will avoid conflicts of interest and biases whenever possible. When my advice is sought, if I have a conflict of interest or bias, I will declare it if appropriate, and recuse myself if necessary.

- *Privacy* — I will access private information on computer systems only when it is necessary in the course of my technical duties. I will maintain and protect the confidentiality of any information to which I may have access, regardless of the method by which I came into knowledge of it.

- *Laws and Policies* — I will educate myself and others on relevant laws, regulations, and policies regarding the performance of my duties.

- *Communication* — I will communicate with management, users, and colleagues about computer matters of mutual interest. I will strive to listen to and understand the needs of all parties.

- *System Integrity* — I will strive to ensure the necessary integrity, reliability, and availability of the systems for which I am responsible. I will design and maintain each system in a manner to support the purpose of the system to the organization.

- *Education* — I will continue to update and enhance my technical knowledge and other work-related skills. I will share my knowledge and experience with others.

- *Responsibility to Computing Community* — I will cooperate with the larger computing community to maintain the integrity of network and computing resources.

- *Social Responsibility* — As an informed professional, I will encourage the writing and adoption of relevant policies and laws consistent with these ethical principles.

- *Ethical Responsibility* — I will strive to build and maintain a safe, healthy, and productive workplace. I will do my best to make decisions consistent with the safety, privacy, and well-being of my community and the public, and to disclose promptly factors that might pose unexamined risks or dangers. I will accept and offer honest criticism of technical work as appropriate and will credit properly the contributions of others. I will lead by example, maintaining a high ethical standard and degree of professionalism in the performance of all my duties. I will support colleagues and co-workers in following this code of ethics."

Other organizations with ethics codes include two engineering groups: the Association for Computing Machinery (ACM, at *www.acm.org*) and the Institute of Electrical and Electronics Engineers (IEEE, at *www.ieee.org*). These organizations focus more on engineering new systems than on managing existing systems, but their sites contain a lot of valuable information. The ethics codes are usually linked from the home page.

One advantage of becoming familiar with a code of ethics geared specifically to system administrators is that it helps you anticipate situations that are most likely to occur in your work as a system administrator, instead of being more generally oriented to good business practices.

 A final comment on the topic of codes of ethics: Think of them as minimum standards of behavior in areas that cannot be easily policed. After pondering these codes, decide what personal impact you want to have and how you can achieve your goals.

7

RISK ASSESSMENT AND SECURITY POLICIES

Computer security presents a paradox: The more secure a system is, the less usable it is. No system is totally secure unless it is totally unusable; if someone can gain access, then the wrong person can gain access as well, given the right information. The trick is to make a system both usable and reasonably secure, or, put another way, to make a system highly secure without undue annoyance to authorized system users.

One security method must be debunked at the outset: so-called "security through obscurity." This method says that if no one knows about your server, or your IP address, or what software you're running, then you are safe. But no one can hide on the Internet. Computers are too fast, software is too widely used, and some crackers are just too clever. The key to good security is not to hope that no one finds your system's security weaknesses, but rather to eliminate those weaknesses.

NOTE Not all crackers are bright; some use prepackaged software "kits" or scripts created by skilled crackers. These scripts let even neophytes break into systems that have not taken basic security precautions. Such crackers are called **script-kiddies**. They are easy to thwart, though many systems remain vulnerable to their standardized attacks.

Understanding System Vulnerabilities

Crackers can attack different parts of a networked computer system:

- The hardware components
- The software programs
- The data used by the software programs
- Availability of services and data

Of these, the most serious threat is to the data. Hardware can be replaced and software can be reinstalled, but data is the lifeblood of many organizations. Even with a good backup policy in place and an emergency response plan worked out, data losses from cracker attacks can cost a company millions of dollars because data is generated on the fly and might not be backed up until the end of the day. If you have not taken minimal precautions by regularly backing up your data, a malicious or careless cracker can destroy several years of work in a few minutes.

Crackers have different goals in breaking in to a system:

- Crackers may steal data for their own use, usually trying to avoid detection. This could include customer sales data, personal information, trade secrets, or similar material. Industrial espionage—though apparently not widely practiced—would use this type of attack. Stolen credit card numbers are another example.

- **Crackers** may corrupt data, either accidentally as they explore files on a system, or on purpose to effect changes in the organization or to damage its credibility or efficiency. Data corruption may be obvious, as with a defaced Web home page, or it may be intentionally hidden, such as bank account figures changed in a way that is unlikely to be discovered until an audit sometime later.

- **Crackers** may try to block access to the system, as in a DoS attack. In such an attack, regular users are unable to reach your Web site because it is overwhelmed with Web page requests from a cracker who is trying to cripple your system.

The majority of security incidents result from the actions of users within an organization's network, not from outside attacks. These could be disgruntled current employees trying to wreak havoc or a technical person who gets caught exploring unauthorized areas. Companies need to have policies in place that clearly state the consequences of unauthorized computer use.

As you may have learned in discussions of system backup procedures and high-availability computing, any time a computer system cannot be used as intended, it is effectively "down." If a DoS attack or corrupted data makes a server unavailable, a cracker has succeeded.

NOTE   Don't confuse high-availability or backup procedures with system security. Security focuses on preventing unauthorized access, which might or might not cause system downtime. (For example, stolen data will not shut down your server.) High-availability hardware and maintenance of good backups help to recover when a security breach causes downtime, but they are also used when hardware failures or natural disasters—unrelated to security concerns—bring down a system.

As with high-availability and backup procedures, security should begin with a careful analysis of the assets you are trying to protect and their value. Consider, for example, the following hypothetical statements that reflect different security concerns:

- A bank manager says: "Our reputation as a secure place to do business electronically is critical to our future. If the public saw a news story that our servers had been broken into, it would be a disaster for us."

- A nonprofit foundation manager says: "Our Web site is a public information service. It doesn't collect any user data, nor is the Web server tied to any other system in our company. If it goes down, we'll look bad to the small number of visitors who were unable to view the site, but nothing beyond that is really at risk, and we can restart the server without much trouble."

- The president of a large insurance company says: "Our Internet servers connect hundreds of our employees to headquarters. If those servers are unavailable, we lose a lot of business because no one can write new insurance policies."

- The founder of an e-commerce company says: "We do business *only* via the Internet. If our servers are unavailable, we lose, on average, nearly $1 million per hour, plus we encourage people to shop elsewhere, because we are unavailable: Our reputation and future are in jeopardy."

No one wants their system to be broken into, but you can better judge the appropriate level of effort to put into security measures if you understand the assets that you are protecting, whether they include reputation, revenue generation, secret data, or other factors. Although security by obscurity is never wise, organizations invest differently based on how vigilant they decide to be. For example, the nonprofit foundation in the previous examples might decide to place a Web server at an ISP's office (this is called **colocating** the Web server), and rely on the ISP's security measures to protect the Web server. However, the bank manager—whose security concerns center on keeping the system running and protecting customers' private data—would likely never choose to co-locate a server at a standard ISP.

Wherever they are located, computers are vulnerable to attack using several standard techniques that you should understand to protect against each one:

- **Password cracking** is a technique in which a cracker obtains a user's password, either by using a program that examines millions of passwords until the correct one is found, or by guessing based on personal knowledge about the user (don't ever use your pet's name as a password). With a valid password in hand, a cracker can log on to your system without any signs of suspicious activity.

- **Trojan horse attacks** can occur when you run a program that you obtained from an untrustworthy source or that was installed on your machine by a cracker without your knowledge. An untrustworthy source may even be a friend or associate who intends you no harm. The program appears to function normally but actually performs hidden tasks that render your system insecure and allow the cracker to gain access. E-mail viruses are a common way for Trojan horse programs to enter a computer system, though these viruses themselves are rarely a problem for Linux servers because of the way that Linux multitasking operates. More common on Linux servers are Trojan horses that run with root access, appearing to be valid system utilities.

NOTE

The term "Trojan horse" comes from Homer's *Iliad*, and refers to the ancient Greeks' siege of Troy. According to the myth, the Greeks built a large wooden horse, then hid their best soldiers inside it and presented the horse as a gift. The Trojans pulled the horse into their fort and were routed after discovering the trick too late. The story is the basis for the saying "Beware of Greeks bearing gifts," or in its modern context, "Beware of geeks bearing gifts."

- **Buffer overflow attacks** rely on a weakness in the design of a program. These weaknesses are usually very difficult to find because they are based on complex logic within a large program (such as a DNS server). However, after being discovered by a skilled cracker, the buffer overflow is generally not hard to exploit as a security hole, and the cracker may also inform others of the problem. A cracker must find a specific sequence of steps, or specific input to give to a program, so that the program becomes confused and tries to use computer memory inappropriately. The buffer, or memory space, reserved for a part of the program overflows. The result can be corruption of system data, a crashed server, or even direct root access, any of which may be the goal of the cracker.

- Denial-of-service (DoS) attacks, mentioned previously, try to overwhelm your system so that valid users cannot access it. This is often done by cracking numerous insecure systems and using all of them at the same time to send requests to a server. Services such as DNS and the Web are among those vulnerable to DoS attacks. Because a server is designed to accept any incoming connection, DoS attacks can be very hard to anticipate and prevent, though features in modern routers and in newer protocols like IPv6 make prevention easier.

After you complete this book, you will not be a security expert, but you will know enough to prevent common security problems from wreaking havoc on your server; you will know enough about how crackers operate to be watchful for new or obscure problems; and you will know where to continue your education about computer security. Security is often divided conceptually into four areas:

- *Physical security* involves physical access to your Linux server. This topic is an important initial step in computer security. Physical access to a server enables crackers to reboot the server using a 3.5-inch disk of their own design, to actually remove the hard disk, or perhaps use an open command-line window with root access. Servers should be locked away so that only the system administrator can access them.

- *User security*, or *password security* means making certain that the person who logs on with a given user account is actually the person authorized to use that account. User security is also concerned with creating appropriate limitations on the activities of authorized users. For example, a user might only be allowed to log on between 9:00 a.m. and 5:00 p.m.

- *File security* means making sure that files are accessed only by those who are authorized to use them, and that changes to system files do not indicate a breach of security. (For example, a changed system utility file might indicate that a Trojan horse program has been added to the system to replace a valid utility.)

- *Network security* is the broadest security topic because it involves dozens of network services, any one of which may present security challenges. Because many network services have root access in Linux, an insecure configuration can allow outside users to have root access to the server via the network service. You have learned about layers in networking protocol stacks; network security can operate at different layers as well. For example, IP packets can be blocked or allowed using a firewall, TCP packets can be controlled using TCP Wrappers, and individual applications can have their own security mechanism, as the access control mechanisms in the Apache Web server illustrate.

Social Security

In one sense, computer security is really about people, about knowing why people act as they do and whom to trust. This is true from the perspective of both the system administrator and the cracker.

System administrators must watch carefully where they obtain the operating system and programs that are run on the server. For all its security features, the fact that Linux includes full source code means that a random copy of a Linux kernel taken from the Internet might have been altered by a cracker to permit access via a special "back door" in the source code.

A **back door** is a method of accessing a program or a computer system that is known to its creator but not to other users of the system. It is undocumented and hidden from everyone except the person who created it. For example, a system administrator might create a second account with root access in case the standard root account is disabled by a cracker. Or, a cracker might send out a system administration utility that permits broad access to a host by sending a special code word via the network.

The official site for the Linux kernel source code is *www.kernel.org*. Many mirror sites are maintained around the world. From this site or its mirrors, you can download the latest version of Linux or any patches. Most users prefer to get updates from the vendor from whom they purchased (or downloaded) their copy of Linux. This has the advantage of keeping you in contact with the security bulletins of your vendor and ensuring that the options set in the kernel closely resemble those you are already using.

Although the Linux kernel is unique among popular operating systems in having full source code available, knowing where your programs are coming from is advisable for any service you intend to run. As a cautionary tale, consider that a few years ago someone broke into the main download archive for a popular FTP server program in Holland and uploaded a corrupted version of the FTP server software. Many people downloaded the compromised software (which would have allowed access to the cracker on any system with that FTP server installed) before the act was noticed.

That was a very unusual circumstance. Generally speaking, downloading server software from its main archive site or a mirror site listed on the main archive site is a very safe way to obtain what you need. Some people consider a Linux vendor such as Novell or Red Hat Software to be a better choice because these companies test each product before burning it to a CD and shipping it. Their Web sites are theoretically still vulnerable to similar attacks when they release updated software via the Web, but apparently no attacks of this type have succeeded.

Either way, the point is to be attentive about where you get the software you run. Be aware that crackers can modify open source software. If they can entice or deceive you into installing it, they have an open door to your systems.

Another social aspect of computer security is a cracker's attitude that people are tools. **Social engineering** refers to manipulating someone to extract needed information about a system. A specific (and all too frequently accurate) example of social engineering occurs when a cracker obtains the name of a user on a system and then calls the user on the phone. The conversation might go something like this:

Cracker: "Hi, this is John down in system engineering. Have you noticed your system slowing down some this morning?" (Because a system might occasionally be slow on many networks, this is a fairly safe line.)

User: "Uh, yeah, a little, I guess. What's wrong?"

Cracker: "We're upgrading the server software and some information in your account appears to have been deleted, but I think if I log on with your regular account name I can recover it."

User: "With my thomasw account?"

Cracker: "Exactly. Can you just spell the password for me so I make sure I get it right?"

Many users, unless instructed otherwise, are helpful and trusting, and offer their password to any stranger over the phone who is bold enough to use such a ruse. Other common social engineering methods are so simple that they have been used in several movies: A walk through an office can yield a harvest of information from people who post their password on a slip of paper at their desk so they don't forget it. People also use their child's or pet's name or spouse's birthday as a password. By learning about a target, a cracker may be able to gain access to a server without using any technology tricks.

After a cracker has gained access to a system using a valid user account, it is much easier to gain root access to the system. The cracker can work without much time pressure and without having all his actions logged, as a Web server or FTP server would do. Unless a system administrator checks logs carefully using specialized security tools, the cracker can work without fear of even being noticed, unless he does something foolish such as logging on in the middle of the night.

Password security begins with educating users and instructing them to take some responsibility for security. No system administrator should ever ask a user for a password. It should never be necessary. As an ethical matter, a system administrator should not know the password of any user, because so many users (foolishly) use the same or similar passwords on their computer at work, their computer at home, their bank account, and numerous other places.

Social engineering lets a cracker play on the ignorance, fear, or trust of users to gain information that he can use to access a computer system. This information might include passwords, numeric access codes, or account usernames.

Creating a Security Policy

One of your first steps as a system administrator in any organization should be to create a solid security policy if one does not already exist. As with other policies for backups, disaster recovery, privacy, and the like, creating a security policy forces you to think through thorny issues and difficult decisions before a crisis strikes. It also helps you to prepare your systems and your end users as thoroughly as possible to avert such a crisis. A security policy is a written document that may do any or all of the following:

- Analyze what assets are at risk and need careful protection through computer security.

- Provide statistics to end users regarding the dangers involved in connecting to the Internet. This information can also serve as justification for spending money on security software, security consultants, and other measures.

- Describe procedures to be followed to keep the operating system and network server software upgraded with the latest security patches.

- Outline access levels, specifying which types of employees or outside personnel (such as independent contractors) are to be allowed access to each part of the organization's information systems.

- List specific tasks that need to be completed to make systems secure, such as specific hardware or software to be installed, with a timeline for completing these tasks.

- Compile specific actions to make the system secure after a reboot. If everything is not automated, these actions would include running required scripts, contacting people who have the passwords to start the system again, and so forth.

- Describe procedures that all end users should follow to help ensure the integrity of the organization's computer systems and data. For example, a procedure for setting passwords should require a minimum length and describe how often they should be changed.

- Outline a procedure to follow when an intrusion by a cracker has been detected. Who should be informed, and how should system data subject to corruption or theft be handled?

- Merge the security policies with plans for disaster recovery in case a cracker causes a massive failure.

As with the many other written plans that a good system administrator will create or be familiar with, a security policy puts managers on notice of the dangers that an organization faces. It provides financial justification for the often expensive steps needed to secure information systems. It also prepares system administrators and users for what is inevitable on all but the smallest networks: Someone will try to break in. Watching a break-in or seeing that it has already happened can be paralyzing for an organization that has not planned for it. The reactions range from "shut everything down" to "let's ignore him and hope he doesn't do too much damage while he's in there." Neither route should be part of your security policy. Instead, prepare your systems and yourself for what might happen, determine how you can respond effectively, and then follow up and execute the plan you have created.

Security-focused Organizations

In addition to the professional organizations for system administrators, such as SAGE, organizations that specialize in security can also help you learn more and implement what you learn. They provide a clearinghouse for recent security information. By regularly accessing this information, you lessen the chance that a cracker will be able to use a newly discovered security hole to exploit a weakness in your Linux server.

Upgrading Your Linux System

Your first goal should be to keep your system upgraded using information from security organizations whenever a security issue is discovered. Issues can arise with both the Linux kernel and the programs that run on Linux. Not every upgrade announcement relates to the security of the system; many only affect which hardware devices are supported, or add new features or documentation to an existing program. In particular, upgrades to the Linux kernel are rarely needed for security reasons. If you manage a Linux system that is running smoothly, you shouldn't feel any need to upgrade the kernel unless a security-specific announcement is made about it.

Most of the software upgrades for security problems come in the form of a patch. A patch doesn't change any of the program features; it only repairs a programming error that lets crackers gain access to your system.

The best way to stay informed about upgrades and patches is to subscribe to the security notification service of a reputable Linux supplier, such as Debian, Red Hat Software, or Novell.

Security upgrades are usually much simpler (and more secure) when you use a distribution that relies on software packages, such as the Debian package format (deb) or the Red Hat package format (rpm). Linux kernel patches are relatively rare—security holes are not infrequent in some server daemons, but they don't occur much in the kernel itself. Red Hat Software offers a service called Red Hat Network. This service informs you of security patches as well as version upgrades to packages you are using by automatically checking the Red Hat Internet site at specific intervals. If you choose to configure this feature, Red Hat Network can automatically download the new software, upgrade the system, and restart the server. This is an excellent way to keep abreast of security upgrades as they are made available—your system would never be subject to security breaches that had been documented but that you had not yet installed. Using a system like Red Hat Network doesn't remove the burden of properly configuring the programs you run. It only means that a break-in is unlikely to be the result of a programming error of which you weren't aware.

NOTE Some have suggested that Linux is a less secure operating system because its source code is openly distributed. Nothing could be further from the truth. Because Linux (and hundreds of other programs) provides source code, patches to repair newly discovered security holes are normally available within a few *hours* of discovery. Compare this to the stalling and excuses that some software companies make while they figure out a patch, leaving customers with nothing to do but shut down their servers or hope that crackers don't discover their vulnerability before the patch comes out, perhaps weeks later.

The Security Experts

The two most prominent computer security organizations are the CERT Coordination Center and the System Administration, Networking, and Security (SANS) Institute.

The **CERT Coordination Center (CERT/CC)** is a federally funded software engineering institute operated by Carnegie Mellon University. It was formerly called the Computer Emergency Response Team, and it focused on handling computer security incidents; most security experts likely still think of it in those terms. The CERT/CC Web site, *www.cert.org*, maintains lists of security vulnerabilities, alerts, incident reports, and so on. Figure 7-2 shows the home page for CERT/CC and illustrates the types of information the site provides.

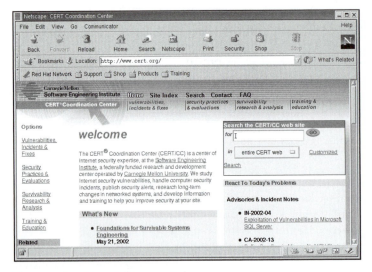

Figure 7-2   The CERT/CC Web site

The **System Administration, Networking, and Security (SANS) Institute** (or simply SANS) is a prestigious and well-regarded education and research organization. Its members include most of the leading computer security experts in the country.

To take advantage of SANS information, start by visiting the Web site at *www.sans.org*. The home page is shown in Figure 7-3. There, you can subscribe to mailing lists of security alerts for various platforms. You can also review information about the SANS Storm Center at *www.incidents.org*. This is a statistical summary of what attacks are taking place at more than 3000 firewalls in more than 60 countries around the world. By analyzing these attacks, SANS security experts are able to provide guidance to other network administrators before new attacks become widespread.

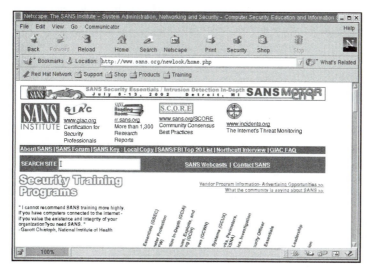

Figure 7-3 The SANS home page

SANS also coordinates with the FBI to provide a Top 20 list of the most widely used strategies being used to attack computer systems. You can review this list to make certain that your systems are protected. For each of the top 20 security issues, the list provides:

- A description of the security issue
- A list of which systems are or might be affected by the issue
- A procedure for determining whether your system is affected
- Steps to protect your system by removing the vulnerability

The information on the SANS Web site is continually updated and includes a number of Linux-specific security resources. Beyond this, SANS maintains a highly regarded hands-on certification program for security professionals: the **Global Information Assurance Certification (GIAC)** program. Related to this effort, SANS provides technical conferences in cities around the world. These are amazing conferences in which top security experts teach hands-on courses to network administrators who face security threats each day. Examples of recent course offerings include the following:

- A multiday series on security essentials
- Investigating incidents (break-ins)

- Managerial and legal issues in security
- Network traffic analysis
- Techniques used by crackers
- Protecting the perimeter of your network with firewalls

The SANS conferences are quite expensive (more than $2000 per person), but SANS operates a volunteer program by which you can attend conference sessions for free in exchange for helping to produce the conference. See the Web site for details.

In addition to CERT/CC and SANS, you should become familiar with the following Web sites:

- *www.securityfocus.com*
- *www.securitymanagement.com*
- *www.insecure.org*
- *www.gocsi.com*

THE U.S. GOVERNMENT AND COMPUTER SECURITY

Because computer security is increasingly viewed as part of our national security, the U.S. government continues to increase its involvement with the computer security industry. For example, the government is prosecuting more computer crimes and has become an information clearinghouse to encourage good security practices.

Security and the Law

When crackers began practicing their craft, U.S. law enforcement agencies had no laws aimed at stopping them. The FBI tried to rely on fraud statutes or other laws related to the damage that a cracker did (such as stealing money by breaking into a bank computer), rather than the specific act of unauthorized computer access.

That situation changed when Congress passed the Computer Fraud and Abuse Act of 1986. This law made it a crime to access a computer without authorization, either for financial gain or to damage U.S. government sites. Penalties include fines and prison terms. Additional laws were passed in more recent years to give the FBI and other law enforcement agencies additional tools to stop the damage that crackers were doing. These laws include the following:

- The Computer Security Act of 1987
- The National Information Infrastructure Protection Act of 1996 (for a good discussion of this law, see *www.usdoj.gov/criminal/cybercrime/1030_anal.html*)
- The PATRIOT Act of 2002

Prosecuting a cracker is different from prosecuting many other criminals. The person investigating the crime might not have a strong initial understanding of the technology involved and so might not realize what damage has been done; the prosecutor might also be uncertain which law provides the best fit and thus gives the best method of stopping the cracker's activities. These problems are greatly reduced when national law enforcement is involved; the FBI and others have special units devoted to these types of crimes. However, the FBI won't get involved if the loss is under a certain amount—$4000 in many locations. Even at the national level, lawmakers can have a hard time keeping up with technology.

Government Agency Resources

Many different parts of U.S. state and federal governments are concerned with proper information security. The following list describes some of the key resources for learning about U.S. government involvement with computer security and computer crime.

- The FBI created a National Computer Crime Squad in 1991 to focus on cases involving crackers (they use the term "hackers"). The FBI maintains extensive online resources related to computer crime. See *www.fbi.gov*.

- The U.S. Department of Justice, Criminal Division, includes a section devoted to Computer Crime and Intellectual Property. This section works with the FBI to prosecute crackers. See *www.usdoj.gov*.

- The Department of the Treasury runs the Secret Service and is responsible for protecting the country against counterfeiting and money laundering. It also operates a separate organization dedicated to protecting against financial fraud (which is now typically done using computers). This group is the Financial Crimes Enforcement Network, or FinCEN, which you can learn about at *www.fincen.gov* or via the U.S. Treasury Home Page at *www.ustreas.gov*.

SECURITY-FOCUSED LINUX PRODUCTS

The popularity of Linux, its freely available source code, and the need for increasingly secure networks has led to the development of several security-focused versions of Linux. These versions are also open source, but they add special features to Linux that make it more like the high-grade secure versions of UNIX used by places like the Central Intelligence Agency and some military installations.

Nevertheless, a word to the wise is in order: Don't accept at face value the claims a company makes for the security of its products. Security is a complex topic, one that has produced as many charlatans as it has experts. Even well-intentioned companies might be unaware of the limitations of their claims of "rock-solid, impenetrable security." Keep your skepticism well-sharpened and be prepared to investigate thoroughly.

As one example, consider the experiences of Microsoft. Its Point-to-Point Tunneling Protocol (PPTP), used to create secure networks between different corporate offices, had been widely praised and received awards. It was later examined by security experts who found five separate flaws in its design and referred to its technology as "kindergarten cryptography." Likewise, in the summer of 1999, Microsoft placed online a server running its Web server, Internet Information Services (IIS), and dared people to crack it as a demonstration of their high-quality, secure products. It lasted less than three hours. Microsoft appears committed to improving its reputation in the area of security, but be wary and test vendors' claims whenever possible.

One of the undoubted leaders in information security is the National Security Agency (NSA), a group that has concerned itself with computer security for decades (either to prevent it or to promote it, depending on the target). A research project at NSA is called security-enhanced Linux, an experimental version of Linux that adds new levels of security to the Linux kernel. Features developed within this project are part of Linux products offered by Red Hat Software and others. You can learn more about security-enhanced Linux and download the source code by visiting *www.nsa.gov/selinux/*.

Another product that provides a more security-conscious Linux is the Bastille Linux hardening package (to **harden** a system is to make it more secure against crackers). Bastille is a set of scripts that can be run on several versions of Linux. Bastille scripts examine your installed Linux system, checking for configurations that present a security hazard. The logic in the Bastille scripts is taken from the SANS Web site and a number of reputable books dedicated to Linux security. Figure 7-4 shows a screen from the Bastille program as it examines a Linux system, provides feedback to the user, and modifies the system as directed.

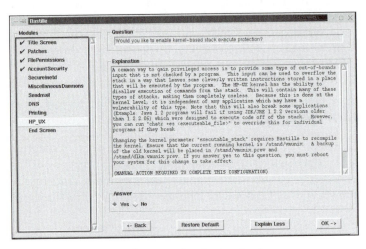

Figure 7-4   The Bastille Linux hardening tool

Using Bastille Linux to harden your Linux system can also help you learn about security because the Bastille scripts instruct you on the security measures being adopted as your system is reviewed and configuration files are altered. To learn more about Bastille Linux and to download the scripts, visit *www.bastille-linux.org*.

CHAPTER SUMMARY

- An amazing number and variety of unauthorized computer attacks continually plague network servers all over the world.

- Computer security is a serious field that pits crackers against administrators seeking to protect their employers' information assets.

- Computer crime statistics are hard to gather, but billions of dollars are spent annually to recover from unauthorized access; people go to prison for committing computer crimes.

- Privacy concerns make computer security a personal issue for anyone using the Internet. A privacy policy is posted on most Web sites and is implemented initially by a system administrator.

- Biometrics for user authentication have significant implications for user privacy.

- System administrators are in a position of great trust and power because of the information they control.

- Codes of ethics help system administrators understand professional expectations that can help them create lasting careers and serve both internal and external customers effectively.

- Difficult security decisions are best made before a crisis arises, based on a considered long-term view of the consequences of each possible course of action.

- Organizations such as SAGE and SANS can help system administrators learn more about security from experts and colleagues.

- A proactive approach to security, rather than "security through obscurity," yields the best results in protecting information systems from attack.

- Hardware, software, and data are all possible subjects of attack, though data is the most likely target. Methods of attack include denial-of-service (DoS) attacks, Trojan horses, buffer overflow attacks, and password cracking.

- Crackers may try to steal data, corrupt data, or deny access to your system by legitimate users. Having a written security policy helps you prepare for all types of attacks by justifying the need for security efforts, informing users of security concerns, and guiding your own actions in defending from or reacting to security breaches.

- Social engineering is a tool of crackers who contact end users and manipulate them to extract needed information.

- You must keep your Linux system upgraded with security patches to prevent attacks that exploit a known problem with software you are using.

- Many laws now exist to allow prosecution of computer crimes. Many government organizations, led by the FBI, are involved in investigating and prosecuting computer crime.

- Security products for Linux may help you improve your security posture, though you must be careful about trusting products that you have not tested.

7

KEY TERMS

back door — A method of accessing a program or a computer system that is known to its creator but not to other users of the system. It is undocumented and hidden.

biometrics — In computer security, user authentication techniques that rely on unique human attributes, such as fingerprints and retina patterns.

buffer overflow attack — A technique for gaining access to a computer system by exploiting a weakness in the design of a computer program. When a cracker follows a specific sequence of steps or provides specific input to a program, the program becomes confused and tries to use computer memory inappropriately. The buffer, or memory space, reserved for a part of the program overflows. The result can be either corruption of system data, a crashed server, or even direct root access.

CERT Coordination Center (CERT/CC) — A federally funded software engineering institute that focuses its attention on computer security issues and provides information to security and system administration professionals around the world; operated by Carnegie Mellon University.

co-locating — An organization's placement of a Web server at the office of its ISP, often to rely on the ISP's security measures to protect the Web server.

computer crime — Unauthorized access to a computer system.

cracker — A person who breaks the law or ethical rules by accessing computer systems without authorization. Some crackers have malicious intentions, but others only want to test their skills by exploring areas that they are not authorized to enter. *See also* hacker.

deface — To alter the text or images on a Web home page.

denial-of-service (DoS) attack — A cracker activity that ties up an attacked server or a particular program with so much bogus network traffic that it cannot respond to valid requests.

Global Information Assurance Certification (GIAC) — A hands-on security certification program run by the SANS Institute.

hacker — A technology expert who enjoys learning about the intricate workings of computer systems and software. To some people's understanding, a technology expert who maliciously attacks others' computer systems. *See also* cracker.

harden — To make a computer system more secure against cracker attacks.

opt-in — A marketing scheme in which users do not receive advertisements unless they specifically request to be added to a list of recipients.

opt-out — A marketing scheme in which users automatically receive advertisements unless they ask to be removed from a list of recipients.

password cracking — An activity by which a cracker obtains the password for a valid user account, either by using a program that examines millions of passwords until the correct one is found, or by guessing based on personal knowledge about the user.

privacy policy — A voluntary statement by an organization about how it will and will not use data that it collects about users or customers, often via a Web site.

script-kiddies — The unskilled crackers who use prepackaged software "kits" or scripts created by skilled crackers to break into systems that have not taken basic security precautions.

social engineering — The process of manipulating someone to extract needed information about a computer system.

System Administration, Networking, and Security (SANS) Institute — A prestigious and well-regarded education and research organization whose members include most of the leading computer security experts in the country. Also known simply as SANS.

Trojan horse attack — A technique for gaining access to a computer system, in which a system administrator executes a program that appears normal but actually creates a security hole for a cracker or destroys data on the host where it is run.

worm — A program that self-replicates and invades networked computer systems. Similar to a virus, but requires less human intervention for continued propagation.

7

REVIEW QUESTIONS

1. Defacing a Web site refers to:

   a. changing the text or graphics on its home page

   b. attempting to crack it

   c. sending derogatory e-mail to the Webmaster

   d. blocking access to the site for valid users

2. Describe the 1988 event that caused many system administrators of Internet servers to begin thinking seriously about security issues.

3. Cracking a system refers to:

   a. gaining unauthorized access to a computer system, usually remotely

   b. giving a password for a system to another user

   c. technical expertise with computers

   d. shutdown of the system

4. Which of the following helps explain why accurate statistics on computer crime are hard to gather?

   a. Crackers cannot erase their tracks after gaining access to a system.

   b. Organizations are not eager to have the public know that their systems were broken into.

   c. Tracking multiple laws used to prosecute crackers can be very challenging.

   d. Many different groups are attempting to collect these statistics.

5. Malicious intentions are:

   a. part of the definition of a cracker

   b. not required to prosecute a cracker who gains unauthorized access to a computer system

   c. restricted to those outside a company being attacked

   d. likely limited to older crackers

6. Personal information is often maintained electronically by businesses to:

   a. prevent theft of that data by crackers

   b. secure new customers and serve existing customers

   c. avoid the need to maintain a privacy policy

   d. prevent government access to that data

7. Describe the purpose of a privacy policy.

8. An opt-in scheme means that:

   a. A user must request to be included on a marketing list.

   b. A user must ask to be excluded from a marketing list.

   c. A user must read a company's privacy policy for it to be effective.

   d. Government officials intend to participate in a security plan.

9. Ethics codes are:

   a. now upheld as laws in many states

   b. completely voluntary and discretionary

   c. not widely known by members of professional groups

   d. an expectation of professionals who belong to professional organizations

10. Name three professional organizations for system administration and security.

11. A script-kiddie refers to a cracker who:

    a. is young

    b. uses only predefined scripts created by more skilled crackers

    c. gains unauthorized access but without malicious intent

    d. attacks sites without any rational motivation for his choices (such as political motives or a grudge against a certain company)

12. To which of the following do crackers present the greatest threat?

    a. data

    b. hardware components

    c. software programs

    d. network connectivity

13. Describe a denial-of-service (DoS) attack.

14. Describe a Trojan horse attack.

15. Describe a buffer overflow attack.

16. Suppose that after gaining unauthorized access to a computer, a cracker created a special user account that only he knew about, so that if discovered, he could later log on using the special user account. This would be an example of:

    a. social engineering

    b. a back door

    c. a denial-of-service attack

    d. firewalling

17. A security policy would probably *not* include:

    a. details on the dangers of lax security

    b. procedures to follow in case a break-in is discovered

    c. expectations of all users regarding use of passwords

    d. descriptions of laws under which crackers could be prosecuted

18. Security advisories:

    a. are created by government agencies under authority of the Computer Fraud and Abuse Act

    b. are provided by Linux vendors and security organizations to help system administrators know how and when they need to update their systems to prevent a break-in

    c. are often a tool of crackers seeking to create back doors or Trojan horses

    d. should not be acted on until a security policy has been revised to include them

19. Name the security certification program developed by the SANS Institute.

20. Name three laws that forbid unauthorized access to computer systems.

21. Besides fingerprints, what other human biometric is unique to each person?

    a. fingernail thickness

    b. retina pattern

    c. pore characteristics

    d. body temperature

22. Which U.S. government agency is primarily responsible for enforcement of computer crime laws?

    a. the FBI

    b. the NSA

    c. the Department of the Treasury

    d. the Secret Service

23. Which U.S. government agency has created publicly available security enhancements to Linux?

    a. the FBI

    b. the NSA

    c. the CIA

    d. the Department of Justice

24. Bastille Linux hardening scripts:

    a. are used by crackers to attack systems using buffer overflow techniques

    b. help system administrators see areas of their system that may be vulnerable to crackers

    c. were created by the NIPC as part of an ongoing program to raise awareness of security issues among government-run Internet sites

    d. are run automatically each time you start your Linux system

25. Computer security for a host is often divided into four areas of concern:

    a. physical, user/password, file, and network

    b. network, firewall, VPN, and tunneling

    c. physical, user, firewalls, intrusion detection

    d. Trojan horse, buffer overflow, password cracking, social engineering

---

HANDS-ON PROJECTS

HANDS-ON PROJECTS

Project 7-1

In this project, you learn how to upgrade a package in which a security hole has been discovered. To complete this project, you should have Fedora Core installed, with networking established, root access to the system, and an Internet connection. This project shows how you would upgrade a package if you *did not* have access to a service such as the Red Hat Network service described in the chapter text. This project also assumes that you know the name of a package on your system that must be updated.

1. Log on as root and open a command-line window.

2. Open a browser and go to *http://fedora.redhat.com*.

3. Click the **Download** link and then click the **Updates** link.

4. Look for the section that discusses downloading security updates and click the relevant link.

5. Click the link for your version of Fedora Core. When this book was printed, the choices were 1, 2, and 3.

6. Click the link for the processor family your computer uses. The i386 link covers 32-bit Intel and Intel-compatible processors such as the Intel Pentium series and AMD equivalents. The x86_64 link covers 64-bit processors such as the AMD Opteron or Athalon64.

7. All the updated packages are listed on this Web page. Click the one you need to download to your computer. Save the file to the /tmp directory.

8. Switch to the command line and change to the /tmp directory.

9. Use the following command to upgrade your system. Substitute the name of the package you downloaded for *packagename*:

```
rpm -Uvh packagename*
```

7

Project 7-2

In this project, you research biometrics. To complete this project, you need a Web browser and an Internet connection.

1. Open a browser and go to *www.bioapi.org*. This is the Web site for the BioAPI Consortium—a group of companies that promote the use of biometrics using a standard called BioAPI. Read the brief introduction.

2. Click the **COMPLIANT PRODUCTS** link and scan the list of biometric products to see what is available. You may want to visit the Web pages of these companies to see how they portray biometrics as a solution for today's security problems.

3. Visit *www.linuxbiometrics.com* and read about plans to support the BioAPI on Linux.

4. To see what Linux geeks think about biometrics, visit a site where you can read many opinions on the subject: Slashdot. Go to *www.google.com* and enter the search term "slashdot linux biometrics". You should see a link to "Slashdot | Linux Biometrics Site Opens Doors". Click the link, then scroll down to see comments from many people who think biometrics is a bad idea.

5. Go to *www.google.com* and enter "microsoft biometrics". The resulting listing takes you to pages that explain biometric support on Windows and why Microsoft embraces biometrics.

Project 7-3

In this project, you research some aspects of the Computer Fraud and Abuse Act. To complete this project, you should have a browser and an Internet connection.

1. Open a browser and go to *www.law.cornell.edu/uscode*.

2. Scroll down the home page until you locate the section titled "Find US Code Materials by Title and Section."

3. Enter **18** in the Title field and **1030** in the Section field. Then click **Go to title and section**.

4. Statutes are not easy to read, but browse down to subsection (c) and review some of the punishments that crackers face when convicted of a computer crime. What are some of the maximum prison terms mentioned?

5. What are some of the circumstances that the law takes into account when deciding on a punishment? (For example, see section 1030(c)(2)(B)(i).)

6. Scroll down to subsection (e)(6) and see how "exceeds authorized access" is defined in this law.

7. Go back to the beginning of the page and notice that the law applies to people who access a computer without authorization or to people whose access exceeds their authorization.

8. Notice in subsection (a)(2)(C) that the law refers to computers involved in interstate communication. This is because the U.S. Constitution limits the topics on which Congress can pass laws (though these limits are usually interpreted very broadly). Can you think of examples of computers that are not tied in any way to interstate commerce (business that crosses state borders)?

9. Go to the Web site *www.findlaw.com* and click the **Search Findlaw** tab.

10. Enter the search query string **Computer Fraud and Abuse Act**.

11. Review the resulting list of items and choose one or two that sound interesting to explore further.

HANDS-ON PROJECTS

Project 7-4

In this project, you research SANS conferences. To complete this project, you should have a browser with an Internet connection.

1. Open a browser and go to *www.sans.org*.

2. Review the list of SANS security conferences that are currently planned. This list may be on the home page, or it may be available by clicking a link from the home page. The list is a large chart with cities and dates in the left column and conference topics marked within squares across each row.

3. Locate a conference near you that includes the SEC401: SANS Security Essentials Bootcamp track (most conferences include this track, referred to in the table as "T1"). Click the link for that city.

4. In the Tracks Offered box on the left side of the page that appears, click the link for **SEC 401: Essentials**.

5. This is a six-part series (one section is devoted to Windows and one to UNIX/Linux). Scroll down the page and review the topics covered in the different sections of the Security Essentials track. You may want to compare some of the topics listed to those presented later in this book. Not all of the essentials are covered here, both because of space limitations and because the SANS security essentials training assumes that you already have experience working as a system administrator.

6. Click the **Back** button on your browser to return to the description of the conference in the city that you selected. Choose another track that sounds interesting and explore the course offerings for that track. (Some conferences offer only two tracks.)

7. Click the **Back** button again to return to the conference home page for the city you selected. Under Conference Links on the left side of the screen, click the **Tuition Fees** link. What are the fees to attend the conference you selected? (Conferences typically last five or six days.) How do you think this fee compares with the value of the conference, based on what you have seen on the SANS site? How could you justify such an expense to a manager to further your technical training in a work environment?

ACTIVITY

Project 7-5

In this project, you research security advisories. To complete this project, you need a browser with an Internet connection.

1. Open your browser and go to *www.cert.org*.

2. On the CERT Coordination Center home page, click the **Search** link (located to the right of the Home link).

3. Uncheck boxes in the Search area so that only Advisories, Incident Notes, and Vulnerability Notes are checked.

4. Enter **bind** in the text entry box and click **Search**.

5. Notice that a large number of security issues related to bind are shown. DNS servers (which provide a name service based on the bind protocol) have been a major source of security holes. Why do you think this is true?

6. Select one of the items listed for bind. Review briefly the Description, Impact, and Solution sections of the document. Does this sound like a problem that might have affected a server for which you were responsible? How would you have learned of this security hole if you had been working as a system administrator?

7. Click the **Search** link at the top of the Web page to return to the Search page.

8. Again, uncheck boxes in the Search area so that only Advisories, Incident Notes, and Vulnerability Notes are checked.

9. Enter **sendmail** in the text entry box and click **Search**.

10. How many items related to sendmail are listed? When was the most recent sendmail problem reported?

11. Click the **Back** button in your Web browser to return to the Search page.

12. Enter **qmail** in the text entry box and click **Search**.

13. How many items related to qmail are listed?

7

14. Why might a person choose `sendmail` when `qmail` is, by all accounts, more secure?

15. Go to **www.us–cert.gov** and explore its contents. Note how it compares with the contents of *www.cert.org*.

CASE PROJECTS

CASE PROJECTS

Case Project 7-1

1. You are working as a system administrator for a financial services company, Safety First Financial Services, Inc., which employs 7000 people. You take care of the computer needs of a group of 75 people. Your supervisor (a nontechnical manager) has just called you into his office. An employee in your group has informed him that another employee has been viewing and storing pornography on his computer at work. Your supervisor asks you to see if this is true without informing the accused person. You can easily check the user's home directory on the server, as well as review logs kept for Internet browsing activity.

   The company has a computer use policy that all employees are to follow. It states specifically that employees cannot visit offensive Web sites and cannot store offensive materials on company computers. However, it also states that the company respects employees' privacy and does not view data stored on their computers or read their e-mail without prior notification and due cause. You are concerned that you might be violating the policy yourself by checking the computer of the accused person as directed, but you also don't want to be in trouble for refusing to do as you are told. If the person is confronted openly, he may erase the offensive files, leaving no basis for disciplinary action or firing, if either became necessary. What should you do? How might you rewrite the company's computer use policy after this incident?

2. Safety First has decided to add a "retirement calculator" to its Web site so that users can enter their age, income, and other factors and see how much they should be saving to retire comfortably, based on various investment styles and lifestyle goals. To use this free feature, a user must register by providing a name and e-mail address. All the information that users enter is stored so that they can return to the site and change the information to explore new retirement scenarios.

   Describe the privacy policy that you would propose for management approval, based on the information that you would be collecting for this feature, the expectations of users of the feature, the needs of the company to market its financial products and services, and other factors you may decide are important. You might decide to visit the Web sites of a few companies and review their privacy policies for ideas. Examples of financial services Web sites include *www.etrade.com*, *www.fidelity.com*, and *www.wellsfargo.com*.

3. You came in to work at Safety First this morning and reviewed your system logs, only to discover that a cracker had broken into the retirement calculator Web site during the night and downloaded the registration details and retirement plan summaries of about 400 customers. What will you do today?

FILE SECURITY

After reading this chapter and completing the exercises, you will be able to:

- ◆ Configure Linux filesystem permissions, attributes, and access control lists
- ◆ Run processes in a `chroot` environment
- ◆ Create and mount loopback filesystems
- ◆ Monitor log files to check for suspicious system activity
- ◆ Automate checks for file integrity and unauthorized modifications

In this chapter, you will learn how to protect files on your Linux system from unauthorized access. This protection starts with standard Linux file permissions and attributes.

Evidence of crackers' activity often appears in system log files. Several utilities can help you track unexpected messages within log files. Further protection is provided by file integrity checkers, which keep track of suspicious changes to any file, not just within log files.

FILESYSTEM SECURITY

Any user who has logged on—with or without authorization—poses a threat to system security, chiefly through the ability to view, delete, or create files. The files stored on your hard disks or other storage media contain system configurations that protect your data, keep your server running smoothly, and hopefully prevent unauthorized entry. In addition, those files contain business and personal data that are the reason for maintaining a system in the first place.

Unauthorized users may want to view files to access data or to see how security settings are configured. They may want to delete data to make it unavailable to you, to disrupt business plans, or to corrupt system configurations. They may want to modify existing files or create new files, either to corrupt your organizational data, to cover signs of their illicit activity in system files, or to establish different security settings that will permit them continued system access.

Ownership

Linux uses the notion of ownership to allow users access to portions of the filesystem. The users can be people and programs. When a person logs on and runs a program, the program is running as the user. When the program creates a file, the file is owned by the user. Here's an example of a user named beth who creates a file called report:

```
-rw-rw----    2 beth    users    4006 Jun 22 21:40 report
```

This file is owned by user beth and by a group called users, of which beth is a member.

Daemons are programs that usually are not run by people—they are run by the system when it starts. These daemons don't have to log on to the system; they are run by the system, which is already running as the root user. If a user logs on and runs a daemon, it runs as that user unless the daemon switches users when it starts.

Daemons that run as the root user have access to the entire filesystem. It's important that these daemons are not compromised by an attacker. A successful attack might mean that the attacker has access to the entire filesystem. To prevent this, daemons should be run as nonroot users whenever possible, and these users should be assigned only the necessary permissions for the daemon to do its job.

Permissions

Permissions give users and the programs they run the ability to access files. For any file or directory, the three standard Linux file permissions are **read** (represented by **r**), **write** (**w**), and **execute** (**x**). These permissions are assigned to the owners of the files. Table 8-1 shows these permissions, with the character and number assigned to each when specifying them for the chmod command.

Table 8-1   Linux file permissions

Permission Name	Character Representation	Decimal Representation	Binary Representation
Read	r	4	100
Write	w	2	010
Execute	x	1	001

Each permission can be assigned to the owner of the file or directory (represented by u, for "user"), to a group defined in /etc/group (g), or to all other users who are logged on to the system but are not the owner or part of the named group (o). These form the standard nine permissions that you see when you use the ls -l command. Table 8-2 describes how each permission affects any user with that permission, either for a file or for a directory.

Table 8-2   File permissions on files and directories

Permission	Effect on a File	Effect on a Directory
Read	Read the file (view and copy it)	List the files in a directory
Write	Update or alter the file	Create and modify files in the directory
Execute	Execute the file	Access files within the directory

Using these nine permissions can become more complicated than it first seems. For example, suppose you have two files in a work directory. One is for your use only—no permissions are granted to the group or other users. The second file is to be read by other users in a managers group that you have created, so it has group permission set to read (r). Because other managers sometimes create files in this working directory, the directory has the write (w) permission set for the group, allowing any member of the group to create files in the directory. The listing for the two files would appear like this (using the ls -l command):

```
-rw-------    1 nwells    users   23411 Jun 22 21:40
private_report
-rw-r--r--    1 nwells    users   21390 Jun 22 21:40
public_report
```

The listing for the directory would appear like this (using the ls -ld command). Note that directory entries always begin with a d:

```
drwxrwx---    2 nwells    users    4096 Jun 22 21:40 reports
```

Now, suppose that another member of the managers group tries to read the private_report file, using this command:

```
$ less private_report
```

She can't because she does not have read permission; only the owner of the file has it. Suppose she tries to copy a file over it using this command:

```
$ cp public_report private_report
```

Once again, the system reports that this is not allowed, this time because she does not have write permission to `private_report`, which is required to overwrite the file using the `cp` command. However, suppose that she instead uses the `mv` command, like this:

`$ mv public_report private_report`

This time, the system checks whether she has permission to create or rename files in this directory, which is controlled by the write permission on the parent directory. In this case, the other manager is part of the group that is granted write permission, including the ability to create new files in the directory. Because that permission also allows renaming files, the operation is permitted. She has not been able to read `private_report`, but she has erased it. You cannot set up a directory for all members of a group to create and share files without this possibility, and you need to understand that it exists.

Several other group-related techniques can help you manage file security, as described in the following sections.

SUID and SGID

The SUID and SGID bits have an effect on programs only. The Set User ID (SUID) bit, which appears as `s` in the Execute bit field for the owner of a file, causes the program to assume the permissions of the file's owner. The SUID bit is necessary for some types of programs, such as `su`. Unfortunately, it presents a real security hazard: If crackers are able to set other system files to have the SUID bit active, they may gain root access to the system simply by running a common system utility.

 SUID is considered so dangerous on script files—because they are so easily modified in any text editor—that the Linux kernel will not honor an SUID bit when set on a script file.

CAUTION

You can also add a Set Group ID (SGID) permission to a file or directory. This gives the person who executes a program file the permissions of the file's group while executing the program. Clearly this isn't very useful, and you rarely hear of SGID being used on a program file. However, adding SGID to a directory does serve a special purpose.

Consider first that when a user creates a new file, the group assigned to that file is normally the primary group for that user, as defined in `/etc/passwd`. For example, on Linux systems using the user private group system described later, a new file lists the same name as both user and group, as shown in this example:

`-rw-rw-r--    1 nwells   nwells    3971 Jun 22 21:44 test1`

You can try this yourself by using the `touch` command to create an empty file and then using `ls -l` to see the ownership and permissions of the file. However, when you set SGID on a directory, any file that is created within the directory is assigned the group of the directory, rather than the group of the user who creates the file. This is a convenient method for creating a working space for a collection of users who should be allowed to create files and read each others' files, all without need for the system administrator to intervene to permit access to each individual file.

To see how this works, suppose you had already created a group called *managers* with a number of users as members. Then, you executed the following commands as root:

```
# mkdir /workspace
# chgrp managers /workspace
# chmod g+rws /workspace
```

If you do a long listing of this new directory, you'll see that SGID is set. This shows up as s in place of the group's x permission:

```
drwxrwsr-x  2 root managers  4096 May 9 13:55  workspace
```

Now suppose that user thomas, a member of the group *managers*, logs on. Within his home directory, he creates a test file and then views its permissions and ownership:

```
$ cd
$ touch test2
$ ls -l test2
-rw-rw-r--  1 thomas   thomas  3971 Jun 22 21:44 test2
```

Then, thomas changes to the /workspace directory, creates a test file, and views its permissions and ownership:

```
$ cd /workspace
$ touch test3
$ ls -l test3
-rw-rw-r--  1 thomas   managers 3971 Jun 22 21:44 test3
```

Because the file that thomas created—test3—is owned by the group *managers*, anyone else in the group can read and edit its contents. Files created by any member of group *managers* will have the same characteristics.

Sticky Bit

The sticky bit is a permission whose original purpose was to keep frequently used programs in memory to avoid the delays of reading them from system storage. This permission is no longer needed on modern operating systems, so the sticky bit has another purpose today. (The name "sticky" has nothing to do with its new function.)

The sticky bit is applied to directories, not files. A directory with the sticky bit set prevents users from deleting files owned by other users, even though all users normally have permission to do so. To set the sticky bit on a directory, enter the following command:

```
chmod +t /workspace
```

The sticky bit shows up as t in place of the x permission for others:

```
drwxrwsr-t  2 root managers  4096 May 9 13:55  workspace
```

Denying Access to Group Members

Another technique allows you to deny access to members of a group. Remember that the "other" permissions on a file or directory still require that a user be logged on to Linux. So this technique allows you to say "the owner has a certain access level, and everyone else on the system has a certain access level, but the members of this group can't access the file or directory."

To set this up, you might use a series of commands like the following, assuming you had created a group called no_finance for whom you wanted to deny access to a particular directory:

```
$ mkdir /finance_data
$ chmod 705 /finance_data
$ chgrp no_finance /finance_data
$ ls -l /finance_data
drwx---r-x 2 nwells no_finance 4096 Jun 22 21:40 finance_data
```

 NOTE   Recall from your introductory Linux training that the "705" represents the file permissions granted for the user, group, and other categories. The 7 is read, write, and execute for the user; 0 is no rights for the group; and 5 is read and execute for others.

No member of the no_finance group can use the cd command to get into the /finance_data directory or list the files it contains. This is effective because Linux computes access rights first by checking whether the user requesting access is the owner and whether the owner's rights permit the access requested. If the user is not the owner, Linux checks to see whether the requesting user is a member of the group assigned to that file or directory. If so, the group permissions of the file or directory are used to assign access (or deny it in this case); the rights assigned to other users are never considered.

User Private Groups

Some Linux distributions, such as Fedora Core, use a technique called **user private groups** to enhance file security. For each user, the idea is to have a group that has the same name as the user. The user is the only member of the group. When a user creates a file, the user and group owner is that user alone—nobody else has access to the file.

To see this concept in Fedora Core, create a user with the useradd command. Use the cat command or a text editor to look at the /etc/group file. You see a group with the same name as the user. No members are listed for the group, but the group number corresponding to the user's name is listed in /etc/passwd as the primary group for the user. As a result, any time the user creates a file, the private group—the one with no members—is assigned as the group for that file. If users want others to have access to the file, they must take deliberate action to create the access.

User private groups are reviewed in a Hands-On Project at the end of this chapter.

Attributes

Filesystem **attributes** are properties of files and directories that indicate how the file or directory should be handled by the operating system, filesystem, and programs. Some attributes determine how files can be accessed (read, write, append-only) or modified (delete, rename, linked). Other attributes determine performance-related criteria, such as not taking the time to update time stamps.

Unlike permissions, attributes have no regard for ownership. The attributes apply regardless of the owner of the file or directory. Even the root user cannot escape the effects of attributes, though the root user can set (turn on) or clear (turn off) attributes. Also, attributes override permissions. In any struggle between permissions and attributes, attributes always win. For example, if a user has permission to delete a file but the file's immutable attribute is set, the file will not be deleted.

The Linux filesystem attributes that are germane to this book include the following:

- A—The `atime` attribute. Can be applied to a file only. When set, the filesystem does not update the file's last accessed time (`atime`) stamp whenever the file is accessed. This is the date and time that the file was last opened for read and/or write access. Normally, `atime` is set to the present date and time when the file is opened. When the A attribute is set, the filesystem has less work to do. You should only use the A attribute for files that do not need to have their `atime` updated.

- a—The append mode attribute. Can be applied to a file only. When set, the file can be opened for write access, but data can only be written to the end of the file. The present contents of the file cannot be overwritten. The practical application is for log files or audit trail files; an attacker cannot change the contents of these files to hide an attack. Only the root user can set or clear this attribute.

- D—The `dirsync` attribute; a subset of the `sync` attribute. When applied to a directory, the following operations are synchronous within the directory tree: create, link, unlink, `symlink`, `mkdir`, `rmdir`, `mknod`, and rename.

- d—The dump attribute. Can be applied to files or directories. When set, the file or directory will not be backed up by the `dump` program, which is a primitive backup program. Other backup programs can use the `dump` attribute in the same way.

- i—The immutable attribute. When set, the file cannot be deleted, renamed, or written to, links cannot be created to the file, the ownership cannot be changed, and date/time stamps cannot be changed. Only the root user can set or clear this attribute.

- j—The journal attribute used with journaling filesystems. Can be applied to a file only. When set, file data is written to the journal first before being written to the file, if the filesystem is mounted with `"data=ordered"` or `"data=writeback"`. If the filesystem is mounted with `"data=journal"`, this attribute is redundant. Only the root user can set and clear this attribute.

8

- S—The sync (synchronous) attribute. Normally, file writes are held in a disk cache (in memory) until the filesystem decides to flush the cache to the disk. This is called asynchronous operation. It could be many seconds before data is flushed to disk. If the system were to crash during this time, the data would be lost—the file on disk would not be updated. If this attribute is set for a file, whenever the file is written to, the data is immediately flushed to disk.

- s—The security erase attribute. Can be applied to a file only. When set, a deleted file has its blocks on disk written with zeros.

- t—The tail-merge attribute. Files seldom consume the entire disk block that holds the data at the end (the tail) of the file. This results in wasted disk space that is often referred to as slack space. The ReiserFS filesystem reduces slack space by having two or more files share a disk block for their tail data. This is called tail-merging. NetWare users know this as block suballocation. When this attribute is applied to a file, its tail is not shared with other files. You set this attribute for files whose size changes often. Tail-merging is not supported by the ext2 and ext3 filesystems.

The a, i, and s attributes are of interest to those who want to use attributes to better secure their Linux system. The A, D, and j attributes affect system performance. Linux has other attributes that are not mentioned here because they are either experimental, not supported by mainstream Linux filesystems, or beyond the scope of this book. Check the chattr man page for details.

You can change the attributes of a file with the **chattr** program. Specify the attributes and the file or directory they apply to, as shown in this example:

```
chattr =i report.txt
```

This sets the i attribute for the file report.txt. You can remove an attribute with the minus sign:

```
chattr -i report.txt
```

Attributes can also be added:

```
chattr +aA report.txt
```

You can change the attributes of all files in a directory tree with the -R option:

```
chattr -R +ia *
```

You can display attributes with the **lsattr** program. If you use the lsattr command with no command-line options, you see a display of all the files and directories in the current directory and their attributes:

```
----i------------ ./dnat.sh
----i------------ ./firewall.sh
```

The $-l$ (lowercase "l") option displays the same information in a friendlier way:

```
./dnat.sh              Immutable
./firewall.sh          Immutable
```

The $-R$ option displays the attributes in a directory tree starting with the current (lsattr $-R$) or specified (lsattr $-R$ /tmp) directory.

File Types and Mount Options

Most new Linux users who install Linux on their computers tend to create a single disk partition for the entire filesystem. After all, this is how it's done with Microsoft Windows. Only after users become familiar with the details of Linux security do they realize that there are benefits to breaking up a disk into many partitions, installing filesystems on the partitions, and using mount options to secure each filesystem.

The reason you would partition disks with Linux and not Microsoft Windows is that Linux follows the time-honored UNIX tradition of keeping files of certain types together in the filesystem hierarchy. Windows does not do this (except for keeping its configuration in its Registry). For example, a well-administered Linux computer has programs stored together in directories such as /bin, /sbin, /usr/bin, and /usr/sbin. System data files are kept somewhere in /var and user data files are kept either in /var or somewhere in the /home directory structure. Files related to configuration are kept in /etc.

This discipline allows an administrator to keep common file types in a separate filesystem from other file types and better secure them by mounting them with appropriate mount options. For example, if a filesystem contains only the /var directory, you can use the noexec mount option to prevent binary programs from executing from this filesystem. It would do an attacker no good to plant a program in /var because it would not be able to run.

 You should already know about mounting filesystems, mount points, mount options, and the use of the mount command. If you don't, refer to Chapter 8 of the *Guide to Linux Installation and Administration* (Course Technology, ISBN 0-619-13095-4).

Another example of the value of partitioning is a filesystem that contains only the /usr directory. If you mounted this filesystem as read-only (ro), attackers would not be able to write to this filesystem and you might prevent an attack. Of course, you won't be able to add or update programs in the directory, but this is easily solved with the remount option. This option allows you to change the filesystem from read-only (ro) to read-write (rw) without having to first unmount the filesystem. Here's an example:

```
mount -o remount,rw /usr
```

To update the filesystem, remount it as read-write, update the programs, and then remount it back to read-only.

Sometimes, you need to use a mount option because of the characteristics of the storage device. Flash memory devices, such as those that connect to a computer's USB port, have limited program/erase cycles. This is called durability; typical flash memory is durable to between 1 and 10 million write cycles. When you exceed this, the device fails—you can't write to it again but you can usually still read from it. When you mount a flash memory device with Linux, it's best to use the `noatime` option to limit the number of times you write to flash memory.

Reserved Disk Space

One way that attackers can disrupt your system is by causing your filesystems to become full. They can cause your log files to grow, cause your printer spools to grow, or exploit security holes in daemons to cause them to consume disk space in some way. If the filesystem becomes full, recovery can be difficult: Nobody can log on if there's no disk space. Under any set of conditions, you want the root user to be able to log on.

To help ensure that there's always disk space for the root user, Linux filesystems have a reserved disk space feature. When you create an ext2 or ext3 filesystem, about 5 percent of the filesystem space is reserved for the root user by default. You can control the amount of reserved disk space by using the −m option when you create the filesystem with the **mke2fs** or `mkfs` program. Here's how you would reserve 2 percent of disk space when you create the filesystem:

```
mke2fs −m2 /dev/hda5
```

The maximum amount of reserved disk space you can specify is 50 percent.

NOTE

If you want to change the reserved disk space on a filesystem that's already been created, you use the `tune2fs` program:

```
tune2fs −m2 /dev/hda5
```

By default, reserved disk space can be used only by the root user. If you want to assign the reserved disk space to another user and group, you must use the `tune2fs` program after the filesystem is created. You can't make this assignment when you create the filesystem. For example, if you want to assign the reserved disk space to user Tricia, use this command:

```
tune2fs −u tricia −g tricia /dev/hda5
```

The root user can see how much reserved disk space exists and who can use it by entering the following command:

```
dumpe2fs -h /dev/hda1|grep eserved
Reserved block count:          100104
```

```
Reserved blocks uid:            0 (user root)
Reserved blocks gid:            0 (group root)
```

The reserved disk space will not be used until all the other disk space has been consumed.

Extended Attributes

Extended attributes or EAs are a recent addition to the Linux kernel. They are name and value pairs that are permanently associated with a file or directory. Think of them as an extension of your filesystem's directory structure that you or your programs control. An EA can be created, deleted, or modified at any time by a user or program.

Practical applications for EAs include adding information to files that describe the content. For example, `lang` could indicate the file's language, `charset` could indicate what character set should be used to properly render the file if it contains text, and `expire` could hold a date and time beyond which the file's contents should no longer be used. The Linux kernel uses EAs for another new kernel feature—access control lists or ACLs. SELinux also uses EAs.

Users manipulate EAs with the **getfattr**, **setfattr**, and `attr` programs. Refer to their man pages for details about their use. For general details on EAs, refer to the man page for `attr` in section 5 of the manual (man 5 attr).

Before you can use EAs, you must enable support in the filesystem using the `user_xattr` mount option. Here's an example of enabling EA support in an already mounted filesystem:

```
mount -o remount,user_xattr /mnt/test
```

An example of an EA name is `user.charset`. The name is in two parts. The first part is called the namespace. There are currently four: security, system, trusted, and user. The security namespace is used by SELinux—an add-on security subsystem for Linux. The system namespace is used by ACLs.

The second part is the specific name, which has the same characteristics and limitations as filenames. The value of an EA is variable-length data whose maximum size on an ext2 or ext3 filesystem is the size of a disk block—typically 1024, 2048, or 4096 bytes. The JFS, XFS, and ReiserFS filesystems allow up to 64 KB. The value is typically used to store file-related **metadata**, not user data, so the size limitations shouldn't be an issue.

You can create EAs with the `setfattr` program. Use the `-n` option to specify the EA name and the `-v` option to specify the value:

```
setfattr -n user.lang -v EN report
```

You can list all the EA names in the user namespace with the `getfattr` program, as shown in the following example:

```
getfattr report
# file: report
user.lang
user.beta
```

You can see the EA values using the following command:

```
getfattr -d report
# file: report
user.lang="EN"
user.beta="456"
```

If you want to see the EAs in other namespaces, use the –m option and specify the namespace followed by a wildcard:

```
getfattr -d -m trusted.* report
# file: report
trusted.alpha="arg"
```

Because extended attributes are a recent addition to Linux, some programs do not yet support the feature. For example, the `tar` program, an archival program commonly used to back up filesystems, does not yet support extended attributes. It does no good to back up a system that relies on extended attributes for its proper operation to a backup facility that cannot restore the extended attributes. The solution is to use the **star** program instead. You can find more information about `star` by searching for it on the Internet.

Access Control Lists

Many Linux administrators have encountered situations in which the simple filesystem permissions that were described earlier don't provide enough granularity to achieve a particular security goal. Seasoned administrators have to spend time designing a directory structure or creating another group to achieve the needed security. Junior administrators who don't know these methods often fail to achieve the needed security and leave their systems vulnerable to attack. Recent Linux kernels now provide a solution.

A new filesystem feature called access control lists or ACLs goes beyond the simple permissions mechanism. You can assign filesystem permissions to anyone—not just the file owners and everyone else. You no longer have to design directory structures that are less than optimal or create additional groups that add confusion and documentation requirements.

ACLs are displayed with the **getfacl** program. Here's an example of what you see for a file that has no ACL:

```
getfacl report
# file: report
# owner: ed
# group: ed
user::rw-
group::r—
mask::r—
other::r--
```

Here's an example of a file that has an ACL with an entry for user bruce:

```
getfacl report1
# file: report1
# owner: ed
# group: ed
user::rw-
user:bruce:r--
group::r—
mask::r—
other::r--
```

You create, delete, and modify ACL entries with the **setfacl** program. Here's how user bruce was assigned his ACL entry in the previous example:

```
setfacl -m u:bruce:r report1
```

The –m option modifies the ACL entries of the file—in this case, a new entry is added. This is followed by the ACL entry (u:bruce:r) and the name of the file. The result is that user bruce can read from the file.

ACLs are based on the new extended attributes feature that was described earlier. The same filesystem support and the same size limitations of extended attributes also apply to ACLs. In addition, the ext2 and ext3 filesystems limit the number of ACL entries to 32 per directory entry (per file).

You can tell which files have ACL entries when you list files with the ls command. These files have a plus sign following their permissions, as shown in the following example:

```
-rw-r-----   0  May  9   09:34   report
-rw-r-----+ 0  May  9   09:36   report1
```

When you copy a file that has ACL entries, the new file does not have the entries unless you use the –p option with the copy command. Some copy command options, such as –a, imply the –p option.

chroot

The **chroot** (short for "change root") feature of Linux and UNIX filesystems allows you to specify a directory that should be seen as the root directory when you run a program. This is sometimes referred to as putting a program "in jail" because the program can't see outside of the chroot directory structure. This is most commonly done by programs that voluntarily restrict themselves to the new root directory, but you can force a program to use the chroot feature.

A good example of a practical use of chroot and daemons is BIND. BIND is a DNS server that has had a number of serious security issues over the years. If BIND is run as root and is successfully attacked, the attacker might have access to all parts of the filesystem. One solution is to run BIND in a chroot environment to limit the damage if it is successfully attacked. Of course, another solution is to use another DNS server.

The primary benefit of chroot is security. If a program running in a chroot environment is successfully attacked and the attacker somehow gains control of the program, the attacker cannot affect anything in the filesystem outside of the chroot directory structure.

Chroot environments must be set up carefully. If you run a daemon in a chroot directory structure and the daemon requires access to one or more libraries in the /lib directory and a configuration file in /etc, you must make sure that these exist in the chroot directory structure. The traditional way of doing this is to create the directories in the chroot environment and then copy the needed files into them. Of course, this consumes disk space.

A program that references lots of files outside the chroot environment might consume quite a bit of disk space. Another Linux filesystem feature comes to the rescue here: bind mounts. A bind mount lets you mount a portion of your real root filesystem into the chroot environment. For the example in the preceding paragraph, you could bind mount the /lib and /etc directories into the chroot environment. This requires no additional disk space. To learn more about bind mounts, refer to the mount man page.

Look at an example of a daemon called chatd that is "chrooted" to the /opt/chatd directory. The daemon requires access to the /etc/chatd.conf file and the /lib/libc.so.6 file. Figure 8-1 shows this environment.

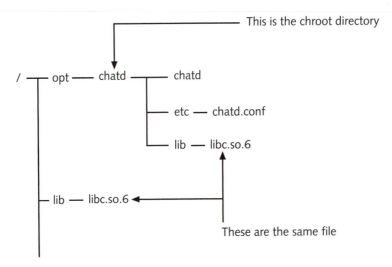

Figure 8-1   An example of a chroot environment

The technique of using chroot to create a program's root directory has applications beyond putting daemons in jail. It can be used when recovering from or troubleshooting a system that won't boot up properly. You boot Linux from a 3.5-inch disk or CD, mount the disk partition that contains the damaged operating system, and then chroot into the mount point.

You can also use `chroot` to put a user in jail. If a user needs access only to a specific application and you don't trust the user to have any other system access, you can `chroot` the user to a small portion of the filesystem.

Loopback Filesystems

Loopback filesystems are virtual disks—filesystems inside of a file instead of on a disk partition. The word "loopback" in the name is unfortunate—it's not clear to most people what "loopback" has to do with a virtual disk. However, everything else about loopback filesystems makes sense eventually. Linux makes it easy to create and use loopback filesystems, and there are numerous practical applications.

One common application is to build a filesystem that you later burn to a CD. You first create an ordinary directory structure on your hard disk and copy files to it for later placement on the CD. Then, you run a program, such as `mkisofs`, that converts the directory structure into a file that is formatted to be an ISO9660 filesystem. This file is then burned onto a CD using a program such as `cdrecord`. The same file can be mounted as a loopback filesystem. You'd do this before burning the CD to be certain that it contains what you need—a CD-ROM (CD-R) can't be changed after it's burned.

To see the commands needed to create a loopback filesystem, refer to Hands-On Project 8-4 later in this chapter.

Now look at another practical application that enhances the security of your system. Suppose you become concerned that log files can grow very large as a result of an attack, and will eventually fill up the filesystem that holds the `/var/log` directory. Rotating your log files periodically might prevent this, but you can't be sure. You can't create another disk partition because you have no free (unallocated) disk space left. You could use the Linux disk quota feature, but it's a complex solution to a simple problem. The simpler solution is to use a loopback filesystem for the `/var/log` directory.

Create a loopback file that's large enough to hold your log files, and then place a filesystem on it. You can choose any filesystem, such as ext2, ext3, ReiserFS, or JFS. The loopback filesystem does not need to match the filesystem in which it resides. You create the loopback file in the `/var` directory. If you want to preserve the existing log files, mount the loopback to a mount point and then copy your log files to it. Unmount the loopback and mount it to `/var/log` using any mount options you choose. Send a SIGHUP signal to the `syslogd` daemon so it logs to the new files:

```
killall -HUP syslogd
```

You're now logging to the loopback filesystem. If the log files ever fill the filesystem, logging will stop, but your system won't fail because it no longer has disk space.

USING THE SYSTEM LOG FOR SECURITY CHECKS

System log files are some of the most important files on your Linux system because they may reveal security problems. These files record the activity of daemons and programs that run on your system. They also record information about successful and failed user logons, packets that were rejected because they were blocked by a firewall rule, and many other conditions.

System messages are usually spread over numerous files in the /var/log directory. Most Linux distributions store general messages in the /var/log/messages file and more specific messages in other files. For example, messages from your e-mail server may be stored in /var/log/maillog. You can see what log files are being used by your system by examining the /etc/syslog.conf file. This is the configuration file for the system logging daemons. In the lines from syslog.conf shown in the following example (taken from Fedora Core), log messages are stored in several different files, depending on which type of program generated the message. The filenames at the end of each configuration line indicate the file where messages are stored. Some lines have been removed from this listing.

NOTE

If you're not already familiar with the format of the syslog.conf file, refer to Chapter 10 of the *Guide to Linux Installation and Administration* (Course Technology, ISBN 0-619-13095-4).

```
.info;mail.none;news.none;authpriv.none;cron.none
                              /var/log/messages
authpriv.*                    /var/log/secure
mail.*                        /var/log/maillog
cron.*                        /var/log/cron
uucp,news.crit                /var/log/spooler
local7.*                      /var/log/boot.log
news.=crit                    /var/log/news/news.crit
news.=err                     /var/log/news/news.err
news.notice                   /var/log/news/news.notice
```

Some daemons do their own logging—they write to their log file directly. They do not use the syslog daemon. Some daemons, like the Apache Web server, give you a choice of using syslog or writing directly to log files.

Messages in the system logs are important because they can leave a trail through which you can see evidence of a cracker's attempts to break into your system, or even evidence of what was done after breaking in.

CAUTION

Skilled crackers will alter log files to hide evidence of their activities. The next section describes how to protect against this.

As an example of how log files can warn you of an impending security crisis, consider what you would think if you found the following message repeated 400 times in succession within /var/log/messages:

```
Jun 21 19:42:13 sundance login[1208]: FAILED LOGIN 1 FROM (null)
    FOR nwells, Authentication failure
```

It's likely that someone is trying hundreds of different passwords to gain access to the system. Admittedly, this would indicate a cracker without much style, but those are the kind you'd prefer to deal with. They're easier to spot before they cause trouble.

NOTE In Chapter 4, you learned how you can have the logging daemons store log entries on a remote computer.

A number of utilities can help you watch for log messages that indicate potential security violations. Not all strange log messages come from crackers; some come from valid users who are experimenting with the system or who don't know how to use a program. However, having a utility that brings these to your attention can allow you to protect your system before an attempted break-in succeeds, or to discover and fix things more quickly if a break-in has already occurred.

Tracking Log Files

The programs running on your Linux system are constantly adding to their corresponding log files. For this reason, you don't normally load a log file into a text editor to review it, though you could. The easiest way to view a log file is to either search it using a command like grep, or view new messages as they are added, using the **tail** program. The grep command would perform a simple search for the word "FAILED" in the system log file:

```
grep "FAILED" /var/log/messages
```

The tail program displays the last 10 lines of any text file. You can change the number of lines displayed using the -n option. To see the last 20 lines of the system log, with new lines appearing on screen as they are added to the file, use this command:

```
tail -f -n 20 /var/log/messages
```

If you are running Linux with a graphical desktop, you can use the **xlogmaster** program to view several system resources, including the system log file. This simple program is not part of most Linux distributions, but you can download it from *rpmfind.net*. Start the program with the command xlogmaster (several command-line options are available, as described in the man page). Figure 8-2 shows the main screen. You can choose one of the buttons on the right side to switch the display window to show different system information.

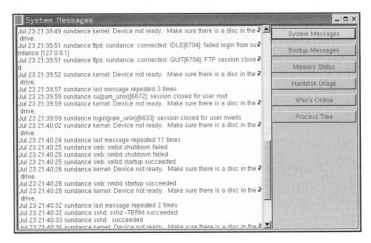

Figure 8-2   The xlogmaster utility

Right-clicking a line in the display window opens a menu where you can choose Customize Entries to set up how you want xlogmaster to display system data. The Customize dialog box is shown in Figure 8-3.

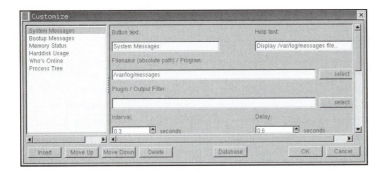

Figure 8-3   Customizing xlogmaster displays

The **logcheck** package does much more than simply display log entries. It checks them hourly for any suspicious entries. If any are found, the entries are e-mailed to the root user (or any other account you select). The logcheck package is not part of most Linux systems, but is available on *rpmfind.net* and other download sites. When you install the logcheck rpm, a cron job file is placed in /etc/cron.hourly so that the logcheck program immediately starts running each hour. The script itself is /usr/bin/logcheck.sh. You can review this file in a text editor to see how it operates. In summary, logcheck refers to a list of words stored in /etc/logcheck/hacking, /etc/logcheck/violations, and a couple of other configuration files. When any of those words appear in a log entry, logcheck e-mails root about it. (Change the line SYSADMIN=root to alter where e-mails are sent.)

You don't need to do anything to get logcheck to function after you have installed the package. You may find it helpful, however, to review the contents of the files in /etc/ logcheck to better understand the types of attacks that logcheck is watching for. You should also review the documentation in /usr/share/doc/logcheck-1.1.1. The following list illustrates some of the words that logcheck watches for in system log files. Not all of these will make sense to you, but see how many you can read, and try to understand what a cracker is attempting when such a log message is generated:

- LOGIN root REFUSED
- rlogind.*: Connection from .* on illegal port
- rshd.*: Connection from .* on illegal port
- sendmail.*: user .* attempted to run daemon
- uucico.*: refused connect from .*
- tftpd.*: refused connect from .*
- login.*: .*LOGIN FAILURE.* FROM .*root
- login.*: .*LOGIN FAILURE.* FROM .*guest
- login.*: .*LOGIN FAILURE.* FROM .*bin
- kernel: Oversized packet received from
- FAILURE
- ILLEGAL
- LOGIN FAILURE
- LOGIN REFUSED
- RETR passwd
- RETR pwd.db
- ROOT LOGIN
- debug
- denied
- deny
- deny host

NOTE

The logcheck utility is based on software originally found in Gauntlet Firewall, from Trusted Information Systems, Inc. For more information, see *sourceforge. net/projects/sentrytools/*.

Another package that is similar to logcheck is **Swatch**. The Swatch package is not part of most Linux distributions, but you can download it from *rpmfind.net* and other sites. Be forewarned, however, that installing Swatch can be challenging. Swatch is a Perl script that requires you to install several additional Perl modules beyond what you are likely to have installed by default; it also requires you to set up a configuration file to specify which logging messages should trigger a reaction from the utility. (Using logcheck, in contrast, you can simply edit the default configuration files instead of creating your own.)

MAINTAINING FILE INTEGRITY

Although log file maintenance and log analysis tools can help you catch potential intruders, they are not foolproof techniques. Sometimes a skillful cracker can gain sufficient access to your system and the log does not indicate a problem. To see evidence of this more sophisticated type of attack, you need to keep track of the state of important files on your system for any unexpected change.

For example, suppose a cracker gained access to your system and replaced your `inetd` superserver daemon with a version that permitted complete access to anyone who connected to a particular port and entered a certain password. You would see no evidence of this in the configuration file—it would be built in to the `inetd` program. Or suppose a cracker replaced your `ls` utility with a new version that failed to list any files beginning with a certain code word. This would allow a cracker to store on the hard disk the configuration files used to disrupt your system, without your being able to see them.

Watching for Rootkits

After a cracker has obtained root access on your system, he wants to maintain that access. A cracker typically uses a **rootkit**, a collection of programs and scripts designed to permit a cracker continued access, even if you discover the original break-in. For example, you might discover that you were using an outdated version of the DNS name server that permitted a cracker to obtain root access. You upgrade the DNS server, so that access point is cut off. However, if the cracker installed a rootkit before you upgraded the DNS server, the cracker will have several more access points that are specifically designed to be much harder to spot. One rootkit, `lrk4`, includes modifications to the programs shown in Table 8-3.

Table 8-3 Examples of how programs are modified by a rootkit

Program	How Altered
`crontab`	Hides certain scheduled tasks from its output
`du`	Doesn't include the size of certain hidden files when reporting disk usage information
`find`	Doesn't list certain hidden files
`ifconfig`	Doesn't display network information that would reveal cracker activity

Table 8-3   Examples of how programs are modified by a rootkit (continued)

Program	How Altered
inetd	Permits automatic access on certain network ports (31337 is commonly used)
killall	Doesn't kill certain processes that the cracker uses to maintain access
login	Permits remote logon without a password to user root
ls	Doesn't list certain hidden files
ps	Doesn't show certain processes used by the cracker

Dozens of rootkits have been developed and are distributed through Internet sites frequented by crackers. You can use the **chkrootkit** package to check your system for evidence of a rootkit. This package includes a script that works much like a virus checker, and though it can report the presence of a rootkit, it cannot eliminate one from your system. It examines system binary files to detect evidence of about 30 different rootkits. The chkrootkit package is not included on most Linux distributions, but you can download it through *rpmfind.net*. It might be more useful, however, to visit *www.chkrootkit.org*, download the package, and review some of the resource links to see how crackers can exploit rootkits to maintain unauthorized access to your system.

The chkrootkit package includes several programming components that you can add to your own software if you choose. These include chklastlog and chkwtmp, which check for modifications of the lastlog and wtmp system files, respectively. These files maintain historical and current data about logons for each user. A rootkit modifies these files to hide their logon activity. Another component of chkrootkit, chkproc, helps you watch for Linux kernel modules that have been installed as part of a rootkit. These modules, referred to by crackers as **LKMs**, provide complete access to your Linux system and can be very difficult to spot, because you don't have to execute any other programs for them to have their desired effect.

If you discover a rootkit on your Linux system, the best course of action is to wipe your disks clean and reinstall the entire system. It's too risky trying to clean up after a rootkit attack because you can't trust anything on the system. You should have backup copies of your data and configuration files made before the attack so you can restore them.

Using Integrity Checkers

Although checking your system for a rootkit is a good idea if you suspect that someone has compromised your system's security, a broader approach is to watch the integrity of files on the system. File integrity checker programs can help you track a large number of files on your system, alerting you to changes that you did not expect. These programs are intrusion detection tools—they alert you to a possible attack. They also might help you see what files have been changed after an attack. The best-known integrity checker is **Tripwire**. You can learn about this commercial software at *www.tripwire.com*.

To use Tripwire, you start with a system that you trust has not been tampered with—ideally one that you have just installed from CDs, before connecting it to any networks. Tripwire creates a baseline or "snapshot" of your critical system files according to a policy that you can configure. Example policy configurations are provided to help you get started. After the baseline has been established, you run Tripwire at regular intervals to see whether the state of the system has changed.

In some cases, the changes will be expected—for example, you may have updated /etc/ passwd because a new employee started working in your division. When the changes are expected, you can update the baseline in Tripwire so that the changes you approve are not marked as potential problems. However, if there is an unexpected change, you can see immediately which files are affected and take corrective actions. In that case, the information provided by Tripwire can show you the changes between the baseline and the current system. This can help you determine how much damage has been done and how to recover.

Tripwire configuration files are protected by a cryptographic signature based on a passphrase that you provide during the initial setup. The encryption prevents intruders from being able to modify your Tripwire policies, configuration, or reports to hide their activities.

 CAUTION   If you lose your Tripwire passphrase, you must reinitialize Tripwire to establish a new baseline. The Tripwire files cannot be used or recovered without the passphrase.

After an integrity check runs, you can review the results using the twprint command and the name of the results database that was created. Here is one example, though the filename on your system will reflect your host name and the times you run the Tripwire checks:

```
twprint -m r --twrfile /var/lib/tripwire/reports/sundance-
    20030622-142613.twr
```

This command displays the report—which can be quite long—on the screen. You may want to direct the output to a file or an e-mail for later review. The first few lines of a Tripwire report are shown here for reference:

```
Note: Report is not encrypted.
Tripwire(R) 2.3.0 Integrity Check Report

Report generated by:          root
Report created on:            Sat 22 Jun 2006 02:26:13 PM EDT
Database last updated on:     Never
===================================================================
Report Summary:
===================================================================
Host name:                    sundance
Host IP address:              127.0.0.1
Host ID:                      None
Policy file used:             /etc/tripwire/tw.pol
```

```
Configuration file used:        /etc/tripwire/tw.cfg
Database file used:             /var/lib/tripwire/sundance.twd
Command line used:              tripwire --check
===================================================================
Rule Summary:
===================================================================
-------------------------------------------------------------------
   Section: Unix File System
-------------------------------------------------------------------
   Rule Name                    Severity Level  Added  Removed  Modified
   -------                      --------------  -----  -------  --------
     Invariant Directories          66           0       0        0
     Temporary directories          33           0       0        0
*    Tripwire Data Files           100           1       0        0
     Critical devices              100           0       0        0
*    User binaries                  66           0       0        1
     Tripwire Binaries             100           0       0        0
*    Critical configuration files  100           0       0        1
     Libraries                      66           0       0        0
     Operating System Utilities    100           0       0        0
     Critical system boot files    100           0       0        0
     File System and Disk Administration Programs
                                   100           0       0        0
     Kernel Administration Programs 100          0       0        0
     Networking Programs           100           0       0        0
     System Administration Programs 100          0       0        0
     Hardware and Device Control Programs
                                   100           0       0        0
     System Information Programs   100           0       0        0
     Application Information Programs
                                   100           0       0        0
     Shell Related Programs        100           0       0        0
     Critical Utility Sym-Links    100           0       0        0
     Shell Binaries                100           0       0        0
     System boot changes           100           0       0        0
     OS executables and libraries  100           0       0        0
     Security Control              100           0       0        0
     Login Scripts                 100           0       0        0
     Root config files             100           0       0        0

Total objects scanned:  17572
Total violations found:   3
```

As with many complex security tools, learning to use Tripwire effectively requires some research and practice. The man pages for Tripwire (`twprint`, `twadmin`, and `twpolicy`) are a good place to begin. The Tripwire package includes limited documentation. You can also consult *www.tripwire.com* for further information.

A second file integrity checker is **Samhain**. (Named after an Irish holiday, this is pronounced "sowen.") Although similar to Tripwire, Samhain has several potential advantages that turn it into a combination of a file integrity checker, a log file checker, and a network monitor:

- It runs as a daemon instead of as a `cron` job, so file changes and logon/logoff events are noted instantaneously.

- It can detect kernel modules that were loaded as part of a rootkit.

- It can operate in a client/server environment to provide centralized monitoring of several systems from one location. Network connections are encrypted using 192-bit AES.

- Reports and audit logs are supported.

- Database and configuration files are signed to prevent intruders from altering them.

- It runs on a number of UNIX and Linux platforms so that you can use it across multiple diverse systems.

- An HTML status page shows information about any client system being monitored.

Samhain is available from *http://la-samhna.de/samhain/* and from *freshmeat.net*. It runs on numerous versions of Linux and UNIX, so you may have to install the source code rather than simply using an rpm.

In Chapter 10, you will learn about using the `md5sum` and `gpg` utilities, plus the `--checksig` option on the `rpm` utility, to validate the integrity of packages.

CHAPTER SUMMARY

- Crackers who break into a system typically want to view or modify the files on that system, either for their own direct use or to cause problems for the organization running the server.

- Linux file permissions do not allow such sophisticated control as some other operating systems because they only permit assigning rights to a file's owner, to a single group assigned to that file, and to all other users on the system.

- Using file permissions can create unexpected results unless you are familiar with their exact consequences. Execute permissions on directories, the SUID bit, and blocking access to a group while allowing access to others are three techniques for using group permissions.

- User private groups enhance security by creating a group for each user account. When users create files, no other group members have access to them.

- Extended attributes allow additional metadata to be associated permanently with files and directories.

❏ Access control lists or ACLs allow finer granularity in assigning users and groups permissions to files and directories.

❏ The Linux `chroot` function allows daemons and programs access to only a portion of the filesystem.

❏ Loopback filesystems allow an entire filesystem to be contained within a single file that is stored in another filesystem.

❏ Reserved disk space ensures that the root user (or another user you specify) still has free disk space when the available disk space to all other users has been depleted.

❏ Log files are important to system security because they may contain evidence of crackers who are attempting to break into a system or of actions by programs running on the system that indicate other potential security problems.

❏ System services continually add lines to the log files. They are often reviewed using not a text editor, but the `grep` search utility or the `tail` program, which displays the last few lines of any text file.

❏ The xlogmaster program displays log file and other system data in a graphical window.

❏ The logcheck utility package watches log files for specific words and phrases that may indicate a security breach has been attempted or has succeeded. The utility can be customized by altering the words that it watches for, as listed in its configuration files.

❏ Crackers can hide their activities by replacing system utilities with new versions designed to ignore special cracker-related files or to prevent reporting the crackers' processes, networking connections, and similar information.

❏ A rootkit helps a cracker easily install a number of programs on a compromised system that permit continued root access even after the initial security hole has been discovered and fixed. Many rootkits are available. The `chkrootkit` package can detect many of these rootkits, much like a virus detector, but cannot remove the rootkit.

❏ The best way to remove a rootkit is to completely reinstall the entire operating system and carefully reconstitute the data on the system.

❏ Regularly checking the integrity of system utilities and configuration files will help you identify changes made by unauthorized users. Tripwire is the most widely used utility for checking the integrity of files and directories.

❏ To use Tripwire, you set up a policy text file and a configuration text file, generate policy and configuration binary files with cryptographic signatures, and then establish a baseline snapshot of system status. Comparison snapshots are then made at regular intervals to determine whether any critical part of the system has been altered unexpectedly.

❏ Another impressive file integrity-checking package is Samhain. This package provides a client/server model to allow maintenance of multiple servers from a central location. Samhain runs continuously rather than occasionally, as Tripwire does.

8

KEY TERMS

attributes — The properties of files and directories that indicate how the file or directory should be handled by the operating system, filesystem, and programs.

chattr — A program that sets and clears filesystem attributes.

chkrootkit — A software package that checks for evidence of more than 30 different rootkits. This package works much like a virus checker, though it can only report the presence of a rootkit; it cannot eliminate one from your system.

chroot — A filesystem feature that allows a program to see a directory as if it were the system's root directory.

execute (x) — A standard Linux file permission—represented in utilities by x—that permits execution of a file as a program or accessing a directory (when assigned to that directory).

getfacl — A program that displays the access control list entries of files and directories.

getfattr — A program that displays the extended attributes of files and directories.

LKM — A Linux kernel module that has been installed as part of a rootkit.

logcheck — A utility package that checks log files each hour for any suspicious entries.

lsattr — A program that displays filesystem attributes.

metadata — In the context of a filesystem, the information about a file or directory, such as its name, size, length, date/time stamps, permissions, attributes, extended attributes, and access control list.

mke2fs — A program that creates an ext2 or ext3 filesystem.

read (r) — A standard Linux file permission (represented in utilities by r) that permits reading the contents of a file or listing the files in a directory.

rootkit — A collection of programs and scripts designed to permit a cracker continued access to a compromised system, even after the original security hole that permitted access has been discovered and closed.

Samhain — A file integrity checker that runs as a daemon and supports client/server configurations.

setfacl — A program that creates, deletes, and modifies the access control list entries of files and directories.

setfattr — A program that creates, deletes, and modifies the extended attributes of files and directories.

star — A program, similar to tar, that can archive filesystems while preserving extended attributes and ACLs.

Swatch — A software package that performs log oversight functions, similar to logcheck.

tail — A program that displays the final 10 lines (configurable) of any text file.

Tripwire — The best-known and most widely used file integrity checker.

user private groups — A security system in which an empty group is created for every user on the system. Files created by a user are assigned to this empty group, meaning that no other users have any default access to the file.

write (w) — A standard Linux file permission—represented in utilities by w—that permits modifying a file or creating new files in a directory (when assigned to that directory).

xlogmaster — A program that displays several system resources, including the system log file, in a graphical window.

REVIEW QUESTIONS

1. File permissions control access based on user accounts that:

   a. are defined in /etc/passwd

   b. are listed in a TCP Wrappers file or similar security configuration file

   c. are part of /etc/services for all network service requests

   d. need not be logged on before accessing data

2. Name the three basic Linux file permissions and the three identities to which each can be assigned for a file or directory.

3. A group that has no members but is assigned as the primary group of a single user within is implementing a security feature called:

   a. file integrity checking

   b. denying group access using file permissions

   c. user private groups

   d. file attributes

4. Which is never shown as a file permission in the output of ls -l?

   a. x

   b. s

   c. w

   d. u

5. Which controls permission to rename a file within a directory?

   a. the execute permission on the file being renamed

   b. the execute permission on the directory containing the file

   c. the write permission on the directory containing the file

   d. the write permission on the file being renamed

6. Setting the SUID bit on a shell script file:

   a. can only be done while logged on as root

   b. is equivalent to setting the SGID bit on the parent directory of the shell script

   c. cannot be done except when a user private group exists for the user who owns the shell script file

   d. will always be ignored by the Linux kernel because it is such a security hazard

8

7. The _____ file configures system logging; system messages are normally stored in _____ .

   a. `/etc/syslog.conf;` `/var/log/messages`

   b. `/etc/message.conf;` `/etc/syslog`

   c. `/etc/log/syslog;` `/var/log/syslog.messages`

   d. `/etc/rc.d/init.d/syslog;` `/var/log`

8. Seeing hundreds of FAILED LOGIN messages in the system log probably indicates:

   a. that one of the users has forgotten her password

   b. that a cracker is trying a brute force attack to gain access to your system

   c. that the system logging daemon is misconfigured

   d. that the logon program PAM modules are misconfigured

9. An administrator has set the read-only attribute for the `pricelist` file, but a user has write permissions to the file. The user is able to write to the file. True or False?

10. Name three types of messages that the logcheck program watches for in its default configuration.

11. If a daemon runs in a `chroot` environment but the daemon must access a library, describe what you must do so the daemon runs correctly.

12. Which mount option allows you to change a mounted filesystem from read-only to read-write without unmounting it?

    a. `sync`

    b. `remount`

    c. `bind`

    d. `noexec`

13. List five files that a rootkit might modify, and describe in general terms how each would be modified to protect a cracker.

14. A rootkit is typically distributed through:

    a. a commercial Linux vendor who can sign the rootkit package to verify its integrity

    b. popular Linux download sites like *rpmfind.net*

    c. developer sites such as *freshmeat.net*

    d. cracker sites that are not publicly advertised

15. Which program allows you to add ACL entries to a file or directory?

    a. `getfattr`

    b. `setfattr`

    c. `getfacl`

    d. `setfacl`

16. To check for evidence of rootkits installed on your system, you can:

    a. Load a kernel module that monitors all network traffic.

    b. Use Tripwire to create a baseline database after a rootkit is suspected.

    c. Use logcheck to see whether a large number of downloaded program files have been modified.

    d. Use `chkrootkit` to look for signs of altered program files and other indications of a rootkit.

17. A loopback filesystem:

    a. is a network filesystem that is accessed through the local loopback (127.0.0.1) network interface

    b. is a virtual disk—a filesystem inside of a file

    c. is the result of mounting a USB flash memory device

    d. is the result of mounting a filesystem over the system's root directory

18. The ext2 and ext3 filesystems allow you to specify that a user besides root can use the reserved disk space on a filesystem. True or False?

19. Which command creates an initial database of system files for Tripwire?

    a. `tripwire --init`

    b. `tripwire --check`

    c. `twadmin --init`

    d. `twinstall.sh`

20. The `dump` attribute is used by the `mount` program to decide which directories to back up. True or False?

21. Which command, with appropriate options, displays a formatted report from a Tripwire integrity check?

    a. `twadmin`

    b. `twprint`

    c. `tripwire`

    d. `twrfile`

22. The ability to work over a secure network connection to manage multiple systems at one time is an advantage of:

    a. `chkroot` over loopback filesystems

    b. Tripwire over Samhain

    c. logcheck over other `binutils` programs

    d. Samhain over Tripwire

23. Which command will display new log messages that are added to the /var/log/
    messages file in real time?

    a. syslog -1 messages

    b. syslog -1 /var/log/messages

    c. tail -f /var/log/messages

    d. head -1 /var/log/messages

24. Using an SGID bit on a directory causes:

    a. users running programs in the directory to have the group permissions of the
       directory's group

    b. no visible change in permissions, because the SGID bit is so rarely used in Linux

    c. access to be denied when any person who is not a member of the group assigned to
       the directory attempts to access a file within that directory

    d. all files created in the directory to be assigned the same group as the directory itself

---

HANDS-ON PROJECTS

HANDS-ON PROJECTS

Project 8-1

In this project, you explore how user private groups affect file permissions on newly created
files. To complete this project, you need root access to a Linux system that also has two
regular user accounts. You can create these accounts using the useradd command. This
project assumes that your version of Linux implements user private groups.

1. Log on as root and open a command-line window.

2. Use su to change to one of the regular user accounts.

    su - username

3. Create a file in the user's home directory by entering a command like the following
   one to copy the contents of another text file instead of typing new material. Don't
   use the cp command, because it preserves the permissions of the file you copy. That
   is not what you want for this project.

    cat /etc/printcap > ~/file1

4. Use the ls -1 command to review the group assigned to this new file and the
   group permissions.

5. Copy your new file to the /tmp directory:

    cp ~/file1 /tmp

6. Exit from the su command so that you are root again.

7. Use su to change to the second regular user account.

8. Go to the /tmp directory and find the file you copied there in Step 3. Look at the file using `ls -l`.

9. Can you read the file (using `more`, for example)? Why?

10. What group would your user need to be a member of to have write permission to the file?

11. Exit `su` so you are root again.

12. Review the /etc/group file to see which group ID corresponds to the group name for the first regular user account. What members are listed?

13. Use the `more` command to review the primary group ID for the first regular user account:

    more /etc/passwd

    Does this number match the number from the /etc/group file?

14. What command could you use to change the permissions assigned to the group when a new file is created?

Project 8-2

In this project, you explore filesystem permissions. To complete this project, you must have two ordinary user accounts and access to the root account.

1. Log on as root and switch to a virtual console by pressing **Ctrl+Alt+F2**. Log on to the virtual console as root.

2. Create a directory called /var/local/share by entering the command **mkdir /var/local/share**.

3. Enter the command **ls -ld /var/local/share** and make sure the share directory has these permissions:

   ```
   drwxr xr x  2  root   root   4096 Aug 18 15:23
   /var/local/share
   ```

If you use the command `ls -l /var/local/share` instead, you see a long listing of the contents of the directory instead of the directory itself.

NOTE

4. If the permissions are different, type the command **chmod 755 /var/local/share**.

5. This project requires two ordinary user accounts. You should already have an ordinary user account set up. This project assumes it's called **justin**. If you don't have a second user account, create a user named beth. (If your first user is named beth, choose another name.) Add the new user by typing **useradd beth**. Next, type **passwd beth** and enter a password that you'll remember.

6. Switch to the virtual console 3 by pressing **Alt+F3**. Log on as user beth. Type **cd /var/local/share**.

7. Switch to the virtual console 4 by pressing **Alt+F4**. Log on as user justin. Type **cd /var/local/share**.

8. Try to create a file with the command **echo "Hello from Justin" > file1**. You see the following error message because you don't have write permission to this directory:

   ```
   bash: file1: Permission denied
   ```

9. Switch to virtual console 2 by pressing **Alt+F2**. You're logged on as root. Type the command **chmod o+w /var/local/share**. You've given all users write permission to the **share** directory.

10. Switch to virtual console 4 by pressing **Alt+F4**. You're logged on as justin. Again, try to create a file with the command **echo "Hello from Justin" > file1**. This time it should succeed and no error message should be displayed.

11. Type the command **ls -l file1**. Notice the permissions on the file as well as the user and group owners:

    ```
    -rw-rw-r--  2 justin   justin    4096 Aug 18 15:23  file1
    ```

12. Switch to virtual console 3 by pressing **Alt+F3**. You're logged on as beth. Type **ls -l** and notice that you see the same results as in Step 11.

13. Type **cat file1**. You see the contents of the file because Beth has read permissions to Justin's file:

    ```
    Hello from Justin
    ```

14. Try to append (write) to the file by typing **echo "Hello from Beth." >> file1**. This command fails, and you see an error message because Beth doesn't have write permissions to Justin's file.

The >> operator tells a program to append to a file rather than to overwrite a file.

15. Switch to virtual console 2 by pressing **Alt+F2**. You're logged on as root. Try to append (write) to the file by typing **echo "Hello from root" >> /var/local/share file1**. This command succeeds because the root user has access to all files and directories on the system, regardless of permissions.

16. Switch to virtual console 3 by pressing **Alt+F3**. You're logged on as beth. Type **cat file1** and watch the following messages appear on your screen:

    ```
    Hello from Justin
    Hello from root
    ```

17. Type **rm file1** and answer **Yes** if you're asked whether you want to remove the file. Type **ls -l** and notice that the file no longer exists. User Beth is able to erase user Justin's files. This doesn't seem right. Beth has only read access to the file. She shouldn't be able to erase it. However, Beth has write access to the /var/local/ share directory, which gives her the power to delete Justin's files. You can solve this security problem by setting the sticky bit on the directory in the next step.

18. Switch to virtual console 2 by pressing **Alt+F2**. You're logged on as root. Type the command **chmod o+t /var/local/share**. Now type **ls -ld /var/local/ share** and you see that the sticky bit (t) has been added (in place of the x bit):

    ```
    drwxr-xrwt  2  root    root    4096 Aug 18 15:23  share
    ```

19. Switch to virtual console 4 by pressing **Alt+F4**. You're logged on as justin. Again, create **file1** with the command **echo "Hello from Justin" > file1**. Verify that the file was created by typing **ls -l**.

20. Switch to virtual console 3 by pressing **Alt+F3**. You're logged on as beth. Again, try to delete the file by typing **rm file1**. You see the following prompt:

    ```
    rm: remove write-protected file 'file1'?
    ```

21. Type **y** and press **Enter**. You see another error message telling you that you can't erase the file:

    ```
    rm: cannot unlink 'file1': Operation not permitted
    ```

Project 8-3

In this project, you experiment with filesystem attributes. To complete this project, you must be logged on as the root user. You should be able to use any Linux distribution.

1. Log on as the root user and open a command-line window. Make sure that your current directory is your home directory.

2. Create a directory called test and make it your current directory:

    ```
    mkdir test
    cd test
    ```

3. Create a file called abc and add some text to it. You can do this with a text editor or with the following command (press Ctrl+Z when you finish entering text):

    ```
    cat>abc
    ```

4. Display the atime (last accessed time) of the file using this command:

    ```
    ls -l --time=atime
    ```

5. Wait a minute or two before continuing. Display the contents of the file with the following command:

    ```
    cat abc
    ```

6. Display the `atime` again using the same command as in Step 4. Note that the time has changed since Step 4 because you displayed (accessed) the file.

7. Set the file's A attribute with this command:

   chattr +A abc

8. Verify that the attribute is set by entering **lsattr**. You should see this:

   ```
   -------A---------  ./abc
   ```

9. Display the file again:

   cat abc

10. Display the `atime` as you did in Step 4. Note that the time has not changed since Step 6 because the A attribute causes Linux not to update the `atime` for files with the attribute set.

11. Set the file's a attribute with this command:

    chattr +a abc

12. Verify that the attribute is set by entering **lsattr**. You should see this:

    ```
    -----a-A---------  ./abc
    ```

HANDS-ON PROJECTS

Project 8-4

In this project, you create a loopback filesystem in your home directory that will be used to hold all the files for a project. You'll be able to copy the loopback file to your USB flash memory so you can take the files from the office and use them on your Linux computer at home. Copying the single loopback file rather than all the project files presumably improves the lifetime of your flash memory by reducing the number of program/erase cycles.

To complete this project, you can be logged on as an ordinary user. You should be able to use any Linux distribution.

1. Log on as the root user and open a command-line window. Make sure that your current directory is the home directory of the user for whom you're building the loopback filesystem. In this exercise, we use user mark as an example.

2. Create a loopback file that is large enough to hold your project files and that will fit on your flash memory. This project assumes that you have created a 30-MB file called loop-project. Use the `dd` command to create the file:

   dd if=/dev/zero of=loop-project bs=1M count=30

3. The loopback file must now be associated with a block device. Use the `losetup` program:

   losetup /dev/loop0 loop-project

4. Place an ext2 filesystem on the loopback:

   mke2fs /dev/loop0

5. You need a directory on which to mount the loopback. Create a directory called `project` in your home directory and assign user mark permissions to it:

```
mkdir project; chown mark.mark project
```

6. Now mount the loopback to the `project` directory:

```
mount -t ext2 -o loop loop-project project
```

7. Go to the `project` directory:

```
cd project
```

8. You're now in your loopback filesystem. Enter `ls`. You'll see the `lost+found` directory that's in the root of every ext2 filesystem.

9. You need to add an entry to your `/etc/fstab` file so the loopback will be auto-matically mounted the next time you boot your computer. Use a text editor to add the following line to the file, substituting your name for *mark*:

```
/home/mark/loop-project    /home/mark/project  auto
loop,defaults,user 0 0
```

10. Reboot the computer and log on as user mark. Go to the `project` directory. You should now be able to copy files here. Place your project files in the directory.

11. When you want to copy the project files to your flash memory, copy the loopback file—not the file within the loopback. On your Linux computer at home, modify its `/etc/fstab` file as you did in Step 9.

CASE PROJECTS

CASE PROJECTS

Case Project 8-1

You are back as a full-time consultant for Snow, Sleet, and Hale. Management asked its part-time technical help to connect the network to the Internet with the assistance of an ISP, but no security measures were put in place. They want you to set up security measures, but do not want you to shut down the servers or disconnect any networking points because the employees have become accustomed to Internet access for their legal research.

On your first day setting up security, you install logcheck and several other programs. On your second day, a logcheck report in your e-mail inbox informs you that the following message was logged late last night (long after you had left work):

ROOT LOGIN

1. What do you suspect has happened? What steps will you take to protect the files on your system? Describe the process you will use to eliminate the danger indicated by this message.

2. As an ethical and practical matter, what will you tell company management? Will you shut down the server or break the network connections? What dangers do you face if you do neither?

3. You had not yet installed Tripwire when this occurred, and you are understandably eager to get it running on your server. You are quite concerned about making an initial database on a system that might already have unknown security problems. How will you proceed?

# CHAPTER 9

USER SECURITY

> **After reading this chapter and completing the exercises, you will be able to:**
>
> ♦ Follow good password security practices
> ♦ Understand Linux pluggable authentication modules (PAM)
> ♦ Use common utilities to promote user security
> ♦ Set up user access to system administration tasks with sudo

In this chapter, you will learn about files and utilities that help you maintain secure user accounts. These include the standard password files and utilities, plus a number of programs that show who is logged on to Linux, that control user access to system administration activities, and similar functions.

In addition, this chapter describes how to use Linux pluggable authentication modules, which let you control how different programs authenticate users (determine their identity) and authorize them to use different services on Linux.

MANAGING USER ACCOUNTS

Users can access services on a Linux system in two fundamentally different ways. First, they can use client software that connects to server software running on Linux. The server software waits for a client connection and accepts or rejects the connection based on a number of factors. A server might reject a connection request because:

- The client is from a domain that is not permitted access.

- The client has an IP host address or network address that is not permitted access.

- The client is using an unsupported version of client software.

- The client is on a blacklist that might be tied to the client's username, e-mail address, domain name, or other information.

- The client does not have the proper credentials.

Even when server software doesn't have the ability to deny access based on these criteria, other software, such as TCP Wrappers, `xinetd`, and the system's firewall, can provide such functionality.

When a person connects to Linux through a network service, access generally consists of limited functionality provided by the server hosting the service. The user does not have broad access to the server because all the user's actions are carried out by the server. For example, a network user connecting from a Web browser does not need an account on the Linux server, but the Web browser knows how to ask the Web server to do something on the user's behalf. Thus, the user's access is limited to the functions performed by the service running on the server.

The second way to access Linux is to log on as a user on that system. To do this, you must have a valid user account on the system.

Managing Linux Passwords

Linux includes several facilities for managing passwords that let you enforce security measures, such as a minimum number of characters, a maximum length of time a password can be used, and other traits.

When you set up a new user account using the `adduser` or `useradd` command (or a graphical utility), a single line is added to the **/etc/passwd** file. A typical entry looks like the following example:

```
nwells:x:500:500:Nicholas Wells:/home/nwells:/bin/bash
```

The fields on this line are separated by colons. The first field is the username; the second field formerly contained the encrypted password for the user, but today the field contains nothing but a placeholder, "x". Because the /etc/passwd file must be accessed by many different programs, it was considered too dangerous to have the encrypted password accessible to all users on the system; it was becoming too easy to crack passwords. Instead, the encrypted password was moved to a file called **/etc/shadow**, which only the root user could access. Each line in this file also corresponds to a single user account, but the fields are related to password management for that account. Specifically, the shadow password file /etc/shadow controls:

- The username to which the entry applies.

- The encrypted password.

- The number of days since January 1, 1970 that the password was last changed.

- The number of days until the user can change the password again. This is relative to the third field.

- The number of days (relative to the third field) until the password must be changed again, at which point it is said to have expired.

- The number of days before the password expires that Linux will warn the user of the upcoming expiration and the need to select a new password.

- The number of days after the password expires that the account will be considered inactive, requiring the system administrator to reactivate the account before a user can log on again.

- The number of days since January 1, 1970 that the account has expired, either as set explicitly by the system administrator or computed from the last password change, and maximum time for password use.

A sample line from /etc/shadow is shown here:

```
nwells:$1$LkrzanmA$/DtzgUGpJa2cTM8rM5WbH1:11844:0:99999:7:::
```

The password in the second field is either encrypted using DES or a one-way hash of the password using MD5. If the password field begins with "1", it is a MD5 hash. Most Linux distributions use the MD5 hash. You can alter this using the authconf utility, in which case DES is used to encode the stored password instead of MD5. When you change from MD5 to DES or vice versa, you need to reenter user passwords.

Each user can change her password using the **passwd** utility. When you enter the passwd command, you are prompted to enter your current password (unless you are working as root), and then you must enter a new password two times. Nothing appears as you type the new password, so entering it twice helps you verify that you entered the correct password. A regular user does not have to specify a username when running the passwd program. When you are logged on as root, you can change any user's password using passwd by adding the username after the command, then entering a new password twice when prompted:

```
passwd nwells
```

The passwd utility performs a few basic checks on the password you enter, based on the configuration of Linux PAM modules (described later in this chapter). However, passwd can't prevent you from using poor passwords.

9

CAUTION

Although root has access to the `/etc/passwd` and `/etc/shadow` files, you should not edit these files directly in a text editor. The danger is too great that you will disable an account (or worse, cause a security hole) because of a typographic error. Instead, use the utilities that follow to edit password data.

If you must edit `/etc/passwd` because the file has become corrupted, use the **vipw** command. This command locks the `/etc/passwd` file before launching the `vi` text editor, which prevents conflicting edits on systems with multiple system administrators.

Similar to `vipw`, the **vigr** command lets you edit the `/etc/group` file, in which all group membership data is stored on Linux. After you edit the `/etc/group` file with `vigr`, you might want to run the **grpck** command to verify that all group memberships are valid user accounts and that no syntax errors were introduced by your edits. Note that in your version of Fedora Core 2 and 3, grpck might be broken. If you use it, you might see the following message, although nothing is wrong with the `/etc/group` and `/etc/gshadow` files:

```
grpck
shadow group bin: no user oot
delete member 'oot'?
```

The shadow password system in `/etc/shadow` is used by default on all major Linux distributions. (You can alter this in the `authconfig` utility of Fedora Core.) The password control information is set using the `useradd` or `passwd` commands. Table 9-1 shows the relevant options for the `passwd` command, and Table 9-2 shows password options you can use with the `useradd` command.

Table 9-1 Command-line options for `passwd`

Command Option	Description
-l	Lock an account so that no one can log on using that username.
-u	Unlock an account that was previously locked using the -l option. The password of the account remains intact.
-d	Disable an account. The account must be enabled again by the root user setting a new password.
-n *days*	Set the minimum number of days that the user must wait before changing the password.
-x *days*	Set the maximum number of days that the current password can be used before it must be changed.
-w *days*	Set how many days before the password expiration date the user will be warned (upon logging on) that the password must be changed to prevent the account from locking up.
-i *days*	Set the number of days after an account is locked before it will become disabled (and its password deleted).

Table 9-2 `useradd` command-line options for password control

Command Option	Description
-e *date*	Set an expiration date for the account. At that time, the password will be deleted and the account will be effectively disabled, though the user's files remain intact.
-f *inactive_days*	Set the number of days after an account is locked before it will be changed to disabled (and its password deleted).

An example of a specialized password system is the single-use password suite designed by Bell Communications Research. This suite, called **S/Key**, requires users to enter a different password each time they log on to the system. It is designed so that the user doesn't have to think of a new password each time, but instead relies on a system-generated password in conjunction with a longer passphrase that the user selects. S/Key is not available on Linux, but a program based on S/Key, called **One-time Password In Everything (OPIE)**, can be compiled for Linux. This suite of utilities was created by the U.S. Naval Research Laboratory.

Selecting Strong Passwords

Counteracting secret cracker tricks can consume a lot of your time as a system administrator, but a cracker's best bet is simply to obtain a valid password for a user on your system. Then, the cracker can log on at his leisure without any of the telltale signs of a forced entry that you watch for on network services. Selecting good passwords and keeping them secure is crucial to good system security. All users need to understand this, and frequently they must have it enforced by rules that a system administrator sets up.

Passwords are sometimes obtained from users by crackers using social engineering tactics, such as posing as a system administrator, looking for notes taped to a person's screen or desk, or looking over someone's shoulder as she types a password (watching the keyboard, not the screen, as the password does not appear as it is typed). Passwords should not be written down, and especially should not be kept anywhere near the computer to which they permit access. They must be chosen carefully so they can be remembered without a written aid. However, they should not include easily guessed words or numbers, such as names of pets, phone numbers, and so on.

Passwords are often given out on purpose by a user who is trying to help a coworker complete some task using his account. The other person might then continue to use the password without specific authorization whenever it is convenient. Or, the other person might not be as careful with the password as the owner would be. Users should be taught never to tell anyone their password, and system administrators must work to make the system operate in a manner that does not encourage people to give out their passwords. For example, everyone needs access to the right hardware and software to do their job.

When users give out their passwords, they violate the idea on which passwords are based: that only one person can access the server using a particular user account and password. Giving out that password also exposes the password's owner to liability for the actions of someone using his account. Helping users understand this liability discourages sharing passwords.

When crackers don't have passwords handed to them on a platter, they might resort to guessing a password based on their knowledge of the account owner. A skilled cracker has a list of password types that users regularly rely on when security is not on their minds:

- Names of children, pets, or spouse
- Company, industry, or product relating to their job
- Combinations of birthdays of the user or user's family
- Commonly used bad passwords like "password," "secret," or the username itself

For each of these, a cracker will try combinations of words, adding numbers, reversing or dropping letters, and trying similar alterations. When users rely on overly simple items as the basis of their passwords, guessing the right one does not take a cracker long. Users should be instructed not to use passwords that draw on readily available personal information; users also should not use a word that is in the dictionary. In fact, the best passwords are composed of random letters, numbers, and symbols, but these can be hard to remember without writing them down. Here are some ideas for creating a good password for a Linux user account:

- It must be long enough; a minimum of eight characters should be sufficient in most situations. Passwords of four letters, for example, are easy to crack, no matter how clever they are.
- Passwords that contain letters should be a mixture of uppercase and lowercase.
- It should include at least one number (a digit) or one symbol (such as @#$%^&*), and preferably a few of them.
- It could include two or three words separated by one or more symbols or numbers, such as red1*?1meat or buda234pest.
- Using multiple words works even better if the words are foreign or altered so that they do not appear in a dictionary (for example, r3d*m3at or rud*muut).
- Using a series of numbers or a pattern of altered letters can make it easier to remember your password. This is especially helpful when you must select a new password frequently and you decide to follow a pattern for subsequent passwords. Just make certain that the pattern is not obvious to someone who might obtain one of your older passwords.

When you use strong passwords and avoid being the subject of social engineering, a cracker must resort to a brute force attack to gain entry to your user account. A **brute force attack** means trying all possible combinations until one succeeds in guessing a password. If a cracker can store the encrypted version of your password on the Linux server, he might be able to devote considerable time to a brute force attack. If he must actually attempt to log on each time he tries a password, a brute force attack is not feasible, because any system administrator will notice repeated unsuccessful logon attempts. A brute force attack can proceed by trying passwords based on a list of words or by trying all possible combinations of letters, numbers, and symbols.

One simple example of a password cracking tool is called **nutcracker**. You can download this program at *www.tucows.com/preview/51035*. Some system administrators use a password-cracking program to randomly test the strength of users' passwords on the systems they manage, perhaps sending a warning e-mail to users whose passwords were easily broken.

CAUTION Be very careful about using a password-cracking program in this way. Get the written approval of your supervisor and be certain you are not violating the company's employee privacy policy. Avoid the appearance of being a cracker who is trying to pry into personal files, even if you have access to them as root. For a real-life example of how important this issue is, use an Internet search engine to find information about Randall Schwartz.

The possibility of a brute force attack points out the need to change passwords frequently. Changing passwords every 30 days is a common security practice, though some organizations require changes weekly. The threat of attack also shows why the encrypted text of passwords must be safeguarded on each Linux system, as described in the earlier section on shadow passwords. Finally, a brute force attack is much less likely to succeed when users create long passwords that include numbers and symbols.

To see why long passwords are more effective in resisting a brute force attack, you must review a little math. If users have four-character passwords composed only from a pool of the 26 capital letters, you have 26 X 26 X 26 X 26, or 26^4 possible passwords: about 457,000. A fast computer can test that many possible passwords relatively quickly to "crack" an unknown password. But what about a password that is six characters long and may include 26 capital and 26 lowercase letters (Linux passwords are case sensitive), plus 32 possible symbols (such as @#$%), and 10 possible digits? That means that each character of the password has 26 + 26 + 32 + 10 = 94 possible values. So, using six characters yields 94^6 possible passwords, or about 690 billion. Using eight characters, as recommended earlier, yields more than 6 quadrillion possible passwords. At that point, a brute force attack may be too time-costly for an attacker.

Aliases for Root

Normally, the root user account is the only one that has the power of the root user. However, sometimes it's desirable to have more than one user with the power of root. Linux doesn't provide an elegant way to do this, but it does allow you to create aliases for the root user; each alias is a unique user account and has its own password. Linux sees these accounts as the same.

The power of the root user doesn't come from the name root. Rather, it comes from the UID (user ID) of zero. If you look at your /etc/passwd file, the first line looks like this:

```
root:x:0:0:root:/root:/bin/bash
```

The third field is the UID; the zero indicates to Linux that this is the root user. The fourth field indicates that the user belongs to the group whose GID (group ID) is zero. If you look at the /etc/group file, you'll see that this is the group called root. These fields give the root user the power of root.

You can create an alias for root by adding a line to the /etc/passwd and /etc/shadow files. Suppose you want to create an alias for root called "admin." You would modify the /etc/passwd file to look similar to the following:

```
root:x:0:0:root:/root:/bin/bash
admin:x:0:0:admin:/home/admin:/bin/bash
```

Remember to create the /home/admin home directory for the admin user; its ownership should be root. You'd modify the /etc/shadow file as well:

```
root:$1$EYT/oBS9$fjnhlLZFFYEf5n5nzFyXY7/:12814:0:99999:7:::
admin::12814:0:99999:7:::
```

Use the passwd command to set a password for the admin account:

```
passwd admin
```

You can now log on to the admin account. When you do, be aware that many programs will not be aware of or expect root alias accounts. For example, if you're logged on as admin and run the whoami program, it will tell you that you are root, because root appears in the /etc/passwd file before admin. If you reverse the lines, whoami will tell you that you are admin whenever you are logged on as either root or admin.

It's possible that you use programs that must run with the power of root and check that you are root when they start. If they check for the user account name (root) rather than the UID (0), they might refuse to run when you're logged on as admin.

USING PLUGGABLE AUTHENTICATION MODULES

The basic UNIX/Linux password architecture described in the previous section includes security that is robust enough for many sites. However, it is not robust enough for all sites, nor does it permit much of the flexibility in configuration that other operating systems have offered for a long time. In addition, adding Linux to a network of other systems (such as Windows NT) can place a real burden on a system administrator, who must then keep two sets of configuration files updated with user information, rather than just one.

The **pluggable authentication module (PAM)** architecture was developed by Sun Microsystems. It is now used on virtually every Linux system to provide improved user-level security, flexibility in managing user authentication, and smoother integration between

Linux configuration data and user information stored on other systems. PAM is an architecture and set of libraries that let a programmer create a module to perform a specific security-related function, such as testing whether an updated password is too short or whether a user is permitted to log on at a certain time of day. System administrators can select, configure, and then use one or more modules to control the operation of any Linux program that is PAM-aware. Because PAM has been in widespread use for several years, many programs recognize PAM as a security mechanism.

You may have already seen PAM at work. If you are using a standard Fedora Core installation, PAM is configured by default. As one example of its operation, you cannot enter a short word (for example, three characters) when you change your password unless you are root. Instead, you see a message that the password is "WAY too short!" and the password is not changed. This message comes from a PAM module (`pam_cracklib`, listed in Table 9-3) that is configured by default in Fedora Core to stop users from entering insecure passwords.

To use PAM, you select which PAM modules you want to control the activity of a particular program. You list those modules in a configuration file for that program, with parameters to set how the module behaves. Some examples will help you see how this is done. You'll also get to practice configuring PAM modules in the Hands-On Projects at the end of the chapter.

PAM is configured using either a single configuration file, `/etc/pam.conf`, or a series of configuration files in the directory `/etc/pam.d`. (The person compiling the software selects which configuration style is used.) Red Hat and many other implementations use the directory method because it makes it simple for a software package to add a file to your system to configure a newly added program. The `/etc/pam.d` directory contains a file with a name matching the program being configured. For example, the text file `/etc/pam.d/login` configures the `login` program. Each file contains a list of one or more modules that PAM uses when that program is run. The file named `other` is used if a program tries to use PAM but no specific configuration file is found in `/etc/pam.d`. The syntax of each line in a file within `/etc/pam.d` is shown here. Each element is described in the following sections:

```
module_type     control_flag     module_path     arguments
```

 Be careful when working with PAM configuration files. If you were to delete the `/etc/pam.d/login` file, for example, you would be unable to log on to your system, even as root.

To discuss these elements, it's helpful to have a sample file to review. The following lines of code are the default `/etc/pam.d/login` file from Fedora Core. Your file might have additional lines that are not shown that refer to `pam_selinux.so`. If you're using another distribution, your file might have absolute path names (`/lib/security/pam_security.so`) to the PAM modules. The lines are numbered for reference here; these numbers are not part of the actual file:

```
1 #%PAM-1.0
2 auth     required   pam_securetty.so
```

```
3 auth      required   pam_stack.so service= system-auth
4 auth      required   pam_nologin.so
5 account   required   pam_stack.so service= system-auth
6 password  required   pam_stack.so service= system-auth
7 session   required   pam_stack.so service= system-auth
8 session   optional   pam_console.so
```

The first element on each line is the **module_type**, which defines when the module will be used. Possible types include the following:

- auth — Authentication modules are used to identify a user, normally by prompting for a password.

- account — These modules manage the user's account after identity has been established by an auth module. These modules typically restrict access—for example, allowing access only during certain times of the day.

- session — These modules manage a user's current session, normally attending to tasks that must be completed before a user is allowed to work, such as creating log files or mounting a filesystem that the user needs.

- password — These modules are executed when a user needs to change a password (or other authentication tokens).

NOTE

Complete documentation on PAM and individual modules is located in /usr/share/doc/pam-0.77 on Fedora Core 3.

When a PAM-compatible program such as login or passwd is executed, it checks to see which applicable modules are configured for a given task. For example, when a user first logs on, login passes control to PAM, which must run all the modules listed as auth modules (lines 2, 3, and 4 in the preceding example file). When multiple modules are listed for a module type, modules are said to be **stacked**. Unless a control_flag dictates otherwise, PAM executes all of the modules in a stack in the order they are listed, and returns a result of Access Permitted or Access Denied based on the modules' results. The **control_flag** element determines how PAM processes stacked modules. The control_flag has two forms; the older and simpler syntax is still used in most configuration files. It supports four possible values:

- required — The module must succeed for the final result to be Access Permitted. Because later modules in the stack are also executed, the user cannot tell which module failed, but the final result will be Access Denied if any required module fails.

- requisite — The module must succeed for the final result to be Access Permitted. If a requisite module fails, remaining modules in a stack are not executed; if a requisite module succeeds, remaining modules are also executed.

- **sufficient** — The final result can be Access Permitted even if this module fails, but if it succeeds, that is sufficient for an Access Permitted result. If a sufficient module succeeds, no other modules are executed; if a previous required module in the stack did not fail, PAM returns immediately with a result of Access Permitted. If a sufficient module fails, later modules are executed without regard to the result of the sufficient module.

- **optional** — The result of an optional module does not affect the final result of a module stack. Optional modules are used to perform tasks such as logging, which are not part of determining access, but are helpful in system administration or meeting user needs.

Figure 9-1 shows several examples of how these control flags would operate together to determine the final outcome after processing a stack of modules.

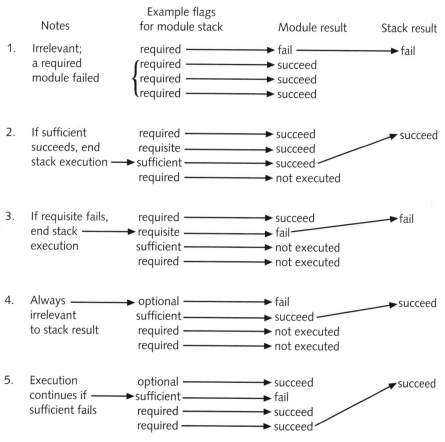

Figure 9-1   PAM control flag processing

As if this system were not sufficiently complicated, PAM also supports another syntax for the control_flag element. You can include one or more sets (separated by spaces) of instructions in the format test=action. The test is one of 30 codes, such as user_unknown or acct_expired. The action can be one of six codes such as ignore, done, or bad; or the action can be a number that indicates how many subsequent modules in the current stack should be skipped. Using this format for the control_flag lets you create a complex stack of PAM modules and control how they are executed based on the results of previous modules. Standard Linux systems don't implement this more complex system in their default configuration files, but you can read about it in the PAM documentation.

The last two elements in a PAM configuration file are the module_path and arguments. The module_path is the complete path and module name to be executed. The arguments are information that should be passed to that module as it is executed. Lines 2, 4, and 8 in the sample file are examples of lines without any arguments. The other lines (besides 1, which is a comment line) have a single argument for the pam_stack module: service=system-auth.

The pam_stack module is a special module that acts like an "include" file. The service listed after a pam_stack module refers to another configuration file in /etc/pam.d. All of the modules listed in the named configuration file are executed at that point. For example, consider the following lines from the previous PAM logon configuration file (again, line numbers are not part of the file):

```
2 auth        required   pam_securetty.so
3 auth        required   pam_stack.so service= system-auth
4 auth        required   pam_nologin.so
```

The file /etc/pam.d/system-auth contains these module configuration lines, which are generated automatically by the authconfig utility based on which security measures you select. This file includes the absolute paths to the PAM modules:

```
auth          required       /lib/security/$ISA/pam_env.so
auth          sufficient     /lib/security/$ISA/pam_unix.so
likeauth nullok
auth          required       /lib/security/$ISA/pam_deny.so
account       required       /lib/security/$ISA/pam_unix.so
password      required       /lib/security/$ISA/pam_cracklib.so
retry=3
password      sufficient     /lib/security/$ISA/pam_unix.so
   nullok use_authtok md5 shadow
password      required       /lib/security/$ISA/pam_deny.so
session       required       /lib/security/$ISA/pam_limits.so
session       required       /lib/security/$ISA/pam_unix.so
```

Given these two files, the `login` command would execute these modules—in this order—as part of the logon process (the `auth` stack):

- `pam_securetty.so`   (from `/etc/pam.d/login`)
- `pam_stack.so`   (from `/etc/pam.d/login`—this module only launches the next three)
- `pam_env.so`   (from `/etc/pam.d/system-auth`)
- `pam_unix.so`   (from `/etc/pam.d/system-auth`)
- `pam_deny.so`   (from `/etc/pam.d/system-auth`)
- `pam_nologin.so`   (from `/etc/pam.d/login`)

The use of each of these modules is described in Table 9-3. Note that some modules support dozens of options. In addition, the file `/usr/share/doc/pam-0.77/html/pam-6.html` in Fedora Core contains reference information for each module, including examples and descriptions of all the supported arguments. These descriptions include information specific to any of the four module types for which the module is supported. For example, the `pam_unix` module can be used for `auth`, `account`, `session`, or `password`.

NOTE   Although you should review the PAM documentation to learn about the operation and options supported by each module, reviewing sample configuration files and the most commonly used modules will help you understand how to configure PAM to meet the needs of your own network. Keep in mind that PAM configurations can be complicated and that misconfigured systems might allow or prevent access in unexpected ways. As you learn about PAM, make changes to configuration files one at a time, testing the results after each change to see what happens.

Table 9-3 Commonly used PAM modules

Module Name	Description
pam_abl	Automatically blacklists hosts from which a large number of failed logon attempts originate.
pam_chroot	Places an authenticated user into a `chroot` environment.
pam_cracklib	Checks the quality of a password and rejects it if it is too short, has been used before, is a dictionary word, or is a minor alteration of the previous password. MD5 password hashing and shadow passwords are implemented through this module.
pam_deny	Always denies access.
pam_env	Sets environment variables as part of the authentication process.
pam_ftp	Checks whether the user is ftp or anonymous; if so, prompts the user for a password.
pam_group	Grants extended group privileges based on a user's ID.

Table 9-3 Commonly used PAM modules (continued)

Module Name	Description
pam_issue	Prepends the /etc/issue file when prompting for the username.
pam_krb4	Provides Kerberos authentication.
pam_lastlog	Maintains the /var/log/lastlog file.
pam_ldap	Authenticates users to LDAP.
pam_limits	Limits the resources to which a user can have access. This module requires additional configuration, but lets you limit a user's CPU time, number of open files, amount of memory, and many other resources.
pam_listfile	Allows or denies services based on the contents of an arbitrary plaintext file.
pam_mail	Informs users whether they have mail.
pam_mkhomedir	Creates a home directory for an authenticated user. The contents of the /etc/skel directory are copied into the new directory.
pam_motd	Outputs the /etc/motd file upon successful logon.
pam_mount	Mounts disk volumes when a user logs on.
pam_nologin	Permits root access, but permits others access only if no file called /etc/nologin exists on the system. Root can create this file to stop users from logging on for a time while completing system administration work.
pam_permit	Always permits access.
pam_rootok	Used where root access is needed but without having to enter a password.
pam_script	Executes a script at user logon and logoff.
pam_securetty	If the user logging on is root, checks whether the /etc/securetty file includes the terminal that the user is logging on from; otherwise, does not permit access.
pam_shells	Figures out whether the user's shell preference (in /etc/passwd) matches an item in the /etc/shells file.
pam_stack	A special-purpose module that uses modules in another configuration file, as described previously.
pam_tally	Allows or denies access based on the number of logon attempts.
pam_time	Sets limits on when a program can be used. When used with login, this module limits the hours during which a user can log on.
pam_unix	Performs standard UNIX-style password logon authentication. Supports many options.
pam_userdb	Authenticates users against a Berkeley DB database.
pam_warn	Logs information as part of the authentication process.
pam_wheel	Only permits root access to members of the wheel group (if it exists) or the GID=0 group.

Table 9-3   Commonly used PAM modules (continued)

Module Name	Description
pam_winbind	Authenticates users against the local SMB domain by accessing the Samba winbindd daemon.
pam_xauth	Forwards xauth tokens between X client and X server to permit graphical programs to operate with PAM authentication.

Shown next is a sample PAM configuration file for the halt command: /etc/pam.d/halt. (Comment lines have been removed.) This command shuts down all Linux services so that you can safely turn your computer's power off.

NOTE   When you press Ctrl+Alt+Del to restart or shut down your Linux system, the init program executes a command to restart the system. Typically, the shutdown command is executed (you can see this in the /etc/inittab configuration file). You can also use the halt or reboot commands at the command line to either shut down or reboot your Linux system.

```
auth        sufficient   pam_rootok.so
auth        required     pam_console.so
account     required     pam_permit.so
```

The auth stack of PAM modules includes rootok and console. These modules operate as follows:

1. The rootok module checks whether the user who is executing the halt command is root (normally by checking whether the User account is 0). If it is, PAM sees that this condition is sufficient and immediately returns an Access Permitted result, so root can execute halt.

2. If the user is not root, the console module checks to see whether the user is working at the console (as opposed to logging on via a remote connection of some kind, such as over a network or modem). If the user is on the console, the user can execute halt. Otherwise, PAM denies access and the command does not execute.

Suppose that you let other users sit at the console of your Linux system, but they cannot log on as root. You don't want them to run the halt command. Because the default action of PAM is to deny access if no module specifically permits access, you could make a change so that only root could run halt by deleting or commenting out the second line in the previous sample file. Then, if the rootok module fails (because the user is not root), the halt command cannot be run. No other checks will be performed.

Many more PAM modules are available than those listed here, with additional modules in development. For example, PAM modules supporting Kerberos authentication are used if you configure Linux to use Kerberos (using authconfig in Fedora Core); modules tied to Samba let your users log on to Linux by authenticating to an existing user account on a

9

Windows NT server; and multiple database modules let users authenticate based on a user entry in SQL database. For information on these, see the module listing in the PAM documentation.

Graphical Logons

Linux desktops that boot into a graphical mode and present the user with a graphical logon screen usually run the gdm program. This program interacts with the user to collect the user's credentials, and then interacts with the system to authenticate and log on the user. If you're running the KDE desktop, you're probably using the kdm program instead. This section focuses on gdm.

You can change the way gdm behaves by editing its gdm.conf configuration file. On Fedora Core systems, you can find it in the /etc/X11/gdm directory.

You can configure gdm to automatically log on a certain user by editing the following statements in the gdm.conf file:

```
AutomaticLoginEnable=true
AutomaticLogin=ed
```

The next time the system boots, gdm automatically logs on user ed. You don't need to enter the user's password. This is possible because gdm runs as root and can spawn a session for the user. To avoid obvious security issues, you cannot log on the root user automatically.

You can also configure gdm to wait for any authorized user to log on, but after a specified delay, log on a certain user. You do this with the following statements in the gdm.conf file:

```
TimedLoginEnable=true
TimedLogin=beth
TimedLoginDelay=15
```

This example displays the gdm logon screen and waits 15 seconds for any user to log on. If no user logs on within 15 seconds, gdm automatically logs on user beth.

You can configure both Automatic Login and Timed Logins with the graphical gdmsetup program. You can run the program by entering the gdmsetup command or by clicking Applications, then System Settings, and then Login Screen from the GNOME menu. Figure 9-2 shows a screen in which Automatic Login is enabled.

When you select the Security tab of the graphical gdmsetup program, you have the following options (see Figure 9-3):

- You can configure gdm not to allow the root user to log on locally by using the AllowRoot=false statement.

- You can control whether the root user is allowed to log on remotely with the AllowRemoteRoot= statement.

- Remote Timed Logins are controlled by the AllowRemoteAutoLogin= statement.

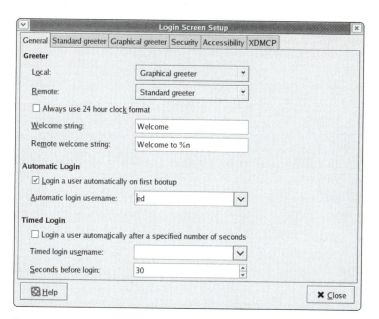

Figure 9-2   Using `gdmsetup` to configure Automatic and Timed Logins

- The `SystemMenu=true` statement enables the Action menu, which allows the user to reboot, shut down, suspend, and configure before being logged on.

- The `DisallowTCP=true` statement prevents remote gdm logins.

- You can determine the number of seconds to wait after a bad logon with the `RetryDelay=` statement (for example, `RetryDelay=3`).

Some security-oriented settings in the gdm.conf file cannot be configured with the graphical gdmsetup program. The `DisplayLastLogin` statement is one of them. If you set this statement to true, it displays the last time the user logged on before prompting for the password. This allows users to decide whether to enter their passwords based on whether the last logon was legitimate. If a user notices that the last logon time was the previous evening when the office was closed, the user can choose not to enter the password and notify the administrator.

The `DoubleLoginWarning` statement, if set to true, detects when a user is logged on already.

The `DisplaysPerHost=` statement determines how many times a person can log on from a single host. This is usually set at 2 in case the server crashes and you want to log on again.

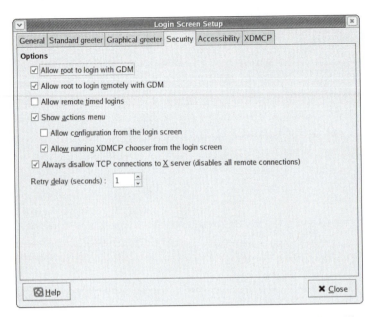

Figure 9-3 Using gdmsetup to configure gdm security settings

SSH Logons

The SSH daemon can be configured to be very secure, as you would expect. This is fortunate because attacks against SSH occur on the Internet all the time, most commonly when an attacker guesses at SSH passwords. The obvious solution is to have robust passwords, but an administrator can't always ensure that users have created secure passwords.

You configure the daemon by editing the /etc/ssh/sshd_config file. The user account that you'd like to protect most is the root user's, of course. However, you're in control of root's password and attackers should not be capable of guessing it. Still, you can prevent SSH logons to the root account by adding the following statement to the configuration file:

```
PermitRootLogin  no
```

You would have to log on to a less privileged account and then su to root.

A better way is to eliminate password logons entirely and instead use keys. The following statement disables password logons:

```
PasswordAuthentication  no
```

Even when you've protected against SSH attacks, attackers will still try because they don't know that you've protected yourself. It's typical to find evidence of SSH attacks in your system logs. These are annoying and consume disk space, so you can significantly reduce them by using a different TCP port. Normally, port 22 is used. Adding the following statement to the configuration file has the SSH daemon listen on port 22222:

```
Port 22222
```

Of course, your SSH clients will have to specify this port. Speaking of logging, the SSH daemon logs using the `auth` facility. You can change this; for example, the following statement creates logging to the `local6` facility:

```
SyslogFacility local6
```

You can further protect from attack using the help of DNS. Using the following statement, you can specify that the SSH daemon should look up the remote host IP address of clients and check that the resolved host name maps back to the same IP address:

```
UseDNS yes
```

Of course, this means that the DNS for your remote SSH clients must be set up correctly. You can specify that certain users cannot log on via SSH:

```
DenyUsers  kenny  lisa  tiffany tyler
```

You can also specify that certain users may log on:

```
AllowUsers jim ann chris danielle
```

The following statement prevents members of certain groups from logging on:

```
DenyGroups sales marketing chess_players
```

Finally, the following statement allows the members of certain groups to log on:

```
AllowGroups engineering support
```

9

Security Tools for Users

This section presents an assortment of security utilities and related files that system administrators and users should be aware of. Some are controlled by PAM modules and are available by default; others are separate packages that you must install and configure before using.

Console and Screen Security

It's not uncommon for a user to simultaneously run multiple browser windows, a word processor, an e-mail reader, an audio CD player, and maybe one or two other programs. The system administrator might also have a collection of utilities running, such as a process monitor, a text editor, and network analysis tool (in addition to Web, e-mail, and a CD player). Linux handles all of this nicely. Shutting down all of these programs and logging off every time you left your desk for a few minutes would be annoying and unproductive, but that is exactly what you should do to protect your system. Otherwise, anyone in the office who happened by your desk (or was waiting for you to step away for a moment) could review your files, delete something, send himself an e-mail containing your files, or otherwise breach the security of your system. Most security problems arise from other employees, not malicious outsiders.

The solution to this dilemma—waste time logging off or leave your system at risk—is to use a screen-locking program. A **screen-locking program** disables input from your keyboard and usually clears or hides the screen so that private information is not visible to passersby. If you are working at a text console (character mode), you can use the **vlock** program to lock the screen you are using or all of the virtual consoles (typically Alt+F1 through Alt+F6). The vlock program is not installed by default on Fedora Core, but it is included in the vlock package on CD 3 and is available for other Linux versions as well.

After you have installed the package, you can lock your current console at any time by using this command:

```
vlock
```

To lock all the consoles (effectively freezing the entire system), use this command:

```
vlock -a
```

You can then unlock the console(s) only by entering either the root password or the password for the user you are logged on as. Until you do, you can't perform any other task at the console.

CAUTION

Be certain that the top of your screen doesn't contain any sensitive information; vlock doesn't clear the screen when you execute it.

If you work in a graphical environment, you're probably using GNOME, KDE, or another desktop that comes with a screen blanker. These include a password option that locks your screen every time the screen saver starts. You can set up the screen saver in GNOME by selecting Applications, then Preferences and then Screensaver. The GNOME screen saver dialog box is shown in Figure 9-4. When you click the "Lock screen after x minutes" check box, the screen saver can only be turned off by entering your password.

The problem with relying on a screen saver is that your screen is locked only after a preconfigured activation time has passed. If you set the screen saver wait period for one minute, you will soon be annoyed with the ever-present screen saver; if you set it to 15 minutes, your system will be insecure for 15 minutes every time you step away from your desk. (The Test button in the KDE screen saver configuration dialog box does not require you to enter a password to end the test, as some versions of Microsoft Windows do.)

Security Files and Utilities

Linux provides several methods of safeguarding or controlling the logon process. Some important methods for system administrators are listed here.

The root user can only log on from terminals that are listed in the file **/etc/securetty**. By default, this file contains only the virtual console terminals, such as ttyl. None of the network devices or other devices, such as a modem on ttyS0, are listed. This means that a

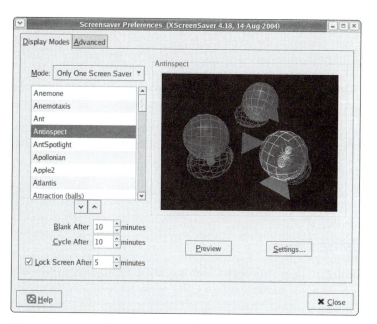

Figure 9-4   Configuring the GNOME screen saver

user dialing into Linux must log on using a regular user account and then use the `su` command to change to root. You can alter this default by adding a device to `/etc/securetty` or by removing some that are already listed, thus limiting the virtual consoles from which root can log on.

If the **/etc/nologin** file exists, only root can log on. No regular users are allowed to log on. This permits root to perform administrative tasks that would be disrupted by having users working on the system (for example, maintenance of key filesystems). The `nologin` file can be empty, but its contents are displayed for any user who tries to log on, so it's a good idea to place an informative message in the file. When you have finished the system administration work, delete `/etc/nologin` to allow users to log on again.

Executable files can have a special permission set that makes them take on the permissions of the file's owner rather than those of the user who executed the file. This file permission is called the **Set UID bit** (also called **SUID**). You can set it for an executable file using the command `chmod o+s filename`. This is done for some utilities such as `su`, which must have root access to run properly, no matter who invokes it. However, having many files with Set UID is a great security risk because any user on the system could easily get root access. You can use the `find` command to search for files with Set UID and see whether they look suspicious.

You can use the PAM module `pam_time` with the `login` program to limit when a user can log on to Linux. Similar time restrictions can be enforced in other ways as well. If you are running the standard shell for Linux—`bash`—you can use the following command to set an environment variable with the number of seconds that the console can sit idle before you are automatically logged off. In the following example, the number 600 means that 10 minutes of inactivity causes the console to be logged off:

```
export TMOUT=600
```

This has value only if you are working in a character-mode console, but it is useful as a backup in case you are called away from your desk suddenly and forget to use `vlock` or log off.

If you are using the `tcsh` shell, the environment variable to accomplish the same thing is shown in the following example. Note that the number refers to minutes of idle time, not seconds:

```
set autologout = 10
```

Whatever shell you are using, you should include the appropriate command in `/root/.profile` so that it is executed each time you log on.

Seeing Who Is Using Linux

Linux includes a number of basic utilities that let you learn about or control user activity on the system. Table 9-4 lists some of these utilities; all system administrators should know how to use them.

Table 9-4   Basic security tools for user accounts

Command	Description
`mesg`	Enables or disables the ability of other users to send a message to your screen using the `write`, `talk`, or `wall` (write all) commands. Entering `mesg` alone prints the status; entering `mesg` with `yes` or `no` as a parameter allows or disallows access, respectively.
`dmesg`	Prints the contents of the kernel ring buffer to standard output (by default, the screen). The **kernel ring buffer** is a memory area that holds messages generated by the kernel. When the buffer is full, the oldest message is discarded each time a new message is generated. Using `dmesg` right after booting Linux is a good way to see all the hardware-related messages generated by the kernel. Any user can run `dmesg`.
`who`	Lists all of the users who are currently logged on the system. The username and terminal are listed. The `-i` option adds the length of time the user has been idle; the `-q` option prints all logged-on usernames on a single line followed by the number of users logged on. A common use of `who` is to see who you are logged on as, using the command `who am i`.
`w`	Lists all users who are currently logged on with their username and terminal. This is similar to `who`, but w also includes the remote location from which the user has logged on, if applicable, the command that the user is currently running, the amount of CPU time that the user's current process is using, the amount of CPU time that all the user's background processes are using, and the time the user logged on.

Table 9-4   Basic security tools for user accounts (continued)

Command	Description
last	Displays a history of user logons and logoffs, plus system reboot information. Use the command alone to list all users' activity; add a user-name as a parameter to list activity for that user; add the word reboot as a parameter to list information about when the system was rebooted.
lastcomm	Displays information about commands that a user has previously executed. This command is part of the process accounting package psacct, which you can search for and download from *www.rpmfind.net*.
ttysnoop	Lets a system administrator capture all of the keystrokes and output from another terminal, effectively watching everything that is happening on another user's screen. This package is not distributed with commercial Linux packages, perhaps because it has not been updated in several years. It is still available from *www.rpmfind.net* or *www.freshmeat.net*.

9

GRANTING ADMINISTRATION PRIVILEGES WITH SUDO

Although you must guard the root account of a Linux system with great care, the system administrators and even regular users might occasionally need to perform tasks that only root is allowed to handle. The **sudo** program lets you assign privileges to any user account to execute only specific programs. Several examples illustrate why the program is useful:

- The system administrator can complete common tasks without needing to su to root.

- Users can mount and unmount 3.5-inch disks or CDs on systems on which they do not have root access.

- Users can kill programs that have crashed or stopped responding.

- Users who don't have root access but who manage a particular service (such as printing or Samba) can access the configuration tools for those programs.

The sudo command uses the **/etc/sudoers** configuration file to determine which users can perform which tasks. Unfortunately, the syntax of this file can be complex. If you don't follow the syntax correctly, sudo refuses to execute at all. (Conversely, you can edit the configuration file using correct syntax but without understanding exactly what actions the file will permit, thus creating a security hole.) The man page for sudoers describes the syntax in exhaustive detail. For those who are new to sudo, skip to the end of the man page and review the examples with explanations instead of wading through the syntax diagrams of all possible configurations. The basic format of a configuration line is:

```
user      host = command_list
```

Part of the power (and possible confusion) of configuring sudo is that you can define aliases, by which a single word might represent any of the following:

- A collection of users who are granted permission

- A collection of hosts on which one or more users' permissions are granted

- A collection of programs for which one or more users are granted permission
- A set of sudo options that are applied to any of the preceding collections

To edit the /etc/sudoers file, you must use the **visudo** program. This program prevents conflicts between multiple open files (assuming multiple users have root access to your system) and checks the syntax of the /etc/sudoers configuration file upon exit. On Fedora Core, you must include the path to this command to execute it:

```
/usr/sbin/visudo
```

The default /etc/sudoers file includes sections in which various types of aliases can be listed, plus a couple of examples. Assume, for example, that you want all users to be able to mount and unmount the CD-ROM drive. The following line in /etc/sudoers will permit it:

```
%users  ALL=/sbin/mount /cdrom,/sbin/umount /cdrom
```

In the preceding line, the %users refers to a group on your system named users; you must create the group or make certain that all users are members of it for this configuration to work correctly. When used in /etc/sudoers, the ALL keyword always matches, so the host field in this example is not controlled. Finally, the two commands that users can execute are /sbin/mount /cdrom and /sbin/umount /cdrom. A user could execute the mount command like this:

```
sudo /sbin/mount /cdrom
```

After checking the /etc/sudoers file, the sudo command executes the command given as a parameter. For this to work properly, you must have an entry in /etc/fstab so that the /cdrom mount point is defined correctly. Assume, for example, that /etc/fstab defines the CD as being mounted at /mnt/cdrom. Because mount /mnt/cdrom is not listed in sudoers, the user will be unable to mount the CD. This points out the need to test sudo configurations carefully, not just for syntax (visudo takes care of this), but for actual effect.

Part of the reason for complex sudo configuration options is that sudo can present security dangers if not properly configured. As with other parts of your system, people should have exactly as much access as their job requires, and no more—everything is on a "need to know basis." The particular risk of sudo is that a clever or malicious user will try to use access to a single command to gain access to other commands. Suppose, for example, that you included the following line in /etc/sudoers to permit a user to edit the printing configuration file:

```
jamesg    ALL=vi /etc/printcap
```

After jamesg is in vi, editing this file with root permission, he simply enters the :!bash command and vi runs a bash command shell—with root permission. This is called **shelling out** of a program. Many programs support shelling out, or at least some limited capacity to execute other programs from within the original program. The sudo program cannot foresee or control all of this; the system administrator must hand out sudo power carefully.

Consider another example: Sarah helps the system administrator with a number of basic Web server administration tasks that require root access. The system administrator creates a subdirectory containing symbolic links that point to the commands Sarah needs to use, and makes the Web user www the owner of those symbolic links. Using /etc/sudoers, the following line grants Sarah access to run any command in that directory on the local machine, all while acting as user www:

```
sarah   myhost = (www) /usr/local/webcommands
```

A single configuration line can assign access to multiple commands, with each assignment pertaining to a different user. By default, a user must enter a password to verify her identity before sudo executes the requested command. However, this can be overridden in /etc/sudoers for one or multiple specific commands. Dozens of other options let you control exactly which tasks a user can perform and how the user can perform them.

CHAPTER SUMMARY

- A user account provides much fuller access to a Linux system than accessing a network service such as a Web server. The network service runs as a user with limited permission on the system and cannot execute commands as the network client chooses.

- Passwords should be guarded carefully to prevent crackers from logging on to a system with the appearance of authorized access. A user should never give a password to anyone.

- System administrators can control how users manage their passwords using features of the shadow password system, as managed by the passwd command.

- Good passwords are hard to guess because they are of sufficient length, do not contain dictionary words, and do not relate in a simple or obvious way to personal information about the user.

- Brute force password attacks attempt to find a password by trial and error. Many programs exist for this purpose, but success is not feasible if a password uses eight or more characters.

- A Linux pluggable authentication module (PAM) lets administrators select from many methods of authenticating users and authorizing access. Modules can be configured for independent control of most relevant Linux utilities, such as login, su, sudo, and halt.

- PAM modules support four types of control: auth for authentication, account for account management, session to initiate or end program use, and password to change authentication tokens (such as a password).

- PAM control flags determine how PAM processes a stack of multiple modules to reach a final determination to permit or deny access. The standard control flags are required, requisite, sufficient, and optional.

- A second method of specifying PAM control flags lets you test the value of one or more of 30 different parameters and process other PAM modules in the stack based on the result.

❑ You can lock a Linux text-mode console while you are away from it for a moment by using the vlock command.

❑ Screen saver programs such as those included with KDE and GNOME offer screen-locking capability, but they cannot be activated until the requisite time expires for the screen saver to start.

❑ The securetty file lists where the root user can log on from; the nologin file, if it exists, stops everyone except root from logging on.

❑ File security includes watching for Set UID bits and reviewing the possibility of using file attributes to protect files from alteration.

❑ Users can be logged off automatically after a period of inactivity when an environment variable is set in the command shell.

❑ Simple utilities such as w, who, last, and lastcomm let users see detailed information about users on the Linux system, including how they are using the system.

❑ The sudo program lets a system administrator allow specific users to execute specific commands while acting as another user (including root). Use of sudo is configured by the /etc/sudoers text file, which must be edited using the utility /usr/sbin/visudo.

❑ Configuration of sudo is potentially complex. Syntax is checked by visudo, but other potential security problems require administrators to set up and test sudo carefully.

Key Terms

/etc/nologin — A file whose existence prevents all users except root from being able to log on. Regular users attempting to log on see the contents of /etc/nologin, if anything.

/etc/passwd — The file in which basic user account configuration data is stored.

/etc/securetty — A file listing all terminals from which root can log on.

/etc/shadow — The file in which users' encrypted passwords and password control data are stored.

/etc/sudoers — A configuration file that determines which users can perform which tasks using the sudo command.

brute force attack — A method of obtaining access to a system by trying all possible combinations until one succeeds in guessing a password.

control_flag — An element of a PAM module configuration that determines how PAM will process multiple modules in a single stack (for example, the auth stack).

dmesg — A utility that prints the contents of the kernel ring buffer to standard output (by default, the screen). Using dmesg right after booting Linux is a good way to see all the hardware-related messages generated by the kernel.

grpck — A utility that verifies that all group memberships are valid user accounts and that no syntax errors exist in the /etc/group file.

kernel ring buffer — A memory area that holds messages generated by the kernel. When the buffer is full, the oldest message is discarded each time a new one is generated.

mesg — A utility that enables or disables other users' ability to send a message to your screen using the write, talk, or wall (write all) commands.

module_type — A characterization of program activity that determines which set of PAM modules will be used to authorize that activity. Possible module_types include auth, account, session, and password.

nutcracker — One of many password-cracking tools.

One-time Password In Everything (OPIE) — A single-user password system available for Linux. OPIE was created by the U.S. Naval Research Laboratory, based on the S/Key program.

passwd — A utility used to change passwords or set password control options that are stored in /etc/shadow (such as a maximum use period for each password).

pluggable authentication module (PAM) — A security architecture designed to improve Linux user-level security, add flexibility in how user access is configured, and permit Linux to integrate smoothly with user information stored on other systems.

S/Key — A specialized, single-use password system designed by Bell Communications Research.

screen-locking program — A program that disables input from your keyboard and usually clears or hides the screen so that private information is not visible to passersby.

Set UID bit — A special file permission that causes executable files (programs) to use the permissions of the user who owns the file rather than those of the user who executed the file. Also called SUID.

shelling out — Starting a command shell from within another program, effectively suspending the first program from executing the shell.

stack — A series of multiple PAM modules accessed in succession to perform a security check.

sudo — A utility that lets a system administrator assign privileges to any user account so that the user can execute only the programs the sudo configuration specifies.

SUID — *See* Set UID bit.

vigr — A special version of the vi editor used to edit the /etc/group file.

vipw — A special version of the vi editor that should be used anytime you must edit /etc/passwd directly (instead of using utilities such as passwd or useradd).

visudo — A special text editor used to edit the /etc/sudoers file; it prevents conflicts between multiple open files and checks the syntax of the /etc/sudoers configuration file upon exit.

vlock — A utility that locks a text-mode console screen.

w — A utility that lists all logged-on users with their username and terminal, plus system usage information.

who — A utility that lists all users who are currently logged on the system.

REVIEW QUESTIONS

1. Describe how logging on to a system with a user account is different from connecting through a Web server.

2. Which of the following is a social engineering method of obtaining a password?

   a. talking your way into an office to deliver a pizza and looking for passwords posted on monitors

   b. guessing at the passwords using a good dictionary

   c. using a cracking program like nutcracker

   d. breaking through a firewall using a combination of knowledge and luck

3. Which action is helpful in creating a good password?

   a. Make the password a single long word found in the dictionary so it will be easy to spell correctly.

   b. Tell the password to a close friend, spouse, or supervisor in case you forget it.

   c. Combine two foreign or altered words with a number or symbol between them.

   d. Include a word with a close relation to the user, such as a pet's name, so it's easy to remember.

4. Using a brute force attack to obtain a password would require:

   a. permission from your target user

   b. that you knew the algorithm used to encode the password

   c. less time than a social engineering method

   d. significant computer processing time

5. Which two files contain user account and encrypted password data on Linux?

   a. /etc/passwd and /etc/group

   b. /etc/passwd and /etc/shadow

   c. /etc/shadow and /etc/pam.conf

   d. /etc/passwd and /etc/vipw

6. The difference between locking and disabling an account is that:

   a. Locking is temporary and preserves the account password; disabling requires that a new password be set.

   b. Disabling is temporary and preserves the account password; locking requires that a new password be set.

   c. Locking is done through command-line tools; disabling uses a graphical interface.

   d. Disabling leaves an unencrypted password where crackers might obtain it; locking deletes the password entirely and is much safer.

7. Which module performs basic password quality checks, such as forbidding short passwords and dictionary words?

   a. `pam_cracklib`

   b. `pam_limits`

   c. `pam_deny`

   d. `pam_unix_auth`

8. The `auth` keyword in a PAM configuration file refers to:

   a. the module type indicating how the named module is being used

   b. the control flag that defines module interaction with the calling program

   c. the parameters passed to the module

   d. whether users must be authorized for the PAM module to be executed

9. Stacking PAM modules refers to:

   a. executing multiple modules of one module type in sequence

   b. the collection of modules of all types listed in a given PAM configuration file

   c. placing PAM data on a fixed memory location where other programs can access it

   d. a user determining the order in which PAM modules are executed to customize logon security

10. What is the difference between a `required` and a `requisite` control flag?

11. The more complex of the two methods of setting up PAM control flags lets you:

    a. skip modules based on any of 30 different testable parameters

    b. allow users to dynamically control which modules are executed

    c. configure PAM in a graphical interface from the GNOME desktop System menu

    d. combine modules of all four types into a single programmable stack

12. Using a screen saver to lock your screen can be a security problem because:

    a. Some screen savers allow the lock to be broken using a random password.

    b. Xauth tokens may not be processed correctly from remote systems when the screen is locked.

    c. The CPU time used for the screen saver can slow down security mechanisms.

    d. The screen saver does not begin working until you have left your system unguarded for a time.

13. What is the purpose of `/etc/securetty`?

14. What is the purpose of `/etc/nologin`?

15. When the SUID bit is set on a program file, Linux:

    a. makes the file completely unchangeable until root removes that bit

    b. allows only the program owner to execute that file

    c. executes the program with the file permissions of the program file's owner

    d. allows that program to be run only using root permission

16. To cause the command shell to automatically log you off if your command line is inactive for a time:

    a. You set an environment variable with the number of minutes or seconds of idle time allowed.

    b. You start the `vlock` program before leaving your console.

    c. You write a small script that regularly checks for activity and executes the `exit` command if needed.

    d. You set up the appropriate configuration file in `/etc/sysconfig`.

17. The `w` command lists information about:

    a. all users currently logged on, with their usernames and additional information about their activities

    b. who is running the program named on the command line as a parameter to `w`

    c. DNS entries from the appropriate domain registrar

    d. all logged printing activities

18. The contents of the kernel ring buffer are viewed using which command?

    a. `dmesg`

    b. `mesg`

    c. `klogd`

    d. `lastcomm`

19. Which command displays a listing of past system reboots?

    a. `lastcomm --reboot`

    b. `who reboot`

    c. `reboot --history`

    d. `last --reboot`

20. The actions of `sudo` are controlled by the file:

    a. `/etc/sudo.conf`

    b. `/etc/visudo`

    c. `/etc/sudoers`

    d. `/etc/sudo/visudoers.conf`

21. The visudo program:

   a. creates default configurations for sudo execution by regular users

   b. lets you safely edit the configuration file for sudo

   c. must be configured by each user who wants to have access to sudo functionality

   d. cannot be accessed without first setting up /etc/sudoers.conf

22. Name at least one danger of sudo.

HANDS-ON PROJECTS

HANDS-ON PROJECTS

Project 9-1

In this project, you set password control information for a user account. To complete this project, you should have Fedora Core installed with root access and at least one regular user account. These steps should work on most Linux systems, though some systems might require different commands to configure user accounts and passwords than those shown in this project.

1. Log on using your regular user account to see that it functions correctly.

2. Log on with root access.

3. Look at the entry for your regular user account in the /etc/shadow file. Notice what the first character of the encrypted password is (the first character after the first colon on that line).

4. Lock your regular user account.

   passwd -l *username*

5. Log off and try to log on using your regular user account.

6. Log on as root and look again at the first character in your encrypted password. The "!!" modifies the encryption and invalidates the password that you enter to log on.

7. Unlock the account.

   passwd -u *username*

8. Check the /etc/shadow file again to see that the !! is gone. You could now log on using the original password.

9. If you are in a lab environment, try using the -d option to disable your regular account and then review /etc/shadow again.

   passwd -d *username*

   When you finish, restore the password for the user account. Enter **passwd *username*** and assign the user the same password as before, if you knew what it was.

9

10. Set the minimum number of days that a password must remain before a user can change it to 100 (this is just an experiment; normally, you would set the minimum at a day or two and the maximum at around 30 to 60).

```
passwd -n 100 username
```

11. Can you spot the field where the minimum number of days is stored in /etc/shadow on the line for your regular account?

12. Log off and log on again with your regular user account. Try to change your password using passwd.

13. Log off, then log on again as root if you want and change the minimum days between password changes back to 0, which lets you change your password as often as you choose.

HANDS-ON PROJECTS

Project 9-2

In this project, you configure PAM settings for a system utility. To complete this project, you should have Fedora Core installed with root access.

1. Log on with root access and open the file /etc/pam.d/system-auth.

2. Locate the line on which the pam_cracklib module is referenced.

3. Change the retry parameter to **5**, add the type parameter with a value of **THE**, and add a minlen parameter with a value of **12**. The line should look like this:

```
password requisite  /lib/security/$ISA/pam_cracklib.
so retry=5 type=THE minlen=12
```

(Note that the minimum length value gives "credit" when a password includes a variety of symbols, mixed case, and digits. So a well-formed password would not need to be 12 characters long.)

4. Locate the line with the pam_unix module (of type password). Add the parameter remember=15. This causes the system to record the previous 15 passwords for each user so that they cannot be used again.

5. Log off and log on using your regular user account.

6. Try changing your password using various lengths and repeating previously used passwords to see how these settings affect what you can do.

HANDS-ON PROJECTS

Project 9-3

In this project, you continue working with PAM by altering the control flag setting for a utility's PAM configuration. To complete this project, you should have Fedora Core installed with root access and should have just completed Project 9-2. You should only complete this project if you are working in a lab where you are not concerned about the security of your system. In addition, note that changing PAM settings incorrectly can completely lock you out of your system. Follow the steps here carefully and use the virtual consoles to check your work, rather than logging off of your main working session. (If you do lock yourself out, reboot the system, press "a" at the boot prompt, and then add an "S" to the boot parameters to start single-user mode. Edit the PAM configuration files to restore their original state and reboot normally.)

1. Log on as root.

2. Edit the file `/etc/pam.d/login`. Change the control flag on the `pam_securetty` line from `required` to **sufficient**.

3. Save the file.

4. Log off and log on again as root. What happened and why?

5. Go back into `/etc/pam.d/login` and change `sufficient` back to **required**.

6. Now edit the `/etc/pam.d/system-auth` file. Just above the lines that begin with `password`, insert this line:

   ```
   password    optional    /lib/security/$ISA/pam_issue.so
   issue=/etc/printcap
   ```

   (You can refer to any brief text file you want instead of the `/etc/printcap` file; this file is used simply as an illustration.) Save your changes and exit the text editor.

7. Switch to a free virtual console (for example, press Ctrl+Alt+F5).

8. Log on. Do you see any differences?

9. Switch back to the graphical environment by pressing **Alt+F7** (or switch to the virtual console you were previously working in).

10. Open the `/etc/pam.d/system-auth` file again in a text editor.

11. Just above the lines that begin with `auth`, insert the following line, then save your changes and exit the text editor.

    ```
    auth optional    /lib/security/$ISA/pam_issue.so
    issue=/etc/printcap
    ```

12. Switch to a free virtual console (for example, press Ctrl+Alt+F5).

13. Log on again by entering your username, but purposely *enter the wrong password*.

14. What do you see?

15. Switch back to the graphical environment or your previous virtual console.

16. Edit the `/etc/pam.d/system-auth` file again and remove the two extra lines you added for this project.

17. Why did the first extra line not have any effect? (See the documentation on the module for the answer.)

18. Why was the optional control flag appropriate here?

Project 9-4

In this project, you experiment with screen-locking programs. To complete this project, you should have Linux installed with root access and a copy of the `xlockmore` package, which you can download from a Web site such as *www.rpmfind.net*.

1. Log on with root access.

2. Download the `xlockmore` package from any of the numerous Web and FTP sites that host it. Install it by entering a command like the following (the download name may vary):

   `rpm -i xlockmore-5.14.1-1.fc3.rf.i386.rpm`

3. Spend a few minutes reviewing the `xlock` man page to see what options the program offers.

   `man xlock`

4. Notice that when `xlock` is active, no new network connections are permitted. Why would that be?

5. Start `xlock`. A randomly selected screen saver is displayed.

6. Press a key to see the prompt for the password. Click the icon to continue the screen lock.

7. Press **Alt+Ctrl+F3** to switch to another virtual console.

8. Log on the console using the same username you used for the graphical environment.

9. Use the **ps** command to see if `xlock` is listed as a process on the system.

   `ps aux | grep xlock`

10. Use the `killall` command to end the `xlock` program.

    `killall -9 xlock`

11. Press **Alt+F7** to switch back to the graphical screen.

12. Why is the ability to kill `xlock` in this way not considered a security hazard?

Project 9-5

In this project, you experiment with attributes and logon control files. To complete this project, you should have Linux installed with root access.

1. Log on with root access.

2. In a text editor, create the /etc/nologin file with the following text in it:

   System locked down for maintenance. Please try again in 15 minutes.

3. Save the file.

4. As explained in Chapter 8, when you set the immutable attribute, a file cannot be deleted, renamed, or written to, links cannot be created to the file, the ownership cannot be changed, and date/time stamps cannot be changed. Only the root user can set or clear this attribute. Use the following chattr (change attribute) command to set the immutable attribute on the file:

```
chattr +i /etc/nologin
```

5. Log off.

6. Try to log on using a regular user account. What happens?

7. Log on as root and delete the file you created:

```
rm /etc/nologin
```

8. What happened?

9. Undo the immutable attribute:

```
chattr -i /etc/nologin
```

10. Remove the file:

```
rm /etc/nologin
```

11. What is the point of having an immutable attribute on a file that only root has permission to alter anyway? Doesn't this just create another step that root has to complete?

9

CASE PROJECTS

Case Project 9-1

CASE PROJECTS

The managing partner at Snow, Sleet, and Hale just attended a special conference titled "Computer Security in Law Firms," and your consulting work is about to increase because of the justifiable concern of your client.

1. One of the security systems that is growing in popularity—Kerberos—was mentioned prominently at the security conference. Although Kerberos was not mentioned in the chapter text about PAM modules, Linux PAM actually has very good support for Kerberos. Review the documentation on this feature, located in a separate directory on Fedora Core (/usr/share/doc/pam_krb5-2.1.2), plus the information listed under Kerberos at *www.us.kernel.org/pub/linux/libs/pam/modules.html*. Write a one-page summary memo of how PAM implements Kerberos and what benefits or concerns this implementation raises for you. You should target your memo to the managing partner, who needs to understand how Kerberos might benefit the organization's LAN, but doesn't want too much technical detail.

2. Snow, Sleet, and Hale has several system administrators helping to manage its office networks. Most do not have root access to the Linux servers. Write a list of policy statements regarding the use of sudo for these system administrators, who must complete specific networking tasks, such as print management, file server maintenance, and e-mail server maintenance. You might want to consult the sudo and sudoers man pages as well as example security policies that you locate on the Internet.

3. The managing partner has asked you to prepare a 15-minute presentation on the best practices for selecting and protecting account passwords. Your presentation could be a collection of 15 to 20 slides in a program such as PowerPoint or OpenOffice Impress. You should include notes for each slide to help you cover important points. Describe the reasons for your recommendations and the actual techniques that compose a "good" password.

CRYPTOGRAPHY

After reading this chapter and completing the exercises, you will be able to:

♦ Explain commonly used cryptographic systems

♦ Understand digital certificates and certificate authorities

♦ Understand how cryptography is used on the Web

♦ Use the PGP and GPG data-encryption utilities

♦ Encrypt files and filesystems

♦ Describe different ways in which cryptography is applied to make computer systems more secure

In this chapter, you will learn how information is secured using a variety of encoding techniques that prevent access by unauthorized users. Similar techniques are also used to authenticate users—to guarantee that users seeking access to a system or system resources are who they claim to be.

You will also learn about applications that implement these techniques, either directly, by encoding data at your command, or indirectly, by creating a channel for secure communication over which many types of data can be sent.

CRYPTOGRAPHY AND COMPUTER SECURITY

Computer security attempts to ensure that only authorized users can access a given computer resource. This is not a new problem. More than two thousand years ago, Alexander the Great had the same concern as he tried to send messages about waging battle to commanders in his empire. In the last hundred years, much military, diplomatic, and political intrigue has focused on transmitting information between members of one group without another group being able to intercept or forge that information. The science of encoding data so that it cannot be read without special knowledge or tools is called **cryptography**.

Cryptography is a key part of many applications running on computer networks, though it is usually hidden from view. Networks transmit data through wires that run in and between buildings, or without wires via radio waves; these may be accessible by unauthorized people. A person with technical skill and the right equipment can tap into a network connection and see the data being transmitted. This is called **sniffing** the network, as illustrated in Figure 10-1. Programs that perform this function—called **sniffers**—are used by many system administrators to troubleshoot difficult networking problems. Though crackers use sniffers to gather information from network packets, it is much more difficult if the payload of those packets has been encrypted.

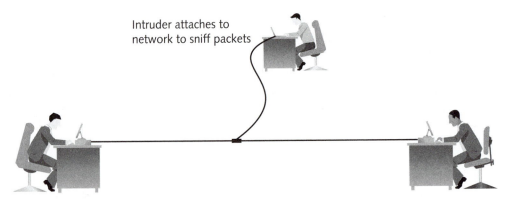

Intruder attaches to
network to sniff packets

Figure 10-1 Sniffing a network connection

Basic Encoding Techniques

The process of cryptography is straightforward. You begin with a message that you want to transmit to another person, called the **plaintext**. Then, you apply a **cipher** to modify the plaintext into **ciphertext** that can't be read by eavesdroppers. This process is called **encryption**.

The most elementary example of encryption is letter substitution. You substitute a different letter of the alphabet for each letter in your message. Suppose that the message you need to encode is:

- ONE IF BY LAND TWO IF BY SEA

You create the following system of substitution—your cipher:

- *Substitute for each letter the letter that follows it in the alphabet.*

The result of encoding the preceding plaintext with this cipher yields the following ciphertext:

- POF JG CZ MBOE UXP JG CZ TFB

Although this is certainly unreadable at first glance, it is an easy cipher to break (decode) without knowing the rule by which it was created. To break a letter-substitution cipher of English plaintext, you would assume that the most frequently occurring letters are vowels. Combinations that recur (such as JG and CZ in the preceding example) must represent common two-letter English words. You can develop more complex letter-substitution rules, but they are all easy to read for an experienced code breaker. Nevertheless, this simple technique illustrates how cryptography can make data less accessible to someone who does not know how the data was encrypted.

TIP
If you are curious and want to experiment with letter-substitution ciphers, you can start with the information that the 10 most often used letters in English, from most to least frequent, are ETAONRISHD. Code breakers use databases of letter and word frequency lists. You can use the frequency of occurrence within encrypted text to determine which letters are substituted for which other letters.

To use letter substitution, the person receiving the ciphertext must know the rule that was used to encrypt the message, or else must figure it out using trial and error, mathematics, or some other technique.

Key Systems

The letter-substitution technique relies on a rule or set of rules for converting plaintext to ciphertext, known as an **algorithm**. Anyone who knows the algorithm you used to encode a message using letter substitution can decode the message. You could also add a level of complexity to the algorithm:

- *Substitute for each letter the letter that follows by X places in the alphabet.*

The X in the algorithm is a **key**, a code necessary to encrypt or decrypt (decode) a message correctly using the algorithm. Most keys are numeric. For example, in the previous cipher, if X = 4, the letter A would be converted to E, B to F, and so on. Even if a person knows the algorithm used for the encryption, the message cannot be decrypted without the key. In the case of letter substitutions, the message is still fairly easy to decrypt using knowledge of the English language, but keys are used in much more complex ciphers with very complex algorithms.

Another method of encryption is called the **one-time pad**. This method is as simple as letter substitution, but it is considered unbreakable using the types of analysis that can break a letter-substitution cipher.

In the one-time pad method, both the person encrypting the message and the person decrypting it have an identical list of random numbers. The random numbers are the key. To encrypt a message using a one-time pad, the message is converted to numbers (for example, A is 1, B is 2, and so on). The first random number is added to the first number of the message, the second random number is added to the second number of the message, and so on. The resulting encrypted message is a list of numbers that looks random to anyone without the key. The recipient subtracts the random numbers on her list and then easily converts the numeric message into letters (for example, 1=A, 2=B, and so on).

The main problem with the one-time pad technique is getting a list of random numbers to both the message creator and the message recipient. This is an issue with the majority of ciphers: How do you get the key to your partner without it being intercepted? You cannot use the same delivery mechanism for the random numbers as for the encrypted messages (such as a radio signal or the mail), because anyone who obtains the random numbers can easily decrypt the message. A one-time pad was used for years in diplomatic and intelligence circles, through which a list of random numbers could be delivered by special courier to the message recipients (such as an embassy in a foreign country). However, in the electronic world there is no efficient and secure way of getting a list of random numbers to a message recipient. If you send the random numbers electronically, they can be intercepted as easily as the encrypted message itself.

Knowing the algorithm—the cipher—used to encrypt a message should not enable someone to read it. Good security assumes that an eavesdropper knows the cipher; the key, however, must be kept secret.

TIP Don't confuse compression with encryption. Compression uses a mathematical algorithm to make a file smaller. It has no key, though some compression programs let you add a password to a compressed file. Encryption uses a mathematical algorithm to make a file unreadable if you don't possess the numeric key. The resulting file might be larger than the original file.

DES

Using computers for cryptography allows you to process very large numbers as part of a cipher. The first widely accepted standard for encryption was developed in the 1970s by IBM and the National Institute of Standards and Technology (NIST, see *www.nist.gov*). This standard is called the **Data Encryption Standard (DES)**. Government-approved standards for information processing are called **Federal Information Processing Standards** or **FIPS**. The site *http://csrc.nist.gov/CryptoToolkit/* contains information on all FIPS, including those described in this chapter. DES is FIPS 46-3, a now obsolete standard.

It uses a 56-bit key to encrypt data using various mathematical alterations of the plaintext message. A 56-bit key means that the key to encode any message consists of 56 digits, each of which is a one or a zero. A DES key would look like this:

- 11001101010011010010100100100100001111101010010110101000

Because each bit can be either one or zero, 56 bits provide for 2^{56} possible keys—roughly 72 quadrillion. Though DES is the most tested and widely used encryption technique in the world, in 1998 John Gilmore and Paul Kocher broke a DES key in 56 hours using a homemade supercomputer with Intel CPUs that they built for $250,000. Their effort was sponsored by the Electronic Frontier Foundation (*www.eff.org*) and by the U.S. government to improve cryptographic methods (because DES was nearly 30 years old). The two winners were awarded a prize of $10,000. Since 1998, the time needed to break a DES key has dropped below 20 hours.

NOTE

Getting a DES key to the recipient of a message is still an issue. It is addressed in the following section on asymmetric encryption.

10

DES is being phased out, but is still widely used for certain transactions. This is true for several reasons:

- Relatively few people have the equipment and patience to crack a DES key.

- 20 hours is still a fairly long time in some circumstances. For example, many transactions require the information to remain secret only for a short time. A typical Web site sale (e-commerce transaction) or a bank wire transfer requires that the data remain secure only for a few minutes. After that, the key is of no use, because a new key is created for each transaction.

- DES was a widely implemented U.S. government standard—inertia keeps it in place in some cases.

Skipjack and Triple DES

There were several responses to the cracking of DES. In one, DES keys were increased to 1024 bits, making the key much more difficult to crack. Another response was the creation of a completely different algorithm called **Skipjack**, which uses an 80-bit key, making it more secure than DES. It is also a government-approved standard (FIPS 185). But until recent changes, products using a key length of more than 64 bits could not be exported by any U.S. company, limiting the usefulness of Skipjack. In addition, though it seemed promising, the Skipjack algorithm had not withstood years of testing, as the DES algorithm had.

Another approach is **Triple DES** or **TDES**. This method is approved for U.S. government use and is documented in NIST Special Publication 800-67. TDES still relies on DES, but encodes each message three times using three different DES keys. The recipient must have all three DES keys and decrypt the message three times in the correct order to obtain the original message.

Triple DES is secure and is considered unbreakable using current techniques and currently available computing power. However, it is not an ideal solution because it is time consuming and resource-intensive both to encrypt and decrypt messages. For every block of text, Triple DES requires the encrypting computer to perform a series of complex mathematical functions three different times. The message recipient must perform the same functions to read the message.

Advanced Encryption Standard

Because Triple DES is so computationally intensive, NIST sponsored a competition in 1997 to create a replacement for DES. The winner was the Rijndael algorithm (pronounced "Rain Doll"), submitted by two Belgians. It is now called the **Advanced Encryption Standard (AES)** and is standardized in FIPS 197.

AES can use three different key lengths: 128 bits, 192 bits, or 256 bits. The 256-bit key length provides roughly 10^{77} possible keys, and NIST expects AES to remain secure for at least 20 more years. AES was approved for use by U.S. government agencies in 2002. Government approval means that many other organizations will feel comfortable using AES as well, and you can expect to see many security products in the coming years that support AES. AES does not have the earlier export restrictions that affected algorithms larger than 64 bits. The U.S. Department of Commerce deals with the export of encryption technology. To learn more about AES, search on the term at *www.nist.gov*.

Several other very good ciphers are commonly used in encryption software. Each has advantages, such as requiring little computing power to decrypt or not being patented (so anyone can use it). Each also has disadvantages, such as making messages much longer after encryption or requiring a lot of computing power (and thus time) to encrypt a message. Some ciphers you might hear about are **IDEA**, **Blowfish**, **Twofish**, **RC2**, **RC4**, **RC5**, and **ElGamal**.

Blowfish, Twofish, and ElGamal are unpatented. IDEA is protected by a U.S. patent until 2010. RC5 is protected until 2015.

Symmetric and Asymmetric Encryption

All of the popular encryption algorithms described thus far—DES, Triple DES, AES, IDEA, Blowfish, ElGamal—use a single numeric key to encrypt and decrypt messages. They are all **symmetric encryption algorithms**, meaning that the same key and the same algorithm are used both to encrypt and to decrypt a message (the algorithm is reversed for decryption). The key used for a symmetric encryption algorithm is called a private key because it must be kept secret for the message to be secure. For this reason, these algorithms are also called **private-key encryption** techniques.

An **asymmetric encryption algorithm** uses one key to encrypt a message and a second key to decrypt it. The algorithm is similar to dropping the message into a box that you lock with one key, but that you open with another key. The advantage to asymmetric encryption is that you can tell everyone how to encrypt the messages they send you, but only you know how to decrypt them. Because the key that you can reveal to everyone is called the public key and the one you must keep secret is called the private key, asymmetric algorithms are often called **public-key encryption**. This model removes the problem of getting a symmetric encryption key to another person without it being intercepted by an eavesdropper.

Asymmetric encryption uses only **prime numbers**—those that are evenly divisible only by 1 and the number itself. For example, the number 24 is not a prime because it can be factored as 2 × 3 × 4. However, 23 is a prime number; you cannot multiply any two numbers except 23 and 1 to get 23. Asymmetric encryption takes two very large prime numbers (between 100 and 300 digits each) and combines them using fairly simple mathematical techniques to yield two keys. When one key is used to encrypt data, the other must be used to decrypt the data. The encryption can be done using either the public or the private key; decryption must be done with the opposite key.

Users who rely on public-key encryption maintain a file that contains the public keys of people they regularly contact. Some users include their public key in their signature file, so it appears at the end of every e-mail message they send. Others have a Web site that includes a link to their public key so that anyone can download and use it to encrypt or decrypt a message as described previously. Some companies also publish a public key on their Web sites. For example, Linux vendors encrypt or sign software packages so users can verify that the package actually comes from the vendor and has not been modified. Vendors must publish their private key so you can verify that their software packages are genuine.

The distribution of public keys is a major concern both to security experts and privacy advocates. (Key management and security are discussed later in this chapter in the section on GPG.) Publicly accessible key servers contain millions of public keys, so you can search for the key of a person you want to contact. One example is *http://www.keyserver.net*. A public key can take many forms, but a typical example resembles the following text. This example has been edited to reduce its size. To see examples of active public keys, you can also visit *web.mit.edu/prz/* and click the link for Phil's Public Keys. (Phil Zimmermann invented PGP, as described later in this chapter, and is a world-renowned cryptography expert.)

```
mQCNAiv8ZoAAAAEEAKc4d45hN5qFM79nWGLkrGWputWmtdxJk0BZEbi0kNRbJBC2p
10ASImd//cCDwLR2alBUSt8O2WGik9PBZgthjMOenoDmzKiG8BkE9AFKonyxvD2lD
nqbydXi+YQmOTsWSw4jTTSb3cflhVkf8hVUVpMFQThafV0CmV5hLjHqWbdAAURtCJ
QaGlsaXAgUi4gWmltbWVybWFubiA8cHJ6QGFjbS5vcmc+iQCVAgUQLB48XPTK
AIGN5yLZAQHWtwP/RBiLPN4dnt8sm9qZtK0HPYV0hfdZ4IiSfR0V52uKKMQsIrBJx
2c5Z2vurBLeKkh8Oecf/X+Zh2mEenrymR/urBCf8xGQnyTPew4t/3IQ5KXsqi2buO
Tysk9Pkk+cqxZTEXJQWixB3fVKrCkR02xbWcRXQ/pPs0ObOE4VLtQT1G2JAGACOd2
oMHwGJI4fy8H7SQSVPHV3BlRZpkIou0/vbEZY9b8WlUm9QEETWZEMmKYgHZTbEzkk
Ftq0zNqgfsuORoe262c/pbYofNrMmnYok7K3vIAoqbUV6JlRRJ0oo3y+8IMifjnNZ
KfgNpGmJDCMTh8M=Hpg1
```

To understand the usefulness of public-key cryptography, consider these three scenarios:

1. If a person wants to send you a message, she can use your public key to encrypt the message. You would have made your public key widely available on your Web site or in other publicly accessible locations. You are the only one who can decrypt the message, using your private key, to which only you have access. Thus, the person sending you a message knows that you are the only person who can read it. This is illustrated in Figure 10-2. Unfortunately, you have no way of knowing who is sending you the message because everyone has access to your public key. Though the person might say she is Sally, it might actually be Brutus.

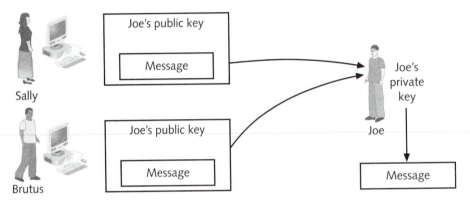

Figure 10-2   Encrypting a message with a recipient's public key

2. To solve this problem, a person could encode a message to you using her private key. You could then be certain that it was from her, because only her public key (which you could find on her Web site or elsewhere) would decrypt the message, as shown in Figure 10-3. Of course, everyone else could also decrypt the message she sent to you.

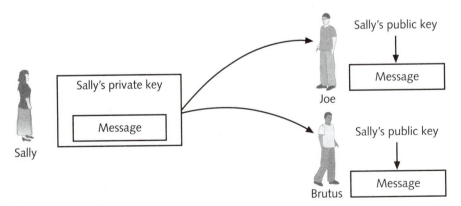

Figure 10-3   Signing a message with your private key

3. To send you an encoded message that only you can decrypt and that you are certain comes from the person who claims to have sent it, a person uses the following steps: First, the person encodes the message using your public key. Then, the person encodes it a second time using her private key. When you receive the message, you first decrypt it using the sender's public key. This tells you for certain that the message came from the person who claimed to send it. Then, you decrypt it a second time using your private key and read it, as illustrated in Figure 10-4. Anyone can use the sender's public key and see that the message could only have come from her, but only you can complete the second step and read the contents of the message.

 NOTE
Most technologies, such as SSL, use a combination of asymmetric and symmetric encryption. Asymmetric encryption is used to encrypt the exchange of a generated symmetric encryption key. Afterward, symmetric encryption is used to encrypt large amounts of data.

10

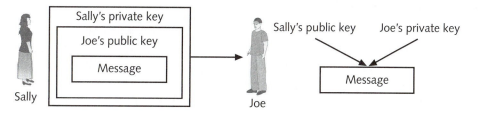

Figure 10-4   Encrypting and signing a document

RSA

The most familiar example of public-key encryption is the **RSA** algorithm, developed by Ronald **R**ivest, Adi **S**hamir, and Len **A**dleman. RSA was the basis for a security product company (see *www.rsasecurity.com*). However, the patent on RSA technology expired in 2000, so other companies can now use the same techniques in their software. (One example is PGP, described later in this chapter.)

RSA technology is used in a number of products from many vendors. RSA Security Inc. uses it for Web server tools, virtual private network (VPN) software (as described in Chapter 11), and for many other situations in which high security is needed. RSA technology is used in popular browsers, including Mozilla and Microsoft Internet Explorer, to make Internet transactions secure. This is done in combination with a symmetrical encryption method such as DES.

As with Triple DES and some other symmetric ciphers, encrypting a message using a public-key encryption algorithm requires a lot of computational power. Because of this, most systems rely on a hybrid: They combine a symmetrical key cipher and a public-key cipher. The public-key technology (such as RSA) is used to encrypt the key for a symmetrical cipher so that the recipient can obtain the key and decrypt the rest of the message. Only the symmetrical key requires the more CPU-intensive effort of public-key encryption. This is how browsers handle secure Web transactions, as illustrated in Figure 10-5.

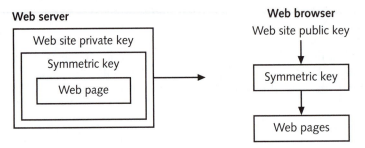

Figure 10-5 A secure Web transaction

Signatures and Certificates

Using public-key cryptography to exchange messages has a potential weakness that might have already occurred to you. How do you know that the public key you have for a person is *really* for that person? When it comes to cryptography, you really can't take anything for granted, but public-key cryptography also lets you verify the integrity of public keys for individuals or organizations. This is done through the process of authentication, using signatures and certificates.

Authentication is the process of proving to a computer system or another person that you are the person you say you are. In real life, you often authenticate yourself using a photo ID, such as a driver's license. Signatures let you authenticate a public key.

You **sign** another person's public key with your own private key to verify that the key really belongs to that person. Others who get the key can see that you trust it, and so they may decide to trust it, or they may verify its correctness themselves, then add their signature by signing the public key with their private key. A public key that has several signatures from people you trust can likely be trusted as a valid public key for the person named as the key's owner.

You can verify a key by contacting a person over the telephone if you feel certain you recognize his voice. Technical conferences often have key signing parties where you can meet people and let them verify a public key so that you can communicate securely with them. ("Fingerprints," described in the next section, provide a shorthand method of referring to public keys.)

The personal connections between you and your colleagues, signing keys that you trust and relying on each others' signatures, form a **web of trust**. You must work to expand this web so that the software described later in this chapter—which implements the encryption algorithms discussed—can be truly useful to you.

NOTE A distantly related concept uses a very similar term: A **digital signature** is a part of an electronic transaction that gives it the same legally binding effect as a document you sign with a pen. Such digital signatures are not used much because the laws controlling them are not settled in many states. One day you may be able to obtain a mortgage or a marriage license without leaving your home or office.

Certificates provide the same type of verification as signatures, and are most often used by organizations engaged in e-commerce. A **certificate** is a numeric code that is used to identify an organization. A certificate is not encryption; it is just a number assigned to you, much like a Social Security number or a driver's license number. The certificate is signed by a **certificate authority (CA)** that has verified the credentials of an organization. To obtain a certificate from a certificate authority, you must prove to the certificate authority that you are who you claim to be, as illustrated in the following scenario.

For example, suppose that XYZ Corp. wants to do business on the Internet. It approaches VeriSign, a large and well-known certificate authority (*www.verisign.com*), and asks for a certificate. VeriSign requires XYZ Corp. to show documents that include articles of incorporation, names of the corporate officers, various addresses and phone numbers, and notarized company letterhead. After VeriSign determines that XYZ Corp. is a real corporation, it issues a certificate, which XYZ Corp. installs on its Web site. When you try to complete a purchase, the XYZ Web server sends you its certificate, which includes a notation about who issued the certificate. Seeing that the certificate was issued by VeriSign, you trust that the Web site you are visiting (and perhaps giving a credit card number to) is run by a valid corporation that was at least stable enough to get a VeriSign certificate. The more you trust the certificate authority, the more you can be certain that the organization providing the certificate is what it claims to be.

Certificates are used in conjunction with public-key cryptography to prevent certificate forgery. Suppose that a user had done business with XYZ and so had a copy of its certificate. That user could, in theory, set up a Web site and pose as XYZ Corp. You could be certain that only XYZ Corp. sent out the certificate if it was signed with the private key of the certificate authority and you decrypted it using the public key of XYZ Corp. Figure 10-6 presents an example of a secure Web transaction with a certificate.

NOTE VeriSign sells different types of certificates based on how well you can prove who you are. The costs of its products range from hundreds to thousands of dollars, and include features such as business insurance in case of problems with a VeriSign certificate.

Fingerprints

Public keys and certificates can be hundreds of digits long. A **fingerprint** is a smaller number that is derived from a public key in such a way that it is hard to forge. A fingerprint is created by hashing the key or certificate. A **hash** is the result of a mathematical function

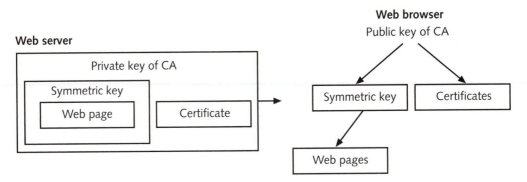

Figure 10-6 A secure Web transaction using a certificate

(loosely called a hashing function) that converts a large number into a smaller number in a predictable way. If the large number is changed, the smaller number (the hash) also changes. Thus, you can compare two hashes of a public key to see whether the key has been modified. Hashes used in this way are also called fingerprints. Two types of hashes are commonly used in computer security: MD5 and SHA-1.

The **message digest hash** (called **MD5**) converts a number of any length to a 128-bit number called a **checksum**. (More generally, a checksum is a computed value that helps you verify that a file or transmission has not been corrupted.) Because 128 bits gives just 32 hexadecimal digits, it is fairly easy to compare the MD5 hash of a key or a file with the expected value. The nature of a hash like MD5 means that if the file or key is altered at all, the resulting hash also changes. Yet it is not possible to extract or derive the original data (the key or the file) by studying the hash.

NOTE

The probability of two messages having the same MD5 hash is about 2^{64} and the probability of creating a message for a given hash is about 2^{128}.

A Linux program called md5sum creates an MD5 hash from any file. The -c option of this utility lets you check a list of existing MD5 checksums against files to see whether any do not match. To use this utility to create an MD5 hash of a file, include the filename after the command:

```
md5sum    filename
```

The utility prints the 128-bit MD5 checksum in hexadecimal, as shown in this sample output:

```
15e10987f891132dc13790ba8e71c3a2    timesheet.doc
```

MD5 is frequently used to help users make certain that downloaded files are not corrupted by a cracker or by download errors. It is also used by most Linux distributions to encrypt passwords in the /etc/shadow file.

To perform this check on an `rpm` file that you have downloaded or have on CD-ROM, run the `rpm` command with the two options `--checksig --nosignature`. For example, suppose you have downloaded a security upgrade to the `bind` package. The following command reports whether the MD5 checksum stored as part of the `rpm` file indicates that the file's integrity is intact:

```
rpm --checksig --nosignature bind-9.1.3-6.i386.rpm
```

The output of the command should look like the following if the package is intact:

```
bind-9.1.3-6.i386.rpm: sha1 md5 OK
```

Another type of hash that is more secure than MD5 is the FIPS-compliant **Secure Hash Algorithm (SHA-1)**. SHA-1 provides a 160-bit hash of any file or key so that you can check whether the message or key was corrupted during transmission. Fingerprints using this hash are used within the public-key encryption utilities described later in this chapter.

A hash like MD5 or SHA-1 is used when you transmit or receive a block of encrypted text. The hash is combined with a public key to create a signature for the transmission. The **Digital Signature Algorithm (DSA)** is a commonly used standard for doing this.

TIP   The Web page *www.redhat.com/security/team/key/* includes Red Hat Software's public key and fingerprint; *fedora.redhat.com/about/security/* includes the public key and fingerprint for The Fedora Project.

CRYPTOGRAPHY AND THE WEB

Cryptography is an important part of the World Wide Web. Web sites, such as e-commerce sites that handle customer credit card numbers, encrypt HTTP so others cannot eavesdrop on your browser's interaction with the Web server.

Whenever you visit a Web page that transmits encrypted pages to your computer, you see a small lock or key in the browser window. Unencrypted pages show this key icon broken into two pieces or show the lock in an unlocked position, as shown in Figure 10-7. Most encrypted Web pages, such as order-entry screens, shopping carts, and account viewing pages, appear with a URL that starts with **https://**. This indicates that the Web server used encryption to transmit the Web page. The encrypted protocol for Web pages is Secure Sockets Layer (SSL).

For a Web server to use SSL to encrypt Web pages, it must have its own certificate, which is based on keys.

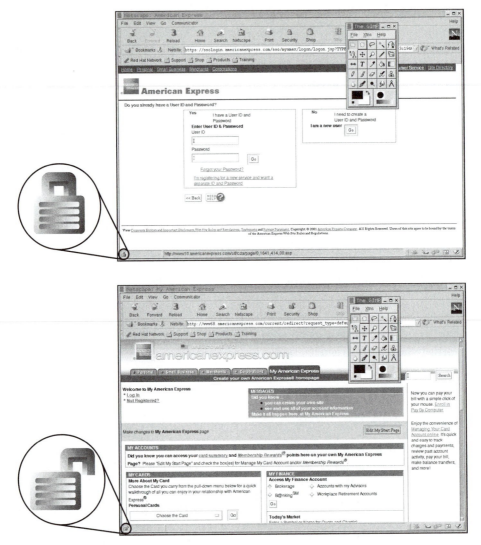

Figure 10-7 Icons to indicate secure and insecure Web pages in Netscape

Server Certificates

To generate a certificate for your Web server, you must generate a private key using the openssl program. Here's how to generate a private key for the *www.alcpress.com* Web server:

```
openssl genrsa -des3 -out www.alcpress.com.key 1024
```

When the program prompts you, enter a passphrase that is reasonably secure. The program generates a private key and saves it in a file called www.alcpress.com.key in the current directory. You should copy this file to a storage medium such as a 3.5-inch disk or USB flash memory device and save it in a physically secure place, along with the passphrase documented on a piece of paper. Storing the file in a bank safe deposit box is a good idea.

Next, you need to generate a Certificate Signing Request or CSR. You send the CSR to your certificate authority so they can generate your public certificate. It's the electronic equivalent of filling out an application for a certificate on paper. You again run the openssl program to generate a CSR:

```
openssl req -newkey www.alcpress.com.key \
-out www.alcpress.com.csr
```

You're prompted to answer numerous questions, the most important of which concerns your common name. The common name is your Web server's name, which is *www.alcpress.com* in the previous example. The common name must match the URL that users enter to access your site. When you finish answering the questions, the CSR is in the www.alcpress.com.csr file in the current directory. The contents of the file look like the following:

```
-----BEGIN CERTIFICATE REQUEST-----
MIIBPTCB6AIBADCBhDELMAkGA1UEBhMCWkExFTATBgNVBAgTDFdlc3Rlcm4gQ2Fw
ZTESMBAGA1UEBxMJQ2FwZSBUb3duMRQwEgYDVQQKEwtPcHBvcnR1bml0aTEYMBYG
A1UECxMPT25saW5lIFNlcnZpY2VzMRowGAYDVQQDExF3d3cuZm9yd2FyZC5jby56
YTBaMA0GCSqGSIb3DQEBAQUAA0kAMEYCQQDT5oxxeBWu5WLHD/G4BJ+PobiC9d7S
6pDvAjuyC+dPAnL0d91tXdm2j190D1kgDoSp5ZyGSgwJh2V7diuuPlHDAgEDoAAw
DQYJKoZIhvcNAQEEBQADQQBf8ZHIu4H8ik2vZQngXh8v+iGnAXD1AvUjuDPCWzFu
pReiq7UR8Z0wiJBeaqiuvTDnTFMz6oCq6htdH7/tvKhh
-----END CERTIFICATE REQUEST-----
```

Send this file to your certificate authority, along with payment; days later you'll receive your certificate, usually via e-mail. If you don't want to wait days before using your site, you can generate a self-signed certificate, meaning that you are acting as your own certificate authority. People can access your site, but their browser will display a message that the certificate is not recognized by any certificate authority known by the browser. Users can choose to access your site anyway.

You generate a self-signed certificate with the following command:

```
openssl x509 -req -days 90 -in www.alcpress.com.csr \
-signkey www.alcpress.com.key \
-out www.alcpress.com.crt
```

This command generates a certificate called www.alcpress.com.crt that expires in 90 days. You can adjust the -days parameter to extend the expiration date. Copy this file to your Web server and then check your Web server documentation to see how to configure the Web server for your certificate. Days later, when your certificate authority sends your certificate, you'll substitute it for the self-signed certificate. You will almost certainly have to restart your Web server for the new certificate to take effect.

10

Kerberos Authentication

The techniques used by browsers for e-commerce are not sufficient for securing all the different services provided for users on an organizational network. A special type of authentication for organizational networks is **Kerberos**. Kerberos was developed at the Massachusetts Institute of Technology (MIT) and is widely used around the world, but not everyone will want to implement it. Kerberos is intrusive, meaning that you must set up all of your other services to work with it. Each of those services must be designed to work with Kerberos, or as MIT says, applications must be "kerberized."

Kerberos secures a network by providing a system that makes users and services prove who they are before they can use a service (such as a file server or a printer). Kerberos uses both public-key cryptography and a symmetric cipher. Signatures and passwords verify actions when users contact a service to perform a task such as printing a document.

 In Greek mythology, Kerberos is the three-headed dog that guards the entrance to Hades.

TIP

A network that uses Kerberos relies on a central Kerberos server on which the private keys of all users and all services are stored. All the users and services whose keys are stored on the Kerberos server constitute the Kerberos **realm**. Kerberos uses the signature techniques described earlier for public-key encryption to ensure that only the "right" user or service can decrypt the information that it sends out.

To use a service, a user on a Kerberos-aware network contacts the Kerberos server and indicates the action that he wants to perform. The Kerberos server checks the identity of the user to see whether that action is permitted. If it is, the Kerberos server grants a **ticket**, which contains the following components:

{sessionkey:username:address:servicename:lifespan:timestamp}

The user sends the ticket requesting service to the daemon that the user wants to access; for example, to a print server daemon. The service decrypts the ticket using its private key. Because the ticket was encrypted on the Kerberos server using the service's public key, only the service can decrypt the ticket to see whether it is valid. If it is, the service grants the user access. This is a simplification of the process presented in Figure 10-8, but it illustrates why Kerberos is considered both a valuable security tool and a labor-intensive system to install and maintain.

Linux supports Kerberos, including all of the common services you are likely to need, such as printing, NFS, FTP, r-utilities, and many others. If you are already operating within a Kerberos realm, you can select Kerberos as an option when you install some versions of Linux. To set up Kerberos after installation in Fedora Core, use the `authconfig` text utility shown in Figure 10-9. This utility has a graphical version that you can start in Fedora Core

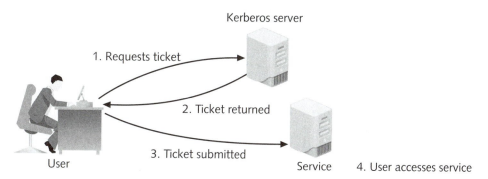

Figure 10-8 The Kerberos ticket-granting process

by opening the GNOME main Applications menu and selecting System Settings, then Authentication (see Figure 10-10). You can run this graphical utility by entering the command `authconfig-gtk`.

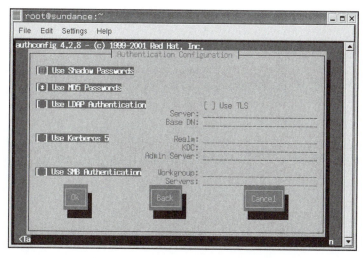

Figure 10-9 The `authconfig` utility in Fedora Core

NOTE

You will see many options in `authconfig` and `authconfig-gtk` that are explained later in this book.

For further information on Kerberos, visit the links under Documentation at the MIT Kerberos site, *http://web.mit.edu/kerberos/www*. A good place to start is *http://web.mit.edu/kerberos/www/dialogue.html*, which gives a conceptual outline of the Kerberos ticket-granting process.

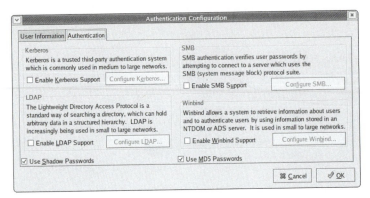

Figure 10-10   The graphical Authentication Configuration utility in Fedora Core

USING ENCRYPTION UTILITIES

You use public-key cryptography when you browse secure Web sites, but you can also use it to encrypt e-mail messages or documents before sending them to others.

Pretty Good Privacy (PGP)

The first utility to provide public-key encryption was the **Pretty Good Privacy (PGP)** program, created by Phil Zimmermann. PGP caused an uproar by making "munition"-grade cryptography—classified by the government as a weapon—available to everyone. Zimmermann endured a three-year government investigation because of his desire to make strong encryption (and privacy, in his view) available to everyone by offering free software.

PGP has not been free since Zimmermann's company was sold to Network Associates. You can learn more about their products by visiting *www.pgp.com*. Another site that links to PGP-related resources is *www.pgp.net*.

Although PGP software was formerly included in every Linux distribution, it has been replaced with another program with similar goals: The Gnu Privacy Guard (GPG) program.

As you learn about GPG in the next section, consider the trade-offs you make with any form of encryption. The more effort you put into securing a document, the more effort it will take an eavesdropper to intercept and read your messages. Some messages are not worth the trouble of using strong encryption techniques, either because their contents are innocuous (for example, a grocery list) or are only valuable for a very short time (for example, a financial transaction that must be completed within seconds or the encryption keys become invalid). Yet, you must create and maintain relationships for secure communications so that when you need them, they work effectively—you must create a web of trust appropriate to your circumstances.

Some users working in financial services or government intelligence, or who are just highly concerned about their privacy, will gladly put the effort into following all the recommendations by security experts for guarding their private keys, signing others' public keys, and otherwise protecting the validity of their security measures. Others do not have such critical information to protect. They assume, perhaps rightly, that no one is likely to spend much time trying to decrypt their messages. You must decide where your security needs fall. All users should be security-conscious, however, and take measures to protect personal data by using secure Internet transmissions. Crackers are always looking for targets for identity theft, credit card fraud, and similar mischief.

Gnu Privacy Guard (GPG)

Gnu Privacy Guard (GPG) is a public-key encryption utility compatible with PGP in many respects, including the ability to use public keys generated by PGP. PGP uses the patented IDEA encryption, whereas GPG uses ElGamal and other nonpatented algorithms. The GPG package is installed by default on Fedora Core and is available for all other Linux systems. For many systems, you can download a software package in rpm or deb format (see *rpmfind.net*). The package name in Red Hat is gnupg. For more information on GPG, see *www.gnupg.org*.

GPG operates from the command line, though graphical utilities are also available, as described later in this section. You use the program by entering gpg followed by various commands and options. The first step in using GPG is to create a key pair for yourself. A **key pair** is a public key that you can hand out to others and a private or secret key that stays on your system—no one else ever sees it. You create a key pair in GPG using the following command:

```
gpg  --gen-key
```

Text like the following appears beneath the command:

```
gpg (GnuPG) 1.2.5; Copyright (C) 2004 Free Software
Foundation, Inc.
This program comes with ABSOLUTELY NO WARRANTY.
This is free software, and you are welcome to redistribute it
under certain conditions. See the file COPYING for details.
gpg: /home/ed/.gnupg: directory created
gpg: new configuration file '/home/ed/.gnupg/gpg.conf' created
gpg: WARNING: options in '/home/ed/.gnupg/gpg.conf' are not
yet active during this run
gpg: keyring '/home/ed/.gnupg/secring.gpg' created
gpg: keyring '/home/ed/.gnupg/pubring.gpg' created
Please select what kind of key you want:
   (1) DSA and ElGamal (default)
```

10

```
 (2) DSA (sign only)
 (4) RSA (sign only)
Your selection?
```

The first time you run gpg, it creates the .gnupg directory below your home directory and creates the key ring files there. You must choose which algorithm GPG will use to create your key. The choices are DSA and ElGamal (the default), DSA, or RSA. Choosing the default lets you both encrypt files and sign them. You must next select a key size. The 1024-bit default should be fine for most users:

```
DSA keypair will have 1024 bits.
About to generate a new ELG-E keypair.
              minimum keysize is   768 bits
              default keysize is  1024 bits
    highest suggested keysize is  2048 bits
What keysize do you want? (1024)
```

You then select an expiration time. Most key pairs should not have an expiration date, because that would require you to inform everyone who had obtained your public key when it was no longer valid, and then redistribute a new public key. For some specialized purposes an expiration time might be a good idea, but generally you should choose "key does not expire." You must confirm this choice to continue:

```
Please specify how long the key should be valid.
        0 = key does not expire
      <n>  = key expires in n days
      <n>w = key expires in n weeks
      <n>m = key expires in n months
      <n>y = key expires in n years
Key is valid for? (0)
```

Next, you must define a user ID for the key pair. This is like naming the key pair and associating it with yourself. The user ID consists of your real name, your e-mail address, and any brief comment you want to add (such as a nickname, title, or organization name). GPG prompts you for these three items, then creates the user ID in a fixed format. When you have entered these and edited them if needed, you can enter O (for Okay) to continue.

```
You need a User-ID to identify your key; the software
constructs the user id
from Real Name, Comment and Email Address in this form:
    "Heinrich Heine (Der Dichter) <heinrichh@dusseldorf.de>"
Real name:Wally
Email address:wally@wallyworld.com
Comment:Save the whales
You selected this USER-ID:
    "Wally (Save the whales) <wally@wallyworld.com>"
Change (N)ame, (C)omment, (E)mail or (O)kay/(Q)uit?
Enter passphrase:
Repeat passphrase:
```

```
We need to generate a lot of random bytes. It is a good idea
to perform some other action (type on the keyboard, move the
mouse, utilize the disks) during the prime generation; this
gives the random number generator a better chance to gain
enough entropy.
+++++++++++++++..+++++...+++++.+++++++++.++++++++++++++++++
+++++++++++++++++++++++++++++++.++++++++++++++++++++++++++++
++++++++++.+++++++++>+++++................+++++
.+++++++++++++++++++++++++++++++++++++++++++++++++++++++++++
.++++++++++.+++++++++++++++++++++++++++++++++++++.+++++.++
+++.++++++++++>+++++..............................+++++^^
^^^
gpg: /home/ed/.gnupg/trustdb.gpg: trustdb created
public and secret key created and signed.
key marked as ultimately trusted.
pub   1024D/3E3D7341 2006-06-14 Wally (Save the whales)
<wally@wallyworld.com>
      Key fingerprint = 0939 8006 B2CF 4A5A D0F2  6C43 24EA
4FFA 3E3D 7341
sub   1024g/C67A4728 2006-06-14
```

Each key pair is stored on your local hard disk so that it can be used to encrypt and sign files as you use the gpg utility. Because this is highly sensitive information, you should assign a passphrase to your key pair. A **passphrase** is a long password. Anytime GPG needs to access the secret key to encrypt, decrypt, or sign a file, you will be prompted to enter the passphrase. It should consist of multiple words, preferably not all words that can be found in the dictionary. It should be very difficult to guess but easy for you to remember, because *you must remember it* or your key pair becomes useless.

Consider the following two example passphrases. Notice that words are intentionally misspelled, but that patterns are used to help you remember the oddities (for example, the left-to-right progression of the nonletter characters on the keyboard). In the second example, English and foreign words are mixed:

- Whan!40@wanters#hav$besized%thy^brow

- Trapani~tromps~Siracusa!ogni!!volta!

GPG then generates the key pair. This takes several seconds. While the key is being generated, move your mouse around or play with the keyboard (Shift, Alt, and Ctrl are good choices). This helps to generate the random data in the operating system that GPG needs to create a secure key.

After the key pair is generated, you can view it with the `--list-keys` command, as shown next.

```
gpg --list-keys
/home/ed/.gnupg/pubring.gpg
-----------------------
pub   1024D/ 3E3D7341  2006-06-14
```

10

```
Wally (Save the whales) <wally@wallyworld.com>
sub  1024g/C67A4728 2006-06-14
```

Notice that only the public key is listed, indicated by pub in the left column. The private key is not shown by the list-keys options. The line labeled sub (for a subordinate key) in the left column is the key for the ElGamal symmetric cipher. The pub key is for public-key cryptography; the subordinate key is for symmetric encryption. GPG will use the following automatic process for encrypting a file:

- Encrypt the file using your symmetric key.

- Encrypt your symmetric key using the public key of the message recipient.

- Sign the resulting ciphertext with the private/secret key of your public-key cryptography pair so the recipient can verify that the message could have come only from you.

You can export your public key so that others can access it using the --export command in GPG. This creates a binary file that you could hand to other people, who could then use the --import command to add the key to their system, allowing them to send you encrypted messages. The collection of public keys that you have stored on your system is called your **key ring**—it's a file on your system that contains all the keys to which GPG has immediate access.

It's common to use the -a option (or --armor in long format) to make GPG convert the output to readable characters, which allows you to include your key in an e-mail or printed document.

As an example, suppose you wanted to exchange keys with a friend. You export your public key with the following command, using your user ID to indicate the key that you want to export. You can use your name or e-mail address and GPG will match them with a key on your key ring. The -o option indicates the output file where the key will be stored:

```
gpg -o wells.key --export wally@wallyworld.com
```

You then receive a key file from your friend and import it to your key ring using this command:

```
gpg --import thomas.key
```

Now when you list your keys using the --list-keys command, the new key is included in the list, and you can encrypt messages for that user.

Suppose that another user included a key within an e-mail message that she sent to you. She used the following command to create the text to paste into her message:

```
gpg -a -o gutowski.key --export pgutowski@xmission.com
```

The text looks something like this:

```
-----BEGIN PGP PUBLIC KEY BLOCK-----
Version: GnuPG v1.0.6 (GNU/Linux)
Comment: For info see http://www.gnupg.org
mQGiBDz5HrMRBACT1vx3gG7v6vB6eYZOcHnl1f56GWxItWNxCPrc5/BOD+jW80q
qwVAvSUfn/Y+aux0G2p1ypWEsB0GAu3PSeygll1nt0S3AuBP+sPT7IT+WlZJu2a
wafRa737aHnP4Be8BV0duRff8CmO2ATeklqY57PTvO5PPKcsx4lessXKikZwCgj
hHoqOZRqI1q0Z/wQHJQtoeH678D/1I6kD6bvy2NsAKqZKDy8WMSm9V4+RCAYsMz
dUK3mWteM0gkYFJr4dVFtV5rAP164acY2anqzHQ0wig/NZlfUuvOkI/itqitggP
5MTwTwWU3O5slkjkJTGXdxIsRYRR6RPRCDMoEwS/hjQL+sV02b5iM9dmudUJUxA
bgUsWDWQaTA/97G1+hxob0SahM/JDWECj3a1c+wNhoBOawJWPP9zqwWaXxU6X/v4
EpzXYC4n9efe2MW8oMzdVyEfEr4HHvpWe3IivWhz5r5e1TGt3dXbp5sxzT4+WBH
oI5qbk60URgv1crrEbhnoaTPyVy0iLHmkOHN76aI4mLGj/k8C5m2L5qjDLQnUGV
0ZXIgR3V0b3dza2kgPHBndXt0b3dkNraUB4bWlzc21vbi5jb20+iFcEExECABcFAj
z5HrMFCwcKAwQDFQMCAxYCAQIXgAAKCRBSx7WA/y+EXIbuAJ9WPzfrOu6Uy0Y9x
8KPZXPCkneEjACggcADA3FeeuamxfZX9CE1+LJj6py5AQ0EPPketxAEAM6zDanG
ygRveThZ+bsOaJI8awGG8rbUSv9h3QnnhEwiDvVwln6OxSi+fJHE5EQCw7E7XUF
7Q6DZZ+pqybe8LPgY0KZytgdj6nivzf6fiLz+iGDjucOKRCMJ8VSDOD4gyilywK
5Ln36gRITahxBphYP66EL3x3K++vopf9hIYj6HAAMFBACjATvzUqkHBgTEqhatq
n6O+kAnnDSkbVJlxkndNKkipyjBqFbcXoBRJpwMA+HNm+xesEeK2zY3WW3g4fT6
/rlmqHQWrqGJUhAB8pKiyMYto8DKyEk5VlkD2IcuyWJ6JwUSFjKzRjp34Ob7Sfu
s+u2cNsp+UWKuSZEUe+2TJo1rgIhGBBgRAgAGBQI8+R63AAoJEFLHtYD/L4RcKT
0An03uYPnqbfCgskKCGhWf5gxoakDzAJ0dIzixzBMx+06Jh2gJuPdT/lhoiJkBo
gQ8+R6zEQQQAk9b8d4Bu7+rwenmGTnB55dX+ehlsSLVjcQj63OfwTg/o1vNKqsFQ
L0lH5/2PmrsdBtqdcqVhLAdBgLtz0nsoJZdZ7dEtwLgT/rD0+yE/lpWSbtmsGn0
Wu9+2h5z+AXvAVdHbkX3/ApjtgE3pJamOez07zuTzynLMeJXrLFyopGcAoI4R6K
jmUaiNatGf8EByULaHh+u/A/9SOpA+m78tjbACqmSg8vFjEpvVePkQgGLDM3VCt
5lrXjNIJGBSa+HVRbVeawD9euGnGNmp6sx0NMIoPzWZX1LrzpCP4raorYID+TE8
E8FlNzubJZI5CUxl3cSLEWEUekT0QgzKBMEv4Y0C/rFdNm+YjPXZrnVCVMQG4FL
Fg1kGkwP/extfocaG9EmoTPyQ1hAo92tXPsDYaATmsCVjz/c6lml8VOl/7+BKc1
2AuJ/Xn3tjFvKDM3VchHxK+Bx76VntyIr1oc+a+XtUxrd3V26ebMc0+PlgR6COa
m5OtFEYL9XK6xG4Z6Gkz8lctIix5pDhze+miOJixo/5PAuZti+aowy0J1BldGVy
IEd1dG93c2tpIDxwZ3V0b3dza2lAeG1pc3Npb24uY29tPohXBBMRAgAXBQI8+R6
zBQsHCgMEAxUDAgMWAgECF4AACgkQUse1gP8vhFyG7gCfVj836zrulMtGPcfCj2
VzwpJ3hIwAoIHAAwNxXnrmpsX2V/QhNfiyY+qcuQENBDz5HrcQBADOsw2pxsoEb
3k4Wfm7DmiSPGsBhvK21Er/Yd0J54RMIg71cJZ+jsUovnyRxOREAsOx011Be0Og
2Wfqasm3vCz4GNCmcrYHY+p4r83+n4i8/ohg47nDikQjCfFUgzg+IMopcsCuS59
+oESE2ocQaYWD+uhC98dyvvr6KX/YSGI+hwADBQQAowE781KpBwYExKoWrap+jv
pAJ5w0pG1SZcZJ3TSpIqcowahW3F6AUSacDAPhzZvsXrBHits2N1lt4OH0+v65Z
qh0Fq6hiVIQAfKSosjGLaPAyshJOVZZA9iHLslieicFEhYys0Y6d+Dm+0n7rPrt
nDbKflFirkmRFHvtkyaNa4CIRgQYEQIABgUCPPketwAKCRBSx7WA/y+EXCk9AJ9
N7mD56m3woLJCghoVn+YMaGpA8wCdHSM4scwTMftOiYdoCbj3U/5YaIg=
=99xI
-----END PGP PUBLIC KEY BLOCK-----
```

You import the key using the same type of command as before:

```
gpg --import gutowski.key
```

Your key ring contains three keys. Consider now how much you trust that the keys you obtained actually belong to the people to whom you think they belong. Maybe someone forged an e-mail message from gutowski so that you would use the key. That person could intercept your e-mails to gutowski, read them, reencrypt them using gutowski's real public key, and then forward the message as if it came from you.

Signing a key indicates that you trust that the key really came from its purported owner; for example, you might have talked to the person on the phone to verify the fingerprint of the key or the person might have handed you a copy of the key on a disk. GPG signs your own key on your behalf at the time it is created. You can list the signatures on a key with the `--list-sigs` command.

Considering the two keys added in the previous example, Thomas handed you his key in person, so you feel very confident that it really is his public key. You decide to sign it to indicate that trust. Others might obtain his public key from you. If they trust your judgment, they may sign the key based on your word. To sign the thomas key that you have added to your key ring, use the `--edit-key` command. This starts an interactive interface in which you can use the `sign` command to add your own signature to the key you are editing, like this:

```
gpg --edit-key thomas@xmission.com
```

The key information for the user ID you entered (thomas@xmission.com here) is displayed, followed by a `Command>` prompt, at which you would enter the command `sign`. You must enter your own passphrase anytime your secret key is accessed, as it must be in this example to sign Thomas' public key.

The gutowski key, however, you are not so sure of, because it came in an e-mail through an insecure Internet connection. To verify it, you print the fingerprint of gutowski's key using this command:

```
gpg --fingerprint pgutowski@xmission.com
```

The output resembles the following:

```
pub   1024D/FF2F845C 2002-06-01
Paula Gutowski <pgutowski@xmission.com>
      Key fingerprint = 6FA2 40FA 9213 366D 6C13  3A02 52C7
B580
              FF2F 845C
sub   1024g/0811249D 2002-06-01
```

Then you call her on the phone. You know where she works, and you know her voice well. You recite the fingerprint over the phone and she verifies that it is correct. Now you feel comfortable signing her key as well.

You can use keys to encrypt documents without having signed them, but signatures indicate that you place a higher level of trust in the key.

To encrypt a document, you specify the recipient and the file to encrypt. The `-o` option gives the filename where the ciphertext will be stored:

```
gpg --encrypt -o report.doc.gpg -r thomas@xmission.com report.doc
```

It's a good practice to sign files you encrypt so the recipient can verify that they came from you. You might use a single command to do the following:

- Encrypt a file with a recipient's public key.
- Sign the encrypted file with your private/secret key.
- Convert the output to a readable format (instead of binary format).
- Store the output in a named file (instead of writing it to the screen).

The following command accomplishes all four of these things; it uses the `-r` option to indicate the recipient instead of adding it after the `--encrypt` command:

```
gpg -o report.gpg -a -r thomas@xmission.com --encrypt
    report.doc
```

NOTE

GPG uses not only commands, such as `--encrypt` and `--fingerprint`, but also options, such as `-a` and `-o`. The option should come before the command.

The person who receives the encrypted file can use the following command to decrypt it, assuming that the key ring on her system includes your public key if you signed the file and the correct secret key to correspond to the key you used to encrypt the file. The decrypted file is printed to the screen or stored in the file that you indicate with the `-o` option:

```
gpg -o report.doc --decrypt report.gpg
```

GPG includes dozens of other commands and options. Useful documentation includes the GPG man page, a mini-HOWTO document, a user manual, and additional technical reference materials. Some of these are available on your Linux system by default when GPG is installed; others are available at *www.gnupg.org*. Table 10-1 summarizes the most common gpg commands.

Table 10-1   Common gpg commands

Command Name	Description
`gpg --gen-key`	Generate a key pair
`gpg --export [UID]`	Export a key
`gpg --import [Filename]`	Import a key
`gpg --gen-revoke`	Generate a revocation certificate
`gpg --list-keys`	Display all keys
`gpg --list-sigs`	Display all keys with signatures
`gpg --fingerprint`	Display key fingerprints

10

Table 10-1 Common `gpg` commands (continued)

Command Name	Description
`gpg --list-secret-keys`	Display secret keys
`gpg --delete-key UID`	Delete a public key
`gpg --delete-secret-key`	Delete a secret key
`gpg --edit-key UID`	Edit key information and sign keys
`gpg --encrypt Recipient [Data]`	Encrypt data
`gpg --decrypt [Data]`	Decrypt data
`gpg --sign [Data]`	Sign data with your key
`gpg --clearsign [Data]`	Sign data with a cleartext result
`gpg --detach-sign [Data]`	Sign data with a detached result

To use GPG correctly, you must fully understand the concepts covered in this chapter. When you do, you can experiment with a graphical interface instead of memorizing all the command-line parameters. Two graphical utilities are the Gnu Privacy Assistant (GPA) and Seahorse. Neither is likely to be included with your Linux distribution, but you can find the source code and (for Seahorse at least) `rpm` packages for some versions of Fedora Core. See *www.gnupg.org/gpa.html* or *seahorse.sourceforge.net*, respectively, for additional information and files to download. Figure 10-11 shows a screen from Seahorse as an illustration of the program's functionality. Figure 10-12 shows a screen from the Gnu Privacy Assistant.

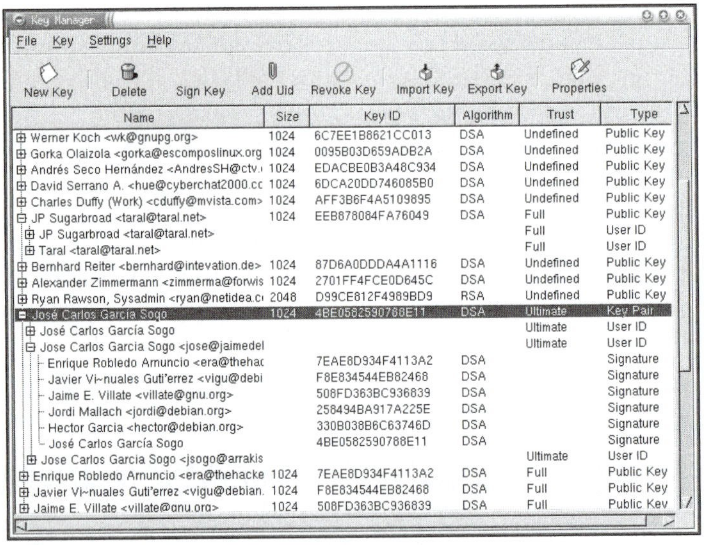

Figure 10-11 The Seahorse graphical interface to GPG

Many other programs are designed to interact with GPG automatically. For example, several e-mail readers such as `pine`, `elm`, and Kmail can be configured to use GPG in the background to encrypt and decrypt messages automatically based on the e-mail address of the sender or recipient.

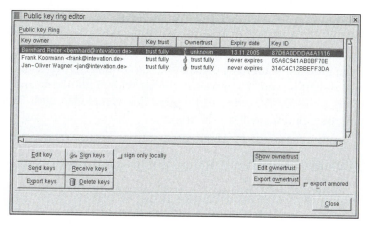

Figure 10-12   The Gnu Privacy Assistant

ENCRYPTING FILES

Linux allows you to encrypt files in a few ways. You can encrypt individual files or entire filesystems. The encrypted filesystems can be entire disk partitions or they can be encrypted loopback filesystems stored within an unencrypted filesystem.

If you only need to encrypt a few files, you can encrypt them individually using a file encryption program like openssl. The openssl program supports a wide range of ciphers, and you must select one when you encrypt a file. To see a list of ciphers, enter the following command:

```
openssl --help
```

You'll see a list like the following as part of the resulting error message:

```
Cipher commands (see the 'enc' command for more details)
aes-128-cbc      aes-128-ecb      aes-192-cbc      aes-192-ecb      aes-256-cbc
aes-256-ecb      base64           bf               bf-cbc           bf-cfb
bf-ecb           bf-ofb           cast             cast-cbc         cast5-cbc
cast5-cfb        cast5-ecb        cast5-ofb        des              des-cbc
des-cfb          des-ecb          des-ede          des-ede-cbc      des-ede-cfb
des-ede-ofb      des-ede3         des-ede3-cbc     des-ede3-cfb     des-ede3-ofb
des-ofb          des3             desx             rc2              rc2-40-cbc
rc2-64-cbc       rc2-cbc          rc2-cfb          rc2-ecb          rc2-ofb
rc4              rc4-40
```

Suppose you have a file called salaries.txt that you want to encrypt. You use a command similar to the following, which uses the 128-bit AES cipher:

```
openssl enc –aes128 –in salaries.txt –out salaries.txt.enc
```

10

You will be prompted to enter a password. Then, the encrypted version of the file is created and called salaries.txt.enc. The original file (salaries.txt) still exists, so you may want to erase it after you have the encrypted version. Of course, if you're going to the trouble of encrypting the file, you probably want to be certain that the contents of the original file can't be recovered from the disk. If so, you can overwrite the file with random data and other data patterns before you erase the file. The `shred` program that is included with Fedora Core and most other Linux distributions will do the trick:

```
shred -v salaries.txt
```

To decrypt the file, use this command:

```
openssl enc -d -aes128 -in salaries.txt.enc -out salaries.txt
```

You will be prompted to enter a password. Next, the decrypted file is created without deleting the encrypted version of the file. If you only read the file and don't make changes to it, you can shred it and delete it when you're finished. If you change the file's contents, you'll have to encrypt it again.

A lot of effort goes into encrypting and decrypting files using programs like `openssl`. Things are much easier if you encrypt entire filesystems.

Encrypting Disk Partitions

You can encrypt an entire filesystem on a disk partition so that you'll be able to access the files normally, without having to specify a password or passphrase each time you access a file. You must configure the filesystem for encryption when you create it. You can't encrypt an existing filesystem that already has files stored on it.

It's good practice to prepare the disk partition by writing random bytes to it. This makes it difficult for an eavesdropper to distinguish between encrypted data and free space. One way to do this is to use the `shred` command:

```
shred -n 1 -v /dev/hda4
```

This writes random data to the fourth disk partition on /dev/hda. Be certain that you specify the correct disk partition. If you specify a partition that has data on it, you will not be able to recover your data.

Next, you need to format the partition to be a loopback device by entering the following command:

```
losetup -e aes /dev/loop5 /dev/hda4
```

You'll be prompted to enter a password or passphrase. Next, place a filesystem on the partition:

```
mke2fs -j /dev/loop5
```

Create a mount point for the encrypted filesystem to use:

```
mkdir /mnt/crypt
```

You can mount the loopback filesystem with the following command:

```
mount /dev/loop5 /mnt/crypt
```

You can now go to the /mnt/crypt directory and use this filesystem as you would any other.

Encrypting Loopback Filesystems

In Chapter 8, you learned about loopback filesystems, which are mounted to loopback devices instead of disk partitions. Now, you'll learn how to encrypt the contents of loopback filesystems.

Start by creating a file large enough to hold all the data you plan to store in the filesystem. After you create the file, you cannot expand its size later without destroying the data stored there. The following command creates a 4-MB file:

```
dd if=/dev/urandom of=/home/justin/secret bs=4096 count=1000
```

Next, you must format the file to be a loopback device. You must be logged on as root to run the next command. You must use a loopback device that is not already in use. In the following example, you use /dev/loop5, in case lower-numbered loopback devices are in use. You must also specify the type of encryption to use (AES in the following example). When you run the losetup command, you'll be prompted for a password:

```
losetup -e aes /dev/loop5 /home/justin/secret
Password:
```

NOTE

The cryptoloop kernel modules must be loaded for this to work. You may have to load them manually with the modprobe cryptoloop command.

Place a filesystem on the loopback device. The following command places an ext2 filesystem on the loopback device:

```
mke2fs /dev/loop5
```

Create a mount point for the encrypted filesystem to use:

```
mkdir /home/justin/diary
```

You can now mount the loopback filesystem with the following command:

```
mount -t ext2 -o loop,encryption=aes /home/justin/secret
/home/justin/diary
```

You'll be prompted to enter a password. This is the same password you used with the `losetup` command. If you forget your password, your data cannot be recovered. You can unmount the encrypted loopback with either of these commands:

```
umount /home/justin/diary
umount /home/justin/secret
```

You can add an entry to the `/etc/fstab` file to make mounting and unmounting easier:

```
/home/justin/secret    /home/justin/diary    ext2
noauto,encryption=aes  0 0
```

Note the `noauto` mount option in the previous line. This means that the loopback will not be mounted automatically at system startup. If it is mounted automatically, the boot process stops and prompts for the password or passphrase of the encrypted filesystem. It's better to have a user manually mount the filesystem when he needs to use it and specify the password then.

If you must have encrypted filesystems mounted automatically, the `pam_mount` module can be used to mount them when users log on. This would be useful if the encrypted loopback filesystem were stored on a USB memory device. This module goes beyond the scope of this book.

The Cryptographic File System

In Chapter 5, you learned about the Network File System (NFS). Although it is potentially a great convenience for users and system administrators, NFS assumes a network environment in which all users can be trusted. The **Cryptographic File System (CFS)** abandons this assumption, enforcing cryptographic authentication on all users who want to share files across the network. Another group has enhanced the work of the original developer of CFS (Matt Blaze) by making it operate transparently to client users on the network. They have renamed their project the **Transparent Cryptographic File System (TCFS)**. TCFS is still in development; to learn more about it, visit *www.tcfs.it*.

OTHER SECURITY APPLICATIONS

GPG is a powerful tool because it lets you manage key rings with a number of specialized commands and allows you to apply public-key encryption to any file you want to transmit securely. You can send a file encrypted with GPG to a recipient using an insecure network without fear of someone sniffing the network and reading your message. However, keep in mind that GPG is only one of many encryption tools available to Linux users. Many other protocols and utilities use the encryption techniques you learned about in this chapter to provide computer security in a number of different contexts.

Some of these security-related utilities are more specialized. For example, the `rpm` command includes a GPG signature that you can verify to see whether a software package came from Red Hat Software without being modified by a cracker. Other utilities are more general purpose, with the goal of securing all communication between two hosts or two networks, without the need to run a utility like GPG explicitly to encrypt a file.

Without the utilities briefly described in this section, networks would be much more dangerous for businesses and individuals to use because of the technologies available to read other users' packets as they traverse the network. Using such utilities makes any school or small-business network as secure as U.S. intelligence networks, provided that both the network administrator and users on the network are willing to follow appropriate steps to create and maintain a secure environment.

Whenever you plan for the security of your network, put yourself in a cracker's shoes for a few minutes. How would you try to break into your own network? Where are the weak points? How would you obtain or falsify a key so that you could read messages sent by network users? For example, if a network is built around a public-key encryption system that all users are committed to, a cracker is unlikely to begin by trying to crack a key. Instead, he will try to falsify a key, steal a laptop containing a secret key, or find a disgruntled employee who has some access to the files he wants. By thinking about the weaknesses of your security—technical or human—you can decide in advance how to thwart efforts to exploit them.

RPM Security

Earlier in this chapter, you read about using the `rpm` command to check the MD5 signature on an `rpm` package and verify its integrity. This verifies that the `rpm` was not damaged during downloading, but says nothing about who created it. To do this, you must add the public key for Red Hat Software from *www.redhat.com/security/team/key/* and then check the public-key signature of an `rpm` to verify that the `rpm` really came from Red Hat. Other companies may use similar techniques; you can obtain their public keys and check the signatures in the same way.

Suppose you had downloaded an `rpm` package from a Web site that you thought was mirroring official Red Hat packages. A check using the command `rpm -qi` listed the packager as Red Hat Software. The package was an update to IP Tables, which is used to create firewalls in Linux (as described in Chapter 11). A knowledgeable cracker could wreak havoc on your security by tampering with IP Tables, so you verify that the package was created by Red Hat Software using the following command:

```
rpm --checksig iptables-1.2.11-3.1.FC3.rpm
iptables-1.2.11-3.1.FC3.rpm:  md5  gpg  OK
```

The OK output on the second line shows that the file is not corrupted (the MD5 checksum is verified) and that the file was signed by the Red Hat Software private key (the GPG key signature is verified).

Other Linux distributions, such as Gentoo, publish an MD5 hash on their download sites instead of using keys.

IP Packet Encryption

Encryption can occur at different points in a network transmission. For example, a user could encrypt a file using GPG before attaching the file to an e-mail message. The data is then encrypted from the moment the e-mail client sees it. Conversely, an e-mail server such as `sendmail` could implement a security measure in which it exchanged keys with another `sendmail` server on the Internet and created a secure connection before transferring any e-mail messages.

Beyond the Web (using HTTP and SSL, as described previously), very few application protocols have standardized encryption mechanisms. For example, POP3, SMTP, FTP, and NFS do not. Instead, developers have created encryption options at the IP packet level.

IPsec (for Secure IP) is a fairly new industry standard for IP packet encryption. IPsec is supported in Linux, but as a standard, IPsec is still not completely settled—issues remain in areas such as key management and integration with higher-layer protocols. When IPv6 becomes widely used, it will have full support for IPsec. For more information, visit *www.rfc-editor.org* and search for RFC 2401.

A less-expensive effort is **Cryptographic IP Encapsulation (CIPE)**, which tunnels IP packets within encrypted UDP packets. CIPE places special effort on being useful immediately (without waiting for complex issues relevant to IPsec to be resolved), and on being compatible with routing techniques used in more complex networks. For details on CIPE, visit *http://sites.inka.de/sites/bigred/devel/cipe.html*.

Secure Shell

The **Secure Shell (SSH)** protocol is probably better known than GPG, though GPG can be used in a broader range of circumstances. The simplest description of SSH is that it is an encrypted version of Telnet—it lets you access a remote host the same way Telnet does, but without the danger that someone sniffing the network can see what you are transmitting. However, such a simple explanation tends to hide the power of SSH; unlike Telnet, SSH has been designed to allow other protocols to ride on top of it (or be encapsulated within it, depending on your preferred metaphor).

For example, protocols like FTP and remote sessions of the X Window System are completely insecure. However, you can start an SSH session and tie an FTP or X session to it, so that all traffic for the FTP or X session is transmitted using SSH—it is completely encrypted.

Like other Linux Internet services, SSH consists of a client utility (`ssh`) and a server daemon (`sshd`). In addition, the SSH package includes utilities to generate keys and the `scp` program that acts like `rcp`, letting you copy files between any two computers on your network with full encryption. SSH is available as a commercial product—see *www.ssh.com*. Linux distributions rely on the free version of SSH, called **OpenSSH**—see *www.openssh.org*. OpenSSH is installed by default on many Linux systems, including Fedora Core. SSH is described in much more detail in Chapter 11.

Virtual Private Networks

The goal of many system administrators using cryptographic products and protocols is to create a **virtual private network (VPN)**. A VPN is a secure organizational network that uses insecure public networks (such as the Internet) for communications. A VPN takes advantage of the high speed and relatively low cost of Internet connectivity while hiding sensitive data from anyone else connected to the Internet. See Figure 10-13.

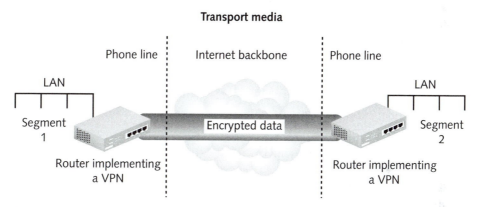

Transport media

Phone line ⋮ Internet backbone ⋮ Phone line

LAN ⋮ ⋮ LAN

Segment 1 — Encrypted data — Segment 2

Router implementing a VPN ⋮ ⋮ Router implementing a VPN

Figure 10-13 A virtual private network (VPN)

VPNs are often created with the aid of specially designed software that integrates many networking functions with cryptographic protocols and system management software. Chapter 11 discusses VPN software in more detail.

NOTE

Some countries restrict the use of encryption technologies in various ways. For example, citizens of France are not allowed to use public-key encryption without special permission. If you intend to move cryptographic products across national borders, you should research what rules apply. The Web site for a package such as OpenSSH contains legal notes on using that package.

CHAPTER SUMMARY

❑ Cryptography is the science of encoding data, typically using a key, so that people without the key cannot read the data. Cryptography uses a cipher to encrypt plaintext into ciphertext.

❑ Cryptography protects computer networks against sniffers, which are programs that allow crackers to see data passing across a network.

❑ Many different algorithms are used to encrypt data. These algorithms are either symmetric (using a single key for encryption and decryption) or asymmetric (using two different keys for encryption and decryption). The use of asymmetric algorithms is commonly called public-key cryptography.

❑ DES was a popular standard algorithm for years. Triple DES and AES have replaced it in many circumstances—both are FIPS (approved for U.S. government work). Several other ciphers such as ElGamal, IDEA, and Blowfish are also popular.

❑ Public-key encryption does not require that you openly exchange a secret key with the recipient of an encrypted message, thus removing a major disadvantage to using encryption on computer networks. Public-key encryption is used for secure transmission of the symmetric key with which a document is encrypted.

❑ RSA is the most familiar public-key algorithm.

❑ Signatures on a document show that the sender is the only one who could have sent the document; signatures on a public key in GPG indicate that the key is trusted by the signer.

❑ Certificates are issued and signed by certificate authorities such as VeriSign to vouch for the identity of the organization holding the certificate.

❑ A hash is a mathematical function that creates a small number from a very large number. Popular hashes are MD5 and SHA-1. A hash is used to create a fingerprint, which lets a user quickly verify the integrity of a public key or other large number or file.

❑ Browsers such as Netscape and Mozilla use cryptography via the Secure Sockets Layer (SSL) protocol to allow secure e-commerce transactions.

❑ To generate a certificate for your Web server, you must generate a private key using the openssl program.

❑ Kerberos provides a network wide user and service authentication scheme to limit network access to authorized users, but it requires a significant time commitment for configuration and maintenance.

❑ PGP was the first freely available public-key encryption software. It was created by Phil Zimmermann and is now owned by Network Associates. PGP remains an industry standard on which GPG is based.

❑ The Gnu Privacy Guard (GPG) is a free public-key encryption utility that lets you manage keys and encrypt, sign, and decrypt documents. Graphical utilities can make it easier to work with GPG. Many utilities such as `pine`, `elm`, and Kmail can integrate access to GPG for sending and receiving messages.

❑ Linux allows you to encrypt individual files or entire filesystems. The encrypted filesystems may be entire disk partitions or encrypted loopback filesystems stored within an unencrypted filesystem.

❑ Keys should be signed only when the identity of the person providing the key has been ascertained with certainty.

❑ The `rpm` utility can check a public-key signature on any package to verify that it came from the person or organization that claims to have created the package.

❑ Other security protocols built on the same principles of cryptography as GPG include IPsec, CIPE, and CFS. Many network administrators use technologies like these or special software to create a virtual private network (VPN) for an organization that spans multiple offices.

❑ The Secure Shell (SSH) provides encrypted remote access via a utility that functions like Telnet. SSH also lets other protocols work with it to create secure connections for many purposes. Both commercial and open versions of SSH are available.

10

KEY TERMS

Advanced Encryption Standard (AES) — A replacement for DES. The next generation of government-approved encryption standards. Uses the Rijndael algorithm (pronounced "Rain Doll").

algorithm — A set of rules or steps that, when followed, result in a predictable outcome.

asymmetric encryption algorithm — An encryption algorithm in which different keys are used to encrypt and decrypt a message. One is kept secret, one is distributed publicly. Often called public-key encryption.

authentication — The process of proving to a computer system or another person that you are who you say you are.

Blowfish — A symmetric cipher.

certificate — A numeric code used to identify an organization.

certificate authority (CA) — An organization that issues a certificate to another person or organization after verifying the applicant's credentials.

checksum — A computed value that helps to verify that a file or transmission has not been corrupted.

cipher — A cryptographic technique or rule that converts plaintext into ciphertext.

ciphertext — A message that has been encoded using a cipher so that it is no longer readable. The end result of encrypting plaintext.

Cryptographic File System (CFS) — A filesystem driver supported by Linux that adds cryptographic features to an NFS-like file-sharing model.

Cryptographic IP Encapsulation (CIPE) — An IP packet encryption protocol. It lacks some features of IPsec but is already fully implemented (while IPsec is not). CIPE operates by tunneling IP packets within encrypted UDP packets.

cryptography — The science of encoding—and trying to decode—data that has been rendered unreadable using special knowledge or tools.

Data Encryption Standard (DES) — The first widely accepted standard for encryption, developed in the 1970s by IBM and the National Institute of Standards and Technology.

digital signature — A part of an electronic transaction that gives it the same legally binding effect as a document signed with an ink pen.

Digital Signature Algorithm (DSA) — A popular algorithm used to sign encrypted files to verify their origin.

ElGamal — A symmetric cipher used by GPG.

encryption — The process of converting plaintext to ciphertext using a cipher algorithm.

Federal Information Processing Standard (FIPS) — A standard for information processing (such as an encryption algorithm) that has been approved for use by government agencies.

fingerprint — A small number that is derived from a larger number (such as a public key) using a hash. The fingerprint provides a convenient test of the integrity of the larger number.

Gnu Privacy Guard (GPG) — A command-line, public-key encryption utility that is compatible with PGP in many respects.

hash — The result of a mathematical function that converts a large number into a smaller number in a predictable way.

https — A code within a Web page URL that indicates the page was transmitted over an encrypted connection.

IDEA — A patented symmetric cipher.

IPsec — An industry standard for IP packet encryption. IPsec is supported in Linux, but as a standard, it is still not completely settled.

Kerberos — A special type of authentication for organizational networks.

key — A code (usually numeric) that can be used to encrypt or decrypt a message.

key pair — The combination of a public key that can be handed out to others and a private or secret key that remains hidden on a user's system (and is protected with a passphrase).

key ring — The collection of public keys stored on a system; a file containing all of the keys to which GPG has immediate access.

message digest hash (MD5) — A hash that converts a number of any length to a 128-bit (32-hexadecimal-digit) number called a checksum.

one-time pad — An encryption method in which a message is converted to numbers, and then random numbers taken from a list are added to each part of the message. The recipient must have the same list of random numbers to decrypt the message. Assuming no one else has the list of random numbers, the encrypted message is considered unbreakable.

OpenSSH — A free version of SSH included in most Linux distributions.

passphrase — A long password.

plaintext — A readable message.

Pretty Good Privacy (PGP) — The first utility to provide public-key encryption. Created by Phil Zimmermann.

prime number — A number that cannot be broken down into factors other than itself and 1. Prime numbers are the core mathematical feature of public-key encryption.

private-key encryption — A form of encryption using a symmetric algorithm.

public-key encryption — A form of encryption using an asymmetric encryption algorithm.

RC2 — A symmetric cipher.

RC4 — A symmetric cipher.

RC5 — A symmetric cipher.

realm — Within a Kerberos-enabled network, all the users and services whose keys are stored on the Kerberos server.

RSA — The most widely known algorithm for public-key encryption. Developed by Ronald Rivest, Adi Shamir, and Len Adleman.

Secure Hash Algorithm (SHA-1) — A hashing algorithm, more secure than MD5, that creates a 160-bit hash of any file or key to help check whether it was tampered with or otherwise corrupted during transmission.

Secure Shell (SSH) — A protocol that provides network connectivity equivalent to an encrypted version of Telnet, plus additional support to allow encryption of other protocols.

sign — To attach your private key to a file to show that the file could only have come from you. Also, the process of attaching your private key to another person's public key to indicate that you trust the validity of that public key.

Skipjack — A government-approved encryption algorithm that uses an 80-bit key.

sniffer — A software package used to sniff the network.

sniffing — Tapping into a network connection to read the packets that other users have sent.

symmetric encryption algorithm — An encryption algorithm in which the same key is used to both encrypt and decrypt a message (the algorithm is reversed for decryption). Also called private-key encryption.

ticket — A set of information provided by a Kerberos server to a user or service that grants the user permission to use the service. A ticket contains the following components: {sessionkey:username:address:servicename:lifespan:timestamp}.

Transparent Cryptographic File System (TCFS) — An enhancement to the Cryptographic File System (CFS) that allows it to operate transparently to client users on the network.

Triple DES (TDES) — A U.S. government-approved encryption algorithm that applies the DES algorithm three times in succession using three different DES keys.

Twofish — A symmetric cipher.

virtual private network (VPN) — A secure organizational network that uses insecure public networks (such as the Internet) for communications.

web of trust — The personal connections between a group of colleagues who have exchanged keys, signed them, and continue to rely on each others' signatures.

REVIEW QUESTIONS

1. Define cryptography.

2. A person using a sniffer would benefit from:
   a. users on the network running unencrypted Telnet sessions
   b. a VPN
   c. the 56-bit key length of a DES cipher
   d. both GPG and PGP

3. Which of the following statements is accurate?
   a. Plaintext and ciphertext differ only in their transmission characteristics.
   b. Cryptography was developed in the 1970s as part of the computer science field.
   c. A cipher is used to encrypt plaintext, yielding ciphertext.
   d. Cipher algorithms cannot use keys if they are to remain secure.

4. For a symmetric cipher to be useful:
   a. The algorithm can be openly known, but the key must remain secret.
   b. The algorithm must be kept secret as well as the key.
   c. The key must be longer than 128 bits.
   d. The government must have approved it as a FIPS.

5. DES is no longer widely used because:
   a. Other ciphers have been better-tested.
   b. DES can now be exported and, thus, is considered an insecure munition.
   c. Patents make it too expensive to implement on a wide scale.
   d. Its key size is too small, allowing specialized computers to crack a DES key in a relatively short time.

6. Name the three alternatives to DES mentioned in the text.

7. Triple DES is not considered a good long-term cipher choice because:
   a. The creators of the algorithm were not government employees.
   b. Asymmetric ciphers are replacing older symmetric ciphers.
   c. Skipjack is much more secure.
   d. Its use of three DES keys applied sequentially requires too much computing power.

8. Which of the following cipher algorithms does AES use?
   a. Rijndael
   b. Skipjack
   c. Blowfish
   d. ElGamal

9. What standard key lengths does AES support?

   a. 128, 192, and 256 bits

   b. 1024 and 2048 bits

   c. 56 bits, three times

   d. 64 bits

10. What is the standard key length for a public key in GPG?

   a. 56 bits

   b. 128 bits

   c. 1024 bits

   d. 2048 bits

11. Name five symmetric cipher algorithms.

12. Define the term "prime number."

13. A document is typically both encrypted and signed:

   a. so that it takes twice the computing power to decrypt it

   b. only when the sender does not know the recipient

   c. unless the recipient does not have the private key of the sender

   d. so that only the recipient can decrypt it and the recipient knows that the named sender sent it

14. The most widely known asymmetric encryption algorithm is:

   a. RSA

   b. DES

   c. Triple DES

   d. GPG

15. A certificate authority (CA):

   a. issues key pairs that can then be imported into programs such as GPG

   b. can read messages encrypted with certificates that it has issued

   c. issues a certificate cryptographically signed by the CA that indicates the CA's verification of the identity of the certificate holder

   d. signs each Web transaction with its public key

16. A hash and a fingerprint of a public key:

   a. are never used at the same time

   b. are effectively the same thing—a hash of a public key is called its fingerprint and allows easy verification of its integrity

   c. cannot be verified except by the GPG program

   d. provide for symmetric encryption

10

17. Name two popular hash algorithms.

18. Within a Kerberos _____ , the Kerberos server grants _____ to users to access services.

    a. realm, tickets

    b. network, keys

    c. program, ciphers

    d. cipher, hashes

19. Within GPG, you must enter a passphrase:

    a. each time GPG decrypts an unsigned document based on the public key of a colleague stored on your key ring

    b. each time GPG contacts a key server

    c. each time GPG accesses your secret key to encrypt or sign something

    d. only when you initially create your key pair

20. The key ring in GPG is:

    a. the collection of all keys that GPG has access to for encryption or decryption

    b. the combination of your secret/private key and your public key

    c. the hash created when you sign another person's public key to verify that you trust it

    d. not accessible except through the GPG command-line utility

21. GPA and Seahorse are:

    a. two symmetric ciphers

    b. two asymmetric ciphers

    c. pseudonyms for the two crackers who broke DES

    d. two graphical utilities that provide GPG functionality

22. Using an `rpm --checksig` command provides:

    a. a fingerprint that you can use to send a file to another user securely

    b. assurance that the purported packager of an `rpm` file actually created the file and that it has not been modified

    c. access to full GPG functionality from within the package file you are installing

    d. a GPG signature check without any MD5 information being provided

23. Name two protocols that encrypt data for network transmission.

24. SSH is commonly used in place of Telnet because:

    a. SSH provides a secure communications channel that is immune to sniffing software.

    b. Telnet patents do not expire for several more years.

    c. SSH is strictly open source and Telnet is not.

    d. SSH protocols use a more robust encryption algorithm than that used by Telnet.

25. Moving cryptographic products across national borders requires care because:

    a. Language barriers can create unexpected results when signing keys.

    b. Different nations use different approved ciphers, which may be incompatible.

    c. Taxes on these products can be very high.

    d. Laws controlling cryptography vary widely between nations and are taken very seriously.

10

HANDS-ON PROJECTS

HANDS-ON PROJECTS

Project 10-1

In this project, you decrypt a letter-substitution cipher. To complete this project, you should have a pencil, paper, and some extra time. You may want to work as a class or in a team so you can more efficiently analyze possible solutions. This type of simple cipher appears regularly in puzzle books, but it provides an excellent chance to understand how more complex ciphers are constructed and how they can be decrypted given patience. Use hints from the chapter text about letter and word frequency as you attack this problem. Remember that having a longer message is helpful because it gives you more data to analyze and test your theories as you work out which letter stands for which other letter. For this cipher, each letter represents a single, different letter of the alphabet. Word breaks in the plaintext have been preserved. The ciphertext follows:

```
QCFW OFQFO: R KFIC MCCX GKZJX RX HKC PRDCG ZP HKC JFW
QCBFWHOCXH F GHFHCOCXH ZP HKC FQELHFXH NCXCWFD HKFH
UZL FWC HKC OZHKCW ZP PRIC GZXG JKZ KFIC QRCQ
NDZWRZLGDU ZX HKC PRCDQ ZP MFHHDC. R PCCD KZJ JCFA FXQ
PWLRHDCGG OLGH MC FXU JZWQG ZP ORXC JKRSK GKZLDQ
FHHCOBH HZ MCNLRDC UZL PWZO HKC NWRCP ZP F DZGG GZ
ZICWJKCDORXN. MLH R SFXXZH WCPWFRX PWZO HCXQCWRXN HZ
UZL HKC SZXGZDPHRZX HKFH OPU MC PZLXQ RX HKC HKFXAG ZP
HKC WCBLMDRS HKCU QRCQ HZ GFIC. R BWFU HKFH ZLW
KCFICXDU PFHKCW OFU FGGLFNC HKC FXNLRGK ZP UZLW
MCWCFICOCXH FXQ DCFIC UZL ZXDU HKC SKCWRGKCQ OCOZWU
ZP HKC DZICQ FXQ DZGH FXQ HKC GZDCOX BWRQC HKFH OLGH MC
UZLWG HZ KFIC DFRQ GZ SZGHDU F GFSWRPRSC LBZX HKC FDHFW
ZP PWCCQZO. - F. DRXSZDX
```

Project 10-2

In this project, you experiment with a hash function to see how changing a large file changes the hash of the file. To complete this project, you should have Fedora Core installed.

1. Log on and open a command-line window.

2. Copy the /etc/termcap file to your home directory under the name test.

   cp /etc/termcap ~/test

3. The termcap file, which you just copied and renamed to test, has more than 17,000 lines of text. Compute an MD5 checksum on the test file using the md5sum command:

   md5sum test

   (You can also include a regular expression to compute checksums on a number of files with one command.)

4. Open the test file in a text editor.

5. Press the Spacebar on the first line of the file (or make some other one-character change to the file).

6. Save the file and exit the text editor.

7. Run another checksum using md5sum:

   md5sum test

8. How do the checksums (the hashes) compare?

Project 10-3

In this project, you review Web page security in a browser. To complete this project, you should have Linux installed with a graphical browser and an Internet connection. This project uses Mozilla Firefox running on Linux, though most browsers have similar functionality.

1. Log on and run Firefox or another graphical browser.

2. Enter *www.americanexpress.com*. When the page appears, notice that there is no lock icon in the lower-right side of the browser window.

3. Click the **Shopping** link. You might have to respond to one or more dialog boxes regarding security issues, such as being transferred to another Web server or moving from an insecure document to a secure document (or vice versa). Why does your browser inform you of these issues?

4. Notice that the URL has changed to begin with https:// instead of http://. A small lock icon appears in the lower-right corner of the window.

5. Choose **Page Info** on the Tools menu. Click the **Security** tab and then click the **View** button.

6. Notice the security information on the page that appears. Try to relate this information to the discussion of certificates in the chapter text.

Project 10-4

In this project, you use the gpg utility to create a key pair and use it to encrypt a file. To complete this project, you should have Fedora Core installed with the gpg utility (which is installed by default). In this project, you work with a partner to share encrypted information. Because you are probably working in a lab environment, do not consider the keys that you create here to be "real" keys that you would distribute to friends outside the classroom. The keys should be discarded after completing the project; you can then create real keys on your personal or office computer.

1. Log on to Linux.

2. Run the gpg command for the first time without any parameters. The program creates needed directories.

    gpg

3. Run gpg again to generate a key pair for your user account. Use the default values for cipher, key length, and no expiration. Enter your name and lab e-mail address when prompted, and decide on a simple passphrase to protect your private key.

    gpg --gen-key

4. View your public key using the --list-keys command.

    gpg --list-keys

5. Export a copy of your public key in binary format. Use your e-mail address as your user ID to specify the key that you want to export (though your key ring contains only one key thus far):

    gpg -o *your_name***.key --export** *your_e-mail_address*

6. Get the .key file you created in the previous step to your lab partner for this exercise, either via a 3.5-inch disk or a network connection (you could e-mail it to her, for example).

7. You and your partner should have exchanged files containing your public keys. Import your partner's key into your key ring:

    gpg --import *partner_key_file*

8. Because the user ID of a key is encoded as part of the key, only the filename is needed, not a username. Check the list of keys on your key ring again to see that the import function worked.

    gpg --list-keys

10

9. Display the fingerprint/checksum for your partner's key.

```
gpg --fingerprint partner_e-mail_address
```

10. Call your partner on the phone or talk across tables. Have her view the fingerprint for her own key (by specifying her own user ID with the --fingerprint command). Review the fingerprint of your partner's key to make certain it is valid.

11. Sign your partner's key by using the edit-key command, then the sign command. Start with the following command, substituting your partner's e-mail address where indicated:

```
gpg --edit-key partner_e-mail_address
```

When the command prompt appears, enter **sign**. Select the default answer when prompted for how carefully you've verified the key. At the Really sign? prompt, type **y** and then press **Enter**.

You are prompted for the passphrase you entered in Step 3 and your partner's key is signed. Exit the gpg program by entering **quit**.

12. Both you and your partner now have a key ring that includes your own key and each other's public key. You can use the text file from the /etc directory used here as an example, or you can create or use any file you choose. Encrypt a document to send to your partner using the --encrypt command:

```
gpg -a -o message.gpg -r partner_e-mail_address --sign
   --encrypt /etc/hosts
```

13. Exchange encrypted files with your partner by FTP, e-mail, 3.5-inch disk, or however your choose.

14. Decrypt and review the file you received from your partner:

```
gpg --decrypt message.gpg
```

**HANDS-ON
PROJECTS**

Project 10-5

In this project, you use the rpm command to verify the signature on an rpm package. To complete this project, you should have Fedora Core installed, root access to the Linux system, and an Internet connection. You should also have completed Project 10-4 so that GPG is installed and you have an active GPG key ring.

1. Log on to Linux.

2. Open a browser and go to *http://fedora.redhat.com/about/security/*.

3. Copy the public key from the Fedora page.

4. Open a text editor and paste the copied text into the editor window. Save the file as **fedora.key**.

5. Import the Fedora Software public key using the --import command of GPG:

```
gpg --import fedora.key
```

6. Verify the import operation by listing all the keys on your key ring:

```
gpg --list-keys
```

7. You need access to an rpm file that was signed by Fedora. You can insert a Fedora Core CD and go to the RPMS directory.

8. Run the rpm command to verify that the package you downloaded was indeed created by Fedora.

```
rpm --checksig package_filename
```

CASE PROJECTS

CASE PROJECTS

Case Project 10-1

1. Using the Web sites mentioned in the chapter text as resources, determine why the Rijndael algorithm was selected for AES. What advantages or disadvantages does it have, compared with other popular symmetric algorithms?

2. Prepare a one-page report on the current issues facing public-key infrastructure—the creation and dissemination of trusted public keys to provide privacy and security to citizens around the world. Use the URLs in the chapter text or Internet search engines to begin your research.

3. Suppose you are the network administrator for a company of 400 employees, each of whom works at a computer all day. Would you encourage use of GPG as much as possible? Why or why not? How would GPG affect the security of your network operations? What other techniques would you want to consider to enhance network security?

10

11

NETWORK SECURITY FUNDAMENTALS

After reading this chapter and completing the exercises, you will be able to:

♦ Examine the types of network security breaches that crackers attempt

♦ Describe how to use special routing techniques to protect local network traffic

♦ Configure a basic Linux firewall

♦ Use networking utilities and techniques that protect network traffic through encryption

In this chapter, you will begin learning about security tools and methods for protecting networks. After reviewing the ways in which crackers attempt to attack your Linux system, you will learn about special routing methods and firewalls that increase network security. The last part of this chapter describes how you can encrypt network traffic using Secure Shell (SSH) and other security tools.

The main network security feature described in this chapter—IP Tables—is part of every Linux kernel. You will learn how to set up these features and how to use graphical tools to ease the work of configuration. You will also learn about several commercial firewall products.

EXAMINING THREATS TO YOUR NETWORK

Previous chapters introduced many of the security threats that a network faces, both from inside your organization and outside. This section describes the threats in more detail.

Trojan Horses

Trojan horses are programs concealed within other programs that you unintentionally download or install on your Linux system. After being installed, the program that "hosts" the Trojan horse appears to do one thing, but actually does something else. For example, it could accept a network connection on a certain port, giving crackers access to your system. Trojan horse programs are hard to spot before they cause damage to your system, unless you use a file integrity program, such as Tripwire or Samhain (described in Chapter 8).

You can protect against Trojan horses by acquiring programs only from trusted sources and by checking the program's cryptographic signature or fingerprint after downloading it.

Viruses and Worms

Viruses and worms are related security threats designed to replicate themselves after they have been installed on your system. A virus usually tries to replicate as part of another program (for example, as an e-mail attachment), whereas a worm attempts to infiltrate other systems on its own. Linux is rarely the target of virus attacks, especially when a Linux system is managed by a security-conscious administrator, because it has a good security architecture.

Seasoned Linux administrators don't allow ordinary users to log on to the system as root, they minimize the number of programs and daemons that run as root, and they seek alternatives when a program or daemon develops a history of security problems. In addition, the most vulnerable viral "carriers"—Microsoft Word, Excel, and Outlook—don't run on Linux.

A few viruses target Linux, but most do little damage to a well-managed Linux system. These viruses represent a tiny percentage of the viruses that plague Windows. It's been suggested that Linux would be just as vulnerable to viruses if it were as popular as Windows, but this is debatable.

Numerous virus scanner programs run on Linux. The most popular open source virus scanner is ClamAV, which can scan for viruses in files on disk, e-mail messages or attachments, or in Web traffic. It can also detect viruses in many compressed and archived file formats. ClamAV is commonly used with e-mail server software such as Postfix and `sendmail`. For more information, go to *www.clamav.net*.

Denial-of-Service (DoS) Attacks

Denial-of-service (DoS) attacks occur when a cracker tries to overwhelm your system, either causing it to shut down or making it unavailable to legitimate users. This can be done in several ways. Two common methods are to overwhelm the network connection with traffic and to execute network requests that fill up the hard disk of the targeted computer. Because a single machine is unlikely to have the capacity to overwhelm a large commercial server, crackers now rely on **distributed denial-of-service (DDoS)** attacks. In a DDoS attack, a cracker infiltrates hundreds or thousands of systems and installs a program that will execute a DoS attack on an assigned target. The administrators of the affected systems may not even realize that a cracker program has been installed on their systems, because the program doesn't attempt to do anything when it is installed. Instead, after many systems have been infiltrated and the DoS program is installed, the cracker sends a signal to all of the systems to begin their DoS attack at the same time. With hundreds or thousands of machines participating in the attack, a server has a hard time knowing which packets are part of the attack and which are from legitimate users.

A DDoS attack is hard to plan for and defeat. Your system might seem altered, and you have no idea of trouble until the attack commences. At that point, you cannot simply reject packets from a certain computer (as you could with a nondistributed DoS attack) because the attack is originating from so many sources.

Although a Linux system might not be damaged by an attack, in the sense that files are altered, the attack still consumes bandwidth. Too little bandwidth might be left for legitimate users to connect to your system. There's little you can do to protect against this, other than ask your ISP to try to block the sources of the attack, but this can be a daunting task if thousands of computers participate in the attack.

As for DoS attacks causing log files to grow so large that the system runs out of disk space, you can easily protect against this by moving the log files to a separate filesystem. If the log file filesystem fills up, the system can still run. To move log files to a separate filesystem, you create another disk partition, place a filesystem on it, mount it to a temporary mount point, copy your existing log files to it, unmount it, and mount it to /var/log. Remember to add the new filesystem to /etc/fstab so it automatically mounts the next time you reboot.

If no space is left on your disk for another partition, you can use a loopback filesystem. For details, see the "Loopback Filesystems" section in Chapter 8.

Buffer Overflow Attacks

A buffer overflow attack refers to the exploitation of a programming flaw to cause a network service to shut down, corrupt data, or provide unexpected (and, therefore, unauthorized) access to a system. Suppose that a program such as an FTP server allocates a block of memory to hold a command such as ls that arrives over a network connection. The command normally is terminated by a newline character. However, if a cracker sends a command that doesn't terminate with a newline character, but instead continues for thousands of characters, the FTP server software (if it is not well designed) just keeps reading in the command. When the command exceeds the space allocated to it in memory, the FTP server crashes. In some cases, a skilled cracker might be able to include information in the extra-long command that is written in certain parts of memory to give the cracker unauthorized access.

Buffer overflow attacks are hard to predict. Obviously, if system administrators knew about a potential buffer overflow, they would fix it immediately. When someone discovers how to create a buffer overflow, a race ensues between crackers who want to exploit it and system administrators who want to get a patch—an update—to fix the problem. Good system administrators don't give a cracker much of a chance; they install updates the same day they are released, which is usually within two days of the problem being discovered by a group such as SANS or CERT/CC. System administrators who don't pay attention to security let old versions of their network service daemons continue running. Crackers are then free to use well-known buffer overflow attacks against them.

You can minimize your exposure to these attacks by using firewall rules to block access to everyone but those who must access your system. For example, if a buffer overflow vulnerability surfaced in the SSH daemon, you would probably not be vulnerable if you blocked the SSH port to all but those few users who needed SSH access. You would still fix the problem, but at your leisure. The situation is different with Web servers and mail servers where you must allow access to anyone. Experienced Linux administrators are more concerned about security problems with daemons that are exposed to the world than those that are exposed to a small population of users.

NOTE

Other types of programming attacks can also crash a server or permit unauthorized access. Buffer overflow is one category of programming errors that permit an attack, and many others are possible. For example, one attack on older versions of DNS causes the `named` daemon to shut down immediately if it receives a particular request.

Spoofing and Man-in-the-Middle Attacks

Spoofing is the forging of information, such as IP addresses. Crackers use IP spoofing and DNS spoofing. In **IP spoofing**, a cracker modifies a packet's source or destination address. For example, if a cracker learns your internal IP address, he might send a packet to your firewall from an outside server, but with the source IP address of your internal network. He hopes that your firewall will let the packet through based on the source IP address. A well-designed firewall would not be fooled: All internal traffic would come through one Ethernet card and all external network traffic through a second Ethernet card. However, IP spoofing can confuse some programs and should be considered as you plan firewall rules and router designs.

DNS spoofing is pretending that a request comes from a particular host instead of its true host. For example, if security is based on domain names, a cracker might be able to subvert the security setting through DNS spoofing; a packet bears the forged address of an authorized domain. Using reverse DNS lookups can help to avoid this problem, because the cracker will have a hard time actually modifying all of the zone information files on the authoritative DNS server. Recall from Hands-On Project 6-2 that you can query a series of DNS servers using dig to determine the authoritative information for a forward or reverse DNS lookup.

Another attack used with DNS is a **cache poisoning attack**. A successful attack causes DNS servers to give the wrong answers to DNS queries. Frequently, the cracker wants to direct HTTP requests to a bogus Web server. The best way to avoid these attacks is to use separate DNS servers for your authority server and for DNS caches. BIND, the most popular DNS server software, combines the authority server and the cache into one. You'd either choose alternative software that separates these two functions, such as djbdns, or you'd run two copies of BIND and configure them for different roles.

Similar to spoofing attacks, **man-in-the-middle attacks** are those in which a cracker intercepts a communication, reads or alters it, and leads the originator of the packet to believe that the intended recipient has received it. Figure 11-1 shows how this attack might operate if a cracker obtained a copy of Sally's private key and used it to intercept all traffic between Sally and a colleague. Private keys are covered in Chapter 10.

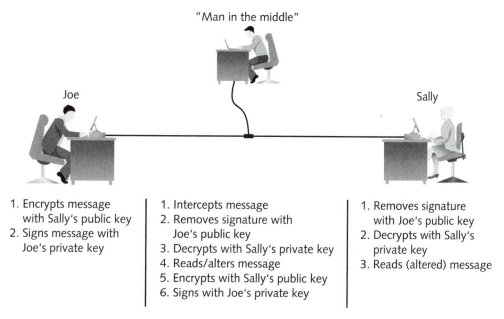

1. Encrypts message with Sally's public key
2. Signs message with Joe's private key

1. Intercepts message
2. Removes signature with Joe's public key
3. Decrypts with Sally's private key
4. Reads/alters message
5. Encrypts with Sally's public key
6. Signs with Joe's private key

1. Removes signature with Joe's public key
2. Decrypts with Sally's private key
3. Reads (altered) message

Figure 11-1   Man-in-the-middle attack using a copy of a private key

The scenario of a man in the middle obtaining Sally's private key is not far-fetched. Private keys must be stored in a secure location on the user's computer. If Sally is running Windows, what secure location does she use? The man in the middle can employ one of many methods to break into Sally's Windows computer and steal her private key.

Another man-in-the-middle attack is **Web spoofing**. In this attack, a cracker deceives users into linking to the cracker's site when they think they are linking to another site. The cracker's server can then begin to intercept every Web request from the user, make the request itself, and alter the response to point all future requests back to the cracker's site.

Using Firewalls

You have learned about numerous ways to control access to your system and keep crackers at bay. For example, you know that many services use TCP Wrappers through the `inetd` and `xinetd` superservers. You can control access to those services by configuring the `/etc/host.allow` and `/etc/host.deny` files. Specific network programs have their own access control mechanisms. For example, the `wu-ftpd` FTP server supports multiple security directives in `/etc/ftpaccess`; Apache supports similar directives in the `httpd.conf` configuration file. These directives let you specify which hosts can access the Web server; they can be as precise as allowing a certain host to access only a single file. Samba and NFS configuration files also support access control mechanisms.

Using any of these per-service configuration files can protect your computer from intruders who try to gain access to that service. You might think of these as application-specific firewalls. However, the term "firewall" usually describes controlling network traffic at a lower level in the protocol stack. You learned back in Chapter 1 about the OSI and Internet networking models, which are shown in Figure 11-2. The middle of the figure shows how different access control mechanisms can protect a network service. A **firewall** typically refers to a packet filter—access control operating at the Network and Transport layers of the networking stack. When a packet reaches the higher layers of the protocol stack, there is a much greater chance that it can gain unauthorized access, either through programming errors or configuration errors. A packet filter can examine and discard packets from unauthorized systems before they have a chance to "attack" applications.

A firewall relies on rules. A **rule** defines the characteristics of a packet and the action to take for any packet that has those characteristics. An example rule might effectively say: "If a TCP packet is destined for port 25, and it comes from any address other than network 192.168.125.0/24, then discard the packet." Another way to protect network services and the clients on a LAN is to use advanced routing techniques. These techniques can effectively "hide" LAN clients from crackers on the Internet, even though the clients can still access the Internet.

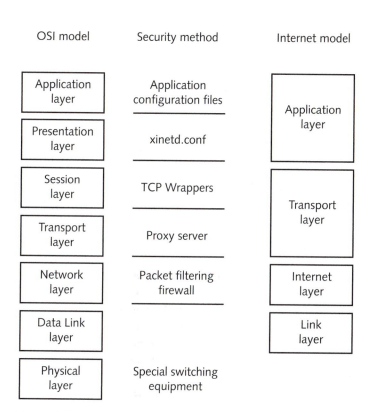

Figure 11-2   Networking models and their access control mechanisms

INTRODUCING NETFILTER AND IP TABLES

Linux has sophisticated packet handling capabilities that are used for building a firewall and for advanced routing. This capability is integrated into the kernel and uses numerous kernel modules. The capability is provided by a framework called netfilter and IP Tables.

Netfilter provides the architecture and **IP Tables** provides the table structure for the rules that allow you to implement these general functions:

- You can filter packets based on their state. You learned in Chapter 1 that TCP is a connection-oriented transport protocol. After a connection is established, all packets that follow are part of that connection until the connection is terminated. Netfilter and IP Tables allow you to write rules based on this stateful nature of TCP. The term "**stateful inspection**" is used to describe this capability.

- You can examine and alter almost any header field of a packet. This is called **packet mangling**.

- You can select packets to be logged based on the value of any header field.

- You can pass packets to regular Linux programs for further processing outside the Linux kernel.

- You can implement intelligent routing based on **Quality of Service (QoS)** features. QoS is a networking feature that lets you guarantee bandwidth to certain users or certain programs. A Linux router with QoS capability could be implemented using the Type of Service bit in the IP protocol or using other parts of a packet that you examine using whatever IP Tables rules you choose.

You configure netfilter and IP Tables by creating rules for its operation. The **iptables** command is used to create, delete, and modify the rules. Each rule describes the characteristics of a packet and how packets that match these characteristics should be handled. You place these rules in lists called **chains**. These lists exist in one of three tables: filter, nat, and mangle. Each table has a different purpose.

 Instead of referring to both netfilter and IP Tables, this book refers to netfilter as the name of the packet filtering and mangling system and `iptables` as the name of the command used to create and modify rules.

NOTE

Firewall Configuration

In netfilter, the filter table is the default table and is used to configure the firewall. Within this table are three chains:

- *Input*—Packets arriving on one of the firewall's interfaces and destined for a program or process running on the firewall pass through this chain.

- *Forward*—Packets coming from outside the firewall that need to be routed to another computer pass through this chain.

- *Output*—Packets sent by a program or process running on the firewall that are destined for other systems pass through this chain.

The basic operation of a chain is shown in Figure 11-3. Each rule in the chain specifies one or more packet characteristics. If a packet matches those characteristics, the packet is handled according to the instruction within the rule. If a packet doesn't match the rule, the next rule is tried. If none of the rules match, a default policy defines what happens to the packet.

The rules can be simple or complex. A simple rule might indicate that the default policy for the input chain is DROP, meaning that if an incoming packet is not processed by one of the rules in the chain, it should be ignored and no response sent back to the sender. This rule is shown here:

```
iptables -P INPUT DROP
```

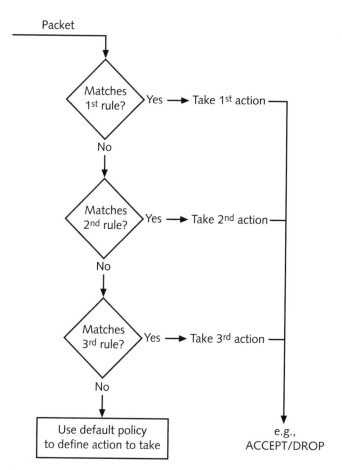

Figure 11-3   Basic operation of an IP chain

An alternative to DROP is REJECT. A rejected packet causes the firewall to send a packet back to the sender as a notification that its packet did not reach the intended destination. In most cases, a REJECT is not the right thing to do because notifying the sender might invite further attack.

Much more complex rules are common, as in this example:

```
iptables -A INPUT -p udp --sport 67:68  --dport 67:68 \
 -i eth0 -j  ACCEPT
```

This command adds a rule to the input chain that says to accept a packet coming from any source IP address and destined for any IP address if it is using UDP, arrives on the eth0 network interface, and uses either port 67 or 68 for the source or destination.

You can list the rules in all chains using the -L option with the iptables command. The -n option tells the command not to try to resolve IP addresses to a name using DNS:

```
iptables -n -L
```

Rules are executed in the order that you place them in the chain. For example, suppose you have the following two rules. The first accepts packets from a single network, and the second drops packets for all networks.

```
iptables -A INPUT -s 192.168.10.0/24 -j ACCEPT
iptables -A INPUT -j DROP
```

Order is important here. If a packet arrives from network 192.168.10.0/24, it is accepted. Packets arriving from any other network are denied. If the order of the two commands is reversed, packets from the 192.168.10.0/24 network are denied as well.

NOTE

Firewall rules usually should progress from specific to more general, with "catch all" rules at the end so that nothing gets through unexpectedly.

Ideally, firewall rules should be in place before networking is started when you boot your system. Otherwise, a cracker has a small window of opportunity between the time networking is activated and the time the firewall rules become active. Because this time is generally a fraction of a second, it is not a significant security concern.

Table 11-1 lists the most commonly used options for the iptables command. All of the options are case sensitive. Refer to the iptables man page for a more complete listing.

Table 11-1 Commonly used options for the iptables command

Option	Description
-A *chain*	Append a rule to the end of the named chain
-D *chain index*	Delete rule number *index* from the named chain
-F *chain*	Flush (delete) all rules from the named chain, or from all chains if no chain is named
-L *chain*	List all the rules from all chains, or from the named chain if given
-N *chain*	Create a user-defined chain
-P *chain policy*	Set the default policy of the named chain to the named policy
-s *address*	Define a source IP address against which to compare a packet
-d *address*	Define a destination IP address against which to compare a packet
-i *interface*	Specify the network interface (such as eth0) that a packet must use to match the rule
-p *protocol*	Indicate the protocol field of the packet that will match the rule; the protocol can be tcp, udp, or icmp
-j *target*	Define an action for packets matching the packet specifications; targets can include ACCEPT, DROP, QUEUE, RETURN, and a few others that may be used when certain kernel modules are loaded

Besides the input, forward, and output chains, you can create your own chains and "call" them like subroutines from within other chains. To create a user-defined chain, you use the -N option:

```
iptables -N http
```

Then add rules to it with the -A option:

```
iptables -A http -s 1.2.3.4/24 -j ACCEPT
iptables -A http -s 192.168.0.0/24 -j ACCEPT
iptables -A http -s 10.0.0.0/24 -j ACCEPT
iptables -A http -j DROP
```

Finally, you can use the -j option within an iptables rule to jump to that chain if the rule succeeds:

```
iptables -A INPUT -p tcp --dport 80 -j http
```

For example, using the following command on a home computer with a dedicated Internet connection (such as DSL or a cable modem) allows you to connect to anyone on the Internet, but any packets trying to establish a connection to your system are ignored ("dropped").

```
iptables -A INPUT -p tcp --syn -j DROP
```

Suppose now that you want to allow SSH traffic (as described below) to reach your computer. This allows you to log on securely to your home computer from remote sites. The following line permits only SSH traffic—it "punches a hole" in the firewall for a single protocol.

```
iptables -A INPUT -p tcp --syn --destination-port 22 -j ACCEPT
```

You would probably want to include both of the previous two examples. First, use the second command to permit SSH traffic, then add the first command so that all other traffic is dropped. Remember that specific rules should come before general rules; the last rules effectively say, "deny packets I haven't specifically allowed before this point."

Network Address Translation

Network Address Translation, or NAT, is a transparent routing technique that alters packet headers to translate packets in one network so they can be used on another network. NAT was originally defined in RFC 1631 in 1994, and in RFC 2663, RFC 2993, and RFC 3022 in 2000 and 2001. In addition, RFC 2766 describes NAT between IPv4 and IPv6 networks. Reading these RFCs will give you a more comprehensive understanding of NAT.

Besides NAT itself, another common form of network address translation is **network address port translation**, or NAPT, in which computers on an internal network appear to be a single computer to outside networks. Figure 11-4 illustrates how this form of NAT works.

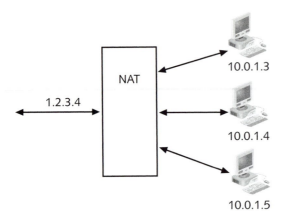

Figure 11-4   Network Address Translation

The diagram shows a network address translator connecting an internal network (on the right side of the translator) with the Internet (on the left side). Three computers are connected to the internal network. Each computer has its own unique IP address on the 10.0.1.0 network. When these computers communicate with remote servers via the Internet, their packets must pass through the translator.

In this example, the translator changes each packet by replacing the source IP address with the address 1.2.3.4. It stores this translation information in a translation table, which is the heart of NAT operation. When a remote server responds, it sends a packet to the 1.2.3.4 address. When the translator receives the packet from the remote server, it refers to the translation table to determine to which of the three computers to send the packet. But how does it distinguish between the computers on the internal network when packets arriving from the outside are all addressed to 1.2.3.4?

The answer is ports. Suppose, for example, that one of the computers is running a Web browser and the user enters a URL. When the Web browser sends the HTTP packet to the remote Web server, it uses a TCP source port that was assigned by the operating system or a library. This is a temporary port (also called an ephemeral port or a private port). These ports were discussed in Chapter 1.

When the three computers on the inside network communicate through the translator, they typically use different source ports. The translator stores these source ports in the translation table. It can now distinguish between the computers by the source port they're using. Of course, it's possible that two computers on the internal network may use the same ephemeral port number at the same time. This would confuse the translator and result in the packet being sent to the wrong computer or dropped entirely. To protect against this, most translators also do port translation to guarantee uniqueness. An example should make this clear. Figure 11-5 shows the path packets take from a Web browser running on one of the computers on the inside network to a remote Web server—and back again.

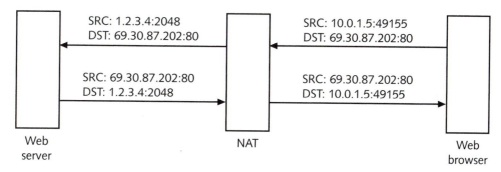

Figure 11-5 NAT address and port translations

The Web browser sends packets whose IP addresses and ports are as follows. Note that 10.0.1.5:49155 refers to the IP address 10.0.1.5 and port 49,155:

```
     Source:  10.0.1.5:49155
Destination:  69.30.87.202:80
```

When this packet reaches the translator, the translator changes the source IP address and the source port before sending the packet to the Internet. It also stores the IP address and source port of the computer in a table with the translated port. When the packet leaves the translator, it looks like the following (where 2048 is an example of the port the translator assigned):

```
     Source:  1.2.3.4:2048
Destination:  69.30.87.202:80
```

The translator now has the following entry in its translation table for this connection:

```
IP               Source port       Translated port
10.0.1.5         49,155            2048
```

The remote Web server responds to this request by sending a packet with the IP addresses and ports swapped, as shown here:

```
     Source:  69.30.87.202:80
Destination:  1.2.3.4:2048
```

When the translator receives this packet, it looks up port 2048 in its table and discovers that the computer that originally sent the request was 10.0.1.5 using port 49,155. The translator replaces the destination address and port and sends the packet to the internal network with these addresses and ports:

```
     Source:  69.30.87.202:80
Destination:  10.0.1.5:49155
```

The Web browser receives the packet and the process is complete. The translator will continue to use the assigned port (2048) for this computer for the duration of the HTTP session.

The computers on the internal network don't know that translation is occurring. It sees the translator as simply the default gateway (router). Similarly, the remote Web server doesn't know that it is exchanging packets with a translator. One benefit of address translation is anonymity. All the computers on an internal network are seen by the outside world as a single machine. The identity of computers on the inside network is hidden from the outside.

In addition, computers on the outside cannot easily access computers on the internal network. If an attacker were to send a packet to the 1.2.3.4 address, the translator may not be able to match it up with any of the translation table entries. Even if the attacker is successful in matching a table entry, other information in their packets will likely be wrong and either the translator or the internal computers will reject them. Successful attacks are not common in a NAT environment.

NAT has problems when higher-layer protocols, such as FTP, place lower-layer addresses, such as IP addresses, in their data fields. An FTP server that receives translated packets will likely be confused by the different addresses. NAT must deal with this by also doing address translation on these upper-layer protocols—something NAT normally doesn't do. The solution is helper applications that assist NAT with handling these tricky protocols. Linux uses helper applications that are implemented as kernel modules. To support a tricky protocol, just load the helper module for that protocol. Here's a list of some of the helper modules:

```
ip_nat_amanda.ko
ip_nat_ftp.ko
ip_nat_irc.ko
ip_nat_quake.ko
```

The amanda module is for disk archiving, the irc module is for Internet Relay Chat, and the quake module is for the Quake game. The use of the ftp module is obvious.

NAT relies on the Linux system operating as an IP router. You need to turn on IP forwarding with the following command:

```
echo "1" > /proc/sys/net/ipv4/ip_forward
```

In Linux, NAT is handled by the netfilter table called nat. Within this table, there are chains called PREROUTING, POSTROUTING, and OUTPUT. You can display this table and chains with the command iptables -t nat --list. If there are no rules in these chains, you see the following:

```
Chain PREROUTING (policy ACCEPT)
target     prot opt source        destination
Chain POSTROUTING (policy ACCEPT)
target     prot opt source        destination
Chain OUTPUT (policy ACCEPT)
target     prot opt source        destination
```

To enable NAT, you use the `iptables` command to add a rule to the NAT table. Here's the command to provide the translation for the example in Figure 11-5:

```
iptables -t nat -A POSTROUTING -o eth0 -j SNAT --to 1.2.3.4
```

This command applies NAT to all the networks connected to your computer. Suppose your system has three Ethernet cards—one is connected to the Internet and the other two are connected to internal networks. Both internal networks will use NAT when creating connections to the outside. You can override this by making the NAT rule more specific. Assume that one inside network is 10.0.1.0/24 and the other is 10.0.2.0/24. This rule will apply only to the 10.0.1.0/24 network:

```
iptables -t nat -A POSTROUTING -s 10.0.1.0/24 \
-o eth0 -j SNAT --to 1.2.3.4
```

Port Forwarding

Port forwarding is another transparent routing capability provided by netfilter. In netfilter terminology, port forwarding is called DNAT, or destination NAT, because the destination IP address of packets is translated. The practical application for port forwarding or DNAT is illustrated in Figure 11-6.

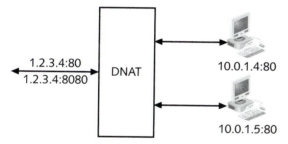

Figure 11-6   DNAT application

The two computers to the right of the translator are running Web servers on port 80. The computer whose IP address is 10.0.1.4 is running a Web server that contains content to be published to the Web. The other computer's Web server has content that should be restricted to employees of the company. It is running on port 80 as well. Both computers are using private IP addresses. These private addresses will be translated to the public 1.2.3.4 address.

The 10.0.1.4 computer should be seen from the outside as running its Web server on port 80. The 10.0.1.5 computer should be seen from the outside as running its Web server on port 8080. This is achieved with the following commands:

```
iptables -t nat -A PREROUTING -p TCP --dport 80 \
-I eth0 -j DNAT --to 10.0.1.4:80
iptables -t nat -A PREROUTING -p TCP --dport 8080 \
-I eth0 -j DNAT --to 10.0.1.5:80
```

When you list the rules in the NAT table PREROUTING chain, you see these lines:

```
Chain PREROUTING (policy ACCEPT)
target      prot opt source        destination
DNAT        tcp  --  anywhere      anywhere      tcpd dpt:80 to 10.0.1.4:80
DNAT        tcp  --  anywhere      anywhere      tcpd dpt:8080 to 10.0.1.5:80
```

If it's important that the content of the Web server running on port 8080 should only be accessible to employees and not the outside world, you can use the firewall to restrict access.

Redirection

Netfilter provides a redirection capability that is similar to port forwarding, but the address you use for forwarding is that of the incoming interface. The packets are redirected to a daemon running on the same computer. The most common practical application is HTTP proxy caching, which has two basic uses. The Web server is insulated from remote Web browsers and remote crackers by a proxy that may provide some protection from attack. It also lightens the load on the Web server by caching Web content. Remote Web browsers fetch some of their content from the proxy cache rather than all requests being handled by the Web server (see Figure 11-7).

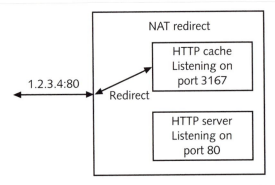

Figure 11-7   Netfilter redirection, server end

When a packet arrives from the Internet with a destination TCP port of 80, netfilter redirects it to port 3167, where the HTTP cache is listening. The cache answers some requests directly. Those requests that can't be answered are sent to the Web server that is listening on port 80. Here's the command to set up the redirection:

```
iptables -t nat -A PREROUTING -i eth0 -p tcp \
--dport 80 -j REDIRECT --to-port 3167
```

Proxy caches can also be used at the Web browser end. There are significant benefits to this:

1. The proxy cache insulates clients from attacks.

2. Users browse the Web in anonymity, just as they would with NAT.

3. An administrator can control access to remote Web sites. Users can be prevented from accessing Web sites whose addresses (URLs) are in a list.

4. The proxy cache reduces traffic over the Internet connection by caching the results of Web server access. This can dramatically improve performance for all users on the local network. Users perceive the remote Web servers to be faster than they really are.

Figure 11-8 illustrates how netfilter handles this caching.

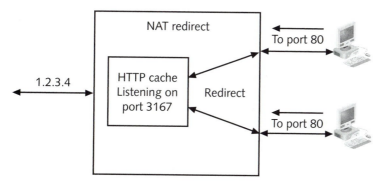

Figure 11-8   Netfilter redirection, browser end

Netfilter redirects client HTTP requests on TCP port 80 to the port the proxy cache is listening on—3167 in this example. The proxy cache then contacts Web servers on the Internet to retrieve the Web site's content. Here's the command to set up the redirection:

```
iptables -t nat -A PREROUTING -i eth1 -p tcp \
--dport 80 -j REDIRECT --to-port 3167
```

This command is remarkably similar to the one in Figure 11-7. The only difference is the interface, but there's another possible difference. In this case, the proxy cache must be listening to the eth1 interface. In the scenario shown in Figure 11-7, the proxy cache is listening to the eth0 interface.

The most widely used Linux proxy cache is **Squid**. The Squid server is officially called an "Internet Object cache," which means it is a caching proxy server for Web requests and other Internet protocols. The Squid Web site is *www.squid-cache.org*.

Normally, you must configure each client (browser) for the IP address and TCP port of a proxy. Netfilter redirects HTTP requests transparently so you don't have to configure clients.

NOTE

GRAPHICAL FIREWALL CONFIGURATION

Although the syntax of the `iptables` command can seem obscure, it's not difficult to use after you become familiar with the options in Table 11-1 and gain some experience using the command. This is a key skill for Linux network administrators.

Several graphical tools are available to help you set up a firewall. Some of these tools are better than others, but none provides complete access to `iptables` functionality. You need to understand how netfilter operates before you can do much useful work with the graphical utilities.

Fedora Core, like many other Linux distributions, includes basic firewall configuration tools to help new users give their systems some level of protection. When you install Fedora Core, you answer basic questions about your network security. These questions are posed using the **lokkit** program, which you can execute at any time from the command line by entering the `lokkit` command.

Two screens make up the `lokkit` text-mode program. It doesn't ask you about rules, but instead sets up reasonable rules based on how secure you want your system to be and any specific protocols that you want to leave more open. Remember that "more secure" means "harder to use" if you are in a trusted environment such as a testing lab, where you want to run many network services without reconfiguring the firewall for each one.

Fedora Core provides a graphical firewall configuration tool called `system-config-securitylevel`. It is used to create simple firewall rules, although some professional administrators consider it too simplistic to be useful. Novice users would use it to protect an individual Linux computer, but it's inappropriate for protecting a network. To start the program, enter the `system-config-securitylevel` command at a command prompt or select System Settings and then Security Level from the GNOME menu. If you're not logged on as root, you will be prompted to enter root's password.

Using the Security level list box, you can enable or disable the firewall. The Trusted services area lets you enable common protocols simply by clicking check boxes. Figure 11-9 shows the HTTP (ports 80 and 443), FTP (port 21), and SSH (port 22) protocols selected. Protocols that don't have a check box are entered in the Other ports area. Figure 11-9 shows that the IMAP (port 143:tcp) and DNS (port 53:udp) protocols have been added. The Trusted devices area lets you choose the interface or interfaces connected to your inside network or networks. Any changes you make to your firewall rules take effect when you exit the program.

NOTE The `system-config-securitylevel` program lets you add protocols by specifying the name that appears in the `/etc/services` file. For example, you can use "imap:tcp" instead of "143:tcp".

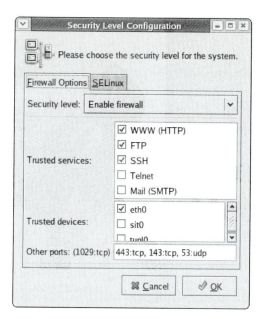

Figure 11-9 The `system-config-securitylevel` firewall window

Firestarter is a much more functional graphical firewall configuration tool. You can download it from *www.fs-security.com.* When you run it for the first time, a Firewall Wizard guides you through firewall setup. If your computer has more than one interface, you can set up NAT for your internal network; Firestarter calls this Internet Connection Sharing. Every time you run Firestarter after the installation, you see the screen shown in Figure 11-10.

The icon in the top portion of the Status tab tells you whether the firewall is active or inactive. You control whether the firewall is active with the Stop Firewall and Start Firewall menus. You might want to stop the firewall temporarily to see if a problem is firewall-related.

NOTE

When the firewall is disabled, the firewall is wide open and you have no protection.

Click the Events tab for a quick indication of firewall-related events that deserve your attention. These events represent packets that have been blocked by the firewall. Figure 11-11 shows seven TCP connection attempts that were blocked by the firewall. If you right-click any of these events, the resulting menu lets you allow or block traffic from the remote host or allow or block connection attempts to the port.

The Policy tab in Firestarter lets you add firewall rules. You can specify hosts or networks from which you want to accept packets, regardless of protocol, and you can specify which ports should allow these packets.

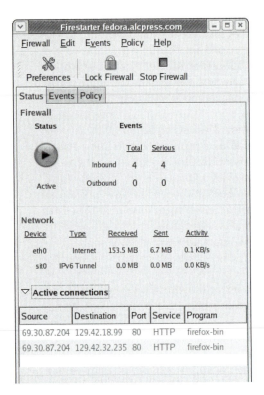

Figure 11-10   The Firestarter Status tab

KMyFirewall is a KDE-based program that lets you set up a "personal firewall" or protect a larger network using IP Tables. It includes a setup wizard for less-experienced users, plus a more advanced interface to help you create complex rules. You can save a copy of your firewall rules to a separate file and then use that file to easily configure other firewalls running KMyFirewall where the same rules should be applied. For information, visit *http://kmyfirewall.sourceforge.net.*

One well-regarded firewall configuration utility for Linux is GuardDog. GuardDog can use either a graphical interface (see Figure 11-12) or its own command-line utility. GuardDog's features include the following:

- A "deny that which is not explicitly allowed" design for more secure systems.
- Script-based rules to permit import and export of rule sets.
- Ability to define firewall "zones": groups of hosts or networks to which rules can be applied.
- Categories of protocols for easier decision making.
- Connection tracking and logging.

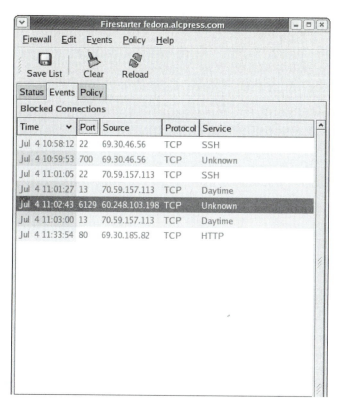

Figure 11-11   The Firestarter Events tab

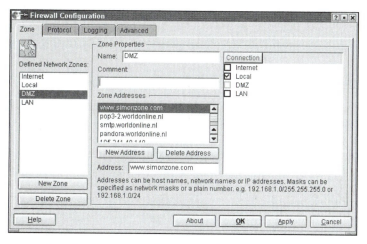

Figure 11-12   The GuardDog firewall tool

11

- Explicit support for many more protocols than other firewall tools (review your /etc/services file). These protocols include X, CORBA, FTP, HTTP, HTTPS, NNTP, POP2, POP3, IMAP, IMAPS, POP3S, ICQ, IRC, MSN Messenger, PowWow, NetMeeting, Gnutella, AudioGalaxy, Real Audio, Diablo II, DirectPlay, Halflife, Quake, QuakeWorld, Quake 2, ping, ICMP Source Quench, ICMP Redirect, traceroute, whois, NetBIOS Name Service, NetBIOS Session Service, DNS, NTP, DHCP, CDDB, finger, Telnet, VNC, SSH, PPTP, ISAKMP, Kerberos, auth, klogin, kshell, Telstra's BigPond Cable, XDMCP, SUN RPC, NFS, NIS, LDAP, LDAP-SSL, SMTP, Linuxconf, Webmin, SWAT, Nessus, Line printer spooler, syslog, SOCKS, Squid, pcANYWHERE stat, PostgreSQL, and MySQL.

ENCRYPTING NETWORK TRAFFIC

Netfilter can help secure your network by isolating clients on a private network from the Internet at large. Even so, the content of client messages sent through the Internet—and indeed the content of every packet sent on your private network—is likely to be unencrypted, or plaintext. This means that a person using a network analysis tool (a sniffer) to view all packets on the local network segment could view the data contained in every packet that you send. Sniffing is sometimes useful for diagnosing stubborn networking problems, and Chapter 12 describes some popular tools that let you do it. But crackers can use the same tools to look for information to help them gain unauthorized access to your servers.

Every unencrypted message that you send might be read by an unauthorized user, either on your local network or on the Internet. SSH is a method of encrypting network traffic. This section explores SSH in more detail and describes other methods of encrypting network traffic, which are all designed to make it difficult for someone gathering packets from your network to extract anything useful about you or your organization.

Using the Secure Shell (SSH)

The SSH package is a client/server protocol. SSH includes a client program called ssh and a server daemon called sshd. The scp program is a secure copy program; it lets you copy one or more files between two machines on the network. All of these programs use the same encryption techniques that you learned about for the GPG program in Chapter 10: They exchange asymmetric keys to establish the identity of a user requesting a connection and to pass a symmetric session key securely. The symmetric key is then used to encrypt all traffic flowing over the secure shell connection.

The OpenSSH implementation of SSH is used on most Linux distributions. On Fedora Core, it is installed by default as five separate packages: openssh, openssh-clients, openssh-server, openssh-askpass, and openssh-askpass-gnome. You can use the rpm command to verify that these packages are installed. The OpenSSH Web site has links to source code, packages, and several types of documentation. On Fedora Core, the OpenSSH documentation is located at /usr/share/doc/openssh-x.y, where x and y make up the current version number. The OpenSSH programs also have lengthy man pages that describe the options that each supports. In particular, the `ssh` and `sshd` man pages are useful.

NOTE OpenSSH was originally written for the OpenBSD operating system and is now available for many variants of UNIX, Linux, Windows, Macintosh, Java, PalmOS, and others.

The SSH protocol in general and the OpenSSH implementation in particular support two versions. SSH protocol version 1 (SSH1) uses a public key encryption system to authenticate each connection, but it does not support strong encryption of the subsequent network traffic. Current releases of OpenSSH support version 1 for backward compatibility. Previously, SSH2 had stricter licensing provisions than SSH1, but SSH2 can now be freely distributed as part of OpenSSH. SSH protocol version 2 (SSH2) uses a more robust authentication process and supports strong encryption of all network traffic. Ciphers currently supported include AES (128-, 192-, or 256-bit), 3DES, Blowfish, CAST128, and Arcfour. 3DES is secure but slow, Blowfish is a good choice for a well-tested cipher that is much faster than 3DES, and 192- or 256-bit AES is a highly secure, government standard cipher.

SSH can authenticate a connection in several ways. The least secure, which is not discussed here, is to rely on the r-utilities files, such as `/etc/hosts.equiv` and `~/.rhosts`. You won't see these files unless you've configured the r-utilities. The SSH documentation recommends against using the r-utilities method. Another alternative is to rely on user passwords. Although using passwords is much better than the `rhosts` method or an unencrypted Telnet session, it still doesn't provide public-key authentication of the session.

To use SSH password authentication, make certain that the `sshd` daemon is running on the system to which you want to connect. The `sshd` daemon is configured in the file `/etc/ssh/sshd_config`. The default configuration in Fedora Core should work well enough to get you started. The SSH protocol uses port 22 by default. This port is listed in `/etc/services`. The `sshd` daemon runs in stand-alone mode; it is not launched on demand by `inetd` or `xinetd`.

To check the status of the `sshd` daemon, use the following command:

```
/etc/rc.d/init.d/sshd status
```

If the daemon is running and no firewall is blocking traffic on port 22 between your client and server computers, you should be able to use the following command on the client to connect to `sshd` on the server:

```
ssh -l username server
```

The `-l` option indicates the account ("l" is for "logon name") on the server that you want to use to connect. Alternatively, you can use this syntax:

```
ssh username@server
```

11

Because the server doesn't know anything about the client at this point, you receive a warning that the server doesn't have a host key for the client:

```
The authenticity of host 'igor (10.0.1.5)' can't be established.
RSA key fingerprint is 3d:c1:c4:b4:24:db:f2:ef:ca:8f:f2:62:34:51:
5a:db.
Are you sure you want to continue connecting (yes/no)?
```

Sometime before you tried to connect to the server, you should know or have been given the server's key fingerprint, shown in the preceding message. The fingerprint is proof that this server is authentic, and that nobody is trying to trick you into logging on to a bogus server where they would capture your password. You would only connect to the server if the fingerprint displayed previously matches the one you were given.

You can enter "yes" to proceed. You are then prompted for the password of the username you entered, and then are logged on to the remote system (the system running sshd).

To use public-key authentication in OpenSSH, you must set up key pairs. The sshd server has a server key pair stored in /etc/ssh. For example, ssh_host_rsa_key.pub contains an RSA-format public key. Both RSA and DSA keys are generated by default in most Linux distributions. To create a key pair for your own user account, you must use the ssh-keygen program and specify a key type of either RSA or DSA using the -t option. The default key length is 1024 bits, but you can alter that length with the -b option (many other options are supported as well—see the man page for ssh-keygen). A sample command looks like this:

```
ssh-keygen -t rsa -b 2048
```

After a few moments, the key pair is generated and you are prompted for the file in which the key pair should be saved. If you accept the default setting by pressing Enter, your private key is stored in ~/.ssh/id_rsa and your public key is stored in ~/.ssh/id_rsa.pub. You must also enter a passphrase (twice) to protect this key pair. You may choose to press Enter to leave the key pair unprotected by a passphrase; you can then create scripts that use ssh without pausing to request your passphrase. This decision depends on who else is using your computer and how you intend to use ssh to access your accounts on remote systems.

After you have a key pair generated on one account, you should place the public key from that account in the authorized_keys file on each system on which you want to log on using ssh. For example, suppose you have an account named alvarez on your principal computer (call it system1). You also have an account named sarah on a second computer (call it system2) that you want to have secure access to via ssh. You could follow these two steps to facilitate the arrangement:

1. While logged on system1 as alvarez, use ssh-keygen to generate a key pair.

2. Using any method you choose (scp, FTP, rcp, e-mail, or 3.5-inch disk), copy the file /home/alvarez/.ssh/id_rsa.pub on system1 to the file /home/sarah/.ssh/authorized_keys on system2. (This assumes that you used a key type of RSA; if you used DSA, the filename is id_dsa.pub.)

If you have only these two accounts, the `authorized_keys` file does not yet exist and you can copy the key file using a command such as the following from system1:

```
scp -l sarah ~/.ssh/id_rsa.pub system2:~/.ssh/authorized_keys
```

To complete this command, you need to enter your password for the sarah account on system2. If you have multiple accounts and had already created an `authorized_keys` file, you could add another key to the end of the `authorized_keys` file using a command such as the following one (recall that the >> operator appends data to the end of an existing file):

```
ssh -l sarah system2 cat ~/.ssh/id_rsa.pub >>
   system2:~/.ssh/authorized_keys
```

After you have the public key from one account listed as an authorized user on another account, you can use `ssh` to log on or `scp` to copy files without entering a password, but you must still enter the passphrase for your private key, unless you use the `ssh-agent` daemon. The keys are exchanged in the background to verify your identity.

NOTE

If you intend to use the SSH suite on a number of systems, review the **ssh-agent** command. This command provides useful tools for managing key pairs and authentication among multiple SSH-capable systems.

11

OpenSSH supports a number of useful features besides replacing Telnet. As mentioned in previous chapters, you can use the `ssh` utility to encrypt other network traffic. This lets you create secure connections for protocols that are not inherently secure. One example is the X protocol for serving remote graphical applications, as you learned in Chapter 3. When the `-X` option is added to the `ssh` command, any graphical program (X clients) launched on the remote system is automatically displayed on the system on which you executed `ssh`. The sshd daemon automatically handles the DISPLAY variable, .Xauthority cookie-based authentication, and transmission of all X protocol data over the encrypted `ssh` connection. To use this feature, follow these steps:

1. Launch a graphical environment on your client system; call it system1.

2. Log on to a remote server using `ssh`. Call it system2. The following command uses the `-X` option to enable X protocol forwarding over the `ssh` connection, as just described. You could also configure this feature to be used automatically for certain hosts. The `-c` option used here indicates, in order of preference, which cipher you prefer to use. (Note that no spaces are used in the list of ciphers.) The server selects the first listed cipher that it supports.

   ```
   ssh -X -l nwells -c aes192-cbc,blowfish-cbc,3des-cbc
   system2
   ```

3. When you have a command prompt on system2, enter the command name of a graphical program that you want to run on system2 but display on system1. Don't include any DISPLAY variable information; the `ssh` and `sshd` programs handle this.

   ```
   gimp &
   ```

4. The program you launched appears after a moment on system1. Any data that you exchange within the program is encrypted. For example, if you executed a word-processing program on system2 that was displayed on system1, all of the document data that you viewed on system1 would have been encrypted as the X protocol passed it from system2 to system1. Figure 11-13 shows how an encrypted remote X connection operates.

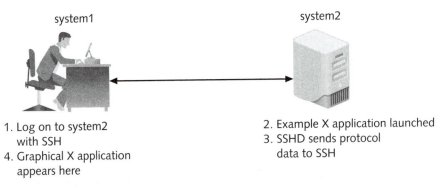

system1

system2

1. Log on to system2
   with SSH
4. Graphical X application
   appears here

2. Example X application launched
3. SSHD sends protocol
   data to SSH

Figure 11-13   Using SSH to encrypt a remote X application

Another important feature of SSH is its port forwarding ability, which lets you encrypt many other protocols over an SSH connection, much as you can encrypt the X protocol to use a graphical application across the network. Consider the following simple example.

Suppose that you have a large LAN with many Samba servers and you want to use SWAT to manage all of them from a single location called client1. You are concerned, however, about using SWAT in your browser because none of the traffic is encrypted, including the password you must enter to access SWAT. You can use SSH in this situation by specifying that any traffic on client1 arriving at port 12,345 (you can pick any port with a high number so that it is unlikely to be used) will be forwarded through ssh to port 901 (the SWAT port) on the remote server, called server1. The following command initiates the connection:

```
ssh -l nwells server1 -L 12345:server1:901
```

After executing this command to set up a secure communications channel, you can start your browser on client1 and enter the URL *http://client1:12345*. The ssh program redirects that request to port 901 on server1, where SWAT is watching for connections. You are then communicating with SWAT over the SSH-encrypted connection. Figure 11-14 illustrates port forwarding. The -R option provides a capability similar to this example, but forwards a remote port (for example, on server1) to a local port (for example, on client1).

Port forwarding allows you to use almost any protocol securely, including SMTP, FTP, or POP3. With more complex configurations, you can even use ssh to tunnel from a remote system through a firewall to an internal server that only permits connections from internal clients.

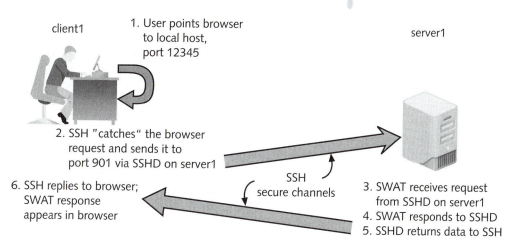

1. User points browser to local host, port 12345

2. SSH "catches" the browser request and sends it to port 901 via SSHD on server1

6. SSH replies to browser; SWAT response appears in browser

SSH secure channels

3. SWAT receives request from SSHD on server1
4. SWAT responds to SSHD
5. SSHD returns data to SSH

Figure 11-14 Port forwarding using SSH

The concept behind using SSH port forwarding is that you can tunnel an insecure protocol inside a secure protocol. Figure 11-15 illustrates this idea. The secure, encrypted protocol provides shielded transportation; even someone who intercepts the data packets cannot read their contents.

11

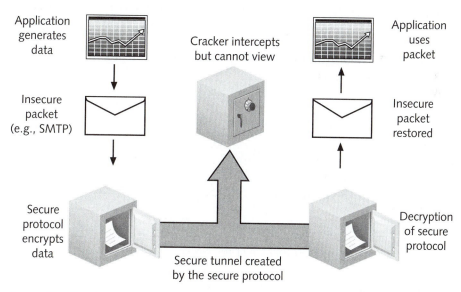

Figure 11-15 Tunneling an insecure protocol in a secure protocol

Tunneling Protocols

Tunneling is the process of transporting one protocol within another. The most obvious need for tunneling is to transport a protocol over a network that only supports another protocol. Figure 11-16 shows how one protocol is transported by another.

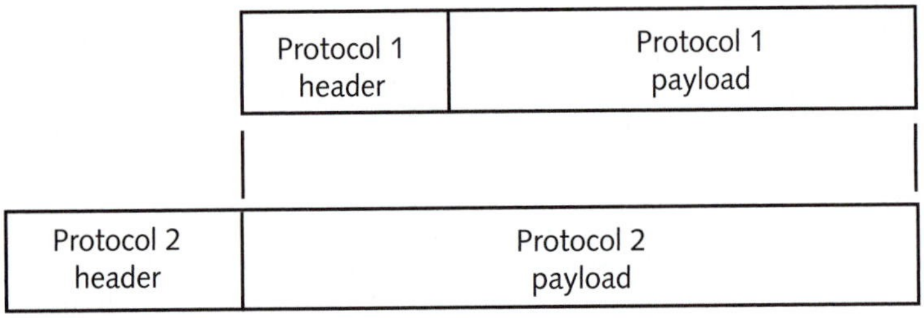

Protocol 1 header	Protocol 1 payload
Protocol 2 header	Protocol 2 payload

Figure 11-16   Tunneling a protocol within another protocol

The Protocol 1 packet, which consists of a packet header and the packet payload, is transported within the Protocol 2 payload. When the packet flows over the Internet, the Protocol 1 header governs this flow.

Figure 11-17 shows an example of connecting two networks running Novell's IPX protocol over the Internet, which runs the IP protocol. The routers take care of the tunneling. Linux supports both IPX and IP and can tunnel IPX over IP. You can use a Linux computer as your router rather than a more expensive commercial router. You'll also need the `ipxtunnel` daemon. More information about IPX tunneling on Linux is in the IPX-HOWTO document at *www.tldp.org*.

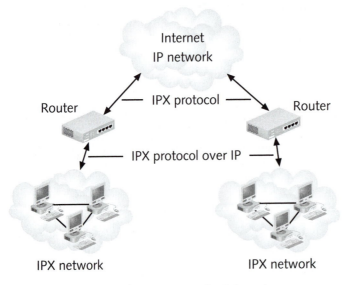

Figure 11-17   Tunneling IPX over the Internet

Another typical example is tunneling the IP protocol over IP. One practical application for this is to connect two networks that use private addressing via the Internet. Packets with private addresses can't flow over the Internet, but the tunnel uses IP addresses that can. Figure 11-18 shows an example.

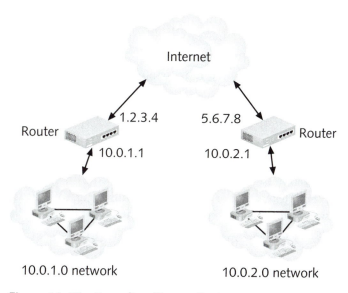

Figure 11-18   Tunneling IP over the Internet

One network uses the private IP network address 10.0.1.0 and the other uses the private network address 10.0.2.0. The router connected to the 10.0.1.0 network has its outside interface configured for the public address 1.2.3.4. The router connected to the 10.0.2.0 network has its outside interface configured for the public address 5.6.7.8. Any computer on the 10.0.1.0 network can communicate with any computer on the 10.0.2.0 network as long as their packets are not blocked by firewall rules.

The computers on each private network must either set their default gateway to the inside interface of the Linux router or an entry must be placed in each computer's routing table. DHCP can easily handle the latter if the computers fetch their IP addresses using DHCP.

To use IP over IP tunneling with Linux, you need to load the `ipip` kernel module. To set up the tunnel shown in Figure 11-18, run the following commands on the Linux router connected to network 10.0.1.0. Assume that address 5.6.7.8 is on a /24 network:

```
ifconfig tunl0 10.0.1.1 pointopoint 5.6.7.8
route add -net 10.0.2.0 netmask 255.255.255.0 dev tunl0
```

Run the following commands on the Linux router connected to the 10.0.2.0 network. Again, assume that address 1.2.3.4 is on a /24 network:

```
ifconfig tunl0 10.0.2.1 pointopoint 1.2.3.4
route add -net 10.0.1.0 netmask 255.255.255.0 dev tunl0
```

The traditional `ifconfig` and `route` commands were used here. The new `ip` command can be used instead, but there are a few more steps. You'd run commands similar to these at each end of the tunnel:

```
ip tunnel add tun10 mode ipip remote 10.0.1.1 local 10.0.2.1
ip addr add 10.0.1.1 dev tun10
ip link set tun10 up
ip route add 10.0.1.1/32 dev tun10
```

The preceding commands set up an IPv4 over IPv4 tunnel. There are limitations, however; the tunnel cannot transport IPv6 traffic and it can't support multicast. For these, you need a more functional tunnel, such as GRE.

GRE Tunnels

General Routing Encapsulation, or GRE, is a tunneling protocol originally designed by Cisco and now specified by RFC 2784. It has more capabilities than `ipip` tunneling. For example, it can handle multicast traffic and IPv6. To use a GRE tunnel, you must first load the `ip-gre` kernel module. Using the example tunneling scenario from the previous `ipip` section, you can use the following commands to set up a GRE tunnel on one side:

```
ip tunnel add tun10 mode gre remote 10.0.1.1 local 10.0.2.1 ttl 255
ip link set tun10 up
ip addr add 10.0.1.1 dev tun10
ip route add 10.0.1.1/32 dev tun10
```

These commands are much like those used to set up an `ipip` tunnel. After you know how to do tunneling in Linux, other tunneling methods are easy. Refer to the Linux Advanced Routing & Traffic Control HOWTO for details on tunneling IPv6.

Using `stunnel`

The Secure Sockets Layer (SSL) protocol is used on nearly all Web browsers to provide secure transmission of Web data for e-commerce. (SSL is used whenever you see "https" at the beginning of the URL.) On Linux, this protocol is supported through the `openssl` package. The **stunnel** package lets you use SSL as a transport protocol for other network traffic instead of just HTTP (Web) traffic. Most Linux distributions install `openssl` and `stunnel` by default.

The `stunnel` man page describes various command-line options that `stunnel` supports, but its basic operation is straightforward. You can start `stunnel` from the `inetd` or `xinetd` superserver to run it on demand. The following is an example of running IMAP using the tunnel (specifically, the last field of the configuration line in `inetd.conf`). The `-d` option indicates the port that should be used; the `-l` option indicates that the program following it is being executed in "inetd mode":

```
stunnel -d 993 -l /usr/sbin/imapd -- imapd
```

NOTE   Port 993 is the standard port for running IMAP over SSL.

If you are using `xinetd`, you can set up a `stunnel` connection using a separate configuration file for the protocol to be encrypted. For example, to encrypt POP3, you could set up a separate configuration file called `/etc/xinetd.d/pop3-redirect` that contains the following lines. The server argument shows that `xinetd` actually runs the `stunnel` program. The `server_args` field includes the arguments for `stunnel`.

```
service pop3
{
    disable   = no
    socket_type     = stream
    wait        = no
    user        = root
    server      = /usr/sbin/stunnel
    server_args     = -c -r pop3s-server.example.com:pop3s
    log_on_success += USERID
    log_on_failure += USERID
}
```

A final example shows how you can start a stand-alone program from a command line and have it use encrypted communications via `stunnel`. The program run here is the PPP daemon, `pppd`. After you establish an encrypted PPP connection using `stunnel`, all network traffic that uses the PPP connection is encrypted.

```
stunnel -d 2020 -L /usr/sbin/pppd -- pppd local
```

In this chapter, you have learned several methods of encapsulating one protocol within another to create a secure communications channel. For example, you can use SSH to encrypt other protocols such as X, FTP, or POP3. As you just learned, you can use `stunnel` to encrypt services such as PPP, POP3, and IMAP.

These are useful options to know, and many Linux users rely on them at some point. However, stacking protocols in this way could be considered a patchwork solution. A better idea is to work on broader network designs that do not require this type of stacking. Technologies such as IPsec and Cryptographic IP Encapsulation (CIPE) can encrypt traffic without the overhead that stacked protocols bring.

Stacked protocols create more network traffic because of the techniques that TCP uses to maintain stable connections. Each packet that TCP transmits must be acknowledged by its recipient. The TCP stack on the transmitting computer adjusts how it transmits based on the acknowledgments it receives from the recipient. For example, if acknowledgments take a long time to return, the sender does not transmit data as fast. This prevents dropped packets and makes better use of network bandwidth. However, when a TCP-based protocol is encapsulated in another TCP-based protocol, the algorithms used to make each of the two

11

connections more efficient can actually work at cross purposes, making the overall connection terribly slow, losing packets, or causing the connection to terminate unexpectedly. This problem is discussed in more technical detail at *http://sites.inka.de/sites/bigred/devel/ tcp-tcp.html.*

Creating a Virtual Private Network (VPN)

Virtual private networks, or VPNs, allow multiple computers to function as part of a single, secure network when parts of the "private" network are actually separated by an insecure public network such as the Internet. A VPN is like a special application of tunneling because it lets a group of computers that can be remote to each other act as a single, secure LAN by tunneling the traffic through specially configured network connections. You can create a VPN in Linux using any of several strategies. Consider the following examples:

■ You want a single filesystem to be available to users on two separate networks that are several miles apart. You want to use NFS to mount the filesystem on a remote server so that users in both offices can use it. Instead of paying for a dedicated connection between the offices, you use a fast Internet connection and SSH with port forwarding to establish an NFS mount for the filesystem. All data passed over the connection (through the Internet) is encrypted by SSH, as represented in Figure 11-19.

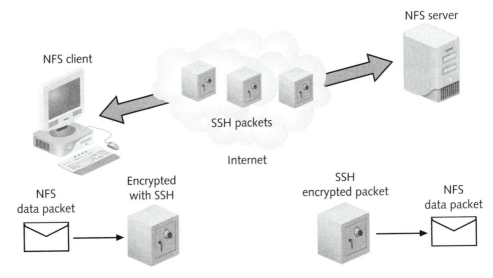

Figure 11-19   Tunneling NFS over SSH

■ You want to be able to dial in to your office network from home. The system administrator sets up PPTP so that you can establish a PPP connection and encrypt all of the transfers between the office server and your home computer. No one on the ISP computer or anywhere else on the Internet can read the network packets that you send and receive. Figure 11-20 illustrates this configuration. (See the next section for more details on using PPTP.)

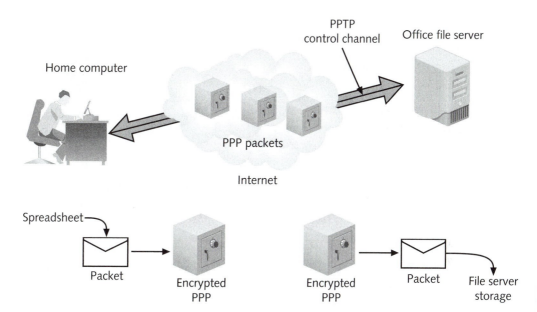

Figure 11-20 A PPTP connection via a modem

- You need to connect four offices into a single network. The traffic volume is low, but the connections must be secure from eavesdropping. You set up a server in each office with a dedicated dial-up connection to the Internet. The server runs either IPsec or CIPE and includes firewall rules (using netfilter) that do not permit any traffic (except for your four offices) into the LAN within each office. All traffic sent out of the LAN is encrypted by IPsec or CIPE and must be destined for one of the other three office network addresses. Figure 11-21 shows this configuration. Notice that, based on the routing and firewalls described, no one in any of the four offices can send or receive e-mail, browse the Web, or have other access to the Internet. Only packets destined for the other offices are routed.

To learn more about setting up a VPN on Linux, consult the Linux documentation on advanced routing and VPNs at *www.linuxdocs.org*, *www.linuxhq.com*, or other Linux download sites. Examples of useful resources that you can find on these sites include the following:

- VPN HOWTO
- VPN Masquerading HOWTO
- Advanced Routing HOWTO
- Linux 2.4 Packet Filtering HOWTO
- Linux Cipe+Masquerading mini-HOWTO

Creating a VPN can be complex, and the dangers of configuration mistakes are usually more serious than mistakes made within your LAN. With a VPN, a mistake can mean that sensitive data from your organization is suddenly visible to anyone on the Internet who

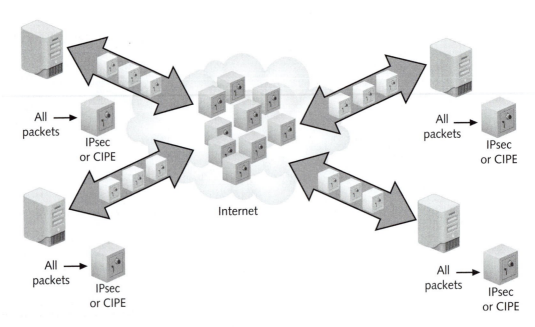

Figure 11-21   Using encrypted IP communications

knows where to look for it. In addition to using standard Linux software to create a VPN, dozens of commercial VPN products are available to help you. Some of these are software products, but most are hardware products. A VPN hardware solution (often called a **VPN router**) acts like a dedicated firewall that connects only to another (usually identical) VPN router at the other end of the public network connection. See Figure 11-22. The software on the VPN router encrypts all traffic from the LAN that it is protecting, and routes traffic between two or more parts of the network as if they were part of a single segment, or a closely allied network.

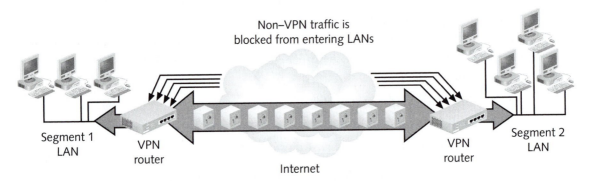

Figure 11-22   VPN routers connecting through the Internet

Using PPTP

The **Point-to-Point Tunneling Protocol (PPTP)** is a standard for creating a VPN. Microsoft had a hand in creating PPTP, and it later became RFC 2637. It allows the Point-to-Point Protocol or PPP to be tunneled through an IP network. The tunneling protocol is GRE.

PPTP is supported on Linux, though it is usually not installed by default. To use PPTP, you need support for the GRE protocol in the kernel and either or both of the PPTP client and server software.

Some security experts have serious concerns about PPTP's viability as a secure protocol. For example, see *www.counterpane.com/pptp.html*.

NOTE

PPTP uses two communications channels between a client and server. The first is a control channel that uses TCP port 1723. The second carries data and can be encrypted. This channel does not use UDP or TCP; it uses the GRE protocol. The data channel is simply a PPP channel, with options such as compression and encryption negotiated when the channel is established, based on the capabilities of the client and server systems.

The client portion of PPTP is available for download at *http://pptpclient.sourceforge.net/*. The PPTP server, called Poptop, is located at *www.poptop.org*. You can use Poptop to create a Linux-based PPTP server that Windows clients can connect to, as if it were another Windows system running PPTP. Windows 95, 98, NT, 2000, and XP are known to work with Poptop.

CHAPTER SUMMARY

- ❑ Trojan horse programs appear to be normal but perform unexpected actions that compromise system security.

- ❑ Viruses and worms are self-propagating security problems. Viruses typically attach themselves to data files; worms work independently of other programs.

- ❑ Denial-of-service (DoS) attacks try to block access by legitimate users. Distributed denial-of-service (DDoS) attacks use many machines to attack a target and are hard to defeat.

- ❑ Buffer overflow attacks rely on a programming oversight to corrupt data or gain unauthorized access by sending unexpected data to a network service.

- ❑ Spoofing attacks forge information to create the false impression that a packet is coming from a trusted service or location. The man-in-the-middle attack is a concern when someone might be able to intercept and read network traffic.

❏ Firewalls filter data packets based on their source, destination, protocol, or other aspects of the packet's makeup. A Linux firewall is controlled through the Linux kernel, which manages all IP packets entering or leaving the system.

❏ Linux firewalls are created using IP Tables (which are part of the netfilter architecture). Both let a system administrator add rules to control which packets are accepted or processed and which are discarded.

❏ IP Tables provides several routing and security features such as packet mangling and support for Quality of Service/Type of Service flags.

❏ Rules used by firewalls define characteristics of IP packets and how to handle matching packets. Rules are always executed in the order in which they are listed within a chain or table. Advanced rules include special actions such as masquerading and redirecting packets.

❏ Network Address Translation, or NAT, is a transparent routing technique that alters packet headers to translate packets in one network so they can be used on another network.

❏ Port forwarding is a routing technique within SSH that can encrypt many other protocols by connecting another service's port to the SSH port.

❏ Redirection in netfilter is similar to port forwarding, but the address you use for forwarding is that of the incoming interface.

❏ Programs for setting up and managing firewall rules are included in Fedora Core. These include `lokkit` and Firestarter.

❏ Many commercial firewall products are available for Linux; some are software and some are dedicated security products.

❏ The Secure Shell protocol (SSH), implemented in the OpenSSH package, provides an encrypted replacement for Telnet, as well as encrypted communications for many other protocols using the port forwarding feature of SSH.

❏ SSH uses either RSA or DSA public-key cryptography plus a symmetric cipher such as AES. To make the best use of SSH, you generate a key pair using an SSH utility called `ssh-keygen`.

❏ The `stunnel` package uses the SSL protocol to encrypt other protocols such as POP3 and IMAP (both used for e-mail retrieval). The `stunnel` package can be used from a superserver or directly on the command line.

❏ Tunneling one TCP-based protocol inside another can cause delays and dropped connections because of the way TCP tries to manage each connection.

❏ Linux security features can be used to create an effective virtual private network (VPN). Many companies sell dedicated VPN products based on Linux.

❏ PPTP was developed by Microsoft to implement a Windows VPN. PPTP uses an encrypted PPP session plus a separate control channel.

KEY TERMS

cache poisoning attack — An attack in which a cracker attempts to block access to a site by uploading erroneous information to a DNS server's cache.

chain — A list of rules that controls how packets are routed or handled in the Linux kernel.

distributed denial-of-service (DDoS) — A special type of attack in which a cracker infiltrates many systems and installs a program that will execute a DoS attack on an assigned target at the cracker's command.

DNS spoofing — Pretending that a request comes from a different host than its true originating host.

firewall — A program that filters (blocks) IP packets based on their characteristics, according to a set of rules.

General Routing Encapsulation (GRE) — A tunneling protocol originally designed by Cisco and now specified by RFC 2784. It has more capabilities than `ipip` tunneling.

IP spoofing — A cracker attack in which special low-level software assigns any address the cracker selects as either the source or the destination address on an IP packet.

IP Tables — The lists of rules associated with one of the programming hooks provided in the networking stacks by the netfilter architecture.

iptables — The command used to manage firewall rules within the netfilter firewall architecture in version 2.4 and later of the Linux kernel.

lokkit — A text-mode program that sets up basic firewall rules according to the level of security protection desired.

man-in-the-middle attack — A general term for any security attack in which a cracker intercepts communication, reads or alters it, and leads the sender to believe that the information was received by the intended recipient.

netfilter — The packet filtering and advanced routing architecture in Linux 2.4 and later kernels.

network address port translation (NAPT) — A routing technique in which the IP addresses and ports in a packet are altered during routing.

Network Address Translation (NAT) — A routing technique in which the IP addresses in a packet are altered during routing.

packet mangling — The altering of packets by a router to change the way they are handled or routed.

Point-to-Point Tunneling Protocol (PPTP) — A standard created by Microsoft for setting up a virtual private network (VPN). PPTP uses two connections, one for control information and one for data.

port forwarding — A routing technique within SSH that can encrypt many other protocols by connecting another service's port to the SSH port.

Quality of Service (QoS) — A networking feature that guarantees bandwidth to certain users or certain programs.

rule — A configuration setting that defines characteristics of an IP packet and an action to take for any packet that has those characteristics.

Squid — The most widely used Linux proxy server.

11

ssh-agent — A part of the SSH suite that helps manage key pairs and authentication among multiple SSH-capable systems.

stateful inspection — The ability of a firewall to make decisions about a packet based on its TCP state. For example, is the packet part of an already established session?

stunnel — A program that uses SSL as a transport protocol to encrypt other network protocols such as POP3 and IMAP.

tunneling — Transporting one protocol within another.

VPN router — A hardware device that acts as a dedicated firewall with VPN capabilities.

Web spoofing — A type of man-in-the-middle attack in which a cracker deceives a user into linking to the cracker's site when the user thinks she is linking to another site. The cracker's server then intercepts every Web request from the user and alters the response to point all future requests back to the cracker's site.

REVIEW QUESTIONS

1. A file integrity program such as Tripwire can protect against Trojan horse attacks by:

   a. automatically deleting Trojan horse programs

   b. helping you catch unexpected changes to a system utility file that might indicate it had been replaced by a Trojan horse

   c. rejecting packets generated by Trojan horse programs

   d. using programming hooks to inform the kernel of Trojan horse behavior

2. Describe the difference between a DoS attack and a DDoS attack.

3. In a cache poisoning attack:

   a. Squid or the Apache proxy server is subject to a buffer overflow attack.

   b. Information in memory is corrupted by a virus or worm.

   c. Erroneous DNS entries are included in the cache of a DNS server.

   d. Netfilter must use IP Chains to reject cached packets.

4. Web spoofing is an example of:

   a. a man-in-the-middle attack, because the user erroneously thinks she is reaching the intended Web site

   b. a Trojan horse attack, because the user's browser doesn't actually attempt to reach the requested site

   c. a worm, because programs on the Web server attempt to infiltrate client sites through the browser

   d. a buffer overflow attack via script programs running on the Web server

5. Linux firewalls consist of _____ organized into _____ or _____ .

   a. commands, packets, datagrams

   b. utilities, secure, insecure

   c. chains, protocols, filters

   d. rules, chains, tables

6. Before the introduction of IP Chains architecture, Linux used the _____ command for firewall configuration.

   a. `ipfwadm`

   b. `netfilter`

   c. `ifconfig`

   d. `stunnel`

7. The three default chains used by netfilter are:

   a. Input, Forwarding, Output

   b. Input, Forward, Output

   c. Deny, Reject, Accept

   d. Netfilter, Iptables, SSH

8. Define the purpose of the following `iptables` options: `-d`, `-s`, `-p`, and `-i`.

9. The difference between REJECT and DENY is that:

   a. DENY informs the sender that the packet was discarded; REJECT provides no feedback to the sender.

   b. REJECT jumps to the next rule in the chain; DENY immediately discards the packet in question.

   c. DENY informs the sender that the packet was discarded; REJECT logs the packet in `/var/log/messages`.

   d. REJECT informs the sender that the packet was discarded; DENY provides no feedback to the sender.

10. Linux port forwarding is also called:

    a. SNAT

    b. DNAT

    c. `stunnel`

    d. redirection

11. Netfilter redirection sends packets to:

    a. a daemon running on the firewall

    b. a computer on the inside network

    c. another computer on the Internet

    d. the input chain for further processing

11

12. By using a transparent proxy configuration, a system administrator can:

    a. Securely transmit packets over the Internet using a variety of ciphers.

    b. Hide logging and other security features from users sending packets through a LAN.

    c. Redirect packets destined for a given port on a remote system to a different port on the router.

    d. Cache packets in the router to provide higher performance for all users on the LAN.

13. Name four Linux firewall configuration tools, and indicate whether they are included with Fedora Core.

14. Which is a new feature that netfilter includes but IP Chains did not include?

    a. routing based on QoS

    b. transparent proxy

    c. IP masquerading

    d. IPsec support

15. Linux is often the basis of dedicated hardware products designed as routers, firewalls, or VPNs. True or False?

16. Name two differences between SSH1 and SSH2.

17. If you use ssh without first creating and storing a key pair on the remote host:

    a. You are prompted for a password to aid authentication.

    b. The sshd program will not permit a connection.

    c. Only the insecure r-utilities method of authentication can be used.

    d. The standard configuration of sshd automatically generates a key pair and sends it back to the client.

18. The command to create a key pair for use by ssh and sshd is:

    a. gpg

    b. ssh-askpass

    c. ssh-keygen

    d. ssh-agent

19. Port forwarding with SSH allows you to:

    a. Use SSH to encrypt protocols that use any TCP port.

    b. Use a proxy server to cache packets.

    c. Pass key pairs between hosts that have not previously communicated with each other.

    d. Use SSH within a superserver configuration file, as with stunnel.

20. PPTP is a VPN solution that:

    a. was developed by Microsoft and uses separate control and data channels

    b. is considered preferable to IPsec and CIPE

    c. is identical to using PPP over `stunnel`

    d. mimics the features found in hardware VPN devices

21. To create a secure communications channel using `stunnel`, you must:

    a. Generate key pairs and store them on the local and remote systems before using the program.

    b. Configure the SSL feature of your browser so that `stunnel` can recognize your certificate authority.

    c. First use the SSH utilities to establish an encrypted channel, then launch `stunnel` to permit another protocol such as POP3 to use the encrypted channel.

    d. Execute the `stunnel` command from a command line or within a superserver configuration file.

22. Describe in detail one method by which Linux security capabilities can be used to create a VPN.

23. Some experts recommend using _____ instead of

    _____ .

    a. IPsec or CIPE, PPP over SSH

    b. `stunnel`, SSH

    c. PPTP, IPsec or CIPE

    d. `ipfwadm`, netfilter

24. Name four of the ciphers that are supported by the latest release of OpenSSH.

25. Quality of Service features let a router:

    a. Control how much bandwidth certain users or programs receive on a busy network.

    b. Log information about how well the router is handling a heavy load.

    c. Monitor when someone sends a packet that matches a particular rule in a firewall.

    d. Reset Type of Service bits, which are not supported in modern routers unless they use IPv6.

11

HANDS-ON PROJECTS

The following projects assume that you are working in a lab environment. **If you are working on a production server or one that contains sensitive data, do not attempt the following projects**.

Project 11-1

In this project, you use netfilter to redirect packets. You should work as a partner with another student or colleague. To complete this project, you should have one computer running Linux with root access. The other computer just needs to be able to run a Web browser.

1. On the Linux system, log on as root.

2. Ensure that the Apache Web server is running. Enter the `ps ax` command to see if `httpd` processes are running. If not, start Apache with the following command:

    `apachectl start`

3. On the Linux computer, enter the `ifconfig` command and make note of the IP address of the eth0 interface.

4. On the Linux computer, start a Web browser and make sure you can access Apache by entering the IP address of the eth0 interface.

5. On the other computer, start a Web browser and enter the IP address of the Linux computer. You should see the same Web page you saw in Step 4.

6. On the Linux computer, redirect TCP port 3333 to port 80 by entering the following command:

    **`iptables -t nat -A PREROUTING -i eth0 -p tcp
--dport 3333 -j REDIRECT --to-port 80`**

7. Verify that TCP port 3333 is now redirected to TCP port 80 by entering the following command:

    `iptables -t nat --list -n`

    You should see a line like the following:

    `REDIRECT   tcp - 0.0.0.0/0   0.0.0.0/0   tcp
dpt:3333 redir ports 80`

8. On the second computer, enter the IP address of the Linux computer immediately followed by :3333, as in the following example:

    `1.2.3.4:3333`

You should see the same Web page as in Step 5. This demonstrates that TCP port 3333 on the Linux computer is being redirected to its port 80 and Apache is answering.

9. To delete the redirection, enter the following command:

```
iptables -F -t nat
```

Project 11-2

In this project, you use `iptables` commands to block `ping` on your system. For this project, you should work as partners with another student or colleague. The two systems mentioned in the steps are your system and your partner's. To complete this project, you should have two Linux systems with root access. The files described here are taken from Fedora Core but should be applicable to most versions of Linux.

1. From the first system, `ping` the second system (substituting the IP address of the second system for 192.168.100.6):

```
ping 192.168.100.6
```

Let the `ping` command continue as you complete the following steps.

2. On the second system, see what firewall rules are in effect using this command:

```
iptables -L -n
```

3. Block ICMP packets (which is how `ping` operates) by executing the following command on the second system:

```
iptables -A INPUT -p icmp -j REJECT
```

4. Notice what has happened on the first system.

5. On the second system, erase all `iptables` rules from the kernel using this command:

```
iptables -F
```

6. Note how the `ping` on the first system responds. (If `ping` has timed out and stopped working, restart it using the command in Step 1.)

7. Use the following command to block ICMP packets again. In place of the IP address shown, include the IP address of the first system:

```
iptables -A INPUT -s 192.168.100.5 -p icmp -j REJECT
```

8. How does the `ping` command on the first system respond?

9. Try pinging the second system from the second system (open a second command-line window). Why does this command succeed?

10. Reinitialize the `iptables` configuration on the second system using this command:

```
/etc/rc.d/init.d/iptables restart
```

11

Project 11-3

In this project, you experiment with the `system-config-securitylevel` graphical tool. To complete this project, you should have Fedora Core 3 installed with root access.

1. Log on as root. Check whether the firewall is currently running by entering the following command:

   `iptables -list -n`

   If you see a line like the following one, the firewall is running:

   `Chain RH-Firewall-1-INPUT (2 references)`

2. Run the `system-config-securitylevel` program from the GNOME menu or from the command line:

   `system-config-securitylevel &`

3. The screen that appears has a Security level setting that shows the firewall as enabled or disabled. If you determined in Step 1 that the firewall is running, the Security level should be set to Enable firewall. Otherwise, it should be set to Disable firewall.

4. If the firewall is enabled, disable it by selecting **Disable firewall** from the Security level list box. Click **OK** and then click **Yes** when you see the warning that the program will end.

5. Verify that the firewall has been disabled by entering the same command as in Step 1:

   `iptables -list -n`

   You should see only three chains, and they should all be set to policy ACCEPT.

6. Run the `system-config-securitylevel` program from the GNOME menu or from the command line:

   `system-config-securitylevel &`

7. Enable the firewall by selecting **Enable firewall** from the Security level list box.

8. Select one or more trusted services by clicking the check boxes.

9. Select an interface from the Trusted devices list.

10. Add the following string to the Other ports text box:

    `666:tcp`

11. Click **OK** and then click **Yes** when you see a warning that the program will end.

12. Verify that a rule for port 666 has been added by entering the same command as in Step 1:

    `iptables -list -n`

You should see a line like the following:

```
ACCEPT   tcp - 0.0.0.0/0   0.0.0.0/0   state
NEW tcp dpt:666
```

Project 11-4

In this project, you configure a key pair and use the ssh command. You should work as partners with another student or colleague. The two systems mentioned in the steps are your system and your partner's. To complete this project, you should have two Linux systems with OpenSSH packages installed. (These are installed by default on Fedora Core.)

1. Log on as a regular user on the first system.

2. Make certain that the necessary SSH packages are installed. (You should have the ssh, sshd, and ssh-keygen programs.)

3. Generate a key pair by entering the following command (do not enter a passphrase):

   ssh-keygen -t rsa -b 2048

4. Copy the public key you just generated to the other system.

   scp ~/.ssh/id_rsa.pub
   **   user2@system2:/home/user2/.ssh/user1key**

   You must enter the password for user2 to complete this command.

5. On system2, if user2 already has an authorized_keys file, append the contents of the user1key file to it using a text editor. If there is no authorized_keys file, rename user1key to authorized_keys.

6. Now try to log on to system2 from system1 using the ssh command.

   ssh system2

7. Why doesn't this work as expected?

8. Try this command to log on:

   ssh -l user2 system2

9. Assuming that you don't always want to enter the logon name on the remote system (or that you work with several systems and can't keep track of multiple usernames), review the man page for ssh to determine how you can set up the ~/.ssh/ config file so that you don't have to include the -l user2 parameter when executing ssh.

Project 11-5

In this project, you build on Project 11-4 to run a graphical program over a secure link using SSH. You should continue to work as partners with another student or colleague. The two systems mentioned in the steps are your system and your partner's. To complete this project, you should have two Linux systems with OpenSSH packages installed. The first system should be running the X Window System (typically GNOME or KDE).

1. Log on to your regular user account on system1. You should be working in a graphical environment.

2. Launch a graphical program, such as gedit, on system2.

   ssh -l user2 -X system2 gedit &

3. Open a second command-line window on system1 and log on as root.

4. Run the ps command to see that the gedit program is not running on system1:

   ps aux|grep gedit

CASE PROJECTS

CASE PROJECTS

Case Project 11-1

1. List the firewall rules that you would want to implement on the main server at Snow, Sleet, and Hale. You can write them out as descriptions rather than iptables commands. For example, one description might be "Block all access to our intranet server except from the networks within the organization." The exact rules you think are warranted will depend on how you have designed the network and how concerned you are about different security threats.

2. Pick a few of the rules that you created in the first case and write them out as iptables commands. Review the documentation for IP Tables to see how you might improve upon your first attempt at creating the needed commands. For example, how might logging or other monitoring help you? What other features seem useful to you?

3. Although the technical committee (a group of partners) at Snow, Sleet, and Hale is impressed with your technical abilities, they are concerned that you have too much to do, overseeing all the other system administrators, implementing Internet connectivity, and now worrying about security configurations. They suggest that instead of configuring all the existing servers, you could just purchase a preconfigured product to use as a VPN or firewall. This might allow you to connect the firm's different offices securely and avoid some of the tedium of setting up rules for IP Tables. Research these products on the Web by searching for appropriate key terms. Many are built on Linux, but not all. Based on your research, write a memo to the technical committee outlining why you might choose to use or avoid such a product. Include reasons for both options so that they know you've considered the issues. Spending money on new technology is not a problem for this law firm, though they want to make wise decisions and not waste money on devices that will not help productivity. What will your final decision be about the product?

12

SECURITY TOOLS

After reading this chapter and completing the exercises, you will be able to:

♦ Use network scanning and packet-sniffing utilities

♦ Understand basic intrusion-detection systems

♦ Perform automated security audits of your Linux system

In this chapter, you will learn about tools that you can use to help secure your systems. You can also prevent cracker break-ins by using security-auditing tools to find weaknesses in your system before a cracker finds them. A security policy is part of security auditing, but the policy should be supplemented by security-auditing utilities, several of which you will learn about in this chapter.

SCANNERS AND SNIFFERS

Previous discussions have shown how crackers might attempt to gain access to your Linux system. In this section, you will learn two more techniques that crackers use:

- **Port scanning**, in which you send packets to a host and gain information about the host from its response. Port scanning normally involves sending packets to many ports or sending malformed packets (as described later) to gain knowledge that the host is not intentionally sharing.

- **Packet sniffing** (also called **network traffic analysis**), in which you examine the headers and data contained within every packet on a network, not just those addressed to your own host.

Network administrators disagree about the legitimate uses of these two network activities. An administrator who is concerned about possible security vulnerabilities on a corporate network can use port scanning to check for security weaknesses. Packet sniffing may serve the same purposes, and is certainly valuable when difficult network troubleshooting tasks arise. For example, if the throughput of the network slows down significantly and no one is sure why, the most effective solution is to examine the network traffic to see what is actually happening "on the wire."

So, when are port scanning or packet sniffing considered security audit or troubleshooting tools? When are they considered an attack? When are they merely harmless exploration of the network? The answer depends on who you are and what network you are scanning or sniffing. The documentation for one of the utilities described in the next section refers to its use by network administrators or "curious individuals." Many people see nothing wrong with scanning any system on a publicly accessible network (such as the Internet); others feel the same way only about examining the traffic on their employer's network. Although these activities are not considered illegal (at least, no one has yet been prosecuted merely for port scanning or sniffing), you run a serious risk of being fired or expelled if someone finds you scanning systems without notifying the administrator first, or if you are discovered sniffing packets on a network for which you are not the network administrator.

If you are a network administrator with responsibility for a network's security, feel free to use the tools in this chapter to learn about your network's weaknesses and improve your security. For other networks, ask before you act.

CAUTION
Regarding the defensive utilities described later in this chapter, a port scan originating from your site might completely block your site from accessing the target of the scan. This might be reason enough to avoid port scans of other networks.

If network administrators don't use the tools described in this chapter, they are at a serious disadvantage in securing their networks because crackers use the same tools every day. To prevent their success, you must plug the holes that these tools locate.

The software described in this chapter is available for many platforms. In fact, a recent survey by a large security consulting firm indicated that 63 percent of attacks on large corporate networks originated from Windows-based computers.

Port Scanning

A port scan begins with the assumption that an attacker does not know where vulnerabilities are on your system. A port scan enables the attacker to identify the type of operating system you are running and any network services that might provide access through a more focused attack. You can think of port scanning as a tool for locating chinks in the armor of a host.

The term "attacker" is used in this context rather than "cracker" because you can perform port scanning on your own systems as a test of system vulnerability.

A port scan typically sends packets with the ICMP, UDP, or TCP protocol. TCP is the most popular choice because the header of a TCP packet contains a section devoted to flags, as shown in Figure 12-1. These **flags** are numeric status indications to establish and track TCP connections.

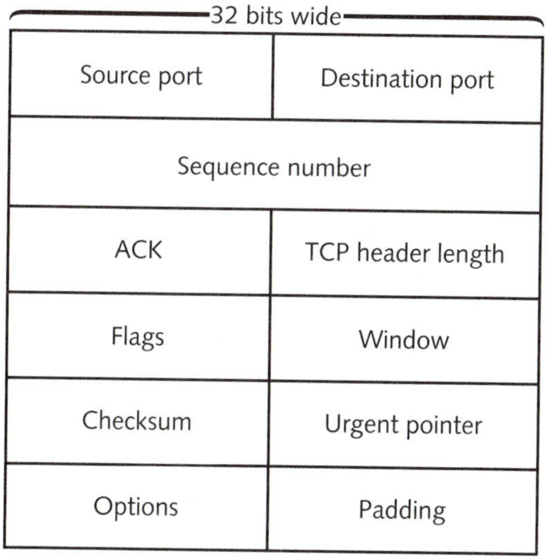

12

Source port	Destination port
Sequence number	
ACK	TCP header length
Flags	Window
Checksum	Urgent pointer
Options	Padding

32 bits wide

Figure 12-1   TCP packet header

For example, when your Web browser contacts a Web server, a TCP connection is established. The three-part process of establishing a TCP connection is as follows:

1. The client sends a packet with the SYN flag set. (SYN stands for synchronize.)

2. If the server can accept the TCP connection, it returns a packet to the client with the SYN and ACK flags set. (ACK stands for acknowledge.)

3. The client sends another packet to the server with the ACK flag set (but not the SYN flag).

At this point, the TCP connection is established and either the client or the server can send data to the other and have it processed in an orderly way. In a basic port scan, a port-scanning utility sends packets with the SYN flag set (commonly called a **SYN packet**) to a range of ports on the targeted host. If the host responds with a SYN+ACK packet, the port scanner knows that the responding port can accept connections. Of course, this doesn't mean that the client can actually connect and perform any tasks; such capabilities might require that the client be from a particular network address or that it provide a password. However, the port scan has identified a place where the targeted host is listening for network connections.

What would happen if a client sent a packet with the ACK flag set before establishing a connection? Or perhaps all the TCP flags at once? What if sending a SYN packet to a host results not in a SYN+ACK packet from the host, but in an ICMP packet stating that the service is unavailable? This is also useful information for an attacker.

Sending a packet with all TCP flags set is called an **Xmas scan**. The name refers to the image of the flags as individual lights. When all the flags are "on," the packet is lit up like a Christmas tree.

TIP

An interesting point is that each operating system—often each version of an operating system—responds differently to these nonstandard network activities. For example, if a client sends an ACK packet before establishing a connection, the targeted host may simply ignore it, or may return it with an error message. The flags set on the returned packet vary by operating system. Although the networking standards documents for IP and TCP specify much of the "correct response," many operating systems do not adhere to these standardized rules. The result is that a port scanner is often used to identify the operating system of a targeted host. This identification process is called **fingerprinting** the host.

Fingerprinting a host is important for a cracker because it tells him what techniques to use to attack your systems. For example, if he knows that you are running a certain version of the Linux kernel, he will also know that if you have not applied a certain upgrade patch, your system is vulnerable to a particular type of attack. Likewise, if he wants to use a certain known weakness in the BIND name server, he knows he may have only one chance to try it. If he knows exactly what software you are running, and if you haven't upgraded your software to fix security bugs, the attack may succeed. If the cracker doesn't know what you're running, he may try an attack that fails; this attempt could alert you to his efforts so that you can block further attempts using software such as PortSentry, described later in this chapter.

Port scans sometimes also use ICMP and UDP packets. They do not provide as much information as TCP scans, but under some circumstances they may provide some information when a TCP scan won't provide any. A diligent cracker will try many tactics to find your network's weak spots.

Packets from port scanners typically have a certain "look" because they are malformed; they include unexpected flags or header option fields. Also, they typically are addressed to ports that are not actively waiting for connections because an attacker is checking thousands of ports looking for a weakness. The utilities described later in this chapter can watch for port scans by "listening" to all the ports on your system. If the utilities detect packets that appear to come from a port scanner, they may update a firewall in real time to block all access to the scanning client. (You can configure or disable such a response.)

More advanced port-scanning software tries to **randomize** port scans, contacting multiple ports in random order. This can make the scan harder to recognize and prevent it from triggering a firewall update to block the scanning site. Other specialized tools distribute a scan among many "drone" clients, each of which scans a small range of ports. Because the packets are coming from a large number of sites instead of a single scanning client, the software watching for port scans is less likely to recognize what is happening. The results from all the distributed partial scans are then correlated into a larger picture of the host's vulnerabilities.

12

Using nmap

The most widely used port-scanning utility is **nmap**, the network mapper. The nmap program is a powerful command-line utility that can use a variety of different scanning methods. It also fingerprints hosts using a number of sophisticated techniques. The nmap program is included with most Linux distributions and is usually installed by default.

To use nmap, you specify the type of scan that you want to perform (that is, which packet types you want nmap to send out), a set of hosts to scan, and a set of port numbers to scan on those hosts. You can include separate options to fingerprint each host, to provide more verbose output, and to configure things like the timing policy (a more erratic timing policy makes detection of the scan much more difficult).

The home page for the nmap utility is *www.insecure.org/nmap*, where you can find a number of interesting security-related articles. One of the most valuable is the list of 75 most popular security utilities, from a survey of hundreds of network administrators. You can find this list at *www.insecure.org/tools.html*. Several examples of using nmap are shown in this section. The following example performs a port scan using SYN packets (via the -sS option) of the host *www.myplace.net*.

```
nmap -sS www.myplace.net
```

The following example performs a port scan using SYN packets for the entire network on which *www.myplace.net* resides:

```
nmap -sS -O www.myplace.net/24
```

The /24 is used to identify the network ID from the IP address for *www.myplace.net*. The -O option also attempts to fingerprint the operating system for each host on that network.

The next example performs a **ping scan**, which reports any hosts that are reachable using ICMP echo packets to perform the ping.

```
nmap -sP 192.129.34-74.*
```

The target here is any IP address beginning with 192.129 and having a third octet between 34 and 74. This scan will attempt to reach 40 subnets (74–34) of 256 hosts each, for more than 10,000 hosts.

Table 12-1 lists the major options of the nmap command.

Table 12-1 Commonly used command-line options in nmap

nmap Option	Description
-sT	Scan by trying to connect via TCP
-sS	Scan by sending a SYN packet without following up with a connection attempt
-sU	Use UDP instead of TCP to scan ports
-sP	Use ping (ICMP) to scan ports
-sF	Use the FIN flag in a TCP packet to scan ports
-sX	Use all flags in a TCP packet to scan ports (an Xmas scan)
-sN	Use no flags in a TCP packet to scan ports (a null scan)
-O	Attempt to fingerprint each listed host, reporting the operating system that the host is running (including the version, if known, such as the Linux kernel version or service pack level for Windows)
-p <range>	Define a range of ports to scan
-P0	Don't ping hosts as part of the scan
-T <policy>	Define a timing policy; the six possible values for <policy> are Paranoid, Sneaky, Polite, Normal, Aggressive, and Insane

Using an nmap Graphical Front End

Although nmap is not difficult to use, the nmap front-end package provides a nice graphical interface that is useful when you are learning to use the utility and when you expect to collect a lot of data that is more easily viewed in a graphical environment. The nmap front-end package is included in many Linux distributions. Both nmap and the nmap front end are available for many versions of Linux from *rpmfind.net*. However, because the **nmapfe** utility in the nmap front-end package is written specifically for GNOME desktops, if you're using strictly KDE, you might want to look on *freshmeat.net* for Knmap, KnmapFE, or Qnmap, all of which are KDE-based graphical front ends for nmap. As one example,

Figure 12-2 shows a view of the Knmap program, which is similar in design to the GNOME program described later. You can learn about Knmap at *http://pages.infinit.net/rewind/*.

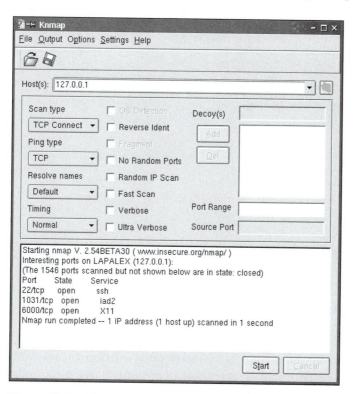

Figure 12-2   The Knmap graphical front end to `nmap`

The Knmap program and the GNOME-based `nmapfe` utility provide graphical access to all nmap command-line options. Both Knmap and `nmapfe` are included with Fedora Core and Red Hat Linux. To launch the `nmap` front-end graphical utility, enter this command:

```
nmapfe
```

Figure 12-3 shows the main window where all nmap activity is displayed. Here, you select features for your port scan, then click the Scan button to begin the scan. The output from the scan is shown in the window below the options. Notice that the line just below the output window is a fully formed nmap command based on the options you select in the graphical interface. This unusual feature teaches you how to use the command-line utility as you use the graphical front end.

Many other port-scanning utilities are available. The nmap utility is considered the standard; it also has good documentation and a large and involved developer community. If you are

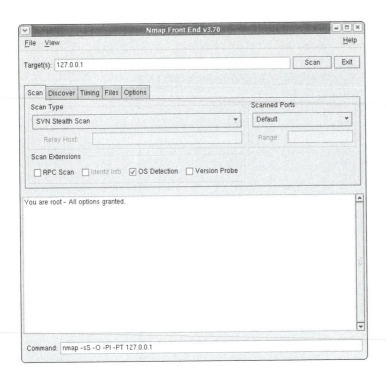

Figure 12-3 A graphical front end to the `nmap` utility

interested in reviewing newer or more specialized port-scanning tools (such as one for performing a distributed port scan, as mentioned previously), search for "port scan" on *freshmeat.net*.

Packet Sniffing

A packet sniffer lets you capture and examine traffic from the sniffer's network interface. Your examination might concentrate on the types of packets being transmitted (the percentage of ICMP, TCP, and UDP packets), or you might examine the payload within individual packets to see what is being sent over your networks. Using the former technique, you can create a statistical picture of your network usage that can be invaluable for planning upgrades, troubleshooting, and providing the best service possible to network users. The latter technique can help you spot security holes, including potentially bad passwords and users who are not following established security procedures.

To understand how a packet sniffer operates, think of the network cable as a stream. Everyone floats their packets down the stream, and each computer plucks from the stream only the packets with that computer's address. You can also instruct your computer to make a copy of everything in the stream; any packet that floats by is available. To do this, your computer must operate in a special mode called **promiscuous mode**.

To run in promiscuous mode, the network card, its software driver, and the operating system must support it. Most Ethernet cards and their software drivers can run in promiscuous mode, but some don't. The operating system supports the mode with **libpcap**, the packet-capturing library. This library is installed on most Linux distributions by default and is available for Windows. If you are downloading software for other systems and see a mention of libpcap or pcap, you may need to find and install that library.

If users can eavesdrop on the packet stream, they can see the contents of all packets on the network segment, which can create security and privacy problems. You must be logged on as root to use promiscuous mode, so all packet sniffers require root access. However, locking down desktop computers so users can't log on as root doesn't solve the problem. In an office environment, anyone can plug a PC into the office network.

Ethernet switches normally prevent users from eavesdropping on the packets of other users. However, you can't rely on this. Some programs are designed to flood the switch with frames that have bogus MAC addresses. The MACOF (MAC Overflow) program is one example. Many switches respond by becoming promiscuous—they send all packets to all ports.

If you are using encryption technologies such as SSH, GPG, and stunnel, as described in previous chapters, the data within your packets is obscured from eavesdroppers.

Many packet sniffers and traffic analyzers are available for Linux. IPTraf, tcpdump, and Ethereal are examined in the following sections, but you can find many other programs by exploring Linux download sites or security Web sites.

12

IPTraf

The **IPTraf** program is a popular tool for viewing network activity on a LAN. It doesn't display the contents (payload) of packets, but instead displays individual network connections, with protocol and other data for each one. It also displays statistics by protocol, interface, host name, or IP address. You can set up filters to track only certain protocols, certain host names, or certain IP addresses. The home page of IPTraf is *http://iptraf.seul.org/*.

> **TIP**
> If you download and install IPTraf, you might also need to install the ncurses package on which the IPTraf interface is built. The ncurses package is a programming library that helps programmers easily create text-mode, menu-based interfaces. You can see this type of interface in programs such as authconfig in Fedora Core.

IPTraf is not installed by default. You can download IPTraf from its Web site or you can find its RPM package (iptraf-2.7.0-11.i386.rpm) on Fedora Core CD 3. Launch it from any command-line window by entering iptraf. Don't use an ampersand (&) after the command name because the program needs to take over the command-line window in which it's launched. Because IPTraf is not a graphical program, you can use it from a text-mode console without running X.

After you press a key to begin, you see the main menu for IPTraf, shown in Figure 12-4. From this menu, you can choose to view overall statistics or a live report of connections and packets as they occur. By default, IPTraf uses nonpromiscuous mode, so only traffic that is originating from or destined for the host on which IPTraf is running is included in the reports. This is perfect when IPTraf is run on a server, gateway, or router. You can also choose the LAN station monitor option on the main menu to view summaries of traffic to and from hosts on your LAN. This option lets you see which users are consuming all the bandwidth if the network suddenly slows down.

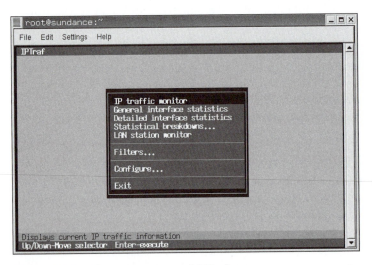

Figure 12-4 The main menu of IPTraf

By choosing Configure on the main menu, you can set up a number of options for how IPTraf processes and displays network information. Figure 12-5 shows this configuration screen. On the main menu, choose General interface statistics to view packet statistics broken down by IP and non-IP categories. The Detailed interface statistics page lists packet volume based on higher-level protocols within IP. For example, the number of packets and bytes for TCP, UDP, and ICMP packets are displayed, both for incoming and outgoing traffic. All of these statistics are updated every few seconds.

Choose IP traffic monitor on the main menu to see a list of connections as they occur, including the protocol, the flags used to make the connection (recall the TCP flags mentioned in the discussion of port scanning), and other details. Figure 12-6 shows this screen.

tcpdump

The **tcpdump** program is a packet capture and decoding program. Using tcpdump, you can examine the headers for each packet and save the information to a file for later analysis. You can also save the data within packets to a file, having tcpdump act as a network sniffer.

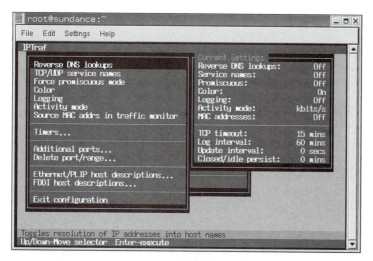

Figure 12-5 The IPTraf configuration screen

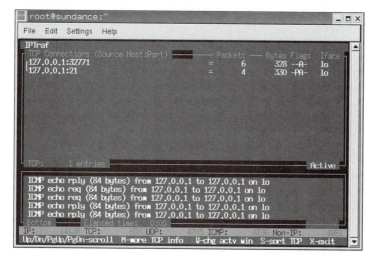

Figure 12-6 The IP traffic monitor screen in IPTraf

You execute `tcpdump` from a command line. If you specify no command-line options or parameters, `tcpdump` captures packets from your first interface and displays the decoded packets to the screen until you press Ctrl+C. Here's an example of `tcpdump` output formatted to fit the limited page width of this book. It will look a little different on your screen:

tcpdump
```
tcpdump: verbose output suppressed, use -v or -vv for full
protocol decode
listening on eth0, link-type EN10MB (Ethernet), capture size
96 bytes
```

```
08:27:40.765312 IP ed.alcpress.com.32895 >
fire.alcpress.com.domain:
25770+ A? www.course.com. (32)

08:27:40.765339 IP fire.alcpress.com.domain >
ed.alcpress.com.32895:
25770 1/0/0 A www.course.com (48)

08:27:40.768023 IP ed.alcpress.com > www.course.com:
icmp 64: echo request seq 0

08:27:40.851309 IP www.course.com > ed.alcpress.com:
icmp 64: echo reply seq 0
```

This output is the result of the host *ed.alcpress.com* pinging the host *www.course.com*. The tcpdump program is running on the *ed.alcpress.com* host, which is configured to use the host *fire.alcpress.com* as its default gateway. Figure 12-7 shows the environment.

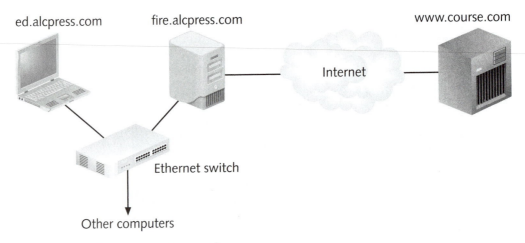

Figure 12-7   Capturing packets with tcpdump

The tcpdump program captured four packets. The first packet is the result of the ping program asking for the IP address of the host *www.course.com*. This packet is a query for the DNS A record. The second packet is the DNS answer—it contains the IP address but tcpdump displays it as *www.course.com*. You'll see later how you can convince tcpdump to show you the address rather than the name.

The third and fourth packets are the ping packets. The third packet is the ICMP Echo Request sent by *ed.alcpress.com*. The fourth packet is the ICMP Echo Reply sent by *www.course.com*.

Because *ed.alcpress.com* is connected to an Ethernet switch, `tcpdump` normally only displays packets that involve this host's transmission or receipt of a packet. Some switches can be configured so a port will expose all packets sent by any host connected to the switch.

All packets begin with a time stamp in *hour:minute:second.decimal* format, where *decimal* is the fractional part of the second to six decimal places. This precision is necessary because many packets can be captured in one second. If you don't want the time stamp to be displayed at all, use the –t option. The –ttt option will instead display the number of microseconds since the previous packet.

Many command-line options and parameters let you control how `tcpdump` captures and processes information. The next example uses the –v option to show more verbose packet decoding. The same four packets as in the previous example are used here:

```
tcpdump -v
tcpdump: listening on eth0, link-type EN10MB (Ethernet),
capture size 96 bytes

08:29:05.003092 IP (tos 0x0, ttl  64, id 3202, offset 0,
flags [DF], length: 60)
ed.alcpress.com.32897 > fire.alcpress.com.domain:
[udp sum ok]  50502+ A? www.course.com. (32)

08:29:05.003270 IP (tos 0x0, ttl  64, id 0, offset 0, flags
[DF], length: 76)
fire.alcpress.com.domain > ed.alcpress.com.32897:
[udp sum ok]  50502 1/0/0 www.course.com. A www.course.com
(48)

08:29:05.005752 IP (tos 0x0, ttl  64, id 0, offset 0, flags
[DF], length: 84)
ed.alcpress.com > www.course.com:
icmp 64: echo request seq 0

08:29:05.093315 IP (tos 0x0, ttl  52, id 6399, offset 0,
flags [none], length: 84)
www.course.com > ed.alcpress.com:
icmp 64: echo reply seq 0
```

The additional details include IP packet header information shown in the first line for each of the four packets. This includes the Time to Live (TTL), the Don't Fragment (DF) flag, and the length of the packet in bytes. The first two packets are UDP packets, and `tcpdump` tells you that the checksum is OK.

12

The next example shows the same four packets captured using the very verbose option (-vv). You see additional detail in the second packet—the DNS answer:

```
tcpdump -vv
tcpdump: listening on eth0, link-type EN10MB (Ethernet),
capture size 96 bytes

08:29:50.922560 IP (tos 0x0, ttl  64, id 49134, offset 0,
flags [DF], length: 60)
ed.alcpress.com.32898 > fire.alcpress.com.domain:
[udp sum ok]  56403+ A? www.course.com. (32)

08:29:50.924307 IP (tos 0x0, ttl  64, id 0, offset 0, flags
[DF], length: 76)
fire.alcpress.com.domain > ed.alcpress.com.32898: [udp sum
ok]
56403 q: A? www.course.com.
1/0/0 www.course.com. A www.course.com (48)

08:29:50.925250 IP (tos 0x0, ttl  64, id 0, offset 0, flags
[DF], length: 84)
ed.alcpress.com > www.course.com:
icmp 64: echo request seq 0

08:29:51.009548 IP (tos 0x0, ttl  52, id 20154, offset 0,
flags [none], length: 84)
www.course.com > ed.alcpress.com:
icmp 64: echo reply seq 0
```

NOTE

The −vvv option displays even more detail, but it affects only specific packets for relatively few protocols.

The −n option prevents tcpdump from resolving IP addresses to names:

```
tcpdump -vv -n
tcpdump: listening on eth0, link-type EN10MB (Ethernet),
capture size 96 bytes

08:55:38.444966 IP (tos 0x0, ttl  64, id 24205, offset 0,
flags [DF], length: 60)
69.30.87.203.32900 > 69.30.87.201.53: [udp sum ok]
1775+ A? www.course.com. (32)

08:55:38.445459 IP (tos 0x0, ttl  64, id 0, offset 0, flags
[DF], length: 76)
69.30.87.201.53 > 69.30.87.203.32900: [udp sum ok]
```

```
1775 q: A? www.course.com.
1/0/0 www.course.com. A 198.80.146.30 (48)

08:55:38.446026 IP (tos 0x0, ttl  64, id 0, offset 0, flags
[DF], length: 84)
69.30.87.203 > 198.80.146.30:
icmp 64: echo request seq 0

08:55:38.537797 IP (tos 0x0, ttl  52, id 29362, offset 0,
flags [none], length: 84)
198.80.146.30 > 69.30.87.203:
icmp 64: echo reply seq 0
```

All the packets now show the IP addresses of the hosts instead of their names. The second packet shows the IP address of *www.course.com* (198.80.146.30) instead of its name. If you want to display the names of your local hosts but the IP addresses of remote (foreign) hosts, use the –f option.

Use the –c option to capture only a given number of packets instead of continuing to capture data until interrupted. For example:

```
tcpdump -c 10
```

Use the –w option to write raw packet data to a file rather than processing it at capture time:

```
tcpdump -c 100 -w trace1
```

The file contains binary information. You can't view the captured packets with a text tool such as a text editor. You can use the tcpdump –r option to read and process previously saved data from a file:

```
tcpdump -r trace1
```

If your computer has more than one interface, you can choose the interface from which to capture packets by using the –i option. Here's how to capture packets from the eth1 interface:

```
tcpdump -i eth1
```

If you want to capture packets from all the interfaces, use the following command:

```
tcpdump -i any
```

If you're not certain which interfaces are in your computer or which ones tcpdump will work with, use the –D option, as in this example:

```
tcpdump -D
1.eth0
2.eth1
3.any (pseudodevice that captures on all interfaces)
4.lo
```

12

Normally, captured packets are decoded starting at the Network layer (IP). The –e option decodes the Data Link layer first:

```
tcpdump –e –c 1
02:03:18.435421 00:0d:87:f1:a3:ed > 0:0d:87:f0:76:1a,
ethertype IPv4 (0x0900),
length 87:
```

This is followed by the remainder of the packet decoding.

You can limit the captured packets to particular protocols, hosts, or networks by adding an expression at the end of the command line. For example, the following command only captures packets when either the source or destination port is 80:

```
tcpdump port 80
```

If you want to capture only packets with a destination port of 80, use a command like this:

```
tcpdump dst port 80
```

If you don't remember TCP and UDP port numbers for infrequently used protocols, you can use the name of the protocol that's in the /etc/services file. These two commands are equivalent:

```
tcpdump port 443
tcpdump port https
```

Suppose that you include the expression dst net 192.168.100 and port pop3. The tcpdump command then captures only packets with a destination IP address within the network 192.168.100.0, which also have a port number matching the POP3 service in /etc/services.

Many other options are described in the tcpdump documentation. The more you know about IP and related Internet protocols, the more tcpdump will aid you in troubleshooting.

Ethereal

If using tcpdump seems uncomfortable, you'll quickly appreciate **Ethereal**, a graphical network traffic analysis tool. If it's not installed on your system and you're using Fedora Core, you can add Ethereal by installing the following two packages:

```
ethereal-0.10.9-1.FC3.1
```

```
ethereal-gnome-0.10.9-1.FC3.1
```

If you're running another Linux distribution, packaged binaries are also likely to be available for your system. Visit the Ethereal home page at *www.ethereal.com* or your favorite Linux download site. To start the program, execute the command ethereal from any graphical command-line window.

TIP

The Ethereal packages also include a text-mode version called `tethereal`. The graphical version is the focus of this discussion.

Ethereal includes several configuration screens. From the Edit menu, choose Preferences to open a configuration dialog box. Figure 12-8 shows the main preferences screen.

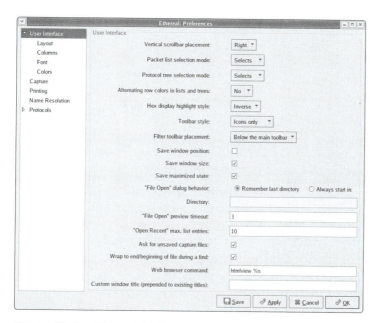

Figure 12-8 Ethereal Preferences screen

To start capturing packets, choose Start on the Capture menu. The Capture Options dialog box opens, in which you set up how the current capture session should operate. A capture session can collect a lot of data; the options in the Capture Options dialog box (shown in Figure 12-9) help you determine how best to start the capture. If you are experimenting with Ethereal, you might want to check the Update list of packets in real time check box to see what is happening from moment to moment on your network.

The Capture section lets you select the interface from which to capture packets. Like `tcpdump`, you can capture packets from all interfaces. If you choose the Limit each packet to option Ethereal will only capture the specified number of bytes instead of the entire packet. Consider using this option when you capture to files. You can specify a capture filter to restrict the packets you capture to those that match certain criteria. The filter is compatible with `tcpdump` expressions. For example, you can specify "dst port 80."

The Capture File(s) section allows you to specify the name of a file to which captured packets will be written. If you choose Use multiple files, you can specify that Ethereal will

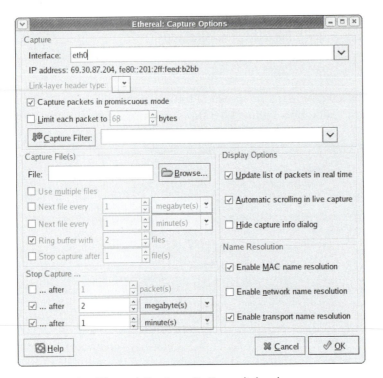

Figure 12-9   Ethereal Capture Options dialog box

close one file and use another after the file has grown to a certain size or a certain period of time has elapsed. This is useful if you're capturing packets over a long period but you want to be able to work with packets that have previously been captured. You can start another instance of Ethereal to examine the files.

When you use multiple files, the filenames will be the name you specify in the File box followed by characters that include the date and time to make the filenames unique. You can choose Ring buffer with or Stop capture after to limit the number of files that are created. The Ring buffer with option continues to capture packets, with the newer packets overwriting those in the oldest file.

The files that Ethereal writes to are compatible with `tcpdump`. You can display an Ethereal file with `tcpdump` by using the `tcpdump -r` option. Similarly, you can use Ethereal to display packets captured by `tcpdump`. In Ethereal, choose File, choose Open, and select the `tcpdump` file.

The Name Resolution section of the Capture Options dialog box controls whether names or addresses are displayed. If you select the Enable MAC name resolution option, MAC layer addresses are displayed like this:

```
Destination: 00:01:02:f0:76:1a (3com_ed:b2:dd)
```

In this example, the first half of the MAC address (00:01:02) is the vendor code for 3COM Corp., the maker of the Ethernet interface. If you choose the Enable transport name resolution option, TCP and UDP packets will have the names of their ports displayed along with the port number, like this:

```
Dst Port: domain (53)
```

If you choose the Enable network name resolution option, the reverse DNS name is displayed instead of the IP address. If an IP address has no DNS PTR record, the address is displayed instead of a name.

The Stop Capture section of the Capture Options dialog box allows you to specify that Ethereal will automatically stop capturing packets based on three criteria:

- After a certain number of packets have been captured
- After a certain amount of packet data has been captured
- After a certain amount of time has passed

Figure 12-9 shows that two of the criteria have been selected. Packet capturing will stop after 2 MB of packet data has been captured or after one minute.

After a capture is started from the Capture menu, you see the Ethereal Capture screen shown in Figure 12-10. This screen shows a graphical depiction of the number of captured packets by major protocol. The figure shows that 401 packets are TCP, 40 are UDP, 27 are ICMP, and three are ARP.

12

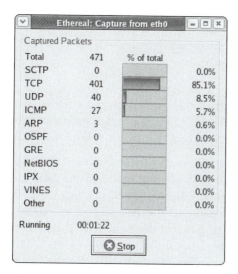

Figure 12-10   Ethereal Capture screen

Figure 12-11 shows a sample capture in progress. The window is divided into three main sections. The top section lists packets. If you are running the capture in promiscuous mode (the default operation), these packets may be passing between any two computers on your network. Each line of data in the top window describes the protocol of the packet, when it was sent, the source and destination addresses on the packet, and additional notes about the packet.

If you don't set up a filter, either by protocol or by host, the packet list can grow to thousands of lines in a matter of moments.

CAUTION

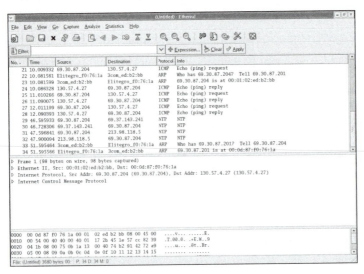

Figure 12-11 Main Ethereal window

You can right-click any line in the top part of the window to see a menu of options for processing the selected packet. For example, you can mark a packet for review later, print its contents, or open one packet in a separate window. This menu is shown in Figure 12-12.

When you select a packet in the top section of the main Ethereal window, the middle section contains *all* the headers from the packet. For example, you can click the small triangle next to the Ethernet II item in this section to see the Ethernet headers. The line labeled Internet Protocol includes the source and destination addresses for the packet; if you click the triangle to the left of this line, you see all the other IP header information for the packet. If you are viewing a TCP packet, you also see a line labeled Transmission Control Protocol that includes the port used by the packet and other relevant information. By clicking the triangle next to this line, you can see all TCP header information, including the state of each flag within the packet (recall the brief discussion about TCP flags earlier in this chapter). Figure 12-13 shows this header information section expanded. (You can click and drag the bar between sections in the Ethereal window to resize each section as needed.)

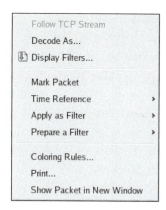

Figure 12-12 Ethereal packet menu

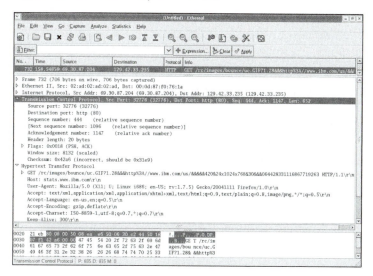

12

Figure 12-13 Viewing packet header information in Ethereal

The bottom section of the main Ethereal window contains the data within the packet—the payload. Packet data is shown in both numeric (hexadecimal) and character formats. This section is where you see users' secrets if they are not using secure protocols. (For an example, see Hands-On Project 12-4.) Figure 12-14 shows a packet capture from an HTTP connection in progress. Notice that the text shows HTTP headers within the packet.

TIP

The Telnet protocol is a popular choice when experimenting with a packet sniffer. If you try it, note that Telnet sends each character that a user types as a separate packet. To see the password that a user enters, you'll need to assemble data from a series of packets.

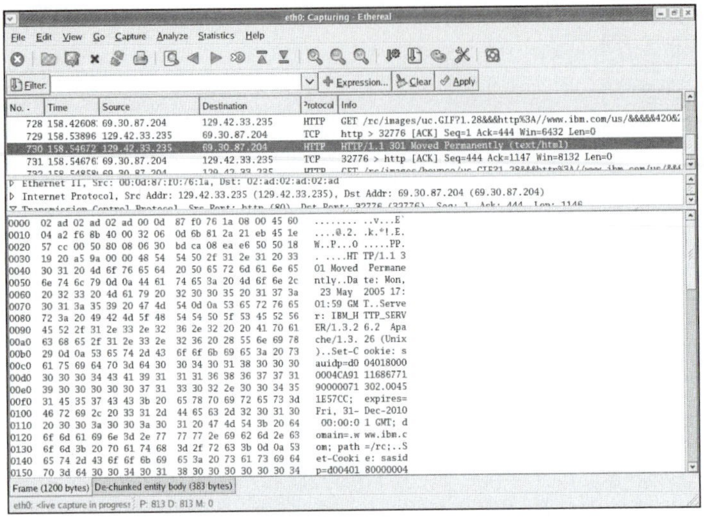

Figure 12-14   Packet data captured in Ethereal

Ethereal also includes several statistical tools similar to those offered by IPTraf. For example, you can view graphs of packets received by time unit, or see a percentage breakdown of packets by protocol. This latter feature is shown in Figure 12-15. Here, 100 percent of the packets are from IP (as opposed to IPX, for example), but within IP, some are TCP and some are ICMP. Further breakdowns by higher-level protocols are also available.

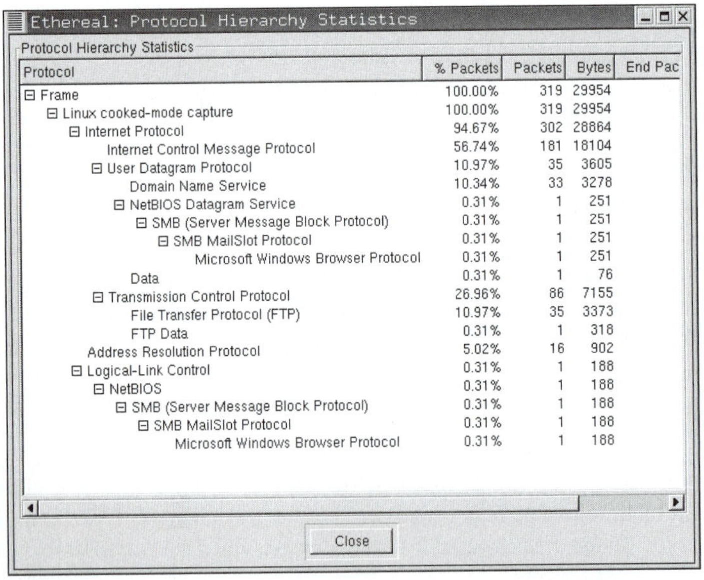

Figure 12-15   Protocol analysis by percentage in Ethereal

You should become familiar with the use of Ethereal, a powerful tool for network troubleshooting as well as for locating potential security problems. If watching other people's data stream by on your screen for a few minutes doesn't convince you to use encrypted protocols, perhaps nothing else will. Dozens of different packet sniffers are available for Linux. Some are graphical, like Ethereal, or the KDE-based program, `ksnuffle`. Others are text based, such as `ettercap` (see *ettercap.sourceforge.net*). To research what is available, start by searching for "sniff" at *freshmeat.net*.

USING INTRUSION-DETECTION SOFTWARE

Using a port scanner, installing a rootkit, and performing other intrusive network activities leave a trace that a skilled network administrator can find. Logs sometimes contain the necessary details, but often the intrusion must be seen by monitoring activity in real time. The process of noticing an attempted or successful break-in to your system is called **intrusion detection**. This section introduces several software tools that help you track and prevent break-ins by watching for signs of impending attack, and taking preventive action when possible. This category of software is called an **intrusion-detection system (IDS)**.

Some IDSs can be configured to try to block an attack when one is detected. Such systems are called intrusion-prevention systems or IPSs.

PortSentry

A port scanner is a popular way for crackers to examine a remote host and determine what methods of attack are most likely to succeed. Network administrators can install a program called **PortSentry** that watches network ports for packets that appear to be port scans, and then takes action based on a configuration file. PortSentry is free software that you can download from *www.sourceforge.net/projects/sentrytools*. PortSentry includes the following features:

- It detects **stealth scans**—port scans that use unexpected flag combinations, including SYN, FIN, none **(null scan)**, and all (Xmas scan).

- The response based on your configuration can include blocking the scanning system by immediately adding it to a packet filter (such as IP Chains or IP Tables) with the DENY instruction, so that the scanning system cannot receive any reply packets of any type from your host.

- Any activity that appears to be a scan is logged so that you can review it. This feature is intended to be used in conjunction with `logcheck`, LogSentry, or a similar program, so that all logged security events are viewed in a coordinated way.

- Systems that have attempted even minimal scanlike activities are recorded by the software so that a port scanner trying to randomize its scan is still likely to be blocked before many ports are contacted.

12

Although PortSentry can be used as part of an intrusion-detection strategy, it is not a true intrusion-detection system.

NOTE

Snort

Snort is the best-known open source intrusion-detection system. It can operate in four modes:

- Sniffer mode
- Packet logger mode
- Network IDS mode
- Inline mode

Each mode is described in this section. For example, Sniffer mode is similar to using tcpdump. You run the program and see decoded packet headers on the screen. In the following example, only one packet is shown:

```
snort -v
06/03-13:09:16.074942 90.0.0.16:1900 -> 239.255.255.250:1900
UDP TTL:4 TOS:0x0 ID:10156 IpLen:20 DgmLen:287
Len: 259
```

If you want to see the data portion of packets as well, use the –d switch:

```
snort -vd
06/03-13:12:10.133449 90.0.0.29:1160 -> 90.0.0.1:139
TCP TTL:128 TOS:0x0 ID:48610 IpLen:20 DgmLen:93 DF
***AP*** Seq: 0x99D18292  Ack: 0x3AC75832  Win: 0xFE8C
TcpLen: 20
00 00 00 31 FF 53 4D 42 2B 00 00 00 00 18 43 C0
...1.SMB+.....C.
00 00 00 00 00 00 00 00 00 00 00 00 FF FF FF FE
................
00 00 FE FF 01 01 00 0C 00 4A 6C 4A 6D 49 68 43
.........JlJmIhC
6C 42 73 72 00                                      lBsr.
```

The –e switch shows the Data Link layer headers:

```
snort -vde
06/03-13:17:47.650842 0:40:CA:54:C2:A6 -> FF:FF:FF:FF:FF:FF
type:0x800 len:0x104
192.168.0.17:138 -> 192.168.0.255:138 UDP TTL:128 TOS:0x0
ID:45205 IpLen:20 DgmLen:246
Len: 218
11 02 E8 75 C0 A8 00 11 00 8A 00 CC 00 00 20 46
...u.......... F
```

```
45 45 4A 45 48 45 46 46 43 43 41 43 41 43 41 43
EEJEHEFFCCACACAC
41 43 41 43 41 43 41 43 41 43 41 43 41 43 41 00
ACACACACACACACA.
20 46 41 45 45 46 49 43 41 43 41 43 41 43 41 43
 FAEEFICACACACAC
41 43 41 43 41 43 41 43 41 43 41 43 41 43 41 42
ACACACACACACACAB
4E 00 FF 53 4D 42 25 00 00 00 00 00 00 00 00 00
N..SMB%.........
00 00 00 00 00 00 00 00 00 00 00 00 00 00 00 00
................
00 00 11 00 00 32 00 00 00 00 00 00 00 00 00 E8
.....2..........
03 00 00 00 00 00 00 00 00 32 00 56 00 03 00 01
.........2.V....
00 00 00 02 00 43 00 5C 4D 41 49 4C 53 4C 4F 54
.....C.\MAILSLOT
5C 42 52 4F 57 53 45 00 01 00 80 FC 0A 00 54 49
\BROWSE.......TI
47 45 52 00 72 00 70 00 63 00 3A 00 5B 00 05 01
GER.r.p.c.:.[...
03 12 01 00 0F 01 55 AA 42 72 75 63 65 27 73 20
......U.Bruce's
63 6F 6D 70 75 74 65 72 2E 00                    computer..
```

The next mode in Snort, Packet logger mode, is more interesting. Captured packets are saved to disk, but not in the same way that tcpdump saves them. Instead of saving all captured packets to one file, Snort sorts them by IP address and saves them in a directory structure. When you run Snort, you specify the directory:

```
snort -ve -l /var/log/snort
```

The -d switch was not used here, to conserve disk space. Within the /var/log/snort directory, there are subdirectories whose names are the IP addresses of captured packets:

```
ls -l /var/log/snort
drwxr-xr-x  21 snort  snort  4096 Jun  3 13:34 .
drwxr-xr-x  12 root   root   4096 Jun  3 07:35 ..
drwx------   2 root   root   4096 Jun  3 13:29 192.168.0.17
drwx------   2 root   root   4096 Jun  3 13:29 192.168.0.21
drwx------   2 root   root   4096 Jun  3 13:30 192.168.0.24
drwx------   2 root   root   4096 Jun  3 13:34 192.168.0.25
drwx------   2 root   root   4096 Jun  3 13:33 192.168.0.26
drwx------   2 root   root   4096 Jun  3 13:28 192.168.0.28
drwx------   2 root   root   4096 Jun  3 13:33 192.168.0.3
drwx------   2 root   root   4096 Jun  3 13:33 192.168.0.32
drwx------   2 root   root   4096 Jun  3 13:33 192.168.0.35
drwx------   2 root   root   4096 Jun  3 13:32 192.168.0.36
drwx------   2 root   root   4096 Jun  3 13:34 192.168.0.37
drwx------   2 root   root   4096 Jun  3 13:28 192.168.0.38
```

12

```
drwx------    2 root   root   4096 Jun   3 13:30 192.168.0.39
drwx------    2 root   root   4096 Jun   3 13:33 192.168.0.4
drwx------    2 root   root   4096 Jun   3 13:31 192.168.0.5
drwx------    2 root   root   4096 Jun   3 13:29 192.168.0.6
drwx------    2 root   root   4096 Jun   3 13:33 192.168.0.7
drwx------    2 root   root   4096 Jun   3 13:32 224.0.1.55
drwx------    2 root   root   4096 Jun   3 13:31 255.255.255.255
-rw-------    1 root   root   3401 Jun   3 13:34 ARP
-rw-------    1 root   root      0 Jun   3 13:28 PACKET_NONIP
```

Each directory contains files that include captured packets. The names of the files are listed by protocol and source-destination port:

```
ls -l /var/log/snort/192.168.0.38
drwx------    2 root    root   4096 Jun   3 13:33 .
drwxr-xr-x   21 snort   snort  4096 Jun   3 13:34 ..
-rw-------    1 root    root    247 Jun   3 13:30 UDP:137-137
-rw-------    1 root    root    250 Jun   3 13:33 UDP:138-138
-rw-------    1 root    root    496 Jun   3 13:33 TCP:33826-80
```

Because packets have both source and destination addresses, Snort might use either to create the directories. Of course, it would be best if the directory name was the remote IP address, not addresses on the local network Snort is monitoring. This is achieved with the –h switch, followed by the local network address:

```
snort -ve -l /var/log/snort -h 192.168.0.0/24
```

Using the –b switch, Snort lets you save packets in a binary form that's compatible with tcpdump and Ethereal. You don't have to specify the –v and –e switches because the entire packet is captured. You also don't have to specify the local network address:

```
snort -b -l /var/log/snort
```

You can read these binary files using tcpdump, Ethereal, or Snort with the –r switch. All three programs let you use filters to display only the packets you're interested in. This example displays only ICMP packets using Snort:

```
snort -ver /var/log/snort/capture1 icmp
```

The third mode in Snort, Network IDS mode, is used for intrusion detection. In this mode, Snort monitors all packets and matches them against a set of rules. The rules are written to detect known attacks. Before you run Snort in this mode, you should edit the snort.conf file, which is commonly in the /etc/snort directory. You start Snort in Network IDS mode as follows:

```
snort -d -l /var/log/snort/ -h 192.168.0.0/24 \
-c snort.conf
```

This command produces a long list of output lines that are similar to the following:

```
Initializing rule chains...
,----------[Flow Config]--------------------
| Stats Interval:  0
| Hash Method:     2
| Memcap:          10485760
| Rows  :          4099
| Overhead Bytes:  16400(%0.16)
`-----------------------------------------------
No arguments to frag2 directive, setting defaults to:
    Fragment timeout: 60 seconds
    Fragment memory cap: 4194304 bytes
    Fragment min_ttl:   0
    Fragment ttl_limit: 5
    Fragment Problems: 0
    Self preservation threshold: 500
    Self preservation period: 90
    Suspend threshold: 1000
    Suspend period: 30
Stream4 config:
    Stateful inspection: ACTIVE
    Session statistics: INACTIVE
    Session timeout: 30 seconds
    Session memory cap: 8388608 bytes
    State alerts: INACTIVE
    Evasion alerts: INACTIVE
    Scan alerts: INACTIVE
    Log Flushed Streams: INACTIVE
    MinTTL: 1
    TTL Limit: 5
    Async Link: 0
    State Protection: 0
    Self preservation threshold: 50
    Self preservation period: 90
    Suspend threshold: 200
    Suspend period: 30
```

When Snort starts in intrusion-detection mode, it creates a file called `alert` in the /var/log/snort directory. Monitor this file so Snort can notify you of possible attacks.

Snort comes with a set of rules that cover many common attacks. The rules are located in a directory such as /etc/snort/rules. You'll find many files there, and each one has rules for a certain type of attack. The rules can be complicated to write, so most people use only the rules that come with Snort. Of course, new attacks are developed frequently; you can download new rules if you register with the Snort Web site. The author of Snort has formed a company that sells subscriptions to new Snort rules. Subscribers receive new rules automatically, five days before nonsubscribers.

12

Inline mode is Snort's intrusion-prevention mode. It works with Linux netfilter and `iptables` to accept or drop packets based on Snort rules, thus actively blocking attacks as they occur. Inline mode is beyond the scope of this book; for more information, visit the Snort Web site at *www.snort.org*.

Host-based Intrusion-detection Systems

PortSentry and Snort are examples of network intrusion-detection and prevention systems. Another type of system detects similar problems with computers or hosts—host intrusion-detection systems or HIDS.

HIDS have the same type of problem that virus scanners have. A host that is suspected of being compromised is asked to diagnose itself, so you can never truly trust the result. In the Linux world, HIDS are generally more than detection systems—they're also intrusion-prevention systems. In this section, you will learn about software and techniques that go well beyond simple intrusion detection.

LIDS

LIDS (or **Linux Intrusion-detection System**) is based on the premise that the root user in Linux is too powerful. If a cracker gets root access, she can do many things to cover her tracks, as well as read and destroy anything on the system at will. LIDS adds a module to the Linux kernel that blocks access to resources for all users—including root—except as configured by LIDS. Specific features of LIDS include the following:

- Port scanner detection within the kernel
- The ability to hide files completely or make them read-only, even to root
- The ability to hide processes completely or block which other processes can send signals to them (effectively blocking the use of the `kill` command to stop or restart an application)
- **Access control lists (ACLs)**, data structures that define access to individual directories and individual programs by specific users or groups
- Time-based restrictions, meaning that a task can only be performed or a file accessed during specific times of the day (this is similar to features offered by services like Pluggable Authentication Modules, but LIDS performs this directly in the Linux kernel)

To download LIDS, visit *sourceforge.net/projects/lids*. LIDS includes a kernel patch and a set of configuration files that are stored in `/etc/lids`. These files are completely hidden when LIDS is running.

CAUTION

Installing and using LIDS requires significant knowledge of the Linux kernel. You can learn about LIDS and how it operates by reviewing the documentation for the LIDS project, but only experienced Linux users should expect to use LIDS effectively. Because of its complexity, you should carefully test the LIDS software before running it on a production server.

NOTE

After LIDS is installed, you can start Linux without using LIDS by adding `security=0` as a kernel boot parameter to the LILO or GRUB boot prompt.

After you install LIDS, you configure it by defining ACLs for files and directories and capabilities for processes that are permitted. A **capability** is a task that the Linux kernel permits a program to perform. LIDS defines several dozen capabilities as used by a default Linux kernel (the capability concept is part of Linux kernel programming terminology). Examples of capabilities include the ability to send broadcast packets to the network and the ability to use the `reboot` command. LIDS also adds a few nonstandard capabilities. To define an ACL for a file or directory, or a capability for a process, use the **lidsadm** command (for "LIDS administration"). This command has a format similar to the `ipchains` command that you've used previously in this book. As with `ipchains` commands, you normally configure a LIDS system by including a number of `lidsadm` commands in the Linux start-up files (such as in `/etc/rc.local`). At the end of this configuration loading process, you include the following command to seal the kernel. After LIDS has sealed the kernel, the LIDS configurations are in effect. No program can then perform any action that is not permitted by your LIDS configuration.

```
lidsadm -I
```

Popular system services may rely on a number of capabilities and other programs to perform their functions. For this reason, it's important to read the LIDS documentation carefully and experiment with your own configuration before attempting to run LIDS on a production server.

After the kernel is sealed, you can still alter the configuration of ACLs and capabilities by starting a **LIDS-free session (LFS)**. This is a command-line session that is free of LIDS restrictions, so you can do anything you choose, just like root could before you installed LIDS. To start an LFS, use this command:

```
lidsadm -S -- -LIDS
```

You must enter the LIDS password you defined during initial LIDS configuration to enter a LIDS-free session. Entering an LFS is similar in concept to using the `su` command to gain access to the root user on a standard Linux system. The difference with LIDS is that you must have both the root password and the LIDS password to access resources to which LIDS has restricted access.

12

Big Brother

A comprehensive program that provides a different level of intrusion detection from LIDS is **Big Brother**. Big Brother uses a client/server model that is similar in some ways to the Simple Network Management Protocol (SNMP) described in earlier chapters. Big Brother includes a server that gathers data from clients on each host within your network. You can define redundant components to make certain that network status information remains available if one part of your system fails.

The results from each client are gathered by the server and displayed as a Web page. Color-coded dots identify the status of each service on each host, which lets you see immediately where attention is needed. Some of the 26 standard services that Big Brother manages include the following:

- DNS
- FTP
- HTTP
- POP3
- SSH
- Telnet

In addition to these services, system resources such as disk space, memory usage, and swap space are tracked. You can use the plug-in architecture to develop new modules that help you monitor any part of your system you need to track remotely. For example, if you have database applications running or need to monitor instruments that are feeding data to a remote system, you could write a Big Brother module to help you keep an eye on that service through Big Brother's Web page on your main server.

Figure 12-16 shows a demonstration Web page from the Big Brother Web site, *www.bb4.org*. You can download Big Brother source code free of charge for Linux and other server platforms. Commercial users need to purchase a license (10 percent of the price is donated to charity). Clients that can interact with the Big Brother server are available for many platforms, including UNIX, Windows 2000, NetWare, Macintosh, AS/400, and OpenVMS.

Big Brother is not as challenging to install as LIDS—you won't need to recompile the kernel. But it will require an hour or two to review the documentation and to get the server and a few clients installed and communicating correctly. Big Brother does not detect intruders in the same way as LIDS or PortSentry. Instead, Big Brother informs you if one of your services is no longer operating or otherwise requires attention (for example, if the hard disks on a remote system are almost full).

Big Brother works best as part of a set of intrusion-detection tools. For example:

- Use nmap to carefully scan your system after you have configured it to see whether any security holes are found.

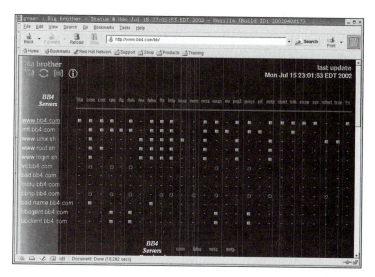

Figure 12-16   A sample of a Big Brother resource management Web page

- Next, use PortSentry to watch for outside hosts trying to port scan your server. Block these hosts using IP Chains or IP Tables, perhaps with the help of a free commercial firewall configuration and management tool.

- Use LIDS to secure your filesystem and processes so that anyone who gains unauthorized access has limited power, even with the root password.

- Use Big Brother to keep a constant eye on services that you are providing on all of your network servers. If anyone causes a problem despite your other efforts (or just because of a nonintrusive computer error), you will know about it immediately and can take corrective action.

NOTE When crackers defaced the Web pages of *USA Today* in July 2002, the fake news stories—including one falsely describing a military attack—were online for 15 minutes before someone alerted the network administrator. The Web site was shut down for three hours while repairs and needed upgrades were made. (The site was running Microsoft's Internet Information Server on Windows 2000.)

Tripwire

Tripwire is an intrusion-detection tool that detects unauthorized changes to files or directories. Assuming that your system is not compromised when you install Tripwire, you can use it to scan your filesystem(s) and compute a cryptographic checksum for all files that should not normally change. After this first scan, you set Tripwire to scan the system periodically, searching for files whose checksum or other characteristics have changed.

Besides the initial checksum, Tripwire also checks file access times, modification times, creation times, permissions, attributes, user owner, group owner, number of links, and other properties. You configure Tripwire by creating a configuration file that specifies which files and directories to watch and which characteristics to check. Then, run the program and tell it to generate the initial database:

```
tripwire -c tripwire.conf -init
```

After the database is created, you must move it to a "secure" place so an attacker can't change it, thus neutering Tripwire's ability to detect changes to files. The problem, of course, is that a truly secure place doesn't exist, short of burning the database to a CD. Some administrators store the database on a 3.5-inch disk or USB memory device and then remove it from the system when it's not being used. The medium must be inserted and mounted before the Tripwire program runs again. This is a problem if you want to run Tripwire from a cron job.

To run a normal scan, use a command similar to the following one. Your database name might be different:

```
tripwire -c tripwire.conf -d /mnt/usb/tw.db
```

If you update files that Tripwire is monitoring, you'll have to notify Tripwire. One way is to use the interactive method:

```
tripwire -c tripwire.conf -d /mnt/usb/tw.db -interactive
```

When Tripwire finds files that have changed, you'll be prompted for an action.

NOTE

The preceding section discussed the open source version of Tripwire, which is available at *sourceforge.net/projects/tripwire*. A commercial version of Tripwire is sold by Tripwire, Inc., and is available at *www.tripwire.com*.

Sealed Systems

Sealed systems are not a security tool. Rather, they are a different way of building Linux-based systems that make them highly resistant to attack. In a sense, they are intrusion-prevention systems built in to the computer system. The core idea is that all programs, static data files, and boilerplate configuration files exist in an immutable filesystem, which cannot easily be changed by either a system user or an attacker.

Sealed systems boot from a trusted boot device, which may be a CD, DVD, or write-protected USB memory device. After the operating system boots, it checks the immutable filesystem (typically stored on a hard disk) with a cryptographic checksum to ensure that it has not been changed while the sealed system has not been running.

Sealed systems offer other benefits besides security, such as rapid deployment and updating, locked-down desktops, and easier backups. For more information, go to *www.sealedsystems.us*.

System Security Audits

After you have used one or more of the utilities described so far in this chapter, you might start to feel fairly confident about the security of your Linux system. The best way to test that confidence is to perform a **security audit**, a review or test of how secure your system really is and what needs to be done to improve its security. Such an audit can take many forms. For example, if you work in an organization that has a well-defined security policy, one type of security audit would consist of a careful review of the policy to see where the systems, system administrators, management team, or end users fall short. This would help to fix procedural problems that might lead to security weaknesses. For example, if management has not fully supported security-related training programs, or system administrators have not installed software that the policy required, corrections could be made before a serious lapse in security occurred.

Another type of security audit is provided by special security-auditing software. These programs use a long list of known security holes, cracker techniques, and networking savvy to poke into every nook and cranny of your networked systems. You receive a detailed report of the problems discovered. Basically, a software security audit performs an attack on your networked computers, letting you know where the weaknesses are. The report might describe the following problems:

- You have not upgraded to the latest software for your DNS server. The version you are using is vulnerable to several known attacks.

- You have not turned off e-mail relaying, which can lead to spammers bouncing e-mail off your system.

- Your firewall has not blocked access to several unneeded ports that are commonly used by cracker-oriented software.

- You are providing Telnet service, which is considered an insecure protocol for remote access.

- An attempt to use r-utilities permitted unauthorized access to some files on your system.

- You permit any host to connect to and use your X server for remote application display.

- Anonymous users can upload files into your FTP directories.

- Filesystems have been exported using NFS without any limiting security parameters.

- A recent advisory from CERT has not been implemented on your system.

One of the first security-auditing programs was called the **Security Administrator Tool for Analyzing Networks (SATAN)**. As with many other program names, the acronym was chosen first and the full name second, but the name did its job: It created a stir in the news and helped to publicize the need for such a tool. You can review this project at *www.porcupine.org/satan/*, but it is no longer in development and has been superseded by a more highly evolved program: the **Security Administrator's Integrated Network Tool (SAINT)**.

SAINT uses a Web browser interface to manage an "attack" on your network and report the vulnerabilities it finds. It is similar to using a port scanner to locate potentially open network ports; SAINT uses different methods and looks for different vulnerabilities than the nmap tool. Figure 12-17 shows some of the configuration options you can set up before beginning a security sweep using SAINT.

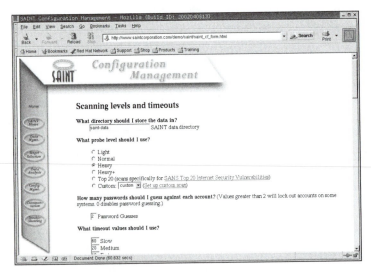

Figure 12-17   Configuring options in SAINT

After auditing (scanning) systems that you have designated, SAINT reports different levels of existing or potential security problems. These are color-coded red, yellow, brown, or green. Reported results in SAINT are correlated with the SANS and FBI Top 20 Vulnerabilities list discussed in Chapter 7. Figures 12-18 and 12-19 show sample Web pages with summary categories and more detailed results that SAINT has reported after performing a security audit.

SAINT was formerly a free software project, but as with many of the tools presented in this book, it has been commercialized to some degree. In the case of SAINT, you must purchase a license before you can obtain the software. To learn about SAINT, go to *www. saintcorporation.com*. The Web site contains quotes from satisfied customers, documentation excerpts, and demos to show you what the product will do.

Another security audit program is an open source scanner called Nessus. You can learn more about it at *www.nessus.org*. Click the DEMO link to see the graphical screens used to configure and initiate the security scans.

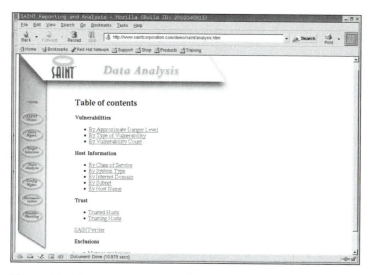

Figure 12-18   Data categories from a security audit using SAINT

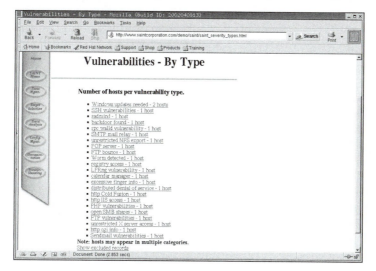

Figure 12-19   Detailed results from a security audit using SAINT

Many other security audit tools are available. Some are free, such as the Tiger and SARA projects (see *freshmeat.net*). Others are expensive commercial tools, complete with consulting services and real-time updates when new vulnerabilities are discovered. Several of these commercial products are mentioned in the list of security products at *www.insecure.org/tools.html*.

CHAPTER SUMMARY

❑ Port-scanning software lets anyone learn about potentially vulnerable network access points on any networked computer. Port scans can use many techniques, but the goal is always to learn about the host being scanned, such as what programs are listening for traffic on a certain port number.

❑ Port scanners use various combinations of TCP flags, UDP packets, and `ping` packets to elicit responses that inform the scanner about services running on the targeted host. Part of the response also permits a good port scanner to identify the type of operating system running on the target.

❑ The most popular port-scanning software is `nmap`. Graphical utilities are available as front ends to `nmap`. Many other port scanners are also available.

❑ Packet sniffers use the promiscuous mode of a NIC to capture all data passing through that node of the network, including all headers and payloads (packet data).

❑ Packet sniffing is just one type—though the most comprehensive—of network traffic analysis. Other programs such as IPTraf help network administrators analyze network traffic patterns based on protocol, point of origin or destination, and other factors.

❑ The `tcpdump` program is a popular packet capturing and decoding program that captures detailed information about network packets.

❑ Ethereal is a powerful and popular graphical packet capturing and decoding program that uses the same capture filters as `tcpdump`. If you know how to use either program, it will take little effort to learn the other.

❑ Ethereal and `tcpdump` use the same data file formats. You can capture packets with the nongraphical `tcpdump` program and examine the packets with the graphical Ethereal program.

❑ Intrusion-detection systems (IDSs) are an important part of modern network security. These software products watch for signs of intruders trying to access your servers and help you respond appropriately.

❑ PortSentry is one piece of IDS software that detects port scans from programs like `nmap`. A more comprehensive IDS package is LIDS, which alters the Linux kernel so that even the root user does not have complete access to files and processes. Therefore, even if an intruder gets root access, she cannot control the server.

❑ Snort is the best-known open source intrusion-detection system.

❑ Big Brother is a simpler IDS that watches the status of network services on multiple servers through a Web page interface.

❑ Tripwire is an intrusion-detection tool that detects unauthorized changes to files or directories.

❑ Security audits using security policies or specialized software can help network administrators see potential security problems and fix them before someone else finds them.

❑ One popular security-auditing software tool is SAINT. Many others are available as well.

Key Terms

access control list (ACL) — A data structure that defines the access permitted for individual directories and individual programs.

Big Brother — An intrusion-detection program that uses a client/server model to gather network service and host resource data from numerous hosts on a network and report that data in a browser-based interface.

capability — A task that the Linux kernel permits a program to perform, such as the ability to send broadcast packets to the network and the ability to use the `reboot` command.

Ethereal — A powerful, graphical network traffic analysis tool.

fingerprinting — Using the results of a port scan to identify the operating system of a targeted host.

flags — The numeric status indications stored within a packet header that are used to establish and track information about the network communication of which the packet is a part.

intrusion detection — The process of noticing an attempted or successful break-in to a system.

intrusion-detection system (IDS) — A type of software that aids network intrusion detection.

IPTraf — A popular "packet sniffer" program for viewing network activity on a LAN.

libpcap — A programming library used for capturing network packets, required by many network traffic analysis utilities.

LIDS-free session (LFS) — A command-line session on a system running LIDS, in which LIDS does not affect the permitted actions.

lidsadm — The administrative command used to control LIDS.

Linux Intrusion-Detection System (LIDS) — A complex and hard-to-use intrusion-detection system that alters the Linux kernel to remove root's comprehensive access to a Linux system.

network traffic analysis — *See* packet sniffing.

nmap — The most widely used port-scanning utility.

nmapfe — A utility that acts as a graphical front end to the `nmap` command; requires the GNOME desktop.

null scan — A method of port scanning in which a TCP packet is sent with no flags set.

packet sniffing — A network activity in which the headers and payload of all packets on the network are captured and examined (also called network traffic analysis).

ping scan — A method of port scanning in which any hosts that are reachable using ICMP echo packets (which are used to ping a host) are reported.

port scanning — A network activity in which packets sent to a host are analyzed to learn about that host.

12

PortSentry — A program that watches network ports for packets that appear to be port scans, then takes action based on a configuration file.

promiscuous mode — A mode of operation for NICs in which any packets that are visible to the NIC are captured and processed, not only those that are addressed to the NIC.

randomization — A method of performing a port scan in which multiple ports are contacted in random order to reduce suspicion.

Security Administrator Tool for Analyzing Networks (SATAN) — One of the first widely known security-auditing programs.

Security Administrator's Integrated Network Tool (SAINT) — A popular security-auditing program that superseded the SATAN program.

security audit — A review or test of how secure a system really is and what needs to be done to improve its security.

Snort — A well-known open source intrusion-detection system.

stealth scan — A port scan that uses unexpected TCP flag combinations, including SYN, FIN, none (null scan), and all (Xmas scan) flags.

SYN packet — A TCP packet sent from a port scanner that has the SYN flag set.

tcpdump — A command-line utility that provides detailed information about packets on a network.

Tripwire — An intrusion-detection tool that detects unauthorized changes to files or directories.

Xmas scan — A method of port scanning in which all flags in the TCP header are turned on (set).

REVIEW QUESTIONS

1. Which of the following statements is true?

   a. A port scanner cannot obtain useful knowledge of a host unless the host responds to a SYN packet.

   b. When a host returns a SYN+ACK packet to a port scanner, this indicates that the sending port can easily be used to gain access to the targeted system.

   c. Even receiving no response at all informs a port scanner about how a targeted host is processing packets sent to a particular port.

   d. Only a null scan should be used on Linux systems.

2. Describe a possible problem when reviewing Telnet packets in a packet sniffer.

3. Fingerprinting of operating systems is possible because:

   a. Most operating systems do not adhere strictly to the detailed standards for networking protocols.

   b. All operating systems are required to report certain information in the networking packets that they propagate.

c. Few networks are inherently as secure as network administrators believe.

d. Most operating systems cannot detect a port scan and so respond with the information necessary to fingerprint the system.

4. Fingerprinting an operating system helps a cracker because:

   a. It defines exactly what software you have installed.

   b. It opens a security-delayed window based on the port being scanned.

   c. It informs the cracker of which vulnerabilities he may be able to exploit on your system.

   d. It doesn't depend on the patches that have been applied to fix existing security holes.

5. A program that defends against a port scanner will attempt to:

   a. Update a firewall rule in real time to prevent the port scan from being completed.

   b. Send back bogus data to the port scanner.

   c. Limit access by the scanning system to publicly available ports only.

   d. Log a violation and recommend use of security-auditing tools.

6. A distributed port scan operates by:

   a. using denial-of-service software against a range of TCP ports

   b. having multiple computers each scan a small number of ports, then correlating the results

   c. blocking access to the targeted host by each of the distributed scanning clients

   d. blocking access to the scanning clients by the targeted host

7. An nmap command that included the host specification of 192.129.34-35.* would scan how many different hosts?

   a. 512

   b. 2

   c. 256

   d. more than 10,000

8. Name three graphical utilities used with nmap.

9. One unusual feature of the nmapfe program is that it:

   a. only includes a limited set of functionality compared to the command-line utility

   b. uses the same graphical interface as Ethereal

   c. can be used on both GNOME and KDE desktops without additional software

   d. includes a line illustrating the command-line parameters that correspond to your selections in the graphical interface

12

10. Which of the following is not a valid reason for using a packet sniffer?

    a. troubleshooting stubborn networking problems

    b. creating statistical data about the protocols being used on your network

    c. auditing security procedures at the managerial level

    d. studying the capacity and bandwidth of the network to plan for upgrades

11. Using a packet sniffer requires root access in Linux because:

    a. Only root should be able to see the payload of other users' packets.

    b. Only root can operate network cards in promiscuous mode.

    c. Any packet available on the network cable requires the root password to access it.

    d. Tools such as nmap and Ethereal are always run as SetUID.

12. Which of the following can protect users' data from packet-sniffing software, even on an internal network?

    a. nmap and tcpdump

    b. SARA or SAINT

    c. IPTraf or PAM

    d. SSH and GPG

13. Which of the following would help you diagnose which user was consuming an inordinate amount of network bandwidth if the network slowed down significantly?

    a. the packet payload section of the Ethereal main window

    b. the timing options in nmap

    c. any of the security-auditing tools, particularly a strong commercial tool like SAINT

    d. the LAN station monitor item in IPTraf

14. Which tcpdump option lets you use data from a previously saved file containing packet data instead of looking at new packets on the network?

    a. -r

    b. -o

    c. --old

    d. -c

15. Using a filter or configuration setting to limit which packets are captured by Ethereal is generally a good idea because:

    a. Without an appropriate filter, firewall rules may block the packets that would be most useful in the traffic analysis.

    b. A busy network can generate thousands of packets per second, which may be too much data to easily find what you're looking for.

   c. Only the packets that are included in the filter are shown onscreen; therefore, if a filter is not configured, the traffic needed for the analysis will probably be missed.

   d. Other utilities such as nmap and tcpdump rely on the filters used by Ethereal to control their interaction with the network administrator.

16. The header information displayed in the middle section of Ethereal includes:

   a. TCP flags

   b. IP source and destination addresses plus TCP flags

   c. application-specific protocol headers plus UDP headers

   d. complete header information for each protocol contained in the packet

17. Define an Xmas scan.

18. Explain the meaning of IDS.

19. Describe how time-based logon restrictions are implemented differently in LIDS versus PAM.

20. How is an LFS different from using the su command to gain root access?

21. Which of the following would not be part of a security audit?

   a. using a program such as SAINT

   b. checking whether end users were complying with the security policy

   c. reviewing old security advisories on CERT/CC

   d. determining whether system software had been upgraded as required by the security policy

22. Big Brother complements other security tools by:

   a. implementing port scans, security-auditing functions, and packet sniffing in a single program

   b. supporting plug-in modules that also work with SAINT

   c. tracking whether network services and resources on multiple servers are running smoothly or require attention

   d. displaying its results in a color-coded Web page format

23. An important benefit of making a program like SAINT available only for a large fee may be that:

   a. Crackers are less likely to use it to identify the vulnerabilities of other users' systems.

   b. Management is more likely to take it seriously as a security tool.

   c. Only commercial programs are continually enhanced when new security issues arise.

   d. End users will feel more comfortable knowing that commercial tools are being used to protect the network.

24. Describe the function of PortSentry.

12

HANDS-ON PROJECTS

The projects presented here assume that you are working in a lab environment. **If you are working on a production server or one that contains sensitive data, do not attempt the following projects.**

The steps that follow assume you are working on a network with a 24-bit network ID: Network addresses in the example commands use "/24" (based on the CIDR address format). If your network uses a different network ID length, you should modify the "/24" in the commands to match your network ID length.

Project 12-1

In this project, you experiment with the nmap port-scanning program. You should work in a lab for this project. In the steps, the host name *target.edu* has been used; replace this with the IP address or host name of any single system in your computer lab. To complete this project, you should have Linux installed and have root access. The second part of the project requires the nmap front-end package, which can only be used on GNOME-compatible systems, such as Fedora Core. *Do not complete this project on a production network; work only in an isolated lab environment.*

1. Use a ping scan to determine which hosts have open ports on your network.

```
nmap -sP target.edu/24
```

This scan might take several minutes to complete, depending on the number of computers on your network. You see a report listing each computer that is detected. This gives you the information you need to start reviewing the services offered by each host.

2. Use the following command to fingerprint the OS of one of the hosts in your network and see a list of ports discovered to be open using a basic port scan. (Replace the address shown with an address for a host on your network.) This scan will take a couple of minutes to complete.

```
nmap -O 192.168.100.45
```

3. You would try a stealthier scan if you were concerned that the default scan might alert the server to your actions and block your subsequent access. For example, you might try a null scan by entering the following command. The resulting list should look the same: You see which ports appear to be open, so that you could try to connect to those ports based on the service they provide to the network.

```
nmap -sN target.edu
```

4. Suppose you knew of a vulnerability in DNS, but didn't know which hosts on the network were running a name server. You could use the following command to scan the DNS port on all systems in your LAN and identify which ones were running a DNS server.

```
nmap -sS -p 53 target.edu/24
```

5. You decide to scan the hosts in the LAN in random order, so you use this command instead:

```
nmap --randomize_hosts -sS -p 53 target.edu/24
```

6. Because you are concerned that someone who may be running PortSentry could block your scans, you decide to slow your scans down in hopes that no one will detect them. Use this command:

```
nmap --randomize_hosts -T 0 -sS -p 53 target.edu/24
```

When you tire of waiting, press **Ctrl+C** and read the man page for nmap to discover how long nmap will wait between each packet sent when the -T 0 timing option is used.

7. Load the nmap front-end package from Fedora Core CD 3 if it is not loaded.

8. Launch the graphical utility:

```
nmapfe
```

9. Use nmapfe to complete any three of the six scans from the preceding steps. Check whether the command-line output for nmap shown just below the output window matches the command you are trying to duplicate from one of the previous steps.

The commands in nmapfe may differ slightly from those in Steps 1 through 7.

Project 12-2

In this project, you download and install a useful network troubleshooting tool called ngrep. This program captures and displays packets just like tcpdump and Ethereal, but it differs in that you can filter packets based on the packet's payload instead of only header fields. You specify the filters using simple strings or regular expressions. You must have Internet access to complete this project.

1. Go to *http://ngrep.sourceforge.net/* and become familiar with ngrep by reading the documentation in the Usage section.

2. Go to the download section and decide whether you want to download ngrep source code or a UNIX binary that will work on your Intel-based Linux computer. By now, you should be able to deal with either without detailed instructions. If not,

you can follow the instructions at ***http://netsecure.alcpress.com/ngrep/***. Download the appropriate file and install ngrep on your computer, and then review the ngrep man page.

Note that you also can download a Windows binary so you can run ngrep on your Windows computer.

3. Enter **ngrep**. You'll see a line of text similar to the following:

```
interface: eth0 (192.168.0.1/255.255.255.0)
```

All incoming packets will be displayed by ngrep. Here's an example of an HTTP packet that was captured by having a Web browser run on the same computer as ngrep:

```
T 192.168.0.1:36653 -> 66.35.250.209:80 [AP]

  GET /favicon.ico HTTP/1.1..Host:
ngrep.sourceforge.net..User-Agent: Mozilla/5.0
(X11; U; Linux i686; en-US;

rv:1.7.10) Gecko/20050720 Fedora/1.0.6-1.1.fc3
Firefox/1.0.6..Accept:
image/png,*/*;q=0.5..Accept-Language: en-
us,en;q=0.5..Accept-Encoding:
gzip,deflate..Accept-Charset: ISO-8859-1,utf-
8;q=0.7,*;q=0.7..Keep-Alive: 300..Connection:

keep-alive..Cookie:
FRQSTR=18701295,18701295,18701295,18701295,18701295;
KIDYMD=#62418:EGVC#67147:EGVF#62542:EGVF#66526:EGVF#66864:
EGVE#62417:EGVB#57492:EGMC#66799:EGMA#62419:EGMA#;
WIDYMD=#8677:EGV#; SESTEST=1; BSUID=1....
```

4. The HTTP protocol is line-oriented, but ngrep runs the lines together, making them difficult to read. You can tell ngrep to display packets in a line-oriented format. Stop ngrep by pressing **Ctrl+C**. Enter **ngrep -W byline**. Refresh your Web browser display. You'll see a packet similar to the following, which makes it easier to read HTTP's line-oriented headers:

```
T 192.168.0.1:36660 -> 66.35.250.209:80 [AP]

GET /favicon.ico HTTP/1.1.
Host: ngrep.sourceforge.net.

User-Agent: Mozilla/5.0 (X11; U; Linux i686; en-US;
rv:1.7.10) Gecko/20050720 Fedora/1.0.6-1.1.fc3 Firefox/1.0.6.

Accept: image/png,*/*;q=0.5.

Accept-Language: en-us,en;q=0.5.
```

```
Accept-Encoding: gzip,deflate.

Accept-Charset: ISO-8859-1,utf-8;q=0.7,*;q=0.7.

Keep-Alive: 300.

Connection: keep-alive.

Cookie: FRQSTR=18701295,18701295,18701295,18701295,18701295;

KIDYMD=#62418:EGVC#67147:EGVF#62542:EGVF#66526:EGVF#66864:
EGVE#62417:EGVB#57492:EGMC#66799:EGMA#62419:EGMA#;

WIDYMD=#8677:EGV#; SESTEST=1; BSUID=1.
```

5. You probably don't want ngrep to display every packet it receives. Typically, you'll want to filter out all packets that don't match a certain criterion. You can specify filters the same way you do with tcpdump, because both use the pcap library. Stop ngrep by pressing **Ctrl+C**. Enter **-W byline port 80**. Now, ngrep will only display packets that are sent from or to port 80.

6. The real power of ngrep is in its ability to filter packets based on the packet's payload rather than headers. You can have ngrep filter out all packets that don't contain a simple string. In the following example, ngrep is searching packets for the word "ethernet." Enter **ngrep ethernet -W byline port 80**. You'll see the following:

```
interface: eth0 (192.168.0.1/255.255.255.0)

filter: (ip) and ( port 80 )

match: ethernet
```

7. Enter *http://netsecure.alcpress.com/ngrep/test1.html* in your Web browser. Switch back to the ngrep screen to see something similar to the following:

```
T 69.30.87.202:80 -> 192.168.0.1:36674 [AP]

HTTP/1.1 200 OK.

Date: Tue, 26 Jul 2005 22:08:06 GMT.

Server: Apache/1.3.28 (Unix).

Cache-Control: max-age=86400.

Expires: Wed, 27 Jul 2005 22:08:06 GMT.

Last-Modified: Tue, 26 Jul 2005 22:07:57 GMT.

ETag: "2f3e4-68-42e6b43d".
```

12

```
Accept-Ranges: bytes.

Content-Length: 104.

Keep-Alive: timeout=15, max=100.

Connection: Keep-Alive.

Content-Type: text/html.


.

<html><head></head><body>

<p>This Web page contains the words Ethernet and
ethernet.</p>

</body></html>
```

8. You can process ngrep output with the traditional grep program. This is useful if you don't want to display the entire packet. Stop ngrep by pressing **Ctrl+C**. Enter the following command:

```
ngrep ethernet -W byline -l port 80|grep ethernet
```

You should use the -l option (make stdout line buffered) if you want to pipe ngrep output to another program such as grep. Strange errors might occur if you don't.

9. Refresh your Web browser display. You see the following message:

```
<p>This Web page contains the words Ethernet and
ethernet.</p>
```

10. Press **Ctrl+C** to exit ngrep.

Project 12-3

In this project, you use the IPTraf program to view network traffic statistics. You should work with a partner on this project. You will establish network connections with a second system, but all work will be done on one system. (Both you and your partner can perform the steps while sitting at your own computer, as long as you permit each other to establish connections as described.) To complete this project, you should have Linux installed and have root access. The second system, to which you will make network connections, should permit ping and FTP or Web connections (these are the default settings in Fedora Core). Other Linux systems should also support this project, but you must at least locate and install the IPTraf package. This project is more interesting if several people on your network are working at the same time, so that multiple connections are visible.

1. Log on as root and install the IPTraf package from Fedora Core CD 3 if it is not already installed.

2. Start the IPTraf program in any command-line window:

   `iptraf`

3. Press a key to reach the IPTraf main menu.

4. Press **Enter** on the IP traffic monitor menu option.

5. Press **Enter** again to select All interfaces.

6. Open a second command-line window.

7. Use the `ftp` *client* command to establish an anonymous FTP connection to your partner's system:

   `ftp partner.lab.edu`

   Use `ftp` and your e-mail address to log on so that you have an `ftp>` prompt.

8. Open a third command-line window and enter a command to ping your partner's system.

   `ping partner.lab.edu`

9. Launch a Web browser and point it to your partner's system or any Web site you choose.

10. Did you notice activity in IPTraf as you completed the previous three steps?

11. Press **X** to exit the IP traffic monitor screen. Choose **Detailed interface statistics** on the main menu. Select the network interface that you have been working with (probably `eth0`).

12. While you watch the summary statistics, switch to the other programs you have running and download another Web page or enter a command such as `ls` in the FTP client. The `ping` command should also still be running. Notice how the numbers update each second based on new network traffic.

13. Press **X** to return to the main menu. Choose **LAN station monitor** on the main menu, choose **All interfaces**, and notice which systems are sending out network data.

14. Press **X** to return to the main menu. Choose **Exit** to close IPTraf.

**HANDS-ON
PROJECTS**

Project 12-4

In this project, you experiment with the Ethereal packet-sniffing program. The steps here do not require that you work with a partner. However, you will find experimenting with Ethereal more interesting if others in the computer lab are also working on projects, which makes a variety of network traffic visible to Ethereal. To complete this project, you need a

Linux system with root access and Ethereal installed. The following steps assume that you are working on Fedora Core, but after Ethereal is installed, the steps should be identical for many versions of Linux.

1. Log on as root and make certain the two Ethereal packages are installed:

   ```
   ethereal
   ethereal-gnome
   ```

2. Execute a command that will generate ongoing network traffic. You can ping another host on your LAN, start a large Web page download, establish a PPP connection, or start another type of connection, such as FTP or SSH. When you establish a connection, network traffic is not constantly flowing, so you might want to switch to the window in which you made the connection and enter a command to generate some interesting traffic for analysis.

3. Launch the Ethereal program from any command line while running a graphical environment.

   ```
   ethereal &
   ```

4. Choose **Start** from the Capture menu.

5. Make certain that the correct interface is selected in the top field of the dialog box (normally you would choose the eth0 interface).

6. In the Display options section, choose **Update list of packets in real time** so that you can see new network traffic as you work.

7. In the Capture File(s) section, enter a filename in the **File** text box. Ethereal will save all captured packets to this file. You can click the Browse button to choose where to save the file.

8. Choose **OK** to begin the capture, and then minimize the Ethereal Capture window.

9. Switch to another screen and launch an FTP session, logging on as an anonymous user with your correct password.

10. Look for a packet labeled with the FTP protocol in the top section of the Ethereal window. See if you can find the packet that contains the password you entered to start your anonymous FTP session. In this case, only your e-mail address is disclosed.

11. Close the FTP session using the **bye** command.

12. Start an SSH session with another host on your LAN that is running sshd, but with which you have not exchanged SSH keys:

    ```
    ssh -l username partnerhost.edu
    ```

13. Notice the packets listed in the top part of Ethereal as the SSH connection was established (or even if it was rejected because you don't have a valid account on the machine you contacted). See if you can locate the packet that contains the password you entered within ssh.

14. Stop the capture by choosing **Stop** on the Capture menu. The capture may take a moment to finish before you can access the Ethereal menus to continue.

15. Choose **Display Filters** on the Analyze menu.

16. Click the **Add Expression** button in the Ethereal: Display Filter dialog box that opens. A list of protocol components appears.

17. In this dialog box, you can set a filter based on any flag or field for any protocol that Ethereal can process. Explore some of the protocol options in this dialog box before closing it. Also close the Ethereal: Display Filter dialog box.

18. Choose **Protocol Hierarchy** from the Statistics menu. Study the resulting percentage breakdowns; different protocol levels are represented by indented lines.

19. If other users are working on your network, continue to explore the Ethereal interface to see how you can process a large number of packets more efficiently by setting up protocol filters, setting values to match for colorization, and using other techniques.

CASE PROJECTS

12

CASE
PROJECTS

Case Project 12-1

1. One of the biggest legal clients of Snow, Sleet, and Hale is an energy company that runs an oil pipeline across the Alaskan wilderness. Recently, a group of antiglobalization protesters traveled cross-country to a remote part of the pipeline and sabotaged it, then made the resulting oil spill public. Snow, Sleet, and Hale are handling the lawsuit against the protest group for property damage and cleanup costs. At the same time, they are trying to press criminal charges and handle the public relations disaster while the energy company cleans up the oil spill.

   Because of the law firm's involvement and public exposure in this case, protesters from various antiglobalization groups around the world have started attacking the law firm's servers. You have just noticed this activity.

   What do you think the protesters' goals are in attacking the systems? Is it too late to use a security-auditing tool? What possible attacks or vulnerabilities are you most concerned about? Which concern you the least? What actions might you take with your network configurations, services, or daily practices to help you weather this attack? How long would you remain in "siege mode"? What are the main costs and disadvantages of operating in constant expectation of a serious attack? Consider the benefits and disadvantages to you as system administrator as well as monetary costs to the firm, and to end users on the firm's networks.

2. One of the legal secretaries in the Fairbanks office is a secret supporter of the largest antiglobalization protest group. Though he doesn't participate in the demonstrations for fear of losing his job, he appears to feel he can contribute to the cause by making your networks more vulnerable to the cyberattacks.

What parts of your well-designed security policy will protect your networks from this employee? If he attempts to attack the network from inside the firm, will your safeguards detect his actions and protect against them? How can you protect the networks against internal attackers without excessively reducing ease of use for everyone and without creating an environment of paranoia at the firm?

3. After the dust settles and the protesters depart, lawsuits are under way (they won't be over for many years) and your success in dealing with this difficult situation is reported in computer trade magazines. As a result, you are asked to join a Presidential commission run in cooperation with the SANS Institute. The commission will study the current landscape of network security and future trends, the increased use of networks around the world, and how both affect corporate and governmental risks.

As an industry luminary, your first task is to prepare brief remarks for a hearing before the Senate Special Committee on Intelligence (see *www.intelligence.senate.gov*).

The Special Committee would like to hear:

- What you feel should be the greatest network security concerns of corporations and government organizations based on current technologies

- What new security-related technologies are in the wings, and their possible effects on corporate and government security efforts

- How international efforts to standardize security protocols and strengthen encryption technologies may affect the work of the U.S. intelligence community (for example, the CIA)

- What government action, if any, you would recommend to make computer networks more secure in the future

LINUX CERTIFICATION OBJECTIVES

The Linux Professional Institute (LPI) is a nonprofit organization sponsored by several major vendors, including IBM and Hewlett-Packard. LPI operates with a board of directors that gathers input from members of the Linux community to develop overall certification goals, testing objectives, and future plans. LPI has planned a three-level certification program. This book addresses the first two levels.

This appendix contains testing objectives for the LPI Level 1 and Level 2 Certification (see *www.lpi.org*). The LPI Level 1 certification encompasses two exams: 101, General Linux, Part 1; and 102, General Linux, Part 2. The LPI Level 2 certification encompasses two additional exams: 201, Advanced Linux Administration; and 202, Linux Networking Administration. A weight ranging from 1 to 10 is assigned to each objective; a higher weight indicates that the topic is covered by more exam questions.

Objectives for Exam 101

Topic 102: Linux Installation and Package Management

1.102.6 Use Red Hat Package Manager (RPM)

Weight of objective: 6

Candidates should be able to perform package management under Linux distributions that use RPMs for package distribution. This objective includes being able to install, reinstall, upgrade, and remove packages, as well as obtain status and version information on packages. This objective also includes obtaining package information, such as version, status, dependencies, integrity, and signatures. Candidates should be able to determine what files a package provides, as well as find which package a specific file comes from.

Key files, terms, and utilities include: /etc/rpmrc, /usr/lib/rpm/*, rpm, grep.

Chapter/Section: Chapter 7/Other Security Applications

Topic 110: The X Window System

1.110.2 Set Up a Display Manager

Weight of objective: 1

Candidates should be able to set up and customize a display manager. This objective includes turning the display manager on or off and changing the display manager greeting. This objective also includes changing default bitplanes for the display manager. It also includes configuring display managers for use by X-stations. This objective covers the display managers XDM (X Display Manager), GDM (GNOME Display Manager), and KDM (KDE Display Manager).

Key files, terms, and utilities include: /etc/inittab, /etc/X11/xdm/*, /etc/X11/kdm/*, /etc/X11/gdm/*.

Chapter/Section: Chapter 3/Running Applications Remotely

A

Objectives for Exam 102

Topic 107: Printing

1.107.4 Install and Configure Local and Remote Printers

Weight of objective: 3

Candidates should be able to install a printer daemon, and install and configure a print filter (for example, `apsfilter`, `magicfilter`). This objective includes making local and remote printers accessible for a Linux system, including PostScript, non-PostScript, and Samba printers.

Key files, terms, and utilities include: `lpd`, `/etc/printcap`, `/etc/apsfilter/*`, `/var/lib/apsfilter/*/`, `/etc/magicfilter/*/`, `/var/spool/lpd/*/`.

Chapter/Section: Chapter 4/Using Administrative Services

Topic 111: Administrative Tasks

1.111.1 Manage Users and Group Accounts and Related System Files

Weight of objective: 7

Candidates should be able to add, remove, suspend, and change user accounts. Tasks include adding and removing groups, and changing user/group information in `passwd`/`group` databases. This objective also includes creating special-purpose and limited accounts.

Key files, terms, and utilities include: `chage`, `gpasswd`, `groupadd`, `groupdel`, `groupmod`, `grpconv`, `grpunconv`, `passwd`, `pwconv`, `pwunconv`, `useradd`, `userdel`, `usermod`, `/etc/passwd`, `/etc/shadow`, `/etc/group`, `/etc/gshadow`.

Chapter/Section: Chapter 9/Managing User Accounts

1.111.3 Configure and Use System Log Files to Meet Administrative and Security Needs

Weight of objective: 3

Candidates should be able to configure system logs. This objective includes managing the type and level of information logged, manually scanning log files for notable activity, monitoring log files, arranging for automatic rotation and archiving of logs, and tracking down problems noted in logs.

Key files, terms, and utilities include: `logrotate`, `tail -f`, `/etc/syslog.conf`, `/var/log/*`.

Chapter/Section: Chapter 4/Logging with `syslogd`

1.111.6 Maintain System Time

Weight of objective: 3

Candidates should be able to properly maintain the system time and synchronize the clock over NTP. Tasks include setting the system date and time, setting the BIOS clock to the correct time in UTC, configuring the correct time zone for the system, and configuring the system to correct clock drift to match the NTP clock.

Key files, terms, and utilities include: `date`, `hwclock`, `ntpd`, `ntpdate`, `/usr/share/zoneinfo`, `/etc/timezone`, `/etc/localtime`, `/etc/ntp.conf`, `/etc/ntp.drift`.

Chapter/Section: Chapter 4/Configuring NTP Time Synchronization

Topic 112: Networking Fundamentals

1.112.1 Fundamentals of TCP/IP

Weight of objective: 4

Candidates should demonstrate a proper understanding of network fundamentals. This objective includes the understanding of IP addresses, network masks, and what they mean (for example, determine a network and broadcast address for a host based on its subnet mask in "dotted quad" or abbreviated notation, or determine the network address, broadcast address, and netmask when given an IP address and number of bits). It also covers the understanding of the network classes and classless subnets (CIDR) and the reserved addresses for private network use. It includes the understanding of the function and application of a default route. It also includes the understanding of basic Internet protocols (IP, ICMP, TCP, UDP) and the more common TCP and UDP ports (20, 21, 23, 25, 53, 80, 110, 119, 139, 143, 161).

Key files, terms, and utilities include: `/etc/services`, `ftp`, `telnet`, `host`, `ping`, `dig`, `traceroute`, `whois`.

Chapter/Section: Chapter 1/Network Software, Chapter 2/Routing Concepts, Chapter 2/Configuring Networking Using Command-Line Utilities and Using Basic Networking Utilities

1.112.3 TCP/IP Configuration and Troubleshooting

Weight of objective: 10

Candidates should be able to view, change, and verify configuration settings and operational status for various network interfaces. This objective includes manual and automatic configuration of interfaces and routing tables. This especially means to add, start, stop, restart, delete, or reconfigure network interfaces. It also means to change, view, or configure the routing table and to correct an improperly set default route manually. Candidates should be able to configure Linux as a DHCP client and a TCP/IP host and to debug problems associated with the network configuration.

Key files, terms, and utilities include: `/etc/HOSTNAME` or `/etc/hostname`, `/etc/hosts`, `/etc/networks`, `/etc/host.conf`, `/etc/resolv.conf`, `/etc/nsswitch.conf`, `ifconfig`, `route`, `dhcpcd`, `dhcpclient`, `pump`, `host`, `hostname` (`domainname`, `dnsdomainname`), `netstat`, `ping`, `traceroute`, `tcpdump`, the network scripts run during system initialization.

Chapter/Section: Chapter 2/Configuring Networking Using Command-Line Utilities

1.112.4 Configure Linux as a PPP Client

Weight of objective: 4

Candidates should understand the basics of the PPP protocol and be able to configure and use PPP for outbound connections. This objective includes the definition of the chat sequence to connect (given a logon example) and the setup commands to be run automatically when a PPP connection is made. It also includes initialization and termination of a PPP connection with a modem, ISDN, or ADSL and setting PPP to reconnect automatically if disconnected.

Key files, terms, and utilities include: `/etc/ppp/options.*`, `/etc/ppp/peers/*`, `/etc/wvdial.conf`, `/etc/ppp/ip-up`, `/etc/ppp/ip-down`, `wvdial`, `pppd`.

Chapter/Section: Chapter 3/Dial-Up Network Access Using PPP

Topic 113: Networking Services

1.113.1 Configure and Manage `inetd`, `xinetd`, and Related Services

Weight of objective: 5

Candidates should be able to configure which services are available through `inetd`, use TCP Wrappers to allow or deny services on a host-by-host basis, manually start, stop, and restart Internet services, and configure basic network services, including Telnet and FTP. Set a service to run as another user instead of the default in `inetd.conf`.

Key files, terms, and utilities include: `/etc/inetd.conf`, `/etc/hosts.allow`, `/etc/hosts.deny`, `/etc/services`, `/etc/xinetd.conf`, `/etc/xinetd.log`.

Chapter/Section: Chapter 4/Daemons on Demand

1.113.2 Operate and Perform Basic Configuration of `sendmail`

Weight of objective: 5

Candidates should be able to modify simple parameters in `sendmail` configuration files (including the "Smart Host" parameter, if necessary), create mail aliases, manage the mail queue, start and stop `sendmail`, configure mail forwarding, and perform basic troubleshooting of `sendmail`. This objective includes checking for and closing open relays on the mail server. It does not include advanced custom configuration of `sendmail`.

Key files, terms, and utilities include: `/etc/sendmail.cf`, `/etc/aliases`, or `/etc/mail/aliases`, `/etc/mail/*`, `~/.forward`, `mailq`, `sendmail`, `newaliases`.

Chapter/Section: Chapter 6/Configuring a Basic E-Mail Server

1.113.3 Operate and Perform Basic Configuration of Apache

Weight of objective: 3

Candidates should be able to modify simple parameters in Apache configuration files, start, stop, and restart `httpd`, and arrange for automatic restarting of `httpd` upon boot. Does not include advanced custom configuration of Apache.

Key files, terms, and utilities include: `apachectl`, `httpd`, `httpd.conf`.

Chapter/Section: Chapter 6/Creating a Linux Web Server

1.113.4 Properly Manage the NFS, `smb`, and `nmb` Daemons

Weight of objective: 4

Candidates should know how to mount remote filesystems using NFS, configure NFS for exporting local filesystems, and start, stop, and restart the NFS server. Install and configure Samba using the included GUI tools or direct editing of the `/etc/smb.conf` file. (Note that this deliberately excludes advanced NT domain issues, but includes simple sharing of home directories and printers, as well as correctly setting the nmbd as a WINS client.)

Key files, terms, and utilities include: `/etc/exports`, `/etc/fstab`, `/etc/smb.conf`, `mount`, `umount`.

Chapter/Section: Chapter 5/File Sharing with NFS, Chapter 5/Windows File and Print Integration with Samba

1.113.5 Set Up and Configure Basic DNS Services

Weight of objective: 3

Candidates should be able to configure host name lookups and troubleshoot problems with local, caching-only name servers. This requires an understanding of the domain registration and DNS translation process. It also requires understanding key differences in configuration files for `bind` version 4 and `bind` version 8.

Key files, terms, and utilities include: `/etc/hosts`, `/etc/resolv.conf`, `/etc/nsswitch.conf`, `/etc/named.boot` (v.4) or `/etc/named.conf` (v.8), `named`.

Chapter/Section: Chapter 3/Name Services, Chapter 6/Setting Up a DNS Name Server

1.113.7 Set Up Secure Shell (OpenSSH)

Weight of objective: Unknown

Candidates should be able to obtain and configure OpenSSH. This objective includes basic OpenSSH installation and troubleshooting, as well as configuring sshd to start at system boot.

Key files, terms, and utilities include: `/etc/hosts.allow`, `/etc/hosts.deny`, `/etc/nologin`, `/etc/ssh/sshd_config`, `/etc/ssh_known_hosts`, `/etc/sshrc`, `sshd`, `ssh-keygen`.

Chapter/Section: Chapter 9/SSH Logons, Chapter 10/Secure Shell, Chapter 11/Using the Secure Shell

Topic 114: Security

1.114.1 Perform Security Administration Tasks

Weight of objective: 4

Candidates should know how to review system configuration to ensure host security in accordance with local security policies. This objective includes how to configure TCP Wrappers, find files with the SUID/SGID bit set, verify packages, set or change user passwords and password aging information, and update binaries as recommended by CERT, BUGTRAQ, and/or a distribution's security alerts. This objective includes basic knowledge of ipchains and iptables.

Key files, terms, and utilities include: `/proc/net/ip_fwchains`, `/proc/net/ip_fwnames`, `/proc/net/ip_masquerade`, `find`, `ipchains`, `passwd socket`, `iptables`.

Chapter/Section: Chapter 2/Using proc, Chapter 4/Daemons on Demand, Chapter 8/Filesystem Security, Chapter 11/Introducing Netfilter and IP Tables

1.114.2 Set Up Host Security

Weight of objective: 4

Candidates should know how to set up a basic level of host security. Tasks include syslog configuration, shadowed passwords, setup of a mail alias for root's mail, and turning off all network services not in use.

Key files, terms, and utilities include: `/etc/inetd.conf` or `/etc/inet.d/*`, `/etc/nologin`, `/etc/passwd`, `/etc/shadow`, `/etc/syslog.conf`.

Chapter/Section: Chapter 4/Daemons on Demand, Chapter 9/Managing User Accounts

1.114.3 Set Up User-Level Security

Weight of objective: 2

Candidates should be able to configure user-level security. Tasks include limits on user logons, processes, and memory usage.

Key files, terms, and utilities include: `quota`, `usermod`.

Chapter/Section: Chapter 9/Using Pluggable Authentication Modules, Chapter 9/Managing User Accounts.

OBJECTIVES FOR EXAM 201

Topic 202: System Start-up

2.202.1 Customizing System Start-up and Boot Processes

Weight of objective: 2

Candidates should be able to edit appropriate system start-up scripts to customize standard system run levels and boot processes. This objective includes interacting with run levels and creating custom `initrd` images as needed.

Key files, terms, and utilities include: `/etc/init.d/`, `/etc/inittab`, `/etc/rc.d/`, `mkinitrd` (both Red Hat and Debian scripts).

Chapter/Section: Chapter 2/Using `proc`, Chapter 2/System Networking Scripts

Topic 203: Filesystem

2.203.1 Operating the Linux Filesystem

Weight of objective: 3

Candidates should be able to properly configure and navigate the standard Linux filesystem. This objective includes configuring and mounting various filesystem types, and manipulating filesystems to adjust for disk space requirements or device additions.

Key files, terms, and utilities include: `/etc/fstab`, `/etc/mtab`, `/proc/mounts`, `mount` and `umount`, `sync`, `swapon`, `swapoff`.

Chapter/Section: Chapter 8/File Types and Mount Options, Chapter 10/Encrypting Disk Partitions, Chapter 10/Encrypting Loopback Filesystems

2.203.2 Maintaining a Linux Filesystem

Weight of objective: 4

Candidates should be able to properly maintain a Linux filesystem using system utilities. This objective includes manipulating a standard ext2 filesystem.

Key files, terms, and utilities include: `fsck` (`fsck.ext2`), `badblocks`, `mke2fs`, `dumpe2fs`, `debuge2fs`, `tune2fs`.

Chapter/Section: Chapter 8/Filesystem Security, Chapter 8/Reserved Disk Space

2.203.3 Creating and Configuring Filesystem Options

Weight of objective: 3

Candidates should be able to configure automount filesystems. This objective includes configuring automount for network and device filesystems. Also included is creating non-ext2 filesystems for devices such as CD-ROMs.

Key files, terms, and utilities include: `/etc/auto.master`, `/etc/auto.[dir]`, `mkisofs`, `dd`, `mke2fs`.

Chapter/Section: Chapter 8/Filesystem Security, Chapter 8/Loopback Filesystems, Chapter 8/Reserved Disk Space

Topic 204: Hardware

2.204.2 Adding New Hardware

Weight of objective: 3

Candidates should be able to configure internal and external devices for a system, including new hard disks, dumb terminal devices, serial UPS devices, multiport serial cards, and LCD panels.

Key files, terms, and utilities include: `/proc/bus/usb`, `Xfree86`, `modprobe`, `lsmod`, `lsdev`, `lspci`, `setserial`, `usbview`.

Chapter/Section: Chapter 2/Interface Drivers

2.204.3 Software and Kernel Configuration

Weight of objective: 2

Candidates should be able to configure kernel options to support various hardware devices, including UDMA66 drives and IDE CD burners. This objective includes using LVM (Logical Volume Manager) to manage hard disk drives and partitions as well as software tools to interact with hard disk settings.

Key files, terms, and utilities include: `/proc/interrupts`, `hdparm`, `tune2fs`, `sysctl`.

Chapter/Section: Chapter 2/Using `proc`

2.204.4 Configuring PCMCIA Devices

Weight of objective: 1

Candidates should be able to configure a Linux installation to include PCMCIA support. This objective includes configuring PCMCIA devices, such as Ethernet adapters, to autodetect when inserted.

Key files, terms, and utilities include: `/etc/pcmcia/`, `*.opts`, `cardctl`, `cardmgr`.

Chapter/Section: Chapter 2/PCMCIA and PC Card Interfaces

Topic 209: File and Service Sharing

2.209.1 Configuring a Samba Server

Weight of objective: 5

The candidate should be able to set up a Samba server for various clients. This objective includes setting up a logon script for Samba clients and setting up an nmbd WINS server. Also included is changing the workgroup in which a server participates, defining a shared directory in `smb.conf`, defining a shared printer in `smb.conf`, using `nmblookup` to test WINS server functionality, and using the `smbmount` command to mount an SMB share on a Linux client.

Key files, terms, and utilities include: `smbd`, `nmbd`, `smbstatus`, `smbtestparm`, `smbpasswd`, `nmblookup`, `smb.conf`, `lmhosts`.

Chapter/Section: Chapter 5/Windows File and Print Integration with Samba

2.209.2 Configuring an NFS Server

Weight of objective: 3

The candidate should be able to create an `exports` file and specify filesystems to be exported. This objective includes editing `exports` file entries to restrict access to certain hosts, subnets, or netgroups. Also included is specifying mount options in the `exports` file, configuring user ID mapping, mounting an NFS filesystem on a client, using mount options to specify soft or hard and background retries, and signal handling, locking, and block size. The candidate should also be able to configure TCP Wrappers to further secure NFS.

Key files, terms, and utilities include: `/etc/exports`, `exportfs`, `showmount`, `nfsstat`.

Chapter/Section: Chapter 5/File Sharing with NFS

A

Topic 211: System Maintenance

2.211.1 System Logging

Weight of objective: 1

The candidate should be able to configure `syslogd` to act as a central network log server. This objective also includes configuring `syslogd` to send log output to a central log server, logging remote connections, and using `grep` and other text utilities to automate log analysis.

Key files, terms, and utilities include: `syslog.conf`, `/etc/hosts`, `syslogd`.

Chapter/Section: Chapter 4/Logging with `syslogd`

Topic 214: Troubleshooting

2.214.2 Creating Recovery Disks

Weight of objective: 1

The candidate should be able to create both a standard boot disk for system entrance and a recovery disk for system repair.

Key files, terms, and utilities include: `/etc/fstab`, `/etc/inittab`, familiarity with the location and contents of the LDP Bootdisk-HOWTO, `/usr/sbin/rdev`, `/bin/cat`, `/bin/mount` (includes `-o` loop switch), `/sbin/lilo`, `/bin/dd`, `/sbin/mke2fs`, `/usr/sbin/chroot`.

Chapter/Section: Chapter 8/`chroot`

2.214.8 Troubleshooting Environment Configurations

Weight of objective: 1

A candidate should be able to identify common local system and user environment configuration issues and common repair techniques.

Key files, terms, and utilities include: `/etc/inittab`, `/etc/rc.local`, `/etc/rc.boot`, `/var/spool/cron/crontabs/`, `/etc/'shell_name'.conf`, `/etc/login.defs`, `/etc/syslog.conf`, `/etc/passwd`, `/etc/shadow`, `/etc/group`, `/etc/profile`, `/sbin/init`, `/usr/sbin/cron`, `/usr/bin/crontab`.

Chapter/Section: Chapter 9/Managing User Accounts

Objectives for Exam 202

Topic 205: Networking Configuration

2.205.1 Basic Networking Configuration

Weight of objective: 5

The candidate should be able to configure a network device to be able to connect to a local network and a wide area network. This objective includes being able to communicate between various subnets within a single network, configure dial-up access using mgetty, configure dial-up access using a modem or ISDN, configure authentication protocols such as PAP and CHAP, and configure TCP/IP logging.

Key files, terms, and utilities include: /sbin/route, /sbin/ifconfig, /sbin/arp, /usr/sbin/arpwatch, /etc/.

Chapter/Section: Chapter 2/Using the ifconfig Command, Chapter 2/Using the route Command, Chapter 2/Using ARP, Chapter 3/Dial-up Network Access Using PPP

2.205.2 Advanced Network Configuration and Troubleshooting

Weight of objective: 3

The candidate should be able to configure a network device to implement various network authentication schemes. This objective includes configuring a multihomed network device, configuring a virtual private network, and resolving networking and communication problems.

Key files, terms, and utilities include: route, ifconfig, netstat, ping, arp, tcpdump, lsof, nc.

Chapter/Section: Chapter 2/Using the ifconfig Command, Chapter 2/Using the route Command, Chapter 2/Using ARP, Chapter 2/System Networking Scripts, Chapter 2/Using ping for System Testing, Chapter 2/Using traceroute to Examine Routing, Chapter 2/Troubleshooting Network Connections, Chapter 12/tcpdump

Topic 206: Mail and News

2.206.1 Configuring Mailing Lists

Weight of objective: 1

Candidates should be able to install and maintain mailing lists using majordomo, and monitor majordomo problems by viewing its logs.

Key files, terms, and utilities include: majordomo.

Chapter/Section: Chapter 4/Using majordomo for Mailing Lists

2.206.2 Using `sendmail`

Weight of objective: 4

Candidates should be able to manage a `sendmail` configuration, including e-mail aliases, mail quotas, and virtual mail domains. This objective includes configuring internal mail relays and monitoring SMTP servers.

Key files, terms, and utilities include: `/etc/aliases`, `sendmail.cw`, `virtusertable`, `genericstable`.

Chapter/Section: Chapter 6/Configuring a Basic E-Mail Server

2.206.3 Managing Mail Traffic

Weight of objective: 3

Candidates should be able to implement client mail management software to filter, sort, and monitor incoming user mail. This objective includes using software such as `procmail` on both the server and client side.

Key files, terms, and utilities include: `procmail`.

Chapter/Section: Chapter 3/Using an E-Mail Filter: `procmail`, Chapter 6/Configuring a Basic E-Mail Server

Topic 207: DNS

2.207.2 Create and Maintain DNS Zones

Weight of objective: 3

The candidate should be able to create a zone file for a forward or reverse zone or root-level server. This objective includes setting appropriate values for the SOA resource record, NS records, and MX records. Also included is adding hosts with A resource records and CNAME records as appropriate, adding hosts to reverse zones with PTR records, and adding the zone to the `/etc/named.conf` file using the zone statement with appropriate type, file, and master values. A candidate should also be able to delegate a zone to another DNS server.

Key files, terms, and utilities include: contents of `/var/named`, zone file syntax, resource record formats, `dig`, `nslookup`, `host`.

Chapter/Section: Chapter 6/Setting Up a DNS Name Server

2.207.3 Securing a DNS Server

Weight of objective: 3

The candidate should be able to configure BIND to run as a nonroot user, and configure BIND to run in a `chroot` jail. This objective includes configuring DNSSEC statements such as keys and trusted keys to prevent domain spoofing. Also included is the ability to configure a split DNS configuration using the forwarder's statement, and specifying a nonstandard version number string in response to queries.

Key files, terms, and utilities include: `SysV init` files or `rc.local`, `/etc/named.conf`, `/etc/passwd`, `dnskeygen`.

Chapter/Section: Chapter 6/Setting Up a DNS Name Server, Chapter 8/chroot

Topic 208: Web Services

2.208.1 Implementing a Web Server

Weight of objective: 2

Candidates should be able to install and configure an Apache Web server. This objective includes monitoring Apache load and performance, restricting client user access, configuring `mod_perl` and PHP support, and setting up client user authentication. Also included is configuring Apache server options such as maximum requests, minimum and maximum servers, and clients.

Key files, terms, and utilities include: `access.log`, `.htaccess`, `httpd.conf`, `mod_auth`, `htpasswd`, `htgroup`.

Chapter/Section: Chapter 6/Creating a Linux Web Server

2.208.2 Maintaining a Web Server

Weight of objective: 2

Candidates should be able to configure Apache to use virtual hosts for Web sites without dedicated IP addresses. This objective also includes creating an SSL certification for Apache and defining SSL definitions in configuration files using OpenSSL. Also included is customizing file access by implementing redirect statements in Apache's configuration files.

Key files, terms, and utilities include: `httpd.conf`.

Chapter/Section: Chapter 6/Creating a Linux Web Server, Chapter 10/Cryptography and the Web

Topic 210: Network Client Management

2.210.1 DHCP Configuration

Weight of objective: 2

The candidate should be able to configure a DHCP server and set default options, create a subnet, and create a dynamically allocated range. This objective includes adding a static host, setting options for a single host, and adding `bootp` hosts. Also included is configuring a DHCP relay agent and reloading the DHCP server after making changes.

Key files, terms, and utilities include: `dhcpd.conf`, `dhcpd.leases`.

Chapter/Section: Chapter 3/Using DHCP

2.210.3 LDAP Configuration

Weight of objective: 1

The candidate should be able to configure an LDAP server. This objective includes configuring a directory hierarchy and adding groups, hosts, services, and other data to the hierarchy. Also included is importing items from LDIF files and adding items with a management tool, as well as adding users to the directory and changing their passwords.

Key files, terms, and utilities include: `slapd`, `slapd.conf`.

Chapter/Section: Chapter 3/Understanding LDAP

2.210.4 PAM Authentication

Weight of objective: 2

The candidate should be able to configure PAM to support authentication via traditional `/etc/passwd`, shadow passwords, NIS, or LDAP.

Key files, terms, and utilities include: `/etc/pam.d`, `pam.conf`.

Chapter/Section: Chapter 9/Using Pluggable Authentication Modules

Topic 212: System Security

2.212.2 Configuring a Router

Weight of objective: 2

The candidate should be able to configure `ipchains` and `iptables` to perform IP masquerading, and state the significance of Network Address Translation and Private Network Addresses in protecting a network. This objective includes configuring port redirection, listing filtering rules, and writing rules that accept or block datagrams based on source or destination protocol, port, and address. Also included is saving and reloading filtering configurations, using settings in `/proc/sys/net/ipv4` to respond to DOS attacks, using `/proc/sys/net/ipv4/ip_forward` to turn IP forwarding on and off, and using tools such as PortSentry to block port scans and vulnerability probes.

Key files, terms, and utilities include: `/proc/sys/net/ipv4`, `/etc/services`, `ipchains`, `iptables`, `routed`.

Chapter/Section: Chapter 11/Introducing Netfilter and IP Tables

2.212.3 Securing FTP Servers

Weight of objective: 2

The candidate should be able to configure an anonymous download FTP server. This objective includes configuring an FTP server to allow anonymous uploads, listing additional precautions to be taken if anonymous uploads are permitted, configuring guest users and groups with `chroot` jail, and configuring `ftpaccess` to deny access to named users or groups.

Key files, terms, and utilities include: `ftpaccess`, `ftpusers`, `ftpgroups`, `/etc/passwd`, `chroot`.

Chapter/Section: Chapter 5/Running an FTP Server, Chapter 8/chroot

2.212.4 Secure Shell (OpenSSH)

Weight of objective: 2

The candidate should be able to configure `sshd` to allow or deny root logons, and to enable or disable X forwarding. This objective includes generating server keys, generating a user's public/private key pair, adding a public key to a user's `authorized_keys` file, and configuring `ssh-agent` for all users. Candidates should also be able to configure port forwarding to tunnel an application protocol over `ssh`, configure `ssh` to support the `ssh` protocol versions 1 and 2, disable nonroot logons during system maintenance, configure trusted clients for `ssh` logons without a password, and make multiple connections from multiple hosts to guard against loss of connection to the remote host following configuration changes.

Key files, terms, and utilities include: `ssh`, `sshd`, `/etc/ssh/sshd_config`, `~/.ssh/identity.pub` and `identity`, `~/.ssh/authorized_keys`, `.shosts`, `.rhosts`.

Chapter/Section: Chapter 9/SSH Logons, Chapter 10/Secure Shell, Chapter 11/Using the Secure Shell

2.212.5 TCP Wrappers

Weight of objective: 1

The candidate should be able to configure TCP Wrappers to allow connections to specified servers from only certain hosts or subnets.

Key files, terms, and utilities include: `inetd.conf`, `tcpd`, `hosts.allow`, `hosts.deny`, `xinetd`.

Chapter/Section: Chapter 4/Daemons on Demand

2.212.6 Security Tasks

Weight of objective: 3

The candidate should be able to install and configure Kerberos and perform basic security auditing of source code. This objective includes arranging to receive security alerts from Bugtraq, CERT, CIAC, or other sources, being able to test for open mail relays and anonymous FTP servers, and installing and configuring an intrusion-detection system, such as Snort or Tripwire. Candidates should also be able to update the IDS configuration as new vulnerabilities are discovered and apply security patches and bug fixes.

Key files, terms, and utilities include: Tripwire, `telnet`, `nmap`.

Chapter/Section: Chapter 8/Using Integrity Checkers, Chapter 12/Using `nmap`, Chapter 2/The Telnet Remote Logon Utility

Topic 214: Network Troubleshooting

2.214.7 Troubleshooting Network Issues

Weight of objective: 1

Candidates should be able to identify and correct common network setup problems. This objective includes knowledge of locations for basic configuration files and commands.

Key files, terms, and utilities include `ifconfig`, `route`, `netstat`, `/etc/network ||` `/etc/sysconfig/network-scripts/`, system log files such as `/var/log/syslog` and `/var/log/messages`, `ping`, `/etc/resolv.conf`, `/etc/hosts`, `/etc/hosts.allow`, `/etc/hosts.deny`, `/etc/hostname || /etc/HOSTNAME`, `hostname`, `traceroute`, `nslookup`, `dig`, `dmesg`, `host`.

Chapter/Section: Chapter 2/Using the `ifconfig` Command, Chapter 2/Using the `route` Command, Chapter 2/System Networking Scripts, Chapter 2/Using `ping` for System Testing, Chapter 2/Using `traceroute` to Examine Routing, Chapter 2/Troubleshooting Network Connections, Chapter 3/Name Services

B

COMMAND SUMMARY

This appendix lists all commands referred to in this book and in the companion volume, *Guide to Linux Installation and System Administration*. The table includes:

- Standard command-line utilities

- Server daemons

- Many specialized utilities that are part of software packages described in the chapter text (for example, the utilities that are part of the Samba Suite)

- Graphical utilities (using their program name, as they would be launched from a graphical command line)

Configuration files are not included in this table. To learn about any of the server daemons or command-line utilities, use the man or info command followed by the name of the program. (In some cases, the man command refers you to the info command for more complete information.) Most graphical programs do not have man pages. For graphical programs, and for many specialized command-line utilities, you can learn more by reviewing the documentation that accompanies the utility. For example, in Fedora Core Linux, the documentation for each package is stored as a subdirectory within /usr/share/doc.

Table B-1   Command-line utilities, server daemons, and graphical configuration programs

Command Name	Description
alias	Assign a new name to a command.
apropos	See a list of man pages that contain a given keyword.
arp	Display stored MAC-to-IP address mappings that were collected using the Address Resolution Protocol.
at	Set up a one-time task for later execution by the atd daemon.
atq	See the list of jobs submitted to atd using the at command.
atrm	Remove a scheduled job from the queue of jobs to be executed by the atd daemon.
authconfig	Text-mode, menu-based configuration tool for setting authentication options in Red Hat Linux and Fedora Core.
authconfig-gtk	Graphical configuration tool for setting authentication options in Red Hat Linux and Fedora Core.
balsa	Graphical e-mail client (message reader) for GNOME desktops.
bash	The default Linux shell.
batch	Set up a scheduled task for future execution by the atd daemon when the processor load falls below a certain level.
bg	Make the current process a background process within the current shell.
bindconf	Graphical tool for setting up zone information files for the named DNS name server daemon.
busybox	A miniature version of dozens of standard Linux utilities in a single compact binary.
cat	Print the contents of a file or files to STDOUT.
cd	Change the current working directory.
chattr	Change the file attributes of one or more files.
chgrp	Change the group assigned to a file or directory.
chkconfig	Turn a system service on or off in a particular run level, so that the service is activated or not activated when the system boots.
chkrootkit	Check systems for signs of a rootkit, much like a virus checker.
chmod	Change the permissions assigned to a file or directory.
chown	Change the user (owner) assigned to a file or directory.
chroot	Specify a directory that should be seen as the root directory by a program.
clear	Clear the screen.
cp	Copy files or directories from one location or filename to another.
cpio	Backup utility, similar to tar.
crond	Daemon that runs programs at regular intervals.
crontab	Submit a script with assigned times for repeated future execution by the crond daemon.
cupsd	The CUPS printer daemon.
date	Display the system date and current time.
dd	Create or copy files.

Table B-1 Command-line utilities, server daemons, and graphical configuration programs (continued)

Command Name	Description
df	Display filesystem information for all mounted standard filesystems (not swap and proc).
dhclient	A DHCP client daemon; used to lease network addresses from a DHCP server.
dhcpcd	A DHCP client daemon; used to lease network addresses from a DHCP server.
dhcpd	The DHCP server.
diald	Daemon that manages dial-up connections (PPP connections), establishing or dropping them as determined by network traffic.
dig	Query a name server for any data the name server maintains in its zone information files.
dmesg	Display the contents of the kernel ring buffer, where certain kernel messages are stored.
du	Display usage information about the size of a directory and its subdirectories.
dump	Back up data in a filesystem.
echo	Display text to STDOUT.
elm	A text-based e-mail client with a menu-style interface.
emacs	A powerful text-mode editor.
ethereal	Powerful graphical utility for analyzing network traffic, including both header details and packet payload (a sniffer); used for GNOME, KDE, or other desktops.
evolution	Graphical e-mail client (message reader).
exit	Log off of a session or window.
export	Make an environmental variable available to other processes.
fetchmail	A simple POP3 mail client for Linux.
fg	Move a process to the foreground of the current shell, so that the output of the process is displayed.
file	Display information about the content and file type of a file.
find	Search for a file with certain characteristics and list them or perform other actions on each one.
findsmb	Display the SMB nodes on a NetBIOS network. This program is part of Samba.
finger	Network service that provides basic status information via the in.fingerd daemon for any user on a system.
firefox	A Web browser based on Mozilla; a sister program to Thunderbird.
firewall-config	A graphical firewall configuration utility.
free	Display the amount of free memory and swap space, with usage details on each.
ftp	The text-mode FTP client.

Table B-1   Command-line utilities, server daemons, and graphical configuration programs (continued)

Command Name	Description
ftpshut	Stop the FTP daemon from accepting new connections after the specified length of time.
gated	Dynamic routing daemon that supports RIP, RIPv2, OSPF, and BGP.
getfacl	Display access control list entries.
getfattr	Display the extended attributes for a file.
getty	A terminal management program. (Others include mgetty and mingetty.) Handle logon via a modem or virtual console.
gftp	Graphical FTP client.
gpg	Manage public key encryption, including generating and managing key pairs and encrypting or decrypting files.
grep	Search for a pattern using a regular expression within a file, group of files, or other input stream.
grpck	Check the /etc/group file to be certain that all members of groups refer to valid user accounts.
gunzip	Uncompress a file that was compressed using gzip.
gzip	Compress a file.
halt	Shut down all processes and halt the system so it can be turned off.
head	Display the first 15 lines of a file.
history	Display recently used commands within the shell.
host	Report basic DNS information about a host name, such as its IP address.
hostname	Display the host name of a system.
httpd	The Apache Web server daemon; more generally, the name used for a Web server daemon.
ifconfig	Use with no parameters to display information on all network interfaces configured in the Linux kernel; use with parameters such as an interface, netmask, and IP address to configure a new interface. System start-up scripts are normally used to configure interfaces instead of directly calling ifconfig.
ifdown	A script used to deactivate a networking interface in an orderly way.
ifup	A script used to activate a networking interface in an orderly way.
IglooFTP	Graphical FTP client.
in.fingerd	Server daemon for the finger network service.
in.ftpd	The standard FTP server daemon.
in.telnetd	The standard Telnet server daemon.
in.tftpd	Server daemon for the Trivial FTP protocol.
inetd	A superserver; used to listen to multiple network ports and start the appropriate network services as needed.

Table B-1   Command-line utilities, server daemons, and graphical configuration programs (continued)

Command Name	Description
init	The master control program in Linux; started by the kernel. All programs are started by either init or one of its children.
innd	The standard Linux news server daemon.
insmod	Load a kernel module.
ip	A replacement for the ifconfig, route, and arp programs.
ipchains	Firewall configuration tool for Linux 2.2 kernels; supported in newer kernels for backward compatibility.
ipfwadm	Firewall configuration tool in old Linux systems.
iptables	Firewall configuration tool in Linux 2.4 kernels.
iptraf	Text-mode, menu-based IP traffic analysis and statistics utility. (Not a packet sniffer.)
ipx_configure	Enable or disable automatic IPX configuration via broadcast information from an IPX server on the same network.
ipx_interface	Add, delete, or check IPX configuration information (similar to the ifconfig command for IP).
ipx_internal_net	Configure an internal IPX network (similar to the loopback device for IP).
ipx_route	Manually modify the IPX routing table (similar to the route command for IP).
iwconfig	Configure wireless interfaces.
iwlist	Display information about a wireless interface's radio.
joe	A full-screen text-mode editor.
kfinger	Graphical finger client for KDE desktops.
kill	Send a signal to a process; often used to end a process.
killall	Send a SIGKILL signal to all processes matching the name given as a parameter.
klogd	A daemon that listens for kernel log messages.
kmail	Graphical e-mail client (message reader) for KDE desktops.
knode	Graphical newsreader client for KDE desktops.
kppp	Graphical utility for configuring and running a PPP dial-up connection.
krn	Graphical newsreader client for KDE desktops.
last	List the last logon time for each user on the system.
lastcomm	List the last command entered by each user on the system.
less	Display STDIN (or a file) one page at a time.
ldapsearch	A text-mode LDAP client program.
lidsadm	Administrative utility to manage LIDS.
links	A text-based Web browser.
ln	Create a link from one file or directory to another (both symbolic and hard links can be created).
locate	Search in the internal index of the filesystem for any files or directories matching the given string.

Table B-1   Command-line utilities, server daemons, and graphical configuration programs (continued)

Command Name	Description
logcheck	Automatically watch for suspicious activity in log files and take action when needed, such as e-mailing root.
login	Log on to the system using a username and password.
logout	End a logon session.
logrotate	Rotate logs automatically via a `crontab` entry.
lokkit	A text-mode, menu-based, simple firewall configuration utility.
losetup	Set up a loopback filesystem.
lpc	Control the `lpd` line printer daemon, setting queuing and printing options for all defined printers.
lpd	The line printing daemon; processes print jobs, including transferring jobs to remote hosts according to `/etc/printcap` configurations.
lpq	Display print jobs within a print queue.
lpr	Print a file.
lprm	Remove a print job from a print queue.
ls	List the contents of a directory.
lsattr	List the file attributes of one or more files.
lsmod	List all modules that are part of the current kernel.
lynx	A text-based Web browser.
m4	Utility that converts the macro language of the `sendmail.mc` file into a standard format configuration file (`sendmail.cf`) for use by the `sendmail` e-mail server.
mail	A text-based, command-line e-mail client.
make	Compile or otherwise assemble the source code of a program into a runnable binary file using a `makefile` as instructions.
makemap	Convert a text file into a hashed database file for use by the `sendmail` e-mail server; used with the access and `virtusertable` files.
makewhatis	Create a database of man pages for use by the `apropos` command.
man	Display an online manual page for the given command.
mars-nwe	A daemon that emulates NetWare 3.x functionality.
mcopy	Copy a file or files to or from the 3.5-inch disk drive.
md5sum	Generate an MD5 hash from a file.
mdel	Delete a file or files from the 3.5-inch disk drive.
mdir	List the files on a 3.5-inch disk drive.
mesg	Enable or disable on-screen text messages from programs such as `talk`.
mgetty	A terminal management program. (Others include `getty` and `mingetty`.) Handle logon via a virtual console.
minicom	A terminal emulator for Linux.
mkdir	Create a new subdirectory.
mke2fs	Format a device with the ext2 filesystem.

Table B-1 Command-line utilities, server daemons, and graphical configuration programs (continued)

Command Name	Description
mkfs	Format a device with the given filesystem.
mksmbpasswd.sh	Script to convert existing Linux user accounts to Samba user accounts.
mkswap	Format a device as swap space (virtual memory on hard disk).
modprobe	Manage Linux kernel modules; most commonly used to add a module and any dependent modules to the kernel.
more	Display STDIN (or a file) one page at a time.
mount	Allow access to a named filesystem via a named directory mount point.
mozilla	A Web browser based on Netscape's code.
mv	Rename or move one or more files or directories.
named	The DNS name server daemon in the BIND package.
named-checkconf	Validate the syntax of the /etc/named.conf configuration file.
neat	Graphical network interface configuration utility for Red Hat Linux and Fedora Core.
netconfig	Text-mode, menu-based network interface configuration utility for Red Hat Linux and Fedora Core.
netscape	Web browser.
newaliases	Convert the /etc/aliases text file into a hashed database file that sendmail can use for processing e-mail name aliases.
nfsd	Daemon to manage filesystem requests from mounted NFS filesystems.
nmap	Comprehensive port-scanning utility.
nmapfe	Graphical front end to the nmap port-scanning utility for GNOME desktops.
nmbd	The NetBIOS name server daemon; used as part of the Samba suite to interact with Windows systems.
nslookup	Query a name server; similar to dig, but this command is not recommended. (Deprecated.)
nsupdate	Dynamically update zone information files for the named daemon.
ntpd	The NTP time server daemon. (Named xntpd in some versions of Linux.)
ntpdate	A client program that synchronizes to a remote NTP time server.
ntpq	A client program that displays information about NTP time synchronization.
ntptrace	A client program that traces a chain of NTP servers back to the primary source.
objdump	Display the contents of a file in any of several low-level formats, such as octal, hex, and ASCII.

B

Table B-1 Command-line utilities, server daemons, and graphical configuration programs (continued)

Command Name	Description
openssl	The command-line tool used with the OpenSSL cryptography toolkit.
pan	Graphical newsreader for the GNOME desktop environment.
passwd	Set or reset the password for a user account.
pico	A full-screen, character-mode text editor with on-screen help.
pine	A text-based e-mail client with a menu-style interface.
ping	Send an ICMP echo packet to see whether a remote host can be contacted via the network.
portmap	Manage network connections based on the RPC system (such as NFS connections).
postfix	A popular and secure SMTP server.
pppd	The PPP daemon; used for dial-up networking.
printconf-gui	Graphical printer configuration tool in Red Hat Linux and Fedora Core.
printtool	Configure printers in Red Hat Linux and Fedora Core.
procmail	An e-mail filtering tool (a Mail Delivery Agent).
ps	Display information about running processes.
pump	A DHCP client daemon; used to lease network addresses from a DHCP server.
pwd	Display the current working directory.
qmail	A popular and secure SMTP server.
rcp	Copy one or more files between any two computers on the network that support the r-utilities.
rlogin	Log on to a remote host that supports the r-utilities.
rm	Delete one or more files or directories.
rmdir	Delete an empty directory.
rndc	Manage the named name server daemon.
route	Use with no parameters to display the kernel routing table; use with parameters such as add -net to add or remove an entry from the kernel routing table. System start-up scripts are normally used to populate the routing table, but some manual reconfiguration with route might be needed for complex networks.
routed	Dynamic routing daemon that supports RIP and RIPv2 routing protocols.
rp3	Graphical utility for establishing a PPP dial-up connection based on a configuration created by rp3-config.
rp3-config	Graphical utility for configuring and establishing a dial-up PPP connection.
rpc.mountd	Daemon to manage mounting of remote NFS filesystems.
rpc.rquotad	Daemon to manage disk storage limits (quotas) for users who have mounted an NFS filesystem.
rpc.rstatd	Daemon to provide statistical data for an NFS filesystem.

Table B-1 Command-line utilities, server daemons, and graphical configuration programs (continued)

B

Command Name	Description
rpm	Manage software packages, including installing new packages and verifying the integrity of package files.
rsh	Execute a command on a remote computer without logging on and seeing a shell prompt.
ruptime	List the uptime for each host on the network that supports the r-utilities.
rwho	List users on the local network who are logged on. (Only those supporting r-utilities are listed.)
sed	Edit files or STDIN input using patterns and commands.
sendmail	Popular MTA (e-mail server).
setfacl	Create, delete, and modify access control list entries.
setfattr	Set the extended attributes for a file.
shutdown	Shut down the system, optionally providing a message or delay for users working on the system.
smbadduser	Add a user to the /etc/samba/smbpasswd Samba user configuration file.
smbclient	Text-mode client for accessed SMB-capable servers (including Microsoft Windows servers).
smbd	The SMB server daemon; used as part of the Samba suite to interact with Windows systems.
smbpasswd	Update the password for a Samba user, which is typically stored in the configuration file /etc/samba/smbpasswd.
smbprint	Text-mode client for printing to SMB-capable servers (including Microsoft Windows servers).
sort	Sort lines in a file according to various options.
ssh	The client utility for establishing a Secure Shell encrypted connection to another host.
ssh-agent	Manage key pairs for users who use SSH on multiple systems.
ssh-keygen	Generate key pairs for use within the SSH suite.
sshd	Server daemon to which the ssh utility can make an encrypted connection.
strings	Display the readable strings found in any file (including binary files).
stunnel	Permit secure network connections of several different protocols (for example, POP3 and IMAP) using the OpenSSL package that Web browsers use.
su	Change to a new user account.
sudo	Execute a command with root privileges; edit the permission configuration with visudo.
SWAT	Browser-based configuration program for the Samba suite.
swatch	A log-watching utility.
syslogd	The system-logging daemon; operates as configured by /etc/syslog.conf.

Table B-1   Command-line utilities, server daemons, and graphical configuration programs (continued)

Command Name	Description
tail	Display the last 15 lines of a file to STDOUT.
talk	A text-based chat client using the talk protocol. Relies on the talkd server daemon.
talkd	The server daemon used for talk-based, text-mode chat sessions.
tar	Create an archive file containing one or more files or directories, optionally compressing them all.
tcpd	The TCP Wrappers daemon; usually called from the inetd superserver; configured by /etc/hosts.allow and /etc/hosts.deny.
tcpdump	Command-line utility for analyzing network traffic.
telnet	Make a remote connection to a system.
tethereal	Text-mode version of the Ethereal network traffic analyzer.
thunderbird	A graphical e-mail client program; a sister program to Firefox.
top	Display the processes running on the system, sorted with the most processor-intensive task listed first.
touch	Update the last accessed time for a file, or create an empty file if the file named does not exist.
traceroute	Determine which routers a packet passes through to reach a destination host.
tripwire	A file integrity-checking program.
trn	A text-mode news reader.
ttysnoop	Capture the output of any tty; useful for teaching situations or spying.
ud	A text-mode LDAP client.
umount	Unmount a filesystem that is currently mounted as part of the Linux directory structure.
unzip	Uncompress a file that has been created using the zip command.
updatedb	Create an index of the entire filesystem for use by the locate command.
useradd	Add a new user to the system or modify the parameters associated with a user's account.
uucp	Use the UUCP protocol to transfer files over a dial-up connection.
vi	A powerful, full-screen text editor.
vigr	Edit the /etc/group file; used when multiple administrators might be trying to access the file at the same time. Locks the file to prevent conflicting edits.
vipw	Edit the /etc/passwd file; used when multiple administrators might be trying to access the file at the same time. Locks the file to prevent conflicting edits.

Table B-1 Command-line utilities, server daemons, and graphical configuration programs (continued)

Command Name	Description
visudo	Edit the configuration file that controls use of the sudo command.
vlock	Lock a text-mode virtual console so that the screen cannot be used without first entering the password of the person who used vlock.
vmstat	Display virtual memory (swap space) statistics.
w	List users who are logged on to the system.
wc	Display the number of characters, words, and lines in a file or STDIN input stream.
Webmin	Browser-based, multifunction system administration utility.
who	List users who are logged on to the system.
whois	Display information from the whois domain name database. (Requires Internet access.)
wvdial	Connect to a server using PPP over a modem.
xauth	Manage permission to access an X server from a remote host using the xauth authentication scheme (based on MIT cookies).
xhost	Set permissions for access to an X server from a remote host using the xhost host name-based authentication scheme.
xinetd	A superserver used to listen to multiple network ports and start the appropriate network services as needed.
xload	Display the current processor load from 0% to 100% as a small graphic.
xlock	Lock a graphical screen so that it cannot be viewed or used without first entering the password of the user who started xlock.
xlogmaster	Graphical program to manage log files.
xlsfonts	Graphical utility in which you choose from installed fonts.
yast	A configuration tool in the SuSE Linux distribution; can be used to configure networking.
zip	Compress one or more files into a single archive (the resulting file is compatible with Zip files on Windows systems).

B

Glossary

--display — An option supported by all graphical programs that defines the X server on which the program's output should be shown and from which input should be collected. Overrides the DISPLAY environment variable.

.nofinger — A file that, when created in a user's home directory, causes the finger program to display no information about that user.

.plan — A hidden file within a user's home directory, the contents of which the finger program displays when queried.

.procmailrc — The configuration file for individual Procmail users. *See also* /etc/procmailrc.

.Xauthority — The file that contains tokens (cookies) used by the xauth security system for displaying graphical programs.

/etc/host.conf — The file that specifies the order in which the resolver should consult resources to resolve the host name to an IP address.

/etc/hosts — The file used to store IP addresses and corresponding domain names for hosts, usually those frequently accessed on a local network.

/etc/hosts.allow — The configuration file that defines services and hosts that should be permitted service by TCP Wrappers.

/etc/hosts.deny — The configuration file that defines services and hosts that should be denied service by TCP Wrappers.

/etc/nologin — A file whose existence prevents all users except root from being able to log on. Regular users attempting to log on see the contents of /etc/nologin, if anything.

/etc/nsswitch.conf — The file that defines the order in which the resolver and many other programs use various local or network resources to obtain configuration information.

/etc/passwd — The file in which basic user account configuration data is stored.

/etc/printcap — The file in which printer definitions are stored.

/etc/procmailrc — The system-wide configuration file for Procmail. *See also* .procmailrc.

/etc/resolv.conf — The file that configures the Linux resolver.

/etc/securetty — A file listing all terminals from which root can log on.

/etc/shadow — The file in which users' encrypted passwords and password control data are stored.

/etc/sudoers — A configuration file that determines which users can perform which tasks using the sudo command.

/etc/sysconfig — The directory in which networking configuration files and scripts are stored, specifically in the subdirectory network-scripts and the file networking.

/lib/modules — The directory in which all of the available kernel modules for Linux are stored.

/var/spool/mail — The default directory for e-mail inboxes on most Linux systems.

A record — A line (a record) within a DNS zone file that provides the IP address for the given host.

access control list (ACL) — A data structure that defines the access permitted for individual directories and individual programs.

Address Resolution Protocol (ARP) — A protocol that broadcasts a message to an entire network segment to obtain a host's MAC address.

Advanced Encryption Standard (AES) — A replacement for DES. The next generation of government-approved encryption standards. Uses the Rijndael algorithm (pronounced "Rain Doll").

afpfs — A software package that lets Linux users access Macintosh resources. This software is still available for download, but because it is not currently being developed, is not supported by the latest Linux kernels.

agent — An SNMP-aware program running on a host. The client that collects data for analysis and transmission using other SNMP software.

algorithm — A set of rules or steps that, when followed, result in a predictable outcome.

anonymous FTP — The use of FTP for public access via a common username, without a user-specific account on the FTP server.

anonymous user home directory — The directory on Linux that anonymous FTP users can access for downloading or uploading files. Typically either `/var/ftp` or `/home/ftp`.

anonymous users — The users logging on to an FTP server who do not have a regular Linux user account and are thus restricted to a specific area of the file system. *See* anonymous FTP.

Apache module — A functionality for the Apache Web server that can be independently loaded on the fly as a shared object.

AppleTalk — The networking protocol used by Apple Macintosh computers. AppleTalk is supported in Linux via the Netatalk package.

ARCnet — An older token-passing network technology that has lost a great deal of its former popularity. ARCnet is reliable, but slower than more modern networking technologies like Token-Ring or Ethernet.

arp — A command that displays or alters the contents of the ARP cache. Used mainly for troubleshooting network connectivity.

ARP cache — A list of IP address-to-hardware mappings maintained by the ARP protocol to assist in routing packets.

asymmetric encryption algorithm — An encryption algorithm in which different keys are used to encrypt and decrypt a message. One is kept secret, one is distributed publicly. Often called public-key encryption.

Asynchronous Transfer Mode (ATM) — A networking technology used for the Internet backbone or other specialized high-speed networks. It is fast (currently 155 Mb/s with 622 Mb/s under development) but also expensive.

attribute — A discrete data element that is part of an object within a directory service database such as LDAP; a property of files and directories that indicates how the file or directory should be handled by the operating system, filesystem, and programs.

authentication — The process of proving to a computer system or another person that you are who you say you are.

authority servers — The DNS servers that are authoritative for particular domains and zones.

back door — A method of accessing a program or a computer system that is known to its creator but not to other users of the system. It is undocumented and hidden.

bandwidth — The amount of information that a network technology can transmit; usually expressed in bits per second (b/s).

Big Brother — An intrusion-detection program that uses a client/server model to gather network service and host resource data from numerous hosts on a network and report that data in a browser-based interface.

bindconf — A graphical utility used to configure zone files.

biometrics — In computer security, user authentication techniques that rely on unique human attributes, such as fingerprints and retina patterns.

bird — An open source routing daemon that supports RIPv1, RIPv2, OSPF, and BGP.

Blowfish — A symmetric cipher.

BOOTP — A protocol used by diskless workstations (prior to DHCP being available) that allowed them to obtain network configuration instructions.

Border Gateway Protocol (BGP) — A widely used external routing protocol.

broadcast address — An IP address in which the host ID consists of all ones, which causes the packet to be sent to every host on the named network.

brute force attack — A method of obtaining access to a system by trying all possible combinations until one succeeds in guessing a password.

buffer overflow attack — A technique for gaining access to a computer system by exploiting a weakness in the design of a computer program. When a cracker follows a specific sequence of steps or provides specific input to a program, the program becomes confused and tries to use computer memory inappropriately. The buffer, or memory space, reserved for a part of the program overflows. The result can be either corruption of system data, a crashed server, or even direct root access.

bus topology — A network topology design in which computers are connected to a single length of cable.

C News — A Linux news server program designed for small networks with low newsgroup volume.

cable modem — A device that supports high-speed networking through a cable television connection, with the cable TV company acting as the ISP.

cache poisoning attack — An attack in which a cracker attempts to block access to a site by uploading erroneous information to a DNS server's cache.

caching name server — A DNS server that contains no preconfigured information on domains (except `localhost`), but simply queries other DNS servers and caches the results.

capability — A task that the Linux kernel permits a program to perform, such as the ability to send broadcast packets to the network and the ability to use the `reboot` command.

CERT Coordination Center (CERT/CC) — A federally funded software engineering institute that focuses its attention on computer security issues and provides information to security and system administration professionals around the world; operated by Carnegie Mellon University.

certificate — A numeric code used to identify an organization.

certificate authority (CA) — An organization that issues a certificate to another person or organization after verifying the applicant's credentials.

chain — A list of rules that controls how packets are routed or handled in the Linux kernel.

Challenge Handshake Authentication Protocol (CHAP) — A security method used by PPP. CHAP maintains username and password data locally but never sends it to the remote computer.

chargen — A network testing service provided by `inetd` on port 19. Whenever queried, `chargen` responds with a stream of characters (the standard character set, in numeric order).

chattr — A program that sets and clears filesystem attributes.

checksum — A computed value that helps to verify that a file or transmission has not been corrupted.

chkrootkit — A software package that checks for evidence of more than 30 different rootkits. This package works much like a virus checker, though it can only report the presence of a rootkit; it cannot eliminate one from your system.

chroot — A filesystem feature that allows a program to see a directory as if it were the system's root directory.

cipher — A cryptographic technique or rule that converts plaintext into ciphertext.

ciphertext — A message that has been encoded using a cipher so that it is no longer readable. The end result of encrypting plaintext.

class — A definition for a type of object within a directory service database such as LDAP. The class defines the attributes of an object as well as its place within a directory service tree.

classes of users — The practice of defining groups of potential FTP clients within an FTP server configuration to aid efficient server configuration.

Classless Interdomain Routing (CIDR) format — A method of indicating the network prefix length of an IP address by writing it with a slash following the address (for example, 192.168.14.45/24).

client — A computer or software program that requests information or service from a server and then processes or acts on the information it receives.

client/server — A model of computing in which information is shared between networked systems by multiple clients requesting information from a server.

CNAME record — A line (record) in a DNS zone file that defines an alias for a given name.

coaxial cable (coax) — A network transmission medium (a cable) made up of a single, thick copper wire encased in thick plastic and foil layers of insulation. Coax is used mostly for video signals, though many people now have Internet access available via a cable modem using coax cable.

collision — The result when two or more Ethernet packets attempt to use an Ethernet cable at the same time.

co-locating — An organization's placement of a Web server at the office of its ISP, often to rely on the ISP's security measures to protect the Web server.

Common Internet File System (CIFS) — The latest extended version of the SMB protocol, used by recent Microsoft operating systems and provided in Linux via the Samba suite.

common name — The name assigned to a leaf object in a directory service database such as LDAP.

Common UNIX Printing System (CUPS) — A replacement for older printing systems used by Linux. CUPS is based on the Internet Printing Protocol or IPP.

compact news file system (CNFS) — A method of storing newsgroup postings within INN using a single file as a buffer for holding multiple individual postings.

computer crime — Unauthorized access to a computer system.

connectionless — A protocol that sends packets without regard to whether they are correctly received by the destination computer. IP and UDP are examples.

connection-oriented — A protocol that keeps track of which packets have been correctly received by the destination computer, resending those that are not received, managing the flow of packets, and reporting errors.

console — The SNMP program that collects and analyzes data from SNMP agents on a network.

container — A special type of Apache configuration directive that activates other directives only if a condition is met or only within a particular context.

container object — Within a directory service database such as LDAP, an object that can have one or more subordinate objects "below it" in the data structure. *See also* leaf object.

control_flag — An element of a PAM module configuration that determines how PAM will process multiple modules in a single stack (for example, the auth stack).

cookie — A token, or long number, used as an identifier by a program such as a Web browser or the xauth X Window System security program.

cost — A measure of how efficient a route is. The route with the lowest cost should always be chosen, other things being equal.

cracker — A person who breaks the law or ethical rules by accessing computer systems without authorization. Some crackers have malicious intentions, but others only want to test their skills by exploring areas that they are not authorized to enter. *See also* hacker.

Cryptographic File System (CFS) — A filesystem driver supported by Linux that adds cryptographic features to an NFS-like file-sharing model.

Cryptographic IP Encapsulation (CIPE) — An IP packet encryption protocol. It lacks some features of IPsec but is already fully implemented (while IPsec is not). CIPE operates by tunneling IP packets within encrypted UDP packets.

cryptography — The science of encoding—and trying to decode—data that has been rendered unreadable using special knowledge or tools.

Data Encryption Standard (DES) — The first widely accepted standard for encryption, developed in the 1970s by IBM and the National Institute of Standards and Technology.

datagram — A network packet sent over a connection-less protocol such as UDP.

daytime — A network testing service provided by inetd on port 13. Returns the current date and time in human-readable form.

deface — To alter the text or images on a Web home page.

default gateway — *See* default router.

default route — An IP address configured on a host computer that identifies the computer to which packets should be sent when their network is not known to the host.

default router — The router to which a packet is sent if a host has no idea where else to send it. Also called the *default gateway*.

denial-of-service (DoS) attack — A cracker activity that ties up an attacked server or a particular program with so much bogus network traffic that it cannot respond to valid requests.

destination port — A port that identifies the application that is to receive the packet.

dhclient — One of the most widely used Linux DHCP client daemons.

dhcpcd — One of the most widely used Linux DHCP client daemons.

dhcpd — The most widely used Linux DHCP server daemon.

diald — A program that manages PPP dial-up connections, initiating a connection only when needed by network traffic and disconnecting when the connection is no longer needed.

dig — A utility used to query specific DNS servers for specific resource records.

digital signature — A part of an electronic transaction that gives it the same legally binding effect as a document signed with an ink pen.

Digital Signature Algorithm (DSA) — A popular algorithm used to sign encrypted files to verify their origin.

digital subscriber line (DSL) — A relatively new digital telephone service that can be added to existing telephone lines in some areas; used for relatively fast Internet connections.

directory service — A database of information about network resources (or other resources) that can be accessed by people throughout a network.

discard — A network testing service provided by inetd on port 9. The discard service acts like /dev/null. Anything sent to the service is discarded without any processing.

DISPLAY — An environment variable that controls the display of graphical programs in X.

distinguished name (DN) — The complete path to an object within the directory tree, traversing (and naming) all the container objects above that object.

distributed denial-of-service (DDoS) — A special type of attack in which a cracker infiltrates many systems and installs a program that will execute a DoS attack on an assigned target at the cracker's command.

dmesg — A utility that prints the contents of the kernel ring buffer to standard output (by default, the screen). Using dmesg right after booting Linux is a good way to see all the hardware-related messages generated by the kernel.

DNS Blacklist (dnsbl) — A list of IP addresses that are known principally as sources of spam and whose messages can be blocked automatically by mail servers such as sendmail.

DNS spoofing — Pretending that a request comes from a different host than its true originating host.

domain name — A name applied to multiple hosts on the Internet that are referred to collectively, such as *ibm.com* or *utah.edu*.

Domain Name Service (DNS) — The name normally used to refer to the name service used by the Internet (BIND).

dotted-quad (dotted-decimal) notation — A method of writing IP addresses as four numbers separated by periods.

dumb terminal — *See* terminal.

Dynamic Host Configuration Protocol (DHCP) — A protocol that allows a server to hand out IP addresses automatically to clients on a network.

dynamic routing — Collecting and updating routing table information automatically using a routing protocol.

echo — A network testing service provided by `inetd` on port 7. The `echo` service parrots back whatever it receives.

ElGamal — A symmetric cipher used by GPG.

elm — A powerful text-based e-mail client (MUA) for reading locally stored e-mail folders.

encryption — The process of converting plaintext to ciphertext using a cipher algorithm.

eth0 — The device name in Linux for the first Ethernet card installed in a host.

Ethereal — A powerful, graphical network traffic analysis tool.

Ethernet — An international networking standard developed in the 1970s by Xerox, Intel, and Digital Equipment Corporation (now part of Compaq Computer Corp.).

execute (x) — A standard Linux file permission—represented in utilities by x—that permits execution of a file as a program or accessing a directory (when assigned to that directory).

exportfs — A command used to activate the contents of /etc/exports.

exports — The /etc/exports configuration file, which defines file systems that NFS can make available to other hosts.

exterior routing protocols — Routing protocols designed for routing packets between networks controlled by different organizations; packets are routed based on administrative policies, which are often controlled by how much a particular organization's routing information is trusted.

Federal Information Processing Standard (FIPS) — A standard for information processing (such as an encryption algorithm) that has been approved for use by government agencies.

Fiber Distributed Data Interface (FDDI) — A networking technology that uses fiber-optic cable in a dual-ring topology. It is highly reliable, but not installed much now because it is slower and more expensive than newer Ethernet technologies.

fiber-optic — A network transmission medium (a cable) made of glass or plastic to transmit light signals; it is capable of extremely fast transmission speeds, immune from electromagnetic interference, and highly secure. It is also very expensive to install.

File Transfer Protocol (FTP) — A protocol used to share files between networked computer systems.

finger — A program that provides brief information about a user.

fingerprint — A small number that is derived from a larger number (such as a public key) using a hash. The fingerprint provides a convenient test of the integrity of the larger number.

fingerprinting — Using the results of a port scan to identify the operating system of a targeted host.

firewall — A program that filters (blocks) IP packets based on their characteristics, according to a set of rules.

fixed wireless — A wireless network communication technology that relies on small transceivers mounted on buildings; it is normally used to connect multiple offices in the same city.

flags — Numeric status indications stored within a packet header that are used to establish and track information about the network communication of which the packet is a part.

forward — The process of sending a packet to a different network than the one from where it originated.

forward lookup — Using DNS to convert a domain name to an IP address.

forwarding name server — A DNS server that forwards all queries to another name server for processing.

fragmentation — The process of breaking up an IP packet into multiple smaller packets for transmission on a different type of network.

frame relay — A technology used to provide dedicated high-speed Internet connectivity via telephone wires.

ftp — The most common text-based client program for accessing FTP servers.

ftpaccess — The main FTP server configuration file.

ftpshut — A command that causes the FTP server to stop allowing connections.

ftpusers — An FTP server configuration file listing user accounts that are not allowed to log on via FTP.

fully qualified domain name (FQDN) — The complete or official name of a network host, including the name of the domain of which the host is a part. More casually, a domain name.

gated — The Linux program that implements OSPF, BGP, and RIPv2 (with classless addressing).

gateway — Generally, a router that can forward packets to other network segments. Also, the default router that acts as a "gateway" or exit point to reach networks outside of a local segment. Also, more technically, a system that can translate between protocols at the Transport and Application layers of a network.

Gb/s — Gigabits per second. 1 Gb/s is 1024 Mb/s or roughly a billion bits per second.

General Routing Encapsulation (GRE) — A tunneling protocol originally designed by Cisco and now specified by RFC 2784. It has more capabilities than ipip tunneling.

getfacl — A program that displays the access control list entries of files and directories.

getfattr — A program that displays the extended attributes of files and directories.

getty — A program (and a type of program) that monitors terminals for activity and processes it, generally to allow a user to log on.

gFTP — A graphical FTP client. Installed by default on many Linux systems.

Gigabit Ethernet — An Ethernet networking technology that can transmit data at either 1 Gb/s or 10 Gb/s.

Global Information Assurance Certification (GIAC) — A hands-on security certification program run by the SANS Institute.

Gnu Privacy Guard (GPG) — A command-line, public-key encryption utility that is compatible with PGP in many respects.

grpck — A utility that verifies that all group memberships are valid user accounts and that no syntax errors exist in the /etc/group file.

guest users — The users logging on to an FTP server who have a regular Linux user account, but are restricted in what they can do while logged on using FTP.

hacker — A technology expert who enjoys learning about the intricate workings of computer systems and software. To some people's understanding, a technology expert who maliciously attacks others' computer systems. *See also* cracker.

hard mount — A method of mounting an NFS file system that causes NFS to wait indefinitely for the NFS server to respond.

harden — To make a computer system more secure against cracker attacks.

hardware address — *See* Media Access Control (MAC) address.

hash — The result of a mathematical function that converts a large number into a smaller number in a predictable way.

header — The highly structured information within a packet that defines how the network stacks should handle the packet.

header checksum — A numeric code within an IP packet header used to ensure the integrity of the header information.

hop — A pass through a router.

host — A device on the network, such as a workstation, server, or printer.

host — A utility used to query specific DNS servers for specific resource records.

host ID — The part of an IP address that designates the host to which the address refers within a certain network.

host name — The name assigned to a host on a network.

https — A code within a Web page URL that indicates the page was transmitted over an encrypted connection.

hub — A device used as a wiring center that allows cables from multiple computers to be concentrated into a single network connection.

IDEA — A patented symmetric cipher.

ifconfig — The interface configuration utility that configures a networking interface within the Linux kernel or that lists all currently configured network interfaces.

ifdown — The script used to shut down individual networking interfaces. Generally used by other scripts such as /etc/rc.d/init.d/network rather than directly by a user.

ifup — The script used to start individual networking interfaces. Generally used by other scripts such as /etc/rc.d/init.d/network rather than directly by a user.

IglooFTP — A popular graphical FTP client.

inetd — The most widely used superserver program. *See also* xinetd.

init — The master control program that the Linux kernel starts right after the system is started.

INN — The most widely used news server software for Linux. Implemented by the innd daemon.

insmod — The command used to install a module into a running Linux kernel. It can include parameters that provide additional information to the module being installed.

Integrated Services Digital Network (ISDN) — A type of telephone service that provides digital signals for higher-speed network connectivity than standard modems.

interface — A computer's networking port or connection.

interior routing protocols — Routing protocols designed for routing packets among networks controlled by a single organization; packets are routed based on mathematical models.

Internet — A collection of many networks around the world that are linked together via high-speed networking connections.

Internet Control Message Protocol (ICMP) — A protocol used by IP to transmit control and error data about IP traffic on a network. Most widely known as the basis of the ping utility, which uses ICMP Echo and Echo-request commands.

Internet Message Access Protocol (IMAP) — A protocol used to interact with a user's e-mail messages that are stored on a remote server, as with many popular Web portals that allow e-mail access via a Web browser.

Internet model — A conceptual model of networking that divides protocols into four layers based on their function. This is the model used by Linux.

Internet Protocol (IP) — The foundation protocol for transporting data across most Linux networks as well as the Internet.

Internetwork Packet Exchange (IPX) — A protocol designed by Novell Inc. based on an older protocol called the Xerox Network System (XNS) protocol. IPX was the dominant protocol on local area networks for many years and is fully supported in Linux. It uses the network hardware address as a host ID, thus simplifying network configuration.

intrusion detection — The process of noticing an attempted or successful break-in to a system.

intrusion-detection system (IDS) — A type of software that aids network intrusion detection.

ip — A program that allows you to change interface names.

IP address — A numbering scheme that allows each computer in the world that wants to use the Internet (or just IP) to have a unique ID number.

IP aliasing — A networking feature that allows a single physical interface to have more than one IP address assigned to it.

ip link — A utility that lists currently configured network interfaces.

IP spoofing — A cracker attack in which special low-level software assigns any address the cracker selects as either the source or the destination address on an IP packet.

IP Tables — The lists of rules associated with one of the programming hooks provided in the networking stacks by the netfilter architecture.

IPsec — An industry standard for IP packet encryption. IPsec is supported in Linux, but as a standard, it is still not completely settled.

iptables — The command used to manage firewall rules within the netfilter firewall architecture in version 2.4 and later of the Linux kernel.

IPTraf — A popular "packet sniffer" program for viewing network activity on a LAN.

IPv6 — The new version of IP that uses 128 bits for addresses instead of 32 bits, and adds numerous other features, including dynamic configuration capabilities, better security options, and more intelligent packet routing. Using IPv6 requires many changes to other protocols, as well as generally more sophistication in networking hardware and software.

ISA bus — The Industry Standard Architecture bus that was developed by IBM in the early 1980s and included in early personal computers. It is also called the AT bus. The ISA bus is obsolete.

iwconfig — The interface configuration utility specific to wireless interfaces.

kb/s — Kilobits per second. 1 kb/s is 1000 bits per second.

keepalive — Maintaining an active network connection after sending a file, based on the theory that a client that has requested one file is likely to request several.

Kerberos — A special type of authentication for organizational networks.

kernel ring buffer — A memory area that holds messages generated by the kernel. When the buffer is full, the oldest message is discarded each time a new one is generated.

key — A code (usually numeric) that can be used to encrypt or decrypt a message.

key pair — The combination of a public key that can be handed out to others and a private or secret key that remains hidden on a user's system (and is protected with a passphrase).

key ring — The collection of public keys stored on a system; a file containing all of the keys to which GPG has immediate access.

kfinger — A graphical version of finger (including talk protocol capability) for KDE.

Knode — A newsreader for KDE.

last mile connection — The connection between a LAN within a home or office and the Internet or other high-speed network.

ldapsearch — A text-mode LDAP client in Linux.

Leaf Node — A Linux news server program designed for small networks with low newsgroup volume.

leaf object — Within a directory service database such as LDAP, an object that cannot have subordinate objects "below it" in the data structure. *See also* container object.

lease — The action a DHCP server takes in assigning an IP address to a client for a specific length of time.

libpcap — A programming library used for capturing network packets, required by many network traffic analysis utilities.

lidsadm — The administrative command used to control LIDS.

LIDS-free session (LFS) — A command-line session on a system running LIDS, in which LIDS does not affect the permitted actions.

Lightweight Directory Access Protocol (LDAP) — A protocol for accessing the lightweight directory service.

Links — A text-based Web browser.

Linux Intrusion-detection System (LIDS) — A complex and hard-to-use intrusion-detection system that alters the Linux kernel to remove root's comprehensive access to a Linux system.

ListProc — A commercial mailing list manager (MLM). See *www.listproc.net*.

LISTSERV — The most widely used MLM in the world. A commercial product available from L-Soft (*www.lsoft.com*).

LKM — A Linux kernel module that has been installed as part of a rootkit.

lo — The device name of the loopback network device.

logcheck — A utility package that checks log files each hour for any suspicious entries.

lokkit — A text-mode program that sets up basic firewall rules according to the level of security protection desired.

loopback interface — Any IP address beginning with 127 (127.0.0.1 is normally used). This address is used only within a computer for testing the network stacks. No packet with a 127 address is ever sent out of the local computer.

lsattr — A program that displays filesystem attributes.

lsmod — The command used to list the modules that are loaded in your kernel at that moment.

Lynx — A text-based Web browser.

m4 — A program that converts a text file containing configuration parameters into a complete `sendmail.cf` file.

mail — A very basic text-mode e-mail client (MUA) for Linux.

Mail Delivery Agent (MDA) — A program that places e-mail in a user's mailbox so that it can be read. This function is often subsumed by an MTA.

Mail Transfer Agent (MTA) — A program that moves e-mail messages from one server on the Internet to another. Also called an e-mail server.

Mail User Agent (MUA) — A program that displays and manages e-mail messages for a user.

mailing list — A group of users who share information on an ongoing basis via e-mail using special management software.

mailing list manager (MLM) — A software package used to create and manage mailing lists, including collections of user information and the messages those users send.

Mailman — A free MLM with many standard list management features.

majordomo — One of the most widely used MLM packages. A free software package consisting of Perl scripts that interact with the `sendmail` e-mail server.

man-in-the-middle attack — A general term for any security attack in which a cracker intercepts communication, reads or alters it, and leads the sender to believe that the information was received by the intended recipient.

map — To create a correspondence between a user ID on an NFS client and user permissions on an NFS server.

master — The authoritative name server for a zone, typically containing database files that provide IP addresses for hosts within that zone.

maximum transmission unit (MTU) — The maximum size for a packet on a given type of network.

Mb/s — Megabits per second. 1 Mb/s is 1000 kb/s, or exactly one million bits per second.

Media Access Control (MAC) address — A unique address assigned to (and programmed into) each Ethernet card in the world.

mesg — A utility that enables or disables other users' ability to send a message to your screen using the `write`, `talk`, or `wall` (write all) commands.

message digest hash (MD5) — A hash that converts a number of any length to a 128-bit (32-hexadecimal-digit) number called a checksum.

metadata — In the context of a filesystem, the information about a file or directory, such as its name, size, length, date/time stamps, permissions, attributes, extended attributes, and access control list.

metric — A value assigned to a network interface to guide dynamic routing decisions about when to use that interface. A higher metric means an interface is less likely to be used if other interfaces are also available.

mgetty — A version of `getty` adapted to use with modems.

mingetty — A minimalist version of `getty`.

minicom — A terminal emulator program used to connect to a remote computer using a modem.

MIT Magic Cookie — The name given to a cookie used by the xauth program for X display authentication.

mke2fs — A program that creates an ext2 or ext3 filesystem.

modprobe — The command to load a kernel module while automatically checking for and loading dependent modules.

module_type — A characterization of program activity that determines which set of PAM modules will be used to authorize that activity. Possible module_types include auth, account, session, and password.

Mozilla — A popular graphical Linux Web browser that began as an open source version of Netscape Navigator.

multicasting — An IP addressing system in which one computer can address a packet to multiple specific hosts.

MX record — A line (record) in a DNS zone file that defines the mail exchanger for the named host. MX records are used by Mail Transfer Agents (MTAs) to find the correct e-mail server to contact when delivering e-mail to a recipient.

name server — A computer running name service software that can translate from IP addresses to names and vice versa.

named — The Linux program that implements the DNS protocol to create a DNS server; part of the BIND collection of programs.

ncftp — A text-based FTP client program similar to FTP, but newer and more refined.

neat — The command-line invocation of the Network Configuration Tool.

Netatalk — A software package for Linux that allows Macintosh computers to recognize Linux (have it show up on the Mac desktop as an available shared resource).

NetBEUI — A protocol within Windows-based computers that implements NetBIOS functionality.

NetBIOS — A protocol that provides a network name resolution service, similar in concept to DNS. Used by Windows operating systems and provided as part of the Samba suite.

netfilter — The packet filtering and advanced routing architecture in Linux 2.4 and later kernels.

network address port translation (NAPT) — A routing technique in which the IP addresses and ports in a packet are altered during routing.

Network Address Translation (NAT) — A routing technique in which the IP addresses in a packet are altered during routing.

Network Configuration Tool — A graphical interface provided in Fedora Core that is used to manage network interfaces. It can be started from the command line using neat.

Network File System (NFS) — A protocol used to share file systems on a network.

network ID — The part of an IP address that designates the network to which the address refers.

Network Information System (NIS) — A protocol that lets hosts share configuration information across a network, so that only one master configuration file need be supported for a number of hosts. *See also* NIS+.

network interface card (NIC) — A hardware device used to connect a computer to a network.

Network News Transport Protocol (NNTP) — The protocol used to transport newsgroup messages (postings).

Network Time Protocol (NTP) — A time management and synchronization protocol used by Linux. Implemented by the ntpd daemon.

network traffic analysis — *See* packet sniffing.

nfsd — A daemon that handles file transfers for a mounted NFS file system, based on the settings that the rpc.mountd daemon has validated.

NIS+ — A more advanced version of the NIS protocol. *See also* NIS.

nmap — The most widely used port-scanning utility.

nmapfe — A utility that acts as a graphical front end to the nmap command; requires the GNOME desktop.

nmbd — The daemon within the Samba suite that provides NetBIOS capability to Linux.

node — A data element within a directory service database such as LDAP. Also called an object.

NS record — A line (a record) within a DNS zone file that defines the authoritative name server for the given domain.

nslookup — A utility used to query DNS servers for resource records.

nsupdate — A utility used to update zone files dynamically at the command line.

ntpd — The Linux daemon that implements NTP. *See also* xntpd.

null scan — A method of port scanning in which a TCP packet is sent with no flags set.

nutcracker — One of many password-cracking tools.

object — A data element within a directory service database such as LDAP. Also called a node.

one-time pad — An encryption method in which a message is converted to numbers, and then random numbers taken from a list are added to each part of the message. The recipient must have the same list of random numbers to decrypt the message. Assuming no one else has the list of random numbers, the encrypted message is considered unbreakable.

One-time Password In Everything (OPIE) — A single-user password system available for Linux. OPIE was created by the U.S. Naval Research Laboratory, based on the S/Key program.

Open Shortest Path First (OSPF) — A protocol that automatically fills routing tables with information about how to reach networks.

Open Systems Interconnection (OSI) reference model — A reference model that divides networking into seven conceptual layers, each assigned a specific task. The OSI model is the basis for much of modern networking theory and system design.

OpenLDAP — The most widely used LDAP server on Linux systems.

OpenSSH — A free version of SSH included in most Linux distributions.

opt-in — A marketing scheme in which users do not receive advertisements unless they specifically request to be added to a list of recipients.

opt-out — A marketing scheme in which users automatically receive advertisements unless they ask to be removed from a list of recipients.

packet — A small collection of data with identifying information (headers) that is destined for or coming from a network.

packet mangling — The altering of packets by a router to change the way they are handled or routed.

packet sniffing — A network activity in which the headers and payload of all packets on the network are captured and examined (also called network traffic analysis).

Pan — A newsreader for GNOME.

Parallel Line Internet Protocol (PLIP) — A protocol that relies on a parallel port to transmit network data, often to connect two computers in a simple, inexpensive network.

passphrase — A long password.

passwd — A utility used to change passwords or set password control options that are stored in /etc/shadow (such as a maximum use period for each password).

Password Authentication Protocol (PAP) — A security method used with PPP. PAP stores pairs of usernames and passwords in a local file and transmits them over the Internet for review by an ISP.

password cracking — An activity by which a cracker obtains the password for a valid user account, either by using a program that examines millions of passwords until the correct one is found, or by guessing based on personal knowledge about the user.

payload — The data that a network packet is transferring. Packets are divided into a header and payload.

peer-to-peer network — A model of networking in which all computers on the network are peers and have the ability to initiate communications, respond to requests for information, and interact with users independent of other computer systems.

pine — A powerful, text-based e-mail client (MUA) for reading locally stored e-mail folders.

ping — The utility used to send ICMP echo packets for network testing.

ping scan — A method of port scanning in which any hosts that are reachable using ICMP echo packets (which are used to ping a host) are reported.

plaintext — A readable message.

pluggable authentication module (PAM) — A security architecture designed to improve Linux user-level security, add flexibility in how user access is configured, and permit Linux to integrate smoothly with user information stored on other systems.

Point-to-Point Protocol (PPP) — A protocol that allows a host to tie directly to a single computer, making a network of two systems. PPP is used most often with a modem providing the underlying physical connection to the second computer.

Point-to-Point Tunneling Protocol (PPTP) — A standard created by Microsoft for setting up a virtual private network (VPN). PPTP uses two connections, one for control information and one for data.

port forwarding — A routing technique within SSH that can encrypt many other protocols by connecting another service's port to the SSH port.

port scanning — A network activity in which packets sent to a host are analyzed to learn about that host.

portmap — The program that watches for RPC requests (such as from NFS daemons) and creates the network connections to make them function.

PortSentry — A program that watches network ports for packets that appear to be port scans, then takes action based on a configuration file.

Post Office Protocol 3 (POP3) — A protocol used to download a single user's e-mail messages that are stored on a remote e-mail server.

Pretty Good Privacy (PGP) — The first utility to provide public-key encryption. Created by Phil Zimmermann.

prime number — A number that cannot be broken down into factors other than itself and 1. Prime numbers are the core mathematical feature of public-key encryption.

privacy policy — A voluntary statement by an organization about how it will and will not use data that it collects about users or customers, often via a Web site.

private-key encryption — A form of encryption using a symmetric algorithm.

proc filesystem — A virtual filesystem that allows you to view and modify kernel settings.

Procmail — A special Mail Delivery Agent (MDA) that filters e-mail messages.

promiscuous mode — A mode of operation for NICs in which any packets that are visible to the NIC are captured and processed, not only those that are addressed to the NIC.

protocol — A formalized system of rules for communication.

protocol stack — The software for maintaining a network protocol. A stack may refer to a single protocol capability or to the collection of protocols supported by a host or server.

PTR record — A line (record) in a DNS zone file that maps an address to a name. Used for reverse DNS lookups.

public-key encryption — A form of encryption using an asymmetric encryption algorithm.

pump — One of the most widely used Linux DHCP client daemons.

Quality of Service (QoS) — A networking feature that guarantees bandwidth to certain users or certain programs.

randomization — A method of performing a port scan in which multiple ports are contacted in random order to reduce suspicion.

RC2 — A symmetric cipher.

RC4 — A symmetric cipher.

RC5 — A symmetric cipher.

rcp — A utility that allows a user to copy files between two hosts. Either or both of the hosts can be remote to the host on which **rcp** is executed.

read (r) — A standard Linux file permission (represented in utilities by r) that permits reading the contents of a file or listing the files in a directory.

real users — Users logging on to an FTP server who have a regular Linux user account.

realm — Within a Kerberos-enabled network, all the users and services whose keys are stored on the Kerberos server.

recipe — A formula used by Procmail to filter or examine an e-mail message and take an action if it matches the given criteria.

Remote Procedure Call (RPC) — A protocol used to allow programs to communicate over a network. RPC acts almost as a superserver, watching for network requests from RPC-capable programs and transferring them to the appropriate transport protocol (such as TCP or UDP).

Request for Comments (RFC) — A document describing a protocol or other technical advance, written by a technical expert and posted on the Internet for review. It then becomes the accepted definition for the protocol or standard it describes.

resolver — The client portion of DNS, which makes requests to a DNS server so that other programs on a host can use the IP address of a named server to make a network connection.

resource record — Information about a name that a DNS server can provide to answer queries. Example resource records include the A record to associate an IP address and host name, the MX record to define a host's mail exchanger, and the PTR record to associate a host name with an IP address for reverse DNS lookups.

reverse lookup — Using DNS to obtain the name that corresponds to an IP address.

ring topology — A network topology design in which multiple computers are linked into a circular shape.

rlogin — A utility that allows a user to log on to another host, much like the telnet command.

rndc — A control program used to manage the named daemon.

root name servers — DNS servers designated as a starting point for DNS queries.

rootkit — A collection of programs and scripts designed to permit a cracker continued access to a compromised system, even after the original security hole that permitted access has been discovered and closed.

route — A command that displays or configures the routing table within the Linux kernel.

routed — The Linux program that implements the Routing Information Protocol (RIP).

router — A device that connects multiple network segments, translating data formats as needed by forwarding packets between segments; also the software program on a computer used for this purpose.

routing algorithm — The software that determines how to process a packet that is sent to the router for forwarding; also called a *routing engine*.

routing engine — *See* routing algorithm.

Routing Information Protocol (RIP) — A protocol that automatically fills routing tables with information about how to reach networks.

routing table — A listing within a router containing network IDs, the network interface by which packets can reach that network, and the IP address of the next router to which the packet should be sent.

rpc.mountd — A daemon used as part of NFS to make new connections, mounting a remote file system after checking relevant permissions to see if the mount is permitted.

RSA — The most widely known algorithm for public-key encryption. Developed by Ronald Rivest, Adi Shamir, and Len Adleman.

rsh — A utility that allows a user to execute a command on a remote host without logging on to that host.

rule — A configuration setting that defines characteristics of an IP packet and an action to take for any packet that has those characteristics.

r-utilities — Short for "remote utilities," the programs that allow a user to access remote hosts to run programs, transfer files, or perform other functions within a trusted network.

S/Key — A specialized, single-use password system designed by Bell Communications Research.

Samba — A suite of programs for Linux and many UNIX operating systems that permits these systems to support Windows protocols such as SMB, CIFS, and NetBIOS.

Samhain — A file integrity checker that runs as a daemon and supports client/server configurations.

schema — The collection of all the possible object classes and their attributes that a directory service supports.

screen-locking program — A program that disables input from your keyboard and usually clears or hides the screen so that private information is not visible to passersby.

screen number — A number used as part of the DISPLAY environment variable for remotely running graphical programs. Most systems have only a single X Window System session, referred to as screen number 0. The screen number is the second zero (the first is the sequence number) in the standard format :0.0.

script-kiddies — The unskilled crackers who use pre-packaged software "kits" or scripts created by skilled crackers to break into systems that have not taken basic security precautions.

Secure Hash Algorithm (SHA-1) — A hashing algorithm, more secure than MD5, that creates a 160-bit hash of any file or key to help check whether it was tampered with or otherwise corrupted during transmission.

Secure Shell (SSH) — A protocol that provides network connectivity equivalent to an encrypted version of Telnet, plus additional support to allow encryption of other protocols.

Security Administrator Tool for Analyzing Networks (SATAN) — One of the first widely known security-auditing programs.

Security Administrator's Integrated Network Tool (SAINT) — A popular security-auditing program that superseded the SATAN program.

security audit — A review or test of how secure a system really is and what needs to be done to improve its security.

segment — A part of a network whose traffic has been isolated from other parts of the network to improve the efficiency of the network as a whole. Each segment's network traffic is only "seen" within that segment unless it is destined for a host outside the segment.

sequence number — The sequential number of the screen on which a graphical program is displayed. Used as part of the DISPLAY environment variable for remotely running graphical programs. Its value is zero (indicated by :0) except on multimonitor systems.

Serial Line Internet Protocol (SLIP) — A protocol that relies on a serial port as the underlying physical connection used to transmit network data, usually over a modem to an ISP.

server — A computer or software program that provides information or services of some type to clients.

Server Message Block (SMB) — The transport protocol used for file and print sharing by Windows systems and the Samba suite.

server-parsed documents — *See* server-side includes.

server-side includes — Statements within a text file that are processed on the fly by a Web server when that document is requested.

Set UID bit — A special file permission that causes executable files (programs) to use the permissions of the user who owns the file rather than those of the user who executed the file. Also called SUID.

setfacl — A program that creates, deletes, and modifies the access control list entries of files and directories.

setfattr — A program that creates, deletes, and modifies the extended attributes of files and directories.

share — A Windows resource for shared use over a network.

shelling out — Starting a command shell from within another program, effectively suspending the first program from executing the shell.

shielded twisted pair (STP) — A type of network transmission media (a cable) made up of several pairs of wires encased in foil-wrapped insulation to block interference by electromagnetic radiation.

sign — To attach your private key to a file to show that the file could only have come from you. Also, to attach your private key to another person's public key to indicate that you trust the validity of that public key.

Simple Mail Transfer Protocol (SMTP) — The protocol by which e-mail is transferred on the Internet.

Simple Network Management Protocol (SNMP) — A protocol designed to provide feedback about how the components of a network are functioning.

Simple Network Time Protocol (SNTP) — A subset of NTP; it does not use the 32-bit value that provides for subsecond precision.

Skipjack — A government-approved encryption algorithm that uses an 80-bit key.

slave — A backup to a master DNS server, containing the same database files as the master DNS server.

SmartList — A free mailing list manager that works in conjunction with `procmail` and `sendmail`.

smbclient — A utility that provides client access to Windows-based hosts or to Samba servers. Part of the Samba suite.

smbd — The daemon within the Samba suite that provides SMB capability to Linux.

smbfs — The file system type designation used to mount a Windows share as part of a Linux file system using the `mount` command.

smbprint — A command within the Samba suite that enables printing to a Windows printer over the network.

sniffer — A software package used to sniff the network.

sniffing — Tapping into a network connection to read the packets that other users have sent.

Snort — A well-known open source intrusion-detection system.

SOA record — The first line (record) in a DNS zone file. Defines the start of authority for the information in the file, describing how to use the information provided for this zone, including a serial number for updates and refresh periods for zone transfers to slave DNS servers.

social engineering — The process of manipulating someone to extract needed information about a computer system.

soft mount — A method of mounting an NFS file system that causes NFS to give up on an operation after waiting for a specified time.

source port — A port that identifies the application that sent the packet.

spam — The unwanted advertisements sent to a large number of e-mail or newsgroup recipients.

spoofing — A technique used by a malicious user to act as another person when contacting a server.

squashing — A security concept used by NFS servers to prevent a user from gaining access to a file system on the NFS server simply by virtue of having the same user ID on the NFS client.

Squid — The most widely used Linux proxy server.

ssh-agent — A part of the SSH suite that helps manage key pairs and authentication among multiple SSH-capable systems.

stack — A series of multiple PAM modules accessed in succession to perform a security check.

star — A program, similar to `tar`, that can archive file-systems while preserving extended attributes and ACLs.

star topology — A network topology design in which multiple computers connect to a single center point, usually a hub or a switch.

stateful inspection — The ability of a firewall to make decisions about a packet based on its TCP state. For example, is the packet part of an already established session?

static routing — Assembling a routing table via entries in start-up scripts or by manually entered `route` commands.

stealth scan — A port scan that uses unexpected TCP flag combinations, including SYN, FIN, none (null scan), and all (Xmas scan) flags.

stratum — A layer within the time server structure of NTP.

stunnel — A program that uses SSL as a transport protocol to encrypt other network protocols such as POP3 and IMAP.

subnet mask — A set of numbers similar in appearance to an IP address, used to denote how many bits of an IP address are part of the network ID. Any bit set (1, not 0) in the subnet mask is part of the network ID; used for class-based IP addressing.

sudo — A utility that lets a system administrator assign privileges to any user account so that the user can execute only the programs the sudo configuration specifies.

SUID — *See* Set UID bit.

superserver — A program that listens on multiple network ports and starts appropriate network service daemons when a client connection arrives for that port. Also called a metaserver. The most widely used superserver program is inetd.

SWAT — A browser-based graphical configuration interface for setting up and managing the Samba SMB server.

Swatch — A software package that performs log oversight functions, similar to logcheck.

switch — A device used to connect other networking devices (such as hosts or printers) into a larger network using built-in intelligence to decide which network packets should be sent to which parts of the network.

symmetric encryption algorithm — An encryption algorithm in which the same key is used to both encrypt and decrypt a message (the algorithm is reversed for decryption). Also called private-key encryption.

SYN packet — A TCP packet sent from a port scanner that has the SYN flag set.

syslogd — The system logging daemon, which can use port 514 to communicate with syslogd on another system to provide remote logging capability.

System Administration, Networking, and Security (SANS) Institute — A prestigious and well-regarded education and research organization whose members include most of the leading computer security experts in the country. Also known simply as SANS.

T-1 — A high-speed transmission format (1.544 Mb/s) available through your local telephone company, usually for a few hundred dollars per month.

T-3 — A high-speed transmission format (45 Mb/s) available through your local telephone company, usually for several thousand dollars per month.

tail — A program that displays the final 10 lines (configurable) of any text file.

talk — A program used with the talkd daemon to initiate and manage a real-time typed conversation with another user.

talkd — The daemon that implements the talk communication system.

TCP/IP model — *See* Internet model.

tcpd (TCP Wrappers) — An application-level access control (security) program that examines incoming network connections when requested by a superserver, then compares the connection details to a configuration file to determine whether the connection is allowed.

tcpdump — A command-line utility that provides detailed information about packets on a network.

telephony — The technology that lets a computer interact with a telephone in such a way that it can serve as an answering machine, call router, voice recorder, and so forth.

Telnet — A terminal emulator program that allows a user to log on to a remote computer as if sitting at that computer's keyboard.

terminal — A screen and keyboard attached to a computer, usually at a distance from the computer. Multiple terminals attached to the same computer allow multiple people to access the computer at the same time; also known as *dumb terminal*.

terminal emulation — A software program that allows a personal computer (or other intelligent device) to act like a terminal in connecting to another computer.

three-way handshake — A procedure used by TCP to establish a connection.

throughput — The amount of useful payload information that can be transmitted on a network.

ticket — A set of information provided by a Kerberos server to a user or service that grants the user permission to use the service. A ticket contains the following components: {sessionkey:username:address:servicename:lifespan:timestamp}.

time — A network testing service provided by `inetd` on port 37. Returns a number corresponding to the current time in a program-readable format, which appears as unreadable characters on screen.

Time to Live (TTL) — A counter within an IP packet header that determines how many hops (routers) a packet can pass through before being discarded as "destination unreachable."

token — An electronic code that is passed from computer to computer to identify which computer on the network has the right to send out a packet at that moment. Used by certain types of networks such as Token-Ring.

Token-Ring — A popular networking technology developed by IBM in the early 1980s. It uses a token-passing technique.

topology — A shape or ordering applied to the connections between systems on a network.

traceroute — A command used to list each router (each hop) that a packet passes through between a source host and a destination host.

Transmission Control Protocol (TCP) — A widely used connection-oriented Transport-layer protocol. TCP is the transport mechanism for many popular Internet services such as FTP, SMTP, and HTTP (Web) traffic.

Transparent Cryptographic File System (TCFS) — An enhancement to the Cryptographic File System (CFS) that allows it to operate transparently to client users on the network.

Triple DES (TDES) — A U.S. government-approved encryption algorithm that applies the DES algorithm three times in succession using three different DES keys.

Tripwire — A popular intrusion-detection tool that detects unauthorized changes to files or directories.

Trivial FTP (TFTP) — A protocol similar to FTP, but designed for downloading an operating system over a network to boot a diskless workstation. Requires less memory and provides fewer features than standard FTP.

trn — The threaded newsreader, probably the most widely used text-mode newsreader for Linux.

Trojan horse attack — A technique for gaining access to a computer system, in which a system administrator executes a program that appears normal but actually creates a security hole for a cracker or destroys data on the host where it is run.

tunneling — Transporting one protocol within another.

Twofish — A symmetric cipher.

unshielded twisted pair (UTP) — A type of network transmission medium (a cable) made up of four pairs of wires encased in plastic insulation. UTP comes in six categories, with Category 6 or CAT6 being the highest quality, and supports the highest speed.

Usenet news — Another name for Internet newsgroups.

User Datagram Protocol (UDP) — A fast, connectionless Transport-layer protocol.

user private groups — A security system in which an empty group is created for every user on the system. Files created by a user are assigned to this empty group, meaning that no other users have any default access to the file.

vigr — A special version of the `vi` editor used to edit the `/etc/group` file.

vipw — A special version of the `vi` editor that should be used anytime you must edit `/etc/passwd` directly (instead of using utilities such as `passwd` or `useradd`).

virtual hosting — A feature of the Apache Web server that lets a single copy of Apache serve documents for several Web sites (several domains).

virtual private network (VPN) — A secure organizational network that uses insecure public networks (such as the Internet) for communications.

visudo — A special text editor used to edit the `/etc/sudoers` file; it prevents conflicts between multiple open files and checks the syntax of the `/etc/sudoers` configuration file upon exit.

vlock — A utility that locks a text-mode console screen.

Voice over IP (VoIP) — The use of IP as a protocol for transport of digitized voice packets, often as a medium for long-distance telephone calls over the Internet.

VPN router — A hardware device that acts as a dedicated firewall with VPN capabilities.

VT100 — The most widely supported dumb terminal standard.

w — A utility that lists all logged-on users with their username and terminal, plus system usage information.

web of trust — The personal connections between a group of colleagues who have exchanged keys, signed them, and continue to rely on each others' signatures.

Web server — A daemon that accepts requests via HTTP and responds with the requested files.

Web spoofing — A type of man-in-the-middle attack in which a cracker deceives a user into linking to the cracker's site when the user thinks he or she is linking to another site. The cracker's server then intercepts every Web request from the user and alters the response to point all future requests back to the cracker's site.

Webmin — A browser-based utility that can manage many system functions, including network configuration.

who — A utility that lists all users who are currently logged on the system.

whois — A utility that queries an Internet database to learn about the person who manages a specific domain.

WINS — Acronym for Windows Internet Naming Service, a host-locating service for Windows systems, similar in function to a DNS server. The Samba suite can act as a WINS server or client.

wireless LAN (WLAN) — A wireless network designed to be used within a small radius of a central transceiver.

worm — A program that self-replicates and invades networked computer systems. Similar to a virus, but requires less human intervention for continued propagation.

write (w) — A standard Linux file permission—represented in utilities by w—that permits modifying a file or creating new files in a directory (when assigned to that directory).

wu-ftp — The Washington University FTP server. The name of the server daemon is `in.ftpd`.

wvdial — A text-mode utility that allows users to configure and initiate dial-up connections easily using PPP.

X client — A graphical program running on a host. *See also* X server.

X server — The screen where a graphical program is remotely displayed (and the keyboard and mouse of that system). *See also* X client.

X.500 — A widely known international standard for a directory service.

xauth — A security system for managing the display of graphical programs on remote computers by sharing a numeric token called a cookie; also the program used in Linux to manage this security system and the numeric cookies associated with it.

XDMCP — A protocol that allows remote hosts to use X running on a Linux system to provide a graphical logon display.

xhost — A program that can control access by X clients to an X server for display of graphical programs. The `xhost` program is not a secure system.

xinetd — A superserver with extended configuration options. Standard on Red Hat Linux instead of the more usual `inetd` program.

xlogmaster — A program that displays several system resources, including the system log file, in a graphical window.

Xmas scan — A method of port scanning in which all flags in the TCP header are turned on (set).

xntpd — A daemon used on some Linux systems to implement NTP. *See also* `ntpd`.

zebra — An open source routing daemon that supports RIPv1, RIPv2, OSPF, and BGP.

zone — A part of the DNS domain tree for which a particular DNS server has authority to provide information.

zone files — The files referred to in `named.conf` that contain detailed information about specific zones; the information that a DNS query seeks.

zone transfer — Exchanging information between a master DNS server and a slave DNS server.

Index